Regulation and Markets

Regulation and Markets

Daniel F. Spulber

The MIT Press
Cambridge, Massachusetts
London, England

© 1989 Massachusetts Institute of Technology

This book was set in Times Roman
by Asco Trade Typesetting Ltd., Hong Kong, and printed and bound by Halliday Lithograph in the United States of America.

Library of Congress Cataloging-in-Publication Data

Spulber, Daniel F.
  Regulation and markets.

  Bibliography: p.
  Includes index.
  1. Trade regulation. 2. Industry and state. I. Title.
  HD3612.S68   1989   338.9   88-11150
  ISBN 0-262-19275-6

To my parents
Pauline and Nicolas Spulber

Contents

IV ANTITRUST: EFFICIENCY AND COMPETITION

V   CONCLUSION

Preface

Regulation, the study of government intervention in markets, should be viewed as a proper field of study in economics. My purpose is to suggest the broad sweep of the field of Regulation and to emphasize the interesting and unique questions that characterize the subject. Regulation involves more than studies of specific regulated industries or of administrative procedure, although these are essential. Rather, its central focus is on the characteristics and consequences of rules and institutions governing markets.

This study considers both normative and positive aspects of government regulation. On the normative side, three broad issues emerge. The first issue is the *choice of policy instruments* to achieve regulatory goals. Regulatory policy instruments range from command-and-control actions and orders issued on a case-by-case basis to broad restrictions that constrain market transactions but rely primarily on the market mechanism for resource allocation. In addition, the objectives pursued by regulators are frequently very diverse. Policy objectives may be simple rules of thumb, politically motivated actions, or various welfare objectives. These goals cannot be specified in general and must be determined for specific models. Often, the goals of regulators are best achieved by extensive interference with the operation of the market mechanism and necessarily result in an inefficient allocation of resources. In many other cases, regulatory objectives are best achieved by reliance on the market mechanism for resource allocation. A theme of the discussion is an emphasis on the ways in which policy objectives may be achieved by implementation of market-type allocation mechanisms or direct reliance on the competitive market.

The second normative issue involves a recognition that markets function within the context of a variety of implicit or explicit *rules*. In many economic models, the assumptions made disguise implicit market rules that are essential to the efficient functioning of the trade mechanism. Market rules are intrinsic to a specification of the context of market models. It must be recognized that the mechanism of resource allocation itself has a technology. There are production possibilities and associated costs for the production of transactions. Market transactions take place within a framework of administrative institutions and legal rules and frequently follow patterns established by custom and standard practice. Regulations applied by government need to be justified as a supplement to the common law of property, tort, and contracts. The judicial system may often adequately handle the problems regulations are meant to address. An important question is how regulation may be designed to provide general rules that promote efficiency in the market allocation of resources.

The third normative issue is the attempt to define areas of *market failure* for which government regulation might enhance allocative efficiency. Market failure is viewed here as a necessary but not sufficient condition for the imposition of regulation. Three broad categories of market failure are proposed: entry barriers, externalities, and internalities. *Entry barriers*, primarily due to sunk costs, may prevent competition in some markets. *Externalities* refers to third-party effects of a transaction unaccounted for in the terms of that transaction. *Internalities* refers to costs or benefits accruing to parties to a transaction that are not fully accounted for in the terms of the transaction. In each area, I examine the potential role for government intervention in markets. This is not meant as an apology for regulation. Rather, I wish to specify the areas where regulation may play a role and areas when it is inappropriate. I do not abstract away from the many potential failures of regulation. Problems in implementing regulatory policy, particularly under asymmetric information, are emphasized throughout.

In terms of positive analysis, I emphasize the particular characteristics of administrative regulation in the United States. The role of administrative procedure, especially public rule-making hearings and adjudication by regulatory agencies, is given some emphasis. I stress the important role played by the process of public hearings in information gathering by agencies and in adversarial interaction by competing interest groups. Regulation is viewed as a *bargaining* process in which market participants form coalitions and negotiate over regulatory policies and their implementation.

Scope of the Book

As government intervention and participation in economic activities has become increasingly diversified and pervasive, so has the study of government in economics. Almost all fields of economics apply the conclusions suggested by economic theory to describe the effects of public policies or to prescribe particular government actions. Thus, for example, fiscal and monetary policy are intrinsic to the study of Macroeconomics and Money. Tariffs, quotas, and other trade policies are studied in International Trade. Tax incidence, government expenditures, and government policy in general are by definition elements of the field of Public Finance. Development examines government policies that promote growth and trade. Given this extensive study of government policy, the justification for the separate study of Regulation must lie in the uniqueness of the questions that are asked as outlined above.

This volume is not directly concerned with the effects of government actions on economic aggregates such as GNP, employment, or inflation. Further, I am not specifically interested in government activities that promote industrial policy or are part of an incomes policy. Also, the effects of government restraint or promotion of international factor movements or terms-of-trade do not enter into the analysis.

I do not propose to cover the entire field of Regulation. A significant omission is the broad subject of financial regulation in banking, securities, bond markets, and insurance. This is an important subject worthy of extensive separate treatment. In addition, I do not cover specific industries that nonetheless have an extensive history of regulation and special economic characteristics, such as airlines or railroads. Institutional issues are not covered in detail. Rather, I attempt to focus on theoretical issues, such as economies of scale or sunk costs, which have general applicability. Finally, little attention is devoted to the large empirical literature on regulation. As an introduction to this area, I recommend MacAvoy's (1979) study.

The present book does not examine *dynamic* models of regulation. Although some discussion of dynamic issues is given, it was felt that this area of regulation is developing very rapidly and is deserving of an extended separate treatment. The strategic interaction of consumers, firms, and regulators over time is a focus of current research. The study of commitment in regulatory policy will undoubtedly play a significant role in future analysis of policy.

The models used in the study of regulation are primarily those of microeconomic theory and game theory. Many regulation models are extensions of models from Industrial Organization. The field of Industrial Organization is concerned with the way in which various economic factors influence market structure (the number and size of firms) and the conduct of firms (competitive strategies). Thus, entry behavior, firm pricing and product strategies, technology, and market demand affect the number and size of firms observed in a market equilibrium. The strategic interaction of firms results in market equilibrium output levels, product differentiation, research and development, product quality and durability, and advertising. In addition, Industrial Organization examines the welfare or "performance" implications of alternative market equilibria along with the effects of government policy on the determinants of firm behavior and market equilibrium.

This study of Regulation attempts to consider the full range of government policies and the role of government actions in the marketplace. It seeks to examine the interaction between administrative regulatory agencies and market participants and to evaluate the welfare implications of regulatory activities. Regulation represents attempts by the state to alter the administrative and legal framework that governs market transactions. Regulation economists must consider the many possible institutions of exchange. Regulation is not limited to the determinants of market structure or the characteristics of firm behavior. Emphasis is placed on the rules under which the market operates.

Intended Audience

This book is intended as both a research monograph and an overview of the field that can be used by researchers and as a textbook in a graduate course on the economics of Regulation. The course can be part of an Industrial Organization sequence. There is sufficient expository material to make the book useful for advanced economics undergraduates as well. In addition, the book may be of value in Regulation courses in Law, Management Science, and Political Science. My approach has been influenced by research in Law and Political Science. I hope that some small part of the debt is repaid here.

The technical level of the book generally requires no more than basic calculus. There is some use of probability, although this usually appears in separate sections or chapters that are specifically labeled as being concerned with "asymmetric information." A reader wishing to avoid these technical issues might skip the relevant sections without losing the main argument. These sections are chapter 11, section 12.4, section 13.4, chapter 15, and sections 19.2 and 19.3.

Acknowledgments

Permission to quote, adapt, or reprint parts of papers by the following publishers and journals is gratefully acknowledged:

Spulber, D. F., "Scale Economies and Existence of Sustainable Monopoly Prices," *Journal of Economic Theory*, 34, October, 1984, pp. 149–163. Copyright © 1984 Academic Press. This paper forms the basis of chapter 4.

Spulber, D. F., "Effluent Regulation and Long Run Optimality," *Journal of Environmental Economics and Management*, 12, 1985, pp. 103–116. Copyright © 1985 Academic Press. This paper is adapted in sections 13.2 and 13.3.

Spulber, D. F., "Bargaining and Regulation with Asymmetric Information about Demand and Supply," *Journal of Economic Theory*, 44, April, 1988, pp. 251–268. Copyright © 1987 Academic Press. This paper forms the basis of chapter 11.

Spulber, D. F., "Capacity, Output and Sequential Entry," *American Economic Review*, 71, June 1981, pp. 503–514. Copyright © 1981 American Economic Association. Material from this paper appears in section 17.5.

Spulber, D. F., "Value Allocation with Economies of Scale," *Economics Letters*, 21, 1986, pp. 107–111. Original publication copyright © 1986 Elsevier Science Publishers B.V., Amsterdam, Holland. Material from this paper appears in chapter 8.

Spulber, D. F., "Optimal Environmental Regulation under Asymmetric Information," *Journal of Public Economics*, 1988. Original publication copyright © 1988 Elsevier Science Publishers B.V., Amsterdam, Holland. Material from this paper forms the basis of section 13.4.

Spulber, D. F., "Second Best Pricing and Cooperation," *Rand Journal of Economics*, 17, Summer, 1986, pp. 239–250. Copyright © 1986 The Rand Corporation. This paper forms the basis of chapter 6.

Spulber, D. F., "Products Liability in a Contestable Market," *Economica*, 1988. Copyright © The London School of Economics and Political Science. Material from this paper appears in section 14.4.

Some of the initial research for the book was undertaken under National Science Foundation grant no. SES-82-19121. The main research for the book was conducted under grant no. SES-86-08115. The research support of the National Science Foundation was indispensable, and it is gratefully acknowledged. I especially thank Misty Chapman and Nadine Deardurff of the Indiana University Department of Mathematics for their very valuable and capable assistance in typing and completing the manuscript. I also thank Victoria Mason of the California Institute of Technology for typing portions of the manuscript.

I would like to thank my students in my graduate course in Regulation at the University of Southern California for their useful discussions and interest in some of the early versions of material presented herein. I also thank friends and colleagues for their helpful comments, which have greatly improved the manuscript: Robert Becker, Sudipto Dasgupta, Tony Marino, Matthew Spitzer, Nicolas Spulber, and Mark Zupan. I thank my editor at The MIT Press, Terry Vaughn, for his able guidance, which made the publication process an enjoyable experience. I also wish to thank several anonymous referees for their very useful suggestions. I thank Sarbajit Sengupta and Anindya Sen for their assistance in preparing the final manuscript and index.

Last, but not least, I thank my family, Sue, Rachelle, and Aaron, for their encouragement and pleasant company.

Regulation and Markets

Introduction

I begin by emphasizing a simple point: Economic regulation is applied to *markets*. Many discussions of regulation speak of government policies directed at business or industry. Regulation often is portrayed as the control of *firms* either as suppliers of goods or employers of labor and resources. However, control over one side of a market, buyers or sellers, will have a corresponding impact on the other side. Restriction of what can be sold is at once a restriction placed on what may be purchased. Intervention by government in the market allocation mechanism may change the production, consumption, and distribution of goods and services. Promulgation and enforcement of market rules alters equilibrium supply and demand decisions. Thus, regulation affects the characteristics of transactions and the terms of contractual relations between buyers and sellers.

Public policy debates generally stress correction of undesirable industry behavior, e.g., mitigating monopoly pricing, reducing environmental pollution, and improving product quality or workplace safety. It is commonly believed that promulgating and implementing rules will be sufficient to achieve desired objectives. Beyond the administrative costs of enforcing a rule, regulations such as price controls, pollution quotas, and safety standards might appear costless to some policymakers. To improve product safety, it is often suggested that the government can simply increase the safety standard. The only costs appear to be the immediate costs to the firm of improving product quality. Economic analysis of such regulatory policies must emphasize the restrictions that are placed on both consumer and firm decisions. Competitive purchasing and selling decisions will be constrained by given regulations. These will in turn determine the market equilibrium price, output, and variety of products. The ultimate consequences of regulation will be the effect on the market equilibrium allocation of goods and services. It is in this context that the full welfare costs of regulation need to be assessed.

The purpose of the discussion is to determine the potential role of government regulation in correcting market failure, to examine the institutional nature of administrative regulation, and to assess the welfare consequences of regulatory intervention in markets. Thus, the study of regulation requires a framework for analyzing market failure. Also, the behavior of regulatory agencies must be observed in an economic context. Finally, an understanding of the interaction between market participants and regulatory agencies is needed to determine the impact of regulatory policy. These concerns are reflected in the outline of the book. I start in part I with an overview of market failure and with an introduction to the administrative regulatory process. The study is structured around three main policy problem areas addressed in parts II, III, and IV: technology, market intervention, and imperfect competition. Part II studies pricing under increasing returns to scale technology in markets without barriers to entry. The section analyzes cost-based pricing, second-best Pareto optimal pricing, discriminatory pricing, optimal pricing, and the design of a franchise competition to achieve these prices. Part III examines administrative regulation of utility rates, environmental quality, product quality, and workplace safety. Part IV studies antitrust policy and enforcement and the welfare implications of government efforts to promote competition. A concluding part, V, extends the discussion to deregulation and the convergence of antitrust and administrative regulatory policies. I now set forth the main themes to be addressed.

1 Economic Efficiency and Administrative Process

Regulation studies markets constrained by administrative agency actions and legal rules. Economic modeling of regulated markets requires consideration of the political and administrative characteristics of regulatory agencies and analysis of alternative legal rules. Chapter 1 surveys definitions of regulation in economics, law, and political science and presents a formal definition of regulation as a field of study. It is observed that traditional definitions of regulation in economics have minimized the role of the administrative process and have modeled government policy choices independently of the institutions charged with implementing those policies. Definitions of regulation in law have identified the importance of administrative process and the legal framework of bureaucratic rule making. In political science, the public choice and administrative policy aspects of regulation have been emphasized. However, these areas have tended to neglect the market despite its being both the *raison d'être* of regulatory policy and the context for regulatory decisions. The view of regulation presented here attempts to integrate models of administrative decision making with those of the market mechanism.

Regulation is viewed primarily as a process of coalition formation and bargaining involving consumers, firms, and regulatory agencies. The implications of administrative procedure for negotiation are considered in chapter 2. This chapter presents an introduction to the structure and characteristics of administrative regulatory agencies. The administrative process involves direct interaction between the agency and consumers and firms through public rule making and adjudicatory hearings. In addition, indirect interaction between the agency and consumers and firms occurs through congressional and executive intervention and judicial oversight. Indirect interaction is the subject of theories of regulatory origin, which are briefly surveyed. My main concern is with direct interaction. The discussion of the regulatory process suggests that the theory of cooperative games provides a natural way to model negotiation in regulated markets.

A classification of types of market failure is presented as a basis for normative analysis. A "market failure test" may be proposed as a guide to determining the desirability of government intervention. The test has essentially three steps. It must first be established that market failure has occurred.[1] *Market failure* is defined as a departure of the market equilibrium allocation from the set of Pareto optimal allocations of goods and services. A *Pareto optimal* allocation is an allocation such that no consumers can be made better off without making another consumer worse off. The optimal allocation may be a second-best optimum subject to institutional, technological, and informational constraints. The second step of the test is to determine whether government regulation can alleviate the misallocation of resources or correct the cause of the market failure particularly when faced with similar institutional, technological, or informational constraints. Finally, it must be shown that the potential benefits of regulatory remedies justify market intervention with any attendant administrative costs and induced allocative inefficiencies. With this market failure test in mind, I turn to applications of government regulation.

2 Increasing Returns to Scale Technology

Natural monopoly generally refers to a property of productive technology, often in conjunction with market demand, such that a single firm is able to serve the market at less cost than two or more firms. Natural monopoly is due to economies of scale or economies of multiple-output production. Increasing returns to scale must occur up to output levels that are significant relative to market demand evaluated at prices that cover the firm's costs. Natural monopoly is generally attributed to utility industries (electricity, telecommunications, natural gas, water) and transportation (railroads, canals). In these industries, multiple entry of firms would result in costly duplication of transmission networks and other facilities (e.g., lines, pipelines, tracks).

Walras (1936) presents an economic analysis of *natural monopoly* regulation with reference to the construction and operation of railroads.[2] His discussion has had a powerful and lasting influence on regulation economics. Walras (1936, p. 223) recommends state intervention in the railroad industry on the grounds that they constitute both a *public good* and a *natural monopoly*. He emphasizes that communication services are a matter of "public interest," anticipating the notion of regulation in the public interest. Walras identifies two forms of state intervention: state ownership and control of the firm or cost-based control of price for a private firm operating a franchise. He argues against separating the management of tracks and operation of railroads because limits on the number of firms that can use the tracks constrain competition. He suggests multiple pricing of railway services based on consumer willingness to pay. Walras recommends procedures that resemble public rate hearings and suggests that regulators be trained professionals. He also mentions auctioning of franchises as a means of regulation, an approach analyzed earlier by Chadwick (1859).

The presence of natural monopoly is often associated with government regulation of prices, service, and entry. However, identification of increasing returns to scale does little more than describe productive technology. This is not sufficient to establish market failure and therefore cannot serve as a basis for regulatory policy. It must be established that economies of scale somehow prevent competition from achieving an efficient allocation of resources and that regulation can provide a remedy. To study competition in markets where firms have increasing returns to scale, we apply the contestable markets framework of Panzar and Willig (1977), Baumol, Bailey, and Willig (1977) and Baumol, Panzar, and Willig (1982). The basic definition of a *contestable market* requires the following:

a. all firms have the same technology, which is used efficiently, and products are homogeneous;

b. there are no barriers to market entry or exit; and

c. perfect information on prices is available to all consumers and firms, and firms have complete demand information.

The textbook model of prefect competition assumes that in addition to free entry, identical technology, and perfect information, there are a large number of price-taking firms. The notion of a perfectly contestable market allows a relaxation of the restriction on the number of firms (market structure) and on the pricing policies of firms (firm conduct). In particular, a market equilibrium in a contestable market may consist of one or a few firms with potential competition provided by the threat of entry. Firms compete by adjusting both prices and output supplied. The forces of price competition and the potential for entry serve to eliminate monopoly rents even with small numbers of firms. The contestable market model allows us to study competition in the presence of significant scale economies.

It is evident that the notion of a perfectly contestable market is an "ideal case," much as the perfectly competitive market represents an abstract ideal. My purpose in studying contestable markets is to isolate the effects of increasing returns to scale on market equilibrium prices and outputs. The extent to which market failure may be attributed to scale economies can then be examined. If contestable markets function well under scale economies, then scale economies cannot serve to rationalize regulation. Merely asserting that technology exhibits natural monopoly will not demonstrate the need for regulatory intervention. On the other hand, if market failure can be shown to result from a combination of scale economies and the departure of markets from the ideal of "contestability," regulatory policy must then respond to a broader range of underlying circumstances. These alternative issues are addressed further in the following section.

Economies of scale pose two dilemmas for economists. First, marginal cost pricing will not yield sufficient revenues to cover firm costs, while average cost pricing or other pricing rules may entail departure from socially optimal output levels. This problem is present whether prices are chosen privately by firms or imposed by regulatory agencies. Second, because production by a single firm yields costs savings, competition may lead to higher production costs or duplication of facilities. Regulation of entry, however, will remove market incentives for productive efficiency and competitive pricing. Regulation of prices and entry under increasing returns to scale must be designed to resolve these two dilemmas. The achievement of alternative regulatory pricing objectives is examined within the contestable markets framework.

In markets characterized by regulated natural monopoly, regulatory authorities often assume responsibility for the selection of prices. Depending upon available information regarding firm technologies and market demand, regulators may choose from an array of pricing policies, which can be listed in order of increasing complexity: (a) cost-based pricing, (b) second-best pricing, (c) second-best price discrimination and nonlinear pricing, and (d) optimal pricing and perfectly discriminatory tariffs. Because of the large informational requirements imposed by any pricing policy, it is in the interest of regulators to use the properties of the market mechanism to aid in the selection of prices and in the enforcement of a particular pricing policy. The regulator may have a number of goals, including efficient production by firms, stimulation of new product and process innovations, and maintenance of product quality. The discipline of the competitive market may provide the regulator with an important policy instrument. Chapters 3–9 study the four types of pricing policies, (a)–(d), and examine conditions under which regulators may use a market mechanism to achieve desired price and allocation objectives. The analysis culminates in the study of how to design auctions in which firms bid for the right to serve the market. For each of the four pricing policies, an equilibrium concept is studied. It is shown how properly managed "competition for the market" may result in each price policy being chosen by firms.

Cost-based pricing is studied in chapter 3. Cost-based pricing refers to pricing policies that rely on the characteristics of firm technology. In the presence of increasing returns to scale, setting prices equal to long-run marginal costs does not allow the firm to break even. Cost-based pricing selects (linear) prices that cover costs. With multiple products that are jointly produced, it is often not possible to attribute costs fully to each output. Often, fixed inputs are also public inputs within the firm and represent nonattributable or joint costs. Various ad hoc rules have been used by regulators to address the problem of attributing costs within firms. An important class of cost-based prices is the set of *subsidy-free* prices. This is the set of prices such that the revenue generated by any subset of output levels does not exceed the stand-alone costs of producing those output levels. Alternatively, the revenue generated by any subset of output levels at least covers the incremental cost of producing those outputs. In this sense, subsidy-free pricing is related to incremental cost pricing.

Zero-profit, subsidy-free prices are the only prices that are *sustainable* against entry in a contestable market. Thus, firms faced with the threat of entry will select prices that are subsidy-free without outside regulation. This is one of the principal insights of the contestable markets literature. Sustainability is studied in chapter 4. It is shown that there exist market clearing subsidy-free prices that deter entry. Thus, if the regulatory objective is simply the elimination of subsidies across goods, and if the market is perfectly contestable, the analysis suggests a greatly limited role for regulation in price setting.

While satisfying a number of desirable criteria, cost-based pricing policies do not consider consumer welfare. Indeed, the elimination of all subsides across goods may eliminate some prices that are desirable in terms of social welfare. The selection of prices that maximize social welfare and allow the firm to break even is examined in chapter 5. These prices are said to be *second-best Pareto optimal prices* and are studied with and without interpersonal income transfers and profit shares. Multiproduct second-best prices are applied to the study of peak load pricing.

My discussion of the regulatory process emphasizes the formation of coalitions of consumers and firms to achieve objectives through the administrative allocation of resources. This approach is particularly applicable to the problem of second-best pricing. In chapter 6, second-best pricing is studied within a cooperative game of joint production that is played by the customers of a multiproduct firm. A solution concept is introduced, referred to as the *second-best core*, which provides a strengthening of the requirements imposed by second-best Pareto optimality. The *second-best core* notion adapts the concept of the core from the theory of cooperative games. Allocations are said to be in the core if they are feasible for the coalition consisting of all consumers and if there does not exist an allocation that is feasible for some subset of consumers and that makes all those consumers better off. *The second-best core* refers to prices for a good that is jointly produced by a coalition consisting of all consumers in a particular market. This is equivalent to a single firm contracting with consumers to serve the market. Prices in the second-best core must be such that no group of customers has incentive to drop off the system or form a separate coalition and produce the outputs on its own. Thus, prices must reflect the bargaining power of all consumer coalitions. No group of consumers may subsidize another. It is shown, however, that these prices are neither subsidy-free across goods nor sustainable with free entry. This does not imply that regulators must set prices. Rather the cooperative game is suggestive of a market-type mechanism that achieves second-best optimal prices in equilibrium.

Chapter 7 studies second-best discriminatory pricing. Both second-best two-part tariffs and general nonlinear pricing are considered. These are pricing policies that offer different average prices based on the size of the consumer's purchase. Consumers reveal their marginal valuations through the size of their purchases. The prices are chosen to maximize consumer welfare subject to a break-even constraint for the firm. Then, a cooperative game is studied for the case of second-best two-part tariffs. It is shown that a core exists for the game of joint production with two-part tariffs. Again the second-best core notion strengthens the second-best Pareto optimality requirement and is suggestive of an equilibrium mechanism that achieves the desired price objective.

Optimal pricing with personalized tariffs is considered in chapter 8. In particular, the prices and personalized fixed charges that support a core allocation under increasing returns to scale are studied. Attention is given to a particular allocation of resources, the Aumann-Shapley value allocation. The Aumann-Shapley value is shown to be an element of the core of the cooperative game of joint production under increasing returns. Thus, prices that support the Aumann-Shapley value yield an allocation of resources in the core.

The analysis of alternative pricing policies comes together in chapter 9. It is shown how regulators can design a market mechanism to achieve optimal prices without direct intervention in firm pricing decisions. By specifying a franchise competition in which firms offer service contracts, regulators can achieve desired pricing objectives. The general principle is that the process of firm solicitation of customers through service contracts resembles the process of coalition formation in a cooperative game. Given the possibility of recontracting, and existence of a core for the cooperative price-setting game, a firm service contract will secure an exclusive franchise if and only if the pricing policy is in the core of the associated cooperative game of joint production. The chapter examines the design of a franchise competition to achieve second-best Pareto optimal pricing, second-best discriminatory pricing, and optimal pricing.

3   Regulation and Market Failure

Regulations may be classified and their effectiveness evaluated on the basis of the market failure they attempt to remedy. Regulation of prices, entry, and quality of service in the utility industries, such as electricity, telecommunications, and pipelines, attempts to address imperfections in competition associated with *barriers to entry*. Environmental regulations directed at air and water pollution or natural resource depletion are aimed at *externalities*, where transactions create costs for third parties. Finally, regulation of product quality, workplace safety, or contract terms is directed at *internalities*, that is, costs or benefits of market transactions that are not reflected in the terms of exchange.

In analyzing direct intervention in markets by administrative agencies, three broad themes emerge. These aspects of regulation are common to regulations whether directed at markets with barriers to entry, externalities, or internalities. First, the welfare effects of regulation must be examined in the context of the market transactions that take place. The decisions of consumers and firms faced with regulatory constraints will determine the resulting allocation of resources. Second, the anticipated results of the regulation will be reflected in the participation of consumer and firm interest groups in the regulatory process. The regulations that are ultimately chosen will reflect the concerns of consumers and firms about the resulting market equilibrium. The administrative process of selecting regulations may be characterized as bargaining and can be usefully represented by economic models of bargaining. Third, imperfect information plays an important role at various stages in the regulatory process. Regulators must establish policies on the basis of incomplete information about firm technology and consumer characteristics. Regulators must implement policy and enforce rules despite the costs of monitoring the behavior of market participants. In addition, market participants themselves operate under incomplete information about prices, product characteristics, technology, or health and safety risks. Market participants are imperfectly informed about the attributes of their trading partners. The consequences of government intervention depend in large part on whether regulation alleviates or exacerbates imperfections in market information.

Regulation of utility rates is studied in chapters 10 and 11. In a full information setting, chapter 10 examines bargaining over the determinants of regulated rates: cost estimates, allowed rates of return, and relative prices. Chapter 11 reexamines rate regulation when firms have private information about costs and consumers have private information about demand. Efficiency losses attributable to asymmetric information are examined.

Regulation of environmental pollution is the subject of chapters 12 and 13. Bargaining over regulatory policies and private bargaining over pollution levels are studied. The effects of property rights assignments and of incomplete information on private bargaining are considered in chapter 12. Chapter 13 turns to policy implementation and the effects of alternative policy instruments on market equilibrium. The analysis concludes with a model of environmental regulation under asymmetric information that explicitly incorporates the final output market.

Regulation of product quality and workplace safety is the focus of chapters 14 and 15. Chapter 14 sets out the framework of the regulatory institutions and examines the performance of legal liability rules under alternative market structures. Chapter 15 presents a detailed analysis of regulation of internalities in the presence of risk and costly contract contingencies, unobservable care in reducing product or workplace risks, and imperfectly observable product or workplace characteristics. The concluding discussion compares market transmission of information via prices, advertising, or contract terms, with such regulatory actions as disclosure rules.

4 Antitrust

By its very name, antitrust suggests actions taken against large firms, the trusts of another era. However, enforcement of the antitrust laws entails extensive intervention in markets. Antitrust affects the types of contracts negotiated between firms (joint ventures, franchises, mergers, cartels) and between firms and their customers. This section emphasizes that antitrust law and enforcement, rather than being simply proscriptive, constitute an elaborate form of market regulation.

Antitrust policy represents the regulation of industry by judicial means. Antitrust agencies have many of the same characteristics as administrative regulatory agencies including rule making and adjudicatory powers. Antitrust agencies influence behavior through announcements of merger guidelines and prosecution policies. Antitrust agencies carry out policy by choosing what type of violations to investigate and prosecute. The administration of antitrust is studied in chapter 16. Antitrust is concerned with both enhancing economic efficiency and promotion of competition. I begin by emphasizing the role of antitrust as a response to market failure. Antitrust enforcement activities are classified by the types of market failure they purport to address. Policies directed at monopoly or attempts to monopolize can only be warranted in the presence of significant *entry barriers*, particularly sunk costs. Similarly, antitrust action against price fixing should require entry barriers since otherwise cartels will not achieve market power. Second, I examine antitrust policy toward what are called exclusionary practices, such as tying and predatory prices. These are often described in terms of *externalities*; that is, incumbent firms are said to take actions that unfairly impede entry. I take the position that exclusionary practices involve competitive market actions, such as price reductions and that enforcement against exclusion can be counterproductive. A possible exception arises in the case of demand and supply bottlenecks involving entry barriers. Finally, I consider antitrust directed at *internalities* in the form of vertical restraints and unfair practices. It is observed that vertical restraints need not in themselves call for antitrust intervention. A role is identified for antitrust enforcement in mitigating internalities when consumers have imperfect information about product quality or contract terms.

Antitrust enforcement is often directed at concentrated industries. The crucial issue of market structure and its connection with economic efficiency is examined in detail in chapter 17 using formal industrial organization models. The role of entry barriers and the differences between competitive price and output strategies are emphasized. This confirms the view that market concentration need not determine economic performance.

Antitrust concern with the effects of price discrimination on competition and welfare is addressed in chapter 18. I emphasize that price discrimination need not impede competition. Indeed, price discrimination is observed in a wide variety of competitive markets. In an oligopoly model with differentiated products, it is shown that social welfare is enhanced if firms offer quantity discounts rather than setting linear prices. Welfare under monopoly is also shown to be greater if the firm chooses quantity discounts rather than linear prices. The chapter concludes with a discussion of Motty Perry's (1984) model of a contestable market with multiple price schedules. Given these price schedules, natural monopoly is sufficient for the sustainability of monopoly. The analysis is extended to show the existence of a sustainable industry structure, again confirming the possibility of price discrimination in a competitive market.

Formal models of public and private antitrust enforcement are presented in chapter 19. I consider the effects of commitment in antitrust enforcement by comparing situations in which the antitrust authority chooses enforcement effort before the cartel chooses its price, after the cartel price, or simultaneously. The antitrust authority is only concerned with social welfare if it can make a credible commitment to enforcement effort. Otherwise, if the antitrust authority acts at the same time or after the cartel, it must be motivated by maximization of some function of the likelihood of detection, such as expected fines. Public antitrust enforcement under asymmetric information is then examined where the antitrust authority can credibly commit to a schedule of enforcement probabilities that is contingent on the cartel's announced price. It is shown that some collusion by low-cost firms is always tolerated but that markups are mitigated by the possibility of prosecution. The discussion of antitrust then compares public and private antitrust enforcement and concludes that the role of public enforcement should be to establish broad guidelines for antitrust actions, while private enforcers may possess superior market information.

5 Deregulation and Reregulation

Who has not heard predictions of the demise of government regulation? What regulatory economist has not been asked "Why study regulation in a period of deregulation; the future lies with competition and laissez-faire policies?" There has indeed been an extensive series of efforts to take the government out of the marketplace. Large-scale deregulation has been observed in communications, railroads, buses, trucking, airlines, crude oil, natural gas, banking, and securities brokerage.[3] Is deregulation the beginning of the end for government regulation? In my view, not at all. The history of regulation is one of shifting emphasis and focus of government activities. As policy objectives change, so do regulatory institutions and the particular markets subject to regulation. Regulation is often an ad hoc response to economic events or to the perception of market failure. The focus might be on, say, airline safety or market structure rather than air fares or route allocation. In fact, the term "reregulation" has come into usage; see, for example, Reagan (1987). A number of legislative proposals for railroad regulation have been referred to as "reregulation" acts. The history of regulation suggests that structural economic change is very often accompanied by new forms of government intervention in the marketplace. Further, regulation by administrative agencies is intrinsic to the nature of government in the United States, particularly since regulatory agencies can be seen as extensions of the congressional decision-making process. Thus, while specific regulatory policies may come and go, the form and structure of regulation may be expected to retain familiar characteristics.

A dynamic analysis of the economic and political factors that create or eliminate regulatory policies is clearly necessary to an understanding of the causes and consequences of economic regulations. The evolution of regulatory policies and institutions is beyond the scope of this book. I focus on the broad economic principles underlying the study of the interaction between market participants and regulatory institutions. It is nonetheless important to review briefly some aspects of regulatory change.

Regulation of markets by administrative agencies can be expected to continue in a recognizable form. The delegation of congressional authority to administrative agencies occurs as a selective mechanism for reducing workloads associated with designing and enforcing regulatory programs. Congress can take advantage of management effort and technical expertise of the regulatory bureaucracy while exercising influence through oversight committees. There is, of course, some variation in procedural rules or legislative constraints placed on agencies.[4] Congress can also choose to delegate some law enforcement functions to the courts. Fiorina (1982, 1986) finds that the choice between delegation to agencies versus courts depends on agency discretion and inherent biases as compared to judicial processes.[5] Despite these caveats, congressional delegation to administrative agencies will continue to be an important mechanism of policy implementation. As subsequent discussion will emphasize, administrative rule making and adjudication are principal components of economic regulation. This feature of policy implementation will remain constant even as changes take place in the intent and focus of regulatory legislation.

Deregulation in particular industries does not signal the end of regulation. Regulation reflects the concerns of Congress and its committees, which may create new agencies or refocus the attention of existing agencies through new legislation or oversight activities.[6] In addition, changes in administrations or in the objectives of the president can affect enforcement and other activities of regulatory agencies.[7] Finally, through lawsuits brought by consumer, industry, or other interest groups, regulatory policies can change in response to judicial oversight.

Changes in regulatory policy will reflect the activities of interest groups exerting influence through legislative, executive, and judicial channels and directly through negotiation with administrative agencies. Noll and Owen (1983) express concern that deregulation will be successfully opposed by its entrenched beneficiaries, in their view regulated firms, even if deregulation would improve consumer welfare: "Competition has only a fragile constituency" (p. 161). They observe that consumers and those firms with small market shares are underrepresented in deregulation debates in such disparate areas as telecommunications, radio and television broadcasting, energy, environmental quality, banking, and transportation. In my view both consumer and firm interest groups may obtain benefits or suffer losses as a result of regulation. Political consensus can result in a changing pattern of regulatory policy while maintaining the basic structure of regulatory procedures and activities.

Regulatory policies change in response to economic events that affect the economy as a whole or that are confined to specific industries. Thus, public concern over recession and unemployment has been translated periodically into a removal of regulatory and antitrust restrictions across the board or focused on specific industries, such as transportation, telecommunications, and manufacturing. Similarly, a trade imbalance as experienced in the 1980s leads to relaxation of regulations and antitrust enforcement in industries that may be expected to compete abroad for exports or to compete domestically against imports. For example, antitrust policy may emphasize productive efficiency over market share and permit more large-scale mergers or joint ventures than would otherwise occur. Inflation can increase regulation and antitrust if market power is perceived to be a source of rising prices. Macroeconomic forces can create a political climate in which changes in regulatory policy extend far beyond the initial response to specific events.

A case in point is the stock market collapse of October 19, 1987. The fall in stock prices had a number of immediate effects on regulatory policy. First, anticipated congressional action on removal of banking restrictions imposed by the Glass- Steagall portion of the Banking Act of 1933 was put on hold. Congress had contemplated elimination of provisions that restricted entry of commercial banks into the securities market. At the same time, Congress faced calls from the public and from the agencies themselves for an increase in the powers, budgets, and enforcement activity of the Securities and Exchange Commission (SEC), which regulates stock markets, and the Commodity Futures Trading Commission (CFTC), which regulates futures markets. The Congress also contemplated new legislation to increase regulation of the stock and futures markets. These proposals range from regulation of the use of computerized trading programs by securities brokerage firms to changes in margin requirements in futures markets to stock price controls. Proposals were advanced to create a commission composed of representatives from the Federal Reserve Board (FRB), the Federal Deposit Insurance Corporation (FDIC), the SEC, the CFTC, and other financial regulatory agencies. The commission would oversee regulatory policies toward financial markets.

Regulation of banking and financial markets was imposed in large part as a response to the stock market collapse of 1929. Some deregulation of financial markets occured though the elimination of fixed brokerage fees by the SEC in 1975. Partial deregulation of banking was achieved by the Depository Institutions Deregulation and Monetary Control Act of 1980 and the Garn-St. Germain Depository Institution Act of 1982. The hesitation shown by Congress in its attempt to revise the Glass-Steagall Act demonstrates how decisions to regulate or deregulate industries can react to economic activity. Perhaps the most interesting reaction to the fall in stock prices was an overall decrease in public confidence in the efficiency of markets in general, not just financial markets. Such public perception that markets are unpredictable and chaotic and therefore inefficient as resource allocation mechanisms may create arguments for increased regulatory intervention in markets outside the financial sector.

Regulatory programs can be initiated or expanded in response to such specific economic events as price changes, quantity constraints, environmental hazards, and a product quality or workplace safety problem. Increased regulation of energy markets accompanied energy price increases in the 1970s, while accelerated deregulation of oil and natural gas prices coincided with price reductions in the 1980s. Increased efforts at regulating environmental pollution and use of environmental resources can occur in response to accidental discharges of hazardous air or water pollutants or can result from an accumulation of damages from environmental pollution. A water shortage or "crisis" can be expected to stimulate public concern and policy responses in the form of environmental regulation. A product failure or workplace accident can lead to increased enforcement activities by the Consumer Product Safety Commission (CPSC) or by the Occupational Safety and Health Administration (OSHA).

The creation, alteration, or elimination of regulations or regulatory institutions can occur as a response to new technology. The partial deregulation of telecommunications was stimulated by new transmission technology. New industries or production processes may lead to new regulatory institutions much as regulation of railroads by the Interstate Commerce Commission (ICC) or regulation of telecommunications by the Federal

Communications Commission (FCC) took place in response to changing markets. Similarly, financial market regulations respond to a perception that problems are created by computerized trading. Environmental regulations result from identification of toxic chemicals not previously employed in production. Regulation may address the effects of the use of computers in the marketplace. New regulations may be created to control applications of innovations in biotechnology. Some regulations may be simply the result of fear of new technology. For example, Tolchin and Tolchin (1983, p. 276) argue for increased government regulation to protect society as "technological and scientific advances lead us into unknown worlds with unimaginable dangers."

Deregulation can be accompanied by new regulations with a different focus. Deregulation of air fares and access to airline routes has given way to regulation of product quality and safety. Legislation has been proposed to address complaints regarding departure delays, cancellation of flights, and lost luggage. Further, suggestions to limit the allocation of airport slots for arrival or departure have been put forward. At the same time there has been increased involvement of the Federal Aviation Administration (FAA) in regulating airline safety by monitoring maintenance and pilot training. Thus, rate regulation is replaced by regulation of product characteristics.

Deregulation can often be partial and can be reversed by subsequent government decisions. The breakup of AT&T and the settlement represented by the Modified Final Judgment implemented in 1984 continue to hold out prospects for continued competition and innovation. However, deregulation of telecommunications has been incomplete and has had some unintended consequences. Divestiture of local telephone service and the distinction between local and long-distance service has increased the scope and power of state regulation. Traditional regulation of rates and quality of service by state regulation has been reinforced. Increased involvement of the courts in regulating the activities of telecommunications companies has resulted from the Modified Final Judgment. Periodic review of industry performance has also entailed the participation of the Justice Department. Finally, the FCC has maintained its involvement in setting long-distance rates and local access charges although proposals for rate ceilings have been advanced. The FCC has also given consideration to promotion of competition in long-distance telephone markets. I return to this instance of deregulation in the concluding chapter.

As regulatory policies change and new regulatory institutions form, regulators can be expected to encounter traditional problems. Price regulation must address such issues as measurement of costs, allocation of joint costs, pricing under economies of scale, and cross subsidization. Environmental regulation must deal with monitoring compliance with pollution restrictions and selection of enforcement mechanisms, such as quotas, taxes, and marketable licenses. Product quality and workplace safety regulation must identify the role of government in mitigating the costs of private contractual agreements. Finally, antitrust policy must contend with the inherent difficulty in government promotion of market competition. The basic issues raised here must be addressed regardless of changes in market outcomes and regulatory policy.

Notes

1. Regulation will generally be modeled as a partial equilibrium phenomenon. Regulators may focus attention on the set of industries under their jurisdiction. Many of the consequences of regulatory activity that are anticipated within a partial equilibrium model may prove invalid when examined in a general equilibrium framework. Thus, many of the predictions made about the effects of regulation in a partial equilibrium setting may prove invalid given adjustment of prices or factor movements in other markets. As a *description* of regulatory policies and the regulatory environment, however, the *ceteris paribus* assumptions of partial equilibrium prove to be useful. Accordingly, I shall generally emphasize the partial equilibrium point of view.

2. Walras's discussion of railroad regulation was first developed in a report written in 1875 and subsequently published in 1897. Walras (1936) is searching for a rigorous theoretical analysis to evaluate the conflicting arguments of the Manchester School proponents of laissez-faire and the German academic socialists who favor government control. His proposed state intervention anticipates many modern developments in the economic analysis of regulation. Mill (1848, vol. 1, chapter 9) emphasizes the wasteful duplication of transmission facilities that can occur in utility services. Mill is frequently credited with introducing the concept of natural monopoly; see the surveys of Lowry (1973), Sharkey (1982a), and Hazlett (1985). Walras (1936, p. 211) refers to Mill's discussion. However, it is Walras who develops the connection between natural monopoly and regulation.

3. The trend toward deregulation and regulatory reform has inspired a series of books on the subject, such as Weiss and Klass (1981), Joskow and Schmalensee (1983), Tolchin and Tolchin (1983), Derthick and Quirk (1985), and Moorhouse (1986). These books seek to explain why deregulation occurred and assess prospects for further reform.

4. See Magat, Krupnick, and Harrington (1986).

5. Fiorina (1986) investigates the effects of legislator uncertainty regarding agency implementation of legislation and systematically relates individual legislator preferences for agency or court enforcement to the legislator's distance from the median position and support or opposition to the legislation. See also Fiorina (1982) and Aranson, Gellhorn, and Robinson (1982).

6. The influence of congressional committee control on regulatory agencies is also emphasized by Weingast and Moran (1983) and Weingast (1984).

7. The effects of executive oversight are stressed by Moe (1982) and Chubb (1983).

I REGULATION AND ECONOMIC ANALYSIS

1 Regulation and Economic Efficiency

The study of regulation requires a consistent framework. The purpose of this chapter is to propose a definition of economic regulation. Regulation is defined formally by explicitly incorporating regulatory constraints within a market model. This allows a classification of regulations in terms of restrictions placed on consumers, firms, and the allocation mechanism. Furthermore, I emphasize a positive approach to the institutional and administrative context of regulation. The regulatory process incorporates the strategic interaction of consumers and firms bargaining over regulatory policy and outcomes. Regulation thus involves the study of both regulated market equilibria and administrative process.

The discussion begins, in section 1.1, with an overview of various definitions of regulation in economics, law, and political science. It is emphasized that while each field has much to contribute to a characterization of regulation, traditional definitions have tended to define regulation outside a market setting, often treating the market as a "black box." An alternative definition of regulation in a *market* setting is presented in section 1.2.

Regulations may have purely redistributive effects, or they may affect allocative efficiency. Therefore, in studying regulation, a normative perspective is needed as well. Evaluation of alternative regulatory policies must involve some standard of comparison. I begin by identifying areas of market failure in which government intervention may improve resource allocation. Of course, market failure in itself is *not* a *sufficient* argument for regulation. As Posner (1977) points out, "government failure" can be a costly alternative. There is no lack of examples of markets in which regulation creates a serious misallocation of resources. Entry regulations in transportation (rail, airlines, trucking, buses, taxis) have raised prices and reduced efficiency. Further, there is no doubt that regulation is often employed by government to achieve various objectives, such as income redistribution and promotion of particular industries, without regard to the consequences for economic efficiency. It is well documented that many regulatory programs are primarily redistributive in nature and are the result of political pressure brought to bear by consumer or industry pressure groups acting out of self-interest. However, the failures of regulation need not discourage the study of regulation in the context of welfare economics. By examining optimal regulation, the shortcomings of actual regulations can be better analyzed and understood. If we view market failure as a *necessary* condition for the establishment of regulation, we may identify conditions under which regulation is unlikely to promote economic efficiency.

A comprehensive overview of market failure and regulation is given in sections 1.3–1.5. I identify and define three types of market failure. These are costs that prevent trade (barriers to entry), absence of legal prerequisites for trade (externalities), and the properties of transactions that create inefficiency (internalities). In each case, I consider regulation and alternative social institutions that might improve allocative efficiency.

1.1   Regulation in Economics, Law, and Political Science

Regulation is extensively examined in the fields of economics, law, and political science. Each of these areas clarifies important aspects of this complex subject. The economics literature has traditionally considered regulation of specific industries or groups of industries. Theoretical developments assess the incentive and welfare properties of alternative policy instruments. The law literature studies enforcement, market rules, and administrative procedure. The political science literature focuses on the political and administrative dimensions of policy formulation and implementation. As my survey of definitions in each field indicates, much discussion has focused on administrative aspects of regulation at the expense of analysis of equilibria in regulated markets. The search for a comprehensive definition remains open and can benefit from consideration of the definitions proposed thus far.

1.1.1   Definitions of Regulation in Economics

The study of regulation in economics has mirrored the broad focus of federal and state regulation in the United States. Theoretical and empirical studies of regulation in economics have traditionally examined the control of prices and entry in particular industries, such as utilities (electricity, pipelines), communications, transportation (trucking, railroads, airlines), and finance (banking, insurance, securities). This type of regulation has become known as "old-style" regulation.[1] Reflecting the broad emphasis of industry studies, economic theory in regulation prior to 1970 has emphasized pricing problems encountered in the utility industries. Much attention has been given to pricing with increasing returns to scale technology. Discussion has also centered on selection of prices to assure the utility of a particular rate-of-return on its capital investment and on the related problem of maintaining incentives for cost minimization. The design of rate structures to allocate consumer demand optimally between peak and off-peak periods of time has been applied to electricity and telecommunications.

Regulation as a field of study requires articulation of general principles both to facilitate formal modeling of regulated markets and to suggest testable hypotheses about regulatory institutions and the consequences of regulatory policy. Unfortunately, as a consequence of rapid development and change in the literature, a broad, workable definition of regulation has failed to emerge. Detailed consideration of specific types of regulation or of specific industries is essential for the evaluation and testing of theories regarding the effects of regulation. However, if the literature is fragmented and specialized, there is a danger that researchers in each area independently "reinvent the wheel" many times. This was often the case with early industry studies. An economic theory of regulation must apply in a general way to the various forms of regulation that are observed. With this in mind, a number of important definitions of regulation in the economics literature are reviewed.

Much of the early regulation literature, up to 1970, has as its focus the regulation of public utilities. The major comprehensive work is the classic text of Kahn (1970, 1971). Kahn (1970, p. 2) identifies the public sector and regulated public utilities as two parts of the economy "that the competitive market model obviously does not describe or even purport to describe." Kahn (1970, p. 20) observes that "the essence of regulation is the explicit replacement of competition with governmental orders as the principal institutional device for assuring good performance." Kahn (1970, p. 3) defines public utility regulation by the actions of regulators, "direct governmental prescription of major aspects of their structure and economic performance ... control of entry, price fixing, prescription of quality and conditions of service and the imposition of an obligation to serve all applicants under reasonable conditions...." Kahn's definition is based on regulatory experience in public utility industries and does not generalize easily to encompass extensions of regulation to such areas as environmental pollution and workplace safety. More significantly, the existence of government institutions that provide a context for the competitive market is viewed by Kahn as being at the "periphery" of markets and is not discussed.[2]

The areas of emphasis in Kahn (1970) are regulated monopoly and rate setting, with particular attention to general principles of marginal cost pricing, long- and short- run marginal costs, and price discrimination.

Institutional considerations in Kahn (1971) include input distortions due to rate-of-return regulation (the Averch-Johnson effect), natural monopoly and economies of scale, and competition in regulated industries (electricity, telecommunications, natural gas, trucking, and so on).

Shepherd and Wilcox (1979, p. 267) state that "regulation is what regulators do." Their regulation text divides "public policies toward business" into antitrust, regulation, and public enterprise. Shepherd and Wilcox concentrate on utilities in the energy sector, communications, transportation, and urban services. Their discussion of public enterprise deals primarily with public ownership and control in the utilities sector. The emphasis is on the policymakers and their interaction with the regulated firms.

An important overview of the field is given by Joskow and Noll (1981), who survey regulation of price and entry in competitive and noncompetitive industries and "qualitative" regulation (environmental, health, occupational safety, product quality). They also emphasize the importance of legislative and bureaucratic theories of regulation that focus on the political and administrative process of regulation.

The broadest definition of regulation is supplied by Stigler (1971, p. 3): "As a rule, regulation is acquired by the industry and is designed and operated primarily for its benefit." Regulation for Stigler is the use, by the state, of its "power to coerce." Thus, regulation can take almost any form to achieve the desired aim of an industry, which is ultimately to increase its profitability. Stigler identifies four principal categories of regulations that are demanded by industry and supplied by the state: direct subsidies of money, control of new entry, policies that promote complementary goods and discourage substitutes, and control of prices. Elsewhere, Stigler (1981) broadens his definition still further to cover "the entire interface of public- private relations," including not only "such old-fashioned fields as public utilities and antitrust policy" but also "public interventions in the resources markets," money raising and disbursement, "public interventions in the production, sale, or purchase of goods and services," as well as legal institutions.[3] In the sense of setting a limit or a boundary, the foregoing definition is overly general for our purposes. Stigler (1981) emphasizes that a theory about the origins of regulation is required before regulation can be properly understood.[4] I return to theories of the origins of regulation in the next chapter.

Regulation economists have also examined those agencies primarily responsible for enforcement of antitrust statutes, the Antitrust Division of the Department of Justice and the Federal Trade Commission (FTC). These studies have employed the methods of industrial organization to examine the effects of antitrust policy on market structure and performance.

Since the founding of the Environmental Protection Agency (EPA) in 1970, emphasis in regulation has shifted in part to regulation of environmental quality, product safety and workplace safety. A change is observed in regulation texts that begin to emphasize "new wave" or "social regulation" applied across industries.[5] A large literature on environmental regulation and policy has developed; see Baumol and Oates (1975, 1979). A large literature on product and workplace safety is forming as well; see Viscusi (1979, 1983). These new areas of interest have significantly broadened the theoretical background in regulation to include welfare economics, public finance, and decision making under uncertainty, and will be reflected in my discussion.

1.1.2 Definitions of Regulation in Law

The study of regulation is based on an elaboration of the characteristics and consequences of alternative forms of government intervention in markets. Government regulation of economic activity involves both *general rules* of market behavior and *specific actions* to achieve short-term policy objectives. Hayek (1960, pp. 220–221) observes that the opposition to government intervention voiced by Adam Smith or John Stuart Mill applied particularly to the "exercise of the coercive power of government which was not regular enforcement of the general law and which was designed to achieve some specific purpose."[6] Regulation involves study of both general market rules and discretionary policy actions.

Markets are a social convention. Rather than being a natural phenomenon, the "invisible hand" of Adam Smith depends on the "visible arm" of the law that regulates exchange. Rules of exchange generally derive from established customs and standard practices, and from the common law. Government regulation of markets provides an additional and at times complementary set of rules that *constrain or enhance* the range of available transactions.

The dependence of orderly market transactions on legal rules is sometimes taken for granted by economists. A main theme in Hayek's *Law, Legislation and Liberty* (1973, vol. 1, p. 4) is that "the rules of just conduct which the lawyer studies serve a kind of order of the character of which the lawyer is largely ignorant; and that this order is studied chiefly by the economist who in turn is similarly ignorant of the character of the rules of conduct on which the order that he studies rests." The study of regulated markets must begin with the study of market rules, a subject at the nexus of law and economics. By studying the *institutional* framework within which markets operate, we may better describe the effects of particular regulatory regimes. Further, we may assess whether regulation can improve market allocations and determine what forms regulation should take.

It is often asserted that market transactions and government regulation of markets constitute alternative methods of resource allocation. This is only true if we restrict regulation to mean direct participation by the government in allocation of resources. This need not be the only form of regulation. In some cases, government regulation may even provide a less costly basis for exchange than the common law. In addressing the problems encountered by market participants, regulation need not be restricted to traditional forms of command and control. Administrative regulation can borrow from the form and procedures of the common law. Regulation may establish rules that allow market-type allocation mechanisms to operate. Further, regulatory agencies may establish a forum where particular rights are enforced and precedents are established in such a way as to avoid specification of particular outcomes or allocations. The argument for regulation then must involve a demonstration that public regulation provides a set of rules that involve lower administration costs and result in a more efficient allocation of resources than judicially administered rules.

An important set of questions in regulation concerns whether any intervention in contractual arrangements is necessary. Private negotiation should yield efficient allocations if individual agents choose to trade voluntarily. Further, contract formation occurs in the context of the common law of contracts, property, and torts. Any assessment of the need for regulatory institutions must take into account alternative legal institutions. For example, market allocations achieved through regulation of product or workplace safety must be compared to those market allocations that would be observed given alternative liability rules. Thus, a major aspect of regulation involves the study of alternative legal institutions.

Another crucial issue in regulation is identification of the means of *enforcing* general rules and specific restrictions. Many of these problems have been addressed in the law and economics literature. An important question is whether rules should be enforced through public or private efforts. A role for administrative regulation may be identified given positive net benefits from public enforcement.

The common law of contracts, tort, and property is generally privately enforced. As Landes and Posner (1975, p. 31) observe, "The state's role is limited to furnishing a court system." Criminal laws are mostly enforced publicly. Antitrust represents an interesting mix of public and private enforcement. The treble-damages penalty provides incentives for private enforcement. Regulatory agencies rely on private complaints or reports of wrongdoing in obtaining information about violations of product quality standards or workplace safety rules. Private provision of information to agencies represents a combination of private and public enforcement efforts.

There is a growing literature on public versus private law enforcement. In an important article, Becker and Stigler (1974) argue that competitive private enforcement can achieve optimal enforcement through incentives generated by fines.[7] Landes and Posner (1975) debate this result by noting that public enforcement may be achieved at lower cost by raising fines above the level of external damages and lowering the probability of apprehension. Given higher fines, however, the private sector would increase the resources devoted to enforcement thus leading to inefficient overinvestment. Polinsky (1980) notes that criminal violations may entail external damages. In this case, private enforcement may lead to underinvestment because of the limited damages that can be collected from violators. Polinsky shows that competitive private enforcement generally leads to less enforcement than public enforcement. Thus, even if public enforcement has a cost disadvantage it may be socially preferable.

In addition to the public good aspects of law enforcement, economies of scale may be present. The legal costs of suit may greatly exceed the damages suffered by a single plaintiff, although total damages across plaintiffs are larger than the potential legal costs of a suit. Posner (1977, p. 449) states that a class action suit aggregates small claims and yields economies of scale in litigation. However, Posner notes that if damages to any individual plaintiff are small and there are many plaintiffs, the costs of compensating individual plaintiffs may be prohibitive. If the class action suit is not filed, however, then society is deprived of the benefits that derive from the deterrent effects of the fine imposed on the violator.

The administrative agency performs the function of aggregating individual claims and imposing punitive damages by responding to complaints from individual consumers. The complaints received need not be contemporaneous, as is necessary for a class action suit, but may be observed over a period of time. Further, the agency can initiate its own investigation based on a small number of complaints. The agency need not accumulate a large amount of complaints before taking action.[8] The public versus private enforcement issue is dependent on whether public or private deterrence of violations is more efficient. By acting on the basis of complaints, an agency may be able to prevent damages from unsafe products before they occur. This system may be less costly than litigation of damages after a large number of violations have occurred. This observation accords with Landes and Posner (1975), who find advantages in public enforcement when the likelihood of detection is less than one.

A significant influence on the economic study of regulation stems from the branch of administrative law concerned with regulation of industry. The law literature and accompanying case histories are essential to understanding the legal framework and evolution of economic regulation. Characterization of feasible actions and regulatory institutions suggests a number of important issues for economists seeking to explain the existence of particular regulations. However, economic analysis should not necessarily be bound by existing institutions or the conceptual framework of law. Rather, economic analysis must be applied to an understanding of the economic impact of regulatory institutions and administrative procedures. Further, the design of efficient institutions and procedures is of interest.

A broad definition of regulation in the law literature is given by Gellhorn and Pierce (1982, pp. 7–8), who state that economic regulation "explicitly substitutes the judgement of regulators for that of either the business or the marketplace." Gellhorn and Pierce (1982) distinguish direct regulation, which is primarily *prescriptive*, from legal restrictions, which are *proscriptive*, noting that "government regulation of industry is but one of many types of legal control on the uses of private economic power."[9] The study of regulation in law focuses primarily on regulatory polices that apply to utilities, particularly rate making, quality of service, and entry restrictions; see Gellhorn and Pierce (1982).

Breyer (1982) implicitly defines classical regulation by emphasizing six principal categories: (1) *cost of service rate making*, which refers to prices chosen to assure the regulated firm of a suitable or "fair" rate of return; (2)

historically based price regulation, under which price controls are calculated on the basis of original costs and often applied across industries; (3) *allocation under a public interest standard,* which entails awarding licenses or the "right to serve" based on a set of market entry criteria rather than on competitive bidding; (4) *standard setting,* which requires promulgation and enforcement of requirements governing environmental pollution, product quality, or workplace safety; (5) *historically based allocation,* which involves allocation of scarce resources based upon previous usage rather than market competition; and (6) *individualized screening,* under which new products (pharmaceuticals, food additives) or new entrants must meet what are often complex technical or scientific criteria applied "on a case-by-case basis."

Breyer (1982, chapter 8) also considers *alternatives* to classical regulation. These include legal institutions, such as antitrust law and tort liability rules, taxes, such as effluent charges in environmental regulation, and allocation of scarce resources through marketable permits or licenses. Breyer (1982, pp. 177–181) also identifies *bargaining* between interest groups as an alternative to classical regulation particularly when decentralization of decision making and of enforcement are desired. My analysis differs from that of Breyer in that I view bargaining between interest groups as a pervasive feature of existing regulatory procedures and institutions.

Heffron (1983) distinguishes three categories of regulation: economic, social, and subsidiary.[10] For Heffron, economic regulation covers market aspects of industry behavior (rates, quality and quantity of service, competitive practices). Social regulation is directed at unsafe or unhealthy products and harmful by-products of the production process. Finally, subsidiary regulation includes regulations associated with implementing various social and benefit programs (Social Security, Medicare, Medicaid, food stamps, veterans' benefit programs). Examples of regulations in this area include restrictions on the health care industry (physicians, hospitals, nursing homes, pharmacies).

A focus of legal discussion is on administrative procedure and judicial controls on agency actions. The administrative process is subject to controls from the legislative branch, the executive branch, and the judiciary. Regulatory agencies must operate within the legal framework of their authorizing statutes and the Federal Administrative Procedure Act. In addition, agencies follow established agency procedures and budget restrictions. The legal and administrative context of regulation has stimulated economic studies of the regulatory process itself. Joskow (1972, 1974) studies the regulatory process in public utility price regulation. Joskow (1972) presents an empirical study in which the regulatory commission's choice of an allowed rate of return depends on the presentations of regulated firms and intervenors. Owen and Braeutigam (1978) focus on the administrative process itself, which they refer to as "the regulation game." They advance and defend two hypotheses. First, the administrative process may be thought of as "a strategic game in which regulated entities and other interested parties struggle to achieve economic rewards." Second, it is asserted that "one major purpose of regulation is to protect economic agents—consumers and firms alike—from too-sudden changes in their economic environment. Thus, for Owen and Braeutigam, the purpose and definition of regulation are closely linked to administrative process. This theme carries over to Noll and Owen (1983, p. 27), who examine the determination of regulatory policy "in the context of organized persuasive activity by competing interest groups." The formal regulatory procedure followed by federal agencies is identified by Noll and Owen as a major factor in explaining observed regulations. Many regulations are seen as the result of strategic manipulation of the regulatory process by industry interest groups. The role of the administrative process in the study of regulation is taken up in chapter 2.

1.1.3   Definitions of Regulation in Political Science

The political science literature stresses the political and administrative context of regulatory decision making. Public input into the regulatory process occurs through lobbying and congressional decision making, which establishes and oversees regulatory agency activity. Further public negotiation occurs in the implementation of regulatory policy.

An important treatise on regulation in political science is Mitnick (1980). Noting that "the concept of regulation is not often defined," Mitnick (1980, p. 7) proposes the following definition: "Regulation is the public administrative policing of a private activity with respect to a rule prescribed in the public interest." The definition is striking in that it seems to carry the controversial assumption that rules are made in the "public interest." This is not the case at all, for in political science the term public interest is broadly defined. Mitnick (1980) surveys the literature and presents a general "typology" of public interest definitions, which range from satisfaction of dictatorial preferences to Pareto optimality to pluralistic aggregation of preferences. Mitnick (1980, p. 271) also allows for determination of the public interest by "group conflict marked perhaps by force or deception, and perhaps characterized by struggle over control of access to policy-determining resources or positions." Thus, the list of definitions of public interest is sufficiently general to encompass both welfare maximization and "capture" theories of regulation. Schubert (1960), as discussed in Mitnick (1980), classifies definitions of the public interest into three categories: "rationalist" (government actions that satisfy a majority of voters), "idealist" (government actions that satisfy the regulator's conscience), and "realist" (where regulators arbitrate conflicting interests). For Mitnick and others, government regulators act as *agents* with consumers or interest groups as their *principal*; see also Goldberg (1976). Mitnick (1980) stresses that justification of regulation by public interest arguments is often purely rhetorical, the object being to give the appearance of a consensus to legislative, administrative and judicial decision making, even when special favors are being granted.

An important aspect of regulation that is given considerable attention in political science is the formulation and implementation of policy.[11] Economists have much to learn in this area. The implementation process is perhaps best summed up by Ripley and Franklin (1986, p. 1): "Bargaining—at the heart of American politics—occurs during implementation." They emphasize that in the United States, government rarely involves command and control.[12] Rather, interest groups participate at each level of policy implementation, particularly through the regulatory agencies.[13] Ripley and Franklin (1986) divide regulatory policies into those that are "competitive" and those that are "protective." The former refer to allocation of franchises or the right to serve by a government agency; the latter "are designed to protect the public by setting the conditions under which various private activities can occur." In both areas, they observe extensive intervention and bargaining in the implementation of regulatory policy.

Meier (1985) defines regulation as "any attempt by the government to control the behavior of citizens, corporations, or subgovernments," and lists price regulation, franchising, standard setting, direct allocation of resources, provision of subsidies and the promotion of fair competition. He emphasizes a multidisciplinary approach that includes economics, law, history, and political science. Meier (1985, p. 8) states that "above all, however, regulation is a political process involving political actors seeking political ends." Meier defines a regulatory *subsystem* consisting of government bureaus, congressional committees, and interest groups.[14] He then poses the interesting question of "whether or not the regulatory bureaucracy dominates the subsystem or if the bureaucracy is reduced to a more passive role of mediating disputes among the active interests." Meier concludes that either outcome may be observed and assigns weight to the resources of the regulatory bureaucracy.

The political science literature can make an important contribution to economic analysis of regulation particularly through its emphasis on *bargaining* between interest groups. The process of policy formation may be characterized in terms of the economic impacts of alternative regulatory programs on market participants. Such a framework would require specification of the objective functions of consumers and firms, the effects of alternative market equilibria on resource allocation, and the relation between regulatory policy and market outcomes. This is the agenda for the economic study of regulation.

1.2   Regulation and Market Transactions

The preceding discussion of regulation in economics, law, and political science has emphasized regulatory policymaking and implementation, administrative process, and legal rules. While it is important to incorporate these aspects of regulation in a general definition, we must be careful not to treat the market as an autonomous mechanism. Accordingly, I broaden the definition of regulation by considering market allocation of resources and decision making by consumers and firms, and the interaction of consumers and firms through regulatory institutions.

1.2.1   What Is Regulated?

My analysis of regulation is based on the following axiom: Every regulatory action that constrains one side of a market has an equal and opposite effect on the other side of the market. A maximum price limit placed on what firms can charge is at once a maximum price that consumers may pay. A minimum quality constraint on which goods can be sold is at once a minimum quality constraint on which goods can be purchased. Any regulation that effectively constrains consumer or firm choices will indirectly affect the market equilibrium. These regulations limit the range of potential market transactions. Other regulations directly interfere with the market

allocation mechanism, such as market-wide price controls. An additional
set of regulations may enhance the range of potential market transactions.
I now give some examples that stress the parallel effects of regulation on
both sides of the market.

Price controls constrain market clearing price adjustment and price
negotiations between buyers and sellers. Price ceilings have existed for
natural resources and other commodities, and price floors for labor
are created by the minimum wage. Price regulations constitute the most
significant form of interference in the market. As noted in a 1923 court
ruling against a minimum wage law, wages are the "heart of the contract."[15] Controlling the price a firm can charge also limits the competitive
bidding opportunities available to consumers. An effective price floor constrains market demand and creates incentives for excess supply of the good.

Price floors that are imposed by law require extensive enforcement costs
to restrict supply or to avoid competitive discounts by suppliers. Price
floors maintained by government subsidies, such as the U.S. agricultural
price support program, entail either costly purchase and storage of excess
supply or subsidies to suppliers and discounts to consumers. Maintenance
of price supports above costs creates incentives for entry, thus increasing
the total subsidies. In the absence of additional entry restrictions, the cost
of price supports to the government continues to increase. Price supports
entail welfare costs equal to the net gains-from-trade forgone due to departure from the market equilibrium output. The well-known allocative effects
of price floors are illustrated in figure 1.2.1 were $\bar{p}$ denotes the price

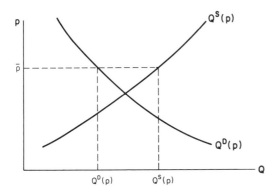

Figure 1.2.1
Price floor.

floor and $Q^D(p)$, $Q^S(p)$ are supply and demand. Conversely, a price ceiling reduces the rationing function of prices on market demand and reduces incentives for increased supply. Price ceilings, such as rent controls, create familiar problems of excess demand, reduction in quantity supplied, black markets, deterioration in product quality, costly queuing, or discriminatory rationing mechanisms.

Rate setting in the utility and transportation sectors constitutes another form of price regulation. Regulation of the *rate structure*, the prices charged by regulated firms for a range of different products or services, may involve both price ceilings and price floors. Such price regulations involve more than wealth transfers across customer classes or between customers and the firm. The prices chosen also affect allocative efficiency by determining the relative quantities of outputs produced by the regulated firm. Similarly, restrictions imposed by antitrust law on firm pricing policies, such as discriminatory pricing and quantity discounts, eliminate the price-quantity options available to buyers as well and alter market equilibrium prices and outputs.

Entry restrictions, applied to the number of firms entering a market or to professionals entering an occupation, limit contractual opportunities for buyers and sellers. In the case of firm entry, consumers are limited in the number of firms from which they can purchase commodities. Firms are limited in terms of markets they may enter and in terms of specific consumers with whom they may contract. Entry restrictions effectively limit the sets of commodities that firms may supply. Also, government entry barriers limit the potential employers available to workers. In the case of occupational entry barriers, firms and consumers are limited in terms of available contracts for labor services. State certification of lawyers, doctors, accountants, pharmacists, architects, and so on limits both the professionals themselves and their potential employers.[16]

Requirements that a firm serve a minimum or maximum number of consumers limit market exchange possibilities. Regulations that impose an *obligation to serve* do not really increase the range of contractual options available to consumers and firms. Rather, they restrict firms to offering those contracts that involve interaction with all potential consumers. Groups of consumers are restricted in their ability to contract exclusively with a single firm. Although it is true that consumers may not be excluded by firms from making a purchase, "common carrier" regulations restrict the contractual alternatives.

Constraints placed on *product characteristics*, such as product quality, quantity, durability, and safety, serve to limit the range of products available to consumers as well as the range of products that may be produced by firms. Thus, constraints on product characteristics limit the range of different goods for which contracts between consumers and firms may be created. The characteristics of a product are as much the "heart of the contract" as the price of the contract. In labor markets, the certification that accompanies occupational licensing restricts quality, however defined, and thus restricts the types of labor that may be employed by consumers and firms. Regulations limiting hours of work per week clearly restrict the quantity dimension of exchange.[17] Exchange is further restricted by regulations requiring complementary products to be provided as a bundle. For example, rules calling for disclosure of product performance, ingredients, or other characteristics require a firm to bundle the product with a particular amount of costly information. This restricts the opportunities of consumers to purchase, and firms to supply, product bundles with less or no accompanying information. If advertising is viewed as a product characteristic, advertising regulations specify the range of product/advertising bundles that may be exchanged.

Regulation of firm *inputs* or *technology* affects the range of available transactions on both input and output markets. On the input market, restrictions on firm inputs or technology, such as those placed on utilities under the Fuel Use Act, affect exchanges between firms and the suppliers of the regulated inputs as well as complementary inputs. On the output market, input or technology restrictions placed on firms function very much like restrictions on product characteristics. Consumers are not able to purchase products containing the restricted inputs or produced using restricted technologies, and firms are not able to supply these products.

Workplace health and safety regulations are also regulations of complementary goods. Restrictions on the workplace environment require workers to offer particular bundles of labor supply characteristics; in particular, the willingness to be exposed to health or safety risks may be constrained. The employer is restricted to particular contracts in which the nature of the various modes of payment (for example, wages versus quality of the work environment) satisfies health and safety regulations. By restricting variation in health and safety, regulations restrict the compensating variation of wage payments in labor contracts.

An example of regulations that may enhance the range of contractual options are *environmental regulations* that create marketable property rights (through emission licenses) where property rights were previously not clearly defined. Without well-defined property rights assigned to either polluter or pollutee, the contractual alternatives of the parties may be constrained. Similar issues arise in connection with other common property resources, such as fishery stocks, game animals, and common pools of oil and natural gas. Market failure may be remedied by creation of new contractual opportunities. Effluent permits may be traded between firms or even purchased by consumer groups or municipalities who choose not to exercise the pollution rights.[18] Regulation of resource extraction in instances of common pool problems, such as fisheries and oil and natural gas extraction, may create transferable property rights and thus enhance the range of available contracts. Patents create property rights that provide incentives for innovative effort and investment. Patents may enhance market opportunities by allowing licensing of product or process innovations.

Contract rules may enhance contractual opportunities by reducing the costs of contract formation and by the provision of remedies for contract breach. Enforcement of contractual promises may allow contractual agreements that would not otherwise occur. This will enhance allocative efficiency by allowing the parties to the contract to capture gains-from-trade. Contracts often involve risk sharing and allow increased investment commitments.

1.2.2 Definitions

I begin by defining regulations and then turn to consideration of the regulatory process. To distinguish between regulation and law, I restrict regulations to those general rules and specific actions imposed on markets by administrative agencies. An *administrative agency* refers to a government unit established by the legislature to carry out policy objectives. In formal models of the economy, such as the Arrow-Debreu model,[19] markets are defined by the exchange of commodities at various prices between two types of economic agents, consumers and firms. Consumers are defined by their preferences, initial endowments of commodities, and ownership shares of firms. Consumers choose to demand or supply commodities and labor by choosing their most preferred commodity bundle given market prices.

Firms are defined by their technology as represented by production possibilities. Firms choose inputs and outputs to maximize profits. Market equilibrium prices are prices that equate total consumer demand with total firm supply.

Within this framework, three types of regulations may be identified following my earlier discussion. First, regulations may directly interfere with the market allocation mechanism. This includes price regulations, property rights regulations, and contract rules. In some markets, the price system may be replaced entirely or in part by administrative allocation of commodities, such as administered pricing for a public enterprise. Second, regulations may affect the market equilibrium through the decisions of consumers. A consumer's budget set is shifted by a tax, subsidy, or other transfer. Direct regulation of consumer choices exist as well in the form of emissions limits on automobile exhaust and insurance purchase requirements. Third, regulations may affect the market equilibrium through firm decisions. This type of constraint includes restrictions placed upon product characteristics, such as quality, durability, and safety. Restrictions on the inputs, outputs, or technology of firms results in a constraint on the firm's production set. For example, environmental regulations involve input constraints (use of low-sulfur fuel oil), output constraints (pollution quotas), and technological constraints (best available technology requirements for pollution abatement). Entry regulations may also be modeled in this way. Taxes and subsidies will affect the profit maximizing decisions of firms and their resulting output supply and input demand. To summarize the discussion, *regulations* are defined as follows.

Definition 1.2.1 *Regulations* are general rules or specific actions imposed by administrative agencies that interfere directly with the market allocation mechanism or indirectly by altering consumer and firm demand and supply decisions.

A regulator is assumed to have a set of available actions that reflects legal or procedural constraints on his activities, such as the Administrative Procedures Act (see chapter 2). This set of actions may be referred to as the *policy set.*[20] The regulator has an initial endowment of resources, which may include staff, plant, and equipment, as well as the agency budget. Various actions in the policy set may entail administrative costs, such as those of formulating and communicating rules and then monitoring and enforcing compliance. The costs of alternative policies will yield an agency *budget set* although in practice this aspect of regulation may be the most difficult to model. The agency budget set is a subset of the agency's policy set.

Next I turn to a definition of the *regulatory process*. One approach is to assume that regulatory agencies select actions from their budget set to satisfy a rule of thumb or to maximize the agency's utility function. This approach is not difficult to characterize since it is the standard social planner model used in many economic analyses.[21] By properly specifying the regulator's preferences, we may select almost any outcome for a regulated market. This "command-and-control" approach is appealing and useful from the modeling standpoint. For now, however, I also wish to give a *positive* characterization of the regulatory process. As emphasized above, creation and implementation of regulations involves extensive public negotiation. While the preferences of the regulatory bureaucracy may play a role, I choose to view the regulatory agency as an arbiter that establishes the rules of negotiation and mediates between consumer and firm interest groups.

Game theory is very useful for describing and modeling the regulatory process. The *players* in the regulatory process are primarily the consumers and firms in the regulated markets. I generally treat regulatory agencies as arbiters or as rule makers for the game rather than as participants. While it might be fruitful to consider regulatory agencies or members of the regulatory bureaucracy as players pursuing specific objectives, I do not choose to do so. This issue is addressed in the next chapter. My object is to focus on the behavior of market participants. I may also wish to consider the participation of interest groups in the regulatory process. An *interest group* refers to a group of consumers and firms that approaches the regulatory agency with a common objective. When interest groups are represented, they are treated as a single player. For convenience, imagine that an interest group represents exclusively either consumer interests or industry interests, although in reality many interest groups have both consumers and firms as supporters. Furthermore, I treat the consumer interest group as a representative consumer and the industry interest group as a representative firm. This approach is used in chapters 10–15. Thus, the players in the game involving interest groups are again simply consumers and firms.

It is reasonable to assume that consumers and firms pursue their self-interest not only in the marketplace but in their interaction with government if government decisions affect their economic well-being. Consumers attempt to obtain preferred bundles of commodities and firms seek to maximize profits. Thus, the *objective functions* of consumers and firms in the regulation game are essentially the same as in standard market models.

The potential actions or *strategies* of players in the regulation game include their actions in the marketplace. For consumers, this refers to demands, and for firms this refers to pricing, production, advertising, research and development, and other activities. The interaction between consumers and firms outside the market, through regulatory agencies, raises the possibility of additional actions. Consumers and firms are presumed to influence regulatory outcomes through communication with the regulatory agency. Communication may take the form of complaints, promises, threats, provision of market data and other information, and testimony at public hearings.

A *game* is defined by the set of players, their objective functions, available strategies, and the set of rules.[22] The regulatory process is viewed here as a game played by the consumers and firms in the regulated market. The set of rules may be given exogenously, as with legal restrictions, or specified by regulatory agency. The regulatory process can be described as a cooperative or noncooperative game, although I shall stress the cooperative aspects. Noncooperative games assume that players act independently without preplay communication. Cooperative games allow for exchange of information and the formation of coalitions. These properties are useful for modeling administrative aspects of regulation; see chapter 2. The preceding discussion is summarized by a definition.

Definition 1.2.2   The *regulatory process* is a game defined by the set of consumers and firms in the regulated market, consumer preferences and firm technologies, available strategies, and the set of rules.

The definition of the regulatory process is meant to be sufficiently restrictive to allow modeling of administrative regulation. The outcome of the regulatory process will determine both what regulations are imposed on the market and what allocation of resources obtains. The regulatory process thus involves both selection of administrative constraints and market equilibrium.

The preceding definitions of *regulations* and the *regulatory process* serve as building blocks for a definition of regulation.

Definition 1.2.3   The field of *regulation* is the study of the regulatory process and of resulting market equilibria in the presence of regulations.

The definition is sufficiently general to accommodate a broad class of market regulations, including price regulation, environmental regulation, and product quality regulation. The determination of regulatory policy through interaction by coalitions of consumers and firms allows regulatory policies that are redistributive in nature or that are directed at eliminating market failure. It should be noted that policies aimed at market failure often turn out to be simply income redistribution programs. I now turn to an analysis of market failure as a basis for normative analysis of regulation, starting each section with a definition of each form of market failure.

1.3   Barriers to Entry

Market power resulting in allocative inefficiency and monopoly rents has traditionally been offered as justification for price regulation and anti-trust.[23] Determination of what constitutes market power is another matter. Concentration of market share in the hands of a few firms and inelasticity of market demand are imperfect indicators of market power. A more promising approach is a determination of market characteristics that may impede competition. The presence of barriers to entry may yield market power for established firms. Market failure stemming from barriers to entry may call for government intervention to remove the barrier to entry or to mitigate its consequences for resource allocation.

1.3.1   A Definition

Identifying a potential task for regulation requires careful definition of what constitutes an entry barrier. An important definition given by Stigler (1968, p. 67) is paraphrased here; see also Baumol and Willig (1981).

Definition 1.3.1 (Stigler)   A *barrier to entry* into a market is a cost of production for an entrant that is not incurred by already established firms.

The major production costs imposed on entrants but not on incumbents are nonrecoverable, market-specific costs, which are referred to as *sunk* costs. It is by incurring these costs that an entrant becomes an established firm. Baumol and Willig (1981, p. 418) state that "the need to sink costs can be a barrier to entry." They observe that sunk costs are viewed by entrants as an incremental cost, and therefore an incremental risk, which must be covered by postentry revenues. The established firm in its current and future decisions does not take into account expenditures that have already been incurred. The extent to which sunk costs create monopoly rents and resource misallocation is not fully understood and is a topic of active research.[24]

A number of barriers to entry are imposed by the government. Stigler (1968) refers to licences, such as taxi medallions, as absolute barriers to entry. Many public utilities are franchises with government regulation of new entry. It would be illogical, however, to consider government-created entry barriers as a basis for recommending rate regulation. Elimination of monopoly rents and resource misallocation from government-created entry barriers can be achieved most easily by permitting new entry. Exclusive resource ownership is certainly an absolute entry barrier, although this situation is unlikely to be observed if new discoveries of the resource are feasible. A special government-created entry barrier is a patent. The monopoly rents accruing to a patent owner provide incentives to innovate while finite patent lives mitigate allocative inefficiency; see Stigler (1968, pp. 123–125).

Bain (1956) defines the major types of barriers to entry as scale economies, product differentiation, and absolute cost advantages. Strictly speaking, these do not satisfy the definition of entry barriers given here. The theory of contestable markets of Baumol, Panzar, and Willig (1982), and a great body of research in industrial organization suggests that economies of scale, and particularly fixed costs, are not barriers to entry. In the contestable markets setting, the productive technology is freely available to potential entrants. With costless entry and exit, firms may enter markets in which profit opportunities exist. The presence of scale economies need not constitute a source of market power. Competition between established firms and the possibility of new entry serve to reduce or eliminate monopoly rents. Scale economies may exacerbate the effects of sunk costs on entry deterrence according to Baumol and Willig (1981), but it is the sunk costs that erect the barrier.

Product differentiation need not constitute an entry barrier. Differences in products may yield monopoly rents, but these rents may create incentive for new product innovations. Furthermore, differences in products may actually facilitate entry since an entrant has available the means to distinguish his own product through advertising, labeling, and so on. An

entrant may compete with an incumbent's product by offering improvements in quality, durability, safety, or other product characteristics, or by
offering more desirable quality-price combinations. The entrant's profit-
maximizing strategy may involve offering products that are similar or very
different from the incumbent. Entry may be deterred if a sufficient variety
of brands already exists and if the establishment of new brands entails
substantial nonrecoverable costs. The problem is, however, the *sunk costs*
of creating brands, not product differentiation itself.

While an absolute cost advantage for incumbent firms will generally
preclude entry, this is not a justification for regulation. The cost advantage
may be due to process innovation or productive efficiency. The rents from
a cost advantage reward a firm for lowering its costs. An entrant may
potentially lower its costs and enter the market as well.

1.3.2   Scale Economies and Regulation

The presence of economies of scale and the characteristics of products as
public goods are frequently given as justification for government intervention in the market. Demonstrations of the existence and optimality of
market equilibria in theoretical market models, such as the Arrow-Debreu
model of general equilibrium, assume that technology exhibits nonincreasing returns to scale, that commodities are perfectly divisible, and that all
goods are private goods. In that setting, economies of scale or public goods
may preclude achievement of a Pareto optimal allocation. The market
equilibrium may not be well-defined.

Given increasing returns to scale for single goods or cost complementarities across goods, there are cost gains from consolidation of production in a single firm. Regulation is often proposed as a means of capturing
the gains from scale economies while mitigating monopoly rents accruing
to a single producer. This is the justification often given for regulation
of "natural monopolies" in electricity, telecommunications, and pipeline
transmission. Regulation has two principal components. First, entry restrictions are imposed to prevent "excessive entry" of new firms. Then, price
controls are imposed to eliminate the monopoly rents created by the entry
barriers.

To evaluate this type of regulation we need to determine whether competitive entry is excessive[25] under increasing returns to scale. This question
remains open. For example, excessive entry is observed in a Cournot model
by von Weizsäcker (1980a, b). With Bertrand-type price competition,

the contestable markets literature shows that in some cases a natural monopoly can be sustained against entry; see Baumol, Panzar, and Willig (1982).

A related issue in rate regulation is that marginal or incremental cost pricing does not cover costs in the presence of economies of scale. In the absence of subsidies, market allocations will not be optimal. As Baumol (1979a) observes, nonoptimal resource allocations in the presence of scale economies is "the price we must pay for a price system."

Restriction of entry to achieve the cost gains from natural monopoly need not entail price regulation. Demsetz (1968) suggests replacement of utility rate regulation by a franchise auction. In the single-product case, competitive entry yields average cost pricing, as in an unregulated contestable market. A deeper problem identified by Williamson (1976) is that with variable quality, the franchise auction may not yield the optimal mix of price and quality.

A major portion of this book, Part II, is devoted to pricing under economies of scale. It is argued that while free entry competition is effective in eliminating monopoly rents, in a multiproduct setting free entry may preclude those relative prices associated with the highest feasible social welfare. Alternative methods of pricing given economies of scale are analyzed. The aim of the discussion is to design market-type mechanisms for franchise allocation. A franchise confers on a firm the right to serve a particular market. By announcing *general rules*, a regulator may establish a *franchise competition* in which firms offer service contracts to groups of consumers. Monopoly rents may be eliminated by competition for franchises. Furthermore, by placing restrictions on the form of the price schedules firms may offer, regulators may achieve desired pricing policies without exercising direct control over rates.

1.3.3 Sunk Costs and Regulation

In the absence of sunk costs, the franchise allocation mechanism may be used repeatedly to assure efficient performance in a market characterized by economies of scale. However, given sunk costs, a franchise system cannot be employed to monitor and enforce desired performance of firms in the market. In this case, traditional forms of rate regulation may be required.

Sunk costs, such as irreversible capital investment and costs of adjustment, impede the ability of economic agents to adapt to changing market conditions. The effects of sunk costs are increased by unforeseen changes in the state of the world. The market response to sunk cost and attendant risks is the long-term contract. Long-term contracts provide for risk sharing and may thus permit an increase in irreversible capital. The gains from this increase in productive investment create incentives for the formation of long-term contractual relations. The market determines the form or terms of the contract, the number of contractual agreements, and the price of each contract. However, there are elements of contractual exchange that are not fully described by the model of market equilibria. These elements are contract enforcement and negotiation of terms.

In market models such as that of Arrow and Debreu, exchange of a commodity bundle at some date for a bundle at a future date differs little from contemporaneous transactions. Thus, contracts in the Arrow-Debreu model are characterized by perfect enforcement. Further, the characteristics of the bundles that are exchanged are known, so that observation and monitoring of performance are feasible. Further, in the presence of uncertainty, contracts are specified for all contingencies. Thus, the need for renegotiation of contract terms does not arise. Finally, the presence of market power is an important factor in contract negotiation between small numbers of economic agents.

Actual contracts involve incomplete specification of contingencies due to the costs of negotiation and identifying potential states of the world. The bargaining process is often characterized by asymmetric information. Performance of contractual specifications may be imperfectly observed. Accordingly, long-term contracts involve general institutions that deal with broadly defined contingencies. Damage penalties exist for breach of contract. Verification procedures, such as auditing, are often specified. Provisions for renegotiation of terms in the presence of unforeseen changes in the costs of production or in opportunity costs for the parties may be present. The common law of contracts provides for compensation or discharge of the contract if contract obligations are not carried out by one of the parties.

Judging by the large number of long-term contracts, sunk costs are a common phenomenon. In industry, investment may be market- or transaction- specific. The investment may be embodied in equipment that is suited for a specific purpose. The firm may acquire knowledge needed to perform a specific task. Expenditures may be undertaken to produce a specific output for a particular customer. Long-term contracts exist that specify prices, product characteristics, dates by which performance is to be achieved, and various rewards or penalties. Workers may also undertake irreversible expenditures for training in a particular field. Employment contracts of some fixed duration are often connected with specific human capital investment.

Many of the problems associated with the negotiation and enforcement of long-term contracts are present in the regulation of industry. Goldberg (1976) defines "administered contracts" as contracts involving both an ongoing relationship and the existence of intermediate agents in negotiation and administration of the contract. Goldberg (1976, p. 429) views regulation as an "implicit contract between the regulated firm(s) and the regulatory agency serving as the collective contract" between the firms and their customers. Goldberg singles out protection of the firms' right to serve as allowing investment in long-lived specialized capital equipment and protection of the consumer's right to be served as allowing consumer investments that rely on supplier performance. Thus, protection of sunk investment provides a justification for these regulatory objectives. Further, monitoring contractual performance and the prevention of contractual holdup leads regulators to monitor performance and to administer the contract through such devices as cost-based pricing. Goldberg suggests that the inefficiencies observed in regulation will also be observed with allocation under privately administered long-term contracts.

The view of regulation as an administered contract need not rely on the regulator's acting as the agent of consumers. Rather, the contractual approach is perfectly consistent with bargaining between consumer and firm interest groups. The regulator may seek to achieve long-term objectives that take into account producer profits as well as consumer preferences. The crucial aspect of the discussion is the trade-off between the mitigation of risk from fixed investment and the preservation of incentives for efficient performance under the contract.

A discussion of regulation as a means of reducing market risks is given by Owen and Braeutigam (1978). They state that voters wish for victims of economic change to be "protected by a mechanism that provides for economic justice." As mentioned previously, Owen and Braeutigam see reliance on administrative procedure as a means of insulating consumers from economic risks—particularly those associated with sunk costs.[26]

Regulations often place obstacles in the path of market adjustment. Changes in consumer demand, input or output supply, productive technology, and government policy may necessitate changes in the plans of consumers and firms. All restrictions placed on prices, entry, product quality, input use, technology, or asset ownership impede adjustments of economic decisions by consumers and firms. If regulation indeed represents an implicit contract to mitigate risks in the presence of sunk cost, the net benefits of publicly administered contracts must be compared with net benefits achieved through private negotiation and enforcement. Regulation may be more efficient if it reduces the costs of negotiation in markets with many consumers. Further, public enforcement of contractual terms may, in some cases, be achieved at lower cost.

1.4 Externalities

The production and supply of commodities, such as environmental pollution in the absence of a directly related economic transaction or compensatory payment, implies that the allocation of resources may fail to be Pareto optimal. Coase (1960) identifies two primary reasons for the absence of an economic transaction bearing on the supply of the externality or on compensatory payments: the absence of well-defined property rights and the presence of transactions costs. This suggests a role for legal institutions or for public regulation in defining property rights or mitigating transactions costs. The mix of judicial enforcement and administrative regulation should depend on the relative costs and effectiveness of these options in improving resource allocation.

1.4.1 A Definition

The starting point for our discussion of environmental regulation is a definition of externalities.[27]

Definition 1.4.1   An *externality* refers to a commodity bundle that is supplied by an economic agent to another economic agent in the absence of any related economic transaction between the two agents.

The point to be stressed about this definition of an externality is that the commodity is transmitted between agents in the absence of any economic transaction between them. This means that there is no negotiation between the supplier and receptor over the extent of the externality and any compensatory payments, at least before the fact. This notion corresponds with that of "accidents between strangers" in tort law, such as those involving a motorist and a pedestrian; see especially Shavell (1980b). Thus, a consumer harmed by air pollution from a factory is not presumed to engage in any directly related transaction with the factory. The definition nonetheless allows for the possibility that the consumer may purchase the factory's output or that the consumer may be an employee of the factory. However, the terms of these transactions are not connected in any direct way with the factory's level of pollution. The distinction is between harm committed between strangers and harm between parties to an economic transaction. The latter includes harm to a consumer from a defective product or harm to a worker from an unsafe work-place. These are classified herein as *internalities*, defined below. The key issue is that the externality may be the only economic connection between the two agents. If the two agents are engaged in other transactions, then the terms of the other transaction have no direct connection to the externality. In the factory air pollution case, it is evident that the factory's supply of goods and the consumer's demand for the factory's final output are dependent upon the level of the externality. However, specification of the level of pollution supplied and compensation payments would not be a meaningful component of the transaction involving the factory's output.

In the above definition of externalities, the emitter or receptor of pollution may be either a consumer or a firm. Externalities may include any set of commodity bundles in the commodity space, broadly defined. If the receptor of the externality is a consumer, externalities may include any object or activity over which the consumer has a preference ranking. The externality may represent air or water pollution. Alternatively, the consumer may be affected by pollution in terms of health or other indirect factors, such as enjoyment of environmental ammenities. The consumer should have a well-defined preference ranking, preferring less pollution to more and being indifferent between various bundles of commodities including pollution. The externality commodity may also include harm from accidents, such as that between a motorist and a pedestrian; discomfort from congestion, such as crowding in a public place; and indirect benefits from another's activity, such as the observation of a neighbor's well-kept house. An alternative approach in which the consumer may mitigate the effects of the externality, such as the use of an air filter to reduce the harm from air pollution, may be modeled using a household production function. If the receptor of the externality is a firm, the externalities may include any object or activity in the space of commodities on which the firm's technological possibilities set is defined. Air or water pollution may thus represent inputs into a firm's production process. In this case, the firm's output may be lowered by pollution taking all other inputs as fixed. Positive externalities (external economies) and negative externalities (external diseconomies) are defined with respect to the receptor of the commodity bundle. Thus, if a consumer prefers less to more of an externality or if a firm's output is reduced by an externality, *ceteris paribus*, it is an *external diseconomy*. The converse is similarly defined.

It is worthwhile to relate the above definition of externalities to the notion of *depletable externalities*, such as common property resources, particularly fisheries and mineral resources; see Bator (1958) and Baumol and Oates (1975) for additional references. In the case of a common pool, the externality should be taken to be the supply of extraction effort by each firm. This is taken as an input into the production of every other firm extracting from the same pool. In the case of oil, this is sufficiently general to take into account competition for the same resource stock or pressure drops from drilling of nearby wells. In the case of fisheries, the definition is sufficiently general to take into account competition for the stock as *well* as congestion externalities from competing vessels. The absence of well-defined property rights, as observed under the rule-of-capture in oil and fisheries, and the presence of transactions costs may preclude an economic transaction. In the absence of a transaction involving adjustment of extraction efforts, the latter therefore constitutes an externality.

1.4.2 Property Rights and Regulation

Without property rights to commodities, it is hard to imagine the formation of markets. Individual demand for commodities is not clearly defined unless all commodities are owned and this ownership is transferable. The demand for commodities is obtained by choosing the most preferred point on the budget set. Commodities not already owned are obtained only by purchase at market prices subject to the individual's wealth constraint. The wealth constraint is formed by the market value of the individual's initial endowment at market prices and the received shares of firm profits. The existence of a well-defined system of property rights is evident in formal market models, such as that of Arrow-Debreu. In microeconomic models, consumers own all of the resources of the economy, the initial total endowment of commodities. Further, consumers entirely own firms and obtain the profits of the firms through given shares. Consumers sell commodities to other consumers as outputs or to firms as inputs. The initial endowments of consumers do not intersect and sum to the total endowment, so that individual ownership of commodities and firms is exclusive and total ownership is complete. Thus, property rights are well-defined. Further, these rights are fully transferable (alienable).[28] The model of market exchange is sufficiently general to allow contracts for time-dependent transactions, such as rental of capital goods, since the services of a good at different dates are distinct commodities.

The market rules implicit in the above discussion are those that establish the initial distribution of rights, the exclusivity of these rights, and the mechanism under which transfers of property rights are effected and recognized. Promulgation and enforcement of these rules may be costly. The manner in which property rights are defined will affect the equilibrium allocation of resources and the existence of market equilibrium.

Consider first the establishment of an initial distribution of rights that is both complete and exclusive. Demsetz (1967) suggests that "property rights arise when it becomes economic for those affected by externalities to internalize benefits and costs." Demsetz identifies communal, private, and state ownership. Cheung (1970) emphasizes that the initial formation of property may be costly particularly due to the "costs of defining and policing exclusivity."

Many aspects of the assignment of rights are covered by the common law of property and tort.[29] However, many situations are not adequately handled by common law. In particular, property rights may not be clearly defined for natural resources, including renewable marine resources, common pools of oil, the atmosphere, water (in oceans, rivers, impoundments, and groundwater aquifers), and the radio spectrum. Here, achieving completeness and exclusivity is often incompatible with a system of private ownership. Unlike manufactured commodities, the natural environment is not divisible in a manner suitable for private ownership. Thus, to achieve completeness of ownership, the government may be seen as the owner of environmental resources[30] or the manager of these resources in the public interest. The government is, of necessity, charged with regulation of the use of the atmosphere, water, and other natural resources. This entails establishment of regulatory agencies as a means to carry out the management of public resources.

Establishing completeness of ownership through government management does not resolve the issue of allocation of resources among competing uses. As Posner (1977, p. 34) observes, "Property rights are never exclusive, if only because exclusive property rights would so often be incompatible." According to Posner, incompatible uses are resolved by the law of property, which assigns a right to the party whose use is more valuable, or by the law of tort, which imposes liability. Unless property rights are both exclusive and exhaustive, markets cannot form and externalities or spillovers are the result. That is, interaction takes place between individuals outside the market framework. Markets cannot form because the property rights basis of exchange is absent.

Consider the "common pool" problem of oil extraction. Under the common law "rule of capture," land owners have mineral rights to oil extracted on their land. If the location of oil reserves were associated with the land in a straightforward manner (as is the case with coal), this land-based definition of mineral rights would be sufficient to achieve both completeness and exclusivity. Unfortunately, many land holdings may cover the same pool or reservoir of oil. Two significant problems arise. First, oil may migrate within the reservoir, so that a landowner may capture some of the oil that was formerly below his neighbor's land. More significantly, all of the landowners with access to a given reservoir have the incentive to race against each other to appropriate the oil in the reservoir. This results in greater expenditures on drilling equipment and oil production than would occur if the pool of oil were owned exclusively by a single individual or if ownership shares were fixed in some way. This results in dissipation of rents to the resource. The second problem is that the percentage of oil in the reservoir that is ultimately recovered often depends upon the rate at which it is extracted. Oil is driven to the surface through water or natural gas pressure. Pumping oil at excessive speed from the reservoir by a greater than optimal extraction rate per well or by a large number of wells results in a dissipation of the well's "natural" or "primary drive," thus affecting the total amount extracted. This implies that competitive extraction from a common pool is wasteful in terms of the resource itself. Additional extraction of oil through artificial injection of water and natural gas may enhance recovery at some cost, but this may not be feasible if the beneficiary of the pressure applied by a landowner is a neighboring landowner who is able to capture the oil driven upward.

From the preceding discussion, it is evident that the "rule of capture" does not create exclusive property rights a priori. Thus, the common law definition of property rights is inadequate as a basis for contractual arrangements between landowners. Indeed, transactions costs in the case of common pools of oil have proved to be quite high.[31] Oil and gas fields are often large, and a great many landowners may have access to the same field. Therefore, federal and state government regulation may prove to be significantly less costly than reliance on private contractual solutions. Unitization, regulated extraction, or an alternative definition of property rights based on land area, characteristics, or location may yield a more efficient use of resources in a regulated regime. Even if the preferred regulatory approach is a set of standard allocation rules, federal or state regulatory agencies may be required to adapt and administer these rules for each oil field. This provides an important example of a case in which an administrative solution to the assignment of property rights dominates the common law solution.

It has been argued following Coase (1960) that a single assignment of property rights is sufficient to correct market failure such as air and water pollution.[32] For example, Aranson (1982, p. 384) states, "The best public policy toward environmental quality is one that creates clear, unambiguous and alienable property rights which are susceptible to judicial protection." Clearly if a complete assignment of exclusive rights is feasible, then the establishment of a market may be considered. However, this does not imply that an assignment of property rights makes government regulation superfluous. Indeed it would be quite misleading to conclude that an assignment of rights is a simple procedure that can be costlessly achieved and, once completed, solves the externalities problem once and for all. The argument that an assignment of property rights makes government intervention unnecessary is ill founded. The assignment of the rights is in itself a formidable and costly enterprise, which might require administrative allocation even if the costs of private negotiation and judicial enforcement were negligible. Further, as Breyer (1982) notes, court-administered liability rules may be costly.[33]

There are three possible problems involved with an assignment of property rights: identification of the least cost avoider, definition of the rights to pollute, and definition of rights to clean air or water; see chapter 12. If property rights to the environment are to be assigned efficiently, the least-cost avoider of environmental pollution must be identified. It is evident that no simple general rules apply if transactions costs are present; see Coase (1960). However, there may be economies from centralization of these decisions within a regulatory agency. Repeated determination of the least-cost avoider of air pollution in each instance through judicial proceedings appears to be a costly and inefficient solution. Further, a high degree of technical knowledge may be required to determine whether abatement expenditures by firms are more or less costly than avoidance costs to consumers. This determination may be made by a single agency able to apply acquired knowledge and experience to diverse industries and locations. Thus, a task of regulatory agencies is determination of the least-cost avoider.

If it is determined that the least-cost avoider in a particular set of markets is polluting firms, there are many reasons why a one-time assignment of pollution rights may not be feasible. First, the number of pollution permits must be chosen. The desirable number of permits may vary over time based on technological change in abatement methods or changes in the damages suffered by victims of pollution. This may require continual reissuance of permits of limited duration. Changes in the supply of substitute or complementary commodities (more or less of another pollutant or a change in avoidance costs) may also affect the optimal permit level. Further, rights to pollute may be quite complex. Complete markets in pollution rights involves identification of every type of pollutant. The number of permits may vary depending upon location, season, or even current climate. The decision as to the number of pollution categories requiring permits, given the costs of operating a system of permits, is itself not a simple decision.

Suppose that rights to clean air are somehow assigned to consumers. Generally the beneficiaries of clean air (as well as polluters) are large in number and difficult to identify. The diffusion of pollutants may render definition of these rights impossible. Even if assignment of property rights to use of the environment may be established by an inexpensive decree, the government may be called upon to establish property rights in related situations. Economies of scale may be obtained by repetition of similar activities by a government agency.

As a final example of property rights definition, consider the set of frequencies of the radio spectrum. In an important paper, Coase (1959) argues that the problem of allocation of the radio spectrum can be solved by the law of property or the law of torts. Commenting on the history of the Federal Communications Commission (FCC), Coase states that "there can be little doubt that left to themselves, the courts would have solved the problems of the radio industry in much the same way as they had solved similar problems in other industries." Coase (1959) suggests that the "usual solution," a mixture of transferable rights plus regulation, could have been adopted for the broadcasting industry. Thus, once rights are established, allocation of these rights by the market is more efficient than allocation of licenses by the FCC on the basis of a complicated set of qualifications.[34] Coase emphasizes that the problem of spectrum allocation should be viewed as one of regulation of the use of transmission equipment. While the market may effectively allocate the rights to use broadcasting equipment in a particular way, rules must be established with regard to interference to ensure exclusivity. Therefore, if regulation has a role to play in broadcasting, it is in the establishment and protection of property rights, not in their allocation.

1.5 Internalities

Many regulations interfere directly with the terms of private transactions and contractual agreements. These regulations include standards applied to product quality and workplace safety and disclosure requirements for product contents or financial agreements. Government intervention of this type cannot be justified by identifying market failure due to barriers to entry or the presence of externalities. Regulation of product characteristics or contract terms often occurs in competitive markets. Also, externalities cannot be said to exist since the costs and benefits of the transactions addressed by this type of regulation affect only the parties to the transactions.

A role for regulation can only be established if transactions are somehow inefficient, due to transactions costs or imperfect information, in a way that can be remedied through government intervention. Many of the imperfections in contractual relations are addressed through the common law. The law is itself subject to controversy and change. The legal process can be costly and often responds slowly to new economic situations. Government regulation may have a role to play in bridging the gaps left by the legal framework and law enforcement. The possible contribution of administrative regulation must be weighed against the efficiency properties of legal rules.[35]

1.5.1 A Definition

Externalities refer to costs and benefits experienced by third parties to economic transactions. It is often asserted that by "internalizing" these costs and benefits through direct transactions, an efficient allocation of resources will result.[36] Coase (1960) argues that in the absence of transactions costs, any assignment of property rights, if these are well-defined, will result in an optimal outcome. I shall argue that this conclusion provides either an overly optimistic view of private bargaining or an assertion of limited applicability since transactions costs are narrowly defined if at all. "Internalization" need not guarantee efficiency. Private bargaining may result in allocative inefficiency under quite general conditions. These inefficiencies are referred to as internalities.[37]

Definition 1.5.1   An *internality* refers to costs and benefits of a transaction experienced by the parties to the transaction that are not accounted for in the terms of exchange.[38]

We may speak of negative or positive internalities[39] to distinguish between internal costs and benefits not reflected in contractual arrangements. An example of a negative internality is the harm to a consumer from product failure where the likelihood and size of the accident were not fully anticipated in the contractual terms. A negative internality may refer to the harm to a party to a contract resulting from breach by the other party. The contract breach case constitutes an internality if the consequences of breach were not explicitly reflected in the contract terms. An example of a positive internality might be informal on-the-job training of an employee that was unanticipated in the labor contract.

Three principal "transaction costs" are sources of internalities: (i) the costs of writing contingent contracts in the presence of risk, (ii) the cost of observing and monitoring actions when behavior is imperfectly observable, and (iii) the cost of information gathering and disclosure when parties to the transaction possess private information. The cost of incorporating alternative uncertain outcomes creates incomplete contingent contracts. The cost of observing actions may lead to inefficient levels of such private activities as accident prevention, a problem known as *moral hazard*. Finally, the cost of observing the characteristics of agents may lead to misrepresentation of preferences or technology and result in contracts that imperfectly distinguish between agents of different types. The possibility that insurance buyers will understate their risks or that workers will overstate their productivity is referred to as *adverse selection*. These problems are by now familiar from the insurance and information economics literature, and each is the subject of a broad literature in itself that need not be repeated here.

My point is that transaction costs or incomplete information may cause parties to a transaction not to allocate fully the net benefits from a transaction. This imperfect allocation of net benefits is referred to as an internality. The presence of internalities causes parties to a transaction not to capture all potential gains-from-trade. I now give several simple examples of internalities.

Consider a standard monopoly pricing problem. The buyer has benefits $v(q)$ of a good, where buyer demand, $q(p)$, solves $v'(q) = p$. The seller has costs $c(q)$. The seller is able to commit himself to a profit-maximizing price offer p^m, where marginal revenue equals marginal cost. The familiar welfare analysis of monopoly shows that the buyer and seller fail to capture all gains-from-trade since output is less than the optimal level, where marginal benefit equals marginal cost. The *internality* in this simple example is due to the fact that the seller does not account for the loss of consumer surplus to the buyer due to pricing above the competitive price, $p^* = v'(q^*) = c'(q^*)$. If we tax the seller by an amount equal to the internality, for $p \geq p^*$

$$T(p) = \int_{p^*}^{p} q(x)\,dx,$$

the seller will choose the competitive price. As is often stated, a two-part tariff will allow perfect price discrimination and lead the monopolist to the optimal output level. The internality here is caused by linear pricing, which may reflect transactions costs of more complicated pricing policies.

A simple contingent contracts problem also illustrates internalities. Suppose that a buyer may have value v_1 with probability η and value v_2 with probability $(1 - \eta)$. A seller has production cost c, where $v_1 > c > v_2$. A noncontingent contract to produce and deliver the good at some price p yields expected net benefits of $\eta v_1 + (1 - \eta)v_2 - c$. A contingent contract, which only requires production if the buyer's value exceeds production costs, yields greater expected net benefits of $\eta(v_1 - c)$. The *internality* associated with a noncontingent contract at price $p = c$ is then equal to the expected losses in the state where the good has lower value, $(1 - \eta)(v_2 - c)$. If the costs of renegotiation or the costs of writing a contingent contract exceed this amount, the parties will not capture all gains-from-trade.

Moral hazard is easily illustrated as follows. A buyer derives value $v(z)$ from a service of quality z. A seller chooses the quality of service at cost z after the contract price p is chosen. Thus, quality is unobservable at the time of contract, and the seller selects the lowest quality level, $z = 0$, rather than optimal quality z^*, where $v'(z^*) = 1$. The net benefits to the buyer of product quality z, $v(z) - v(0)$, are not accounted for in the terms of exchange thus creating an internality. If product quality were observable, a contract might specify a payment to the buyer as a function of quality.

1.5.2 Transaction Costs and Regulation

Transaction costs are present in immediate exchange as well as long-term contracts. The simplest barter of goods of known characteristics may involve negotiation over the terms of trade. The negotiation process may have at least three costs. First, there may be disutility from effort spent in negotiation. This might include the costs of communication or of providing information about the transaction. Second, the time spent bargaining has an opportunity cost for each party. Third, the delay in securing the benefits from the transaction is costly in that the parties discount future utility.[40]

If there are many traders, locating potential trading partners imposes additional costs. Coordination of multiple traders through a price system may also be costly. A price system requires traders to be informed about relative prices. This may involve costly communication.[41] Advertising of product characteristics entails additional costs. Market prices may require time to adjust to equilibrium levels. Trading out of equilibrium results in costly misallocation of resources. Even if trading only occurs at equilibrium prices, delays in price adjustment are costly if future benefits are discounted. If markets involve brokers or auctioneers, the services of these agents are a cost of effecting transactions.

It is incorrect to assert that the market functions efficiently if this belief is based on standard models of general equilibrium, such as the Arrow-Debreu model, in which there are no explicit transaction costs. There is a single price in each market. Markets clear immediately and simultaneously. A costless medium of exchange or numeraire commodity is present. Firms are described by a production possibilities set without explicit attention to problems of communication and control that may exist within the firm. Because markets are established costlessly, there is a complete set of markets. Thus, separate markets exist for all commodities, for all of the time and location indices in the commodity space. In the presence of uncertainty, contingent markets are costlessly established for all possible states of the world. Because allocation is achieved by the price mechanism, explicit contracts are not required. For economic models to predict accurately, the efficiency properties of market equilibrium require incorporation of transaction costs.

One approach to modeling transaction costs explicitly in a general equilibrium framework is to treat transactions as a set of perfectly divisible commodities with a given production technology. Thus, the resource costs of market exchange may be viewed as simply those required to produce a complementary commodity, such as transportation of goods. The production of brokerage services, wholesale or retail services, or the actions of arbitrageurs may be viewed as equivalent to other productive activities. Brokerage services may be consumed directly, or they may be an intermediate good used in production. By a suitable relabeling of the commodity space, the allocation of resources to the process of exchange may be examined. Feasible transactions are then the outcome of decisions of consumers and producers. The nonexistence of a market can then be equated to the zero output point in a production set.[42] An objection to this approach might be that transaction costs are specific to a particular exchange. Further, a transaction cost may represent a fixed cost for a given transaction, and thus production of transactions may involve nonconvexities in technology. These objections do not present problems in modeling the resource costs of transactions. They simply refer to the properties of the production technology, and as such, they apply equally to the treatment of other goods (such as dams or bridges) whose production entails scale economies.

Even if transactions may be handled formally as commodities, however, the importance of the process of exchange does require attention to institutions that may facilitate communication and negotiation between agents. There may be a role for regulatory agencies in reducing the resource costs of exchange. The costs of government intervention in exchange must be compared to the costs of private negotiation and judicial intervention.

It is evident that there are a large number of private institutions that facilitate exchange. The primary activities of wholesale and retail firms, excluding transportation and storage of commodities, may be seen as mediation of transactions between manufacturers and purchasers. Brokerage is performed by agents in insurance, travel, freight transportation, and real estate. Privately established exchanges exist for stocks, bonds, commodities, and futures. Banks perform an important role as intermediary between large numbers of borrowers and lenders. Auction houses are good examples of costly price mechanisms.

The firm itself, as Coase (1937) points out, is a means of mitigating the "cost of using the price mechanism," particularly the "costs of negotiating and concluding a separate contract for each exchange transaction." According to Coase, the size of the firm (or extent of vertical integration) will depend on the relative costs of internal and market transactions. Williamson (1975, p. 26) defines *opportunism* as "self-interest seeking with guile" through "strategic manipulation of information or misrepresentation of intentions." He identifies the advantages of internal organization in reducing incentives for *opportunism*, in making auditing more effective and in settlement of disputes. *Bounded rationality* refers to imperfect decision making by individuals as a result of the costs of processing and communicating information; see Simon (1957, 1972) and March and Simon (1958). Williamson (1974) posits *bounded rationality* and *opportunism* as sources of transaction costs in negotiation. Further, Williamson considers market uncertainty and bargaining among small numbers of agents as sources of costs in contracting and exchange.

The previous discussion of property rights emphasized that there may be costs associated with the establishment of a system of property rights. Cheung (1970) notes that in addition there may be "costs associated with negotiating and enforcing contracts for the exchange or transfer of property rights." By allowing the exchange of certificates of ownership (titles, deeds, shares of stock), governments may reduce the costs of transactions. If enforcement of property rights has the characteristics of a public good, there may be benefits from centralized enforcement. Finally, by recording certain transfers of rights (as with houses or cars), government participation may reduce private costs of verifying whether the seller is actually transferring ownership of an asset.

There are a number of ways in which the common law of property and contracts provides rules that assist in private minimization of transaction costs. It is here that we consider the applicability of alternative administrative regulations. Posner (1977, p. 69) identifies two ways in which the law of contracts reduces the costs of contracting: "The first is to reduce the complexity and hence cost of transactions by supplying a set of normal terms that, in the absence of a law of contracts, the parties would have to negotiate explicitly. This function of the law is similar to that performed by a standard or form contract. The second function is to furnish prospective transacting parties with information concerning the many contingencies that may defeat an exchange, and hence to assist them in planning their exchange sensibly." If one grants these beneficial aspects to the law of contracts, then in both cases one may discern potential roles for administrative regulation as well. In markets with new product characteristics or new technologies of production, there may not yet exist standard procedures or contractual forms. In other markets, standard procedures that have evolved over time may prove inadequate.

Standard contracts are offered by sellers in many markets, such as insurance, banking, and transportation. One-sided contracts exist as well. For example, manufacturers commit themselves to remedy product failures through standard warranties. In these markets, firms may compete both through product quality and price and through contract terms. A firm may increase its sales by offering contract terms that are more advantageous to consumers. The contracts offered by a firm are standardized because they apply to a large number of purchases and it would be costly to renegotiate contract terms for each purchase. For market competition to produce an efficient set of contracts implies that the costs to firms of designing these contracts and the costs to consumers of comparing contract terms across firms are not excessive. It may be that the design and enforcement of guidelines for contract terms, such as product warranties, may reduce the private costs of agreement on standard contractual terms.

In their study of prorationing regulations in oil extraction, Libecap and Wiggins (1984, p. 97) conclude that "detailed analysis of bargaining among firms is essential for insight into the emergence of various institutional forms." They find that "without recognition of the heterogeneities among firms and the impact on contracting efforts to increase rents, the observed prorationing arrangements observed in Oklahoma and Texas cannot be explained." Thus, while it is generally acknowledged that prorationing may allow inefficient dissipation of resource rents,[43] the policy tool may be optimal given the costs of negotiation. Thus, the presence of transactions costs provide an explanation of such second-best allocation rules.

High transaction costs may result in nonexistence of markets. In this case, the benefits of government allocation of resources must be weighed against administrative costs. In environmental regulation, even if property rights are clearly defined, the costs of implementing a transferable permits system must be compared with the costs of a system of effluent fines and standards. While transferable effluent permits present advantages in that the price of permits is set by competitive bidding, establishing a system of permits and monitoring their use may be costly. Thus, policy instruments that are inferior in terms of setting a correct price (such as effluent fees) may present advantages in terms of administrative costs.

Costly Contingencies   Long-term contracts are formed in the presence of
market risks. The absence of immediate exchange may require formal
specification of contract terms and costly negotiation. Taking many contingencies into account involves both effort and communication between
the parties. The delays in carrying out the contract may involve costly
monitoring and enforcement of the contract's provisions.[44] Determining
which state of the world has occurred may be costly; see Radner (1968).
The parties to the contract may undertake expenditures to demonstrate
their commitment to carry out the contract terms. Those expenditures that
are incidental to the exchange may be seen as a cost of contracting.

Contract law provides a means of reducing the costs of planning for
contingencies.[45] Shavell (1980a, p. 468) notes that "damage measures for
breach of contract can serve as a kind of substitute for complete contingent
contracts." Simpler contracts may reduce the time and effort involved in
negotiation. The purpose of penalties for breach of contract is to allow the
parties to the contract to make efficient choices between performance of
the contract and paying compensation for damages sustained if the terms
of the contract are not carried out. Penalties for breach should be designed
so that efficient reliance expenditures are made. A similar role may be
identified for regulation of markets in which explicit contracts are not
present. It may be that breach of an implied contract is a frequent occurrence. Rather than resorting to costly litigation in each instance of
breach, it may be preferable to have standard penalties for breach that are
established and enforced by a regulatory authority.

Tort law also provides remedies for accidents and serves as a substitute
for contract contingencies. Shavell (1984a) compares liability in tort with
regulation of safety. Shavell notes that the regulatory instrument of fines
is similar to the legal instrument of liability in that both reduce risk by
imposing penalties on the party causing the damages. However, a fine may
result in lower transactions costs "where suits would not be brought due
to difficulty in establishing causation or where harms are widely dispersed, as in many environmental and health cases" (Shavell, 1984a, p. 373).
Similarly, the regulatory instrument of safety standards is comparable to
the legal instrument of the injunction. Shavell (1984a, p. 374) concludes
that "... safety regulation would be more attractive where parties are not
easily able to assess dangers or where many parties are involved and 'free
rider' and associated problems make it difficult to coordinate a collective
action...."[22] Shavell emphasizes that the costs of the tort system must be

compared with the administrative costs of direct regulation. The principal difference is that in the case of regulation "administrative costs are incurred whether or not harm occurs." Because of these costs, a *combination* of liability and regulation may be required to reduce the risks of product failure and unsafe working conditions.

Moral Hazard   When the actions of parties to a contract are not directly observable, they are not subject to negotiation and cannot be incorporated in the terms of the contract. This creates the incentive problem known as *moral hazard* and constitutes an important source of internalities. Moral hazard was identified by Arrow (1963, 1965) as the result of incentives created by risk-sharing arrangements, such as insurance policies. The presence of moral hazard complicates the design of contracts in the principal-agent relationship.[46]

As Arrow (1965) observes, incomplete risk shifting, such as coinsurance, provides a partial remedy for moral hazard that trades off incentives for efficient behavior with the benefits of risk-sharing. The difficulties that arise in insurance markets appear in a wide range of transactions in labor and product markets. There may be imperfect incentives for employers or manufacturers to prevent accidents. Similarly, consumers may use products carelessly if their risks are covered by insurance contracts, such as warranties. Workers covered by workers' compensation may not devote sufficient effort to avoiding accidents on the job. The possibility of market failure in product and labor markets suggests that there may be a role for social institutions that mitigate the costs of risk-sharing. It should be noted, however, that government programs, such as medical insurance, are subject to the same moral hazard problems as private contracts.

Cooter (1985) proposes a unified approach to torts, contracts, and property based on the notion of *precaution*, that is, actions that reduce harm. For accidents, precaution refers to the care taken by injurers and victims to reduce harm. In the case of nuisance, precaution refers to abatement by the injurer and prevention by the victim. In the case of contract breach, precaution refers to the care of the promiser in avoiding breach and reduction in reliance by the relier. Finally, precaution in the taking of property refers to conservation by the government and reduced improvements by the property owner.[47] If precaution is unobservable, as is often the case in tort liability and contract performance, it is likely that legal remedies are subject to moral hazard problems.[48]

The moral hazard problems observed in liability are also present in regulatory alternatives, such as government provision of insurance.[49] Product and workplace safety standards and inspection programs are in part designed to address the unobservability of manufacturer and employer care levels. The administrative costs of these regulatory programs must be balanced against the system of market insurance and liability in the absence of standards. In addition, the inefficiencies associated with command and control regulations, such as standards, must be seriously considered.

Asymmetric Information   If agents possess incomplete and asymmetric information, the market mechanism may not achieve an efficient allocation of resources. In the Arrow-Debreu framework, consumers and firms have access to the same information regarding prices, product characteristics, and contract terms. Even if the state of the world is uncertain, agents have identical perceptions of the likelihood of events. The presence of asymmetric information may create a role for regulation of market transactions.

Given symmetric information, individuals may fully insure against the risk of accidents or unsafe products. Arrow (1963) examines the risks associated with medical care. Arrow (1963) concludes that government intervention in labor or product markets through licensing, or alternatively through the production of information, may be required if information is imperfect and costly.[50] Public production of information may benefit from economies of scale and the public good aspects of information transmission and use. However, private production of information may yield benefits through competition to produce product information as well as tailoring information to specific market requirements.[51] The problem of public supply of information is the classic difficulty of correctly assessing public demand.

The presence of asymmetric information about preferences, endowments, or technology requires a redefinition of efficiency. Hölmstrom and Myerson (1983) define *ex ante, interim,* and *ex post efficiency* on the basis of the information available to economic agents see chapter 11. *Ex ante efficiency* is defined for the state in which agents are not yet informed about their own individual characteristics. An allocation is *interim efficient* if all agents are informed about their own characteristics but do not yet know the characteristics of other agents. Finally, *ex post efficiency* corresponds to the state in which agents possess full information about their own characteristics and those of others. The presence of asymmetric information implies that market allocations may fail to be *ex post* efficient.

Consider the simple model of bargaining over an object between a buyer and seller in Myerson and Satterthwaite (1983). They show that if buyer and seller have private information about their valuation of the object, trade may not occur in some cases even though the buyer's valuation exceeds that of the seller. Thus, ex post, there are gains from trade that could have been realized if each party possessed better information about the other's preferences. The parties refrain from revealing this private information to maintain an advantage in bargaining. There is a wide class of outcomes to the bargaining problem that are *interim efficient*. However, in concealing their information, both parties may be worse off because they do not capture all of the rents from exchange that are available under full information. An internality is present because neither party has incentive to reveal private information.

The ex post inefficiency of resource allocation due to asymmetric information occurs in competitive markets as well. Asymmetry of information is present in many markets in which one or both parties to a transaction possesses superior information. The classic example is Akerlof's 1970 "market for lemons" in which the differential between the prices of new and used cars reflects the greater possibility of obtaining a bad car (a lemon) if a used car is purchased. This occurs because owners of bad used cars are more likely to sell their cars than are owners of good used cars. The presence of adverse selection has been noted in many markets. In insurance markets, firms may have an interest in distinguishing between customers with high or low probabilities of accidents. To induce individuals to reveal their private knowledge about their likelihood of having accidents, insurance policies must be designed in such a way that consumers select policies on the basis of risk. The result is that the set of policies chosen by a firm with market power reflects the inclusion of incentives for revelation of knowledge.[52] Riskier individuals are given incentives to purchase greater insurance coverage. In competitive insurance markets, not only does asymmetric information create departures from optimality, but the market equilibrium may fail to exist as well.[53] Similar asymmetries of information exist in labor markets, where employees have private information about their abilities and employers have private information about workplace safety. On product markets, firms may have private information about product quality or safety that is not available to consumers.

The inefficiency of market equilibria in the presence of asymmetric information is not sufficient, in itself, to justify public intervention. As noted by Oi (1973) and others, publicly set standards of product quality or safety may reduce consumer well-being by eliminating product variety and thus restricting choice. There may be a role for government in the production or subsidization of information in markets if the incentives for revelation of information are imperfect. However, the welfare gains from improved information must be compared with the costs of government production of information. If regulation sets standards for labeling or private information production, high costs may be imposed on firms. This may also reduce product variety and restrict choice. The need for regulation in markets with asymmetric information may thus depend on the trade-off between the costs of information production and the costs of inefficient transactions.

Schwartz and Wilde (1979) see competition as mitigating the effects of imperfect information.[54] They conclude that public policy should thus not be directed at information production or contractual terms but rather at the promotion of competition through provision of comparative data on prices and contractual terms and the requirement that prices and terms be presented to the consumer in a form that is easily understood and allows comparisons. Schwartz and Wilde (1979, p. 679) observe that because "judicial power is limited to striking an offending term or price," it follows that "courts would remain poor institutions to resolve information problems."[55] They note that their view is consistent with the delegation of enforcement to administrative agencies of the Truth-in-Lending Act and Magnuson-Moss Act.

The creation of a set of normal contractual terms may provide an explanation for mandated *disclosure* in securities, banking, or product quality regulation. Disclosure requirements may also serve to assist consumers and firms in accounting for contractual contingencies and effectively planning exchange. In the absence of transactions costs, it is arguable whether market competition will lead to appropriate disclosure of information. However, in the presence of transactions costs, there may be efficiency gains from a standardization of disclosure formats and from a uniformity in what information is disclosed. Thus, the establishment of disclosure regulations may be efficient if the standards that are imposed could not have been achieved through priviate negotiation unless at greater costs.[56]

The preceding discussion has identified a role for administrative regulation in the presence of asymmetric information. Economic agents may fail to achieve available gains from trade with information asymmetries. Regulatory agencies may supply information to the market if they are the least-cost provider or if there are public good aspects to the information that prevent private supply. Private solutions to asymmetric information include private research organizations, brokers, agents, and other financial intermediaries. As discussed in the preceding section on transactions costs, regulation may standardize disclosure in such a way as to reduce consumer search costs. Further, by promoting competition, administrative agencies may create incentives for firms to supply useful product information. The desirable regulatory policy is to set general rules for disclosure or contract provisions and to rely on market forces for disclosure of private information.

My discussion of the various forms of market failure has attempted to define a role for government regulation of markets. It should again be emphasized that the presence of market failure is a necessary precondition for regulation. It is not sufficient to require government regulation. Regulation may entail high administrative costs. The formulation and implementation of regulation may entail policies that not only are redistributive in nature but that interfere with allocative efficiency. Regulation of markets is subject to all of the problems that attend economic planning. The regulator operates with imperfect information. Regulatory policies may be second best, reflecting rules of thumb, administrative procedures, and institutional constraints. Even well-intentioned public policies can create incentives for inefficient private behavior. Accordingly, I take up the institutional setting for the regulatory process in the following chapter.

Notes

1. See the books by Kahn (1970, 1971), Bonbright (1961), Phillips (1969), Bailey (1973), Shepherd and Wilcox (1979), and Crew and Kleindorfer (1979) for overviews of the vast theoretical and applied literature.

2. According to Kahn (1970, p. 2), institutions that operate at the "periphery" of markets include "regulating the supply and availability of money, enforcing contracts, protecting property, providing subsidies or tariff protection, prohibiting unfair competition, providing market information, imposing standards for packaging and product content, and insisting on the right of employees to join unions and bargain collectively." Furthermore, externalities are mentioned only in passing (1970, pp. 193–195) as they apply to pollution by public utilities. Needless to say, these issues have moved to center stage with deregulation in communications and transportation and the contemporaneous increase in social regulation.

3. Stigler (1981, p. 73) asserts that public regulation as a field "includes most of public finance, large parts of monetary and financial economics and international trade, large sectors of labor economics, agricultural and land economics and welfare economics," and then adds the economic theory of contracts, torts, and property. Stigler (1981, p. 74) asks rhetorically, "Can this vast array of public policies be usefully viewed as a single subject?" Need it be said that the scope of regulation as a subject that is proposed by Stigler is far too broad?

4. Stigler (1981, p. 76) remarks, "If one cannot explain why some regulations appear and some regulations do not appear one simply cannot deal with the fundamental questions of regulation."

5. The texts include MacAvoy (1979), Weidenbaum (1980), Needham (1983), and Asch and Seneca (1985).

6. Hayek distinguishes between rules that are generally applied and specific government decisions. Hayek notes that "[h]ow well the market will function depends on the character of particular rules" (1960, p. 229). Hayek (1960, p. 224) emphasizes that "a free system does not exclude on principle all those general regulations of economic activity which can be laid down in the form of general rules specifying conditions which everybody who engages in a certain activity must satisfy."

7. See also Becker (1968), Stigler (1970), and Friedman (1984).

8. Posner's (1977, p. 272) objection to this system is that firm's competitors have incentive to make nuisance complaints to the FTC, while defrauded consumers have less incentive to complain. However, the commission should be able to discern the reliability of complaints by considering their sources.

9. Antitrust laws involve a proscriptive approach to the promotion of competition; they are not generally considered in law as part of regulation.

10. See also Wiedenbaum (1977, 1980).

11. Edelman (1967, p. 103) observes that "to draft a law is not to reflect a public will; it is only through subsequent bargaining and administrative decision-making that values find some sort of realization in policy."

12. Ripley and Franklin (1980, p. 219) state that in the United States "it is also assumed that at all stages of the policy process various groups and individuals should have access to policymakers and policy implementers to try to influence what they do and how they proceed."

13. Lowi (1969) laments the emphasis on bargaining over each decision on a case-by-case basis rather than bargaining over the form of laws or general rules. Lowi attributes the "crisis in public authority" in part to the system of regulation. He observes that "a good law eliminates the political process at certain points" (1969, p. 127).

14. For additional references and further discussion, see Meier (1985, p. 10).

15. See *Adkins* v. *Children's Hospital*, 261, U.S. 525, 554 (1923). This case is quoted in Kahn (1970, pp. 5, 20).

16. See Stigler (1971) on occupational licenses as a barrier to entry.

17. In the case of *Adkins* v. *Children's Hospital*, 261 U.S. 525, 554 (1923) the Court found that "laws fixing hours of labor. ... [have] no necessary effect on the heart of the contract, that is, the amount of wages"; see note 15. This statement is, of course, inconsistent from an economist's point of view.

18. Note that any restriction of a firm's pollution activities restricts contractual alternatives in the firm's output markets, as occurs with any restriction of inputs or productive technology.

19. See Arrow (1951), Arrow and Debreu (1954), and Debreu (1959). In the Arrow-Debreu model consumer preferences are defined on the set of commodities available to the consumer, called the *consumption set*. Firm technology is described by a set of input and output vectors called the *production possibilities* set. The choice by the firm of an element of its production set is referred to as that firm's supply. An allocation of resources refers to a vector listing the net consumption vectors of consumers and the net output vectors of firms. An allocation of resources among consumers and firms refers to a product bundle in a set that is the cross product of consumption sets and production sets. Regulations such as product quality rules may be represented as constraints on the consumption set. Output, input, or technology restrictions can be represented as constraints on the firm's production possibilities set.

20. In the case of direct interference with the allocation mechanism, the simplest policy is a restriction of the set of prices. More complex policies might involve a correspondence that maps messages from consumers and firms into the space of resource allocations. Here, the policy set is the set of these correspondences.

In the case where regulations affect consumer decisions, regulations may be constraints on consumption sets. Regulatory constraints are then a correspondence from the consumer's choice set into itself. Alternatively, the regulator's actions may take the form of personalized transfers or nonlinear tax schedules that affect the consumer's budget constraint. The policy set is then a set of these instruments.

In the case where regulations affect firm decisions, regulations may take the form of constraints placed on production sets. Also, taxes and other transfers will alter the firm's profit function. The regulator's policy set may include these instruments.

21. In many regulation models, it is assumed that a regulatory agency behaves as a single individual with well-defined preferences. Thus, the regulator is a third type of economic agent in addition to consumers and firms. Regulatory preferences are assumed to be given exogenously and to be represented by a weighted sum of the preferences of consumers and rankings given by the profit functions of firms. Thus, the regulator is only concerned with the effects of allocations on the well-being of consumers and firms. The introduction of distinct agents called regulators requires a modification of the definition of economic equilibrium. For example, given resource allocation by a price system, the market equilibrium consists of the equilibrium demand of consumers, equilibrium supply of firms, and equilibrium regulations chosen by regulators. Given an administrative system of resource allocation, the equilibrium consists of the constraints imposed on the allocation mechanism by the regulator and the equilibrium consumption of consumers and production of firms.

22. See Shubik (1982, 1984) for a wide-ranging exposition of theory and applications of game theory in the social sciences. See also Friedman (1977, 1986) and Owen (1982) on formal representations of games.

23. See, for example, Breyer's (1982) discussion and critique of the "typical justifications" given for regulation.

24. Von Weizsäcker (1980a, p. 400) defines a barrier to entry as a production cost borne by entrants but not incumbents, *which results in social welfare losses.*

25. The issue of excessive entry is sometimes related to "excessive competition." The latter concept has been used to justify regulation of airlines, trucks, and ocean shipping. The notion of excessive competition, as Breyer (1982) rightly points out, is not well defined and is certainly not applicable to competitive industries with small economies of scale.

26. Owen and Braeutigam (1978, p. 21) state that "noneconomists are great respectors of sunk costs; the transformation of useful physical and human capital into an irrelevant sunk cost by market or technological forces is a process that is easily viewed as unjust or even inhumane." Examples are given of cable television, radio formats, local service airlines, passenger railroads, and natural gas.

27. Compare this definition with that of Baumol and Oates (1975) or Mishan (1971). I emphasize that externalities are commodity bundles rather than real variables in consumer utility functions or firm production functions. This is done to avoid any confusion that might arise from the interpretation of an externality as affecting the individual's preferences, as, for example, a taste parameter in the utility function. I take the consumer's underlying preferences to be given. This is not to deny that consumer choices are affected by the actions of others such as by advertising. However, I would choose instead to interpret advertising as a commodity. Similarly, I take the firm's technology as fixed and unaffected by externalities such as pollution. In the sense that observation of another firm (or stealing secrets) may allow a firm to improve its production process, I would interpret this situation as an input of information into the firm's production function broadly defined to include technological data as inputs. I do not wish to treat externalities as a technological parameter in the firm'

production function. My definition is consistent with the formal analysis in Baumol and Oates (1975).

28. An understanding of the importance of the context of market transactions may be obtained by careful consideration of formal models of the market. In particular, the Arrow-Debreu model (see note 19) provides a basic framework that defines market equilibrium and states sufficient conditions under which that equilibrium exists. Further, welfare economics provides a criterion by which the efficiency of market allocation of resources may be evaluated. The two fundamental theorems of welfare economics demonstrate sufficient conditions under which a market equilibrium is Pareto optimal and under which any Pareto optimal allocation may be attained by the market mechanism given a suitable redistribution of endowments. The rules of exchange that underlie these basic results may be inferred by a careful consideration of the implicit and explicit assumptions of the Arrow-Debreu model. The object of the analysis is *not* to question the realism or applicability of the Arrow-Debreu model. Instead, the focus is on the role that government regulation and the common law play in facilitating exchange and in providing the conditions under which markets may form and achieve efficient allocations. The Arrow-Debreu model serves to provide a formal framework for the present discussion. In the rest of the book, I shall rely primarily on partial equilibrium models as a descriptive assumption.

29. Statutory penalties also exist for criminal activities such as theft.

30. See Dales (1968).

31. Wiggins and Libecap (1985) analyze the failure of landowners to agree on management of a common reservoir by a single firm (unitization). They attribute contractual failure to imperfect and asymmetric information due to different private information on the value of leases and different interpretations of publicly available data.

Regulatory policy with regard to oil field contractual arrangements is studied in Libecap and Wiggins (1984, 1985). The federal government regulation encourages unitization; see Libecap and Wiggins (1984). Further, Libecap and Wiggins (1985) examine the impact of regulatory policy on the extent and rate at which unitization agreements are achieved in Oklahoma, Texas, and on federal lands. Elsewhere, Libecap and Wiggins (1984) study prorationing regulations as a solution to the common pool problem.

32. See Coase (1960), Demsetz (1967), and Aranson (1982).

33. Breyer (1982, p. 24) states that "government officials must determine the precise shape and location of liability rules. This in itself may prove a herculean task." Breyer (1982) notes the difficulty of determining which party is best able to calculate the relevant costs. Assignment of liability to this party is suggested by Calabresi (1970).

34. Breyer (1982, pp. 72–73) notes that only 0.1% of the electromagnetic spectrum is allocated for major commercial broadcast rules. Breyer (1982) lists the extensive information that applicants for licenses must provide to the FCC. This information includes legal, financial, and engineering qualifications and proposed programming.

35. Posner (1977, p. 271) states that "the choice is rarely between a free market and public regulation. Ordinarily the choice is between two methods of public control, the common law system of privately enforced rights and the administrative system of direct public control. The choice between them should depend upon a weighting of their strengths and weaknesses in particular contexts. The concept of 'market failure' needs to be balanced by one of 'government failure.'"

36. See, for example, Coase (1960) and Cheung (1970).

37. To my knowledge, the term "internalities" has not been previously used in economics; nor has it been given the definition stated here. Webster's *New World Dictionary*, 2nd college edition gives the definition of "inner, intrinsic, or essential quality or attribute" for internality. Externality is defined as "the quality or state of being external." An analogous definition may be given for internality.

38. An alternative definition consistent with our earlier definition of an externality is the following: An *internality* refers to a commodity bundle exchanged between parties to an economic transaction that is not accounted for in the terms of exchange.

39. Alternatively, one may speak of internal diseconomies or internal economies.

40. In dynamic bargaining models, transactions costs have been associated with discounting the future net benefits of trade; see, for example, Rubinstein (1982).

41. There may be equilibria with a distribution of prices for the same good requiring costly search for the lowest price. This issue is examined in the large literature on search in labor and commodity markets; see for example, Stigler (1961), Rothschild (1973), and Wilde and Schwartz (1979).

42. The zero output point is termed "possibility of inaction" by Debreu (1959, p. 40). If brokerage activities are inputs to the production of a commodity, then transactions costs may be counted as part of total production costs.

43. See Adelman (1964) and Libecap and Wiggins (1984).

44. See Dye (1985) for a model of labor contracts with costly contingencies.

45. See Shavell (1980a), Rogerson (1984), and the references therein.

46. There is a large literature on the principal-agent problem; see especially Shavell (1979a, b) and Holmström (1979).

47. This list of activities that represent precaution appears in Cooter (1985). Cooter does not directly address the issue of moral hazard since precaution expenditures are observable.

48. For example, Epstein (1985) emphasizes that products liability rules should be designed to reflect the contractual forms observed in private transactions.

49. Note the many criticisms of workers' compensation insurance. On the other hand, Trebilcock (1985, p. 675) notes that there are high administrative costs in the present liability system, so that "victims receive between 20 and 30 percent of all resources entering the system" as compared to "80 to 90 percent of revenues received" for market insurance.

50. See also the discussion in Oi (1973).

51. Posner (1977, p. 84) notes that property rights to consumer product information could be recognized so as to provide incentives for its private production.

52. See Stiglitz (1977a).

53. See Rothschild and Stiglitz (1976).

54. The analysis of Schwartz and Wilde (1979) is based on a model of markets in which consumers search, or "comparison shop," for the best prices and products. See also Stigler (1961), Rothschild (1973), Salop and Stiglitz (1977), and Wilde and Schwartz (1979) on models of search.

55. Schwartz and Wilde (1979, p. 681) identify three advantages of administrative agencies over courts in handling problems of asymmetric information: "First, the agency could be given the resources to investigate market conditions adequately; second, it could be given the power to order the remedies that are likely to make the markets behave more competitively; third, it would be more effective in policing disclosure schemes."

56. A similar argument may be made for regulations that set *standards* of product quality, durability, and safety and workplace safety. As evidence of the high costs of privately negotiating standards, one need only consider the difficulties encountered by the computer industry in achieving compatible programs and equipment. In a study of the industry, Brock (1975, p. 144) concludes that "most of the progress that has taken place in computer standards has been as a result of government pressure."

2 Regulation and the Administrative Process

Government regulation of markets involves both *direct* and *indirect interaction* between the regulatory agency and buyers and sellers. *Direct interaction* occurs through public hearings and the rule-making process, which involves both consumers and firms. *Indirect interaction* refers to the attempts by consumer and firm interest groups to influence regulatory decisions through legislative, administrative, and judicial channels. Understanding the direct and indirect interaction of consumers and firms in regulated markets with regulatory agencies requires an examination of administrative law. This is a broad and complex subject. My object here is not to attempt a comprehensive review. Rather, I seek to highlight a few aspects of the administrative process that appear to be significant for economic modeling of regulated industries. The direct interaction of consumers and firms with regulators occurs in the context of administrative procedure, particularly the Administrative Procedures Act (APA). I begin by an examination of the organization of regulatory agencies in section 2.1. I consider the economic implications of direct interaction of regulators, with consumers and firms in section 2.2. The role of agencies in gathering information and negotiating regulatory policy with consumers and firms is emphasized. It is argued that the theory of cooperative games provides a natural approach to modeling the regulatory process.

Although the focus of the present discussion is on direct interaction of regulators with consumers and firms, most theories of the origins of regulation examine indirect interaction as the source of regulatory rules, procedures, and decisions. Indirect interaction occurs in the context of legislative and executive control of agency activities and judicial review of agency decisions. My approach in later chapters is to take these indirect influences on regulators as *givens* and to suggest ways to embody indirect interaction within a "reduced form" model of direct interaction. By specifying the regulators' preferences or legal and procedural constraints on regulatory policies, attention may be focused on price regulations, entry controls, or other specific actions. The reduced form models may then be useful to the study of broader questions about the determinants of regulatory objectives and institutions. Thus, a positive theory is sought that explains why particular market equilibria are observed as a consequence of regulatory institutions, rules, and decisions. Also a normative theory is sought that evaluates how well regulatory objectives are achieved by various policy instruments. The literature on indirect interaction is briefly examined in section 2.3.

Section 2.4 discusses how the regulatory process can be represented using game theory. The players in the regulatory game are consumers and firms. Examples of cooperative and noncooperative games are given.

2.1 Administrative Agencies

2.1.1 Legislative Aspects

Regulation in the United States, at least at the federal level, is a century-old phenomenon whose beginning is generally traced to the establishment of the Interstate Commerce Commission (ICC) in 1887. State regulatory commissions originated with a Rhode Island law of 1839 (Gellhorn and Pierce, 1982). Administrative agencies are created by Congress to carry out broadly defined policies. Regulatory agencies take many forms.[1] Yet most have extensive powers and significant latitude in formulating policy and independence of action. As early as 1937, a president's committee on administrative management referred to the independent regulatory commissions as a "headless 'fourth branch' of the Government, a haphazard deposit of irresponsible agencies and uncoordinated powers."[2]

Agencies are ad hoc instruments of congressional policy. Congress determines the agency's purpose, procedures, and powers. The existence of agencies can be explained in part by the costs of legislative decision making and the returns to scale in agency production of decisions. The legislative system is characterized by the formation of committees and subcommittees. The committee system brings the benefits of specialization of function and division of labor to the decision-making process. Further, smaller numbers of decision makers in committees may reduce the costs of negotiation and communication. The formation of administrative agencies is in part explained by the limits on congressional time and resources. By specifying policy objectives and periodically reviewing agency actions, Congress may delegate authority to the administrative agencies. Agencies achieve economies from specialization. They are able to form a professional staff that may devote its attention to a particular industry or group of industries over a long period of time and thus learn about its characteristics. Agencies may thus yield economies in information gathering. Agencies may perform specific tasks many times, such as regulation of pollution in different industries by the EPA.

The dilemma faced by Congress in establishing regulatory agencies is that a dual purpose is envisioned. Regulatory agencies must be accountable to the Congress or the Executive and represent an exercise of congressional and executive power. However, it is desired that regulatory agencies proceed fairly, that they accord individuals the due process of law, and that their decisions are consistent with judicial review. Unfortunately, achieving these two purposes within any single agency may be inconsistent or problematic at best. This basic conflict has been reflected in studies of regulation as will be seen.

The multiple goals that Congress attaches to the regulatory process has resulted in a broad range of powers for regulatory agencies and diverse instruments for carrying out the agency's mandate. Agencies create laws and standards in the form of administrative rules. Agencies enforce laws by monitoring compliance with laws and imposing legal sanctions. Agencies perform arbitration of conflicting interests and allocate resources as in a court of law. Thus, the powers and procedures of regulatory agencies resemble those of the legislative, executive, and judicial branches of government.[3] It has frequently been pointed out that this combination of functions violates, at least in principle, the constitutional objective of separation and delegation of powers.

Consider first the legislative and executive powers of regulatory agencies. Because Congress cannot fully specify the detailed rules that are required to achieve various regulatory objectives, Congress has delegated some rule-making powers to administrative agencies.[4] At the same time, agencies must perform a variety of executive tasks from information gathering to law enforcement. The issue is then how to enforce congressional policy objectives while giving the agency sufficient leeway and flexibility to carry out its task. The goal of accountability and control is partly reflected in the location of agencies, some of which are within the executive branch either as independent agencies or in cabinet departments and some of which are entirely outside of the direct control of the executive. There has been much speculation as to apparent inconsistencies in the location of agencies in the federal administration. Cushman (President's Committee, 1937, p. 207) states that "if Congress has followed any consistent principle in choosing between these two methods, it has failed to disclose what that principle is." There is naturally a struggle between the Congress and the president over control of regulatory agencies. Cushman presents a strong argument for executive control based on the role of the executive in coordinating policy and on the responsibilities of the president in proposing legislation. Whether Congress or the president exercises oversight and control of agencies, it is apparent that agency actions are subject to political control and the influence of interest groups. This is a basic consequence of the fact that agency power is delegated power. Responsibility for regulatory actions must rest with elected officials, either the Congress or the president. Thus, the determination of regulatory policy independent of political influence is in itself contradictory. This need not constitute a criticism of the regulatory institutions, however. Rather, it is a direct consequence of a representative form of government. Congressional representatives and the president are subject to the pressures of public opinion and interest groups. Regulatory agencies are themselves instruments of policy. Thus, of necessity, the actions taken by regulatory agencies reflect the concerns of elected officials.

At the same time, Congress intended for agencies to carry out a judicial role. This is reflected in the process of case-by-case adjudication of particular issues or the function of agencies as a court of law. Indeed, the rule-making process itself, under the Administrative Procedures Act, has the nature of a courtroom proceeding with a formal written record and testimony from parties of opposing viewpoints. However, as has long been recognized, the quasi-judicial nature of agency proceedings need not imply that agency decisions are impartial. Although agency decisions and procedures are subject to judicial review, this is not sufficient to guarantee the impartiality of an independent court. One issue is the combination of the functions of prosecution and adjudication. Even though hearings are often conducted under the auspices of an administrative law judge, Heffron (1983, p. 280) notes that a majority of cases are appealed by either the party or the agency itself, with the appeal being made to the director of the agency. As Heffron (1983, p. 281) observes, "The initial decision becomes part of the record, a part that must be carefully considered but that is in no way binding on the agency. The Supreme Court has consistently held that the final decision power rests with the agency."

Cushman (Brownlow Committee, 1937) suggested that a resolution of the dual objectives of achieving "political responsibility" and "judicial independence" is to place all of the agencies within the executive branch to achieve direct control by the president, while breaking commissions into an independent "Judicial Section" and an "Administrative Section." Administrative and rule-making functions would go to the administrative component, while quasi-judicial functions would go to the judicial component. The difficulty lies in the large number of formal and informal actions that involve a mixture of functions. The proposal of Cushman would delegate these functions to the administrative section with extensive review of these decisions by the judicial section. Cushman notes the dangers of political control of agencies by industry pressure groups (this is far from being a new discovery by economists) but emphasizes the necessity of discretionary power and the impartiality of career public administrators. In the second half-century of regulation following the Brownlow Committee's report, little has changed in the nature of the regulatory process and in the criticisms thereof.

The conflicting purposes of regulatory agencies has led the economic literature to emphasize separately two different aspects of regulation. Discussions of indirect interaction consider the effects of interest groups, political pressure groups, and public opinion as exercised through political representatives. Discussions of direct interaction refer to the administrative process itself through the agency's direct contact with consumers and firms. Direct contact occurs through the agency's information-gathering and law enforcement functions as well as through rule making and adjudication. Our primary concern is with the process of direct interaction.

2.1.2 Agency Functions

I now classify federal and some state regulatory agencies by the market failures that they are intended to address. I divide the agencies into those concerned with barriers to entry, externalities, and internalities.

A wide variety of alternative social institutions have been created to address the problem of cost minimization for industries with high levels of sunk costs. A common solution in the United States and abroad is direct government ownership and control. Examples in the United States include the Tennessee Valley Authority (TVA) and state and local public utilities in electricity, the postal system, and the Amtrak railroad. An important means of regulation quite frequently observed in many countries but not in the United States is the mixed enterprise that combines both public and private ownership and control.[5] Experience with government divestiture or "privatization" in the United States and abroad has shown that the terms of sale constitute a source of government control. The conditions imposed by the government for the transfer of publicly held assets to private hands is often a form of regulation itself. In what follows, we narrowly define regulation to apply to those industries in which firms are privately owned and controlled but that operate in the presence of government restrictions.

As noted previously, sunk costs can create entry barriers that impede competition. In industries with relatively minimal costs of market entry and exit, market competition should provide an effective allocation mechanism in the absence of administrative interference. These industries include buses, trucks, and barges that have nonetheless been regulated by the ICC. Furthermore, ICC regulation of railway rates, despite the high level of sunk costs required to establish a railroad, is also likely to be unnecessary due to extensive "intermodal" competition from trucks, barges, and pipelines. The competition faced by railroads lies behind the partial deregulation provisions of the Railroad Revitalization and Reform Act (1976) and the Staggers Rail Act (1980); on railroad regulation see MacAvoy and Snow (1977a), Keeler (1983), and Friedlaender and Spady (1981), and see MacAvoy and Snow (1977b) on truck regulation. The existence of competition in airline markets was a major factor in the deregulation of airlines through elimination of the Civil Aeronautics Board (CAB) under the Airline Deregulation Act of 1978. There is a large literature on the regulation and deregulation of the airline industry. See particularly Douglas and Miller (1974), MacAvoy and Snow (1977c), Bailey and Panzar (1981), Meyer and Oster (1981), and Bailey, Graham, and Kaplan (1985).

Table 2.1.1 lists those regulatory agencies that have primarily been involved in rate regulation. We classify those agencies engaged in "possibly appropriate" rate regulation where significant sunk costs are present and

Table 2.1.1
Rate regulation

Possibly appropriate	Inappropriate
Interstate Commerce Commission (1887) (Pipelines)	Interstate Commerce Commission (1887) (rail, bus, trucks, barges)
Federal Energy Regulatory Commission, Department of Energy (1980)	Federal Maritime Commission (1936)
State regulatory commissions (electricity, natural gas, telephones)	Federal Communications Commission (1934) (Long-distance telephone rates)
	Civil Aeronautics Board (1938–1984)
	Energy Regulatory Administration (1974)
	Postal Rate Commission (1970)
	Copyright Royalty Tribunal (1976)
	State regulation of airlines, trucks, and rail

Source of agency names and year established: MacAvoy (1979).

there may not exist competitive provision of close substitutes. These areas include pipeline regulation by the ICC and Federal Energy Regulatory Commission (FERC) and state regulation of electricity, natural gas, and local telephone service. A rather longer list of "inappropriate" applications of regulation is given. Regulation as applied to industries with low sunk costs, such as airlines, buses, trucks, and barges, would be expected to interfere with the efficient operation of the competitive market. The same distortions are to be expected in railroads due to the presence of closely substitutable services offered by trucks and barges. Technological change in long-distance telecommunications allows competition without sunk costs in overland transmission facilities and makes rate regulation super-fluous. Regulation of oil and natural gas prices by FERC is clearly not required since prices may be set on competitive spot and futures markets, as has been observed since deregulation. Many of the inefficiencies observed in pricing, supplies, and contract formation in natural gas markets are the result of piecemeal deregulation under the Natural Gas Policy Act of 1978; see MacAvoy (1983).[6]

Breyer proposes an interesting normative approach to regulatory institutions. This consists of evaluating whether regulatory policies are matched or mismatched to the market failure they are supposed to remedy. For example, Breyer describes a partial mismatch between standard setting and the problem of environmental pollution and suggests that effluent taxes or marketable permits yield a better match. Breyer (1982, p. 197) identifies a mismatch when "classical price and entry regulation is applied to a structurally competitive industry," particularly under the questionable rationale of "excessive competition." This approach to evaluating regulation can be useful in practice but lacks an underlying classification of market failure as presented here.

Table 2.1.2 lists agencies concerned with externalities. The Federal Communications Commission (FCC) is included since access to the radio spectrum must be controlled to prevent interference in communications. Interference and crowding of the radio spectrum are externalities of the type that result from free access to a common property resource. The most active federal agency involved with externalities is the Environmental Protection Agency (EPA). Its activities are discussed in chapters 12 and 13. Those agencies concerned with externalities in highway and rail transport are the Federal Highway Administration, the National Highway Traffic Safety Administration, and the Federal Railroad Administration. These

Table 2.1.2
Externalities

Federal Communications Commission (1934)
Federal Highway Administration, Department of Transportation (1966)
Environmental Protection Agency (1970)
National Highway Traffic Safety Administration, Department of Transportation (1970)
Federal Railroad Administration, Department of Transportation (1970)
Nuclear Regulatory Commission (1974)

Source of agency names and year established: MacAvoy (1979).

agencies are primarily responsible for the establishment of safety standards. I include the Nuclear Regulatory Commission (NRC) since a large part of its activities constitutes setting safety standards for nuclear reactors so as to reduce population health and safety risks.

Agencies that regulate environmental quality and product and workplace safety are often grouped together in the category of social regulations or "new-wave" regulations. However, I find the distinction between those agencies primarily concerned with *externalities*, that is, harm done to "third parties," and those concerned with *internalities*, harm done within a contractual relation, to be quite useful. Although many of the agencies concerned with product and workplace safety pursue other objectives as well, I list them under "internalities" in table 2.1.3 to emphasize their direct intervention in market transactions. Food safety is a concern of the Packers and Stockyards Administration, the Agricultural Marketing Service, and the Food and Drug Administration (FDA). The FDA is involved with the regulation of food additives and the testing, approval, and marketing of pharmaceuticals (see chapter 14). The National Highway Traffic Safety Administration is included in table 2.1.3 (in addition to table 2.1.2) since it sets safety standards for automobiles. The major regulatory agency that sets product standards is the Consumer Product Safety Commission. The Occupational Safety and Health Administration (OSHA) has established a complex set of standards that attempts to control workplace accident and health risks; see chapter 14 for an extended discussion.

The subject of financial regulation requires extensive analysis of financial markets and the investment decisions of consumers and firms. This subject

Table 2.1.3
Internalities

Product quality and safety
Packers and Stockyards Administration, Department of Agriculture (1916)
Food and Drug Administration, Department of Health and Human Services (1931)
Agricultural Marketing Service, Department of Agriculture (1937)
Federal Aviation Administration, Department of Transportation (1948)
National Highway Traffic Safety Administration (1970)
Consumer Product Safety Commission (1972)

Workplace safety
Mining Enforcement and Safety Administration, Department of the Interior (1973)
Occupational Safety and Health Administration, Department of Labor (1973)

Source of agency names and year established: MacAvoy (1979).

is deserving of separate treatment and is beyond the scope of the present book. A complex system of federal financial regulations is enforced by a number of agencies whose policies have interrelated and at times conflicting effects. The agencies concerned with financial regulation and the dates they were established include the following:

Board of Governors of the Federal Reserve System (1913),

Federal Home Loan Bank Board (1932),

Federal Deposit Insurance Corporation (1933),

Securities and Exchange Commission (1934),

Securities Investors Protection Commission (1970),

Farm Credit Administration (1971),

Commodity Futures Trading Commission (1975).

It is more difficult to classify financial regulation because of the significant connections between capital markets and the monetary system. Regulations that are concerned with financial disclosure may be seen as addressing internalities. However, regulations that are concerned with solvency may be seen as part of government management of the monetary system. For example, regulations such as portfolio restrictions, capital adequacy requirements, and Regulation Q restrictions are directed at the solvency of depository intermediaries.[7] In this sense, solvency regulations are directed at the externalities within the financial system that would be caused by bank failures.

2.2   Direct Interaction: Administrative Process

2.2.1   Policy Instruments

Agency actions are governed by restrictions imposed by statutory law and the Constitution. The Constitution imposes broad requirements that decisions allow individuals due process of law, equal protection, and the core constitutional rights.[8] The requirement of due process of law is reflected in the authorizing legislation for the agency, the agency's own procedural rules, and the Administrative Procedures Act (APA).[9] Similarly, at the state level agency procedures follow authorizing legislation, the agency's own procedural rules, and, for many states, statutory requirements that follow the model State Administrative Procedure Act.[10]

The APA provides a number of formal definitions that are of great usefulness in the study of regulation. The following definitions are paraphrased or adapted from section 551 of the APA. These are meant to establish a framework for use of these terms in subsequent discussion and are not meant as legal definitions. The first five definitions describe agency policy instruments.

Definition 2.2.1   A *rule* is an agency statement that implements, interprets, or prescribes law or policy or that describes the organization, procedure, or practice requirements of the agency.

Definition 2.2.2   A *license* is an agency permit, certificate, approval, registration, charter, membership, statutory exemption, or other form of permission.

Definition 2.2.3   An *order* is an agency decision in the form of a statement of policy or injuction applying to a particular case.

Definition 2.2.4   A *sanction* is an agency (a) prohibition, requirement limitation, or other condition affecting the freedom of a person; (b) withholding of relief; (c) imposition of penalty or fine; (d) destruction, taking, seizure, or withholding of property; (e) assessment of damages, reimbursement, restitution, compensation, costs, charges, or fees; (f) requirement, revocation, or suspension of a license; or (g) taking other compulsory or restrictive action.

Definition 2.2.5   *Relief* is a (a) grant of money, assistance, license, authority, exemption, exception, privilege, or remedy; (b) recognition of a claim, right, immunity, privilege, exemption, or exception; or (c) taking of other action on the application or petition of, and beneficial to, a person.

The five categories of policy instruments listed, rule, license, order, sanction, and relief, are refered to by the APA as *agency actions*. The procedure by which an agency arrives at a particular policy depends on the policy actions in question. Different procedural guidelines apply. In particular, a *rulemaking* process is distinguished from *adjudication*, which is a process for formulating orders, and licensing. The imposition of sanctions or granting of relief may also be through adjudication. The difference between rule making and adjudication is that rules have a general applicability. Adjudication refers to orders for specific cases although these may establish precedents that have general applicability.

It is important to emphasize that most of the actions of agencies are informal and do not follow the explicit procedures associated with rule making and adjudication.[11] Studies of regulation must attempt to identify a consistent pattern of informal actions by an agency (if one exists). Agency activities, even if informal with regard to administrative procedure, nonetheless affect resource allocation in regulated markets.

2.2.2 Information Gathering

A principal activity of regulatory agencies is information gathering. The expenditures made by agencies to acquire and process information are quite high.[12] These expenditures clearly illustrate the high cost of information collection by nonmarket participants. Further, the costs of providing information to regulatory agencies that are incurred by consumers and firm are even greater.[13] The expenditures incurred by market participants in gathering information attests to the presence of incomplete information in markets. The private costs of communicating with administrative agencies and of complying with agency requests for information must be included as a cost of regulation.

The gathering of vast amounts of information by federal, state, and local agencies is an integral part of regulation for a number of reasons. First, production of information in itself may be the agency's goal. The agency may be charged with providing information to the general public, such as consumer product information or technical information for industry. Federal agencies may be required to obtain information for Congress or the Executive branch. Second, the collection of information is a significant aspect of the rule-making process as mandated by the Administrative Procedures Act. Judicial oversight sets requirements on the information that must be collected.[14] Third, information is required by the agencies to monitor compliance with laws and administrative rules and to carry out enforcement.[15] Fourth, market information is required for most direct regulation. Thus, setting or approving rates, allocating routes, licenses or franchises and setting standards for product quality or workplace safety necessitate detailed market data.

On the one hand, the presence of incomplete information in markets provides a justification for the system of administrative regulation. As noted in the previous chapter, asymmetric information may result in market transactions that do not appropriate all of the rents from exchange. The ex post inefficiency of these transactions implies the presence of possible welfare gains from provision of information by a third party to the transactions, either a private broker or a public agency. Some types of information may be costly to produce, but may be relatively less costly to disseminate and may provide benefits to a large number of consumers. The nature of information as a public good argues strongly for the production of information by a government agency. Otherwise, due to free rider effects, private production of information may be at less than efficient levels. Thus, the fact that the regulatory process generates large amounts of information need not in itself be cause for alarm if the sum of private valuations of that information is greater than or equal to the marginal cost of producing the information.

On the other hand, the high cost of gathering information faced by agencies may be the strongest argument against the system of administrative allocation of resources. Command and control regulation requires intimate knowledge of the firm's technology and management.[16] In the extreme case, complete control would require, at least, administrative duplication of the management apparatus of the firm. Even if regulators seek to satisfy "simple performance criteria," they encounter complex monitoring problems; see McKie (1970). Further, attempts by regulatory agencies to supplant the market allocation mechanism may involve extensive amounts of data regarding consumer demand and firm technology. The distinctive feature of markets, that individual traders need only focus attention on summary data such as prices, is lost in administrative allocation. For rate setting or allocating leases or property rights, regulatory agencies may significantly reduce their information requirements by employing market type mechanisms, such as auctions and transferable property rights.

Therefore, we must attempt to distinguish carefully between useful and unnecessary production of information by agencies. If particular product or technical information has the nature of a public good and can be provided at lower than private cost by an agency, then information gathering may be useful. If information gathering is required to enforce rules, then it may also be useful although the cost of that information gathering must be netted out from the benefits of compliance with the rules. However, if information gathering occurs simply in the service of administrative allocation of resources where a market mechanism could be employed to achieve desirable results, then the information gathering process may be identified as unnecesary and inefficient.[17]

The provision of information to various regulatory agencies is a time-consuming and expensive task for individual consumers and firms. The regulatory process leads to private information gathering for a number of reasons. First, individuals must supply information to agencies to comply with legal requirements. For example, firms must report compliance with standards for product quality, environmental quality, or workplace safety. Second, individuals choose to supply information to regulators as part of the regulatory process. Intervenors in rate hearings seek to influence the outcome of the regulatory process by their presentation of relevant information. Because adequate information is crucial to regulatory decision making, the private production of information that is then supplied to agencies illustrates the concept of rent seeking. Rent seeking is defined as "the expenditure of scarce resources to capture an artificially created transfer"; see Tollison (1982) for a survey. A wasteful private allocation of resources to information gathering and communication may be expected if the regulatory process generates appropriable rents. The extensive literature on rent seeking considers the political influence over economic regulation by interest groups. If the provision of information influences regulatory outcomes,[18] it is to be expected that sufficient resources will be also devoted to supplying information to regulators to capture rents.[19] In the limit, competition will drive information production to the point where private expenditures equal publicly created rents. Third, information is supplied to legislatures by lobbyists for particular regulatory programs and is thus an ancillary cost of regulation. The supply of information is an important component of the lobbying costs of industry groups and professional associations. Fourth, the judicial oversight of regulatory proceedings necessitates a large quantity of information gathering both by agencies and by private parties that challenge agency decisions.

Information is gathered by administrative agencies on a routine basis through voluntary reporting as well as through formal investigatory procedures. Heffron (1983, chapter 7) extensively discusses formal procedures that include (i) records and reports, (ii) physical inspections of firms and households, (iii) legislative hearings, and (iv) subpoenas for testimony and documents enforced by the courts. Information is supplied by consumers and firms both voluntarily and under compulsion.

The preceding discussion of information gathering suggests a number of general hypotheses for models of regulated markets. (1) Incomplete and asymmetric information is present for regulators with regards to market data and the characteristics of consumers and firms. (2) Regulators engage in information gathering, and consumers and firms supply information to regulators. (3) Information gathering is costly for regulatory agencies and participants in regulated markets. These hypotheses imply that informational considerations should be an important component of economic models of regulated markets.

2.2.3 Rule Making

Regulatory agencies create laws and standards in the form of administrative rules. Rule making by regulatory agencies is the most specific delegation of legislative powers by the Congress. Rules made by agencies serve to fill in the details in authorizing statutes. Rules provide a policy instrument for achieving specific agency objectives. The selection and enforcement of rules by agencies are what is generally meant by regulation in economic models and includes rate making and standard setting. The immediate focus of the discussion is on the rule-making process itself.

The rule-making process is defined by authorizing legislation, established agency procedures, and the APA. The flavor of rule making is that of congressional hearings on proposed legislation. The first requirement imposed by the APA is that general notice of a proposed rule making be given (in the *Federal Register*) (APA, section 553): "The notice shall include

(1) a statement of the time, place, and nature of public rule-making proceedings;

(2) reference to the legal authority under which the rule is proposed; and

(3) either the terms or substance of the proposed rule or a description of the subjects and issues involved."

The APA makes exceptions to the notice requirement for "interpretive rules, general statements of policy, or rules of agency organization procedure, or practice" unless these are required by statute. Also, notice need not be required if it is impracticable or contrary to the public interest. Rule-making procedures may be *formal*, with hearings on the record resembling a court trial. Rule making may be *informal*, without a hearing on the record but with notice of the rule-making and public comments. "Hybrid" forms of these two types of rule-making procedures have become common; see Williams (1975), and Magat, Krupnick, and Harrington (1986).

Concerned parties are given access to the rule-making procedure after notice is given. What is more, concerned parties may initiate rule making. The APA requires that "each agency shall give an interested person the right to petition for the issuance, amendment, or repeal of a rule" (APA, section 553). The agency must allow interested individuals "an opportunity to participate in the rulemaking through submission of written data, views, or arguments with or without opportunity for oral presentation."

The rule-making process has been criticized as being costly to both the agency holding public hearings and to the concerned parties presenting their views. Further, the process is viewed as cumbersome and involving unnecessary delays. It is therefore worthwhile assessing the reasons why the rule-making process has been established and whether the criticisms are justified.

The primary justification for the established rule-making procedure is to assure individuals in regulated markets that rules that affect their well-being are arrived at in a consistent manner. The establishment of formal procedures with opportunity for expression of differing viewpoints is motivated by the desire for due process of law. Although rules generally affect the "life, liberty, and property" of broad *classes* of individuals, administrative procedures allow concerned individuals to be represented and to present evidence on the effects of agency actions and on questions of fact. By expressing their viewpoints, interested individuals add to the formal record of the hearing. In announcing a rule, the agency must then record the relevant opinions expressed and where necessary respond to public criticism.

The hearing is primarily a mechanism for information gathering by the agency. As noted above, a large part of agency activity is devoted to the collection of information. By basing decisions on privately supplied information, the agency creates incentives for private data collection and research. This shifts the costs of information gathering to private individuals and firms and reduces the costs of information gathering to the agency. Of course, private individuals need only supply information that is relevant and supportive of their position. It is often emphasized that regulatory agencies are subject to manipulation by intervenors capable of producing convincing testimony.[20] Whether or not agencies are consistently influenced by particular firms or interest groups is an empirical issue. It is generally acknowledged that information gathering does influence ultimate rule making. It may be that the competitive supply of information by individuals of opposing views yields a balanced presentation overall.[21]

There are a number of important aspects of information generated by hearings on proposed agency rules. The information is sometimes of a technical nature regarding market data, such as firm technology, product characteristics, and consumer preferences and buying habits. The hearing may produce insights into unforeseen consequences of the agency rule. What is of special significance is the reactions that bear specifically on the ultimate adoption of the rule. The hearing indicates to the agency points of contention that firms or individuals might raise through court challenges. A desire to avoid a rule being overturned in the courts may determine the form of the rule that is finally adopted. The public reaction generated through hearings alerts the agency to possible reactions to the rule on the part of Congress or the president. A strong lobbying effort against an agency ruling indicates future congressional interest and subsequent opposition to the ruling.

Because the hearings are public, arguments presented before the agency are also made available to parties of opposing views. Thus, the hearing on a proposed rule effectively constitutes a debate between interested parties. This debate may be interpreted as a process of *negotiation* with the agency in the role of mediator. A significant aspect of rule making is that it is an adversarial procedure whereby opposing parties compete to influence the agency.[22] However, the competition involves a certain amount of communication *between the parties themselves.* In many cases, the rules that emerge may represent a consensus between the consumer and firm interest groups. Rules reflect the interests of consumers to maintain future participation in the market. Rules reflect the interests of regulated firms to assure the viability of those firms and to reduce the costs of enforcement.

An important aspect of the rule-making process that is often criticized is the presence of long delays inherent in public hearings and the associated high costs of information gathering and communication. This criticism must be answered by questioning whether delays are long relative to alternative procedures. Relative to judicial proceedings, regulatory hearings may not appear inordinately long. Relative to executive actions, the hearings appear slow. However, there may be benefits from delay. One benefit is observance of due process in allowing individual interests to be expressed. More significantly, delays in the rule-making process serve to warn markets of impending changes in the regulatory regime. This gives consumers and firms time to react to future rules. The reaction time is important because of the high costs of adjustment of consumption and investment decisions. For example, airline deregulation resulted in costly adjustment of travel patterns, labor contracts, and airline investment as well as entry and exit of airlines. The benefits of deregulation must be balanced against cost savings that might be achieved by advance notice of future rule making followed by a period of gradual adjustment. This is not to say that rules must be adjusted gradually. The gradual adjustment of some natural gas prices (and not others) created severe problems for pipelines and suppliers under long-term contract. Rather, the delay in implementing a rule change allows the market to select a rate of adjustment in advance of the new regime.[23]

An additional aspect of the delays imposed by administrative procedure is that rule making is at least somewhat removed from any immediate objectives of the regulatory authority. Thus, the response of the regulatory agency to a particular market equilibrium is limited. The agency is prevented from "fine-tuning" by the foreseeable delays of hearings. This reduces the agency's flexibility and to some extent requires the formulation of rules that have general applicability and are not designed to address specific allocations. This is not to say that regulatory agencies necessarily pursue broadly defined objectives. Rather, the constraints imposed by formal rule making may serve to limit the exercise of command and control type policies.[24]

The rule-making process is evolutionary. A contrast is often made between the interference in market processes by regulatory agencies and common law solutions. However, the rule-making process with comments from market participants on proposed rules and on previously established rules allows the set of rules passed by an agency to emerge from a process of revision of previous rules and creation of new ones. This is not to say that the process will proceed without errors. Rather, the hearing process over time may involve a long series of errors, public comments, and revision of rules. The process may result in evolution toward market rules that are superior to those established by agency fiat.[25]

In criticizing government regulation of industry one must be careful to distinguish between arguments against intervention itself and criticism of the procedures followed by regulatory agencies. It is true that some markets would function more efficiently with limited government intervention. However, given that regulatory intervention is to occur, it should not be asserted that regulation always takes the form of "command and control." A contrast is often made between the law, which is a system of rules that have evolved over time, and regulations, which are the product of human design. This contrast may not be so clearly defined.

The distinction between social institutions that are the product of human actions and those that are the result of conscious design is central to Hayek (1973). Hayek (1973, vol. 1, p. 13) stresses that "most of the rules of conduct which govern our actions, and most of the institutions which arise out of this regularity, are adaptations to the impossibility of anyone taking conscious account of all of the particular facts which enter into the order of society." Thus, "spontaneous" institutions such as the common law are superior to those institutions that are the product of human design because the latter "greatly restrict the utilization of available knowledge." (1973, vol. 1, p. 5). This criticism of rules that are designed certainly applies to *specific* rules selected by regulatory agencies. The agency cannot hope to make use of all of the available information used by market participants in making innumerable decisions. Indeed, Hayek emphasizes that "the gist of the argument against 'interference' or 'intervention' in the market order" is that "although we can endeavour to improve a spontaneous order by revising the general rules on which it rests, and can supplement its results by efforts of various organizations, we cannot improve the results by specific commands that deprive its members of the possibility of using their knowledge for their purposes" (1973, vol. 1, p. 51). Hayek distinguishes between commands and rules, which, "unlike commands, create an order even among people who do not pursue a common purpose" (1973, vol. 1, p. 99).

The issue is whether the rules created by agencies have the nature of commands or more general rules of conduct. It is often the case that the rules promulgated by an agency are intended to achieve a specific objective in a given situation. There is an attempt by regulatory agencies to design regulations in a rational manner so as to obtain what are often very precise desired allocations of resources. In this sense, some agency rules take the form of commands and as such may greatly impede market performance. However, the rules promulgated by agencies are subject to intense scrutiny and public comments. The distortions and inefficiencies that they create result in reactions that ultimately amend the rules or result in new rules. Thus, the dynamic process of regulation, through repeated hearings and rule making, results in a pattern of regulation that may be far removed not only from the agency's authorizing statutes but far removed from the agency's direct control as well. Often, the pattern of rule making by an agency may result in rules that could not have been foreseen or effectively designed by the agency itself a priori.

As a case in point, consider the partial deregulation of natural gas prices at the wellhead under the Natural Gas Policy Act (NGPA). The Federal Energy Regulatory Commission (FERC) initiated public proceedings by a Notice of Inquiry (NOI) in Docket No. RM85-1-000. In the period December 1984 to March 1985, FERC received 200 detailed comments from participants in the natural gas markets as noted in the Notice of Proposed Rulemaking (Docket No. RM85-1-000). As is typical in regulatory proceedings FERC acknowledges the "NOI comments, judicial decisions, comments of both the legislative and executive branches of the Federal Government—and our own experience." The public comments, the decisions of the reviewing courts of appeal, and comments by congressmen and policymakers in the executive branch (such as the Department of Energy) lead FERC (Docket No. RM85-1-000, pp. 2–3) to the conclusion that the present regulatory framework for the natural gas transmission industry may not be as well adapted as it could be to the economic realities of the industry as they exist today and are likely to evolve in coming years. As pointed out by the commentors, the partial removal of wellhead price controls mandated by the NGPA has been responsible in large part for the economic forces that have fundamentally changed the behavior of the various segments of the natural gas industry. This natural evolution in the industry appears to have been impeded to some degree by a regulatory framework which, while well adapted to the earlier period, has not been sufficiently adjusted to promote adequately the public interest in the newer, evolving economic environment.

In reaction to complaints and public comments FERC proposed a complex new set of rules and amendments to existing rules. These proposals are themselves subject to change after hearings. An attempt is made to react to market distortions and conflicts generated by rulings. Furthermore, an attempt is made to identify points of agreement among commentors. For example, FERC identifies a "broad consensus" among commentors over long-term regulation of natural gas transmission given sufficient opportunity by market participants to adjust long-term contracts.

Detailed study of the case of natural gas regulation and other industries indicates that the pattern of rule making and subsequent revision is a common one. Thus, the complex of rules that emerges can be said to evolve from the interaction between regulators and interested market participants. Rules that generate conflict or severe inefficiencies will be altered. Rules that are subject to reversal by courts of appeal will no longer apply. Rules that are implemented generate large amounts of information about market performance particularly through the observations of market participants. Thus, the body of rules that are applied by an agency will represent the outcome of a complex series of (a) hearings on proposed rules, (b) issuance of rules, (c) observations of market equilibria under the new rules, and (d) proposals of revisions to existing rules. It cannot be said that the body of rules is then strictly the product of agency design. Rather, the set of rules that emerges must reflect a consensus of market participants as well as rules that are useful in the mitigation of conflict. The rules that remain viable are therefore related to legal principles that emerge from the judicial system of conflict resolution and creation of precedents.

The discussion given above suggests that it might be incorrect to conclude that regulation is inefficient from observation of a specific set of rules. Some attention must be given to the dynamics of the rule-making process. What must be addressed is whether the interaction between rule making and observations of market equilibrium may lead to improvement in regulations. Thus, it must be examined whether the rule-making process tends to equilibria and whether the equilibrium rules support efficient allocation of resources by the competitive market.

In summary, the preceding discussions suggests a number of hypotheses about the rule-making process. (1) Hearings are a means of gathering information about market data, which may be otherwise incomplete and costly to attain. (2) The hearing process involves an exchange of information not only between the market participants and the regulator but also among market participants themselves. (3) The hearing process involves identification of a consensus among interested parties. (4) Finally, the rule-making process is dynamic. The body of rulings evolves in a manner that responds to the existence of conflict between market participants and to observations of the complex effects of existing rules on resource allocation.

2.2.4 Adjudication

Regulatory agencies arbitrate some conflicts in a manner resembling courts of law. Most agency actions may be seen as informal adjudication in the sense of decisions on the claims of individuals. In issuing orders, agencies, in some cases, must act through a formal court-type proceeding. As in the case with formal rule making, adjudication requires on-the-record exchange of information between the interested parties and the agency. Like a trial, the process is adversarial, with the agency as an interested party. However, the presence of outside intervenors may make adjudication procedures similar to rule making. Formal adjudication may be time consuming, with evidence presented on the record through lengthy hearings. As with rule making, the primary concern is for due process of law.

Formal adjudication by agencies requires a hearing on the record. As with rule making, the APA requires that interested parties be informed of

1. the time, place, and nature of the hearing;

2. the legal authority and jurisdiction under which the hearing is to be held; and

3. the matters of fact and law asserted

(APA, ¶554,b). The agency must give interested parties opportunity for the "submission and consideration of facts, arguments, offers of settlement, or proposals of adjustment" (APA ¶554,c). The hearing is presided over by members of the agency and one or more administrative law judges. Public intervenors may often participate. The agency may be represented by counsel. The agency often performs a prosecutorial role. The agency or the administrative law judge may not communicate separately with any of the interested parties; see APA ¶557,d on *ex parte* communication. Further, if any such communication occurs, it is to be made a part of the public record of the proceeding. Although the administrative law judge makes a decision at the hearing, the outcome is subject to appeal by either the affected parties or the agency itself. The final decision thus rests with the agency directly. On reviewing the appeal, the APA (¶557,b) states that "the agency has all the powers which it would have in making the initial decision except as it may limit the issues on notice or by rule."

There is no question that *specific* agency orders that result from adjudication may reflect agency policy. In this sense, some precedents are established. In fact, as Heffron (1983, p. 265) observes "Even if an administrative agency is required by statute or the Constitution to provide an opportunity for hearing, it may still bypass that requirement in some instances by promulgating rules of general applicability." Adjudication represents a class of agency policy instruments. However, the *process* of agency decision making and issuance of orders through adjudication is evolutionary. The body of adjudicatory decisions and related rules is influenced by the sequence of hearings and the particular circumstances of each case. Thus, the overall pattern of agency rulings may not reflect any particular agency intention or deliberate policy.

Consider, for example, the effect of the initial MCI decision in telecommunications.[26] Microwave Communications, Inc. (MCI), applied to the FCC for licensing. The initial decision of the hearing examiner made clear that the decision in favor of the application did not necessarily reflect the policy of the FCC. Rather, the examiner (and later the commission) intended the grant of licenses as a means of gathering information about resulting market equilibria, the demand for the services provided by MCI, the actual costs and quality of service, and the reaction of other market participants. The hearing examiner stated that "any such grant [of certification] should not be construed as indicating that the Commission would favorably regard similar proposals between other major markets by MCI or others. The instant proposal should be given a reasonable opportunity to become established and thereby afford the Commission an opportunity to observe the results and consequences of its operations in terms of the demand generated for its services, its ability to operate efficiently and profitably, and its effect.[27]" The decisions on the specific case of MCI lead to large numbers of additional license applications. As Kahn (1971, p. 135) observes, "And so, also, within the year, the FCC staff was calling for a radical generalization of the *above* -890 and *MCI* decisions into a bold policy of free entry into the field of specialized communications services." A major policy shift toward competition and away from protection of natural monopoly in telecommunications was thus partly a result of a limited decision on a specific case and observation of the resuling market reactions.

The evolutionary nature of the regulatory process has been widely criticized. The fact that adjudication is often reactive implies that it does not allow a clear articulation of agency policy.[28] Others see adjudication as preventing government planning of regulatory policy.[29] Similar criticisms might be made of the process of adjudication by the courts. There, the long-term evolution of common law doctrines is sometimes seen as a strength rather than a weakness; see Posner (1977). The arbitration of conflict creates situations in which the economically inefficient aspects of previous agency decisions or rules are continually reexamined. Economically inefficient regulations should create market responses that circumvent those rules or that make apparent their restrictive nature. Thus, regulations that do not properly mediate between interested parties will lead to conflict and challenges. The process of meeting these challenges on a case-by-case basis may substantially affect overall agency policy.

The case-by-case system of adjudication often creates severe inefficiencies when regulation directly interferes with the internal decision making of firms. Thus, attempts to control the prices, technology, outputs, inputs, product quality, or assets of firms leads to a misallocation of resources due to the inflexibility of the adjudicatory process. Generally, cost-of-service rate making adjusts poorly to demand or costs changes. Thus, the process of rate hearings creates costs of price adjustment. Attempts to adjust to competition from substitute goods or shifts in consumption patterns are hindered by regulatory delays and rigidities in the decision processes of rate-setting commissions. Attempts to reduce the costs of adjustment may distort the input decisions of firms and thereby create additional inefficiency. For example, automatic pass-throughs of fuel cost increases by electric utilities have been said to create a bias toward more fuel intensive technologies (see chapter 10). The rate-hearing process creates costs of adjustment in the presence of inflation although regulatory lag has been identified as providing incentives for short-run cost savings in between rate hearings. In the case of the assets of regulated firms, the obstacles created by the ICC for railroads that wish to abandon track may be an important factor in the decline of many railroads. The underlying issue in these cases may not be adjudication itself. Rather, the direct interference in decisions by market participants, combined with the inherent delays of the administrative process, imposes high costs on market adjustment. This results in distortions of relative prices and interferes with cost minimization by firms. The principal conclusion to be drawn is that the administrative process is a poor substitute for decision making by market participants. The design of regulatory policy should, where possible, attempt to formulate general rules rather than adjudicate specific economic decisions.

Posner (1977, p. 485) argues that the administrative process reflects the "politicization of regulation" rather than "efficient legal regulation." Posner observes that the combination of prosecution and adjudication within an agency creates bias not present in courts. In particular, agencies have incentives to issue remedial orders rather than dismiss complaints. For Posner (1977, p. 482) bias exists if "the agency weights the costs of an erroneous decision to dismiss a complaint more heavily than the costs of an erroneous decision to enter a remedial order against the respondent." The bias may be tempered by the requirements of the APA and the possibility of judicial review.[30] There is, as always, a trade-off between the pursuit of agency objectives and achieving impartial adjudication. The indirect influences on agency decisions are discussed in the next section.

2.3 Indirect Interaction: Positive Theories of Regulation

The preceding section has examined direct interaction between administrative agencies and market participants through agency gathering of information, rule making, and adjudication. Regulatory agencies are subject to controls and oversight from the legislative, executive, and judicial branches of government. This section briefly examines the extensive literature on indirect interaction between regulators and market participants that occurs through controls on agency activities.

Indirect interaction between regulatory agencies and economic agents is often defined by the political influence that consumer and firm interest groups exercise through elected officials. Indirect interaction also includes consumer and firm influence on members of the regulatory agency's bureaucracy. Finally, indirect interaction may include legal actions or the threat of legal actions by consumers and firms to create or alter particular regulations. The study of these indirect interactions is the subject of political and administrative "theories of regulation." These *positive* theories seek to explain why particular regulatory agencies are established, and why these agencies pursue various objectives.[31]

A large political science literature on the origins of regulation exists; see Mitnick (1980) for a comprehensive survey. Posner (1974) comments on "capture" theory in political science. An analysis of legislators as intermediaries between constituents appears in Fiorina and Noll (1978). On models of bureaucratic behavior see Downs (1957), Tullock (1965), and Niskanen (1971, 1975). On public choice theory and regulatory decision making see the survey of Romer and Rosenthal (1985).

Stigler (1971, p. 3) asserts that regulation is a set of government favors demanded and controlled by industry. An industry is said to purchase government regulation with financial or in-kind campaign contributions.[32] To this, Posner (1974) adds the observation that the coercive powers of the state provide industry with a more efficient means of cartelization. Elsewhere, Posner (1975) identifies the welfare losses from monopoly as equal to the total monopoly rents, not just the welfare triangle that is traditionally identified with deadweight welfare losses. The reasoning is that if entry barriers are created by the government, competition to become the monopolist or to influence the government to create monopoly rents by firms will lead to expenditures that equal potential profits. That is, competitive bidding for political influence will lead to the dissipation of potential monopoly rents through wasteful expenditures to acquire those rents. Thus, competition to obtain rents from government regulation generates social costs that in the limit may exhaust monopoly profits.[33]

Posner (1971) argues that the presence of internal cross-subsidies in the pricing structure of multiproduct regulated firms constitutes a form of taxation. Higher rates are set on some regulated goods to subsidize production of other goods that the market might not supply otherwise. Thus, Posner views regulation as a means of public finance, subject to political influences similar to other tax and subsidy programs.

Peltzman (1976) develops a political or legislative model of regulation in which legislators make regulatory decisions to maximize their expected

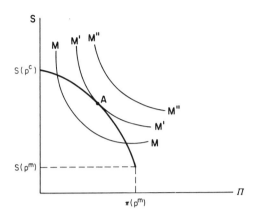

Figure 2.3.1
The Peltzman model.

voting majority. Peltzman (1976) extends Stigler's (1971) model by giving a role to politicians in the formation of interest groups and by positing an objective function for politicians. The objective function is a "majority-generating function" that depends on the wealth levels of interest groups. For price and entry regulation, the interest groups can be consumers and firms. Let $S = S(p)$ represent consumer surplus and let $\Pi = \pi(p)$ represent industry profits as a function of the market price p. The political production function is then

$$M = M(S, \pi), \tag{2.3.1}$$

where $M_1 \equiv \partial M/\partial S > 0$ and $M_2 \equiv \partial M/\partial \pi > 0$. Consumer surplus is greatest at the competitive price p^c, $\pi(p^c) = 0$, and smallest at the monopoly price p^m, $\pi'(p^m) = 0$. We can derive a political production possibilities frontier

$$S = S(p(\Pi)) = S(\pi^{-1}(\Pi)), \tag{2.3.2}$$

where Π take values between $\pi(p^c)$ and $\pi(p^m)$; see figure 2.3.1. Assuming that M exhibits diminishing marginal rate of substitution, the "isomajority curves" resemble the MM curves in figure 2.3.1. Then, a politician will select a regulatory regime that maximizes the voting majority and yields an equilibrium such that the marginal rate of political substitution equals the marginal rate of transformation of firm profits to consumer surplus. The regulated price solves

$$\max_p M(S(p), \pi(p)),$$ (2.3.3)

subject to $p \in [p^c, p^m]$. Therefore, the regulated price $\bar{p}$ satisfies

$$\frac{M_2(S, \Pi)}{M_1(S, \Pi)} = \frac{-S'(\bar{p})}{\pi'(\bar{p})},$$ (2.3.4)

where $S = S(\bar{p})$, $\Pi = \pi(\bar{p})$. This corresponds to point A in figure 2.3.1 and yields a price that may be strictly between the competitive and monopoly prices.

The work of Stigler and Peltzman is extended in a set of case studies in Wilson (1980a). Wilson (1980b, pp. 367–370) focuses on the distribution of the costs and benefits of regulation and the resulting political coalitions that form to promote or oppose prospective policy. Thus, the demand side of the "market for regulation" includes narrow interest groups that favor (or oppose) regulation if the net benefits (or costs) are concentrated or wider constituencies if net benefits are broadly dispersed. As Shepsle (1982) points out, this approach has a tendency to minimize the supply side, including public sector rule-making technology and administrative law procedures.

Regulatory controls may support a cartel; see MacAvoy (1965). The substitution of government coercion for private cartel enforcement has been modeled by Lee (1980). Following Stigler's (1971) insight that the social costs of cartel enforcement may be less than private costs, Lee (1980b) identifies welfare gains to be shared between consumers and firms. Let p^0 be the price in a cartelized market free of government regulation. Again let $S(p)$ represent net consumer surplus. Let $\pi(p)$ represent cartel profits exclusive of enforcement costs. Then, let K^G represent the costs of cartelization by the government (i.e., regulation) and K^P the private costs of cartelization. Then, net surplus and firm profits under regulation must exceed net surplus and firm profits in the absence of regulation. Thus, the regulated price must be such that

$$S(p) - K^G \geq S(p^0) \qquad \text{and} \qquad \pi(p) \geq \pi(p^0) - K^P.$$ (2.3.5)

Thus, a Pareto frontier much like that given in figure 2.3.1 is defined along which the welfare of consumers cannot be improved without reducing the profits of firms. The inequalities generate an upper bound on prices, p'', referred to as the social concession price, and a lower bound on prices, p', referred to as the industry concession price, $S(p'') - K^G = S(p^0)$, $\pi(p') =$

$\pi(p^0) - K^P$. Lee (1980b) refers to the Nash bargaining equilibrium of the cooperative game between the consumers (or regulator) and the cartel as the "fair" or "just" price. However, any price satisfying (2.3.5) might be similarly characterized. To find the Nash bargaining equilibrium, maximize the product of consumer and firm net benefits over p;

$$\max_p [(S(p) - K^G) - S(p^0)][\pi(p) - (\pi(p^0) - K^P)]. \tag{2.3.6}$$

The regulated price, $\bar{p}$, solves

$$\frac{[S(\bar{p}) - K^G] - S(p^0)}{\pi(\bar{p}) - [\pi(p^0) - K^P]} = \frac{-S'(\bar{p})}{\pi'(\bar{p})}. \tag{2.3.7}$$

Compare equation (2.3.7) with the voting model solution in equation (2.3.4).

Another approach to the study of regulatory agencies is to examine the nature of incentives for members of the administration of the agencies. Noll (1971, p. 40) identifies two success indicators for regulatory agencies. First, rules or decisions are successful from the point of view of regulators if they are not overridden by Congress or by the courts. Second, the viability of firms in the regulated sector is seen as important, or at least the avoidance of service interruptions that might be attributable to regulation. The fear of being overridden by the courts or by Congress may have two effects. It might make regulators overly cautious or it might make regulators subject to influence by well-organized or well-financed industry or consumer groups. These groups can threaten to challenge decisions through the courts or through Congress. Even if the regulatory agency followed legal guidelines and pursued its statutory purpose in its decisions, the risks of being over-turned are present nonetheless. It is not apparent that regulators derive their primary motivation from the fear of legislative or judicial reversal. Unlike court rulings, regulatory decisions need not create precedent. Concern for the viability of the regulated industry appears innocuous. In normative economic models, such as Ramsey pricing, prices are set to maximize net consumer welfare subject to a break-even condition on firm profits. In practice, however, concern for industry viability may translate into giving positive weight to firm profits in agency welfare calculations. This may greatly alter agency decision making and lead to actions that cause income transfers from consumers to regulated firms and create efficiency losses.

An interesting view is that regulators may have altruistic or publicly interested goals; see Kau and Rubin (1979), Kalt (1981), and Tullock (1982).

Kalt and Zupan (1984, 1986) emphasize the possibility of "slack" in the political process that influences the decisions of regulators and legislators. This slack may be due to regulators taking various actions for ideological reasons or self-interest.

The theories of regulation discussed above attempt to describe observed behavior of regulatory agencies. In addition, these theories are expressed in reaction to the "public interest" theory of regulation.[34] The public interest view is that the objectives of regulation are the maximization of social welfare. The clearest statement of criticism of this view is by Joskow and Noll (1981): "As a positive theory of regulation, the normative theory of welfare economics is obviously incorrect." The failure of regulators to serve the public interest is thus seen to make criticisms of regulatory policies on welfare grounds redundant or beside the point. It is argued that if regulators are not pursuing welfare maximization, then it is no accident that regulatory decisions result in departures from economic efficiency and losses in social welfare.

In my view, one should not readily abandon the methods of welfare economics. If the interests of firms or specific interest groups are given weight by regulators in their decisions, it should be possible to incorporate these indirect influences in a representation of regulatory preferences. As a positive theory, this approach lends itself to testing in the manner pioneered by McFadden (1975).[35] McFadden (1975) suggests that the outcomes of regulatory decisions, if properly anticipated by regulators, may be examined empirically. Then a test may be made whether "there exists an implicit choice criterion such that the bureaucracy behaves *as if* it is attempting to follow this choice rule. Thus, using revealed preference analysis, the outcomes of regulatory decisions may be used to attempt to recover regulatory preferences.[36] By analyzing the decision-making behavior of regulators, it is possible to improve our understanding of regulatory objectives. In his study of the regulatory process in rate hearings for public utilities, Joskow (1972, p. 644) concludes that "decision rules for legal decision making units (whether they be regulatory agencies, other types of administrative agencies, or courts) should be observable, may be specified in a simple way, and can be estimated by collecting data from a sample of cases and using standard statistical techniques." The specification of the decision rules of regulators need not be inconsistent with the methods of welfare economics. All agency decisions will result in winners and losers. Specifying agency policies within a framework of relative weights on the well-being of economic agents allows the study of the impacts of alternative policy objectives.[37]

In general, studies of the economic effects of regulation may require embedding the regulator-market interaction within a model with explicit attention to the choice mechanisms of agencies and the effects of external control. For example, Weingast and Moran (1983) examine the effects of congressional influence on decision making by the FTC. In particular, Weingast and Moran consider the influence of the Subcommittee on Consumer Affairs, the Senate Commerce Committee, and the House Committee on Interstate and Foreign Commerce subcommittee overseeing the FTC. The influence of congressional *preferences* over the distribution of cases selected by the FTC is examined using logit analysis as in Joskow (1972) and McFadden (1975, 1976). The work of Weingast and Moran (1983) appears to support the view that FTC decisions are sensitive to the composition of congressional oversight subcommittees. The effect of this analysis is to push back the source of agency preferences to the level of the congressional subcommittee. A stimulating empirical analysis of agency behavior using the revealed preference approach is carried out by Magat, Krupnick, and Harrington (1986) for the case of industrial effluent standards established by the Environmental Protection Agency. They apply Peltzman's (1976) model to examine the effects of "external signals" from consumers and firms on the stringency of environmental quality standards. One interesting conclusion of their empirical analysis is that considerations of equity or economic efficiency were not sufficient to explain the stringency of environmental standards.

2.4   Regulation and Game Theory

Models of the administrative process yield interesting predictions regarding the types of regulations that are chosen and the effects of those regulations on the market equilibrium. Different game theoretic tools can be applied to study alternative aspects of regulatory procedures. Consumer and firm interest groups often act independently in choosing the strategies they will use in interaction with a regulatory agency. Given its adversary nature, the regulatory hearing process may be modeled as a *noncooperative* game played by consumer and firm interest groups under rules designed by the administrative agency. Direct interaction through the hearing process described above may also involve exchange of information between interested parties and in some cases results in a consensus. The process then may be usefully modeled as a *cooperative game*. Cooperative games allow for preplay communication and the formation of contracts. The analysis will emphasize cooperative games.

2.4.1 Noncooperative Games

Two examples of noncooperative regulatory games are now considered. A model of the rule-making process can be obtained by applying noncooperative bargaining games such as Rubinstein (1982).[38] Suppose that exchange of goods between a consumer and firm requires approval by a regulatory agency. The firm might be a utility seeking a license to serve from a regulator. Suppose further that the regulator will only grant such a license after the consumer and firm agree on a price. Regulatory hearings can then be viewed as a bargaining process. Suppose that the consumer and firm exchange a sequence of offers. Each party can accept the other's offer or make a counteroffer. The consumer and firm discount future gains from exchange with the same discount factor $\delta, 0 < \delta < 1$. The consumer derives benefit v from the good and the firm's production costs are c. Suppose that the consumer makes the first offer. Then the consumer obtains net benefits equal to $(v - c)/(1 + \delta)$ at the perfect equilibrium of the bargaining game; see Rubinstein (1982). The regulated equilibrium price is therefore

$$p = c + (\delta/(1 + \delta))(v - c).$$

The regulated price reflects consumer benefits, production costs, and bargaining costs in the form of the discount rate. This application can be generalized to allow asymmetric information about demand and costs by applying models of bargaining under asymmetric information. Given that rate hearings are usually long and costly procedures, a dynamic bargaining model yields predictions regarding the effects of impatience and transactions costs on the prices that are ultimately selected by regulatory agencies. This analysis can of course be applied to other problems, such as setting environmental pollution quotas and product quality standards.

Another example of a noncooperative regulation game is a static game involving two players, interest groups 1 and 2. They can devote expenditures or persuasive efforts $x^i, i = 1, 2$. Depending upon their expenditures, the regulatory process creates payoffs $g^i(x^1, x^2), i = 1, 2$, for the two interest groups. A Nash noncooperative equilibrium for this simple game is a pair of expenditure levels (x^{1*}, x^{2*}), which solve $\max_{x^1}[g^1(x^1, x^{2*}) - x^1]$ and

$\max_{x^2}[g^2(x^{1*}, x^2) - x^2]$. Such an approach requires careful specification of what constitutes a noncooperative strategy, such as persuasive effort, and the ways in which these strategies affect regulatory outcomes. The preceding discussion has been in terms of a single regulatory agency. Many markets are subject to the actions of several regulators. For example, a single firm may obey worker safety, environmental pollution, and product quality rules. Thus, it is possible for regulatory agencies themselves to interact strategically. Two agencies may choose to set their policies in either a cooperative or noncooperative manner. In this case, the attainable allocations for an agency will depend on the strategic choice of the other agency. Baron (1985) presents a noncooperative game theory approach to competition between environmental and utility regulators.

2.4.2 Cooperative Games

Administrative regulation involves communication and negotiation among market participants. The outcome of this bargaining process can include market rules, reallocation of resources, and constraints on consumer and firm decisions. Cooperative games are useful in modeling negotiation and in assessing the bargaining power of coalitions of consumers and firms. The players are the set of market participants or interest groups that represent them.[39] The objective functions are utility functions for consumers and profit functions for firms. The set of feasible outcomes reflects both technological feasibility and constraints on policy instruments available to the regulatory agency. These constraints reflect legislative restrictions, agency budgets, and in some cases oversight by Congress, the Executive, and the Judiciary. The outcome of the cooperative game represents the consensus achieved through the process of rule making, adjudication, and enforcement of regulations. I consider both cooperative bargaining and the core of cooperative games.

The outcomes of a cooperative game of regulation are assumed to be Pareto optimal for the players. This means that those consumers and firms that are involved in direct interaction achieve a consensus that reflects their own interests. Of course, such an outcome need not be Pareto optimal in the sense that the term is used in welfare economics. Inefficiency may occur for several reasons. In welfare economics, an allocation is efficient or Pareto optimal if there do not exist alternative allocations that make some consumers better off without making other consumers worse off. Regulated outcomes can fail to be efficient because the profits of firms are taken into account in the regulation game. For example, entry barriers increase firm profits but harm consumers. A number of other factors can lead to inefficiency in the regulated market. The players may be interest groups that imperfectly represent consumer interests. The outcome of regulatory hearings can depend on the particular intervenors involved and the characteristics of their presentations. Unlike the competitive market, rule making and adjudicatory processes are far from anonymous. Also, the allocations that result from regulatory actions may fail to be efficient due to constraints on the regulator's actions. Specific policy instruments may involve a trade-off between economic efficiency and other objectives, such as income redistribution. Finally, the preferences of the regulators themselves may play a role in determining the regulated outcome.

The regulatory agency may have preferences that reflect the benefits obtained by consumers and firms in the regulated market.[40] These preferences could be represented by a standard social welfare function except for the inclusion of firm profits.[41] Of course, there may not exist social welfare functions that satisfy various desirable criteria. However, regulation need not be an ideal social choice scheme. Recall that there are strong "filters" between social preferences and the regulator's ranking. The expressed preferences of the regulator are influenced by Congress, and so are one step removed from voting constituents. Consumer and firm pressure groups have uneven strength. Less powerful coalitions may not make their influence felt. As noted above, the actions of the regulator are subject to the constraints of judicial review and the restrictions of administrative procedure and the agency's governing statutes. The notion of regulatory preferences allows a framework that is sufficiently general to encompass various views of regulation. In particular, exclusive weighting of consumer preferences may be interpreted as satisfying the *public interest* view of regulation. Exclusive weighting of the profits of a group of firms may be interpreted as consistent with the *capture theory* of regulation. Of course, a wide range of preferences may exist between these two extremes.

The analysis will not emphasize regulator's preferences although I do not wish to deny their significance. Rather, I stress the role of regulatory agencies as arbitrators between consumers and firms in the bargaining process. It is assumed that regulators follow specific decision rules in mediating between interest groups in regulated markets. Luce and Raiffa (1957, p. 121) suggest that an arbitrator may wish to announce basic principles that underlie his choices:

We may suppose that the arbiter sincerely envisages his mission to be 'fairness' to both players; however, there are not, as yet, any simple and obvious criteria of 'fairness,' so, in effect, he is being asked to express a part of his ethical standards when resolving the game. The arbiter can be assumed to want to suggest a solution which will seem 'reasonable,' both because he is sincere and because he may wish to be hired for such tasks in the future. Thus, for example, he would be mistaken to suggest a solution having an obvious alternative which is preferred by both players. Or suppose there are two different conflict situations and that everyone agrees player 1 is strategically better off in the first than the second; then the arbiter should not give player 1 less in the first than the second. In short, an arbiter will (or should) try to satisfy some consistency requirements. In addition, as with most adjudicators, he will be anxious to defend his suggested solutions with some fairly good rationalizations. All of this means that he should be prepared to formulate and to defend the basic principles which lie behind his suggested compromises— they should not be completely arbitrary!

In reading this description of arbitration, one is struck by its applicability to the administrative regulatory process. In particular, the agency often pursues vaguely defined objectives in reaching decisions that are "fair" or "reasonable." Often, ethical judgments must be applied to resolve conflicts. The regulator must formulate general rules but must be prepared for adjudication in a variety of conflict situations. Finally, regulatory agencies present extensive formal explanations of general principles underlying rule making or adjudicatory decisions. Regulators may set prices or standards to satisfy a specific set of criteria.

A particular set of criteria that the regulator may follow is the well-known axioms that are satisfied by the Nash (1950, 1953) bargaining solution. Chapter 10 presents a discussion of rate hearings as a bargaining process that applies the Nash bargaining solution. I illustrate my approach with a simple bargaining problem. Suppose that a representative consumer and a regulated firm bargain over output Q and total payment R. The consumer obtains benefits $u(Q)$ from good Q. The firm produces at cost $C(Q)$. *Pareto optimality* requires that output be chosen in such a way that marginal benefit equals marginal cost, $u'(Q^*) = C'(Q^*)$. *Individual rationality* requires that both consumer and firm obtain nonnegative gains-from-trade, $u(Q^*) \geq R \geq C(Q^*)$. This allows a wide range of alternative choices for the total payment. The payment given by the Nash bargaining solution solves

$$\max_R (u(Q^*) - R)(R - C(Q^*)).$$

Thus, the payment equals $R = (u(Q^*) + C(Q^*))/2$ and the consumer and firm evenly divide the total gains-from-trade.

The Nash bargaining solution can be used to calculate a *second-best* price for our example. The output level will depart from its Pareto optimal level if the price must both ration consumer demand and allocate gains-from-trade between the consumer and regulated firm. Let $Q(p)$ be the consumer demand that solves $u'(Q) = p$. The second-best price given by the Nash bargaining solution solves

$$\max_p (u(Q(p)) - pQ(p))(pQ(p) - C(Q(p))).$$

Solving the maximization problem and rearranging terms, we obtain an expression for the relative markup above marginal cost,

$$\frac{p - C'(Q)}{p} = \frac{1}{\eta(Q)}[1 - (pQ - C(Q))/(u(Q) - pQ)],$$

where $\eta(Q) = -pQ'(p)/Q$ is the elasticity of demand.

The concept of the core is useful to identify regulated outcomes that reflect the bargaining power of all subcoalitions of consumers and firms. The core can be viewed as a minimum standard of social stability. In a market setting, the core conditions guarantee that groups of consumers and firms do not form subcoalitions that might choose to not participate in the regulated market. The core accounts for all potential strategies and opportunities available to each coalition of consumers and firms. I illustrate my applications of the core with an example. The example is related to benefit games studied by Littlechild (1975a) and Sharkey (1982b).

Consider an economy with three consumers who derive benefits $v^i, i = 1$, 2, 3, from consuming a particular commodity. The commodity may be produced by any group or coalition of consumers. Let $c^i, i = 1, 2, 3$, be the *stand-alone cost* of supplying consumer i. Let $c^{ij} = c^{ji}, i, j = 1, 2, 3, i \neq j$, be the cost of supplying any two consumers i and j. Finally, let c be the cost of supplying all three consumers. The net benefits of coalitions are defined as follows:

$$V(\{i\}) = v^i - c^i, \qquad i = 1, 2, 3,$$

$$V(\{i,j\}) = v^i + v^j - c^{ij}, \qquad i \neq j, \qquad i, j = 1, 2, 3,$$

$$V(\{1, 2, 3\}) = v^1 + v^2 + v^3 - c.$$

We assume that all coalitions obtain positive net benefits. Payoffs or imputations are represented by V^i, $i = 1, 2, 3$, and are determined by personalized prices p^i, $i = 1, 2, 3$,

$$V^i = v^i - p^i.$$

The *core* is a set of imputations V^i that is defined by the following conditions. The first condition is feasibility:

$$V^1 + V^2 + V^3 \leq v^1 + v^2 + v^3 - c.$$

This essentially requires that prices cover production costs, $p^1 + p^2 + p^3 \geq c$. Second, core allocations must be Pareto optimal, $V^1 + V^2 + V^3 = v^1 + v^2 + v^3 - c$. This implies that prices exactly equal production costs, $p^1 + p^2 + p^3 = c$. Third, core allocations must satisfy *individual rationality*, that is, $V^i \geq v^i - c^i$, so that individuals have incentive to join the coalition that includes all consumers. This requires prices to be less than stand-alone costs:

$$p^i \leq c^i.$$

Finally, core allocations cannot be improved upon by any coalition of two consumers,

$$V^i + V^j \geq v^i + v^j - c^{ij}, \qquad i \neq j, \qquad i, j = 1, 2, 3.$$

This reduces to the requirement that the payments by any two consumers not exceed their joint stand-alone costs,

$$p^i + p^j \leq c^{ij}, \qquad i \neq j, \qquad i, j = 1, 2, 3.$$

Formal definitions of the core are given in chapters 3 and 8.

The costs of production are assumed to be increasing, $c^i < c^{ij} < c, i \neq j$, $i, j = 1, 2, 3$. Furthermore, we define *natural monopoly* as follows:

$$c \leq c^{ij} + c^k, \qquad i \neq j \neq k, \qquad i, j, k = 1, 2, 3,$$

$$c^{ij} \leq c^i + c^j, \qquad i \neq j, \qquad i, j = 1, 2, 3.$$

Because the cost function exhibits *natural monopoly*, it is in the interest of the consumers to cooperate in jointly producing the commodity. If prices satisfy the requirements associated with a core allocation, no consumers or pairs of consumers will be able to improve their positions by producing the good on their own. I interpret core prices as regulated prices. Let $c - c^{12}$

be the *incremental cost* of producing good 3 for the grand coalition, let $c^{13} - c^3$ be the incremental cost of producing good 3 for coalition $\{1, 3,\}$, and so on for other coalitions. Let incremental costs be nonincreasing,

$$c - c^{ij} \leq c^{jk} - c^j, \qquad i \neq j \neq k, \qquad i, j, k = 1, 2, 3.$$

It is now shown that nonincreasing incremental cost is a sufficient condition for existence of core allocations. It is actually sufficient for only one incremental cost condition to hold, for example, $c - c^{13} \leq c^{23} - c^3$. Then, the following prices yield a core allocation:

$$p^1 = c - c^{23}, \qquad p^2 = c^{23} - c^3, \qquad p^3 = c^3.$$

First, note that Pareto optimality is satisfied since $p^1 + p^2 + p^3 = c$. The allocation satisfies individual rationality, $p^i \leq c^i, i = 1, 2, 3$, by the natural monopoly assumption. The allocation cannot be blocked by any coalition of two members. By definition, $p^2 + p^3 = c^{23}$. By natural monopoly, $p^1 + p^2 = c - c^3 \leq c^{12}$. By decreasing incremental costs,

$$p^1 + p^3 = c - c^{23} + c^3 \leq c^{23}.$$

So, (p^1, p^2, p^3) supports a core allocation.

In chapter 6 I introduce the concept of the *second-best core*. This is the *core* of a game in which we restrict allocations to those that are supported by a price system. In my example, this means that all consumers must pay the same price for the good. The zero profits requirement implies that the Pareto optimal price must equal average cost, $p = c/3$. A sufficient condition for the second-best core to exist is for average costs to be nonincreasing, $c/3 \leq c^{ij}/2 \leq c^i, i \neq j, i, j = 1, 2, 3$. It is easy to see how the second-best core is empty if this condition is not satisfied. If $c^1 = c/4$, then the second-best core allocation does not satisfy individual rationality for consumer 1. Suppose further that $c^2 = c^3 = 3c/5$, $c^{12} = c^{23} = c^{13} = 4c/5$. Natural monopoly will still hold, but the benefits from joint production will not be attainable due to the uniform pricing constraint. The second-best core notion provides a link between cooperative games and market models. It will be useful in the analysis of franchise competition in chapter 9.

General versions of the preceding examples of cooperative games will be used throughout the analysis. The presentation is meant to be suggestive of the manner in which cooperative games may be used to model the regulatory process. By carefully specifying the strategies and objectives pursued by consumers and firms, cooperative games can lead to greater understanding of the connections between the administrative process and equilibrium in regulated markets.

Notes

1. Heffron (1983) identifies five principal forms of regulatory agencies: independent regulatory commissions, agencies in cabinet departments, independent agencies, government corporations, and agencies in the executive office of the president.

2. See President's Committee on Administrative Management (1937, p. 40), also referred to as the Brownlow Committee.

3. This observation is commonplace in administrative law; see Posner (1977), Breyer (1982), Heffron (1983), Gellhorn and Boyer (1981), and President's Committee (1937).

4. The congressional delegation of power to independent agencies or agencies in the executive branch may be unconstitutional in that it is contrary to the separation and delegation of powers doctrine. This problem is closely identified with regulation. Lowi (1969, p. 128) states that "delegation of power did not become a widespread practice or a constitutional problem until government began to take on regulatory functions."

5. See Eckel and Vining (1985) and Eckel and Vermaelen (1986).

6. See also MacAvoy and Noll (1973) and MacAvoy and Pindyck (1975).

7. See Koehn (1979) for additional discussion.

8. See Heffron (1983, p. 52).

9. See Breyer (1982), and Breyer and Stewart (1979).

10. See Heffron (1983, p. 96, and appendix II).

11. Heffron (1983, chapter 8) lists informal actions as including summary actions, creation of publicity, policy statements, negotiated settlements, processing of applications, and "friendly persuasion." Heffron (1983, p. 215) emphasizes that most informal actions are "marked by a seeming absence of compulsion" but are always backed and made effective by the possibility of formal action. Informal actions have the advantage of speed and "flexibility."

12. The costs to the federal government for the year 1976 were over $18 billion for handling and processing forms. In 1976, the government distributed approximately 4,418 different forms; see Heffron (1983, p. 173). The processing of forms is just one part of the information-gathering activities by federal agencies.

13. One estimate gives a figure of $100 billion for total public and private costs of completing forms required by the federal government for the year 1976 alone; see Heffron (1983, p. 173).

14. Harrington and Frick (1983, p. 537n) note that in the courts "the current trend is to increase the amount of information which an agency must consider before promulgating a regulation or taking other actions."

15. See the discussion in Heffron (1983). Heffron also notes the role of information gathering by agencies in preparing legislation for recommendation to Congress.

16. McKie (1970) gives a summary list of the many decision variables available to a firm and observes that "control over these variables by the management of the enterprise itself is never complete, even with full access to information and complete internal authority."

17. The information advantages of the market mechanism over administrative allocation are well known. The benefits using market mechanisms to achieve regulatory objectives is one of the themes of this book.

18. Joskow (1972) finds that the presence of consumer or firm intervenors in electricity rate cases has an effect on the allowed rate of return. See also Lee (1980b, pp. 858–860).

19. It is suggested by attorneys Harrington and Frick (1983, p. 537–538) that "it is not only a person's right but his duty to provide agencies with his position on the issues under consideration, an analysis of the legal framework of the proposed regulation, and hard technical data and scientific information on the proposal and its economic effect." It may go without saying that these duties are primarily fulfilled by industry representatives and public interest groups with a stake in the outcome.

20. Owen and Braeutigam (1978, p. 235) assert that industries make strategic use of information: "Agencies can be guided in the desired direction by making available carefully selected facts." Further, Owen and Braeutigam find that firms may obtain delays in agency procedures by providing information in large amounts or in highly technical form. Further, they suggest that industries may coopt "experts, especially academics" by hiring them or providing research grants.

21. It is frequently asserted that those parties with the most resources will have the greatest influence over the hearing process because they will be able to spend more on legal representation and research. It is rather those parties who stand to gain or lose the most from agency decisions who will have incentive to invest in formal presentations at rate hearings. One expects that the marginal return to investment in presentations is decreasing beyond some level.

22. Posner (1977, p. 400) observes that "the legal process, like the market, is competitive." The same may be said for the regulatory allocation process, although regulators need not have the "aloof disinterest" that Posner ascribes to judges. See Susskind and McMahon (1985) on negotiated rule making with application to the EPA. Regulatory rule making is studied by Krupnick, Magat, and Harrington (1983) and Magat and Estomin (1981).

23. Owen and Braeutigam (1978, p. 18) argue that "the effect of administrative procedure ... is to slow down or delay the operation of market forces." They argue that Congress (and voters) intend for the administrative process to achieve economic justice or fairness through delay, and "the grant to individuals and their interest groups of equity rights in the status quo" (p. 20). In their model, regulation exists "in order to slow down the rate at which the free market redistributes income, thus reducing the market risks faced by voters" (p. 26). This is an accurate description of regulatory policy in some cases. However, this differs from the point we are making, which is that delay allows the market to adjust to changes in *regulatory policy itself.*

24. Hayek (1973, p. 32) observes that "liberalism ... restricts deliberate control of the overall order of society to the enforcement of such general rules as are necessary for the formation of a spontaneous order, the details of which we cannot foresee." By the formulation of general rules, the regulatory agency is thereby constrained a bit in taking actions that have an easily predictable effect. Of course, the informal rule making and informal adjudication carried out by agencies do give more latitude for economic tinkering.

25. A number of studies have focused on tendencies toward efficiency in common law through challenges to inefficient precedents; in particular, see Priest (1977), Rubin (1977, 1982), and Landes and Posner (1979). Tullock (1980) and Rubin (1982) consider the effects of competing interests on the efficient evolution of statutes and regulation.

26. See FCC, *In re Applications of Microwave Communications, Inc.,* Docket No. 16509, Initial Decision of the Hearing Examiner, October 17, 1967. See Kahn (1971, pp. 132–136) for a discussion of the particulars of the case.

27. This is quoted in Kahn (1971, p. 134) and is taken from Docket No. 16509. Kahn notes that the commission makes a similar observation in its statement *In the Matter of Establishment of Policies and Procedures for Consideration of Applications to Provide Specialized*

Common Carrier Services in the Domestic Public Point-to-Point Microwave Radio Service, etc., Docket No. 18920, Notice of Inquiry to Formulate Policy, etc., July 15, 1970 (par. 37).

28. For example, Kahn (1971, p. 87) states that "preponderantly, regulation has been a negative process, with the initiative coming from the companies themselves; private parties act, and commissions react. From this fact follows most of the other severely criticized characteristics of the regulatory process: it proceeds on a case-by-case basis, on issues usually framed and a record made up by contesting parties, rather than on occasions and issues formulated by the government itself in terms of its own independent judgement of the public concern." Kahn (1971, pp. 87–88) asserts that case-by-case adjudication "reinforces the tendencies to restriction of competition and protectionism."

29. On planning of regulatory policy, see Trebing (1967a,b).

30. See Posner (1972b, 1977) on the behavior of regulatory agencies.

31. See also Stigler (1971, 1974, 1975), Posner (1971, 1974, 1975), Noll (1971), and Joskow and Noll (1981).

32. An important model due to Peltzman (1976) analyzes regulation as the outcome of vote maximization. See Becker (1983) on the influence of pressure groups.

33. This idea is related to the general theory of the rent-seeking society; see Tullock (1967) and Krueger (1974). A survey of this literature is given by Tollison (1982).

34. The public interest view of regulation is portrayed by the Chicago School as "naive" in contrast to the "sophisticated" (or cynical) view of interest group theories of regulation.

35. McFadden (1975, 1976) applies revealed preference analysis to study freeway route selection by the California Division of Highways. McFadden tests the form of the benefit-cost calculation used by the bureaucracy, its evaluation of benefits and costs, and the influence of political interest groups on bureaucratic decisions.

36. See also a related study by Davis, Dempster, and Wildavsky (1966) of the federal budget process.

37. As frequently occurs in social choice theory, a problem arises if the decision-making procedures of congressional committees or regulatory commissions lead to behavior that cannot be represented by consistent preferences.

38. Rubinstein (1987) gives a survey of the sequential bargaining literature.

39. An alternative regulatory framework is given by Sharkey (1986), which explicitly describes coalitions of agents as interest groups and employs a cooperative game theory approach. Sharkey (1986) shows that the core of the regulation game can easily fail to exist and studies an alternative solution concept.

40. The regulator's preferences need not always reflect the preferences of the consumers and firms in the regulated market. For example, the Drug Enforcement Agency's mission is diametrically opposed to the consumers and firms in the regulated market. However, if we include the negative externalities generated by the drug trade, the potential group of consumers with an interest in the regulation of this market widens as a result.

41. Luce and Raiffa (1957, p. 332) use the following terms synonymously: social welfare function, constitution, arbitration scheme, amalgamation method, and voting procedure. These terms refer to a rule that associates a social preference ordering to a profile of individual preference orderings.

II COMPETITION AND PRICING UNDER INCREASING RETURNS TO SCALE

3 Cost-Based Pricing

Productive technology, as represented by the firm's cost function, often provides both the *reason* given for regulation and the *method* of price regulation. The productive technology in such industries as electricity, telecommunications, railroads, and pipelines generally yields returns to consolidation of production. Thus, the properties of the technology in these industries are often used to explain or justify imposition of government regulation of prices, inputs, outputs, quality of service, market entry, and the choice of the technology itself. At the same time the properties of the firm's cost function are used by regulators to set prices. This is referred to as *cost-based pricing*. Various cost-based pricing methods have been proposed in the economics and operations research literature and applied by regulatory agencies. This chapter examines properties of firm cost functions and related cost-based pricing methods, including subsidy-free prices and fully distributed cost allocation.

Cost-based methods of price regulation generally ignore social welfare considerations. There may exist alternative prices that enhance the well-being of consumers and cover the costs of the firm. Even if cost-based prices are market clearing, they may involve incorrect signals to consumers about the incremental costs of production and incorrect incentives for the regulated firm. The chapter concludes with a discussion of economic inefficiencies associated with cost-based pricing.

3.1 The Firm's Cost Function

There are three principal technological reasons for consolidating production. First, cost savings may be obtained through *diversification* of outputs. *Economies of scope* refers to the cost gains achieved by joint production of multiple goods. Second, cost savings may be obtained by *expansion* of the firm's size through growth or horizontal merger. *Economies of scale* refers to the total cost gains achieved by unification of production. Third, cost savings may be achieved by combining the production of inputs and outputs through vertical integration. I introduce the concept of *economies of sequence* to analyze the cost gains achieved by combining a sequence of production stages.

The properties of the firm's cost function that imply that consolidation of production is desirable are at once the properties that create difficulties for cost-based regulation of prices. When *economies of scope* are present, the regulator faces the problem of selecting relative prices that allocate nonattributable or joint costs between the firm's outputs. Prices equal to marginal or incremental costs will not fully allocate total costs. When *economies of scale* exist, marginal cost pricing will not yield revenues sufficient to cover total costs. Average cost prices do not convey correct signals to consumers about the firm's marginal costs. In the multiproduct case, average costs may not be easy to define. Finally, under *economies of sequence* difficulties in pricing intermediate inputs may complicate pricing of outputs and prevent decentralization of production by regulated firms. In this section, I set forth a number of important properties of cost functions.

3.1.1 Economies of Scope

An important issue in regulation is the determination of *relative prices* for the goods and services produced by regulated firms. In utility industries, the *rate structure* affects the pattern of consumer demand and firm production decisions. Regulated firms are often characterized by multiproduct technology. The properties of multiproduct cost functions are a major determinant of relative prices when regulators employ cost-based pricing rules. Multiproduct technology is also a crucial factor in explaining market structure and the extent of horizontal integration in many industries.

The firm's technology is described by a cost function $C(Q; w)$, where $Q = (Q_1, \ldots, Q_m)$ is a nonnegative vector of outputs and $w = (w_1, \ldots, w_r)$ is a positive vector of input prices. Inputs are assumed to be purchased at constant prices on competitive factor markets. Thus, my analysis of output prices and economies of scale is partial equilibrium in nature. I generally suppress input prices and write $C(Q)$ to indicate the firm's cost function. Let $C(Q)$ be twice continuously differentiable, positive, and nondecreasing for $Q \gg 0$, $C(0) \geq 0$, and let $C_l(Q) \equiv \partial C(Q)/\partial Q_l$, $l = 1, \ldots, m$. Define $C(0, \ldots, Q_l, \ldots, 0)$ as the *stand-alone* cost of good l.

The first issue to be addressed is whether multiproduct production yields cost savings. A useful benchmark is *nonjoint production*.[1] A theorem of Hall (1973) as modified by van den Heuvel (1986) serves as our definition of *nonjoint* technology.

Definition 3.1.1 The firm's technology is *nonjoint* if and only if the cost function can be written as the sum of stand-alone costs, that is,

$$C(Q; w) = \sum_{l=1}^{m} C(0, \ldots, Q_l, \ldots, 0; w). \tag{3.1.1}$$

for all Q and w.

Thus, if technology is nonjoint, production may be organized efficiently with single-product firms. For multiproduct production to yield cost efficiencies there must be returns to common or joint production of outputs.[2] A minimum requirement is that there exist *economies of scope*; see Willig (1979b) and Baumol, Panzar, and Willig (1982). Let $M = \{1,\ldots,m\}$ represent the product set and let S be some subset of M. Let Q_S represent the output vector Q with outputs Q_l not in the set S equal to zero.

Definition 3.1.2 The cost function $C(\cdot)$ exhibits *economies of scope* if for any nonempty subsets S, T of M, $S \cap T = \varnothing$,

$$C(Q_S) + C(Q_T) > C(Q_{S \cup T}).$$

A simple example of economies of scope is the cost function $C(Q_1, Q_2) = F + C^1(Q_1) + C^2(Q_2)$, where F is a fixed cost of an input used by both production processes. A regulator setting prices on the basis of costs faces the problem of allocating fixed costs between the firm's markets for goods 1 and 2. Define *incremental costs* of good l as the costs of producing l when all other goods are already being produced,

$$IC^l(Q) \equiv C(Q) - C(Q_1,\ldots,Q_{l-1},0,Q_{l+1},\ldots,Q_m).$$

Define the incremental cost of producing any subset of goods S jointly with another distinct subset of goods T as $IC^S(Q_{S \cup T}) \equiv C(Q_{S \cup T}) - C(Q_T)$. Economies of scope implies that the stand-alone costs of any subset of goods exceed their incremental costs when produced jointly with any other distinct subset of goods, $C(Q_S) > IC^S(Q_{S \cup T})$.

Returns to joint production of commodities are conceptually distinct from economies of scale although in practice the size and scope of a firm's activities are closely related. We can illustrate the connection between size and scope with two goods. Suppose that given some level of good Q_2, stand-alone costs for good 1 are below incremental costs for good 1 up to some output level $\bar{Q}_1(Q_2)$ but above incremental costs thereafter. This is shown in figure 3.1.1. Then, given Q_2 we may think of output $\bar{Q}_1(Q_2)$ as the minimum efficient output of good 1 at which joint production is efficient.

3.1.2 Economies of Scale

The principal implication of economies of scale is that marginal cost pricing will result in losses for the firm.

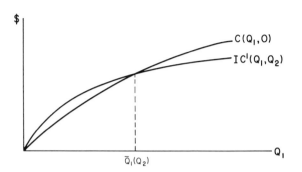

Figure 3.1.1
Minimum efficient output for joint production.

Definition 3.1.3   The cost function exhibits *increasing returns to scale* if $C(Q) > \sum_{l=1}^{m} C_l(Q)Q_l$.

Given $C(0) = 0$, note that strict concavity of the cost function is sufficient, but not necessary, for increasing returns to scale. In the presence of economies of scale, alternatives to marginal cost pricing must be found.

Consider the one good case with costs given by $C(Q) = F + V(Q)$, where V represents variable costs. Suppose that $V(0) = 0$ and $V'(Q) > 0$. The regulator faces the problem of allocating fixed costs F across the units of output produced. Average cost pricing simply assigns a consumer a share of F proportional to the output purchased. Various regulatory formulas exist that yield two-part tariffs by allocating a proportion of fixed costs to the entry fee and the remainder to the per unit charge. Alternatively, consumers are charged per unit of "capacity" required to serve them and per unit of the good purchased. In the long run, with variable capacity, the production of the good and of service capacity may be treated as two separate commodities, so that the problem is one of multiproduct pricing (e.g., peak and off-peak prices). For a consumer's capacity requirements to differ from his purchases requires either uncertainty about a future purchase or variation in repeated purchases over time.

Average costs are not clearly defined for the multiproduct firm. Thus, the concept of decreasing average cost does not have a counterpart for the multiple product case. A very special type of increasing returns to scale may be defined for a particular set of output vectors with the same fixed proportions.[3]

Definition 3.1.4   The cost function $C(\cdot)$ exhibits *decreasing ray average costs* (subhomogeneity) at Q if for all scalars λ, $0 < \lambda < 1$, $C(\lambda Q) \geq \lambda C(Q)$.

Baumol, Panzar, and Willig (1982, p. 175) state that increasing returns to scale up to Q imply (strictly) decreasing ray average costs up to Q. In particular,

$$\frac{\partial}{\partial \lambda} C(\lambda Q)/\lambda = (1/\lambda^2)\left[\sum_{l=1}^{m} C_l(\lambda Q)\lambda Q_l - C(\lambda Q)\right] < 0.$$

A stronger definition of average costs that arbitrarily weights the output vector is as follows.

Definition 3.1.5   The cost function $C(\cdot)$ exhibits *generalized decreasing average costs* if there exists a vector $a \in \mathbb{R}_+^m$, $a > 0$, such that $C(Q)/aQ$ is nonincreasing in Q.

Clearly for any scalar λ, $0 < \lambda < 1$, for a cost function exhibiting generalized decreasing average costs, $C(\lambda Q)/\lambda aQ > C(Q)/aQ$, thus implying subhomogeneity.

The concept of *natural monopoly* refers to the case where a single firm may produce any output more efficiently than any number of smaller firms. This concept relies on the implicit assumption that an allocation mechanism exists such that the costs savings from joint production translate into net welfare benefits. Complicated price-transfer mechanisms may be required to allocate total costs. A local definition of subadditivity is considered.

Definition 3.1.6   (Natural Monopoly)   The cost function $C(\cdot)$ exhibits *subadditivity* on the comprehensive set $K^C = \{Q \in \mathbb{R}_+^m : Q \leq Q^0\}$ if for $Q' + Q'' = Q \in K^C$,

$$C(Q') + C(Q'') > C(Q).$$

Clearly natural monopoly implies that economies of scope are present.

It is important to emphasize the difference between economies of scale and natural monopoly. In the single good case, declining average cost is sufficient for subadditivity. From declining average cost, it follows that

$$C(Q') > Q'\frac{C(Q' + Q'')}{Q' + Q''} \qquad \text{and} \qquad C(Q'') > Q''\frac{C(Q' + Q'')}{Q' + Q''}.$$

Adding the two equations yields $C(Q') + C(Q'') > C(Q' + Q'')$. However, subadditivity does not require economies of scale to be present. Consider a cost function with the traditional U-shaped cost curve, $C(Q) = F + Q^\alpha$ where $\alpha > 2$. The minimum average cost is attained at $Q_{\min} = (F/(\alpha - 1))^{1/\alpha}$. However, the cost function is subadditive up to $\tilde{Q} = (F/(1 - 2^{1-\alpha}))^{1/2} > Q_{\min}$. In the example, natural monopoly is due to the avoidance of multiple fixed costs by consolidating output up to $\tilde{Q}$. For total outputs larger than $\tilde{Q}$, rising marginal costs make production by multiple firms more efficient.[4]

Cost complementarities are said to exist if increased production of any output lowers marginal costs for all of the firm's outputs.

Definition 3.1.7 The cost function $C(\cdot)$ exhibits *cost complementarities* if $C_{lk}(Q) \leq 0$ for all $l, k = 1, \ldots, m$.

Cost complementarities are a particularly strong requirement for firm cost functions. For example, cost complementarities are a sufficient condition for (weak) increasing returns to scale,

$$C(Q) = \sum_{l=1}^{m} \int_0^1 C_l(tQ)Q_l \, dt + C(0) \geq \sum_{l=1}^{m} C_l(Q)Q_l.$$

Further, cost complemetarities imply not only economies of scope but (weak) subadditivity as well, as shown by Sharkey (1982a, proposition 4.4). By the definition of cost complementarities

$$C(Q') + C(Q'') \geq \sum_{l=1}^{m} \int_0^1 C_l(t(Q' + Q''))(Q'_l + Q''_l) \, dt + 2C(0)$$

$$\geq C(Q' + Q'').$$

The property of cost complementarity stems from public inputs (Baumol, Panzar, and Willig, 1982, p. 77) and other economies of joint production. Cost complementarity will be important for our subsequent analysis of cost-based pricing. Realization of cost savings from consolidation of production of different goods requires regulators to pay close attention to the product mix of regulated firms.

3.1.3 Economies of Sequence

Beginning with Adam Smith's discussion of the division of labor in a pin factory, economists have recognized that production by a single firm may involve a *sequence* of steps.[5] This can include processing raw materials, assembling inputs, or the sequence of design, production, and marketing.[6]

Stigler (1961) suggests that we can "partition" the firm not among the markets in which it buys inputs but among the functions or processes that constitute the scope of its activity. In antitrust cases and regulatory policies regarding vertical mergers, a crucial issue often involves determination of potential cost savings from vertical integration. In this section, I introduce a cost test for assessing the benefits of vertical integration.

Consider a two-stage production sequence where a scalar Q denotes final output and a scalar X denotes a produced intermediate good. As before, w is an r-vector of primary input prices for input vector Z. Let $C^U(X;w)$ be the upstream cost function and let $C^D(Q;X,w)$ be the downstream cost function given that X units of the intermediate good are used in production. The best available technology for a vertically integrated firm is represented by $C(Q;w)$.[7] As a benchmark, I introduce the concept of *nonlinked* technology.

Definition 3.1.8   The technology (C, C^U, C^D) is *nonlinked* if and only if the cost of production by separate upstream and downstream firms equals the cost of the integrated firm,

$$C(Q;w) = \min_X [C^U(X;w) + C^D(Q;X,w)]$$

for all Q and w.

A number of properties of nonlinked production processes are easily derived. By Shephard's lemma and the envelope theorem, total amounts of each input demanded with vertically integrated production must equal total amounts of each input with decentralized production,

$$Z_j(Q;w) = Z_j^U(Q;w) + Z_j^D(Q, X^*(Q;w), w), \qquad j = 1, \ldots, r,$$

where $X^*(Q;w)$ minimizes costs $(C^U + C^D)$. Further, the marginal cost of the integrated firm equals the marginal cost of the downstream firm evaluated at the optimal input level, $C_Q(Q;w) = C_Q^D(Q; X^*(Q;w), w)$. It should be noted that efficient pricing of the intermediate input requires price to equal upstream marginal cost, $C_X^U(X^*;w) = -C_X^D(Q; X^*, w)$, where $X^* = X^*(Q;w)$. If economies of scale exist upstream, marginal cost pricing will not cover upstream costs, which may complicate the choice between purchasing and producing inputs for the downstream firm.

If technology is *nonlinked*, decentralized production is efficient. In contrast, there may be returns to vertical integration of production. To represent this case, I introduce the notion of economies of sequence.

Definition 3.1.9   The technology (C, C^U, C^D) exhibits *economies of sequence* at output Q if and only if

$$C(Q; w) < C^U(X; w) + C^D(Q; X, w)$$

for all X and for all w.

The definition of *economies of sequence* is local since it applies to a particular output level. If economies of sequence are global, then vertically integrated production will be efficient. This possibility is referred to as *natural hierarchy*.

Definition 3.1.10   The technology (C, C^U, C^D) is that of a *natural hierarchy* if it exhibits economies of sequence at all output levels.

Economies of sequence may arise from public inputs as with economies of scope. Let the integrated technology be described by

$$X = f(K^1, L^1; K^2), \qquad Q = F(X, K^2, L^2),$$

where the capital from the downstream process increases production of the upstream output. Then economies of sequence will occur.

    The vertical production model provides useful restrictions on the internal transfer pricing of intermediate inputs. Let ρ be the internal transfer price of the input X. Then the transfer price cannot exceed average stand-alone costs of producing the input, $\rho \leq C^U(X; w)/X$. Otherwise, nonintegrated production of the input would appear desirable. Also, the transfer price must be sufficient to cover the average internal cost of producing the intermediate input, $\rho \geq [C(Q; w) - C^D(Q; X, w)]/X$. It follows that such transfer prices exist under economies of sequence. Regulators are concerned with the possibility of vertical cross-subsidization within regulated firms. I return to this issue again in chapter 10.

3.2   Subsidy-Free Prices

3.2.1   Subsidy-Free Prices and Support Prices

Selection of relative prices by regulatory agencies reflects consideration of social equity and economic efficiency. Changes in relative prices affect the distribution of income as well as the pattern of demand for the regulated firm's products. The present section focuses on the definition and interpretation of *subsidy-free* prices. These are prices such that the revenues generated by any subset of the regulated firm's outputs cover the costs of producing those outputs. This criterion is entirely based on the form of the regulated firm's cost function. It will serve as the basis for subsequent analysis of competition in a contestable market.

Government regulation of industry must address the two fundamental problems of entry and pricing. Should a particular activity such as electricity generation or construction of a bridge be undertaken? What should be the price charged for the output of the regulated activity? How should electricity rates or tolls for passage across the bridge be chosen? Answering these questions involves a number of complexities that are put aside for the purposes of the present chapter.

The first problem is to determine the desired level of the activity through analysis of marginal benefits and costs. Policy decisions are often presented as all-or-nothing propositions, such as the choice of whether or not to build a bridge. In practice, most projects allow some variation in terms of quality, durability, safety, and output that calls for marginal analysis. For the present, ignore such considerations by asking which activities are desirable or not at given levels of output.

The second problem is measurement and aggregation of consumer benefits. Estimating consumer demand and deriving a monetary measure of benefits (e.g., equivalent variation) can be problematic. In addition, policy decisions may have distributional effects that are not reflected in the aggregate measure of benefits. These considerations may preclude application of a simple benefit-cost criterion for evaluating policy choices.

It may be necessary to assess the desirability of economic activities in the absence of direct benefit measures. Suppose that the outputs of the activity can be rationed among consumers by a price system. Then, suppose that given particular prices, consumer demand equals or exceeds the produced outputs. Thus, the revenues generated by the activity provide at least a minimum measure of benefits, excluding, of course, consumer surplus. Hence, an economic activity is socially desirable at some price vector p and output vector Q if the revenues it generates exceed its costs, $pQ > C(Q)$. Thus, profitability of an activity is a *sufficient* but not necessary condition for production of a good to be socially desirable. Cost-based pricing methods essentially use revenues as an imperfect proxy for consumer benefits.

In regulated industries, the simple cost-benefit criterion is further complicated by benefit and cost complementarities associated with multiple product demand and technology. The benefit-cost test cannot be applied directly to specific outputs because of benefits or costs that are incurred jointly with other outputs. Suppose, for example, that local and long-distance telephone service are provided by a single regulated firm. Suppose that $W(Q_1, Q_2)$ represents the monetary value of consumer benefits from local service Q_1 and long-distance service Q_2. If benefits exceed costs, $W(Q_1, Q_2) \geq C(Q_1, Q_2)$, then the bundle of services (Q_1, Q_2) is desirable. It is important, however, to evaluate whether each activity is socially desirable. This involves verifying whether the *incremental* benefits of each activity are greater than or equal to incremental costs, that is, for good 1

$$W(Q_1, Q_2) - W(0, Q_2) \geq C(Q_1, Q_2) - C(0, Q_2),$$

and similarly for good 2. It is reasonable to suppose that the revenues generated by each good do not exceed incremental benefits to consumers. Thus, if both goods are purchased, at prices p_1 and p_2,

$$W(Q_1, Q_2) - p_1 Q_1 - p_2 Q_2 > W(0, Q_2) - p_2 Q_2,$$

so that $W(Q_1, Q_2) - W(0, Q_2) \geq p_1 Q_1$, and similarly for good 2. Therefore, a *sufficient* condition for the incremental benefits of each good to exceed incremental costs is for revenues to exceed or equal incremental costs, $p_1 Q_1 \geq C(Q_1, Q_2) - C(0, Q_2)$ and $p_2 Q_2 \geq C(Q_1, Q_2) - C(Q_1, 0)$. These inequalities are referred to as the *incremental cost test*. Prices that satisfy the incremental cost test yield revenues that cover the incremental production costs. In general, the *incremental cost test* is stated as

$$P_T Q_T \geq C(Q) - C(Q_{M-T}), \tag{3.2.1}$$

where T is any subset of the set of products M and $M - T$ is the complement of T in M.

In regulated industries, prices are often chosen in such a way that regulated firms break even. Zero-profit prices which satisfy the incremental cost test are said to be *subsidy-free*.[8] In the simple two-goods example, the incremental cost test states that the revenue from good 1 and the stand-alone cost of good 2 exceed total cost, $p_1 Q_1 + C(0, Q_2) \geq C(Q_1, Q_2)$. Thus, if the prices yield zero profits, it follows that the revenues generated by good 2 must be less than stand-alone costs, $p_2 Q_2 \leq C(0, Q_2)$. This implies that the price for good 2 when supplied jointly with good 1 is less than the break-even price if good 2 is supplied independently. Thus, given prices that yield zero profits and satisfy the incremental cost test, all consumers benefit from joint production.

In general, zero-profit prices that satisfy the incremental cost test always yield revenues for any subset of goods that are less than or equal to stand-alone costs for that subset of goods. To see this, just subtract (3.2.1) from the zero profit equation $pQ = C(Q)$. This gives

$$p_S Q_S \leq C(Q_S) \qquad \text{for all } S \subseteq M. \tag{3.2.2}$$

This implies that the costs to consumers independently purchasing a subset of goods exceeds their payments with subsidy-free pricing. The definition of subsidy-free prices is stated in terms of stand-alone costs.

Definition 3.2.1 Let $B(Q)$ denote the *set of subsidy-free prices* evaluated at output level Q,

$$B(Q) = \{p \in \mathbb{R}^m_+ : pQ = C(Q), p_S Q_S \leq C(Q_S) \text{ for all } S \subseteq M\}. \tag{3.2.3}$$

For a price p to be subsidy-free across commodities does not, of course, guarantee that groups of consumers are not providing subsidies for other groups of consumers, since consumption bundles generally differ.[9] A stronger notion of subsidy-freeness is the absence of subsidies across all consumption bundles. This is the Sharkey and Telser (1978) definition of prices that *support* a cost function C.

Definition 3.2.2 (Sharkey and Telser)[10]   The cost function $C(\cdot)$ is *supportable* at Q if there exist prices $p > 0$ such that $pQ = C(Q)$ and $pQ' \leq C(Q')$ for all $Q' \in \mathbb{R}^m_+$, $Q' \leq Q$.

Definition 3.2.3 Let $\Gamma(Q)$ denote the *set of support prices* of $C(\cdot)$ at Q,

$$\Gamma(Q) = \{p \in \mathbb{R}^m_+ : pQ = C(Q), pQ' \leq C(Q'), Q' \leq Q\}. \tag{3.2.4}$$

Clearly, as before, the stand-alone cost test given zero profits is equivalent to an incremental cost test for product bundles less than Q,

$$pQ'' \geq C(Q) - C(Q - Q'') \qquad \text{for all } Q'' \leq Q. \tag{3.2.5}$$

Sharkey and Telser (1978) provide an extensive analysis of supportability.[11]

It is easy to see that if a price vector p supports the cost function C at Q, then p is subsidy-free. Since p supports the cost function at Q, $pQ' \leq C(Q')$

for all outputs Q' less than or equal to Q, including output vectors Q_S for all S in M. Thus, $\Gamma(Q) \subseteq B(Q)$. While supportability is generally more restrictive than subsidy-freeness, the two definitions are equivalent under some conditions. Given *cost complementarities*, subsidy-free prices are also support prices, $\Gamma(Q) \supseteq B(Q)$, so that $\Gamma(Q) = B(Q)$.[12] Therefore, given cost complementarities, the set of subsidy-free prices is the same as the set of support prices.

3.2.2 Cost-Sharing Games

The concept of subsidy-free prices is closely related to cost-sharing games. Suppose that there are m players, where each player l obtains benefits v_l from purchasing good Q_l, $l = 1, \ldots, m$. Then y_l is an imputation in the core of the cost-sharing game if it satisfies the core conditions,

$$\sum_{l \in M} y_l = \sum_{l \in M} v_l - C(Q),$$

$$\sum_{l \in S} y_l \leq \sum_{l \in S} v_l - C(Q_S) \qquad \text{for all } S \subseteq M.$$

(3.2.6)

This game is equivalent to a cost allocation game where the "players" are directly associated with the m outputs or m divisions of the firm producing Q. Let $E_l = v_l - y_l$. Then the core conditions are the same as $\sum_{l \in M} E_l = C(Q)$ and $\sum_{l \in S} E_l \leq C(Q_S)$ for all $S \subseteq M$; see Faulhaber (1975). The *imputation* to each output l is simply the revenue generated by that output, $E_l = p_l Q_l$, $l = 1, \ldots, m$. Clearly, the core conditions of the cost-sharing game are precisely the conditions for prices to be subsidy-free. The set $B(Q)$ is the core of the cost-sharing game. Similarly, the concept of support prices is comparable to a cooperative cost-sharing game where the set of *output bundles* $[0, Q] \subset \mathbb{R}^m_+$ represents a continuum of players and where $\Gamma(Q)$ represents the core of the game.

Given that the set of subsidy-free prices is equivalent to the core of a cost-sharing game, it is of interest to calculate particular imputations in the core. A useful approach involves application of the Aumann-Shapley imputation. The *Aumann-Shapley* imputation is an allocation of benefits that reflects the bargaining power of all coalitions that have the same composition as the coalition involving all players. The Aumann-Shapley imputation has been applied to the cost-sharing game by Mirman and Tauman (1982), Billera and Heath (1982), and others.[13] In a cost-sharing game the Aumann-Shapley imputation reflects the marginal costs of each output bundle that has the same output mix as a given output level. The imputation is calculated by means of a simple "diagonal formula," where $C(0) = 0$ and C is continuously differentiable,

$$AC^l(C,Q) = \int_0^1 C_l(tQ_1,\ldots,tQ_m)\,dt, \qquad l = 1,\ldots,m. \tag{3.2.7}$$

The imputation for good l is thus $AC^l(C,Q)Q_l$. The term $AC^l(C,Q)$ may be interpreted as an *average cost* although it is more accurately an *average of marginal costs* along the ray tQ. It is now shown that if the cost function $C(Q)$ exhibits cost complementarities, then prices $p_l = AC^l(C,Q)$ are in the set of support prices $\Gamma(Q)$, or equivalently, the imputations $p_l Q_l$ are in the core of the cost-sharing game.

Let $AC(C,Q) = (AC^1,\ldots,AC^M)$. Clearly average costs times output sums to total costs, $\sum_{l=1}^m AC^l(C,Q)Q_l = C(Q)$, so that the Aumann-Shapley "prices" are zero-profit prices. Given cost complementarities it is then easy to show that revenues do not exceed stand-alone costs,

$$\sum_{l \in S} AC^l(C,Q)Q_l = \sum_{l \in S} Q_l \int_0^1 C_l(tQ)\,dt$$

$$\leq \sum_{l \in S} Q_l \int_0^1 C_l(tQ_S)\,dt$$

$$= C(Q_S). \tag{3.2.8}$$

So the average cost price is in the core of the cost-sharing game. Therefore, *given cost complementarities the set of subsidy-free prices is nonempty.*[14] The Aumann-Shapley average cost prices will be studied further in chapter 4.

The core of the cost-sharing game is easily represented in the two-goods case. Let $AS^1 = C(Q_1,0)/Q_1$ represent average stand-alone costs for good 1 and let $AIC^1 = [C(Q_1,Q_2) - C(0,Q_2)]/Q_1$ represent average incremental costs for good one (and similarly for good 2). By economies of scope incremental costs are less than stand-alone costs, so that $AIC^l < AS^l$, $l = 1, 2$. Then, the set of subsidy-free prices can be represented as a weighted sum of average stand-alone costs and average incremental costs,

$$p_1 = \lambda AS^1 + (1 - \lambda)AIC^1, \qquad p_2 = (1 - \lambda)AS^2 + \lambda AIC^2, \tag{3.2.9}$$

where λ takes all values between 0 and 1. The set of subsidy-free prices, or equivalently, the core of the cost sharing game $\Gamma(Q_1,Q_2)$, is represented by

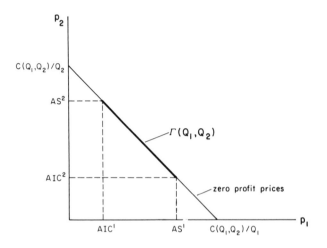

Figure 3.2.1
The set of subsidy-free prices.

the shaded line segment in figure 3.2.1. For this simple two-goods case, the weight associated with Aumann-Shapley pricing is

$$\lambda(Q_1, Q_2) = [AC^1(C, Q_1, Q_2) - AIC^1]/[AS^1 - AIC^1]. \qquad (3.2.10)$$

Consider also the Nash bargaining solution for the two-goods cost-sharing game. Choose prices to maximize $(p_1 Q_1 - S^1)(p_2 Q_2 - S^2)$ subject to the zero-profit condition $p_1 Q_1 + p_2 Q_2 = C(Q_1, Q_2)$. Then prices equally weight average stand-alone and average incremental costs,

$$p_l = (1/2)AS^l + (1/2)AIC^l, \qquad l = 1, 2. \qquad (3.2.11)$$

3.2.3   Anonymous Equity

The existence of subsidy-free support prices depends strictly on the properties of the cost function. A more important issue is whether there exists *market-clearing support prices*, which Faulhaber and Levinson (1981) refer to as *anonymously equitable prices*.[15] Let $D: \mathbb{R}^m_+ \to \mathbb{R}^m_+$ represent market demand.

Definition 3.2.4   A price vector p is said to be *anonymously equitable* given the cost function $C(Q)$ and market demand $D(p)$ if for all $Q = D(p)$, $p \in \Gamma(Q)$.

Anonymously equitable prices will be useful in our discussion of market

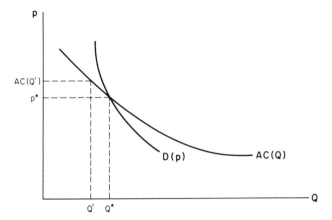

Figure 3.2.2
Anonymous equity of price p^*.

equilibrium prices in contestable markets. For the one-good case with downward-sloping demand and decreasing average costs, the market-clearing average cost price is the unique anonymously equitable price. This is represented by price p^* in figure 3.2.2. Note that $p^*Q' \le C(Q')$ for $Q' \le Q^*$.

Existence of anonymously equitable prices is shown by ten Raa (1983).[16] A preliminary result characterizes the set of support prices.

LEMMA 3.2.1 (ten Raa, 1983) *For a supportable cost function, $\Gamma(Q)$ is an upper semicontinuous convex-valued correspondence. It is bounded on $\{Q \in \mathbb{R}^m_+ : Q \ge \varepsilon\}$ for $\varepsilon \gg 0$.*

So $\Gamma(Q)$ is a closed convex set for each Q. Using the lemma and Kakutani's fixed point theorem, ten Raa (1983) shows that with an uppersemicontinuous demand correspondence and threshold demand levels for all goods, $Q \ge \varepsilon$, $\varepsilon \gg 0$, there exist *market-clearing support prices*. In other words, continuous market demand and a supportable cost function are sufficient to guarantee the existence of anonymously equitable prices.

3.3 Fully Distributed Cost Pricing

Regulators often employ various ad hoc rules for allocating the costs of joint production in multiple-product industries. Fully distributed cost-pricing rules allocate costs on the basis of relative output levels, revenues, or attributable costs. In this section, the preceding discussion of subsidy-free prices is applied to study these cost allocation rules. I show that fully distributed cost-pricing rules can be chosen that are consistent with subsidy-free pricing.

In the single-product case, cost-based multipart pricing rules attempt to recover arbitrary shares of fixed costs through lump sum entry fees and per unit charges. In rate regulation of natural gas pipelines, for example, the entry fee is called the demand charge and the per unit fee is called the commodity charge. Various allocation formulas include (1) the fixed-variable method in which 100% of fixed costs are recovered by the demand charges, (2) the Atlantic Seaboard formula in which 50% of fixed costs are covered by the demand charges, (3) the United formula in which 25% of fixed costs are covered by the demand charges, and (4) the volumetric method in which all costs are recovered by the commodity charge.

I now consider standard linear pricing in multiproduct industries. Let the multiproduct cost function $C(Q)$ have the form

$$C(Q) = F + V(Q) \tag{3.3.1}$$

for $Q \geq 0$, $Q \neq 0$, where $F > 0$, $V(0) = 0$, V is continuous for $Q \geq 0$, and $V(Q) \geq 0$ for all $Q \geq 0$, $Q \neq 0$. Assume that the cost function C exhibits weak cost complementarities. The regulator must allocate both joint fixed cost F and nonattributable components of variable cost $V(Q)$ as well. If variable costs represent nonjoint technology, $V(Q) = \sum_{l=1}^{m} V(0, \ldots, Q_l, \ldots, 0)$, then the regulator's problem reduces to allocation of fixed costs across outputs.

I solve the regulator's problem in two steps. First, choose *internal subsidy-free prices* $\gamma = (\gamma_1, \ldots, \gamma_m)$ that fully allocate variable costs $V(Q)$, that is, $\sum_{j=1}^{m} \gamma_j Q_j = V(Q)$ and $\sum_{j \in S} \gamma_j Q_j \leq V(Q_S)$ for all $S \subseteq M$. Clearly the subsidy-free prices γ_j exist since V exhibits weak cost complementarity. Further, each γ_j exceeds product j's average incremental costs. I restrict attention to continuous functions $\gamma(Q)$. This is possible since the correspondence $\Gamma(Q)$ is upper-semicontinuous and thus admits a continuous selection. Clearly, if the technology is nonjoint, γ_j equals average stand-alone costs for each good j.

Now let f_j be product j's share of fixed costs F, where $0 \leq f_j \leq 1$, $\sum_{j=1}^{m} f_j = 1$. Then let prices p_j be *fully distributed cost* (FDC) *prices* such that

$$p_j Q_j = f_j F + \gamma_j Q_j. \tag{3.3.2}$$

Clearly $\sum_{j=1}^{m} p_j Q_j = C(Q)$. The following statement shows how the presence of fixed costs creates a wide range of subsidy free prices.

PROPOSITION 3.3.1   *The FDC prices p given by (3.3.2) are subsidy-free for any arbitrary choice of weights f_j, $0 \le f_j \le 1$, $\sum_{j=1}^{m} f_j = 1$.*

Proof   Choose any product set $S \subseteq M$. Then

$$\sum_{j \in S} p_j Q_j = \sum_{j \in S} f_j F + \sum_{j \in S} \gamma_j Q_j$$

$$\ge \sum_{j \in S} f_j F + V(Q) - V(Q_{M-S}) \tag{3.3.3}$$

by γ subsidy-free for V. But since $C(Q) - C(Q_{M-S}) = V(Q) - V(Q_{M-S})$ for all $S \subseteq M$,

$$\sum_{j \in S} p_j Q_j \ge C(Q) - C(Q_{M-S}). \tag{3.3.4}$$

Thus, p is subsidy-free.   QED

Therefore, any arbitrary rule of thumb or administrative procedure may be used to select the weights f_j as long as the internal prices γ are subsidy-free. First consider the simple rule that bases the shares of fixed costs on *relative output* levels,

$$f_j^0 = Q_j / \sum_{l=1}^{m} Q_l, \qquad j = 1, \dots, m. \tag{3.3.5}$$

As Kahn (1970, p. 150) notes, rate making by public utility commissions involves dividing costs of serving customer classes into attributable and joint costs and then distributing joint costs "on the basis of some common physical measure of utilization, such as minutes, circuit-miles, message-minute-miles, gross ton-miles, MCF, or kwh." In our framework, under the *relative output rule*,[17] the price of service j equals

$$p_j = F / \sum_{l=1}^{m} Q_l + \gamma_j, \qquad j = 1, \dots, m. \tag{3.3.6}$$

Another common FDC pricing method is to base the shares of fixed costs on *relative revenues*. This approach is commonly used in transportation regulation by the ICC.[18] Thus the *relative revenue rule* is

$$f_j^R = p_j Q_j / \sum_{l=1}^{m} p_l Q_l, \qquad j = 1, \dots, m. \tag{3.3.7}$$

In our framework, the output prices must satisfy

$$p_j = \gamma_j / \left[1 - F / \sum_{l=1}^{m} p_l Q_l \right]$$

$$= \gamma_j (F + V(Q))/V(Q), \qquad j = 1, \ldots, m, \tag{3.3.8}$$

since $\sum_{l=1}^{m} p_l Q_l = C(Q)$ by the zero-profit requirement. The rule simply involves rescaling the internal subsidy-free prices.

The final FDC rule to be considered bases the share of fixed costs on *relative attributable costs*. This is usually applied for the case of nonjoint variable costs by setting shares equal to the ratio of stand-alone variable costs to total variable costs, $f_j^V = V(0, \ldots, Q_j, \ldots 0)/V(Q)$, see Braeutigam (1980). Using internal subsidy-free prices, this rule may be extended to allow for cost complementarities. Letting $\gamma_j Q_j$ represent the variable costs attributed to good j gives

$$f_j^V = \gamma_j Q_j / V(Q). \tag{3.3.9}$$

Given this approach, the output prices satisfy

$$p_j = F\gamma_j / \sum_{l=1}^{m} \gamma_l Q_l + \gamma_j, \qquad j = 1, \ldots, m,$$

$$= \gamma_j (F + V(Q))/V(Q). \tag{3.3.10}$$

Surprisingly, the attributable cost rule given here is identical to the revenue rule.

Mirman, Samet, and Tauman (1983) propose a set of axioms for cost allocation rules when fixed costs are present. They derive a cost allocation formula that uniquely satisfies their axioms. Their formula may be directly obtained in a straightforward manner by applying the general attributable cost rule. Let γ_j represent the Aumann-Shapley prices at Q, $\gamma_j = \int_0^1 V_j(tQ)\,dt$. Then from the attributable cost rule,

$$p_j = \int_0^1 V_j(tQ)\,dt\, F/V(Q) + \int_0^1 V_j(tQ)\,dt, \tag{3.3.11}$$

which is the desired formula.

It is useful to check whether the three FDC pricing rules are *demand compatible*. Since these prices are subsidy free by proposition 3.3.1, demand compatibility implies anonymous equity.

PROPOSITION 3.3.2   *Given strictly positive demand for all goods $Q \geq \varepsilon \gg 0$, internal subsidy-free prices $\gamma(\cdot)$ can be chosen such that the fully distributed cost-pricing rules based on relative outputs, revenues, or attributable costs are market clearing.*

The proof is given in the appendix. Therefore, under any of the fully distributed cost rules, as formulated here, anonymous equity is achieved.

3.4   Inefficiency of Cost-Based Pricing

3.4.1   Subsidy-Free Prices versus Ramsey Prices

If prices are subsidy-free, the revenues from any subset of goods covers their incremental costs. I have stated that this provides a sufficient condition for the regulated activity to be socially desirable. It was also seen that market-clearing, subsidy-free prices could be chosen. These prices are called anonymously equitable prices, which carries the implication that a standard of fairness or distributional equity is observed. However, subsidy-free pricing and other cost-based pricing methods do not directly consider consumer welfare. Cost-based pricing rules can fail to be efficient in two ways. These may be some subsidy-free prices that are better than others in terms of some social welfare criterion. Thus, regulators need not be indifferent between all subsidy-free prices. Second, there may be prices that are not subsidy-free but that improve social welfare. The criterion of subsidy-freeness will constrain regulators seeking to achieve efficient pricing.

It has been seen that fully distributed cost rules for allocating fixed costs can be used to achieve subsidy-free pricing. This approach required all variable costs to be attributable or that regulators select internal subsidy-free prices. If all variable costs are allocated by internal subsidy-free pricing, *any* allocation of fixed costs preserves subsidy-freeness. Thus, a very large set of subsidy-free prices may exist. The choice of prices from this set by regulators may have significant welfare effects. Consider the problem of choosing from the set of market-clearing subsidy-free prices. The *set of anonymously equitable prices*, A, is defined by

$$A = \{p : p \in \Gamma(Q), Q = D(p)\}. \tag{3.4.1}$$

For ease of presentation, I assume that market demand is a continuous function. The set A may be described by the following equations:

$$pQ(p) - C(Q(p)) = 0,$$
$$p_S Q_S(p) \leq C(Q_S(p)), \qquad S \subset M. \tag{3.4.2}$$

The set A is nonempty by lemma 3.2.1 and is compact under the following conditions.

PROPOSITION 3.4.1   *For a supportable cost function, the set of anonymously equitable prices A is compact for $Q \geq \varepsilon$, $\varepsilon \gg 0$.*

The proof is stated in the appendix. Thus, given cost complementarities and threshold demand levels, A is compact.

Let $W(p)$ be the regulator's indirect social welfare measure. If the regulator is constrained to select anonymously equitable prices, the regulator chooses p to maximize $W(p)$ subject to p in the set A. Given $W(p)$ continuous, the regulator's problem is well defined since A is a compact set. Consider the special case of two goods with independent demands. Suppose that income effects are not significant and that the welfare measure equals aggregate consumer surplus, $W(p) = \int_{p_1}^{\infty} Q_1(p_1') \, dp_1' + \int_{p_2}^{\infty} Q_2(p_2') \, dp_2'$. The regulator's problem may be solved as a Kuhn-Tucker-Lagrange problem,

$$L = W(p) - \lambda[p_1 Q_1 + p_2 Q_2 - C(Q_1, Q_2)]$$

$$+ \sigma_1[C(Q_1, 0) - p_1 Q_1]$$

$$+ \sigma_2[C(0, Q_2) - p_2 Q_2]. \tag{3.4.3}$$

Rearranging the first-order conditions and noting that $\partial W(p)/\partial p_l = -Q_l(p_l)$, $l = 1, 2$, give the following relative markups above marginal costs:

$$(p_l - C_l)/p_l = (1 + 1/(\lambda + \sigma_l))(1/\eta_l), \qquad l = 1, 2, \tag{3.4.4}$$

where $\eta_l \equiv -(dQ_l/dp_l)(p_l/Q_l)$ is elasticity of demand for good l.

Generally, given strict economies of scope, $C(Q_1, 0) + C(0, Q_2) > C(Q_1, Q_2)$, and the zero profit constraint, it is evident that at most one constraint is binding, i.e., either $\sigma_1 = 0$ or $\sigma_2 = 0$. Suppose, for example, that $\sigma_1 = 0$, $\sigma_2 > 0$, and the revenues from good 2 equal stand-alone costs for good 2. Then the ratio of relative markups is greater than the reciprocal of the ratio of demand elasticities,

$$((p_1 - C_1)/p_1)/((p_2 - C_2)/p_2) > \eta_2/\eta_1.$$

Compare subsidy-free prices with Ramsey prices. *Ramsey prices* maximize $W(p)$ subject to a zero-profit constraint for the firm. Thus Ramsey prices are said to be "second-best" optimal prices. The ratio of relative markups equals the reciprocal of the ratio of demand elasticities. Ramsey prices are subsidy-free only if both inequality constraints in (3.4.3) are nonbinding. One can easily obtain examples where Ramsey prices fail to be subsidy-free.[19] Suppose that the cost function has the form $C(Q_1, Q_2) = F + F_1 + c_1 Q_1 + c_2 Q_2$. Suppose that stand-alone costs are $C(Q_1, 0) = F + F_1 + c_1 Q_1$ and $C(0, Q_2) = F + c_2 Q_2$, where joint fixed cost is less than attributable fixed cost for good 1, $F < F_1$. Let market demand for each good exhibit unitary elasticity. Then relative markups are equal for the two goods and the Ramsey prices equal $p_1^*/c_1 = p_2^*/c_2 = 2/(2 - F - F_1)$. But revenue for each good equals one, which is greater than stand-alone cost for good 2.

$$F + c_2 Q_2(p_2^*) = 1 + (F - F_1)/2 < 1.$$

Therefore, the requirement that prices be subsidy-free is actually quite stringent. Choosing welfare maximizing prices from the set of anonymously equitable prices involves a "third-best" notion of optimality, which may entail avoidable welfare losses. For this reason, cost-based pricing does not appear to be desirable regulatory policy. An alternative approach is taken in chapter 6, where it is shown that there may exist Ramsey prices that do not involve cross-subsidies between groups of consumers.

3.4.2 Imperfect Information and Transaction Costs

As noted at the outset, price and entry regulation is often viewed as a means of achieving cost economies from horizontal and vertical consolidation of production. However, information constraints and transaction costs may not permit regulators to achieve their objective. In addition, cost-based price regulations may create welfare losses that outweigh the gains from cost efficiency.

Welfare losses from price and entry regulation occur if cost-based pricing fails to be even second-best optimal. Rather than simply emphasizing cost efficiency, the proper standard of comparison for the unregulated market equilibrium is welfare under cost-based pricing. Indeed, with cost-based pricing, natural monopoly is not sufficient to imply that welfare is greatest with production by a single firm. The competitive market may also achieve cost gains associated with multiproduct production, economies of scale, and vertical integration. Private contractual agreements may realize cost efficiencies. Competition from potential entrants may result in one or a few firms serving the market efficiently, as will be seen in the next chapter. If cost economies and concentrated market structure do not inevitably entail market power, it is no longer sufficient to assert that large-scale cost economies require regulation of some industries. Furthermore, even if entry regulation is perceived as being required to obtain cost economies, this need not entail price regulation. As will be shown in chapter 9, entry regulations can be designed in such a way as to eliminate monopoly rents through firm competition for the right to serve the market.

Cost-based pricing may fail to be efficient if regulators have imperfect information about firm production costs or market demand. Not only may regulators fail accurately to perceive total costs, but what is even more likely, estimates of incremental costs or stand-alone costs may be wide of the mark. This will complicate selection of subsidy-free prices. It may be difficult for regulators to distinguish between joint and attributable costs, thus worsening pricing distortions associated with fully distributed cost pricing and other administrative pricing rules.

Cost-based pricing may create the wrong incentives for firms. If prices allocate total costs, the firm may not have an incentive to minimize total costs. Regulated firms may not select the best technology, or they may not choose efficient input levels. Cost-based pricing may distort input choices. Average cost pricing in the natural gas utility industry may have been responsible for utility purchases of costly supplies of gas that were priced significantly above average market prices in the period following partial decontrol of gas prices.

A serious problem with the cost efficiency basis of regulation arises if the costs of the firm are not well represented by a cost function based on production technology. Williamson (1985, p. 87) cautions that "rarely is the choice among alternative organization forms determined by technology." Thus, for Williamson (1975, 1985) and Coase (1937) there may exist transaction costs of using markets that yield returns to consolidation of production. Alternatively, there may exist transaction costs of contracting which limit these returns. Williamson (1985, p. 90) views asset specificity as the main determinant of transaction costs associated with vertical integration. Teece (1980, 1982) argues that without transaction costs of market contracting, the multiproduct firm cannot be explained. Therefore, I conclude that production-based economies of scope, scale, and sequence are not sufficient to justify price and entry regulation. It must be verified that total costs of production and transaction are minimized by consolidation of production.

Appendix

Proof of Proposition 3.3.2   I state the proof for $D(p)$ upper-semicontinuous and convex valued. The proof employs arguments similar to those in ten Raa (1983). Define the set of subsidy-free prices for V by $\Gamma(Q; V)$. Given supportability of V by weak cost complementarities, $\Gamma(Q; V)$ is an upper-semicontinuous convex-valued correspondence bounded on $\{Q \in \mathbb{R}^m_+ : Q \geq \varepsilon\}$ by lemma 3.2.1. Thus, a continuous function γ may be chosen that is bounded on $\{Q \in \mathbb{R}^m_+ : Q \geq \varepsilon\}$. Define the functions $p^0(\cdot)$, $p^R(\cdot)$, and $p^V(\cdot)$ by

$$p_j^0(Q) = F / \sum_{l=1}^{m} Q_l + \gamma_j(Q), \qquad j = 1, \ldots, m, \tag{1}$$

$$p_j^V(Q) = p_j^R(Q) = \gamma_j(Q)(F + V(Q))/V(Q), \qquad j = 1, \ldots, m. \tag{2}$$

Clearly, V is continuous for $Q > 0$, $Q \neq 0$. The functions $p^0(Q)$, $p^V(Q)$, and $p^R(Q)$ are continuous and bounded. Thus, p^0, p^V, and p^R take values in a compact set $\mathcal{H}$ for $Q \geq \varepsilon$. Given that the demand correspondence $D(p)$ is an upper-semicontinuous convex-valued correspondence from $\mathbb{R}^m_+$ to $\mathbb{R}^m_+$, $D(\mathcal{H})$ is contained in a compact, convex set $\mathcal{D}$. It follows that the mapping $p^0 \times D$ takes the compact convex set $\mathcal{D} \times \mathcal{H}$ into itself. Thus by Kakutani's fixed point theorem, $p^0 \times D$ has a fixed point (p^*, Q^*) with $p^* = p^0(Q^*)$ and $Q^* \in D(p^*)$.   QED

Proof of Proposition 3.4.1   I state the proof for $D(p)$ continuous. By lemma 3.2.1, $\Gamma(\{Q \in \mathbb{R}^m_+ : Q \geq \varepsilon\})$ is bounded. Thus, A is bounded. To check if A is closed, let $\{p_n\} \in A$, with $\lim_{n \to \infty} p_n = \bar{p}$. By continuity of $D(p)$, if $Q_n = D(p_n)$ and $\bar{Q} = D(\bar{p})$, $\lim_{n \to \infty} Q_n = \bar{Q}$. By upper-semicontinuity of $\Gamma(Q)$, if $p_n \in \Gamma(Q_n)$ and $\lim_{n \to \infty} Q_n = \bar{Q}$, then $\lim_{n \to \infty} p_n = \bar{p}$ implies that $\bar{p} \in \Gamma(\bar{Q})$. Therefore, since $\bar{Q} = D(\bar{p})$, $\bar{p} \in A$, and so A is closed.   QED

Notes

1. Nonjoint production is examined by Samuelson (1966), Hanoch (1970), Hall (1973), Diewert (1973), and van den Heuvel (1986).

2. Kahn (1970, p. 79, Vol. 1) distinguishes common costs from joint costs as follows. If output proportions can be varied, then separate marginal production costs can be identified and costs are said to be common. If outputs are produced only in fixed proportions, then there are no separate incremental cost functions and costs are said to be joint. No such distinction is made here.

3. This concept involves a definition of the *ray average cost* of a composite good $C(\gamma Q^0)/\gamma$, where the scalar γ is the number of units of the unit bundle and where Q^0 represents an arbitrary unit bundle. See Baumol, Panzar, and Willig (1982) for an extensive analysis of this and other cost function characteristics.

4. Multiproduct economies of scale, even combined with economies of scope, are not sufficient for subadditivity; see Baumol, Panzar, and Willig (1982, proposition 7C1), and Sharkey (1982a, chapter 4).

5. See Chenery (1953), Frisch (1965), and Danø (1966) on the engineering basis of production models. Danø refers to plants that are organized as a "sequence of processes (stages)" (1966, p. 149).

6. The classic example of public inputs in vertical integration refers to reuse of energy used to make heat when iron smelting is combined with steel refining; see Bain (1959).

7. Let the underlying technology have the form

$$X = f(Z^1; Z^2), \qquad Q = F(X, Z^2; Z^1),$$

where Z^1 and Z^2 are r-vectors of inputs. The effects of Z^2 on the output of X and of Z^1 on the output of Q are "externality" or "public input" effects. Then we define C^U, C^D, and C as follows:

$$C^U(X; w) \equiv \min_{Z^1} wZ^1 \quad \text{subject to } X = f(Z^1; 0),$$

$$C^D(Q, X; w) \equiv \min_{Z^2} wZ^2 \quad \text{subject to } Q = F(X, Z^2; 0),$$

$$C(Q; w) \equiv \min_{Z^1 + Z^2} (Z^1 + Z^2)w \quad \text{subject to } X = f(Z^1; Z^2) \quad \text{and} \quad Q = F(X, Z^2; Z^1).$$

8. Baumol (1986, p. 114) traces the incremental cost test for subsidy-freeness back at least to Hadley (1886) and others. Willig (1979a) and Faulhaber (1975) give formal definitions of subsidy-free prices.

9. This issue is discussed further in chapter 6.

10. Sharkey and Telser (1978) define a supportable cost function as one that is supportable for all $Q > 0$.

11. Panzar and Willig (1977) show that given $C_{lk} \le 0$ for $l \neq k$, the set of subsidy-free prices is nonempty. Sharkey and Telser (1978) devise a number of important results including the following. Necessary conditions for the supportability of $C(\cdot)$ include (1) $C(\cdot)$ is subadditive, (2) $C(\cdot)$ is subhomogeneous, and (3) $C(\cdot)$ exhibits (weak) increasing returns to scale. Sufficient conditions for the supportability of C include (1) cost complementarities and (2) generalized decreasing average costs. Finally, if C is concave and differentiable, then for C to be supportable it is necessary and sufficient for cost complementarities to hold for all $Q \ge 0$. These results involve rather straightforward applications of the cost definitions.

12. See Mirman, Tauman, and Zang (1985) and Faulhaber and Levinson (1981, proposition 6).

13. Mirman, Tauman, and Zang (1983b) refer to the pricing rule derived from the Aumann-Shapley diagonal formula as an average cost price. See in addition Samet and Tauman (1982), Mirman, Samet, and Tauman (1983), Bös and Tillman (1983, 1984), and Young (1985) for axiomatic treatments.

14. Panzar and Willig (1977) show that weak cost complementarities imply the existence of subsidy-free prices. Given $C_{lk} \leq 0$, it follows that

$$C(Q_{S \cup T \cup R}) - C(Q_{S \cup T}) \leq C(Q_{S \cup R}) - C(Q_S),$$

where S, T, and R are disjoint subsets of M. One may then define the characteristic function of the cost-sharing game by $v(S) = -C(Q_S)$, which is convex by the properties of C. Then, by a well-known theorem of Shapley (1971), the core is nonempty.

15. See a discussion of anonymous equity in Willig (1979a).

16. Existence of market clearing Aumann-Shapley prices is shown by Mirman and Tauman (1982). Market-clearing cost-based prices are also studied by Bös and Tillman (1984). See also Spulber (1984c).

17. See Bonbright (1961) and Braeutigam (1980).

18. See Friedlander (1969) and Braeutigam (1980).

19. This is contrary to Baumol, Bailey, and Willig (1977), who give sufficient conditions for Ramsey prices to be subsidy-free. Sharkey (1981) provides another counterexample.

4 Contestable Markets and Sustainable Monopoly Prices

The *contestable market* equilibrium proposed by Baumol, Panzar, and Willig[1] is closely linked to the concept of subsidy-free prices discussed in the previous chapter. A market is said to be *contestable* in the absence of barriers to entry. The notion of *sustainable prices* refers to a set of market equilibrium prices such that incumbent firms make nonnegative profits and there are no incentives for new entry. A *sustainable monopoly price* refers to a market-clearing price vector such that the monopolist is able to break even and additional entry is unprofitable. Given free entry and competitive-pricing strategies, sustainable market equilibrium prices must be subsidy-free. If prices are not subsidy-free, then revenues for some output or set of outputs exceed their stand-alone production costs. This would provide an incentive for rival firms to provide those outputs at competitive prices, thus contradicting their sustainability.

Free entry competition thus provides a market mechanism for achieving subsidy-free prices without the need for price regulation. Also, the possibility of competitive entry limits the profits of incumbent firms. Furthermore, if the incumbent firm's technology is that of a natural monopoly, the market achieves the cost gains from consolidation of production without the need for entry regulation. If a market is contestable, this suggests that an absence of regulation is preferable to cost-based price regulation. However, subsidy-free prices need not achieve even second-best optimality, as shown in the preceding chapter. Ramsey prices maximize consumer benefits subject to the constraint that the regulated firm breaks even. Ramsey prices may involve cross-subsidies and thus generally are not sustainable.[2] This implies that an important trade-off exists. If price regulation yields Ramsey prices, social welfare may be higher in a regulated market. The welfare gains from price regulation net of the costs of regulation must be compared with the welfare level achieved in a market equilibrium with subsidy-free prices.

Determination of how firms compete for access to markets is a significant problem for the economics of regulation. This issue is effectively addressed by the theory of contestable markets, which represents an attempt to extend the definition of perfect competition to allow for economies of scale and natural monopoly. The perfectly contestable market has no barriers to entry in the form of sunk costs. The productive technology is known and freely available. Competition is provided by firms in the industry and potential entrants. This ease of entry is essentially the same assumption present in standard economic models of perfect competition. The underlying assumption is the costless movement of factors of production across markets. Free availability of technology is a reasonable hypothesis in a deterministic model. The contestable markets literature has generally focused on a static equilibrium with complete information regarding prices, outputs, demand, and costs. The admittedly ideal case presented by the theory of contestable markets is both useful and important for the study of regulation since it provides a standard of comparison against which market equilibria with entry barriers can be judged. The presence of entry barriers (due to regulation or sunk costs), differentiated products, technological differences, or asymmetric information clearly would require modification of the outcome predicted for a contestable market. However, in many cases it is apparent that the degree to which the market outcome departs from that observed for a contestable market is directly related to such factors as the height of entry barriers.

A frequently heard criticism of the contestable market model is that even a small sunk cost faced by entrants will prevent the "hit-and-run" entry needed to discipline firms in the market.[3] Dynamic entry models with irreversible investment are not well understood. Much additional research remains to be done to characterize equilibria in markets with sunk costs.[4] A competitive model with sunk costs must also incorporate demand and cost uncertainty. In a deterministic model, potential entrants have no reason to regret investment decisions, so that sunk costs do not create significant risks for entrants.[5] The present chapter uses the contestable markets framework to provide a useful benchmark for comparing free entry equilibrium prices with regulated markets.

This chapter presents an analysis of the sustainability of monopoly prices. The model and all of the discussion in section 4.1 is based on Panzar and Willig (1977) and Baumol, Panzar, and Willig (1982). Sections 4.2, 4.3, and 4.4 are based on Spulber (1984c). Existence of a sustainable monopoly price vector is shown for firm cost functions that are, respectively, separable and nonseparable across goods. The sustainable market equilibrium is compared with Cournot quantity competition in section 4.4.

4.1 Sustainable Prices: Definition and Necessary Conditions

Given free entry and a common technology, consider a multiproduct market in which firms may choose both prices and quantities. Assume that firms may produce any subset of a set of nondifferentiated products.

The model has the flavor of simple Bertrand price models. An important difference is the ability of entrants to ration their output. Defining a Nash equilibrium in price quantity pairs creates a number of consistency problems. In particular, how is demand for a good l to be divided between two or more firms with identical prices for good l? It is assumed that firm quantity offers cannot exceed market demand. Thus, each firm fulfills its quantity plan. Second, it is assumed that firms may not make losses. Finally, it is assumed that for any good l, the lowest-price firms may capture all market demand. This is analogous to the perfect price elasticity of demand in the competitive market model. Consumers evaluate the price of each good separately and purchase each once at the lowest price. Therefore, there can only be a single market price vector in equilibrium if no quantity constraints are binding. There may potentially exist multiple prices for a commodity if quantity constraints are effective.

Assume that there are m commodities and n firms in the market. Let $\bar{p} = (p^1, \ldots, p^n)$ represent price vectors offered by n firms, $p^i \in \mathbb{R}_+^m, i = 1, \ldots, n$. Let $\bar{q} = (q^1, \ldots, q^n)$ represent vectors of quantity offers. Define

$$Q(p^i; \bar{p}^{(i)}, \bar{q}^{(i)})$$

as the demand at price vector p^i given that other firms are offering price-quantity pairs $(p^j, q^j), j \neq i$. A Bertrand-Nash equilibrium with free entry is defined as follows:[6]

i. The price-quantity pairs chosen by firms must constitute a Nash equilibrium. As in Bertrand equilibria, no consumer will purchase a commodity at a particular price if the commodity is available at a lower price.

ii. All firms make nonnegative profits.

iii. There are no incentives for additional entry.

Formally stated, the equilibrium is defined as follows.

Definition 4.1.1 A *Bertrand-Nash equilibrium with free entry* is an integer number of firms n^*, a set of quantity vectors $\bar{q}^*$, and a set of price vectors $\bar{p}^*$ such that

a. $p^{i*}q^{i*} - C^i(q^{i*}) \geq p^i q^i - C^i(q^i)$ for all (p^i, q^i), where $q^i = Q(p^i; \bar{p}^{(i)*}, \bar{q}^{(i)*})$

and

b. $p^e q^e \leq C(q^e)$ for all (p^e, q^e) such that $q^e \leq Q(p^e; \bar{p}^*, \bar{q}^*)$.

We restrict our attention to price-setting equilibria that result in mono-poly. Let $D(p)$ represent market demand. A price-quantity pair is said to be a *sustainable monopoly equilibrium* if the incumbent firm supplies all output demand and earns revenues that are greater than or equal to costs. Also, there does not exist a price-quantity entry plan such that an entrant is able profitably to undercut the incumbent's price on a subset of goods and supply output less than or equal to market demand.

Definition 4.1.2   The price-quantity pair (p^*, q^*) is a *sustainable monopoly equilibrium* if

a. $p^*q^* - C(q^*) \geq pq - C(q)$ for all (p, q), where $q = D(p)$, $q^* = D(p^*)$

and

b. $p^e q^e \leq C(q^e)$ for all (p^e, q^e) such that $p_S^e \leq p_S^*$ for any subset of products $S \subseteq M, M = \{1, \dots, m\}$, and $q^e \leq D(p_S^e, p_{(S)}^*)$.

The definition differs slightly from Baumol et al. (1982) in that firms are assumed to maximize profits. This brings out in a clear way the competitive effects of potential entry.

The remainder of this section presents conditions which must be satisfied at a sustainable monopoly equilibrium. The necessary conditions are from Panzar and Willig (1977), Baumol, Panzar, and Willig (1982) and Sharkey and Telser (1978). Sufficient conditions for the existence of a sustainable monopoly equilibrium are explored in sections 4.2 and 4.3. Conditions 1, 2, 4, and 5 are due to Panzar and Willig (1977), and condition 3 is due to Sharkey and Telser (1978). The sustainability definition places important restrictions on the equilibrium price vector.

CONDITION 1   *At a sustainable monopoly equilibrium, profits are zero.*

Otherwise, with positive profits, an entrant would be able to slightly undercut the established firm. As Baumol, Panzar, and Willig (1982) point out, if entry barriers are present that give the established firm a cost advantage, the monopoly rents cannot exceed the cost advantage. The zero-profit condition is of particular importance since it states that *competition for the market* eliminates monopoly rents. This is an important implication of the price competition assumption. The elimination of monopoly rents is due to potential competition. Thus, if a market is sufficiently contest-able, the observed degree of market concentration need not be positively associated with monopoly rents contrary to the traditional structure-conduct-performance paradigm of industrial organization. This implies that market structure in itself cannot provide a basis for regulation or antitrust enforcement. Rather, an assessment of entry barriers and the availability of technology must accompany market share data. The elimination of rents may not obtain with alternative behavioral descriptions of competitive strategies employed by firms. This issue is discussed further in section 4.4.

The following holds as a corollary to condition 1.

CONDITION 2   *At a sustainable monopoly equilibrium, prices are greater than or equal to marginal costs.*

Consider an entry plan (p^e, q^e) where $p^e = p^*$ and q^e differs from q^* by Δ for the lth commodity, $q^e = q^* - \Delta_l$, $\Delta_l = (0, \ldots, \Delta, \ldots, 0)$. Then, since $p^*(q^* - \Delta_l) \leq C(q^* - \Delta_l)$ by definition, and $p^*q^* = C(q^*)$,

$$p_l^* \geq [C(q^*) - C(q^* - \Delta_l)]/\Delta_l.$$

Taking the limit as Δ_l goes to zero, it follows that $p_l^* \geq C_l(q^*)$.

The following condition is the most significant in terms of characterizing the market equilibrium.

CONDITION 3   *At a sustainable monopoly equilibrium, prices must support the cost function.*

Otherwise, if $p^*q > C(q)$ for some $q \leq q^* = D(p^*)$, an entrant could profitably supply q. Thus, prices are subsidy-free for all output vectors. As noted in the preceding chapter, the set of support prices is equivalent to the set of prices that are subsidy-free across goods in the presence of cost complementarities. The importance of this condition is the intuitively appealing result that price competition eliminates cross-subsidies. If a subset of commodities or a subset of total sales generates revenues in excess of stand-alone costs, there are obvious opportunities for new entry. These returns to entry are inconsistent with the free entry Bertrand-Nash equilibrium. It must be emphasized that elimination of cross-subsidies should not be considered an efficiency result unless this is the specified regulatory objective.

The existence of sustainable monopoly prices entails a number of necessary conditions on technology. First, condition 3 implies that the cost function must be supportable. The technology must also be that of a natural monopoly.

CONDITION 4   *For a sustainable price vector to exist, costs must be subadditive.*

For any arbitrary division of outputs such that $\sum_{j=1}^{J} q^j = q^*$, the free entry condition implies $p^* \sum_{j=1}^{J} q^j \leq \sum_{j=1}^{J} C(q^j)$. Given $p^* q^* = C(q^*)$, $C(q^*) \leq \sum_{j=1}^{J} C(q^j)$.

Nondecreasing returns to scale are implied by the following condition.

CONDITION 5   *For a sustainable price vector to exist, costs C must exhibit subhomogeneity.*

An entrant can enter the market by selling a proportion of output λ, $0 < \lambda \leq 1$. Then, since $p^* \lambda q^* \leq C(\lambda q^*)$ and $p^* q^* = C(q^*)$, it follows that $C(\lambda q^*) \geq \lambda C(q^*)$.

4.2   Existence of Sustainable Prices: Nonjoint Technology

The essential problem posed by the literature on natural monopoly is that while a monopoly may produce more efficiently than two or more firms, there may not exist prices that deter rival entry. This section addresses the crucial issue of existence of sustainable prices. It is argued that the principal requirement for entry-deterring prices to exist is that the *size of the firm*, as represented by its minimum efficient scale, be *sufficiently large relative to market demand*. The analysis provides an appealing sufficient condition for sustainability that is easily verified from cost and demand data. The emphasis on firm size relative to demand allows a relaxation of global restrictions on the cost function.[7]

4.2.1   The Size of the Firm

It should come as no surprise that the form of the cost function cannot in itself determine whether entry-deterring prices exist. Clearly the existence of sustainable prices must depend upon the characteristics of both market demand and firm costs. To formalize the notion of the size of the firm, I rescale the firm's cost function.[8] Let $q = (q_1, \ldots, q_m)$ be the firm's output vector.

Definition 4.2.1   An α-size firm corresponding to $C(\cdot)$ is a firm with cost function $C_\alpha(q) = \alpha C(q/\alpha)$.

The effect of cost and demand specifications on existence of sustainable prices is made explicit by the following definition.

Definition 4.2.2 Let $S(\alpha, C, D)$ represent the set of monopoly price vectors that are sustainable given the cost function $C_\alpha(\cdot)$ and market demand $D(\cdot)$. A price vector in $S(\alpha, C, D)$ is said to be (α, C, D) sustainable.

Given *nonjoint technology*, the firm's cost of producing a vector of outputs is equal to the sum of their stand-alone costs. Let $C^j(q_j)$ represent the *stand-alone* costs of good j, and define average costs by $AC^j(q_j) \equiv C^j(q_j)/q_j$, $j = 1, \ldots, m$. The stand-alone cost function for each good is assumed to have a well-defined *minimum efficient scale* (*MES*) and increasing marginal cost.

ASSUMPTION 4.2.1   The cost functions C^j are continuously differentiable for $q_j > 0$, $C^{j'}(q_j) > 0$ and $C^j(q_j) > 0$ for $q_j > 0$, $C^j(0) \geq 0$, for $j = 1, \ldots, m$.

ASSUMPTION 4.2.2   There exists an interval $[\tilde{q}_j, \tilde{\tilde{q}}_j] \subset (0, \infty)$, $\tilde{\tilde{q}}_j \geq \tilde{q}_j$, such that $AC^j(q_j) = AC^j_{\min} > 0$ for $q_j \in [\tilde{q}_j, \tilde{\tilde{q}}_j]$ and $AC^j(q_j) > AC^j_{\min}$ for $q_j \notin [\tilde{q}_j, \tilde{\tilde{q}}_j]$. Also, $AC^j(\cdot)$ is nonincreasing for $0 < q_j \leq \tilde{q}_j$. Without loss of generality let $\tilde{q}_j = 1$, $j = 1, \ldots, m$.

ASSUMPTION 4.2.3   Let average cost be bounded for small outputs, $\lim_{q_j \to 0} AC^j(q_j) \leq b < \infty$, $j = 1, \ldots, m$.

Assumption 4.2.2 normalizes efficient scale. Define $MES(AC^j)$ as the *minimum efficient scale* of the average cost function. Thus, $MES(AC^j) = \tilde{q}_j = 1$. The assumption allows flat bottomed average cost curves of the type discussed in Baumol, Panzar, and Willig (1982). Average costs satisfying assumptions 4.2.1–4.2.3 need not have the traditional smooth U-shape. Assumption 4.2.3 rules out fixed costs. The effect of relaxing this assumption in the single-product case will be examined.

The rescaled cost function for the α-size firm is $C_\alpha(q) = \sum_{j=1}^n \alpha C^j(q_j/\alpha) = \sum_{j=1}^n C^j_\alpha(q_j)$. By the definition of average cost,

$$AC^j_\alpha(q_j) \equiv C^j_\alpha(q_j)/q_j = C^j(q_j/\alpha)/(q_j/\alpha) = AC^j(q_j/\alpha). \qquad (4.2.1)$$

The *minimum efficient scale* for each good j equals the scalar α, since

$$MES(AC^j_\alpha(q_j)) = MES(AC^j(q_j/\alpha)) = \alpha, \qquad (4.2.2)$$

for $j = 1, \ldots, m$. Also, the minimum average cost is not affected by α,

$$AC^j_{\alpha \min} = AC^j_{\min} = AC^j(1). \qquad (4.2.3)$$

The effect of an increase in the size of the firm is to flatten the average

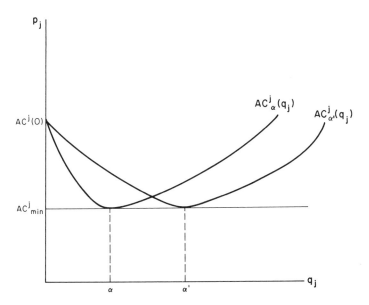

Figure 4.2.1
Rescaling the cost function.

cost curve to the left of minimum efficient scale. Given marginal costs $MC_\alpha^j(q_j) = \alpha \, \partial C^j(q_j/\alpha)/\partial q_j = C^{j'}(q_j/\alpha)$,

$$\partial AC_\alpha^j(q_j)/\partial \alpha = (1/\alpha)[AC_\alpha^j(q_j) - MC_\alpha^j(q_j)],$$

$j = 1, \ldots, m$, which is positive for output less than minimum efficient scale. If assumption 4.2.3 holds, an increase in the size of the firm shifts out average costs for each good j as in figure 4.2.1.

4.2.2 The Single-Product Case

Global increasing returns to scale imply subadditivity of costs and yet are *not* sufficient for the existence of sustainable prices. In figure 4.2.2, for example, where $D(p)$ is market demand and $AC(q)$ is average cost at output q, there are no sustainable prices. Any price below p_2 will cover the costs of supplying the market demand, so p_2 is not sustainable. While the price p_1 is *locally* sustainable, an entrant may still select prices below p_2, draw the demand away from the established firm, and earn positive profits. The problem illustrated by figure 4.2.2 is that at the *last crossing* of inverse demand and average costs, demand crosses average costs from *below* and

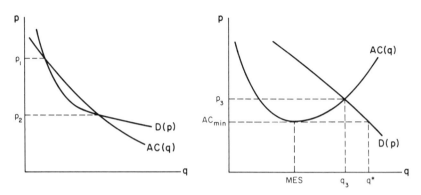

Figure 4.2.2 (left) and 4.2.3 (right)
Prices p_1, p_2, and p_3 are not sustainable.

is everywhere above average costs for larger outputs. To ensure that at the last crossing demand crosses average costs from above, assume that average costs have a well-defined *minimum* and that market demand is positive and bounded at a price equal to minimum average costs. If decreasing returns to scale eventually set in, demand will cross average costs from above at the intersection at which output is greatest. This situation is depicted in figure 4.2.3.[9] Although it is important for the monopoly cost function to exhibit increasing returns for small output levels, it is unreasonable to require that they hold globally. This would imply that existing technology places no limits on the size of an enterprise and that reductions in average costs can always be achieved by further expansion. In figure 4.2.3, however, the price p_3 is not sustainable since it occurs in a region of decreasing returns. The entrant can charge a price below p_3, thus increasing demand and produce less than output q_3, thus lowering average costs below p_3. The source of the problem in figure 4.2.3 is that *the size of the firm is small relative to market demand.* There is a well-defined minimum average cost AC_{min}, and inverse demand equals minimum average costs at a positive output q^*. *Existence of sustainable prices is obtained if the minimum efficient scale of the firm, MES, is greater than the output at which inverse demand equals minimum average costs q^*.*

We now state sufficient conditions for existence of a sustainable monopoly price in the single-product case. Let market demand be continuously differentiable and downward sloping with inverse demand $F(q)$. There exists an output q^* such that inverse demand equals the minimum level of average cost, $F(q^*) = AC_{min}$. Also, $\lim_{q \to 0} F(q) = \infty$. The set of sustainable prices is nonempty if the size of the firm is neither too large nor too small relative to market demand.

PROPOSITION 4.2.1   *Given assumptions 4.2.1 and 4.2.2, there exist α^*, α^{**}, $\alpha^{**} > \alpha^*$, such that for all $\alpha \in [\alpha^*, \alpha^{**})$, $S(\alpha, C, D)$ is nonempty.*

Proof Let $\alpha^{**} = \sup\{\bar{\alpha} : AC_\alpha(q) > F(q)$ for all q, for all $\alpha > \bar{\alpha}\}$. Let $\alpha^* = q^*/\tilde{\tilde{q}}$ with $\tilde{\tilde{q}}$ given in assumption 4.2.1 and q^* given in assumption 4.2.2. By the continuity of $AC_\alpha(q)$ in q and α, $\alpha^{**} > \alpha^*$. Then for each $\alpha \in [\alpha^*, \alpha^{**})$, there is an output q such that $F(q) = AC_\alpha(q)$, $q \leq q^* = \alpha^* \tilde{\tilde{q}}$. Thus, $q/\alpha^* \leq \tilde{\tilde{q}}$, so that demand crosses average cost from above in the region of nonincreasing returns to scale. Thus, for all $p' < F(q)$ and $q' \leq D(p')$, $p' < AC_\alpha(q')$.   QED

The idea of the proof is to guarantee that the scale of the firm is sufficiently large so that the demand curve intersects average costs either at a minimum average cost output or at an output less than the minimum efficient scale. The upper bound α^{**} may be finite if there is a scale at which average costs exceed inverse demands at all outputs. This situation is ruled out if average costs are bounded for small outputs.

PROPOSITION 4.2.1a   *Given assumptions 4.2.1–4.2.3, there exists α^* such that for all $\alpha \in [\alpha^*, \infty]$, $S[\alpha, C, D)$ is nonempty.*

Therefore, if the firm's minimum efficient scale is sufficiently large relative to market demand at the minimum average cost price, there exists a sustainable monopoly price.

4.2.3 Multiple Products with Nonjoint Technology

Existence of sustainable monopoly prices is now examined for the multiple-product firm with nonjoint technology. Let $D(p)$ represent the vector of market demand functions $D^j(p)$, $j = 1, \ldots, m$. Also, $F(q)$ represents the vector of inverse demand functions, $F^j(q)$, $j = 1, \ldots, m$. The demand function has the following properties.

ASSUMPTION 4.2.4   Demands $D^j(p)$ are continuously differentiable and downward sloping, $D_j^j(p) \equiv \partial D^j(p)/\partial p_j < 0$, $j = 1, \ldots, n$. Also, inverse demands are asymptotic to the y axis; $\lim_{q_j \to 0} F^j(q) = \infty$ given $q_i > 0$, for all $i \neq j$.

ASSUMPTION 4.2.5 Products are weak substitutes, $D_i^j(p) \equiv \partial D^j(p)/\partial p_i \geq 0$, $i \neq j$. Demands are bounded above; $D^j(p) \leq D^j(p_j) < \infty$ for all $p_j > 0$, where $D^j(p_j)$ is a downward-sloping continuous function of p_j.

The assumption that inverse demands are asymptotic to the y axis is made to guarantee that small output levels may be profitably produced if average costs are bounded. The assumption of weak substitutes permits demands for each good to be independent. The upper bound on market demand for any given price is due to consumers having budget constraints with fixed income levels. Define q_j^* such that

$$D^j(AC_{\min}^j) = q_j^*, \qquad j = 1, \ldots, m. \qquad (4.2.4)$$

This is the *size of the market* for good j at the minimum average cost price.

With additively separable costs, only average cost prices are sustainable, since any other monopoly price can be undercut by entry in any single market. To show that average cost prices are sustainable, note that demand for each good j is shifted down if $p^e \leq p^m$ since the products are substitutes, see figure 4.2.4. Thus, good j can only be supplied at a loss. This intuition is used to prove the following result.

PROPOSITION 4.2.2 *Given assumptions* 4.2.1–4.2.5 *and nonjoint technology, there exists* α^* *such that for all* $\alpha \in [\alpha^*, \infty)$, $S(\alpha, C, D)$ *is nonempty.*

The proof is given in the appendix. If α^* is the smallest scale such that the

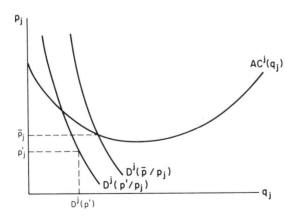

Figure 4.2.4
Sustainability of the price vector $\bar{p}$ with nonjoint technology.

monopoly is sustainable, α^* can be interpreted as the *minimum sustainable size*.

4.3 Existence of Sustainable Prices: Cost Complementarity

As noted above, a necessary condition for sustainability is that prices are subsidy-free across all product bundles; that is, a sustainable price vector must support the cost function. Accordingly I focus on a particular price vector, the Aumann-Shapley cost allocation discussed in chapter 3. The effect of rescaling on multiproduct average costs resembles the single-product case. Recall that the Aumann-Shapley cost allocation prices are zero-profit prices.

The following assumptions on the general multiproduct cost function $C(q)$ are useful. Define $AC^j(C, q) = \int_0^1 C_j(tq)\, dt$ as in chapter 3.[10]

ASSUMPTION 4.3.1   The cost function $C(q)$ is twice continuously differentiable for all $q \in \mathbb{R}^m_+$ and $C(0) = 0$. Let $C_j(q) \equiv \partial C(q)/\partial q_j, j = 1, \ldots, m$. Also $AC^j(C, q) \geq AC^j_{\min} > 0$ for all q, where $AC^j_{\min}$ is independent of q, and $\lim_{q_j \to 0} AC^j(C, q) < \infty$ for $q_i > 0$, $i \neq j$, $i, j = 1, \ldots, m$.

It is assumed that cost complementarities exist for small outputs.

ASSUMPTION 4.3.2   The cost function exhibits local cost complementarities, $C_{ij}(q) \leq 0$ for all i, j for all outputs q in a compact, convex, and comprehensive set $K^C \subset \mathbb{R}^m_+$.

A *comprehensive set*[11] is a set such that if some output q is in the set all smaller outputs are also in the set. We assume that K^C contains positive output levels for each good j. Assumption 4.3.2 guarantees that there exist support prices for all outputs within the set K^C. Assumption 4.3.2 places no restrictions on the cost function outside of the set K^C although the average cost allocation must be bounded below by assumption 4.3.1.

The local cost complementarity assumption can be understood by allowing outputs to be cost substitutes for large outputs, $C_{ij}(q) > 0$ for all i, j and for all $q \notin K^C$. Then, we can define a set of outputs, larger than outputs contained in K^C, that constitutes the exact multiproduct analogue to *minimum efficient scale* for single-product cost functions.[12] Let $q^{(j)}$ be the vector of outputs $(q_1, \ldots, q_m)$ excluding q_j. Then, we may define a corresponding output $MES^j(q^{(j)})$ as the minimum efficient scale for output

$q^{(j)}$. This is the output q_j at which the Aumann-Shapley average cost will then be U-shaped.

The multiproduct α-size firm has the cost function $C_\alpha(q_1,\dots,q_n) = \alpha C(q_1/\alpha,\dots,q_n/\alpha)$ for a scalar $\alpha > 0$. Thus, the rescaled Aumann-Shapley average costs are

$$AC^j(C_\alpha, q) = \int_0^1 C_j(tq/\alpha)\, dt = AC^j(C, q/\alpha). \tag{4.3.1}$$

Furthermore, where the minimum efficient scale is well defined,

$$MES_\alpha^j(q^{(j)}) = \alpha MES^j(q^{(j)}/\alpha). \tag{4.3.2}$$

Clearly $AC_{\alpha\,\min}^j = AC_{\min}^j$ by assumption 4.3.1. Finally, $q \in K^{C_\alpha}$ if $q/\alpha \in K^C$. We illustrate these concepts with an example.

Example   Consider now an *example* of a cost function satisfying assumptions 4.3.1 and 4.3.2,

$$C(q) = \left(\sum_{i=1}^m a_i q_i\right)^\beta + \left(\sum_{i=1}^m a_i q_i\right)^{\beta+1}, \tag{4.3.3}$$

where $0 < \beta < 1$, $a_i > 0$, $i = 1,\dots,m$. To verify whether assumption 4.3.2 is satisfied, calculate C_{ij}:

$$C_{ij}(q) = a_i a_j\left[\beta(\beta - 1)\left(\sum_{i=1}^m a_i q_i\right)^{\beta-2} + (\beta + 1)\beta\left(\sum_{i=1}^m a_i q_i\right)^{\beta-1}\right]. \tag{4.3.4}$$

Thus $C_{ij}(q) \gtrless 0$ as $\sum_{i=1}^m a_i q_i \gtrless (1 - \beta)/(1 + \beta)$, and so $K^C = \{q \in \mathbb{R}_+^m : \sum_{i=1}^m a_i q_i \leq (1 - \beta)/(1 + \beta)\}$. Next, calculate average costs,

$$AC^j(C, q) = a_j\left[\left(\sum_{i=1}^m a_i q_i\right)^{\beta-1} + \left(\sum_{i=1}^m a_i q_i\right)^\beta\right]. \tag{4.3.5}$$

Then $\partial AC^j(C, q)/\partial q_j \gtrless 0$ as $\sum_{i=1}^m a_i q_i \gtrless (1 - \beta)/\beta$. For $\sum_{i \neq j} a_i q_i < (1-\beta)/\beta$, AC^j has a minimum at

$$MES^j(q^{(j)}) = \left[(1 - \beta)/\beta - \sum_{i \neq j} a_i q_i\right]\Big/a_j. \tag{4.3.6}$$

Thus,

$$AC_{\min}^j(C, q^{(j)}, MES^j) = a_j(1 - \beta)^{\beta-1}/\beta^\beta = AC_{\min}^j, \tag{4.3.7}$$

where $AC^j(C, q) \geq AC_{\min}^j$ for all $j = 1,\dots,m$ and for all q. The multiproduct analogue to *minimum efficient scale* is therefore $\bar{H} = \{q \in \mathbb{R}_+^m : \sum_{i=1}^m a_i q_i = (1 - \beta)/\beta\}$. Rescaling the cost function, we have the average cost for the α-size firm,

$$AC^j(C_\alpha, q) = (a_j/\alpha^\beta)\left[\alpha \left(\sum_{i=1}^m a_i q_i \right)^{\beta-1} + \left(\sum_{i=1}^m a_i q_i \right)^\beta \right], \qquad (4.3.8)$$

where for $q \in K^C$

$$MES_\alpha^j(q^{(j)}) = \left[\alpha(1 - \beta)/\beta - \sum_{i \neq j} a_i q_i \right]/a_j. \qquad (4.3.9)$$

An increase in the firm's size α shifts the average cost curve upward and to the right as in figure 4.2.1.

It is now shown that for the size of the firm sufficiently large, there exist market-clearing Aumann-Shapley average cost prices[13] such that there are cost complementarities at the market output vector.

PROPOSITION 4.3.1 *Given demand assumptions* 4.2.4 *and* 4.2.5 *and cost assumptions* 4.3.1 *and* 4.3.2, *there exists* $\alpha^* > 0$ *such that for each* $\alpha \in [\alpha^*, \infty)$ *there exist positive market-clearing Aumann-Shapley prices and quantities* (p^m, q^m) *satisfying* $q^m = D(p^m)$ *and* $p_j^m = AC^j(C_\alpha, q^m), j = 1, \ldots, n$, *such that* $C_{\alpha ij}(x) \leq 0$ *for all* $x \leq q^m, x \in \mathbb{R}_+^m$.

The proof is given in the appendix. Note that since the Aumann-Shapley prices support the cost function, the proposition implies that these prices are *anonymously equitable* for $\alpha \geq \alpha^*$; see definition 3.2.4.

Given existence of supportable Aumann-Shapley prices, the main sustainability result is now obtained. Mirman, Tauman, and Zang (1985, proposition 5) show that *global* cost complementarities, weak substitutes in demand, and inelastic demand for $p \leq \bar{p}$ are sufficient for a price $\bar{p}$ in the core of a cost game to be sustainable.[14] The proof of the following result follows their proof, but weakens the cost requirement and shows the *existence* of a specific sustainable price vector, the Aumann-Shapley prices. The exposition is clarified by the properties of Aumann-Shapley prices.

PROPOSITION 4.3.2 *Given demand assumptions* 4.2.4 *and* 4.2.5 *and cost assumptions* 4.3.1 *and* 4.3.2, *there exists* α^* *such that for all* $\alpha \in [\alpha^*, \infty)$, *there exist sustainable Aumann-Shapley prices* p^m, *and thus* $S(\alpha, C, D)$ *is nonempty, if* $D_j^j(p)p_j/D^j(p) \geq -1$ *for each* $j \in N$ *and* $p \leq p^m$.

Proof For $\alpha \geq \alpha^*$, let $AC^j(q) \equiv AC^j(C_\alpha, q)$. Let $p_j^m = AC^j(D(p^m))$, $j \in N$. The entrant's profit is given by

$$\pi^e = p_M^e D_M(p_M^e, p_{N\setminus M}^m) - C_\alpha(D_M(p_M^e, p_{N\setminus M}^m)), \tag{4.3.10}$$

where $p_M^e \leq p_M^m$ $M \subseteq N$. Let $M_1 = \{ j \in M : D^j(p_M^e, p_{N\setminus M}^m) \leq D^j(p^m)\}$ and $M_2 = M \setminus M_1$. By increasing costs,

$$C_\alpha(D_M(p_M^e, p_{N\setminus M}^m)) \geq C_\alpha(D_{M_1}(p_M^e, p_{N\setminus M}^m), D_{M_2}(p^m)). \tag{4.3.11}$$

Since $C_\alpha(q) = \sum_j AC^j(q)q^j$ by definition, and $C_{\alpha ij}(q') \leq 0$ for $q' \leq D(p^m)$, given $\alpha \geq \alpha^*$,

$$C_\alpha(D_{M_1}(p_M^e, p_{N\setminus M}^m), D_{M_2}(p^m)) \geq \sum_{j \in M_1} AC^j(D(p^m))D^j(p_M^e, p_{N\setminus M}^m)$$

$$+ \sum_{j \in M_2} AC^j(D(p^m))D^j(p^m). \tag{4.3.12}$$

But, since $p_j^m = AC^j(D(p^m))$, $j \in N$, and $p_M^e \leq p_M^m$,

$$C_\alpha(D_M(p_M^e, p_{N\setminus M}^m)) \geq \sum_{j \in M_1} p_j^e D^j(p_M^e, p_{N\setminus M}^m) + \sum_{j \in M_2} p_j^m D^j(p^m). \tag{4.3.13}$$

Thus, from (4.3.10)

$$\pi^e \leq \sum_{j \in M_2} [p_j^e D^j(p_M^e, p_{N\setminus M}^m) - p_j^m D^j(p^m)]. \tag{4.3.14}$$

By weak substitutes in demand and $p_M^e \leq p_M^m$,

$$\pi^e \leq \sum_{j \in M_2} [p_j^e D^j(p_j^e, p_{N\setminus j}^m) - p_j^m D^j(p^m)]. \tag{4.3.15}$$

By $D_j^j(p)p_j/D^j(p) \geq -1$, for each $j \in N$, $p \leq p^m$, $\pi^e \leq 0$.   QED

Thus, without imposing global restrictions on the cost function, subsidy-free prices are sustainable against the entry of rival firms. Monopoly is sustainable if the efficient scale of the firm is sufficiently large relative to market demand.

4.4 Quantity Sustainability

As emphasized in section 4.1, the contestable markets literature and the analysis of sustainability are predicated on particular behavioral assumptions about the nature of strategic competition between firms. When these vary, the implications of the model vary as well. It should be noted that only noncooperative static equilibrium strategies are discussed here. Based upon the analysis of Grossman (1981b) of Nash equilibria with supply function strategies, Sharkey (1982a) and M. Perry (1984) have reexamined the notion of sustainability for more complex pricing policies in single-product models. This is discussed more fully in chapter 18. Perry's analysis shows that elimination of rents by potential entry need not occur when more sophisticated pricing strategies are used to deter entry by shifting residual demand to the left of average costs.

Brock and Scheinkman (1983) offer the concept of quantity sustainability as a means of verifying whether a vector of output levels set by a monopolist can deter entry in a subset or in all of the markets served by the monopolist. Brock and Scheinkman (1983, p. 232) suggest that "Cournot's notion is 'dual' to that of Bertrand in that entrants anticipate that the monopolist's quantities remain fixed but that prices adjust to absorb the extra output of the entrant. This motivates a 'dual' notion of sustainability." Quantity sustainability thus involves entering firms making the conjecture of Cournot firms that rivals will hold their output constant.[15] The following definitions are based upon the Brock and Scheinkman (1983) definition of quantity sustainability.

Definition 4.4.1 Given C, F, and $\alpha \in (0, \infty)$, the monopoly price vector p^m and quantity vector $q^m = D(p^m)$ are (α, C, F) *quantity sustainable* if for every set of products $S \subseteq M$,

$$\sum_{j \in S} F^j(q^m + q_S^e)q_S^e - C_\alpha(q_S^e) \leq 0 \tag{4.4.1}$$

for all entrant output levels $q_S^e \geq 0$ for all $S \subseteq M$. It is also required that $p^m q^m - C_\alpha(q^m) \geq 0$.

Definition 4.4.2 Let $QS(\alpha, C, F)$ represent the set of (α, C, F) quantity sustainable monopoly prices.

The quantity sustainable output vector essentially shifts residual demand to the left of average costs in the single-good case. Brock and Scheinkman (1983) have shown quantity sustainability to be a weaker requirement than price sustainability.

PROPOSITION   (Brock and Scheinkman)   *Given downward sloping demands and weak substitutes, price sustainability implies quantity sustainability.*

Clearly by the proposition, $S(\alpha, C, F) \subseteq QS(\alpha, C, F)$. Thus, for the size of the firm α sufficiently large, the set of quantity sustainable prices will be nonempty. Define *Aumann-Shapley quantities* as the market-clearing quantities for Aumann-Shapley average cost prices,

$$\bar{q}_j = D^j(AC(\bar{q})), \qquad j = 1, \ldots, m. \tag{4.4.2}$$

Given α^* as in proposition 4.3.2, the following is obtained.

PROPOSITION 4.4.1   *Given the conditions of proposition 4.3.2, there exists $\bar{\alpha}^* \leq \alpha^*$ such that for $\alpha \in [\bar{\alpha}^*, \infty)$, Aumann-Shapley quantities are quantity sustainable and thus $QS(\alpha, C, F)$ is nonempty.*

Clearly, from the definition of quantity sustainability, increasing average costs are consistent with existence of a quantity sustainable output. In figure 4.4.1, q^* is sustainable since the incumbent's residual demand is shifted to the left of the average cost curve. Further, the quantity sustainable output level generally involves positive profit. Indeed, the quantity sustainability condition in the single-product case is related to the free entry condition in the Cournot-Nash model of Novshek (1980a); see chapter 17. Thus, the Cournot-Nash equilibrium with multiple firms making positive profits is quantity sustainable. Indeed, it is shown in chapter 17 that with fixed costs sufficiently large, the profit-maximizing monopoly output is quantity sustainable.

Brock and Scheinkman (1983) argue against petitions for denial of entry made to regulatory commissions that are based on claims of nonsustainability of natural monopoly. They show that if the one-plant Ramsey optimum is not quantity sustainable, there exist two plants that both break

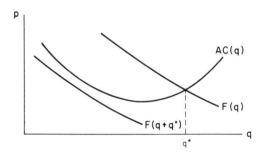

Figure 4.4.1
Output q^* is quantity sustainable.

even and yield social surplus that is greater than at the one-plant Ramsey optimum. This suggests that evaluation of petitions for entry restrictions by regulators must depend upon careful evaluation of the competitive strategies employed by firms even if a static model is appropriate. As indicated earlier, additional work on dynamic entry strategies in the presence of sunk costs is needed to evaluate entry restrictions imposed by regulatory commisions.

Appendix

Proof of Proposition 4.2.2   First, the existence of market-clearing average cost prices is shown. Let $AC_\alpha(q) = (AC_\alpha^1(q_1), \ldots, AC_\alpha^m(q_m))$, $Q = [0, q_1^*] \times \cdots \times [0, q_m^*]$ and $A = [AC_{\min}^1, b] \times \cdots \times [AC_{\min}^m, b]$ with q_j^* given by (4.2.4). Then $AC_\alpha(q)$ is a continuous mapping from the compact set Q into the compact set A. The demand function $D(p)$ is a continuous mapping from A to Q. Define the mapping $\Gamma: A \times Q \to A \times Q$ by

$$\Gamma(p, q) = AC_\alpha(q) \times D(p).$$

Then the mapping Γ has a fixed point by Brouwer's theorem, $\Gamma(p^m, q^m) = (p^m, q^m)$.

Now it is shown that for α sufficiently large, the equilibrium (p^m, q^m) occurs in the region of nondecreasing returns for each $C^j(\cdot)$. Let $\alpha_j^* = q_j^*/\tilde{\tilde{q}}_j$, $j = 1, \ldots, m$, where $\tilde{\tilde{q}}$ is given in assumption 4.2.2. Let $\alpha^* = \max\{\alpha_1^*, \ldots, \alpha_m^*\}$. Then, for each $\alpha \geq \alpha^*$, for all q such that $q = D(p)$ and $p_j = AC_\alpha^j(q_j)$, $j = 1, \ldots, m$, the following holds:

$$q_j \leq \alpha_j^* \tilde{\tilde{q}}_j \leq \alpha^* q_j, \qquad j = 1, \ldots, m.$$

Thus, given $\alpha \geq \alpha^*$, $q_j^m/\alpha \leq \tilde{\tilde{q}}_j$ and $AC_\alpha^j(x)$ is nonincreasing for $x \leq q_j^m$, $j = 1, \ldots, m$.

Finally, it is shown that there exists a vector of *sustainable* average cost prices. For $\alpha \in [\alpha^*, \infty)$ given, let p^m be a vector of undominated average cost prices, i.e., there does not exist $p' \leq p^m$ for p^m, p' in $G(\alpha)$, where $G(\alpha) = \{p \in \mathbb{R}_+^m : p_j = AC_\alpha^j(q), q_j = D^j(p)\}$. Let $p_S^e \leq p_S^m$, $S \subseteq M$. Let $p^{(j)}$ be the vector p excluding p_j. Then for all $j \in S$,

$$D^j(p_S^{e(j)}, p_{M-S}^m, p_j) \leq D^j(p^{m(j)}, p_j)$$

for all p_j by assumption 4.2.4. Thus, since average costs are nonincreasing and bounded below and $p_j^e \leq p_j^m, j \in S$,

$$p_j^e \le AC_\alpha^j(q_j)$$

for all $q_j \le D^j(p_S^e, p_{M-S}^m)$ for all $j \in S$. Thus $p_j^e q_j^e \le C_\alpha^j(q_j^e)$ for all $j \in S$, $S \subseteq M$, and so p^m is sustainable.   QED

Proof of Proposition 4.3.1   First, the existence of market-clearing Aumann-Shapley prices is shown. Then it is shown that for α^* chosen appropriately, the market equilibrium outputs lie in the set K^{C_α} for $\alpha \ge \alpha^*$. Let $q_j^* = D^j(AC_{min}^j)$ as in (4.2.4) and $q^* = (q_1^*, \dots, q_m^*)$. Let $Q^j = [\varepsilon, q_j^*]$ and $Q = Q^1 \times \dots \times Q^m$ for some $\varepsilon > 0$. Since $AC^j(C_\alpha, q)$ is continuous in q by assumption 4.3.1, so is $AC_\alpha(q) = (AC^1(C_\alpha, q), \dots, AC^m(C_\alpha, q))$. Since Q is a compact set and $q > \varepsilon$, there exists a number B such that for each j and $q \in Q$, $AC_{min}^j \le AC^j(C_\alpha, q) \le B$. Consider the set $A = [AC_{min}^1, B] \times \dots \times [AC_{min}^m, B]$. Then $AC_\alpha(q)$ is a continuous map from Q to A. Given assumptions 4.2.4 and 4.2.5, $D(p)$ is continuous and there exists an $\varepsilon > 0$ such that $D(p)$ is a mapping from A into Q. Define a mapping $\Gamma: A \times Q \to A \times Q$ by

$$\Gamma(p, q) = AC(C_\alpha, q) \times D(p).$$

Since the mapping is continuous, Γ has a fixed point by Brouwer's theorem, $\Gamma(p^m, q^m) = (p^m, q^m)$. Thus, $p^m = AC(C_\alpha, q^m)$ and $q^m = D(p^m)$.

Since $C_{\alpha ij}(q) = (1/\alpha)C_{ij}(q/\alpha)$, $C_{\alpha ij} \le 0$ at q if $C_{ij} \le 0$ at q/α. Choose α^* such that $q^*/\alpha \in K^C$ for $\alpha \ge \alpha^*$. Thus, $q^* \in K^{C_\alpha}$ for $\alpha \ge \alpha^*$. Since $q^m \le q^*$, $C_{\alpha ij}(x) \le 0$ for all $x \le q^m$, $x \in \mathbb{R}_+^m$.   QED

Notes

1. See Baumol, Bailey, and Willig (1977), Panzar and Willig (1977), and Baumol, Panzar, and Willig (1982).

2. Sharkey (1981) argues that if the industry is a natural monopoly and if free entry is taken as a *given*, then, unless the price vector is sustainable (and therefore subsidy-free), "some form of inefficient multiple firm production would result." However, the argument is predicated on free entry. An absence of entry barriers or restrictions exists in few markets. Furthermore, free entry need not be an end in itself. For many economists involved in regulatory debates, it is elimination of cross-subsidies through complete deregulation that is seen as the desired objective. However, as emphasized in the preceding chapter, this is a cost-based notion of price setting that may preclude even second-best optimality. Sharkey (1981) presents a simple counterexample showing that for an affine cost function Ramsey prices generally are not sustainable prices. Baumol, Bailey, and Willig (1977) place conditions *jointly* on cost and revenue functions that guarantee the existence of Ramsey prices that are a sustainable market equilibrium. These joint conditions are difficult to verify from cost and demand data. In particular, Baumol, Bailey, and Willig (1977) require that the total cost function including entry costs be supported at the Ramsey output by a "pseudorevenue hyperplane"; see also Baumol, Panzar, and Willig (1982, chapter 8).

3. The theory of contestable markets has generated considerable controversy. Critical comments include Schwartz and Reynolds (1983), Weitzman (1983), and Shepherd (1984). For review articles see Brock (1983) and Spence (1983).

4. The contestable markets analysis has not been extended satisfactorily to allow a general dynamic analysis. The equilibrium definition is static in nature. Thus, Baumol's (1979b) policy prescription that strategic responses of established firms be inhibited by regulatory intervention to render price changes quasi-permanent lacks the foundation of a dynamic entry model. If cost complementarities are present over time (that is, between goods produced in different periods), future entry cannot fully discipline future performance of the established firm. A more restrictive sustainability notion is required that specifies sustainable prices relative to entry opportunities over time. Thus, in a two-period entry model, without entry in the first period, monopoly revenues in the second period cannot exceed one-period stand-alone costs.

5. In a deterministic model, all costs are sunk once a production decision has been made, whether costs are fixed or variable in relation to output. On the other hand, nonstationarity in demand or input prices will result in a variation in capacity requirements over time.

6. See Novshek (1980a) for an analogous definition of a Cournot-Nash equilibrium with free entry.

7. In the multiproduct case, a frequent assumption in the literature on sustainable prices and on allocation of multiproduct costs is that global cost complementarities exist between outputs; that is, an increase in the output of any product lowers the marginal cost of all other products—see, for example, Panzar and Willig (1977), Sharkey and Telser (1978), and Mirman, Tauman, and Zang (1983b). However, in Baumol, Bailey, and Willig (1977) transray convexity is assumed to hold only at the sustainable output point.

8. Novshek (1980a) employs the definition of an α-size firm to examine the existence and approximate competitiveness of a single-product Cournot-Nash equilibrium when the size of firms is *small* relative to market demand. In my framework, the scale of the firm is increased relative to market demand to examine the existence of a sustainable monopoly equilibrium. It is appealing that small minimum efficient scale, MES, results in existence of a competitive equilibrium, while large MES results in existence of a monopoly equilibrium. This provides a natural economic explanation of the sustainability results.

9. A figure similar to figure 4.2.2 is in Mirman, Tauman, and Zang (1985). A figure similar to 4.2.3 is in Baumol, Panzar, and Willig (1982, p. 30).

10. Given assumption 4.3.1, the average cost function $AC^j(C, q)$ is continuously differentiable in q. This assumption is made for convenience and may be relaxed. The assumption excludes fixed costs although these may be approximated.

11. X is a *comprehensive set* if for any $q \in X$, $X_q \subseteq X$, where $X_q = \{x \in \mathbb{R}^m_+ : x \leq q\}$.

12. Let $\bar{K}^C$ be the set of undominated vectors in the set K^C. This is well defined since K^C is compact and comprehensive. Then we may define the scalar function $t(q)$, $0 < t(q) < 1$, such that for any output $q \notin K^C$, $\bar{q} = t(q)q$ is an element of $\bar{K}^C$. Then for any $q \notin K^C$, since $C(0) = 0$,

$$C(q) = \sum_{j=1}^{m} \left[\int_0^{t(q)} C_j(tq)q_j\,dt + \int_{t(q)}^1 C_j(tq)q_j\,dt \right].$$

Since $C_{ij} > 0$ for all i, j and $q \notin K^C$,

$$C(q) < \left[C(t(q)q) - \sum_{j=1}^{m} C_j(q)t(q)q_j \right] + \sum_{j=1}^{m} C_j(q)q_j.$$

By increasing q, the term in brackets can be made arbitrarily small, so that corresponding to any q' on the boundary of K^C there exists $q \notin K^C$ such that C exhibits decreasing returns to scale at q. Further, we can show that if C exhibits decreasing returns to scale at q, then decreasing returns to scale are present for all $\tilde{q} = q/t$, $t \leq 1$. This implies that there exists a comprehensive set $H \supset K^C$ such that C exhibits increasing returns to scale for all $q \in H$ and decreasing returns to scale for all $q \notin H$. Let $\bar{H}$ represent the set of undominated outputs in the set H. Then $\bar{H}$ is the exact multiproduct analogue to *minimum efficient scale* for single-product cost functions.

13. Mirman and Tauman (1982) prove that there exist demand compatible Aumann-Shapley cost-sharing prices. Their analysis is more general in the sense that market demands are derived from individual consumer maximization. They do not consider the issues raised here regarding the effect of firm size.

14. By weak substitutes in demand and by a result of Mirman, Tauman, and Zang (1985), one only needs to consider the case where the entrant supplies all of the demand in the market it enters, $q_S^e = D(p_S^e, p_{M-S}^m)$, $S \subseteq M$.

15. The quantity sustainable output is a multiproduct version of the entry-deterring limit quantity discussed elsewhere by Bain (1956), Sylos-Labini (1969), Modigliani (1958), and others. The belief on the part of entrants that an established firm will keep its output constant is referred to as the Sylos Postulate. See Spulber (1981a) and chapter 17 for an evaluation of the Sylos and Excess Capacity Hypotheses. Note that the quantity sustainability condition for an industry is related to the Cournot-Nash entry condition in Novshek's model (1980a).

5 Second-Best Pareto Optimal Pricing

Suppose that a regulator must choose prices for a regulated utility subject to the following restrictions:

1. The outputs Q are rationed among consumers by a linear price mechanism.

2. Only one firm is allowed to supply the goods Q.

3. The firm is required to break even.

4. Other than direct payments for purchases of the outputs Q, there are no other direct or indirect payments between consumers and the firm.

5. Transfers between consumers are not permitted.

Suppose further that the regulator must choose prices that are Pareto optimal within the set of prices satisfying (1)–(5). This is the second-best pricing problem associated with Ramsey (1927) and others. This chapter reviews the second-best pricing problem in a general multiconsumer framework. Section 5.1 characterizes the optimal markups above marginal cost that are chosen by the regulator. Section 5.2 relaxes the last restriction by allowing lump sum transfers between consumers. The selection of second-best prices given consumer ownership of profit shares is examined in section 4.3. Finally, in section 4.4, the insights obtained regarding second-best optimal markups are applied to the problem of peak load pricing under increasing returns to scale.

Given increasing returns to scale, marginal cost pricing does not generate sufficient revenue to cover production costs. In the absence of multipart pricing or subsidies, the regulated firm must set some prices above marginal cost in order to break even. A large literature exists on the selection of prices that maximize welfare subject to a break-even profit constraint. The literature on public sector pricing parallels the literature on proportionate commodity taxation dating back to Ramsey (1927) and Samuelson (1951). A synthesis and historical survey is given in Baumol and Bradford (1970). Ramsey pricing generally refers to prices (or proportionate taxes) that maximize an aggregate measure of consumer surplus subject to a nonnegative profit constraint.[1] The literature on regulated pricing has emphasized the aggregate welfare gains that may be achieved by raising prices for goods with relatively low demand elasticities and lowering prices for goods with relatively higher demand elasticities.

A general analysis of the second-best pricing problem was first given by

Boiteux (1951a, 1956). Accordingly, in later chapters, I sometimes refer to second-best Pareto optimal prices as Ramsey-Boiteux prices.[2] For additional extensions see Diamond and Mirrlees (1971a,b) and subsequent papers by Diamond (1975), Mirrlees (1975), Atkinson and Stiglitz (1976), and Guesnerie (1975b, 1979, 1980). Guesnerie (1980) presents a discussion of general principles of second-best Pareto optimality in an economy with government intervention.

The analysis of second-best pricing in the present chapter lays the groundwork for the analysis of a cooperative game of joint production given in the next chapter. Chapter 6 shows that prices in the core of the cooperative production game with linear prices must be second-best Pareto optimal.

5.1   Second-Best Pareto Optimality

5.1.1   Second-Best Pricing and Social Welfare Maximization

The market served by the regulated firms is described by a set of consumers $N = \{1, \ldots, n\}$ with endowments $\omega^i \in \mathbb{R}_+$ and utility functions $U^i(q^i, x^i)$, where $q^i \in \mathbb{R}_+^m$ is the vector of goods purchased from the regulated firms and $x^i \in \mathbb{R}_+$ is a numeraire good purchased in a competitive market. Consumers choose (q^i, x^i) to maximize utility subject to the budget constraint $pq^i + x^i = \omega^i$, where ω^i is the consumer's money endowment. Consumer endowments are assumed to be strictly positive, $\omega^i > 0$. Define an *indirect utility function* V^i as follows:

$$V^i(p, \omega^i) \equiv \max_{(q^i, x^i)} U^i(q^i, x^i) \tag{5.1.1}$$

subject to

$$pq^i + x^i = \omega^i.$$

Solution of problem (5.1.1) yields demands $(q^i(p, \omega^i), x^i(p, \omega^i))$. The following assumptions on utility are useful.

ASSUMPTION 5.1.1   (a) U^i is twice continuously differentiable; (b) U^i is increasing and strongly monotonic in (q^i, x^i); (c) U^i is strictly quasi-concave in (q^i, x^i); (d) all goods (q^i, x^i) are consumed in positive quantities for all p.

Given our assumptions, the indirect utility function is decreasing in p, increasing in ω, and convex in p. Given positive price vectors $p \in \mathbb{R}^m_+$, the demand vectors $(q^i(p, \omega^i), x^i(p, \omega^i))$, $i \in N$, are continuous and single valued.

For each consumer, writing (5.1.1) as a Lagrangian problem gives

$$L(q^i, x^i, \xi^i; p, \omega^i) = U^i(q^i, x^i) + \xi^i(\omega^i - pq^i - x^i). \tag{5.1.2}$$

The first-order necessary conditions are as follows:

$$U^i_{q_l}(q^i, x^i) - \xi^i p_l = 0, \qquad l = 1, \ldots, m, \tag{5.1.3}$$

$$U^i_x(q^i, x^i) - \xi^i = 0, \tag{5.1.4}$$

$$\omega^i - pq^i - x^i = 0. \tag{5.1.5}$$

Applying the envelope theorem gives the important relations

$$V^i_l(p, \omega^i) = \partial L/\partial p_l = -\xi^i q^i_l, \qquad l = 1, \ldots, m, \tag{5.1.6}$$

$$V^i_\omega(p, \omega^i) = \partial L/\partial \omega^i = \xi^i, \tag{5.1.7}$$

where $q^i_l = q^i_l(p, \omega^i)$. Combining (5.1.6) and (5.1.7) allows the statement of Roy's identity,

$$q^i_l(p, \omega^i) = -V^i_l(p, \omega^i)/V^i_\omega(p, \omega^i). \tag{5.1.8}$$

The firm has a multiproduct cost function $C(Q)$ that exhibits increasing returns to scale. Thus, costs are not covered by marginal cost pricing for any output level $Q = (Q_1, \ldots, Q_m)$,

$$\sum_{l=1}^{m} Q_l C_l(Q) < C(Q).$$

Further, we require the following:

ASSUMPTION 5.1.2   The cost function $C: K \to \mathbb{R}_+$ is twice differentiable and increasing in Q, where $K \subset \mathbb{R}^m_+$ is a compact set. Also, $C(0) \geq 0$.

Given that the firm is a monopolist and that outputs are rationed among consumers by a price mechanism, the firm faces market demands $Q(p) \equiv \sum_{i \in N} q^i(p, \omega^i)$. The absence of government subsidies or lump sum transfers requires the firm to cover its costs with its revenues.

Definition 5.1.1   The price vector p is *feasible* if the firm does not make a loss,

$$\Pi(p) \equiv pQ(p) - C(Q(p)) \geq 0. \tag{5.1.9}$$

The feasible price vector p supports an allocation of consumer demands (q^i, x^i), $i \in N$, such that the firm makes no losses. Given the consumer budget constraints, the feasibility condition is equivalent to the standard requirement,

$$\sum_{i \in N} (\omega^i - x^i) - C\left(\sum_{i \in N} q^i\right) \geq 0,$$

where $q^i = q^i(p, \omega^i)$, $x^i = x^i(p, \omega^i)$.

Given the definition of feasible prices, second-best Pareto optimal prices may be defined following Ramsey (1927) and Boiteux (1956). See also Baumol and Bradford (1970) and Guesnerie (1980). Due to the subadditivity of costs, the definition requires a single firm to serve all consumers. By focusing attention on the jointly produced goods, the definition also allows study of the partially regulated second-best problem; see Braeutigam (1979). Given restrictions (1)–(5), the regulator's objective is to find a price vector p^* for which no Pareto superior price vector exists. This is now defined formally.

Definition 5.1.2   The price vector p^* is *second-best Pareto optimal*, or equivalently, *Ramsey-Boiteux*, if it is feasible and if there does not exist another feasible price vector p' such that

$$V^i(p', \omega^i) \geq V^i(p^*, \omega^i)$$

for all $i \in N$ and strictly greater for some $i \in N$.

It must be emphasized that the second-best (s.b.) Pareto optimal price vector p^* is not necessarily unique. Further, we associate with each price vector p^* an allocation q^*, $q^* = (q^1(p^*, \omega^1), \ldots, q^n(p^*, \omega^n))$. A second-best Pareto optimal state allows zero consumption for some individuals by demand compatibility. To rule out boundary problems, I assume that all consumers choose to make positive purchases of the regulated firm's output. Given this restriction, I verify that second-best Pareto optimality is well defined.

PROPOSITION 5.1.1   *Given assumptions 5.1.1 and 5.1.2 and threshold aggregate demands $Q \geq \varepsilon$, $\varepsilon \gg 0$, there exists a second-best Pareto optimal price vector.*

The proof is given in the appendix and uses a fixed point argument similar to that in ten Raa (1983).

Second-best Pareto optimality may be studied using calculus. The following proposition and proof are similar to Varian's (1978) analysis of unconstrained Pareto optimality.

PROPOSITION 5.1.2 *The price vector p^* is second-best Pareto optimal if and only if p^* solves the problems*

$$\max_{p} V^i(p, \omega^i) \tag{5.1.10}$$

subject to

$$V^j(p, \omega^j) \geq V^j(p^*, \omega^j), \qquad j \neq i, \quad j = 1, \ldots, n,$$

and

$$pQ(p) - C(Q(p)) \geq 0$$

for all $i \in N$.

Proof Suppose that p^* solves all of the problems but is not second-best Pareto optimal. Then there must exist p' that makes everyone better off, which yields a contradiction. If p^* is second-best Pareto optimal, but does not solve one of the problems, then it must be possible to find a feasible price vector that increases one consumer's indirect utility without making any other consumers worse off. QED

Proposition 5.1.2 allows us to solve for second-best Pareto optimal prices using a Kuhn-Tucker-Lagrange expression. This is similar to the approach taken by Boiteux (1956) in a general equilibrium framework. Let λ^i, $i \in N$, be the shadow prices on the minimum utility constraints and let γ be the shadow price on the nonnegative profit constraint,[3]

$$L = \sum_{i \in N} \lambda^i(V^i(p, \omega^i) - \bar{V}^i) + \gamma[pQ(p) - C(Q(p))], \tag{5.1.11}$$

where $\bar{V}^i = V^i(p^*, \omega^i)$. To obtain any problem in (5.1.10) simply set $\lambda^i = 1$ for any $i \in N$.

The first-order *necessary* conditions include the following:

$$\sum_{i \in N} \lambda^i V_l^i(p^*, \omega^i) + \gamma \left[Q_l^* + \sum_{k=1}^{m} (p_k^* - C_k) \partial Q_k^* / \partial p_l \right] = 0, \qquad l = 1, \ldots, m, \tag{5.1.12}$$

where $Q_l^* = Q_l(p^*)$ and $C_k = \partial C(Q^*)/\partial Q_k$. In addition, the nonnegative profit constraint and the minimum utility constraints for $n - 1$ consumers must hold.

To complete the welfare analysis, suppose that there exists a social welfare function $W: \mathbb{R}_+^n \to \mathbb{R}_+$ that is dependent upon the vector of indirect utilities V^i, $W = W(V^1(p, \omega^1), \ldots, V^n(p, \omega^n))$. Suppose that W is monotonically increasing in its arguments. One may then represent the social welfare function by a function of the price vector $B(p) \equiv W$ for a given distribution of income ω. The following result is similar to well-known results for Pareto efficient allocations; see, for example, Varian (1978).

PROPOSITION 5.1.3   (a) *If p^* maximizes a social welfare function $B(p)$ subject to a nonnegative profits constraint, then it is a second-best Pareto optimal price.* (b) *If p^* is a second-best Pareto optimal price, then there is a choice of weights b^{i*} such that p^* maximizes $\sum_{i \in N} b^{i*} V^i(p, \omega^i)$ subject to the feasibility constraint, $pQ(p) - C(Q(p)) \geq 0$, $Q(p) = \sum_{i \in N} q^i(p, \omega^i)$, given $Q \geq \varepsilon \gg 0$.*

Given the monotonicity of W and V^i, $i \in N$, part (a) is obvious from the previous discussion of the calculus approach to second-best optimality. Part (b) follows immediately from the Lagrangian problem (5.1.11) by setting $b^{i*} = \lambda^i$, for all $i \in N$.

5.1.2   Second-Best Optimal Mark-Ups

A number of interesting interpretations of the optimality condition for second-best prices are considered. In equation (5.1.12), the bracketed expression represents the firm's marginal profit,

$$\partial \Pi(p)/\partial p_l = Q_l + \sum_k (p_k - C_k) \partial Q_k/\partial p_l, \qquad l = 1, \ldots, m.$$

The term $\sum_{i \in N} \lambda^i V_l^i(p^*, \omega^i)$ represents the marginal social benefits due to a lowering of the price of good l given a particular distribution of wealth $\omega = (\omega^1, \ldots, \omega^n)$ and the shadow prices on the indirect utility constraints in problem (5.1.10). Thus, the marginal social valuation of a price change is proportional to the firm's marginal return. Taking ratios of the first order conditions gives the following expression:

$$\frac{\sum_{i \in N} \lambda^i V_l^i(p^*, \omega^i)}{\sum_{i \in N} \lambda^i V_k^i(p^*, \omega^i)} = \frac{\partial \Pi(p^*)/\partial p_l}{\partial \Pi(p^*)/\partial p_k}, \qquad l, k = 1, \ldots, m. \tag{5.1.13}$$

The term on the left side of (5.1.13) represents a ratio of weighted averages of consumer indirect marginal utilities with respect to price. Thus, the term on the left represents a marginal rate of substitution in terms of prices for goods l and k. The term on the right side of (5.1.13) is a ratio of marginal profits due to price increases.

The nonnegative profits condition gives rise to a set of break-even prices. The zero-profit prices form the boundary of this set. An increase in the price of a good l must be balanced by a change in the price of another good k to keep profits equal to zero. In this sense the right side of (5.1.13) is the marginal rate of price transformation between the prices for products l and k along the zero-profit frontier. Therefore, second-best optimality requires the social marginal rate of substitution in prices to equal the marginal rate of price transformation.

To interpret further the necessary conditions for second-best Pareto optimality, (5.1.12), apply Roy's identity, (5.1.8). Then

$$\sum_{i \in N} \lambda^i V_\omega^i(p^*, \omega^i) q_l^i(p^*, \omega^i)$$

$$= \gamma \left[Q_l^* + \sum_{k=1}^{m} (p_k^* - C_k) \partial Q_k^* / \partial p_l \right], \qquad l = 1, \ldots, m. \qquad (5.1.14)$$

Letting $V_\omega^i(p^*, \omega^i) = \xi^i$ from (5.1.7), this may be rewritten to obtain

$$\sum_{k=1}^{m} (p_k^* - C_k)(\partial Q_k^* / \partial p_l)$$

$$= (1/\gamma) \sum_{i \in N} \lambda^i \xi^i q_l^{i*}(p^*, \omega^i) - Q_l^*, \qquad l = 1, \ldots, m. \qquad (5.1.15)$$

Equation (5.1.15) may be used to solve for the optimal markups above marginal cost. Let G be the matrix of own- and cross-price effects,

$$G \equiv \begin{bmatrix} \partial Q_1^* / \partial p_1 & \cdots & \partial Q_m^* / \partial p_1 \\ \partial Q_1^* / \partial p_m & \cdots & \partial Q_m^* / \partial p_m \end{bmatrix}.$$

Suppose that G is invertible. Then from (5.1.15),

$$(p_1^* - C_1, \ldots, p_m^* - C_m)^T$$

$$= G^{-1} \left((1/\gamma) \sum_{i \in N} \lambda^i \xi^i q_1^{i*} - Q_1^*, \ldots, (1/\gamma) \sum_{i \in N} \lambda^i \xi^i q_m^{i*} - Q_m^* \right)^T, \qquad (5.1.16)$$

where ^{T} indicates the transpose.

Therefore, in the two good case, the optimal markups for the regulated goods are given by

$$p_1^* - C_1 = (1/|G|)\left[(\partial Q_2^*/\partial p_2)\left((1/\gamma) \sum_{i \in N} \lambda^i \xi^i q_1^{i*} - Q_1^* \right) \right.$$

$$\left. - (\partial Q_2^*/\partial p_1)\left((1/\gamma) \sum_{i \in N} \lambda^i \xi^i q_2^{i*} - \gamma Q_2^* \right) \right],$$

where $|G| = [(\partial Q_1^*/\partial p_1)(\partial Q_2^*/\partial p_2) - (\partial Q_1^*/\partial p_2)(\partial Q_2^*/\partial p_1)]$, with a similar expression for good 2. It is apparent from (5.1.16) that prices may be *below* marginal cost for some goods depending upon the sign and magnitude of cross-price effects. The marginal costs of production for the regulated firm represent the marginal social costs of producing the second-best outputs. Thus, the optimal markups represent optimal departures of prices from the (marginal) social costs of the outputs produced by the regulated firm. In the two-goods case, the relative markups may be expressed as

$$\frac{p_1^* - C_1}{p_2^* - C_2}$$

$$= \frac{[(\partial Q_2^*/\partial p_2)(\sum_{i \in N} \lambda^i \xi^i q_1^{i*} - \gamma Q_1^*) - (\partial Q_2^*/\partial p_1)(\sum_{i \in N} \lambda^i \xi^i q_2^{i*} - \gamma Q_2^*)]}{[(\partial Q_1^*/\partial p_1)(\sum_{i \in N} \lambda^i \xi^i q_2^{i*} - \gamma Q_2^*) - (\partial Q_1^*/\partial p_2)(\sum_{i \in N} \lambda^i \xi^i q_1^{i*} - \gamma Q_1^*)]}.$$

The ratio of markups thus depends on own- and cross-price elasticities as well as the welfare weights λ^i.

Suppose there is only one consumer. Let the consumer's demands for the goods be separable or "independent." Then we have the familiar inverse elasticity rule,

$$\frac{p_l^* - C_l}{p_l^*} = \frac{\xi - \gamma}{\gamma \eta_{p_l}}, \qquad \eta_{p_l} \equiv (\partial q_l/\partial p_l) \cdot (p_l/q_l), \qquad l = 1, \ldots, m.$$

This type of equation leads to the frequently made policy recommendation to set markups higher on those goods that have lower elasticity of demands. The complex form of equation (5.1.15) or (5.1.16) serves to provide a caution against simplifying assumptions, such as independent demands, constant and equal consumer weights λ^i, and constant and equal marginal valuations of income ξ^i. These types of assumptions underlie the models that maximize the sum of consumers' surplus. See Boiteux (1956) for further comments comparing the consumer surplus approach to general second-best Pareto optimality.

In the absence of lump sum transfers across consumers, relative prices for the regulated good may have significant distributional impacts.[4] Substitute into (5.1.12) for $\partial q_k^{i*}/\partial p_l$ using the Slutsky equation,

$$\partial q_k^{i*}/\partial p_l = \partial h_k^i(p^*, V^i(p^*, \omega^i))/\partial p_l - q_l^{i*} \, \partial q_k^{i*}/\partial \omega^i, \qquad (5.1.17)$$

where $h_k^i(p^*, V^i)$ is the *Hicksian compensated demand* for good k and $\partial h_k^i/\partial p_l$ equals the own price effect for $l = k$ and the substitution term for $l \neq k$. This yields after rearranging terms

$$\sum_{k=1}^m (p_k^* - C_k) \sum_{i \in N} \partial h_k^i/\partial p_l$$

$$= -\left[n\bar{Q}_l - \sum_{i \in N} \lambda^i V_\omega^i q_l^i/\gamma - \sum_{k=1}^m (p_k - C_k) \sum_{i \in N} q_k^i \, \partial q_k^i/\partial \omega \right], \qquad (5.1.18)$$

where $\bar{Q}_l = \sum_{i \in N} q_l^i/n$ denotes average consumption of good l. Let the net marginal social valuation of consumer i's income, β^i, be defined by

$$\beta^i = \lambda^i V_\omega^i/\gamma + \sum_{k=1}^m (p_k - C_k) \partial q_k^i/\partial \omega^i. \qquad (5.1.19)$$

Then (5.1.18) is rewritten as

$$\sum_{k=1}^m (p_k - C_k) \sum_{i \in N} (\partial h_k^i/\partial p_l)/n\bar{Q}_l = -\left[1 - \sum_{i \in N} \beta^i q_l^i/n\bar{Q}_l \right]. \qquad (5.1.20)$$

Compare with Atkinson and Stiglitz (1980, equation 12-55) for the Ramsey taxation problem. They interpret the left-hand side of (5.1.20) as a proportional reduction in commodity l along the compensated demand schedule, since $\partial h_k^i/\partial p_l = \partial h_l^i/\partial p_k$ by symmetry of the Slutsky substitution terms. Let $\bar{\beta} = \sum_{i \in N} \beta^i/n$ be the average social valuation and let $\zeta_l = (1/n)\sum_{i \in N} q_l^i \beta^i/\bar{Q}_l\bar{\beta}$. The term ζ_l is the generalized distribution characteristic of Feldstein (1972a,b) and $(\zeta_l - 1)$ represents the "normalized covariance between the consumption of the kth commodity and the net social marginal valuation of income" (Atkinson and Stiglitz, 1980, p. 388). Rewriting (5.1.20) yields

$$(1/\bar{Q}_l) \sum_{k=1}^m (p_k - C_k) \sum_{i \in N} (\partial h_k^i/\partial p_l)/n = -[1 - \bar{\beta} - \bar{\beta}(\zeta_l - 1)]. \qquad (5.1.21)$$

This shows the dependence of the markups of the m goods on the distribution of income and the welfare weights λ^i.

5.1.3 Second-Best Prices Proportional to Marginal Cost

An important question is whether second-best prices can ever be proportional to marginal cost. In other words, should relative prices equal the ratio of marginal costs (the marginal rate of transformation) at the second-best optimum? Prices proportional to marginal costs are suggested by Frisch (1939), Allais (1948), Lerner (1970, p. 285), and others. Lerner (1970) observes that maintaining prices proportional to marginal cost "is appropriate where the shifting [of resources] is only to another part of the taxed sector (as would be the case if all uses of resources could be, and were, taxed)." We study this assertion by assuming that all consumers spend a constant share of their income ω^i on the numeraire commodity. Sufficient conditions are obtained under which prices proportional to marginal cost are a second-best optimum.

From (5.1.16) it is apparent that markups generally vary across goods depending upon own- and cross-price elasticities of demand. The issue of whether setting all prices equal to a constant proportion of marginal cost yields an optimal allocation has generated some controversy. I consider two special cases in which prices that are proportional to marginal costs, $p_k^* = M \cdot C_k$, are second-best Pareto optimal. Suppose first that the weighted marginal indirect utilities of income are constant across consumers,

$$\lambda^i V_\omega^i = 1,$$

for all i. Further, suppose that each consumer i devotes a *constant* share of income, $z^i > 0$, to the numeraire good x. Then, from the consumer's budget constraint $pq^i + x^i = \omega^i$ and $x^i = z^i \omega^i$, consumer demand must satisfy

$$\sum_{k=1}^{m} p_k \frac{\partial q_k^i}{\partial p_l} = -q_l^i,$$

$$\sum_{k=1}^{m} p_k \frac{\partial q_k^i}{\partial \omega^i} = 1 - z^i. \tag{5.1.22}$$

Then, given $p_k^* = M \cdot C_k$, relative markups are given by $(p_k^* - C_k^*)/p_k^* = (M - 1)/M$. Thus,

$$\sum_{k=1}^{m} (p_k^* - C_k)\,\partial Q_k^*/\partial p_l = ((M-1)/M)\sum_{k=1}^{m} p_k^*\,\partial Q_k^*/\partial p_l$$

$$= ((M-1)/M)\sum_{i \in N}\sum_{k=1}^{m} p_k^*\,\partial q_k^{i*}/\partial p_l$$

$$= -((M-1)/M)Q_l^*.$$

From (5.1.14), it follows that constant markups are second-best optimal. Further, the markup factor exactly equals the value of the nonnegative profits constraint,

$$M = \gamma. \tag{5.1.23}$$

Note also from (5.1.19) that the social valuation of each consumer i's income equals $1/\gamma$ plus the proportional markup times the proportion of income spent in the regulated sector, $(1 - z^i)$,

$$\beta^i = 1/\gamma + \sum_{k=1}^{m} (p_k - C_k)\,\partial q_k^i/\partial \omega^i$$

$$= 1/\gamma + ((M-1)/M)(1 - z^i). \tag{5.1.24}$$

Alternatively, without restrictions on $\lambda^i V_\omega^i$, prices proportional to marginal cost may be obtained by assuming that marginal costs are constant. Let $C(Q)$ be given by the affine cost function $C(Q) = F + \sum_{k=1}^{m} c_k Q_k$. Let $p_k^* = Mc_k$ for all k, where

$$M = \frac{\sum_{i \in N}(\omega^i - z^i)}{\sum_{i \in N}(\omega^i - z^i) - F}. \tag{5.1.25}$$

First, note that the price vector p^* yields zero profits. By the definition of M,

$$\sum_{k=1}^{m} p_k^* Q_k^* = \frac{\sum_{i \in N}(\omega^i - z^i)}{\sum_{i \in N}(\omega^i - z^i) - F}\sum_{k=1}^{m} c_k Q_k^*. \tag{5.1.26}$$

Since consumers spend all of their income, $\sum_{k=1}^{m} p_k^* Q_k^* = \sum_{i \in N}(\omega^i - z^i)$. Thus, (5.1.26) implies that $\sum_{i \in N}(\omega^i - z^i) = F + \sum_{k=1}^{m} c_k Q_k^*$, and so the firm's profits equal zero. Suppose that another feasible price vector p' exists that Pareto dominates p^*, that is, $V^i(p', \omega^i) \geq V^i(p, \omega^i)$ for all i and is strictly greater for some i. Then, by revealed preference arguments, it follows that

$$p^*Q' > \sum_{i \in N} (\omega^i - z^i),$$

where $Q' = \sum_{i \in N} q^i(p', \omega^i)$. Substitution for p^* implies that

$$\frac{\sum_{i \in N} (\omega^i - z^i)}{\sum_{i \in N} (\omega^i - z^i) - F} \sum_{k=1}^{m} c_k Q'_k > \sum_{i \in N} (\omega^i - z^i).$$

Rearranging terms, and noting that $p'Q' = \sum_{i \in N} (\omega^i - z^i)$, it follows that

$$p'Q' < F + \sum_{k=1}^{m} c_k Q'_k,$$

which contradicts the feasibility of p'. Thus, p^* is a second-best Pareto optimal price vector.

Summarizing the preceeding discussion gives the following.

PROPOSITION 5.1.4   *Suppose that the consumer devotes a constant share of income to the numeraire good* x, $z^i > 0$. *Then prices proportional to marginal cost are second-best Pareto optimal if either one of the following conditions holds:*

a. $\lambda^i V_\omega^i(q^i, \omega^i) = 1$ *for all* q^i, ω^i, *for all* i.

b. $C_k(Q) = c_k > 0$ *for all* Q, *for all* k.

The proposition implies that under condition (a) or (b) relative prices equal the ratio of marginal costs, $p_k^*/p_l^* = C_k/C_l$. More significantly, the result gives sufficient conditions for prices for all goods to exceed marginal cost.

5.2   Interpersonal Transfers

The second-best pricing problem is now modified to allow lump sum transfers between consumers, $t = (t^1, \ldots, t^n)$. The transfer program must satisfy $\sum_{i \in N} t^i = 0$. The introduction of transfers is considered to highlight the distributional impact of second-best pricing.[5] The first four restrictions considered in the previous section still apply. Given the transfer t^i, consumer i's indirect utility is $V^i(p, \omega^i + t^i)$ for any price p.

Definition 5.2.1   The price transfer mechanism (p^*, t^*) is second-best Pareto optimal if p^* is feasible and there does not exist another feasible price vector p' and transfer program t' such that

$V^i(p', \omega^i + t^{i\prime}) \geq V^i(p^*, \omega^i + t^{i*})$

for all $i \in N$ and $V^i(p', \omega^i + t^{i\prime}) > V^i(p^*, \omega^i + t^{i*})$ for some $i \in N$.

As in proposition 5.1.2, the price transfer mechanism can be characterized using calculus. In particular, the second-best Pareto optimal price transfer mechanism (p^*, t^*) must solve the following problems for all $i \in N$:

$$\max_{p, t} V^i(p, \omega^i + t^i)$$

subject to $\qquad V^j(p, \omega^j + t^j) \geq V^j(p^*, \omega^j + t^{j*}), \qquad j \neq i, \quad j \in N,$

$$pQ(p) - C(Q(p)) \geq 0,$$ (5.2.1)

$$\sum_{i \in N} t^j = 0.$$

Given the transfers t^i, the solution to (5.2.1) simply involves adding the following necessary conditions to those obtained in the previous section:

$$\lambda^i V_\omega^i + \gamma \sum_{k=1}^m (p_k^* - C_k) \partial q_k^{i*} / \partial \omega^i = \sigma, \qquad i = 1, \ldots, n, \qquad (5.2.2)$$

where σ is the shadow price on the net transfers constraint, $\sum_{i \in N} t^i = 0$. Since the left-hand side of (5.2.2) divided by γ is the marginal social valuation of individual i's income, it is clear that the transfers serve to equalize the marginal social valuations of income across consumers,

$$\beta^i = \sigma / \gamma,$$

for all $i \in N$. Substituting for β^i in (5.1.20) yields

$$\sum_{k=1}^m (p_k^* - C_k) \sum_{i \in N} (\partial h_k^i / \partial p_l) / n \bar{Q}_l^* = -[1 - \sigma/\gamma], \qquad l = 1, \ldots, m. \qquad (5.2.3)$$

Thus, the proportional reduction in commodity l along the compensated demand curve is equal across all goods.

Rewrite (5.2.3) in matrix terms to solve for the optimal markups. Let H^i be individual i's matrix of substitution terms for the goods $k = 1, \ldots, m$,

$$H^i = \begin{bmatrix} \partial h_1^i / \partial p_1 & \cdots & \partial h_m^i / \partial p_1 \\ \vdots & & \vdots \\ \partial h_1^i / \partial p_m & \cdots & \partial h_m^i / \partial p_m \end{bmatrix}.$$

Thus, H^i represents the Slutsky matrix excluding the row and column involving the numeraire good x. Let $H = \sum_{i \in N} H^i$. Then equation (5.2.3) may be rewritten as follows:

$$(p_1^* - C_1, \ldots, p_m^* - C_m)^{\mathrm{T}} = ((\sigma - \gamma)/\gamma)H^{-1}Q^{*\mathrm{T}}, \tag{5.2.4}$$

where $Q = (Q_1, \ldots, Q_m)$. Let $\bar{h}_{lk}$ represent a term in the matrix H^{-1}. Then (5.2.4) represents

$$p_l^* - C_l = ((\sigma - \gamma)/\gamma) \sum_{k=1}^{m} \bar{h}_{lk} Q_k^*, \qquad l = 1, \ldots, m. \tag{5.2.5}$$

Thus, given interconsumer transfers, equation (5.2.5) provides an expression for the optimal departure of price from the marginal (social) cost of the outputs of the regulated firm. To characterize further the optimal markups, multiply both sides of (5.2.4) by output,

$$Q(p_1^* - C_1, \ldots, p_m^* - C_m)^{\mathrm{T}} = ((\sigma - \gamma)/\gamma)QH^{-1}Q^{*\mathrm{T}}. \tag{5.2.6}$$

Then, giving increasing returns to scale and the negative profits requirement, note that $\sum_{k=1}^{m} (p_k^* - C_k)Q_k > \sum_{k=1}^{m} p_k^* Q_k - C(Q) \geq 0$. Thus, the marginal social valuation of income is less than one, $\beta^i = \sigma/\gamma < 1$.[6]

Let the commodities Q supplied by the regulated firm be substitutes in the sense that $\partial h_k^i/\partial p_l \geq 0$ for $l \neq k$, for all consumers i. Then the following result, which is proven in the appendix, is obtained.

PROPOSITION 5.2.1 *Given nonnegative compensated cross-price effects for all i, $\partial h_k^i/\partial p_l \geq 0$, $l \neq k$, the optimal markups $p_l^* - C_l$ are nonnegative for all regulated goods $l = 1, \ldots, m$.*

This result has implications for the peak load pricing problem in section 5.4.

5.3   Profit Shares

Suppose that a simple general equilibrium formulation with a single firm and many consumers is considered. Suppose that a single input L is employed in the production of the outputs Q given the production relation $G(Q, L) = 0$. In units of X, the production constraint may be rewritten as $L = C(Q)$, where C is the cost function defined above. Suppose that each consumer is endowed with positive amounts of the good L (say, labor) and a share, θ^i, in the profits of the single firm, $\pi(p) = pQ - C(Q)$. The firm is required to break even, $\pi(p) \geq 0$, as before to avoid sharing of losses.

The price vector p^* is then second-best Pareto optimal if it is feasible and if there does not exist another feasible price vector p' such that $V^i(p', \omega^i + \theta^i\pi(p')) \geq V^i(p^*, \omega^i + \theta^i\pi(p^*))$ for all $i \in N$ and $V^i(p', \omega^i + \theta^i\pi(p')) > V^i(p^*, \omega^i + \theta^i\pi(p^*))$ for some $i \in N$. Note that from the consumer budget constraints, $L = C(\sum_{i \in N} q^i)$, where $L = \sum_{i \in N} (\omega^i - x^i)$.

Given a second-best optimal price vector, the firm's profit may now be positive due to the income value of profit to consumers. The Lagrangian for the welfare maximization problem is restated for convenience,

$$L = \sum_{i \in N} \lambda^i(V^i(p, \omega^i + \theta^i\pi(p)) - \bar{V}^i) + \gamma\pi(p), \qquad (5.3.1)$$

where $\bar{V}^i = V^i(p^*, \omega^i + \theta^i\pi(p^*))$, and $\pi(p) = pQ(p) - C(Q(p))$. The first-order necessary conditions are then

$$\sum_{i \in N} \lambda^i V_l^i(p^*, \omega^i + \theta^i\pi(p^*))$$

$$+ \left[\sum_{i \in N} \lambda^i V_\omega^i(p^*, \omega^i + \theta^i\pi(p^*))\theta^i + \gamma \right] \frac{\partial\pi}{\partial p_l}(p^*) = 0, \qquad l = 1, \ldots, m.$$

$$(5.3.2)$$

Note that γ is a Kuhn-Tucker multiplier on the nonnegative profit constraint. Given positive profits $\pi(p^*)$, $\gamma = 0$ and the bracketed term in (5.3.2) represents the income value of profits. The problem may be recast by restricting profits to equal or exceed $\pi(p^*)$ and ignoring their income value,

$$L = \sum_{i \in N} \lambda^i(V^i(p, I^i) - \bar{V}^i) + \eta[\pi(p) - \pi(p^*)]. \qquad (5.3.3)$$

The first-order conditions for (5.3.3) will be identical to those for (5.3.2) if income, I^i, is correctly evaluated at $I^i = \omega^i + \theta^i\pi(p^*)$. In particular, the value of the shadow price on the profit constraint, η, will equal the income value of profits.

This discussion serves to emphasize why regulators might allow positive profits for the regulated firm. The income value of profits is thus an important consideration in determining the "fair" price for the regulated firm. Breyer (1982, p. 398) notes that the Supreme Court has stated that rates are "just and reasonable" that "enable the company to operate successfully, to maintain its financial integrity, to attract capital, and to compensate its investors for the risks assumed" (*Federal Power Commission* v. *Hope Natural Gas Co.*, 320 U.S. 591, 605 (1944)). In our simple framework, the just price requires equating the marginal addition to profits from a price increase to the effect on indirect utility of a higher price weighted by the income value of profits,

$$\frac{\partial \pi(p^*)}{\partial p_l} = \frac{-\sum_{i \in N} \lambda^i V_l^i(p^*, \omega^i + \theta^i \pi(p^*))}{\eta}. \tag{5.3.4}$$

The analysis is easily extended to examine multiple firms. The problem of regulating a number of multiproduct firms each with a break-even constraint is termed a "viable firm Ramsey optimum" by Baumol, Panzar, and Willig (1982, pp. 337–343); see also Braeutigam (1984). As noted by Baumol, Panzar, and Willig, the viable firm Ramsey optimum does not minimize industry costs when some good is produced by more than one firm, since marginal costs will differ across firms. Consider the implications of shareholding for the multiple firm case where θ^{ij} represents consumer i's share of firm j's profits, $i = 1, \ldots, n, j = 1, \ldots, J$. Let $\eta^j = \sum_{i \in N} \lambda^i V_\omega^i(p^*, \omega^i + \sum_j \theta^{ij} \pi^j(p^*))\theta^{ij} + \gamma^j]$. Then

$$-\sum_{i \in N} \lambda^i V_l^i(p^*, I^*) = \sum_{j=1}^{J} \eta^j \frac{\partial \pi^j(p^*)}{\partial p_l}, \qquad l = 1, \ldots, m. \tag{5.3.5}$$

The second-best Pareto optimal prices set for the regulated sector will reflect the ownership distribution of the shares of the regulated firms among consumers and thus the income effects of the distribution of profits across firms. The analysis suggests that the weight η^j given to the profit of firm j should reflect the welfare effects of profits for the shareholders of firm j. Thus, at a second-best Pareto optimum, the direct benefits of lower prices must be balanced against the impact of lower profits on the firms' shareholders.

Another approach to second-best pricing is considered in chapter 10. There it is assumed that firms have bargaining power vis-à-vis consumers in setting rates. It is assumed that the firm's customers are not the firm's shareholders. Positive profits are then observed as a consequence of the bargaining power of the regulated firm.

5.4 Peak Load Pricing

This section considers the peakload pricing problem using the preceding analysis of second-best Pareto optimal pricing. Important contributions to the peak load pricing problem include Boiteux (1949), Houthakker (1951), Davidson (1955), Steiner (1957), Hirschleifer (1958), Williamson

(1966), and Panzar (1976). Much of the traditional literature relies on a fixed proportions technology with capital investment determining productive capacity without affecting marginal cost. Further, the early literature emphasizes the issue of determining the appropriate allocation of the marginal cost of production in peak and off-peak periods and the selection of peak capacity to maximize social welfare. This section departs from the traditional approach by using neoclassical technology as in Panzar (1976) and by characterizing second-best prices. If the firm is required to break even, then peak load prices must reflect income effects and other welfare considerations in the allocation of costs across time periods.

Suppose that $Q = (Q_1, \ldots, Q_m)$ represents (steady-state) electricity demands in subperiods 1 through m of a particular time period. Suppose that Q is produced using a public input of capital K purchased at a competitive rental $\rho > 0$. Suppose that, aside from the capital input, all other inputs are product specific. Then product specific or short-run cost functions can be defined,

$$c^l(Q_l, K), \qquad l = 1, \ldots, m.$$

Thus, total costs $C(Q)$ are given by

$$C(Q) = \min_K \left[\sum_{l=1}^m c^l(Q_l, K) + \rho K \right]. \tag{5.4.1}$$

The peak load pricing technology considered here is a cost function representation of the neoclassical production technology presented in Panzar (1976).[7] In particular, given a neoclassical production function $f^l(x_l, K)$, where x_l is a vector of inputs with prices w,

$$c^l(Q_l, K) \equiv \min w x_l \qquad \text{subject to} \quad Q_l = f^l(x_l, K).$$

As Panzar notes, the traditional peak load pricing literature has emphasized a constant returns to scale production technology of the form $f(x_l, K) = \min(x_l/a, K)$ leading to an aggregate cost function of the form

$$C(Q) = b \sum_{l=1}^m Q_l + \rho \max_l \{Q_l\}.$$

This form of the cost function leads to the well-known result that peak users bear all of the costs of capacity $K = \max_l\{Q_l\}$. Panzar (1976) examines *optimal* peak load pricing by maximizing the sum of consumer surplus given independent demands. I generalize his results to allow *second-best pricing* and general consumer preferences. As noted above, given increasing returns to scale, optimal pricing is unlikely in the absence of government subsidies or transfers between consumers and the firm. Formally, I make the following assumption on the *attributable cost function* c^l.

ASSUMPTION 5.4.1   The *attributable cost function* c^l is twice differentiable, increasing in Q_l, and decreasing in K. Further, c^l exhibits short-run (weakly) decreasing returns to scale, $c^l_Q(Q_l, K)Q_l > (\geq) c^l(Q_l, K)$.

Thus, the choice of capacity affects attributable costs and average attributable costs are upward sloping.

The Lagrangian for the second-best pricing problem may be rewritten by explicitly solving for the public input K. Then the additional necessary condition for the second-best problem, (5.1.11), is

$$\sum_{l=1}^{m} c^l_K(Q^*_l, K^*) + \rho = 0. \tag{5.4.2}$$

An important issue in setting peak load prices is the contribution each period makes to the cost of capacity, ρK^*. The total contribution made by the purchasers of good l to capacity costs equals the difference between revenue and attributable costs Y_l,

$$Y_l \equiv p_l Q_l - c^l(Q_l, K). \tag{5.4.3}$$

Given a constant proportion of income devoted to the numeraire good, $z^i \omega^i$, each period is shown to make a positive contribution to capacity if $\lambda^i V^i_\omega = 1$ for all i, or alternatively if short-run marginal costs are constant, $c^l_Q(Q_l, K) = c^l(K)$.

PROPOSITION 5.4.1   *Given that consumers devote a constant share of income to the numeraire good, then if either of the following conditions holds, all periods make a positive contribution to the cost of capacity, ρK:*

i. *Short-run costs exhibit weakly decreasing returns to scale and $\lambda^i V^i_\omega = 1$ for all consumers $i \in N$.*

ii. *Short-run marginal costs $c^l_Q(Q, K)$ are constant in Q.*

Proof   By proposition 5.1.4 all markups are positive. Thus,

$$p_l Q_l - c^l(Q_l, K) \geq p_l Q_l - c^l_Q(Q_l, K)Q_l > 0,$$

for all $l = 1, \ldots, m$.   QED

The contribution made by each good l (or period l) is also positive when lump sum transfers take place between consumers.

PROPOSITION 5.4.2 *Given nonnegative compensated cross-price effects* $\partial h_l^i / \partial p_k \geq 0$, $l \neq k$, *optimal transfers between consumers, and short-run decreasing returns to scale, all periods make a positive contribution to the cost of capacity*, ρK.

Since short-run decreasing returns are present, $p_l Q_l - c^l(Q_l, K) > p_l Q_l - c_Q^l(Q_l, K)Q_l$. The result follows from proposition 5.2.1 since markups above marginal cost are nonnegative. Thus, when optimal lump sum transfers are feasible, and the regulated goods are substitutes, each period pays a positive share of capacity.

Consider again the second-best pricing problem without transfers and suppose that demands in each period are independent. The assumption of independent demands is made throughout the peak load pricing literature. To formalize this notion suppose that all consumers purchase from the monopolist in a single period and then partition the set of consumers N according to the good purchased $\{N_l\}$. Thus, consumers $i \in N_l$ purchase only good Q_l. Then the first-order necessary condition for second-best pricing (5.1.12) can be written as

$$p_l^* - c_Q^l(Q_l^*, K) = -\left[(1/\gamma) \left(\sum_{i \in N_l} \lambda^i V_l^i \right) + Q_l^* \right] (\partial Q_l^* / \partial p_l). \qquad (5.4.4)$$

From (5.4.4), the markup above marginal cost is ambiguous. Thus, given second-best pricing, independence of demands is not sufficient for prices to exceed marginal costs. The distributive effects of prices may require that some periods not contribute to capacity costs.

Appendix

Proof of Proposition 5.1.1 The following argument is similar to a previously cited result of ten Raa (1983). It is sufficient to show existence of a zero-profit feasible price vector. Consider the set of zero-profit prices for an arbitrary output allocation vector q, $G: \mathbb{R}_+^{n \cdot m} \to \mathbb{R}_+^m$,

$$G(q) = \left\{ p \in \mathbb{R}_+^m : p \sum_{i \in N} q^i = C \left(\sum_{i \in N} q^i \right) \right\}.$$

Given $q \geq \varepsilon$, $\varepsilon \gg 0$, G is bounded. Clearly, $G(q)$ is a compact, convex set given by an isorevenue surface. Given C continuous, G is a continuous correspondence. By assumption 5.1.1, demand $Q^i(p, \omega^i)$ is a continuous function of p. Let $F(p)$ represent the vector of individual demands, $F: \mathbb{R}_+^m \to \mathbb{R}_+^{n \cdot m}$. A compact, convex set Γ contains $G(\{q \in \mathbb{R}_+^{n \cdot m} : q^i \geq \varepsilon\})$. By continuity of $F(\cdot)$, a compact convex set B contains $F(\Gamma)$. Let $B \subseteq \{q \in \mathbb{R}_+^{n \cdot m} : q^i \geq \varepsilon\}$. Let $p \in \Gamma$ and $q \in B$. Then $G(q) \subset G(B) \subset G(\{q \in \mathbb{R}_+^{n \cdot m} : q^i \geq \varepsilon\}) \subset \Gamma$ and $F(p) \subset F(\Gamma) \subset B$. Thus, the continuous correspondence $G \times F$ maps the compact, convex set $\Gamma \times B$ into itself and has a fixed point (p^*, q^*) with $p^* \in G(q^*) \subset \mathbb{R}_+^m$ and $q^* \in F(p^*) \subset \mathbb{R}_+^{n \cdot m}$.   QED

Proof of Proposition 5.2.1   Fiedler and Pták (1962, theorem 4.3) show that for a square matrix A with nonpositive off-diagonal elements and with all principal minors positive, the inverse A^{-1} has all nonnegative elements. Letting $A = -H$, write (5.2.4) as $(p_1^* - C_1, \ldots, p_m^* - C_m)^T = -((\sigma - \gamma)/\gamma)A^{-1}Q^{*T}$. Thus, $p_l^* - C_l \geq 0$ since each term in A^{-1} is nonnegative and $\sigma/\gamma < 1$.   QED

Notes

1. See also Manne (1952), Fleming (1953), Rees (1968), and Dixit (1970).

2. Feldstein (1972a) also refers to second-best pricing as the Ramsey-Boiteux rule.

3. It is assumed that the second-best optimal price vector can be obtained from the first-order conditions. Note, however, that the regulator's problem involves maximizing a convex function on a compact set since V^i is convex in p and the set of market-clearing prices that yield nonnegative profits is closed and bounded. The solution will occur on the boundary (of the convex hull) of the set of break-even prices; see Rockafeller (1970, theorems 32.2 and 32.3). I thank Robert Becker for this reference. The solution need not be unique. In general, multiple second-best optimal prices exist. The zero-profit prices are bounded away from zero, so the solution will be interior.

4. Feldstein (1972a, p. 32) observes that "in practice, optimal lump sum redistribution is impossible and the distributional impact of public pricing is an important policy consideration." My interpretation of the first-order conditions (5.1.12) is similar to the extension of Feldstein (1972a,b) given in Atkinson and Stiglitz (1980, pp. 386–388).

5. Boiteux (1956) considers optimal lump sum income transfers.

6. Since the Slutsky matrix is negative semidefinite, the principal submatrix H^i is negative semidefinite with nonzero determinant. Thus, the inverse of H^i is well-defined. The matrix H retains the properties of the H^i matrices. Given $QH^{-1}Q^{*T} < 0$, it follows that $(\sigma - \gamma)/\gamma < 0$, or $\sigma/\gamma < 1$.

7. We can also allow each period l to use capacity k_l up to the capacity constraint K. Then $c^l(Q_l, K)$ is defined by $c^l(Q_l, K) \equiv \min_{x, k_l} wx_l$ subject to $Q_l \leq f^l(x_l, k_l)$ and $k_l \leq K$.

6 Second-Best Pricing and the Core

Traditional approaches to pricing for public enterprises such as Ramsey (1927), Boiteux (1956) and Baumol and Bradford (1970) have emphasized second-best prices, which allow the firm to break even and are not Pareto dominated by another feasible price vector. These prices can be chosen by a regulator through maximization of some measure of social welfare. This approach makes sense only if there is a single regulated firm that exclusively owns the productive technology or if the government restricts entry of new firms into the market. Otherwise, it is not clear whether second-best Pareto optimal prices will be attained by the market when the technology is freely available to all potential entrants. It might pay for a firm to enter the market by offering contracts at prices that Pareto dominate the second-best price for a subgroup of consumers. What is lacking is a description of a *market mechanism* that allows revenues to cover costs for firms with economies of scale and multiproduct economies of scope and that takes into account consumer preferences.

To answer these questions, this chapter introduces the concept of the *second-best core*. The second-best core is the core of a cooperative game of joint production played by consumers in which the only allocation mechanism is that of linear market prices that ration the goods among consumers. The notion of a second-best core for private goods considered here is closely related to the excellent analysis of Guesnerie and Oddou (1979, 1981), who study second-best taxation for public goods using cooperative games. The second-best core refers to a set of feasible price vectors. A price vector is said to be feasible if the total of market demands at that price vector allow the firm to make nonnegative profits. A price vector is in the second-best core if it is feasible and if there does not exist a coalition of consumers for whom a preferable, feasible price may be found. Clearly, the second-best core is a (possibly empty) subset of the set of second-best Pareto optimal or Ramsey price vectors. Determining the existence of a second-best core provides the answer to whether there may exist *market equilibrium* Ramsey prices. In particular, are there prices for the public enterprise such that no group of consumers has incentive to object by breaking away from the grand coalition to produce the vector of goods on its own? Thus, prices in the second-best core will reflect the relative bargaining strengths of all subcoalitions of consumers.

The second-best core provides a framework that is helpful for the design of a franchise allocation mechanism. As will be shown in chapter 9, the second-best core provides a natural way to study the free entry of firms that offer their customers a *contract* to supply a vector of goods at an announced price vector. A blocking coalition is then equivalent to a feasible (nonnegative profit) price vector offered by a potential entrant to a set of consumers.[1] This provides a more realistic description of entry in terms of informational requirements than the core of a game in which all feasible allocations are considered. In that case, the core requires an entering firm to offer a complex set of contracts to a group of consumers possibly involving personalized prices or interpersonal transfers of wealth.

The second-best core also provides an alternative description of market price formation to that given in the contestable markets literature; see Baumol, Panzar, and Willig (1982).[2] As in the contestable markets literature, the technology is freely available to all potential entrants. However, the definition of a *sustainable* monopoly or oligopoly price vector requires that there not exist *lower* price vectors such that an entrant can break even.[3] In chapter 9, it is shown that a franchise competition may be established such that the entry of firms parallels the bargaining implicit in the second-best core. In particular, an entering firm may offer a feasible price vector that is preferred by a set of consumers. This price vector can then *Pareto dominate* an established firm's price vector even if it *exceeds* the established firm's price vector in some components so long as consumers are compensated by relatively lower prices on other goods. Consumers are not allowed to split their purchases among different producers, so that coalitions do not interact and the cooperative equilibrium is well-defined. It should be emphasized that in the second-best core problem, a potential entrant (or blocking coalition) is offering a contract to a group of customers that implicitly spells out that the purchases will actually be made. This differs from an announced price posted by a firm.

The second-best core is characterized by means of a series of necessary conditions. These conditions show the relation of the second-best core definition to a number of important concepts in the literature, including consumer subsidy free prices (Willig, 1979a; Faulhaber and Levinson, 1981), sustainability (Baumol, Panzar, and Willig, 1982), supportability (Sharkey and Telser, 1978), and natural monopoly.

6.1   The Second-Best Core

Consider a cooperative game played by a group of consumers $N = \{1, \dots, n\}$. The consumers wish to produce jointly a vector of goods $Q \in \mathbb{R}_+^m$. The technology is described by a multiproduct cost function $C(\cdot)$ and is freely available to any group of consumers.[4] Each coalition must choose a price $p \in \mathbb{R}^m_+$ to allocate the jointly produced goods. It is required that the value of the goods produced by a coalition using the market price p must exceed the cost of production. Let the individual consumption decisions be given by equation (5.1.1) where $V^i(p, \omega^i)$ represents consumer i's indirect utility given endowment ω^i and where $q^i(p, \omega^i)$ represents his consumption of the jointly produced goods and $x^i(p, \omega^i)$ the consumption of the numeraire good. Consumer utility is assumed to satisfy assumption (5.1.1).

The production technology exhibits subadditivity (natural monopoly), increasing returns to scale, and satisfies assumption (5.2.1). The technology is freely available to any group of consumers. Since the cost function exhibits subadditivity, a feasible price vector for a single firm in relation to the group of consumers $S \subseteq N$ to whom the contract is offered may be defined.

Definition 6.1.1 A price vector p is *feasible* for $S \subseteq N$ if at the demands $(\tilde{q}^i, \tilde{x}^i) = (q^i(p, \omega^i), x^i(p, \omega^i))$, $i \in S$, profits are nonnegative,

$$\Pi = p \sum_{i \in S} \tilde{q}^i - C\left(\sum_{i \in S} \tilde{q}^i\right) \geq 0. \tag{6.1.1}$$

The feasible price supports consumer demands (q^i, x^i) in such a way that the firm makes no losses. Given the consumer budget constraints, the feasibility condition (6.1.1) is equivalent to the standard condition,

$$\sum_{i \in N} (\omega^i - \tilde{x}^i) - C\left(\sum_{i \in N} \tilde{q}^i\right) \geq 0. \tag{6.1.2}$$

For the grand coalition of consumers to agree on a price vector it must be the case that no subcoalition can break off and produce on its own at a preferable feasible price vector.[5] Note that no transfer payments may be made within a coalition. Otherwise (first-best) core allocations could be supported on the demand side by a uniform price given appropriate transfers. The core concept is a natural equilibrium solution concept for a game of joint production. Due to subadditivity and increasing returns to scale, there are incentives for consumers to cooperate in producing the vector of goods. Because of the efficiency loss resulting from coalitions leaving the grand coalition to produce on their own, prices must be set in such a way that there are no incentives for any consumers to stop purchasing from a firm serving the entire market. Note that coalitions do not interact (through consumers splitting their purchases across firms). This is a standard assumption in cooperative games. In my framework, if consumers split their purchases across, say, two firms, then the customers of the two firms would be treated as a single coalition. To keep the analysis of consumer contracts as simple as possible requires a single price vector within each coalition. By subadditivity, any price p that yields nonnegative profits for two or more firms serving a given group of consumers yields nonnegative profits for a single firm. Thus, given $Q' + Q'' = Q$, $pQ' \geq C(Q')$, and $pQ'' \geq C(Q'')$, it follows that $pQ \geq C(Q)$. Therefore, a firm is identified with the set of consumers that it serves.

The second-best core is now defined formally.

Definition 6.1.2   A price vector p is in the *second-best (s.b.) core* if it is feasible for the grand coalition N and there is no $S \subseteq N$ such that $S \neq \varnothing$ and for some price vector p'

$$p' \sum_{i \in S} q^i(p', \omega^i) - C\left(\sum_{i \in S} q^i(p', \omega^i) \right) \geq 0$$

and

$$V^i(p', \omega^i) \geq V^i(p, \omega^i)$$

for all $i \in S$ and $V^i(p', \omega^i) > V^i(p, \omega^i)$ for some $i \in S$.

The definition requires group rationality (second-best Pareto optimality— P.o.) to be satisfied by a price in the second-best core. Thus, if it is nonempty, the *second-best core is a subset of the set of Ramsey-Boiteux prices*. The existence of a second-best core will determine whether or not the market equilibrium will be characterized by monopoly. Note that the second-best P.o. prices are not necessarily individually rational. To determine individual rationality, these prices must be compared to the feasible autarky prices for each consumer producing the goods independently.

The concept of the second-best core as given by definition (6.1.2) serves to provide a caution against the standard Ramsey prices, which are often recommended to regulatory authorities by economists. In particular, if these Ramsey prices are not in the second-best core, powerful incentives may exist for groups of consumers to seek to leave the system and set up their own utility or contract with another firm. Unless the regulatory authority places entry restrictions on other firms and legally prohibits internal production of utility services by groups of consumers, the regulated utility will experience loss of demand, and potentially, its rates will have to be increased to cover fixed costs. If restrictions against entry are enforced, the rate structure that does not reflect second-best core prices may lead to political pressures on the regulatory authority to revise those rates. The pressure for changes in the rate structure would come from coalitions of customers (households or businesses) who would stand to gain from production by another firm charging preferable rates. To illustrate these arguments, compare the second-best core prices with second best Pareto optimal prices obtained by a regulator maximizing social welfare subject to a break-even constraint.

PROPOSITION 6.1.1   (i) *Even if a price vector p^* maximizes a social welfare function, subject to a nonnegative profits constraint, it is not necessarily in the second-best core.* (ii) *If p^* is in the second best core, then there is a choice of weights a^{i*}, $i \in N$, such that p^* maximizes*

$$\sum_{i \in N} a^{i*} V^i(p, \omega^i)$$

subject to $pQ(p) - C(Q(p)) \geq 0$, where $Q(p) = \sum_{i \in N} q^i(p, \omega^i)$.

Part (i) holds whether the second-best core is empty or is a proper subset of the set of second-best Pareto optimal prices, since any second-best price may be attained by properly chosen weights. The same reasoning implies part (ii). Thus, unless the government or regulatory authority controls entry, an arbitrary choice of weights for the Bergsonian social welfare function may create incentives for coalitions of consumers to recontract with another firm. If there are departures of groups of consumers (blocking coalitions), the prices chosen by maximizing the social welfare function may be no longer second-best Pareto optimal.

Clearly, since second-best Pareto optimality is necessary for a price to be in the core of the second-best market game, any price selection method chosen by regulators that does not accurately reflect *individual* consumer preferences is vulnerable to entry. Thus, if the regulator's "welfare" definition is based upon aggregate consumer surplus or presumes that interpersonal transfers take place, the resulting regulated prices are vulnerable to competitive entry. Even if entry can be restricted, these prices may not reflect the relative bargaining strengths of the regulated firm's customers. Thus, unless entry is restricted, the preceding analysis implies that the use of estimated Ramsey numbers in calculating prices for the public enterprise will create incentives for groups of consumers to seek alternative sources of supply. In chapter 9, it is shown that the second-best core allocation may be attained by a franchise competition managed by a regulatory agency.

6.2 Necessary Conditions

6.2.1 Prices

Consider now a number of necessary conditions that are satisfied by an allocation in the second-best core. These necessary conditions serve to characterize conditions that must be met by the Ramsey-Boiteux prices set by the grand coalition. The first four conditions are on the second-best price itself. The next three conditions impose requirements on the firm's cost function.

If conditions that guarantee an interior solution are imposed, the first condition follows as an immediate consequence of second-best Pareto optimality. The first condition implies that free entry eliminates monopoly rents.

CONDITION 6.2.1   *Given p^* in the second-best core, the firm's profits Π^* are zero.*

The proof is given in the appendix.

Willig (1979a) and Faulhaber and Levinson (1981) introduce the notion that a price is *consumer subsidy-free* if total revenues exactly cover costs and no group of consumers can produce on its own at lower costs. In the present framework, this definition may be restated as follows.

Definition 6.2.1   A price vector p is *consumer subsidy-free* if

$$p \sum_{i \in N} q^i(p, \omega^i) = C\left(\sum_{i \in N} q^i(p, \omega^i) \right) \tag{6.2.1}$$

and

$$p \sum_{i \in S} q^i(p, \omega^i) \leq C\left(\sum_{i \in S} q^i(p, \omega^i) \right) \tag{6.2.2}$$

for all $S \subseteq N$.

CONDITION 6.2.2 *Given that p is a price vector in the second-best core, p is consumer subsidy-free. However, a consumer subsidy-free price vector need not be in the second-best core.*

Proof Suppose that p is in the second-best core. Then, by second-best Pareto optimality, revenues equal costs. Suppose that

$$p \sum_{i \in S} q^i(p, \omega^i) > C\left(\sum_{i \in S} q^i(p, \omega^i) \right).$$

Then by monotonicity of utility and continuity of the demand and cost functions, there exists p' feasible such that $V^i(p', \omega^i) \geq V^i(p, \omega^i)$ for all $i \in S$ and is strictly greater for some $i \in S$. This contradicts the assumption that p is in the second-best core.

An example is sufficient to show that not all consumer subsidy-free prices are in the second-best core. Suppose that there are only two consumers and that these consumers are identical. Then consider the set of zero-profit prices $Z = \{p : 2pq(p, \omega) = C(2q(p, \omega))\}$. By the subadditivity of costs, it follows that $pq(p, \omega) \leq C(q(p, \omega))$ for all $p \in Z$. Thus, the set of zero-profit prices coincides with the set of consumer subsidy-free prices. But not all zero-profit prices are in the second-best core. To see this last statement, let utility be Cobb-Douglas,

$$U(q_1, q_2, x) = a \ln q_1 + b \ln q_2 + (1 - a - b) \ln x,$$

and let the cost function be an affine,

$$C(q_1, q_2) = F + c_1 q_1 + c_2 q_2,$$

where $a + b < 1$ and $a, b, c_1, c_2,$ and F are positive. Then it can be shown that the (unique) second-best P.o. prices are $p_1^* = c_1/(1 - F/2(a + b)\omega)$ and $p_2^* = c_2/(1 - F/2(a + b)\omega)$. These prices are in the s.b. core. All other zero profit prices yield strictly lower indirect utility and are thus not in the s.b. core. In particular, it is easy to show that the prices $p_1 = (2a/(a + b))c_1/(1 - F/2(a + b)\omega)$ and $p_2 = (2b/(a + b))c_2/(1 - F/2(a + b)\omega)$ are zero-profit prices and yet yield strictly lower indirect utility than (p_1^*, p_2^*).   QED

Thus, the concept of the second-best core is a more restrictive notion than the requirement that no group of consumers subsidize another.

The definition of a consumer subsidy-free price implies that the total of payments by any coalition is less than the stand-alone production costs for that coalition. This implies the following result when weak cost complementarities are present, that is, $C_{lk}(Q) \leq 0$ for all $l, k = 1, \ldots, m$.

CONDITION 6.2.3   *Given that p is a price vector in the second-best core, and the cost function exhibits weak cost complementarities, each consumer's payment exceeds the product of his consumption vector times marginal costs.*

Proof   By the conditions for p to be consumer subsidy-free,

$$pq^j(p, \omega^j) \geq C\left(\sum_{i \in N} q^i(p, \omega^i) \right) - C\left(\sum_{i \in N, i \neq j} q^i(p, \omega^i) \right)$$

$$= \sum_{l=1}^{m} \left(\partial C\left(\sum_{i \in N} q^i(p, \omega^i) - z \right) \Big/ \partial Q_l \right) q_l^j(p, \omega^i),$$

where $0 \leq z \leq q^j(p, \omega^j)$. By weak cost complementarities,

$$\partial C\left(\sum_{i \in N} q^i(p, \omega^i) - z \right) \Big/ \partial Q_l \geq \partial C\left(\sum_{i \in N} q^i(p, \omega^i) \right) \Big/ \partial Q_l.$$

Thus

$$pq^j(p, \omega^j) \geq \sum_{l=1}^{m} \left(\partial C\left(\sum_{i \in N} q^i(p, \omega^i) \right) \Big/ \partial Q_l \right) q_l^j(p, \omega^i). \quad \text{QED}$$

The existence of a monopoly price sustainable against entry has been studied by Panzar and Willig (1977) and Baumol, Bailey, and Willig (1977). The definition of sustainability rules out all *lower* feasible price vectors by the force of competitive entry. However, the sustainability criterion is based upon free entry competition vis-à-vis a given *aggregate demand* and as such ignores disaggregated welfare effects. Thus, in my framework, a firm may profitably enter the market by offering a group of consumers a contract at a price p that gives each consumer greater indirect utility than at a sustainable price. The notion of entry blocking or sustainable prices is therefore quite different from that of second-best core prices.

CONDITION 6.2.4   (i) *Sustainable prices need not be in the second-best core.* (ii) *Second-best core prices need not be sustainable.*

Proof   Let costs be separable and assume that there are two goods, $C(Q) = \sum_{l=1}^{2} C^l(Q_l)$,

$$C^l(Q_l) = F^l + c_l Q_l, \qquad l = 1, 2,$$

where $F^l > 0$, $c_l > 0$, $l = 1, 2$. Suppose that consumers are identical. Let consumer utility be Cobb-Douglas, $U = a \ln q_1 + b \ln q_2 + (1 - a - b) \ln x$, where $a > 0$, $b > 0$, and $a + b < 1$. Then, total consumer demands for goods 1 and 2 are $Q_1(p_1) = na\omega/p_1$ and $Q_2(p_2) = nb\omega/p_2$.

As is well-known, given separability of costs, the only sustainable prices are average cost prices. Thus, in the example, the *unique* sustainable prices (p_1^S, p_2^S) solve $p_1^S = (F^1/Q_1(p_1^S)) + c_1$ and $p_2^S = (F^2/Q_2(p_2^S)) + c_2$. The sustainable prices are then

$$p_1^S = \frac{c_1}{1 - F^1/a\omega n}, \qquad p_2^S = \frac{c_2}{1 - F^2/b\omega n}.$$

The *unique* second-best Pareto optimal prices (i.e., those that maximize consumer indirect utility subject to a nonnegative profit constraint) are

$$p_1^* = \frac{c_1}{1 - (F^1 + F^2)/(a + b)\omega n}, \qquad p_2^* = \frac{c_2}{1 - (F^1 + F^2)/(a + b)\omega n}.$$

Generally, unless $F^1/F^2 = a/b$, the sustainable prices (p_1^S, p_2^S) and the second-best core prices (p_1^*, p_2^*) do not coincide.   QED

If we restrict the definition of sustainability to exclude (i) entry of firms in any proper subset of markets and (ii) split purchases by consumers, then a price vector p is sustainable if for all $p' \le p$, $p' \ne p$ and $S \subseteq N$, $S \ne \emptyset$,

$$p'Q^S(p') < C(Q^S(p')),$$

where $Q^S(p') = \sum_{i \in S} q^i(p', \omega^i)$. In this case, if a price is in the second-best core, it is also sustainable.

CONDITION 6.2.5   *If entry of firms into any proper subset of markets is excluded and if consumers cannot split purchases across firms, then, given that p is a price vector in the second-best core, it is sustainable.*

Proof   Suppose not. Then, given p in the second-best core, there exists a price $p' \le p$, $p' \ne p$, and a set $S \subseteq N$, $S \ne \emptyset$, such that $p'Q^S(p') \ge C(Q^S(p'))$. By assumption, there exists a price p'' such that $V^i(p'', \omega^i) \ge V^i(p, \omega^i)$ for all $i \in S$ and is strictly greater for some $i \in S$, which contradicts the definition of the second-best core.   QED

Note also that by second-best Pareto optimality, prices in the second-best core are undominated in the sense of Baumol, Panzar, and Willig (1982,

p. 194); i.e., *there does not exist a lower price vector yielding greater profits for the firm.*

6.2.2 Costs

The following conditions characterize the core given a continuum of agents. While analogous conditions can be obtained given a finite number of consumers, the continuum assumption serves to emphasize the effect of large markets on prices that reflect cooperative arrangements. Suppose that the triple (I, Ω, F) represents the measure space of agents I, the Borel σ-algebra on I, and the measure F defined on Ω. Suppose that there are n types of consumers. Let $\{S^i\}$, $i \in N$, be a partition of the space I such that if $s \in S^i$, consumer s is of type i with utility function $U^i(q^i, x^i)$ and endowment ω^i. This essentially replicates the economy studied thus far. Define the real-valued vector measure $\mu = (\mu^1, \ldots, \mu^n)$ by

$$\mu^i(S) = F(S \cap S^i), \quad S, S^i \in \Omega, \quad i \in N. \tag{6.2.3}$$

The real number $\mu^i(S)$ represents the number of type i consumers in the set S. A coalition can be represented by a value of μ.

Given a continuum of agents, the second-best core implies a number of restrictions on the common technology.

CONDITION 6.2.6 *Given a continuum of consumers and p^* in the second-best core, C must exhibit decreasing ray average costs (subhomogeneity) at $Q^* = \sum_{i \in N} \mu^i q^i(p^*, \omega^i)$, $\mu^i = \mu^i(I)$.*

Proof Suppose that a coalition $S \in \Omega$ with composition $\lambda\mu$, $0 < \lambda < 1$, $\mu = \mu(I)$, charges prices p^* to its members. Then by the definition of a s.b. core allocation and the strict monotonicity of U^i,

$$p^* \left(\sum_{i \in S} \lambda\mu^i q^{i*} \right) \leq C \left(\sum_{i \in S} \lambda\mu^i q^{i*} \right)$$

for $q^{i*} = q^i(p^*, \omega^i)$. Otherwise, a feasible price p' could be found for the coalition S such that $V^i(p', \omega^i) > V^i(p^*, \omega^i)$ for all $i \in S$. Since p^* is in the s.b. core,

$$p^* \sum_{i \in N} \mu^i q^{i*} = C \left(\sum_{i \in N} \mu^i q^{i*} \right). \tag{6.2.4}$$

Multiply both sides by λ:

$$p^* \sum_{i \in N} \lambda \mu^i q^{i*} = \lambda C\left(\sum_{i \in N} \mu^i q^{i*} \right). \tag{6.2.5}$$

Thus given $Q^* = \sum_{i \in N} \mu^i q^{i*}$,

$$\lambda C(Q^*) \le C(\lambda Q^*). \quad \text{QED} \tag{6.2.6}$$

Consider the set of allocations of an output vector q that are associated with subgroups of consumers, $S \in \Omega$,

$$\Gamma(q) = \left\{ Q \in K : Q = \sum_{i \in N} a^i q^i, 0 \le a \le \mu, \mu = \mu(I) \right\}. \tag{6.2.7}$$

Now examine the shape of $\Gamma(q)$. Suppose that there are two consumer types and two goods q_l, $l = 1, 2$. There are μ^i consumers of type i and each consumer purchases $q^i, i = 1, 2$. Thus, $q = ((q_1^1, q_2^1), (q_1^2, q_2^2))$. Then Γ has the shape given in figure 6.2.1. When the q^i are very different, in terms of the proportion of goods q_1 and q_2, the set Γ approaches the comprehensive set $X = \{0 \le x \le q^1 + q^2\}$. With the q^i similar, the set Γ approaches the diagonal $[0, q^1 + q^2]$.

CONDITION 6.2.7   *Given a continuum of consumers and p^* in the second-best core, C must be subadditive at $Q^* = \sum_{i \in N} \mu^i q^i(p^*, \omega^i), \mu^i = \mu^i(I)$, on the set $\Gamma(q^*)$.*

Proof Suppose not. Then there exists Q', Q'' such that $Q' + Q'' = Q^*$, $C(Q' + Q'') > C(Q') + C(Q'')$, and $Q', Q'' \in \Gamma(q^*)$. Then there exist a', a'' such that $\sum_{i \in N} a^{i'} q^{i*} = Q', \sum_{i \in N} a^{i''} q^{i*} = Q''$, and $a' + a'' = \mu$. By the zero-profit condition,

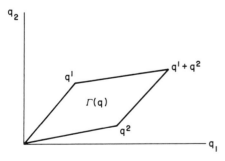

Figure 6.2.1
The set of output allocations with two consumer types.

$p^*Q' + p^*Q'' > C(Q') + C(Q'')$.

Thus, for one of the coalitions there exists a feasible price vector that dominates p^*. This contradicts the definition of the s.b. core.   QED

The restricted defintion of subadditivity does *not* require C to exhibit economies of scope, i.e., $C(Q) < C(Q_1, 0) + C(0, Q_2)$, in the two-goods case, since this would require that each consumer type be associated with a single good.

Given the set of output allocations within the grand coalition $\Gamma(q^*)$, the Faulhaber-Levinson definition of a consumer subsidy-free-price for a continuum of agents may be rephrased. Equation (6.2.2) becomes

$$p \sum_{i \in N} a^i q^i \leq C\left(\sum_{i \in N} a^i q^i \right) \tag{6.2.8}$$

for all coalitions defined by the distribution a, $0 < a \leq \mu(I)$. This requirement may be used to examine supportability of the cost function as defined by Sharkey and Telser (1978).

CONDITION 6.2.8   *Given a continuum of consumers and p^* in the second-best core, C must be supportable at Q^* on $\Gamma(q^*)$.*

Proof   By condition 6.2.3 all prices in the second-best core are consumer subsidy-free. Thus, equation (6.2.8) holds at the output vector q^*. Let Q' be any output in the set $\Gamma(q^*)$. Thus, there exists a coalition a' such that

$$\sum_{i \in N} a^{i'} q^{i*} = Q'$$

and therefore $p^*Q' \leq C(Q')$.   QED

Since p is a subsidy-free price on Γ, subsidies across goods become less likely when the product ratios of consumer purchases q_l^i/q_h^i vary greatly across coalitions and the set Γ approaches the comprehensive set $\{0 \leq x \leq \sum_{i \in N} q^{i*}\}$.

6.3   Natural Monopoly and Existence

Subadditivity of costs (natural monopoly) is not sufficient for production by a single firm to be efficient in a *second-best* world, where interpersonal transfers are not permitted. Consider a simple one-good average cost $AC(Q)$ that is subadditive up to output $\bar{Q}$. Suppose that there are two

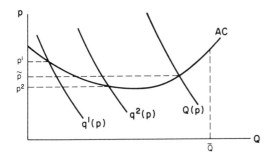

Figure 6.3.1
The second-best core is empty.

consumers with demands $q^1(p)$, $q^2(p)$, where total demand equals $Q(p) \equiv q^1(p) + q^2(p)$. Let $\tilde{p}$ be the zero profit market-clearing average cost price given by $\tilde{p} = AC(Q(\tilde{p}))$. As shown in figure 6.3.1, player 1 faces a higher average cost price $p^1 > p^2$ under autarky and player 2 faces a lower average cost price $p^2 < \tilde{p}$ under autarky. Thus, without a transfer payment, it does not pay for player 2 to join player 1, since this would effectively raise the price of the good for player 2. Thus, while $\tilde{p}$ is the Pareto optimal break even price, it is not individually rational. Thus, it cannot be concluded that production by a single firm is efficient. Production by two firms, charging *different prices*, is the efficient solution, given the second-best requirements of linear pricing, nonnegative profits, and no transfers between consumers.

Declining average costs in the single-product case is *not necessary* for existence of a second-best core. Let average costs be given by $AC(Q) = 2 - Q$ for $0 \le Q \le 1$, and $AC(Q) = Q$ for $Q \ge 1$, where minimum efficient scale (MES) equals 1. Let there be two consumers with Cobb-Douglas utility $U^i(q^i, x^i) = a^i \ln q^i + (1 - a^i) \ln x^i$, $i = 1, 2$, and endowments ω^i, $i = 1, 2$. Then, demands equal $q^i = a^i \omega^i / p, i = 1, 2$. Let $a^1 \omega^1 = 1/2$ and $a^2 \omega^2 = 3/4$. Then, $p^1 = 1 + 1/\sqrt{2}$, $p^2 = 3/2$, $\tilde{p} = \sqrt{5/4}$. Thus, $\tilde{p} < p^1 < p^2$ and $\tilde{p}$ is the second-best core price. Outputs are $q^1(p^1) = 1/(2 + \sqrt{2})$, $q^2(p^2) = 1/2$, $Q(\tilde{p}) = q^1(\tilde{p}) + q^2(\tilde{p}) = \sqrt{5/4}$. Thus, Q is greater than MES and $q^1(p^1)$, $q^2(p^2)$ are less than MES.

Clearly, with average costs $AC(Q)$ everywhere nonincreasing, the undominated[6] *average cost price* is the *unique* element of the second-best core. Thus, *given a single good Q and $AC(Q)$ nonincreasing, the second-best core is nonempty*. To see this, let $p^* = AC(\sum_{i \in N} q^i(p^*, \omega^i))$ be the undominated average cost price. Suppose $p' \le p^*$ is feasible for a coalition $S \subset N$. Then

$$p' \geq AC\left(\sum_{i \in S} q^{i*}(p', \omega^i)\right) > AC\left(\sum_{i \in N} q^i(p', \omega^i)\right).$$

Thus, there exists a price $p'' < p'$ such that profits are zero. This contradicts the assumption that p^* is the undominated average cost price.

Another problem with existence of a core may arise in the case of multiple goods if the change in relative prices due to cooperation makes some consumers worse off despite the fall in total costs.[7] Given identical consumers and many goods, the s.b. core is easily seen to exist.

PROPOSITION 6.3.1   *Given identical consumers, and C subhomogeneous, the second-best core is nonempty.*

Proof   Let p^* be second-best P.o. Suppose that p' is feasible for $S \subset N$, $S \neq \emptyset$, and $V^i(p', \omega^i) > V^i(p^*, \omega^i)$ for all $i \in S$. By symmetry, p' is preferred for all $i \in N$. Let $q^i(p', \omega^i) = q'$, $i \in N$. Let $s = |S|$ and $n = |N|$. Since p' is feasible for S, $p'sq' \geq C(sq')$. Subhomogeneity implies that p' is feasible for the grand coalition since $0 < s/n < 1$,

$$(n/s)C(sq') \geq C(nq').$$

Thus, $p'nq' \geq C(nq')$, which implies that p' Pareto dominates p^*, which is a contradiction.   QED

Recall that subhomogeneity is neither necessary nor sufficient for subadditivity.

An existence result for the multiproduct case is now given. Let utility, $U^i(q^i, x^i)$, be Cobb-Douglas for all consumers $i \in N$. Then it follows that each consumer allocates a fixed expenditure, β^i, $0 < \beta^i < \omega^i$, to the *numeraire* good x^i.[8] This confines the effects of changes in relative prices to the market for jointly produced goods as noted in the preceding chapter. Let $\omega \equiv \sum_{i \in N}(\omega^i - \beta^i)$ represent total expenditures in the monopoly sector.

Let costs be given by affine cost function, $C(Q) = F + \sum_{l=1}^{m} c_l Q_l$. Then there is a unique zero-profit price vector p^* such that price ratios p_l/p_k equal marginal cost ratios c_l/c_k, $l, k = 1, \ldots, m$,

$$p_l^* = c_l/(1 - F/\omega), \qquad l = 1, \ldots, m. \tag{6.3.1}$$

To see this, note that $\omega = \sum_{l=1}^{m} p_l Q_l = (p_k/c_k)\sum_{l=1}^{m} c_l Q_l$ from the consumer's budget constraint and $p_l/p_k = c_l/c_k$. Given the zero-profit condition, $\omega = F + \sum_{l=1}^{m} c_l Q_l$. Thus, $\omega = (p_k/c_k)(\omega - F)$, which yields (6.3.1) after rearranging terms.

It is now shown that p^* is in the second-best core. Since p^* yields zero profits, it is feasible. Suppose that for some coalition $S \subseteq N$, $S \neq \varnothing$, there exists p' feasible for S such that $V^i(p', \omega^i) \geq V^i(p^*, \omega^i)$ for all $i \in S$ and is strictly greater for some $i \in S$. Then, by revealed preference, $p^* \sum_{i \in S} q^i(p', \omega^i) > \omega^S$, where $\omega^S = \sum_{i \in S}(\omega^i - \beta^i)$. By the definition of p^*, this inequality implies

$$\sum_{l=1}^{m} c_l \sum_{i \in S} q_l^i(p', \omega^i) > \omega^S - (\omega^S/\omega)F. \tag{6.3.2}$$

From the consumer budget constraints, $\omega^S = \sum_{l=1}^{m} p_l' \sum_{i \in S} q_l^i(p', \omega^i)$. Further, note that $(\omega^S/\omega) \leq 1$ by definition. Thus, rearranging (6.3.2) yields

$$F + \sum_{l=1}^{m} c_l \sum_{i \in S} q_l^i(p', \omega^i) > \sum_{l=1}^{m} p_l' \sum_{i \in S} q_l^i(p', \omega^i), \tag{6.3.3}$$

which contradicts the feasibility of p' for S. Thus, p^* is an element of the second-best core.

The preceding result is easily generalized as follows.

PROPOSITION 6.3.2   *Suppose that consumers devote a constant share of income to the* numeraire, β^i, *and the cost function is given by* $C_h(Q) = h(F + \sum_{l=1}^{m} c_l Q_l) + (1-h)V(Q)$, *where h is a scalar,* $0 \leq h \leq 1$, *and V is continuous and increasing in Q. Then there exists* h^*, $0 < h^* < 1$, *such that for all h,* $h^* \leq h \leq 1$, *the second-best core is nonempty.*

The proof is given in the appendix. A similar weighted cost function appears in Baumol, Panzar, and Willig (1982) in a somewhat different context.

6.4 Multiple-Firm Equilibria

As shown in the preceeding section, the cooperative second-best pricing game may easily fail to be superadditive. Further, the second-best core may fail to exist for general technologies. Guesnerie and Oddou (1979, 1981) consider a cooperative game of production for a public good in which equilibrium is defined by a *stable set of coalitions*, each producing the public good independently.[9] Thus, even if the core is empty, a stable and efficient arrangement may be achieved by separation of consumers into independent coalitions. Guesnerie and Oddou (1981, p. 73) state that "in the language of the theory of local public goods, the grand city made of A and B will split and two 'small' cities A and B will emerge each one producing locally its own public good." As noted by Guesnerie and Oddou (1981, p. 69), the interpretation of separate production "reflects the maximin threat of a coalition." Further, the interpretation fits with the notion of geographically distinct cities producing independently as in a Tiebout model.

The formation of multiple coalitions in a cooperative game with private goods produced with increasing returns to scale technology is analogous to the formation of multiple communities or cities observed in equilibria with local public goods. The production of public goods reflects non-convexities in that the marginal costs of supplying the good to an additional individual are equal to zero.[10] The coalition structure in a private goods economy may be seen as a reason for the existence of multiple firms in industries where large economies of scale are present. Also, regulated utility markets are divided into multiple service areas. Clubs, such as health spas, often provide a mixture of both excludable public goods (such as a swimming pool) and private goods (such as swimming lessons). The theory of clubs has focused on excludable public goods. On the theory of clubs, see Buchanan (1965), Ng (1974), and Berglas (1976, 1981).[11] Clubs have been studied in a cooperative games setting by Pauly (1967), Stiglitz (1977b), and Wooders (1978, 1980), who generally find that a core fails to exist.

The framework of Guesnerie and Oddou (1979, 1981) is adapted here to represent the multiproduct, private good case. Further, the second-best pricing issue is addressed. Let p_S be a price vector that is feasible for the coalition S, $S \subseteq N$. Define a *coalition structure*, $\mathscr{S} = (S_1, \ldots, S_J)$, as a partition of the set of consumers N into distinct coalitions, $S_j \cap S_k = \varnothing$, $j \neq k$. Define a *price structure associated with* $\mathscr{S}$, $P_{\mathscr{S}} = (p_{S_1}, \ldots, p_{S_J})$, as the vector of prices p_{S_j} that are feasible for each coalition $S_j, j = 1, \ldots, J$.

Definition 6.4.1 An allocation structure, $\mathscr{A} = ((p_{S_1}, S_1), \ldots, (p_{S_J}, S_J))$ is a vector of prices and coalitions such that $\mathscr{S} = (S_1, \ldots, S_J)$ is a coalition structure and $(p_{S_1}, \ldots, p_{S_J})$ is a price structure associated with $\mathscr{S}$.

Consider an allocation structure such that no other coalition may form and find feasible prices that improve the well-being of all of its members. This concept generalizes the second-best core idea to allow independent contracting between distinct groups of consumers with different firms. This is meant to describe a situation in which different utilities serve distinct (sometimes geographically overlapping) groups of consumers with possibly different rate structures.

Definition 6.4.2   An allocation structure $\mathscr{A}^*$ is said to be *stable* if there does not exist any set $S \subseteq N$ such that $S \neq \varnothing$ and for some p_S (p feasible for S),

$$V^i(p_S, \omega^i) > V^i(p_{S_j}, \omega^i),$$

where j is such that $S_j \supseteq \{i\}$ for all $i \in S$.

It is evident that if the second-best core is nonempty, the only stable allocations are core allocations, (p^*, N). To illustrate the idea of a stable allocation structure consider again figure 6.3.1. The stable allocation structure is given by the efficient solution with each player producing the good separately and paying the average cost price. Thus, $\mathscr{A}^* = ((p^1, \{1\}), (p^2, \{2\}))$.

The stable allocation structures $\mathscr{A}^*$ must satisfy several necessary conditions. The first condition emphasizes that for an allocation structure to be stable requires that each coalition select a price that is internally efficient.

CONDITION 6.4.1   *If $\mathscr{A}^*$ is a stable allocation structure, then p_{S_j} is in the second-best core for the cooperative game played by the set of consumers S_j for all (p_{S_j}, S_j) in $\mathscr{A}^*$.*

Thus, each coalition's price vector p_{S_j} must satisfy all of the necessary conditions for the second-best core of the subgame played by consumers in S_j. These necessary conditions are discussed above in section 5.2. Another necessary condition that must be satisfied by a stable allocation structure is that gains from trade between coalitions are exhausted. This is evident from definition 6.4.2, which rules out any merging of coalitions in equilibrium. A simple implication is that two coalitions cannot have the same price if costs are strictly subadditive. Otherwise, the two coalitions could merge and lower the price. A stronger assertion is the following.

CONDITION 6.4.2   *If $\mathscr{A}^*$ is a stable allocation structure, then, if i wishes to join coalition S_j,*

$$p_{S_j} \tilde{q}^i < C(\tilde{q}^i),$$

where $\tilde{q}^i = q^i(p_{S_j}, \omega^i)$ for $i \notin S_j$.

Otherwise, if $p_{S_j} \tilde{q}^i \geq C(\tilde{q}^i)$, it follows from subadditivity and the break-even condition for coalition S_j that

$$p_{S_j} Q_{S_j} + p_{S_j} \tilde{q}^i \geq C(Q_{S_i} + \tilde{q}^i),$$

where Q_{S_j} is the output produced by coalition j. This would mean that individual i could join S_j, contradicting the assertion that $\mathscr{A}^*$ is stable. Thus, individual i cannot cover the stand-alone costs of what he would demand at price p_{S_j}. Put differently, individual i could not cover the incremental costs he would impose on coalition S_j. This may be expressed as "Any club that i would like to join would not have him as a member." Conversely, "Any club that would have i as a member, i would not like to join." If i could reach an agreement with coalition S_j, this would contradict the stability of the allocation structure $\mathscr{A}^*$.

Multiple coalitions may constitute an efficient outcome in the single-good case if decreasing returns to scale set in for large outputs. With multiple goods, the differences in individual preferences over relative prices may be sufficient to prevent the existence of a core even with global increasing returns to scale. The formation of communities with homogeneous preferences postulated by Tiebout (1956) need not occur in the case of private goods. The presence of cost complementarities in production argues for benefits to be derived from having heterogeneous markets for the private goods. There appears to be a trade-off between the costs savings that will result from diversity in consumer demand and the welfare losses due to the "distortion" of relative prices.

Appendix

Proof of Condition 6.2.1 Suppose not. Let $\Pi^* = \varepsilon > 0$. Then $\Pi^* = \sum_{i \in N} (\omega^i - x^i(p^*, \omega^i)) - C(\sum_{i \in N} q^i(p^*, \omega^i)) = \varepsilon$. By continuity of $(q^i(\cdot, \omega^i), x^i(\cdot, \omega^i))$ in p, one can choose $\delta_1 > 0$ such that $p' = p^* - (\delta_1, \ldots, \delta_1)$ and

$$\left| \sum_{i \in N} (x^i(p^*, \omega^i) - x^i(p', \omega^i)) \right| < \varepsilon/2.$$

Further, given $C(\cdot)$ continuous, one can choose $\delta_2 > 0$ such that $p'' = p^* - (\delta_2, \ldots, \delta_2)$ and

$$\left| C\left(\sum_{i \in N} q^i(p^*, \omega^i) \right) - C\left(\sum_{i \in N} q^i(p'', \omega^i) \right) \right| < \varepsilon/2.$$

Let $\delta = \min(\delta_1, \delta_2)$ and $p = p^* - (\delta, \ldots, \delta)$. Then, given

$$\Pi = \sum_{i \in N} (\omega^i - x^i(p, \omega^i)) - C\left(\sum_{i \in N} q^i(p, \omega^i)\right),$$

it follows that

$$|\Pi - \Pi^*| \le \left| \sum_{i \in N} (x^i(p^*, \omega^i) - x^i(p, \omega^i)) \right|$$

$$+ \left| C\left(\sum_{i \in N} q^i(p^*, \omega^i)\right) - C\left(\sum_{i \in N} q^i(p, \omega^i)\right) \right|$$

$$< \varepsilon/2 + \varepsilon/2 = \varepsilon.$$

Thus, since $\Pi^* = \varepsilon$, $\Pi' \ge 0$. Thus, p^* is Pareto dominated by p', which is feasible, which is a contradiction. Thus $\Pi^* = 0$.   QED

Proof of Proposition 6.3.2 It is sufficient to show that there exists a feasible price p^* that is not blocked by any subcoalition $S \subset N$. Let $\omega = \sum_{i \in N} (\omega^i - \beta^i)$ and $\omega^S = \sum_{i \in S} (\omega^i - \beta^i)$. Then let p^* be given by

$$p_l^* = k c_l \omega / [\omega - (kF + (1 - k)V(Q^*))], \tag{1}$$

where $Q_l^* = \sum_{i \in N} q_l^i(p^*, \omega^i)$. By the consumer budget constraints and the definition of p^*, it follows that

$$\omega = \sum_{i \in N} p^* q^{i*}(p^*, \omega^i) = C_k(Q^*). \tag{2}$$

Thus, p^* is feasible.

Suppose that for some coalition $S \subset N$, $S \ne \varnothing$, there exists p' feasible such that $V^i(p', \omega^i) \ge V^i(p^*, \omega^i)$ for all $i \in S$ and is strictly greater for some. Then, by revealed preference,

$$p^* \sum_{i \in S} q^i(p', \omega^i) > \omega^S.$$

By definition of p^*,

$$k \sum_{l=1}^{m} c_l Q_l' > \omega^S - (\omega^S/\omega)(kF + (1 - k)V(Q^*)), \tag{3}$$

where $Q_l' = \sum_{i \in S} q^i(p', \omega^i)$. Adding $(kF + (1 - k)V(Q'))$ to both sides yields

$$C_k(Q') > \omega^S + [(1 - \omega^S/\omega)kF - (1 - k)((\omega^S/\omega)V(Q^*) - V(Q'))]. \tag{4}$$

If the term in brackets is nonegative, then $C_k(Q') > \omega^S$, thus contradicting the feasibility of p'.

Since V is continuous on K, $V(Q)$ and $V(Q_0) - V(Q)$ are uniformly bounded on K by some upper bound $B > 0$. Define $\omega_{\min} = \min_{i \in N}\{\omega^i - \beta^i\}$. Then, choose k^* such that

$$k^* = B\omega/(F\omega_{\min} + B\omega). \tag{5}$$

Clearly $0 < k^* < 1$. Then, for all k such that $k^* \le k \le 1$,

$$(\omega_{\min}/\omega)kF \ge (1 - k)B.$$

Thus,

$$((\omega - \omega^S)/\omega)kF \ge (1 - k)B$$

for all $S \subset N$. By definition of B,

$$B \ge V(Q^*) - V(Q') \ge (\omega^S/\omega)V(Q^*) - V(Q').$$

Therefore, for all k, $k^* \le k \le 1$,

$$((\omega - \omega^S)/\omega)kF \ge (1 - k)[(\omega^S/\omega)V(Q^*) - V(Q')]$$

for all $S \subset N$, which implies that the bracketed term in (4) is nonnegative.
QED

Notes

1. A similar point is made by Mas-Colell (1982, p. 15) in the context of the core of a perfectly competitive market in the tradition of Edgeworth (1881).

2. Baumol, Bailey, and Willig (1977) (see also Baumol, Panzar, and Willig, 1982) give sufficient conditions for Ramsey prices to be a sustainable monopoly equilibrium.

3. As Baumol, Panzar, and Willig (1982, p. 198) state, "Potential entrants can only hope to lure customers from the monopolist if they match (or *slightly* undercut) his price."

4. The analysis is partial equilibrium in nature. However, the cost function can easily be derived endogenously by assuming that x^i is a single numeraire commodity as well as a productive input and that total outputs $Q = \sum_{i \in N} q^i$ and the total input $X = \sum_{i \in N} x^i$ must lie in a closed, nonempty production set Y. Then define C by $C(Q) = \min\{X : (Q, X) \in Y\}$. See Spulber (1989) for a general equilibrium analysis.

5. This is a significant consideration for firms with economies of scale where the volume of service affects average costs.

6. With multiple crossings of aggregate demand and average costs, the lowest average cost price must be chosen. See Spulber (1984c) for a related discussion. I assume away corner solutions within the set K.

7. The game may easily fail to be superadditive. For an enlightening discussion of the failure of superadditivity in second-best games, see Guesnerie and Oddou (1979, 1981).

8. A similar assumption is used by Sharkey (1979) to establish existence of the core with increasing returns.

9. Guesnerie and Oddou (1981, p. 69) assume that (a) "the technology is available to any coalition," (b) "the coalition alone cannot benefit from the public good produced by other coalitions," and (c) "institutional constraints on tax schemes are the same within each coalition where the public good is financed through a linear wealth tax." This framework is equivalent to that of Westhof (1977) for a set of cities.

10. Baumol, Panzar, and Willig (1982, p. 302) assert that there "is no essential difference between the case of fixed costs and the case of public goods"; see also Baumol and Ordover (1977). The reason is that a public good involves a high level of cost to supply the good to anyone with a negligible cost to supply additional persons. These cost conditions are seen as a limiting case of a private good with high fixed cost but low marginal cost. The analogy is appropriate if the private good is supplied in a fixed amount to all consumers, as occurs with a public good. Otherwise, consumption of the private good varies across persons. An additional difference arises if the public good is subject to congestion externalities, as occurs with roads, parks, or museums.

11. See also Scotchmer (1985a,b). A survey is given by Sandler and Tschirhart (1980). A comprehensive and useful overview is given in Cornes and Sandler (1986).

7 Second-Best Price Discrimination

Although economies of scale and cost complementarities generate gains from joint production, uniform pricing may not create incentives for consumers to cooperate. With uniform pricing, consumers' marginal willingness to pay levels are equalized. This may fail to capture variations in consumer marginal willingness to pay for fixed costs, such as productive capacity. As with public goods, it may be desirable to raise revenue through price discrimination. The present chapter examines various forms of price discrimination that allow the regulated firm to break even.

Price discrimination can lead to welfare improvements over uniform Ramsey-Boiteux pricing in a number of ways. By distinguishing customer classes (residential, commercial, industrial), utilities can charge different prices for similar services. In the same way that Ramsey prices are higher for those goods with relatively less elastic demand, discriminatory prices can capture rents across customer groups for each good. Section 7.1 considers Pareto-optimal price discrimination across customer classes where revenues cover costs. Then quantity-based price discrimination through two-part tariffs is studied. The Ramsey-Boiteux model is applied to obtain second-best unit prices and entry fees. The use of a two-part tariff allows per unit prices to reflect marginal costs more closely since the entry fee recovers some nonattributable costs.

In section 7.2, two cooperative games with joint production are studied. First is considered a second-best core for a game in which price discrimination across customer classes is feasible. If consumers each purchase only a single good, there are prices in the second-best core and these prices are subsidy-free. Next, a cooperative game with two-part tariffs is defined. If all consumers make positive purchases with prices equal to marginal cost and entry fees equal to per capita fixed costs, then this two-part tariff yields an allocation in the second-best core. Unfortunately, entry fees equal to per capita fixed costs often exclude low-demand consumers. It is shown how consumer incentives to cooperate may be restored by giving consumers a choice between a high linear price and a two-part tariff with a lower per unit charge.

The issue of exclusion of consumers through fixed fees is examined in section 7.3 when there is a continuum of income levels. It is shown how to select optimally a simple nonlinear tariff of the type proposed by Willig (1978).

Section 7.4 examines second-best Pareto optimal nonlinear price schedules. These quantity-based outlay schedules are a general form of declining block tariffs. They combine elements of both third-degree price discrimination and second-degree price discrimination. Thus, nonlinear pricing both discriminates across customer classes and captures consumer surplus as do two-part tariffs.

7.1 Second-Best Tariffs

The analysis of second-best Pareto optimal prices in chapter 5 and 6 demonstrated that welfare improvements over cost-based pricing were feasible by making a selection from the set of break-even prices. Ramsey-Boiteux prices maximize welfare over the set of break-even prices. Prices in the second-best core are Ramsey-Boiteux prices that reflect the opportunities and bargaining power of coalitions of consumers. The task in this section is a preliminary examination of whether further welfare improvements can be achieved if the regulated firm engages in some form of price discrimination. Two types of price discrimination commonly observed in markets served by regulated utilities are considered: pricing by customer class and multipart tariffs.

7.1.1 Customer Classes

In section 5.4 it was shown that Ramsey-Boiteux pricing could be applied to the peak load pricing problem in electricity supply. By treating the electricity supplied in each period as a different commodity, the requirement of second-best Pareto optimality leads to different prices for electricity depending upon the elasticity of demand in each period and consideration of the effects on income distribution. To the extent that electricity is more costly to produce in peak periods due to the addition of generators and increased use of capacity, peak load pricing reflects the costs of production. However, across some periods, costs of production are relatively similar but differences in second-best prices reflect the need to raise revenue to cover nonattributable costs. One may interpret Ramsey-Boiteux prices as discriminatory in the sense that price ratios need not equal relative marginal costs.[1] This type of discrimination may be referred to as discrimination across goods and is generally inevitable if second-best pricing is to be used. As noted before, the peak load pricing literature generally assumes independent demands across time periods. This generally implies that each consumer only purchases electricity during a single time interval within any period of time. Thus, if demands are independent, the second-best peak load prices may be said to discriminate across consumers.

Rather than employing time-of-use pricing or peak load prices, utilities often distinguish customer classes (residential, commercial, industrial); see Davidson (1955), Schmalensee (1981b), and Eckel (1985). This is clearly an example of *third-degree* price discrimination, and to the extent that demand elasticities are similar within each customer class, there may be welfare gains from segmenting the market in this manner. The selection of discriminatory prices across customer classes can be approached within the second-best pricing framework. Simply relabel goods as different commodities depending on whether they are purchased by residential, commercial or industrial customers. Suppose that q^i, $i = R, C, I$, represents a vector of m services purchased by a representative member of each class, $q^i \in \mathbb{R}^m_+$. One can easily generalize the problem to allow for diversity within each class. The second-best price discrimination problem is to select a price vector $p* = (p^{R*}, p^{C*}, p^{I*})$ that is Pareto optimal across customer classes and allows the regulated firm to break even. Proceding as in the discussion of Ramsey-Boiteux prices in chapter 5, the regulator's Lagrange problem is defined by

$$L = \sum_i \lambda^i (V^i(p^i, \omega^i) - \bar{V}^i) + \gamma \left[\sum_i p^i q^i(p^i, \omega^i) - C\left(\sum_i q^i(p^i, \omega^i) \right) \right]. \quad (7.1.1)$$

The term $\bar{V}^i = V^i(p^{i*}, \omega^i)$, $i = R, C, I$, represents consumer indirect utility evaluated at the second-best discriminatory price. The shadow price on each customer class's indirect utility constraint is λ^i and the shadow price on profits is γ. As before set $\lambda^i = 1$ for a given customer class R, C, or I. A second-best optimal discriminatory price vector must solve all three variations of problem (7.1.1).

The first-order necessary conditions for problem (7.1.1) include the following:

$$\lambda^i V^i_l(p^{i*}, \omega^i)$$

$$+ \gamma \left[q^{i*}_l + \sum_{k=1}^m (p^{i*}_k - C_k) \partial q^{i*}_k / \partial p_l \right] = 0, \quad l = 1, \ldots, m, \quad i = R, C, I,$$

$$(7.1.2)$$

where $q^{i*} = q^i(p^{i*}, \omega^i)$. Recalling Roy's identity, it follows that for each customer class, the ratio of demands equals the ratio of price effects on profits obtained from that customer class,

$$q_l^{i*}/q_s^{i*} = \sum_{k=1}^{m} (p_k^{i*} - C_k)(\partial q_k^{i*}/\partial p_l^i)$$

$$\bigg/ \sum_{k=1}^{m} (p_k^{i*} - C_k)(\partial q_k^{i*}/\partial p_s^i), \qquad l, s = 1, \dots, m, \quad i = R, C, I. \tag{7.1.3}$$

Thus, the trade-offs between prices for any two goods are fully internalized within each customer class. The pricing rule in (7.1.3) is a standard Ramsey pricing formula obtained by maximizing aggregate consumer surplus; see Baumol and Bradford (1970). The rule is obtained as a result of discriminatory pricing, assuming equal welfare weights or interconsumer transfers. This property will again vanish with heterogeneity within the customer class.

Recall the marginal social valuation of the income of a type i consumer, β^i, given in equation (5.1.19),

$$\beta^i = \lambda^i V_\omega^i/\gamma + \sum_{k=1}^{m} (p_k - C_k)\,\partial q_k^i/\partial \omega^i.$$

Applying the Slutsky equation (5.1.17) and noting by symmetry that $\partial h_k^i/\partial p_l = \partial h_l^i/\partial p_k$, (7.1.3) is rewritten as

$$(1/q_l^{i*}) \sum_{k=1}^{m} (p_k^{i*} - C_k)\,\partial h_l^i/\partial p_k$$

$$= -(1 - \beta^i), \qquad l = 1, \dots, m, \quad i = R, C, I. \tag{7.1.4}$$

Therefore, for *each* customer class, the proportionate reductions along the compensated demand schedule for any good l due to a change in relative prices just equals $-(1 - \beta^i)$ for all goods. Distributional considerations are absent since these are handled by price discrimination. Note, however, that unlike the case of interpersonal lump sum transfers in section 5.2, the marginal social valuations are not equalized in general, $\beta^R \neq \beta^C \neq \beta^I$.

If each customer class purchases a single service k from the regulated utility, the analogue to the Ramsey pricing rule with independent demands follows:

$$(p_k^{i*} - C_k)/p_k^{i*} = (\lambda^i V_\omega^i - \gamma)/\gamma \eta_k^i, \qquad i = R, C, I, \tag{7.1.5}$$

where $\eta_k^i = -(p_k^{i*}/q_k^{i*})(\partial q_k^{i*}/\partial p_k^i)$ is demand elasticity.[2]

7.1.2   Two-Part Tariffs

Given economies of scale, welfare improvements over linear pricing can be achieved by two-part tariffs.[3] The fixed fee allows the firm to recover some of the consumer surplus and so is a form of *second-degree* price discrimination. As a simple form of quantity-dependent pricing, two-part tariffs allow some recovery of fixed costs through the entry fee. However, the second-best two-part tariff need not lead to marginal cost pricing. Optimal departures from marginal cost pricing occur even with fixed fees; see Ng and Weisser (1974) and Feldstein (1972b). The fixed charge or entry fee has two effects. First, the entry fee affects the purchases of consumers in the market through income effects, thus affecting variable revenues. Second, the entry fee may exclude some consumers from purchasing the good altogether, thus affecting the number of entry fees that are collected. Ng and Weisser (1974) observe that the optimal price may be above or below marginal cost given consumer exclusion from the market. They demonstrate that the unit price is greater than (less than) marginal cost if average consumption is greater than (less than) the consumption of a marginal consumer. A marginal consumer is a consumer with net gains from trade equal to zero given the two-part tariff.

The second-best pricing model is now modified to accommodate two-part tariffs. Suppose that consumers purchase a numeraire good x^i and a vector of jointly produced goods q^i. The jointly produced goods have unit prices $p \in \mathbb{R}^m_+$ as well as a positive scalar fixed fee E. The consumer's indirect utility is a function of prices, the fixed fee and the initial endowment. Indirect utility is defined as follows:

$$V^i(p, E, \omega^i) \equiv \max_{(q^i, x^i)} U^i(q^i, x^i) \tag{7.1.6}$$

subject to

$$pq^i + \delta_{q^i}E + x^i = \omega^i,$$

where $\delta_{q^i} = 1$ if $q^i \neq 0$, $q^i \geq 0$, and $\delta_{q^i} = 0$ if $q^i = 0$. Given $q^i \neq 0$, the envelope theorem and first-order conditions for (7.1.6) yield the following:

$$V^i_{p_l}(p, E, \omega^i) = -\xi^i q^i, \tag{7.1.7}$$

$$V^i_E(p, E, \omega^i) = -\xi^i = -V^i_\omega(p, E, \omega^i). \tag{7.1.8}$$

Clearly, $V^i_{p_l}(p, E, \omega^i) = V^i_\omega(p, E, \omega^i)q^i$ for all l and for all i as before.

The entry fee is assumed to apply to the right to purchase the entire vector of jointly produced goods Q. This is reasonable for markets in which a single firm offers a broad range of services. For example, an electric utility charges customers a single entry fee for connection to the transmission or distribution network. In the well-known example of the amusement park (Oi, 1971), diverse rides are available at different unit prices after payment of a single joint entry fee. The entry fee essentially "bundles" the goods together even though they may be purchased in any proportion. The analysis can be extended to analysis of separate entry fees for each good; see Calem and Spulber (1984).

The definition of *feasibility* for a two-part tariff (p, E) is given by the nonnegative profits condition,

$$\Pi(p, E) \equiv pQ(p, E) + \sum_{i \in N} \delta_{q^i} E - C(Q(p, E)) \geq 0, \tag{7.1.9}$$

where $Q(p, E) = \sum_{i \in N} q^i(p, E)$. Given feasibility, the second-best Pareto optimal two-part tariff may be defined.

Definition 7.1.1   The two-part tariff (p^*, E^*) is *second-best Pareto optimal* if it is feasible and if there does not exist another feasible two-part tariff (p', E') such that

$$V^i(p', E', \omega^i) \geq V^i(p^*, E^*, \omega^i)$$

for all $i \in N$, and $V^i(p', E', \omega^i) > V^i(p^*, E^*, \omega^i)$ for some $i \in N$.

As with Ramsey-Boiteux prices, the optimal two-part tariffs may be obtained by constrained maximization.

Consider the regulated firm's choice of second-best two-part tariffs,

$$L = \sum_{i \in N} \lambda^i (V^i(p, E, \omega^i) - \bar{V}^i) + \gamma \left[pQ(p) + \sum_{i \in N} \delta_{q^i} E - C(Q(p)) \right], \tag{7.1.10}$$

where $\bar{V}^i = V^i(p^*, E^*, \omega^i)$. Given $q^i \neq 0$, the first-order necessary conditions are as follows:

$$\sum_{i \in N} \lambda^i V_l^i(p^*, E^*, \omega^i) + \gamma \, \partial \pi(p, E)/\partial p_l = 0, \qquad l = 1, \ldots, m, \tag{7.1.11}$$

$$\sum_{i \in N} \lambda^i V_E^i(p^*, E^*, \omega^i) + \gamma \, \partial \pi(p, E)/\partial E = 0. \tag{7.1.12}$$

The effects of prices and the entry fee on profits are defined by the following:

$$\partial \pi(p, E)/\partial p_l = Q_l + \sum_k (p_k - C_k) \partial Q_k/\partial p_l, \qquad (7.1.13)$$

$$\partial \pi(p, E)/\partial E = \sum_{i \in N} \delta_{q^i} + \sum_k (p_k - C_k) \partial Q_k/\partial E. \qquad (7.1.14)$$

Consider the optimal markup of the per unit price over marginal cost in the case of a single good. From (7.1.11)–(7.1.13),

$$p^* - C'(Q^*) = \frac{\sum_{i \in N} \lambda^i V_\omega^i [Q^* - q^{i*} \sum_{j \in N} \delta_{q^{j*}}]}{\sum_{i \in N} \lambda^i V_\omega^i [q^{i*} \partial Q^*/\partial E - \partial Q^*/\partial p]}. \qquad (7.1.15)$$

Thus, the size of the markup reflects the relative income effects of prices and entry fees. The numerator weights income effects by the deviation of each consumer's output from the average. The denominator weights income effects by the individual's consumption times the effect of entry fees on total demand net of the effect of price on total demand. With identical consumers it is apparent that $p^* = C'(Q^*(p^*, E^*))$ and $E^* = [C(Q^*) - C'(Q^*)Q^*]/n$ if consumers choose to purchase from the firm at this tariff. Suppose, for example, that consumers are given equal weight, $\lambda^i = 1$, for all i. Further suppose that consumers have identical Cobb-Douglas utility functions $U^i = q^\alpha x^{1-\alpha}$ for all i. Then, even if consumers have different incomes, they have the marginal utility of income $V_\omega^i = (\alpha/p)^\alpha (1 - \alpha)^{1-\alpha}$ for all i. Suppose that E^* is less than income for all consumers. Then all consumers purchase the good from the firm. From (7.1.15), the second-best optimal per unit price equals marginal cost.

When consumers differ, the two-part tariff separates consumers on the basis of the average price paid. This case is discussed further in section 7.3. The welfare weights can have significant effects. Suppose that substitution effects dominate income effects in such a way that the denominator in equation (7.1.15) is positive.[4] Then, if buyers whose purchases are below average are given greater weight, the price will be above marginal cost and a correspondingly smaller share of revenues is obtained from fixed fees. Conversely, if greater welfare weight is placed on buyers with above average purchases, price is set below marginal cost and a relatively larger share of revenues is obtained through fixed fees. If residential customers make smaller purchases than commercial or industrial customers, then regulatory policy favoring residential customers would raise prices above marginal costs and lower entry fees.

Returning to the first-order conditions (7.1.11) and (7.1.12), apply Roy's identity and define the marginal social valuation of income as before in equation (5.1.19). Then, from equation (7.1.12), assuming that all consumers purchase from the firm ($\sum_{i \in N} \delta_{q^i} = n$), it follows that the average social valuation of income equals one,

$$\bar{\beta} = (1/n) \sum_{i \in N} \beta^i = 1.$$

In this case, the entry fee functions as an optimal lump sum tax.

Application of the Slutsky equation to (7.1.11) yields

$$(1/\bar{Q}_l) \sum_{k=1}^{m} (p_k - C_k) \sum_{i \in N} (\partial h_k^i / \partial p_l)/n = \zeta_l - 1, \qquad l = 1, \ldots, m, \qquad (7.1.16)$$

where $\zeta_l = (1/n) \sum_{i \in N} q_l^i \beta^i / \bar{Q}_l$ is the distribution characteristic of Feldstein (1972a,b); see also Atkinson and Stiglitz (1980). This formulation is closely related to our preceding discussion of second-best pricing. Simply set the social valuation of income, $\bar{\beta}$, equal to 1 in equation (5.1.21). The per unit price component of the two-part tariff can thus be expressed in terms of Slutsky substitution terms.

The set of second-best Pareto optimal two-part tariffs can be quite large. In the next section, a selection from this set that reflects the bargaining power of consumers is examined using a cooperative game of joint production. Under additional assumptions, the second-best core allocation may be attained by setting the per unit charge equal to marginal cost and the entry fee equal to per capita fixed costs.

Many regulated firms practice both second- and third-degree price discrimination by offering different two-part tariffs to various customer classes. This situation can be described by merging the discussions of customer classes and two-part tariffs in this section. In addition, utilities may offer multipart tariff schedules in which customers with similar characteristics self-select through the size of their purchases. I defer discussion of this issue until section 7.4.

7.2   The Second-Best Core with Price Discrimination

7.2.1   Customer Classes and the Core

Consider again price discrimination across customer classes. Suppose that there are heterogeneous consumers within each class but that each consumer purchases only *one good* from the regulated firm. Thus, one may associate each customer class (e.g., residential, commercial, industrial) with the type of good purchased. If two customer classes purchase the same good at different prices, simply relabel the purchases as different goods. Partition the set of consumers N into subsets $\{N_l\}$, $l = 1, \ldots, m$, in such a way that a consumer $i \in N_l$ purchases only good l. Then refer to the m groups of consumers as customer classes. Observe that the demand for any good will be *independent* of prices for all other goods. Thus, for $i \in N_l$, $V^i(p, \omega^i) = V^i(p_l, \omega^i)$. With this restriction, the definition of the *second-best core* (definition 6.1.2) is applicable to the case of price discrimination across customer classes.

Given independent demands, the necessary conditions for a price vector to be in the second-best core are strengthened as follows.

CONDITION 7.2.1 *With independent demands, sustainable monopoly prices are second-best core prices.*

To see this suppose that p^* is sustainable but not in the second-best core. Then there exists p' and $S \neq \emptyset$ such that $V^i(p'_l, \omega^i) \geq V^i(p^*_l, \omega^i)$ for all $i \in N_l \cap S$, $l = 1, \ldots, m$, and strictly greater for some $i \in S$, and where $\sum_{l=1}^m p'_l Q^s_l(p'_l) \geq C(\sum_{l=1}^m Q^s_l(p'_l))$. This implies that $p' \leq p^*$, $p' \neq p^*$, and (p', q') is a feasible entry plan, $q' = \sum_{l=1}^m Q^s_l(p'_l)$. But this contradicts the sustainability of p^*, so p^* is in the second-best core.

In addition, with independent demands, consumer subsidy freeness implies the absence of subsidies across goods; see equation (3.2.2).

CONDITION 7.2.2 *With independent demands, given p^* in the second-best core, p^* is subsidy-free (across goods).*

This follows immediately from the definition of subsidy-freeness across goods and condition 6.2.2. Recall that given cost complementarities, the set of subsidy-free prices coincides with the set of support prices. Thus, since second-best core prices clear the market, it follows that all prices in the second-best core are anonymously equitable.

CONDITION 7.2.3 *With independent demands, given p^* in the second-best core, p^* is anonymously equitable.*

Following a conjecture of Sharkey (1981), ten Raa (1984) shows that given independent demands, Q bounded, cost complementarities, and profitability at all output levels, there exist undominated, anonymously equitable prices that are sustainable. See Baumol, Panzar, and Willig (1982, proposition 8D2) for a related result. Since sustainable prices are in the second-best core for independent demands, this constitutes a proof of existence of the second-best core for independent demands and cost complementarities.

Using Scarf's proof of nonemptiness of the core under increasing returns to scale, a direct proof may be given that the second-best core is nonempty for the independent demands case. Assume that costs satisfy generalized decreasing average costs (definition 3.1.3). This property of the cost function is suggested by Sharkey (1979) as a sufficient condition for generalizing Scarf's proof of existence of a core with increasing returns to scale to the multiple-goods case. Note that generalized decreasing average costs implies both subadditivity and subhomogeneity (Sharkey, 1979). I do not impose the stronger requirement of cost complementarity across goods.

PROPOSITION 7.2.1   *Given independent demands across customer classes and generalized decreasing average costs, the second-best core is nonempty.*

The proof is given in the appendix and uses Scarf's (1973) approach for balanced games. Recall that second-best core prices support consumer demands and yield zero profits for the firm. No interconsumer or consumer-to-firm transfers are permitted. It must be emphasized therefore that allocations obtained through second-best core prices do *not* correspond to allocations in the *core*.

7.2.2   Two-Part Tariffs and the Core

As with second-best pricing, a Pareto optimal two-part pricing mechanism may create incentives for groups of consumers to recontract with another firm, leading to a decrease in the customer base for the regulated firm. To study this problem, the cooperative game of joint production with a price mechanism to allocate outputs across consumers may be extended to the two-part pricing case. I shall focus attention on the case where the per unit fee is set equal to marginal cost and the entry fees exactly cover fixed costs.

The second-best core notion in a game with two-part tariffs may be thought of as a problem of cooperative formation of "clubs." Many clubs, such as health spas, have a dues structure consisting of a fixed annual membership fee and a per unit rental charge for use of specific facilities.[5] The membership fee serves to limit the total number of members and covers at least part of fixed costs. The per unit charges allocate the facilities while covering part of variable costs and fixed costs. Given large fixed costs, it is desirable to have as many members as possible. However, if individual preferences differ sufficiently, it may be desirable to form multiple clubs, some with relatively high membership fees and low usage charges and others with the reverse. Similarly, in electric utility markets, consumers may have different preferences over whether the recovery of nonattributable costs should be achieved primarily through access charges or per kilowatt charges.

A two-part-tariff (p, E) is said to be *feasible* for a coalition $S \subseteq N$ if the regulated firm is able to break even,

$$p \sum_{i \in S} q^i(p, E) + \sum_{i \in S} \delta_{q^i} E - C\left(\sum_{i \in S} q^i(p, E)\right) \geq 0.$$

With this notion of feasibility we may define a second-best core with two-part pricing.

Definition 7.2.1 A two-part tariff (p, E) is in the *second-best core* if it is feasible for the grand coalition N, and there is no $S \subseteq N$ such that $S \neq \varnothing$ and for some two-part tariff (p', E'),

$$p \sum_{i \in S} q^{i\prime} + \sum_{i \in S} \delta_{q^i} E' - C\left(\sum_{i \in S} q^{i\prime}\right) \geq 0, \tag{7.2.1}$$

for $q^{i\prime} = q^i(p', E', \omega^i)$ and

$$V^i(p', E', \omega^i) \geq V^i(p, E, \omega^i)$$

for all $i \in S$ and $V^i(p', E', \omega^i) > V^i(p, E, \omega^i)$ for some $i \in S$.

Clearly, all two-part tariffs in the second-best core must be second-best Pareto optimal tariffs. A number of the necessary conditions for prices to be in the linear pricing second-best core studied in chapter 6 carry over to the two-part pricing case. These conditions include (i) zero profits, and (ii) the absence of cross-subsidies between groups of consumers,

$$p \sum_{i \in S} q^i + E \sum_{i \in S} \delta_{q^i} \leq C\left(\sum_{i \in S} q^i\right). \tag{7.2.2}$$

Further, (iii) the two-part tariff in the second-best core (p, E) cannot be dominated by another feasible tariff $(p', E') \leq (p, E)$, $(p', E') \neq (p, E)$, so that all (p, E) in the second-best core are sustainable given entry in all markets. Finally, (iv) given a continuum of agents, subhomogeneity of the cost function and subadditivity on a restricted set of outputs may be established.

Consider an *example* with an *affine* cost function $C(Q) = F + \sum_{l=1}^{m} c_l Q_l$. A classic article of Coase (1946, 1947) makes the suggestion that prices be set equal to marginal costs with fixed fees covering fixed costs. Thus, let $p_l^* = c_l$, $E^* = F/n$, if n consumers purchase the good. This immediately yields the following result.

PROPOSITION 7.2.2 *Given an affine cost function, if all consumers purchase from the firm given the two-part tariff* $p_l^* = c_l$, $l = 1, \ldots, m$, *and* $E^* = F/n$, *then* (p^*, E^*) *is in the second-best core.*

Proof Note that (p^*, E^*) yields zero profits and is therefore feasible. It remains to show that there is no two-part tariff (p', E') feasible for any coalition S that dominates (p^*, E^*). Suppose (p', E') is such a tariff. Then, by revealed preference,

$$p^* q^{i\prime} + x^{i\prime} + E^* > \omega^i,$$

for all $i \in S$. Substituting for (p^*, E^*) and summing over i,

$$\sum_{l=1}^{m} c_l \sum_{i \in S} q^{i\prime} + \sum_{i \in S} x^{i\prime} + (s/n)F > \sum_{i \in S} \omega^i,$$

where $s = |S|$ and $n = |N|$. Thus,

$$C\left(\sum_{i \in S} q^{i\prime}\right) > \sum_{i \in S} (\omega^i - x^{i\prime}).$$

But this implies that $C(\sum_{i \in S} q^{i\prime}) > p \sum_{i \in S} q^{i\prime} + \sum_{i \in S} \delta_{q^{i\prime}} E'$, thus contradicting the feasibility of (p', E'). Since (p^*, E^*) is undominated for $S \subseteq N$, it is in the second-best core of the two-part pricing game. QED

The preceding result can be generalized using a weighted cost function as in the last chapter,

$$C_h(Q) = h\left(F + \sum_{l=1}^{m} c_l Q_l\right) + (1 - h)H(Q),$$

where h satisfies $0 \le h \le 1$ and $H(Q)$ is continuous and nondecreasing. Define the two-part tariff $p(h)$, $E(h)$ by

$$p_l(h) = hc_l, \qquad E(h) = (hF + (1 - h)H(Q))/n.$$

Then, if consumers strictly prefer to purchase from the firm at the tariff $p(1)$, $E(1)$, there is some $h' < 1$ such that all consumers purchase the good at the tariff $p(h)$, $E(h)$, $h' \leq h \leq 1$. Then it can be shown that there exists $h' \leq h^* \leq 1$ such that for all h, $h^* \leq h \leq 1$, the second-best core is non-empty. Thus, if entry fees do not exclude consumers and the cost function approximates an affine, consumers will set tariffs cooperatively and production will be carried out by a single firm.

The second-best core can easily fail to exist if consumers are excluded from the market by the entry fee. The size of the market is the subject of the next section. Consider a one-good case with affine costs $C(Q) = F + cQ$. Suppose that there are two consumers and that consumer 1, given $p = c$, $E = F/2$, will choose not to purchase from the firm,

$$U'(q'(p, E, \omega^1), \omega^1 - pq'(p, E, \omega^1) - E) < U^1(0, \omega^1),$$

while the converse is true for consumer 2. Then, $p = c$, $E = F/2$ is not feasible. In the absence of income effects, one may represent this problem graphically; see figure 7.2.1. The entry fee E that splits fixed costs is greater than consumer 1's net surplus abc, but less than consumer 2's net surplus dec. An alternative presentation is given in figure 7.2.2. Let I^1, I^2 represent the indifference curves that go through the zero consumption point for consumers 1 and 2, respectively. The indifference curve for consumer 1 is everywhere below the revenue line for two-part tariffs, while consumer 2 strictly prefers to purchase the good and will reach a level of net benefits represented by indifference curve $I^{2'}$. Thus, consumer 1 will not agree to

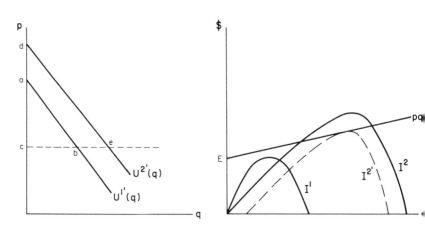

Figure 7.2.1 (left) and 7.2.2 (right)
Nonexistence of the second-best core with two-part tariffs.

join with consumer 2 in jointly producing the good. Due to the absence of transfers, the cooperative game fails to be superadditive in this instance and the second-best core is empty.

Ng and Weisser (1974) and Littlechild (1975b) find that a shift to two-part tariffs from uniform price raises aggregate welfare. However, Willig (1978) observes that in the absence of transfers, this shift to two-part tariffs may harm consumers with small demands while benefiting those with large demands. Willig shows that a Pareto improvement of a given price is achieved by a continuous schedule of the form

$$R(q) = \begin{cases} p^1 q & \text{for} \quad q \le E/(p^1 - p^2) \\ E + p^2 q & \text{for} \quad q > E/(p^1 - p^2), \end{cases}$$

where $p^1 > p^2$. Willig's result may be adapted to show that *second-best* Pareto optimal improvements are obtained by a shift from a Ramsey price to a nonlinear outlay schedule. Using figure 7.2.3, it is shown informally how a nonlinear outlay schedule of this form accommodates both low and high demanders. Suppose that $\bar{p}$ is a break-even price. Then construct a schedule $R(q)$ such that both consumers are made strictly better off and the increased revenues earned from the high-demand consumer 2 cover the

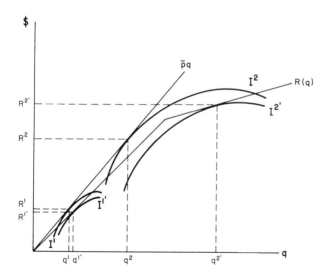

Figure 7.2.3
Two-part tariffs are Pareto superior to linear pricing.

reduced revenues earned from the low-demand consumer 1. In figure 7.2.3, let q^1, q^2 represent consumption levels at the uniform price $\bar{p}$ and $q^{1\prime}$, $q^{2\prime}$ represent consumption vectors with the nonlinear schedule $R(q)$. Revenues earned from the consumers at $\bar{p}$ are $R^1 = \bar{p}q^1$ and $R^2 = \bar{p}q^2$, while, given $R(q)$, $R^{1\prime} = p^1 q^{1\prime}$ and $R^{2\prime} = E + p^2 q^{2\prime}$. To show that the two-part tariff yields a (second-best) Pareto improvement, observe that as in figure 7.2.3, the welfare of any consumer—the high-demand consumer in this case—can be increased by lowering his marginal price while raising revenues through a fixed fee.[6] Let $\bar{p}$ be the average cost price. Let $R(q)$ be such that the lower price equals marginal cost, $p^2 = c$, and choose E such that

$$E + cq^2 > R^2 = \bar{p}q^2.$$

The change in profits generated by this tariff is positive,

change in profits $= (R^{2\prime} - R^2) - c(q^{2\prime} - q^2) = E + cq^2 - \bar{p}q^2$.

The additional revenue generated by the tariff exceeds the additional production costs. To maintain zero profits, simply lower the price charged to the low demand consumer, $p^1 < \bar{p}$.

The preceding discussion has important implications for the two consumers. They have incentive to cooperate in joint production of the good with payments determined by a nonlinear price schedule. The schedule yields an outcome that dominates any linear pricing equilibrium. Further, although the Coase solution was not feasible, at least the high-demand consumer pays a per unit price equal to marginal cost. The nonlinear schedule treats the two consumers as separate customer classes, charging discriminatory tariffs. Thus, both second- and third-degree price discrimination are present. Consumers select the appropriate tariff through the size of their purchase.

7.3   Two-Part Tariffs and Market Size

7.3.1   The Marginal Consumer

Consider now the effects of two-part tariffs on the number of customers that purchase from the regulated firm. For simplicity let consumers differ only in terms of income ω^i. Let there be a continuum of consumers with incomes distributed in $[\underline{\omega}, 1]$ according to the cumulative distribution

$F(\omega)$ where $\bar{\omega} > 0$. Let $F(1) = 1$, $F(\underline{\omega}) = 0$, and $dF(\omega)/d\omega = f(\omega) > 0$. Assume that the regulated firm supplies a single good. Also, require $U_{qx}(q, x) \geq 0$.

Let $q(p, E, \omega) > 0$, $x(p, E, \omega) > 0$ equate the consumer's marginal rate of substitution to the price of q and satisfy the budget constraint for income level ω,

$$U_q(q, x)/U_x(q, x) = p, \qquad (7.3.1)$$

$$pq + E + x = \omega. \qquad (7.3.2)$$

Then the purchase q^* of a consumer with income ω is positive if and only if $U(q(p, E, \omega), x(p, E, \omega)) \geq U(0, \omega)$. Given this framework, it follows that there exists a marginal consumer with income $\omega^0 \in [\underline{\omega}, 1]$ such that $q^* = q(p, E, \omega) > 0$ for all $\omega \geq \omega^0$ and $q^* = 0$ for $\omega < \omega^0$. To see this, suppose that $U(q(p, E, \omega'), x(p, E, \omega')) \geq U(0, \omega')$ for some ω'. By the envelope theorem,

$$\Delta(\omega) = \frac{\partial}{\partial \omega}[U(q(p, E, \omega), x(p, E, \omega)) - U(0, \omega)]$$

$$= U_x(q(p, E, \omega), x(p, E, \omega)) - U_x(0, \omega). \qquad (7.3.3)$$

By the concavity of U, $U_x(q(p, E, \omega), x(p, E, \omega)) > U_x(q(p, E, \omega), \omega)$. Further, given $U_{qx} \geq 0$, $U_x(q(p, E, \omega), \omega) \geq U_x(0, \omega)$. Thus, $\Delta(\omega) > 0$, which implies that $U(q(p, E, \omega), x(p, E, \omega)) > U(0, \omega)$ for all $\omega > \omega'$. Thus, low-income customers are excluded from the regulated market.

Given a *marginal consumer* $\omega^0 \in (\underline{\omega}, 1)$, such that $U(q(p, E, \omega^0), x(p, E, \omega^0)) = U(0, \omega^0)$, consider the effects of the price and entry fee on the size of the firm's market, $[\omega^0, 1]$ by examining the marginal consumer,

$$\omega_p^0(p, E) = q^0 \omega_E^0(p, E) = q^0 U_x(q^0, x^0)/\Delta(\omega^0),$$

where $\omega_p^0 \equiv \partial \omega^0/\partial p$, $\omega_E^0 \equiv \partial \omega^0/\partial E$ and where $q^0 = q(p, E, \omega^0)$, $x^0 = x(p, E, \omega^0)$. Therefore, the effect of the per unit price on the marginal consumer equals the effect of the entry fee on the marginal consumer times his purchase, $\omega_p^0 = q^0 \omega_E^0$. Clearly, either higher per unit prices or higher entry fees reduce the size of the regulated firm's market.

Let $Q(p, E) = \int_{\omega^0(p, E)}^{1} q(p, E, \omega) dF(\omega)$ represent total sales and let $n(p, E) = \int_{\omega^0(p, E)}^{1} dF(\omega)$ represent the number of customers served by the regulated firm. The effects of the price and entry fee on total sales are easily obtained,

$$Q_p(p, E) = q^0 n_p(p, E) + \int_{\omega^0}^1 q_p(p, E, \omega^0) \, dF(\omega), \tag{7.3.4}$$

$$Q_E(p, E) = q^0 n_E(p, E) + \int_{\omega^0}^1 q_E(p, E, \omega^0) \, dF(\omega), \tag{7.3.5}$$

where $n_p(p, E) = -f(\omega^0)\omega_p^0(p, E)$ and $n_E(p, E) = -f(\omega^0)\omega_E^0(p, E)$ are reductions in the number of total customers resulting from increases in the price and entry fee.[7] Note that given (7.3.4) and (7.3.5), the reduction in customers due to a price increase equals the reduction in customers due to an entry fee increase times the marginal consumer's purchase, $n_p(p, E) = q^0 n_E(p, E)$.

The regulated firm's profits are defined by

$$\pi(p, E) = pQ(p, E) + n(p, E)E - C(Q(p, E)). \tag{7.3.6}$$

The effects of the per unit price and entry fee on profits are then

$$\pi_p(p, E) = pQ_p(p, E) + Q(p, E) + n_p(p, E)E - C'(Q(p, E))Q_p(p, E), \tag{7.3.7}$$

$$\pi_E(p, E) = pQ_E(p, E) + n(p, E) + n_E(p, E)E - C'(Q(p, E))Q_E(p, E). \tag{7.3.8}$$

These expressions reflect both substitution and income effects for inframarginal consumers and the departure of marginal consumers from the market.

The second-best two-part tariff is solved for using the following Lagrange problem,

$$L = \int_{\omega^0(p, E)}^1 \lambda(\omega)V(p, E, \omega) \, dF(\omega) + \gamma\pi(p, E), \tag{7.3.9}$$

where $\lambda(\omega)$ is the weight given to consumer with income ω. The first-order conditions are closely related to our earlier analysis of second-best Pareto optimal pricing. Including the zero-profit constraint $\pi(p, E) = 0$ gives

$$\left[\int_{\omega^0}^1 \lambda(\omega)V_p(p, E, \omega) \, dF(\omega) + \lambda(\omega^0)V(p, E, \omega^0)n_p(p, E) \right] + \gamma\pi_p(p, E) = 0, \tag{7.3.10}$$

$$\left[\int_{\omega^0}^1 \lambda(\omega)V_E(p, E, \omega) \, dF(\omega) + \lambda(\omega^0)V(p, E, \omega^0)n_E(p, E) \right] + \gamma\pi_E(p, E) = 0. \tag{7.3.11}$$

These conditions equate the weighted average of consumer welfare losses associated with an increase in the price or entry fee to the effect of an increase of the price or entry fee on the firm's profits weighted by the shadow price γ. The term in brackets in (7.3.10) represents the welfare effects of a price increase on inframarginal consumers purchasing from the firm plus the social value of the marginal consumer's indirect utility times the change in the number of customers. The bracketed term in (7.3.11) is the corresponding welfare effect of the entry fee. A ratio of (7.3.10) and (7.3.11) shows that the rate of substitution between the price and the entry fee effects on consumer welfare equals the ratio of the price and entry fee effects on profit. To see this clearly, suppose that the marginal consumer's indirect utility is zero,[8] $V(p, E, \omega^0) = 0$. Recalling that $V_p = qV_E = -qU_x(q, x)$, yields

$$\int_{\omega^0}^1 \lambda(\omega) U_x q \, dF(\omega) \bigg/ \int_{\omega^0}^1 \lambda(\omega) U_x \, dF(\omega) = \pi_p/\pi_E. \tag{7.3.12}$$

Thus, the ratio of marginal profits from the price and entry fee equals a weighted average of consumer demands.

Return to the optimality conditions for the second-best tariff. Combine (7.3.10) and (7.3.11) to eliminate the entry fee terms and the marginal consumer's indirect utility.[9] The relative markup over marginal cost is then

$$\frac{p - C'(Q)}{p}$$

$$= \frac{\int_{\omega^0}^1 \lambda(\omega) V_p \, dF(\omega) - (n_p/n_E) \int_{\omega^0}^1 \lambda(\omega) V_E \, dF(\omega) + \gamma[Q - (n_p/n_E)n]}{p\gamma[-Q_p + (n_p/n_E)Q_E]}. \tag{7.3.13}$$

Define aggregate demand elasticities with respect to the price and entry fee, $\eta_p = -(Q/p)Q_p$ and $\eta_E = (Q/E)Q_E$. Also, define corresponding elasticities for the number of customers of the firm, $\alpha_p = -(n/p)n_p$ and $\alpha_E = -(n/E)n_E$. Then (7.3.13) simplifies somewhat,

$$(p - C'(Q))/p = -\left(\frac{1}{\gamma Q}\right) \int_{\omega^0}^1 (\lambda(\omega) U_x - \gamma)(q - q^0) \, dF(\omega) / [\eta_p - (\alpha_p/\alpha_E)\eta_E]. \tag{7.3.14}$$

The denominator in (7.3.14) is positive[10] and represents a modified aggregate demand elasticity. In the standard two-product Ramsey pricing model with independent demands, relative markups are proportional to the reciprocal of the demand elasticity. In the model of two-part pricing for a single product, the price elasticity of aggregate demand is reduced by subtracting the income elasticity of demand weighted by the ratio of price and income effects on the number of customers. This reflects the additional revenue generated by the entry fee and the reduction in the number of customers resulting from increases in the per unit price and entry fee.

The main implication of condition (7.3.14) is that marginal cost pricing need not be socially optimal with diverse consumers. The condition illustrates in an interesting way the familiar trade-off between consumer welfare and the need to cover production costs. If the weighted social value of each consumer's marginal utility of income $\lambda(\omega)U_x$ is less than (greater than) the shadow price on the profit constraint γ, then the relative markup will be positive (negative). Suppose, for example, that consumers are weighted equally, that is, $\lambda(\omega) = 1$ for all income levels ω. Given diminishing marginal utility of income $V_{\omega\omega} < 0$, then, if the marginal consumer's marginal value of income is less than or equal to the shadow price on the profit constraint, $U_x(q^0, x^0) \leq \gamma$, it will be so for inframarginal consumers as well and price will exceed marginal cost. The entry fee will cover less than nonattributable costs $C(Q) - C'(Q)Q$. A necessary condition for marginal cost pricing is that the weighted sum of consumer demands equal the marginal consumer's demand, $\int_{\omega^0}^{1} (\lambda U_x - \gamma)q\, dF / \int_{\omega^0}^{1} (\lambda U_x - \gamma)\, dF = q^0$.

7.3.2 A Simple Nonlinear Tariff

Two-part tariffs can be controversial in practice if the fixed fee excludes some consumers from the market. This problem is addressed by Willig's (1978) simple nonlinear tariff, which offers consumers a choice between a linear price p^1 and a two-part tariff (p^2, E). As was seen, the second-best tariff must be such that the per unit price p^2 equals marginal cost. The framework of the preceding section is now adapted to obtain second-best optimal values for p^1 and E.

Let the cost function be affine, $C(Q) = FC + cQ$. Define the indirect utility $V(p, \omega)$ as before. Let $V(c, \omega - E)$ represent the indirect utility of making a purchase using the two-part tariff (c, E). Assume that the marginal indirect utility of income is nonincreasing, $V_{\omega\omega} \leq 0$, and that a higher price lowers the marginal indirect utility of income, $V_{p\omega} < 0$. A consumer chooses the linear tariff p^1 if and only if $V(p^1, \omega) \geq V(c, \omega - E)$.

Given our assumptions consumers choose the price p_1 if and only if their income is below a critical value.

PROPOSITION 7.3.1   *If $V_{\omega\omega} \leq 0$ and $V_{p\omega} < 0$, consumers with low incomes, $\omega \in [\underline{\omega}, \tilde{\omega}]$, choose the linear price p^1 and consumers with high incomes, $\omega \in (\tilde{\omega}, 1]$, choose the two-part tariff (c, E), where the marginal consumer's income $\tilde{\omega}(p^1, c, E)$ solves $V(p^1, \tilde{\omega}) = V(c, \tilde{\omega} - E)$.*

The partition of consumers follows by noting that

$$(\partial/\partial\omega)[V(p^1, \omega) - V(c, \omega - E)] = V_\omega(p^1, \omega) - V_\omega(c, \omega - E)$$

$$\leq V_\omega(p^1, \omega - E) - V_\omega(c, \omega - E)$$

$$< 0. \tag{7.3.15}$$

Thus, if a given consumer prefers the two-part tariff, so do all consumers with higher income levels.

Given proposition 7.3.1, the second-best optimal schedule (p^1, c, E) solves

$$\max_{p^1, E} \int_{\underline{\omega}}^{\tilde{\omega}} \lambda(\omega) V(p^1, \omega) \, dF(\omega) + \int_{\tilde{\omega}}^{1} \lambda(\omega) V(c, \omega - E) \, dF(\omega) \tag{7.3.16}$$

subject to a zero-profit constraint,

$$\pi = (p^1 - c) \int_{\underline{\omega}}^{\tilde{\omega}} q(p^1, \omega) \, dF(\omega) + E \int_{\tilde{\omega}}^{1} dF(\omega) - FC = 0.$$

Fixed costs are shared between low-income and high-income consumers. Low-income consumers cover fixed costs by paying more than marginal cost per unit, while high-income consumers pay for fixed costs through entry fees. A trade-off exists between the size of the markup and of the entry fee, $\partial E/\partial p^1|_{\pi=0} = -\pi_{p^1}/\pi_E$, where[11]

$$\pi_{p^1} = \int_{\underline{\omega}}^{\tilde{\omega}} q(p^1, \omega) \, dF(\omega) + (p^1 - c) \int_{\underline{\omega}}^{\tilde{\omega}} q_p(p^1, \omega) \, dF(\omega)$$

$$+ [(p^1 - c)q(p^1, \tilde{\omega}) - E] f(\tilde{\omega}) \, \partial\tilde{\omega}/\partial p^1, \tag{7.3.17}$$

$$\pi_E = 1 - F(\tilde{\omega}) + [(p^1 - c)q(p^1, \tilde{\omega}) - E] f(\tilde{\omega}) \, \partial\tilde{\omega}/\partial E. \tag{7.3.18}$$

Raising the markup can increase revenue from lower-income consumers but causes a shift to the two-part price for some consumers at the margin. Similarly, higher-entry fees increase the number of consumers choosing the linear tariff. The second-best optimal linear price equates the marginal cost of a price increase for low-income consumers to the marginal benefits of the corresponding increase in the entry fee for higher-income consumers. Thus, the relative marginal welfare effects for low- and higher-income consumers equals the marginal rate of substitution between the price and entry fee in generating profits,

$$\frac{-\int_{\omega}^{\tilde{\omega}} \lambda(\omega) V_p(p^1, \omega) \, dF(\omega)}{\int_{\tilde{\omega}}^{1} \lambda(\omega) V_{\omega}(c, \omega - E) \, dF(\omega)} = \frac{\pi_{p^1}}{\pi_E}. \tag{7.3.19}$$

In general, welfare may be improved by offering consumers a menu of choices of two-part tariffs; see Faulhaber and Panzar (1977). With declining block tariffs, consumers are able to lower their per unit charge by selecting a higher fixed charge. It should be apparent that the number of choices offered need not exceed the number of consumer types. In the limit, as the distribution of consumer types approaches a continuum, a continuous schedule of quantity discounts is second-best Pareto optimal. This is the subject of the next section.

7.4   Second-Best Nonlinear Pricing

Consider a pricing policy that makes full use of the available information regarding consumer preferences. It is assumed that the firm (or the regulator) knows the characteristics of consumers and their distribution in the relevant market. However, the firm cannot identify the characteristics of the consumer being served for the purpose of optimal price discrimination. The firm must design a price mechanism in which consumers self-select according to their individual characteristics by the size of their purchase. Self-selection is induced by means of a quantity-dependent outlay schedule offered by the firm. The consumer faces a nonlinear outlay schedule $P(q)$. This may represent declining block tariffs in utility rate schedules or other forms of quantity discounts and premiums.[12]

Assume away income effects. Consider the single-good case in which consumer utility has the form $U^i(q^i, x^i) = \int_0^{q^i} u^i(q) \, dq + x^i$, where u^i represents consumer i's marginal willingness to pay. Assume that consumers differ in a systematic way according to a taste parameter μ that affects the consumer's valuation of the good q relative to income as well as the marginal valuation of q, $u^i(q) = u(q, \mu^i)$ for all i. Define $U(q, \mu) \equiv \int_0^q u(q', \mu) \, dq'$. Suppose that there is a continuum of consumers and that the taste parameter μ is distributed on $[0, 1]$ according to a continuously differentiable cumulative distribution $F(\mu)$ with positive density $f(\mu) \equiv dF(\mu)/d\mu$. Assume that $F(1) = 1$, $F(0) = 0$, $F(\mu) > 0$ for $\mu > 0$ and $f(\mu) > 0$ for $\mu \in [0, 1]$. The continuum case is considered for ease of comparison with later analysis of rate regulation in the presence of asymmetric information about demand and costs (see chapter 11).

The consumer marginal willingness to pay, $u(q, \mu)$, is positive, strictly decreasing, and concave in q and increasing and weakly concave in μ. The requirement that μ is increasing in the taste parameter implies that consumption of the good is normal in the taste parameter. Assume further that consumption and the parameter μ have complementary effects on marginal willingness to pay, $u_{q\mu} \geq 0$.

Restrict attention to schedules that are (piecewise) continuously differentiable. Define the marginal price schedule by $p(q) = dP(q)/dq$. The indirect utility for a consumer of type μ is defined by

$$V(\mu) \equiv \max_q \left[\int_0^q u(q', \mu) \, dq' - P(q) \right]. \tag{7.4.1}$$

Let $q(\mu) = q(\mu, P(\cdot))$ represent the demand of a consumer of type μ facing the nonlinear outlay schedule $P(\cdot)$. If the consumer's problem is well-defined, $q(\mu)$ is an interior solution to the maximization problem (7.4.1),

$$u(q(\mu), \mu) - p(q(\mu)) = 0. \tag{7.4.2}$$

This is refered to as a self-selection condition since a consumer *indirectly* reveals his type by revealing his marginal willingness to pay through the size of his purchase $q(\mu)$. For example, suppose that the marginal price schedule, p, is downward sloping, thus yielding quantity discounts. Then consumers with greater marginal willingness to pay will purchase a larger quantity from the firm. As shown in figure 7.4.1, a higher value for the taste parameter ($\mu^2 > \mu^1$) shifts out the marginal willingness-to-pay schedule, which crosses the marginal price schedule at a higher output.

The choice problem for the consumer may be recast to emphasize the revelation of preferences through the size of purchases. Rather than announcing a quantity-dependent price schedule $P(q)$, the firm can announce an output and payment schedule that depends on each consumer's declaration of his taste parameter, $(q(\mu), R(\mu))$. For any quantity-dependent schedule $P(\cdot)$, one can always construct the equivalent revelation schedule. Let $q(\mu, P(\cdot))$

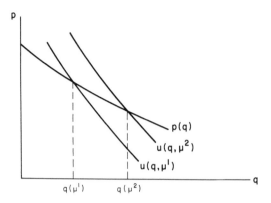

Figure 7.4.1
Consumers self-select by the quantity that they purchase.

be the consumer optimal demand schedule. Then define (q, R) by $q(\mu) = q(\mu, P(\cdot))$ and $R(\mu) = P(q(\mu, P(\cdot))$. The consumer will thus have incentive to reveal correctly his type μ, since (q, R) was constructed using the consumer demand schedule. This equivalence is an illustration of the *revelation principle*.[13] Although our primary objective is to characterize the firm's quantity-dependent outlay schedule P, it is more useful to consider the parameter based schedule (q, R).

A schedule (q, R) for which the consumer announces his taste parameter μ is referred to as a *direct revelation mechanism*. The requirement that truth telling is optimal for consumers is referred to as *incentive compatibility*. Define $V(\mu, \hat{\mu})$ as the indirect utility of reporting $\hat{\mu}$ obtained by a consumer whose true type is μ,

$$V(\mu, \hat{\mu}) = \int_0^{q(\hat{\mu})} u(q', \mu)\, dq' - R(\mu). \tag{7.4.3}$$

Thus, *incentive compatibility* requires (q, R) to be such that

$$V(\mu, \mu) \geq V(\mu, \hat{\mu}) \qquad \text{for all } \mu, \hat{\mu} \in [0, 1]. \tag{7.4.4}$$

Let $V(\mu) \equiv V(\mu, \mu)$ for all $\mu \in [0, 1]$. For a consumer to participate in the market, he must obtain positive gains-from-trade. The opportunity cost of nonparticipation is normalized to zero. Thus, *individual rationality* requires (q, R) to be such that

$$V(\mu) \geq 0 \tag{7.4.5}$$

for all $\mu \in [0, 1]$. A mechanism (q, R) that is incentive compatible and individually rational is referred to as *feasible*. Attention is restricted to (piecewise) continuously differentiable mechanisms.

By now standard arguments, due to Mirrlees (1971), incentive compatibility requires

$$\int_0^{q(\mu)} [u(q', \mu) - u(q', \hat{\mu})] dq' \geq V(\mu, \mu) - V(\hat{\mu}, \hat{\mu})$$

$$\geq \int_0^{q(\hat{\mu})} [u(q', \mu) - u(q', \hat{\mu})] dq'. \qquad (7.4.6)$$

Dividing equation (7.4.6) by $(\mu - \hat{\mu})$ and taking limits as $(\mu - \hat{\mu})$ goes to zero, it follows that the marginal indirect value of the taste parameter is

$$V'(\mu) = \int_0^{q(\mu)} u_\mu(q', \mu) dq', \qquad (7.4.7)$$

where $u_\mu(q, \mu) \equiv \partial u(q, \mu)/\partial \mu$. Thus, $V(\mu)$ is nondecreasing in μ and it is sufficient to require $V(0) \geq 0$ to guarantee individual rationality for all consumer types μ in $[0, 1]$.

An important implication of (7.4.6) is that the consumption schedule $q(\mu)$ is nondecreasing in the taste parameter μ. Given $\mu \geq \hat{\mu}$, $u(q, \mu) - u(q, \hat{\mu})$ is positive and nondecreasing in q. Thus, $q(\mu) \geq q(\hat{\mu})$.

For market exchange to be feasible requires in addition that the firm can earn nonnegative profits, $\Pi \geq 0$. Let costs be given by the affine $C(Q) = cQ + FC$. Then the firm's profits are given by

$$\Pi = \int_0^1 [R(\mu) - cq(\mu)] dF(\mu) - FC. \qquad (7.4.8)$$

From the definition of integration and equation (7.4.7) consumer indirect utility is given by

$$V(\mu) = V(0) + \int_0^\mu \left(\int_0^{q(\mu')} u_\mu(q', \mu') dq' \right) d\mu'. \qquad (7.4.9)$$

Then observe that $V(\mu) = \int_0^{q(\mu)} u(q', \mu) dq' - R(\mu)$. Therefore, the sum of the smallest consumer indirect utility and firm profits may be written as follows:

$$V(0) + \Pi = \int_0^1 \left[\int_0^{q(\mu)} u(q', \mu) \, dq' - cq(\mu) \right.$$

$$\left. - \int_0^\mu \left(\int_0^{q(\mu')} u_\mu(q', \mu') \, dq' \right) d\mu' \right] dF(\mu) - FC. \qquad (7.4.10)$$

Integration by parts allows simplification of (7.4.10),

$$V(0) + \Pi = \int_0^1 \left[\int_0^{q(\mu)} u(q', \mu) \, dq' - cq(\mu) \right.$$

$$\left. - \int_0^{q(\mu)} u_\mu(q', \mu) \, dq' \left(\frac{1 - F(\mu)}{f(\mu)} \right) \right] dF(\mu) - FC. \qquad (7.4.11)$$

Given the definition of feasibility for the consumer and firm, the full set of feasible mechanisms may now be characterized.

PROPOSITION 7.4.1   *The mechanism* $(q(\mu), R(\mu))$ *is feasible if and only if* $q(\mu)$ *is nondecreasing in* μ *and*

$$\int_0^1 \left[\int_0^{q(\mu)} u(q', \mu) \, dq' - cq(\mu) \right.$$

$$\left. - \int_0^{q(\mu)} u_\mu(q', \mu) \, dq' \left((1 - F(\mu))/f(\mu) \right) \right] dF(\mu) - FC \geq 0. \qquad (7.4.12)$$

Proof Let (q, R) be feasible. Then, as shown above, q is nondecreasing in μ. Also, by feasibility, $V(0) + \Pi$ is defined by (7.4.11). Further, $V(0) \geq 0$ and $\Pi \geq 0$ implies inequality (7.4.12).

Now let q be nondecreasing in μ and assume that constraint (7.4.12) is satisfied. Consider the consumer's marginal indirect utility,

$$V'(\mu) = u(q(\mu), \mu) \, \partial q(\mu)/\partial \mu + \int_0^{q(\mu)} u_\mu(q', \mu) \, dq' - \partial R(\mu)/\partial \mu. \qquad (7.4.13)$$

For incentive compatibility it is necessary that $V'(\mu) = \int_0^{q(\mu)} u_\mu(q', \mu) \, dq'$; thus it is necessary that

$$u(q(\mu), \mu) \, \partial q(\mu)/\partial \mu = \partial R(\mu)/\partial \mu. \qquad (7.4.14)$$

Define $R(\mu)$ by

$$R(\mu) = \int_0^\mu u(q(\mu'), \mu')(\partial q(\mu')/\partial \mu) \, d\mu' + \int_0^{q(0)} u(q', 0) \, dq'.$$

This is nonnegative since $\partial q(\mu')/\partial \mu$ is nonnegative. It follows that (q, R) is incentive compatible, since $\partial V(\mu, \hat{\mu})/\partial \hat{\mu}|_{\hat{\mu}=\mu} = 0$. Thus, equation (7.4.11) applies. Further, $V(0) = \int_0^{q(0)} u(q', 0)\, dq' - R(0) = 0$. So, by (7.4.11) and (7.4.12), $\Pi \geq 0$. Thus, (q, R) is a feasible mechanism. QED

The second-best nonlinear price schedule is now considered. Each nonlinear price schedule is associated with a second-best Pareto optimal direct mechanism. A direct mechanism (q, R) is *second-best Pareto optimal* if it is feasible and if there does not exist another feasible mechanism (q', R') such that $V(\mu, q', R') > V(\mu, q, R)$ for all $\mu \in [0, 1]$. As before, solve the pricing problem by constrained maximization. In particular, (q, R) is second-best Pareto optimal if and only if there are nondecreasing welfare weights $\lambda(\mu)$, $\mu \in [0, 1]$, such that $\lambda(1) = 1$, $\lambda(0) = 0$, and such that (q, R) maximizes

$$\int_0^1 V(\mu)\, d\lambda(\mu) \tag{7.4.15}$$

subject to equation (7.4.12), $\Pi \geq 0$, and $q(\mu)$ nondecreasing in μ. Let the break-even constraint be strictly binding, $\Pi = 0$. Then, equation (7.4.11) specifies the minimum net consumer benefit, $V(0)$, for any output schedule. Also, integrating by parts gives

$$\int_0^1 V(\mu)\, d\lambda(\mu)$$
$$= V(0) + \int_0^1 ((1 - \lambda(\mu))/f(\mu))\left(\int_0^{q(\mu)} u_\mu(q', \mu)\, dq'\right) dF(\mu). \tag{7.4.16}$$

Substituting for $V(0)$ from (7.4.11) immediately characterizes the regulator's maximization problem

PROPOSITION 7.4.2   *The second-best Pareto optimal nonlinear price schedule is obtained from the following problem,*

$$\max_{q(\mu),\, \mu \in [0, 1]} \left[\int_0^1 I(q, \mu)\, dF(\mu) - (1 + \gamma)FC \right] \tag{7.4.17}$$

subject to $\partial q(\mu)/\partial \mu \geq 0$, where γ is the multiplier for constraint (7.4.12) *and where*

$$I(q, \mu) = (1 + \gamma)(U(q, \mu) - cq)$$
$$- [((1 + \gamma)(1 - F(\mu)) - (1 - \lambda(\mu)))/f(\mu)]\, U_\mu(q, \mu). \tag{7.4.18}$$

Let $\eta(\mu)$ represent the bracketed term in (7.4.18), $\eta(\mu) \equiv ((1 + \gamma)(1 - F(\mu)) - (1 - \lambda(\mu)))/f(\mu)$. Assume that $\eta(\mu) \geq 0$ for all μ. This places a bound on the difference between the welfare weight $\lambda(\mu)$ and the cumulative distribution, $(1 - \lambda)/(1 - F) < 1 + \gamma$. This is satisfied, for example, if the welfare weights and the distribution of consumer types coincide. This guarantees that $I(q, \mu)$ is strictly concave in q. Since $u_{q\mu} \geq 0$ and $u_q < 0$,

$$I_{qq} = (1 + \gamma)u_q(q, \mu) - \eta(\mu)u_{\mu q}(q, \mu) < 0.$$

Given the second-best optimal output schedule $q^*(\mu)$, one may characterize the associated nonlinear price schedule. Recall that the consumer chooses the size of his purchase in such a way that marginal willingness to pay equals the marginal price schedule, $u(q, \mu) = p(q)$. Let $\mu(x)$ represent $\min\{\mu : q(\mu) = x\}$; see, for example, Spence (1977c) and Maskin and Riley (1984). Then the nonlinear price schedule can be represented in the standard form.

PROPOSITION 7.4.3   *The second-best optimal nonlinear price schedule is given by*

$$P(q) = \int_0^q u(x, \mu(x))\, dx, \tag{7.4.19}$$

where $q^*(\mu)$ *solves the maximization problem* (7.4.18).

Consider first the optimal output schedule in the absence of the boundary condition imposed by incentive compatibility, $\partial q/\partial \mu \geq 0$. Let $\bar{q}(\mu)$ represent the unconstrained output schedule. Then, $\bar{q} > 0$ solves

$$(1 + \gamma)(u(q, \mu) - c) - \eta(\mu)u_\mu(q, \mu) = 0. \tag{7.4.20}$$

If

$$(1 + \gamma)(u(0, \mu) - c) - \eta(\mu)u_\mu(0, \mu) < 0, \tag{7.4.21}$$

then $\bar{q}(\mu) = 0$. With some restrictions, the unconstrained output schedule is second-best optimal.

PROPOSITION 7.4.4   *Given* $\eta(\mu)$ *nonnegative and nonincreasing in* μ, *the unconstrained output schedule* $\bar{q}(\mu)$ *is equivalent to second-best optimal schedule* $q^*(\mu)$.

Proof It is sufficient to verify that $\partial\bar{q}(\mu)/\partial\mu \geq 0$. For $\bar{q} > 0$, $\partial\bar{q}/\partial\mu = -I_{q\mu}/I_{qq}$. By concavity, $I_{qq} < 0$. Note that $I_{q\mu} = (1 + \gamma)u_\mu(q, \mu) -$

$\eta(\mu)u_{\mu\mu}(q,\mu) - (\partial\eta(\mu)/\partial\mu)u_{\mu}(q,\mu)$. Since $u_{\mu} > 0$, $\eta(\mu) \geq 0$, $u_{\mu\mu} < 0$, and $\partial\eta(\mu)/\partial\mu \leq 0$, it follows that $I_{q\mu} > 0$. Also, if $\bar{q}(\mu^0) = 0$, then $\bar{q}(\mu) = 0$ for all $\mu \leq \mu^0$. Thus, $\partial\bar{q}(\mu)/\partial\mu \geq 0$. QED

Under the condition of proposition 7.4.4, those consumers purchasing from the firm exactly reveal their type through the size of their purchase. Thus, the proposition characterizes a *separating* equilibrium. An example satisfying the conditions in proposition 7.4.4 is easily obtained by letting the welfare weights equal the population distribution function, $\lambda(\mu) = F(\mu)$. Then $\eta(\mu) = \gamma(1 - F(\mu))/f(\mu)$ is nonincreasing in μ. This holds, for example, for the uniform and exponential distributions.

The monotonicity requirements may be weakened considerably to obtain a general characterization of the second-best optimal output schedule $q^*(\mu)$. The proposition follows from the analysis of Guesnerie and Laffont (1984, theorem 4).

PROPOSITION 7.4.5 *Given $\eta(\mu)$ nonnegative, if $(\partial\eta(\mu)/\partial\mu)$ changes sign a finite number of times, then the second-best optimal output schedule, $q^*(\mu)$, is nondecreasing and piecewise continuously differentiable. Also, $q^*(\mu)$ coincides with $\bar{q}(\mu)$ except on a finite number K of disjoint intervals $J^k = (\mu_0^k, \mu_1^k)$, $k = 1, \ldots, K$, μ_0^k increasing in k, where $q^*(\mu) = q^k$ for all $\mu \in J^k$.*

The proposition specifies the optimal degree of *pooling* given by the nonlinear outlay schedule. In other words, given the second-best outlay schedule, consumers with different taste parameters may choose to purchase the same output from the regulated firm.

The second-best optimal nonlinear price schedule involves departures from marginal cost pricing. Turning again to the unconstrained optimum, let $\mu = 1$. Since $\eta(1) = 0$, equation (7.4.20) implies that $p(q(1)) = u(q(1), 1) = c$. All other consumers will pay a marginal price in excess of marginal cost for $\eta(\mu) > 0$, since

$$p(q) = c + \eta(\mu(q))u_{\mu}(q, \mu(q))/(1 + \gamma). \qquad (7.4.22)$$

If, however, $\eta(\mu) < 0$ for some values of μ, then some consumers may pay a marginal price below marginal cost. These results are analogous to those for two-part tariffs and represent the inefficiency of second-degree price discrimination.

The second-best optimal marginal price schedule exhibits quantity discounts if strong conditions are imposed on the weights $\eta(\mu)$. The proof is given in the appendix.

PROPOSITION 7.4.6   *Given $\eta(\mu)$ and $u_q(q,\mu)/\eta(\mu)$ nonincreasing, the price schedule exhibits quantity discounts.*

Thus, since consumers with higher values of the demand parameter make larger purchases, the marginal price paid is smaller.

It may be desirable to exclude some consumers from the market at the second-best optimum. It is of interest to solve explicitly for the demand parameter value of the marginal consumer. Let $\tilde{\mu}$ be the marginal consumer, where $V(\tilde{\mu}) = 0$. Thus, $P(q;\tilde{\mu}) = \int_0^q u(q',\tilde{\mu})\,dq'$ for $q \le q(\tilde{\mu})$, and the marginal consumer's payment is such that $P_{\tilde{\mu}}(q(\tilde{\mu}),\tilde{\mu}) = \int_0^{q(\tilde{\mu})} u_\mu(q',\tilde{\mu})\,dq'$. Then the marginal consumer is chosen to maximize social welfare,

$$
\max_{\tilde{\mu}} \left\{ \int_{\tilde{\mu}}^1 \left[U(q(\mu),\mu) - P(q(\mu);\tilde{\mu}) \right] d\lambda(\mu) \right.
$$

$$
\left. + \gamma \left[\int_{\tilde{\mu}}^1 \left(P(q(\mu),\tilde{\mu}) - cq(\tilde{\mu}) \right) dF(\mu) - FC \right] \right\}. \tag{7.4.23}
$$

PROPOSITION 7.4.7   *At the second-best optimum, the marginal consumer $\tilde{\mu}$ is chosen to satisfy*

$$
[P(q(\mu)) - cq(\tilde{\mu})]\,f(\tilde{\mu}) = \int_0^{q(\tilde{\mu})} u_\mu(q',\tilde{\mu})\,dq' \left[(1 - \lambda(\tilde{\mu})) - \gamma(1 - F(\tilde{\mu})) \right]/\gamma.
$$

$$
\tag{7.4.24}
$$

The condition in proposition 7.4.7 equates the marginal effect on profits of increasing the market size to the marginal indirect value of the taste parameter for the marginal consumer, weighted by $[(1 - \lambda(\tilde{\mu})) - \gamma(1 - F(\tilde{\mu}))]/\gamma$.

Finally, note a result of Panzar and Postlewaite (1984) for a finite number of consumer types. They study nonlinear pricing in a contestable markets setting and show that when marginal costs are constant, and a nontrivial second-best optimal outlay schedule exists, there exists one such schedule that is consumer subsidy-free. Let (P_i, q_i), $i = 1, \ldots, n$, represent the payment schedule with n discrete consumer types. A *consumer subsidy-free* schedule satisfies

$$
\sum_{i \in S} P_i \le FC + c \sum_{i \in S} q_i,
$$

for all $S \subseteq N = \{1, \ldots, n\}$; that is, no group of consumers pays more than its stand-alone costs. Panzar and Postlewaite (1984) show that any zero-profit subsidy-free optimal tariff is sustainable as a market equilibrium.

This is an important generalization of the result that under free entry price competition, average cost prices are sustainable. However, they give an example with declining marginal costs that shows that sustainability may no longer hold, since in this case optimal outlay schedules are susceptible to entry by firms serving high-demand consumers. I return to discriminatory pricing in a contestable market setting in chapter 18.

Appendix

The proof of proposition 7.2.1 employs the well-known technique of Scarf (1973, theorem 8.5.5). Let u be a vector of utility levels u^i, $i \in N$. Then the second-best cooperative allocation game may be defined by (N, W), where for each $S \subset N$,

$$W_S = \left\{ u : u^i \leq U^i(q^i_l(p_l), x^i(p_l)), \quad i \in S \cap N_l, \quad l = 1, \ldots, m, \right.$$

$$\left. \sum_{l=1}^{m} p_l Q^S_l(p_l) \geq C\left(\sum_{l=1}^{m} Q^S_l(p_l) \right) \right\},$$

(1)

where $Q^S_l(p_l) = \sum_{i \in S \cap N} q^i_l(p_l, \omega^i)$. Scarf (1973) shows that a sufficient condition for a core to exist is that a game (N, W) be balanced. A collection $T = \{S_1, \ldots, S_t\}$ of subsets of N is a *balanced collection* if there are non-negative weights δ_S satisfying the equation $\sum_{S \in T, S \ni \{i\}} \delta_S = 1$ for each $i \in N$. The game (N, W) is *balanced* if for every balanced collection T,

$$\bigcap_{S \in T} \tilde{W}_S \subseteq W_N,$$

where $\tilde{W}_S$ is the set of all vectors $u = (u^1, \ldots, u^n)$ whose projection u^S is in W_S. The following proof is based on Scarf (1973).

Proof of Proposition 7.2.1   For ease of presentation, the proof is sketched for the case where each good is uniquely associated with a single consumer $i \in N$. Thus, the vector of total outputs is given by the allocation vector $q = (q^1, \ldots, q^n)$. Given independent demands and strict monotonicity of preferences, one can uniquely associate with each price vector p a vector of utility levels $u(p) = (V^1(p^1, \omega^1), \ldots, V^n(p^n, \omega^n))$. Thus, if $u \in \bigcap_{S \in T} \tilde{W}_S$, there is an associated price vector p such that $u(p) \in W_N$, $u(p) \geq u$, if p is a feasible price vector for N.

Let $q_S(p) \in \mathbb{R}^n_+$ be an output vector containing $q^i(p^i)$, $i \in S$, and zeros elsewhere. Let

$$A_p(S) \equiv C(q_S(p))/aq_S(p)$$

denote the generalized average cost for coalition $S \subseteq N$, $p > 0$.

Suppose that p is feasible for all $S \in T$ but not for N, where T is a balanced collection of coalitions,

$$\sum_{i \in N} p^i q^i(p^i) < C(q(p)).$$

Since p is feasible for all $S \in T$, it follows that

$$\sum_{i \in G} p^i q^i(p^i) \geq C(q_G(p))$$

for $G \in T$. Thus,

$$\sum_{i \in N \setminus G} p^i q^i(p^i) < C(q(p)) - C(q_G(p)).$$

Therefore, by generalized decreasing average costs,

$$C(q_G(p))/aq_G(p) \geq C(q_G(p) + q_{N \setminus G}(p))/a(q_G(p) + q_{N \setminus G}(p)).$$

Thus, combining the previous two equations yields

$$\sum_{i \in N \setminus G} p^i q^i(p) < A_p(G) aq_{N \setminus G}(p). \tag{2}$$

Partition T into $T_1 = \{S_1, \ldots, S_k\}$ and $T_2 = \{S_{k+1}, \ldots, S_t\}$ and assume (following Scarf, 1973, 8.5.6) that $\delta_{S_1} + \cdots + \delta_{S_k} = 1$. Define probabilities following Scarf's rule (1973, 8.5.11) such that G is selected at random from T_1 with probability δ_G, $G \in T_1$ and for each i not in G, S is selected at random from T_2. Thus, taking the expectation over the left-hand side of (2) yields

$$\sum_{S \in T_2} \delta_S \left(\sum_{i \in S} p^i q^i(p) \right) \geq \sum_{S \in T_2} \delta_S C(q_S(p))$$

$$= \sum_{S \in T_2} \delta_S aq_S(p) A_p(S)$$

by feasibility of p for $S \in T$ and the definition of $A_p(S)$. Applying the expectation to the right-hand side of (2), by independence of the choice of S, yields

$$\sum_{G \in T_1} \delta_G A_p(G) \sum_{S \in T_2} \delta_S aq_S(p).$$

Thus, letting $\gamma = \sum_{S \in T_2} \delta_S aq_S(p)$, one obtains normalized weighted sums,

$$\sum_{S \in T_2} (\delta_S aq_S(p)/\gamma) A_p(S) < \sum_{G \in T_1} \delta_G A_p(G).$$

Ordering the sets $S_j \in T$ such that $A_p(S_1) \leq A_p(S_2) \leq \cdots \leq A_p(S_t)$ yields a contradiction. QED

Proof of Proposition 7.4.6 From the first-order condition (7.4.20),

$$\partial q/\partial\mu = \frac{[-(1 + \gamma)u_\mu + \eta'(\mu)u_\mu + \eta u_{\mu\mu}]}{[(1 + \gamma)u_q - \eta u_{\mu q}]}. \tag{3}$$

Since $u_q < 0$, $u_{\mu q} \geq 0$, $u_{\mu\mu} < 0$, note that $\partial q/\partial\mu > 0$. From the consumer's decision problem, $\partial p/\partial q = u_q + u_\mu/(\partial q/\partial\mu)$. Substituting from (3) gives

$$\frac{\partial p}{\partial q} = \frac{[u_\mu(\eta' u_q - \eta u_{\mu q}) + \eta u_q u_{\mu\mu}]}{[-(1 + \gamma)u_\mu + \eta'(\mu)u_\mu + \eta u_{\mu\mu}]}. \tag{4}$$

The denominator in (4) is negative. By hypothesis, $(\eta' u_q - \eta u_{\mu q})$ is positive, so that $\partial p/\partial q < 0$. QED

Notes

1. It should be noted that the issue of whether peak load prices should be viewed as discriminatory was the subject of a debate in the literature. Steiner's (1957, 1958) view that peak load pricing was discriminatory was contested by Hirschleifer (1958), Ekelund and Hulett (1973), and Demsetz (1973). This controversy is discussed in Phlips (1983). The Hirschleifer (1958) argument that peak prices reflect the marginal cost of increased capacity is answered by Steiner (1958), who questions the characterization of marginal cost. This issue is certainly moot in the case of second-best prices.

2. Eckel (1985) gives conditions under which second-best prices are less than monopoly prices when there is price discrimination across customer classes.

3. Optimal two-part tariffs for regulated monopolies have been studied by Feldstein (1972b), Ng and Weisser (1974), Littlechild (1975b), Mitchell (1978), and others. Profit-maximizing two-part tariffs are analyzed in Gabor (1955) and Schmalensee (1981a). Profit-maximizing two-part tariffs with multiple goods under monopoly and duopoly market structures are considered in Calem and Spulber (1984).

4. Then the sign of the mark up $p^* - C'(Q^*)$ depends on the difference between average output and the weighted average of purchases, $[Q^*/n - \sum_{i \in N} \lambda^i V_\omega^i q^{i*}/\sum_{i \in N} \lambda^i V_\omega^i]$, where $n = \sum_{i \in N} \delta_{q^{i*}}^i$ is the number of buyers.

5. The use of "two-tier" pricing of club facilities is studied by Scotchmer (1985a,b). Scotchmer's analysis emphasizes congestion externalities and the observed number of clubs in a free entry market equilibrium.

6. In fact, Willig (1978, p. 65) shows that "any nonlinear outlay schedule can be strongly Pareto dominated if the marginal price it offers at the largest purchase does not equal marginal cost."

7. Schmalensee (1981b) derives similar formulas in a setting without income distribution effects in the welfare measure.

8. Suppose, for example, that the consumer has Cobb-Douglas utility $U = q^{\alpha_1} x^{\alpha_2}$. Then the indirect utility function equals $V = p^{-\alpha_1} A (\omega - E)^{\alpha_1 + \alpha_2}$, where $A = (\alpha_1)^{\alpha_1} (\alpha_2)^{\alpha_2} (\alpha_1 + \alpha_2)^{-(\alpha_1 + \alpha_2)}$. If $\omega^0 \in (\underline{\omega}, 1)$, then $\omega^0 = E$ and $V(p, E, \omega^0) = 0$. In general, if output q is essential, $U(0, x) = 0$, then, if $E \in (\underline{\omega}, 1)$, $V(p, E, \omega^0) = 0$. Note that $n_p = 0$ and $q^0 = 0$ in this case.

9. The indeterminacy of the sign of the relative mark up is partly due to the partial equilibrium setting. More specific results are obtained in a similar setting by Ng and Weisser (1974) in which consumers supply a labor input. However, the demand side in their framework is not fully specified.

10. First note that since consumer purchases are increasing in income, $q(p, E, \omega) > q^0$. Further, note that

$$[Q_p - (n_p/n_E)Q_E] = \int_{\omega_0}^{1} (q_p + q^0 q_\omega) \, dF(\omega)$$

by (7.3.4) and (7.3.5), $q_0 = (n_p/n_E)$ and $q_\omega = -q_E$. But $q_p + q^0 q_\omega < q_p + q q_\omega < 0$ for all $\omega > \omega^0$, since the pure substitution effect is negative. So, $[-Q_p + (n_p/n_E)Q_E] > 0$.

11. By the definition of $\tilde{\omega}$, we have $\partial \tilde{\omega}/\partial p^1 = -V_p(p^1, \tilde{\omega})/(V_\omega(p^1, \tilde{\omega}) - V_\omega(c, \tilde{\omega} - E))$, $\partial \tilde{\omega}/\partial E = -V_\omega(c, \tilde{\omega} - E)/(V_\omega(p^1, \tilde{\omega}) - V_\omega(c, \tilde{\omega} - E))$.

12. The nonlinear pricing model derives in large part from the optimal taxation framework of Mirrlees (1971). Principal early references include Spence (1977c), Willig (1978), Stiglitz (1977a), Mussa and Rosen (1978), and Roberts (1979). For applications of nonlinear pricing in a spatial model see Spulber (1981b, 1984a), and for a monopoly with advertising see Spulber (1984b). Extensions of the monopoly pricing problem appear in Guesnerie and Laffont (1984), Maskin and Riley (1984), and Matthews and Moore (1984). A weighted sum of consumer's surplus and profits is used in an analysis of socially optimal nonlinear pricing by Spence (1980).

13. On the revelation principle, see Myerson (1979), Dasgupta, Hammond, and Maskin (1979), Gibbard (1973), and Harris and Townsend (1981).

8 Optimal Pricing

The recommendation that the output of regulated firms be priced at long-run marginal costs has been stressed by regulation economists. If marginal cost prices cover costs, then this recommendation may be implemented. However, if the firm's technology exhibits increasing returns to scale at its long-run output level, then marginal cost pricing entails losses that must be made up by direct transfers from consumers to the firm or by indirect transfers in the form of government subsidies. The preceding chapters have emphasized alternative pricing policies designed to allocate costs in the absence of subsidies. In particular, I have examined various cost-based pricing rules, second-best pricing, and second-best price discrimination. In this chapter, I examine the optimal set of interpersonal transfers and subsidies to the firm that support the optimal allocation of resources.

The optimal allocation of resources need not entail marginal cost pricing when economies of scale are present. These issues are briefly discussed in section 8.1. In section 8.2, the optimal set of uniform prices and personalized transfers that support a core allocation are examined. If marginal cost pricing is optimal, then the uniform prices that support the core allocation will be marginal cost prices.

In section 8.3, a cooperative game with transferable utility is examined for a large market with a finite number of consumer classes. A particular allocation of resources is studied: the Aumann-Shapley value allocation. The explicit characterization of the Aumann-Shapley value allocation is used to identify the personalized net transfers that must be made, given that marginal cost pricing is used. In section 8.4 it is shown that given cost complementarities in production and demand complementarities, the Aumann-Shapley value is in the core. Thus, the value is useful in obtaining an explicit characterization of the net transfers that support a particular core allocation. Given the presence of consumer classes for regulated industries in large markets, the analysis allows approximation of the optimal fixed fees that support marginal cost pricing.

8.1 Marginal Cost Pricing

Assertion of the optimality of marginal cost pricing has a long history in economics.[1] The marginal cost-pricing principle is often associated with the classic work of Dupuit (1969) and Hotelling (1938);[2] see Samuelson (1960). Kahn (1970, vol. 1), in particular, argues strongly for the use of marginal cost pricing in single or multiproduct regulated industries as the "central policy prescription of microeconomics."[3] The marginal cost price generally refers to the *market-clearing* marginal cost price.[4] The marginal cost price signals to consumers the costs of producing the last unit of the good. The price in turn signals to competitive producers the marginal benefits of the good to consumers. The marginal cost price is thus distinct from strictly cost-based pricing rules.

The traditional problem of pricing a facility such as a bridge can be illustrated with a simple example. The bridge should be built if benefits exceed costs. Marginal cost pricing and recovery of fixed costs through fixed fees or government subsidies guarantee that the correct decision will be made regarding whether or not to build the bridge. Let market demand for the services of the bridge be linear, $P(Q) = a - bQ$. The costs of constructing the bridge are F and the marginal costs of operating the bridge are c. The optimal usage of the bridge is $Q = (a - c)/b$, which occurs at the marginal cost price. The bridge should be built if consumer surplus, $(a - c)^2/2b$, exceeds fixed costs F. On the other hand, if we require the revenues of the bridge to cover its total costs, the bridge may not be built with linear pricing. Suppose that $(a - c)^2/2b > F > (a - c)^2/4b$. Then, even though building the bridge is warranted, average costs exceed demand for all outputs, or equivalently, fixed costs exceed operating profits at any price. It is apparent that marginal cost pricing is desirable to the extent that lump sum transfers from consumers to the firm can be implemented.

It is useful to distinguish between marginal and incremental costs. Given nonincreasing marginal cost, the incremental cost of producing a good exceeds the marginal cost times the output of the good, $IC^l(Q) \geq C_l(Q)Q_l$. More generally, given cost complementarities, the incremental cost of producing a set of goods S jointly with a set of goods T exceeds the marginal costs of producing the set S, $IC^S(Q_{S \cup T}) \geq \sum_{l \in T} C_l(Q_{S \cup T})Q_l$. Thus, requiring prices to exceed incremental cost is a more stringent standard than coverage of marginal cost in the presence of cost complementarities and diminishing marginal cost.

Kahn (1970) stresses that short run marginal cost (SRMC) is the proper basis for efficient pricing of public utility services and that any fixed costs of capacity (depreciation, property, income taxes, and return on investment) should not be reflected in price. Kahn provides a thorough discussion of the many practical difficulties of implementing SRMC pricing in a regulated industry. Not least of these is the measurement of marginal costs. When SRMC is less than average total costs over the range of outputs relevant to the market, Kahn stresses that this provides a justification for perfect price discrimination to cover costs. The distinction between short- and long-run marginal costs illustrates the problem of commitment in regulated industries. After capacity costs have been incurred, the static optimum requires setting the price equal to the SRMC. This rule will affect the regulated firm's incentives to invest in capacity, however. Given risk due to demand or input price fluctuations, pursuit of static efficiency can lead to underinvestment. Regulators cannot expect to pursue static efficiency without compensating the regulated firm for investment.

The general problem of selecting optimal prices is now considered for a market with multiple consumers. In chapter 5, the second-best pricing problem with interconsumer transfers yielded the following expression for optimal markups:

$$p_l^* - C_l(Q^*) = ((\sigma - \gamma)/\gamma) \sum_{k=1}^{m} \bar{h}_{lk} Q_k^*, \qquad l = 1, \ldots, m, \qquad (8.1.1)$$

where $\bar{h}_{lk}$ is a term in the inverse of the matrix H of Slutsky substitution terms. Given that the problem has a well-defined solution, a necessary condition for marginal cost pricing to be optimal is for the shadow price on the consumers' net transfer constraint σ to equal the shadow price on the firm's profit constraint γ. This will not occur in general unless consumers subsidize the firm and the net transfers cover the firm's losses,

$$\sum_{i \in N} t^i = pQ(p) - C(Q(p)). \qquad (8.1.2)$$

Given marginal cost pricing, it is difficult to specify the firm's supply decision when its technology exhibits increasing returns to scale. Consider a simple one consumer economy with m outputs Q, a single input X (say, labor), and an initial endowment ω. The production relation is $G(Q, X) = 0$, which is satisfied for $X = C(Q)$. Then

$$U_l(Q, \omega - X)/U_\omega(Q, \omega - X) = -G_l(Q, X)/G_X(Q, X) = C_l(Q). \qquad (8.1.3)$$

Note that pricing the goods Q at marginal cost does not imply that optimal outputs maximize profits $pQ - C(Q)$. If the isocost line is convex, this may be a *minimum* for the firm. In general, one cannot even expect that marginal cost prices will support the cost function at minimum profits.

Pareto optimality in a general equilibrium framework is defined by the Pareto equalities given sufficiently smooth preferences and technology. The goal of marginal pricing is equality of marginal rates of technical substitution for inputs across firms and equality of marginal rates of transformation in production with marginal rates of substitution in consumption for produced outputs. As pointed out in an important discussion by de V. Graff (1967), a great number of assumptions are needed to establish the optimality of the marginal cost pricing rule,[5] including absence of uncertainty, externalities, and distortionary government taxes and regulations. In the presence of incomplete or asymmetric information, marginal cost pricing may also fail to be optimal. Regulation in the presence of incomplete or asymmetric information will be analyzed in later chapters.

The presence of technological nonconvexities, an important aspect of regulated industries, raises additional issues beyond the existence of a market equilibrium. The regulatory authority faces the additional problem that there may not exist a marginal cost-pricing equilibrium that is Pareto efficient.[6] Brown and Heal (1979) show that in the presence of increasing returns to scale it is no longer possible to judge distributions of endowments strictly on the basis of equity since attaining the welfare frontier may require transfers of initial endowments. Thus, existence of a Pareto efficient marginal cost-pricing equilibrium may be determined by the distribution of initial endowments. For an analysis of these issues within a model of marginal cost pricing combined with fixed fees, see Brown and Heal (1980).

When lump sum redistributions of wealth are not feasible, de V. Graff (1967, p. 155) suggests that "the simplest way of securing the distribution of wealth we desire is *through the price system*" (emphasis in original). de V. Graff (1967, p. 155) recommends that consideration be given to the "just price": "I suggest that the only price a public enterprise or nationalized industry can be expected to set is what we may well call a *just price—a price which is set with some regard for its effect on the distribution of wealth* as well as for its effect on the allocation of resources." It is not clear what the "just price" really means beyond value judgments about "fairness" on the part of legislators or regulatory agencies. As has been emphasized, rate hearings and regulatory bargaining reflect consideration of the effects of regulated prices on the distribution of income. Economists generally avoid recommendation of pricing strategies to achieve a redistribution of income or wealth. The efficiency of the price system as an allocative mechanism need not be abandoned simply because marginal cost pricing equilibria do not exist in the presence of increasing returns to scale. The next section examines allocation by a price system when personalized tariffs are set optimally.

8.2 Optimal Two-Part Pricing and the Core

Without basing the pricing mechanism on the marginal equivalences generally associated with the Pareto optimum, it is still possible to consider optimal pricing. Let the optimal pricing mechanism be a system of prices and personalized tariffs that support core allocations. The core solution to cooperative games is an appealing optimality concept for reasons given in preceding chapters—particularly the absence of subsidies across consumers. I abandon the requirement that the price mechanism decentralize firm decision making, but retain the requirement that demand be rationed by price.[7] If personalized tariffs are not a feasible alternative, then the regulator must fall back on a second-best pricing mechanism.

Consider the core of a cooperative game of cost sharing by consumers with nontransferable utility. An allocation (q, x) is a vector of outputs $q^i \in \mathbb{R}_+^m$, and money $x^i \in \mathbb{R}_+$, $i = 1, \dots, n$. Consumers have positive initial endowments of money ω^i, $i = 1, \dots, n$. An allocation (q, x) is said to be feasible for a set of consumers $S \subseteq N$ if

$$\sum_{i \in S} (\omega^i - x^i) \geq C\left(\sum_{i \in S} q^i\right).$$

An allocation (q^*, x^*) is in the core of the cost-sharing game if it is feasible and there does not exist a group of consumers $S \subseteq N$, $S \neq \emptyset$, and an allocation (q', m') that is feasible for S such that

$$U^i(q^{i\prime}, x^{i\prime}) \geq U^i(Q^{i*}, x^{i*})$$

for all $i \in S$, strictly for some i. Scarf (1973) shows existence of a core for this game and his result is restated by Sharkey (1979) for multiple outputs.

THEOREM (Scarf) *Given generalized decreasing average costs and C nonnegative and nondecreasing and given U^i monotonic and finite valued, the core is nonempty.*

Given existence of a core, it is then of interest to find a price mechanism that supports core allocations.

A personalized two-part price mechanism (p, E) denotes a common per unit price $p \in \mathbb{R}_+^m$ and a vector of personalized fixed fees $(E^1, \dots, E^n)$.

Definition 8.2.1 A personalized two-part price mechanism (p, E) *supports* an allocation (q, x) if (a) (q^i, x^i) maximizes U^i subject to $pq^i + E^i + x^i = \omega^i$. The consumer takes E^i as a given before choosing q^i. (b) Profits (losses) are fully allocated, $\sum_{i \in N} E^i = \Pi$, where

$$\Pi = p \sum_{i \in N} q^i - C\left(\sum_{i \in N} q^i\right). \tag{8.2.1}$$

By a relatively straightforward application of the basic efficiency theorem of welfare economics (see Arrow and Hahn, 1971, theorem 4.4, p. 194), it can be shown that all individually rational Pareto optimal allocations are supported by a corresponding personalized two-part pricing arrangement. Thus, the following assertion holds.

PROPOSITION 8.2.1 *If (q^*, x^*) is in the core, it is supported by a corresponding two-part pricing arrangement (p^*, E^*).*

The proof is given in the appendix. This result makes explicit the information structure that is needed to achieve a core allocation at least on the demand side. It must be emphasized that if marginal cost pricing is optimal, the prices p^* will be equal to marginal cost.

An important implication of the definitions of the core and of the two-part price mechanism is that no group of consumers subsidizes another, that is,

$$\sum_{i \in S} (p^* q^{i*} + E^{i*}) \le C\left(\sum_{i \in S} q^{i*}\right).$$

Otherwise, if revenues covered stand-alone costs, the consumers in coalition S could produce on their own and improve their welfare by lowering all of the fixed payments below E^{i*}, $i \in S$. Alternatively, given (8.2.1), the payments of a coalition cannot be less than its incremental cost,

$$\sum_{i \in N-S} \left(p^* q^{i*} + E^{i*}\right) \ge C\left(\sum_{i \in N} q^{i*}\right) - C\left(\sum_{i \in S} q^{i*}\right).$$

Again, the principle of anonymous equity (absence of cross-subsidy between groups of consumers) is illustrated by the core.

8.3 Optimal Pricing in Large Markets

8.3.1 The Cooperative Game

Optimal pricing may be appropriate for regulated firms operating in large markets that identify broad customer classes (e.g., industrial, commercial, and residential customers). Fixed fees may apply uniformly to customers within a particular class. If customers' demand characteristics are similar within a class, the two-part pricing approach may be *approximately* optimal. The discriminatory or personalized fixed fee may not impose such high information costs if there are a relatively small number of customer classes. This section gives an example of optimal pricing where strong assumptions are used to guarantee existence of a marginal cost-pricing equilibrium.

This section studies optimal pricing by means of a transferable utility cooperative game.[8] A particular solution, the Aumann and Shapley (1974) value allocation, is considered and shown to be in the core of the transferable utility benefit game using a technique developed by Mirman, Tauman, and Zang (1983a). The Aumann-Shapley value is an allocation of total net benefits across consumers. I consider an economy with a finite number of consumer types, but many consumers of each type. The Aumann-Shapley value restricts attention to all subgroups of consumers having the same proportions of each type of consumer as the general population. Each consumer then receives an *average* of his *marginal contribution* to each subgroup of consumers.

The Aumann-Shapley value allocation is used to calculate explicitly the regulated firm's optimal pricing policy. The pricing policy that we derive has an interesting economic interpretation based on the bargaining power of coalitions of consumers. In particular, if optimal outputs are rationed by the firm, then the optimal prices for each type of consumer are *average marginal cost* prices. These prices equal a weighted average of marginal costs in all subcoalitions (with the same composition as the grand coalition). The average marginal cost prices are then used to calculate discriminatory fixed charges. Given these charges, a marginal cost pricing equilibrium is in the core.

Suppose that there are n consumer types in the regulated market. Let I represent the set of consumers and let Ω represent the set of all consumer coalitions $S \subseteq I$. There is a continuum of consumers of each type. Let $\mu(S) = (\mu^1(S), \mu^2(S), \ldots, \mu^n(S))$ represent the number of consumers of each type in the coalition S. The *total* number of all types of consumers is given by the vector $\mu(I) = \bar{\mu} = (\bar{\mu}^1, \bar{\mu}^2, \ldots, \bar{\mu}^n)$. Any coalition may be conveniently represented by its composition μ.

Let $U^i(q^i)$ represent type i's utility in money terms.[9] Let U^i be twice continuously differentiable, increasing, and concave, and let $U^i_I(q^i) \equiv$

$\partial U^i(q^i)/\partial q^i_l$, $l = 1, \ldots, m$, and $U^i(0) = 0$ for all $i = 1, \ldots, n$. Let $U^i_{ll}(q^i) < 0$ for all $l = 1, \ldots, m$.

The technology of the regulated firm $C(\cdot)$ is assumed to be freely available to any group of consumers. Define a cooperative net benefit game (N, v), where $N = \{1, \ldots, n\}$ is the set of players and a coalition of consumers $S \in \Omega$ chooses goods $\{q^i\}$ to maximize consumer surplus,[10]

$$v(S) = \max_{\{q^i\}} \left[\sum_{i=1}^{n} \mu^i(S) U^i(q^i) - C\left(\sum_{i=1}^{n} \mu^i(S) q^i \right) \right]. \tag{8.3.1}$$

This represents the maximum net benefits available to a coalition of consumers S and is referred to as the *characteristic function* of the game. Consumers face the problem of allocating net surplus. I shall study the Aumann and Shapley (1974) value allocation as well as the core for this game.

A relatively strong assumption is made to assure that the maximum problem (8.3.1) is well defined. In particular, define W by

$$W(q, \mu) = \sum_{i=1}^{n} \mu^i U^i(q^i) - C\left(\sum_{i=1}^{n} \mu^i q^i \right) \tag{8.3.2}$$

for $q^i \in \mathbb{R}^m_+$, $\mu \in \mathbb{R}^n_+$, and q an $n \cdot m$ vector of the consumption vectors q^i, for each type $i \in N$. Then assume that

$$v^T \nabla_{qq} W(q, \mu) v < 0 \tag{8.3.3}$$

for all $v \in \mathbb{R}^{n \cdot m}$, $v \neq 0$, for all $\mu = \mu(S)$, $S \in \Omega$. This condition implies that $W(q, \mu)$ is *strictly concave* in q (but the converse does not hold). It must be emphasized that my goal is not to examine existence of a nonempty core in an increasing returns economy. This has been considered elsewhere (see Sharkey, 1979). Rather, I wish to characterize the Aumann-Shapley value allocation given increasing returns. Given additional assumptions, condition (8.3.3) will be shown to be a sufficient condition for the Aumann-Shapley value to be in the core.

Condition (8.3.3) guarantees existence of a unique maximum of $W(\cdot, \mu)$ at $\tilde{q}^i = q^i(\mu)$, $i = 1, \ldots, n$, where $\nabla_q W(\tilde{q}, \mu) = 0$. Further, $q^i(\mu)$ is continuously differentiable by the implicit function theorem. Now substitute the optimal output vectors for a coalition of composition μ, $q(\mu)$, back into W to obtain the net benefits for coalition μ,

$$B(\mu) = W(q(\mu), \mu) = \sum_{i=1}^{n} \mu^i U^i(q^i(\mu)) - C\left(\sum_{i=1}^{n} \mu^i q^i(\mu) \right). \tag{8.3.4}$$

Note that the characteristic function for any coalition S is given by $v(S) = B(\mu(S))$ for all $S \in \Omega$.

8.3.2 The Aumann-Shapley Value

The marginal contribution of an individual of type i to a coalition of composition μ is simply the marginal effect of increasing the number of type i consumers on the coalition's net benefits. Define the *marginal contribution of a type i consumer* by $B_i(\mu) \equiv \partial B(\mu)/\partial \mu^i$. To compute the marginal contribution, I state the first-order conditions for the vector of output allocations $q(\mu) = (q^1(\mu), \ldots, q^n(\mu))$ that solves the maximization problem in (8.3.1) for any coalition $\mu = \mu(S)$,

$$U_l^i(q^i) = C_l\left(\sum_{j=1}^{n} \mu^j(S) q^j \right), \qquad l = 1, \ldots, m, \quad i = 1, \ldots, n. \tag{8.3.5}$$

Let $q^{i*} = q^i(\mu(I))$ be the solution to (8.3.5) for the grand coalition.

Applying (8.3.5) and the envelope theorem, the marginal net benefit to the coalition due to additional consumers of type i is given by

$$B_i(\mu) = U^i(q^i) - \sum_{l=1}^{m} C_l\left(\sum_{j=1}^{n} \mu^j q^j \right) q_l^i, \tag{8.3.6}$$

where $q^i = q^i(\mu)$ for a coalition of composition μ. Thus, the marginal value of an additional member of type i is just *consumption benefits net of marginal cost of goods consumed.*

Computation of the Aumann-Shapley value may be obtained from the diagonal formula of Aumann and Shapley (1974, 3.1, 3.2, p. 23). The total allocation received by any subset of the grand coalition $S \in \Omega$ is given by the mapping $\phi(B \circ \mu)$,

$$\phi(B \circ \mu)(S) = \sum_{i=1}^{n} \mu^i(S) \int_0^1 B_i(t\mu(I)) \, dt. \tag{8.3.7}$$

An individual of type i in the grand coalition receives

$$\phi(B \circ \mu)(ds) = \mu^i(ds) \int_0^1 B_i(t\mu(I)) \, dt. \tag{8.3.8}$$

Clearly, a coalition represented by $t\bar{\mu}$, $0 \leq t \leq 1$, has the same proportional composition as the coalition of the whole. The range of the scalar t traces the "diagonal" line between 0 and $(\bar{\mu}^1, \ldots, \bar{\mu}^n)$. Integrating B_i over t averages the marginal contributions of type i.

To characterize the Aumann-Shapley value, substitute for the marginal net benefit $B_i(t\bar{\mu})$. Then, within the grand coalition, any subgroup S receives benefits equal to

$$\phi(B \circ \mu)(S) = \sum_{i=1}^{n} \mu^i(S) \int_0^1 \left[U^i(q^i(t\bar{\mu})) \right.$$

$$\left. - \sum_{l=1}^{m} C_l \left(\sum_{j=1}^{n} t\bar{\mu}^j q^j(t\bar{\mu}) \right) q_l^i(t\bar{\mu}) \right] dt, \qquad (8.3.9)$$

where $\bar{\mu} = \mu(I)$ and where $q^i(t\bar{\mu})$ solves

$$U_l^i(q^i) = C_l \left(t \sum_{j=1}^{n} \bar{\mu}^j q^j \right), \qquad l = 1, \ldots, m, \quad i = 1, \ldots, n. \qquad (8.3.10)$$

The allocation for an individual ds in S^i, that is, of type i, is obtained from (8.3.9),

$$\phi(B \circ \mu)(ds) = \mu^i(ds) \int_0^1 \left[U^i(q^i(t\bar{\mu})) \right.$$

$$\left. - \sum_{l=1}^{m} C_l \left(\sum_{j=1}^{n} t\bar{\mu}^j q^j(t\bar{\mu}) \right) q_l^i(t\bar{\mu}) \right] dt. \qquad (8.3.11)$$

Thus, an individual simply receives an "average" of his consumption benefits net of the marginal cost of output times his consumption, which represents his contribution to the subcoalitions.

8.3.3   Average Marginal Cost Prices

Suppose that the optimal quantities for the grand coalition $q^{i*} = q^i(\bar{\mu})$, $\bar{\mu} = \mu(I)$, are rationed or directly distributed to individual consumers. This section shows that there are per unit charges for the goods such that the total allocation of benefits given by the Aumann-Shapley imputation is attained. These per unit charges are referred to as *average marginal cost prices* (AMC). These prices allocate total costs among consumers and take into account the side payments implicit in the Aumann-Shapley allocation. The prices are discriminatory and therefore may involve subsidies across goods and between consumer types. Let $y^{i*} = \int_0^1 B_i(t\bar{\mu}) \, dt$, $\bar{\mu} = \mu(I)$, $i = 1, \ldots, n$, represent the Aumann-Shapley imputation. Then the prices that yield the Aumann-Shapley imputation satisfy

$$y^{i*} = U^i(q^{i*}) - \rho^{i*} q^{i*}. \qquad (8.3.12)$$

PROPOSITION 8.3.1   *The prices that yield the Aumann-Shapley imputation are given by*

$$\rho_l^{i*} = \int_0^1 C_l\left(\sum_{j=1}^n t\bar{\mu}^j q^j(t\bar{\mu})\right) \xi_l^i(t)\, dt, \tag{8.3.13}$$

where the $\xi_l^i(t)$ are normalized weights.

The proof is given in the appendix.

Therefore, the Aumann-Shapley allocation is attained by discriminatory prices ρ_l^{i*} that are explicitly calculated from the cost function given the weights ξ_l^i. The prices ρ_l^{i*} have an interesting economic interpretation. In any subcoalition $t\bar{\mu}$, the consumer's marginal cost prices would be given by $C_l(\sum_{j\in N} tq^j(t\bar{\mu})\bar{\mu}^j)$. Thus, the price ρ_l^{i*} is a *weighted average* of the marginal cost price that the consumer would pay in any smaller coalition (of the same composition). This is related to the game theory interpretation of the Aumann-Shapley value as an *average* of the individual's marginal contributions to all smaller coalitions.

Clearly, since $C(0) = 0$, the prices ρ_l^{i*} allocate the total costs,

$$\sum_{l=1}^m \sum_{i=1}^n \bar{\mu}^i \rho_l^{i*} q_l^{i*} = C\left(\sum_{i=1}^n \bar{\mu}^i q^{i*}\right). \tag{8.3.14}$$

The weights ξ_l^i may be rewritten as $\xi_l^i(t) = (1 + \eta_l^i(t))(q_l^i(t\bar{\mu})/q_l^{i*})$, where $\eta_l^i(t)$ represents the elasticity of demand $q_l^i(t\bar{\mu})$ with respect to t evaluated at $t\bar{\mu}$, $\eta_l^i(t) = td \ln q_l^i(t\bar{\mu})/dt$. Thus, the marginal cost terms C_l are weighted by individual demand elasticities.

Suppose that there is only one type of consumer and the total cost function is additively separable, $C = \sum_{l=1}^m C^l(q_l)$. Then the price of good l equals the *average cost* of good l,

$$\rho_l = \int_0^1 C^{l'}(t\bar{\mu}q(t\bar{\mu}))\left[(q_l(t\bar{\mu})/q_l^*) + (t\bar{\mu}/q_l^*)(dq_l(t\bar{\mu})/d\mu)\right] dt.$$

After integration, $\rho_l = C^l(q_l^*)/q_l^*$.

8.3.4   Marginal Cost Prices

Since the outputs q^{i*} maximize welfare, *the only demand compatible prices are marginal cost prices*. However, if there are increasing returns to scale, marginal cost prices do not cover total costs. There are two ways for the

firm to cover its losses at a marginal cost-pricing equilibrium. One way is
to assign a discriminatory fixed fee to each class of consumers. The other
way is to assign "profit shares" to each class of consumers. These may be
explicitly calculated using the Aumann-Shapley value and the average
marginal cost prices ρ_l^{i*}.

The firm's profit (loss) with marginal cost pricing is given by

$$\pi = \sum_{l=1}^{m} c_l \sum_{i=1}^{n} \bar{\mu}^i q_l^{i*} - C\left(\sum_{i=1}^{n} \bar{\mu}^i q^{i*} \right), \tag{8.3.15}$$

where $c_l = C_l(\sum_{i=1}^{n} \bar{\mu}^i q^{i*})$. This can be allocated using personalized fixed
fees $E_l^{i*} = (\rho_l^{i*} - c_l)q_l^{i*}$,

$$E_l^{i*} = \left[\int_0^1 C_l\left(\sum_{j=1}^{n} t\bar{\mu}^j q^{j*} \right) \xi_l^i(t)\, dt - c_l \right] q_l^{i*}, \tag{8.3.16}$$

where $q^j = q^j(t\bar{\mu})$. Clearly, $\sum_{l=1}^{m} \sum_{i=1}^{n} E_l^{i*} = \pi$.

Alternatively, consider the allocation of profit using profit shares and
marginal cost pricing. If profits equal zero under marginal cost pricing,
the profit share is not well-defined, as in the case of C homogeneous of
degree one. If profits are nonzero, the profit shares β^{i*} are given by
$\beta^{i*} = -\sum_{l=1}^{m} E_l^{i*}/\pi$, $i = 1, \ldots, n$. The preceding discussion is summarized
as a corollary to proposition 8.3.1.

COROLLARY 8.3.1   *A market equilibrium with marginal cost pricing coincides
with the Aumann-Shapley value allocation given either*

i. *fixed fees* E_l^{i*}, $i = 1, \ldots, n$, $l = 1, \ldots, m$,

ii. *if* $\pi \neq 0$, *profit shares* β^{i*}, $i = 1, \ldots, n$.

The value allocation is now compared to the competitive allocation for
the case of constant returns to scale. Let C be homogeneous of degree one.
This implies that marginal costs are homogeneous of degree zero. Then the
first-order conditions (8.3.10) imply that outputs $q^i(\mu)$ are homogeneous of
degree zero as well. Then, from equation (8.3.13), prices ρ_l^{i*} equal marginal
costs C_l for all $i = 1, \ldots, n$, $l = 1, \ldots, m$. This yields an additional equivalence
result (see Aumann, 1975; Mas-Colell, 1977; Hildenbrand, 1980), but one
based on the cost function. See Baumol, Panzar, and Willig (1982, pp. 52–
57) for the relations between attributes of multiproduct cost functions and
of the underlying technology set.

PROPOSITION 8.3.2 *Given constant returns to scale, the Aumann-Shapley value allocation coincides with the competitive equilibrium.*

Note that given $C_{lk} \leq 0$ for all l, k, homogeneity of degree one implies that C is linear and additively separable. Then the competitive allocation is in the core. However, proposition 8.3.2 allows more general cost functions such as the CES form, $C(Q) = (\sum_{l=1}^{m} Q_l^{\alpha})^{1/\alpha}$, where $C_{lk}(Q) \gtreqless 0$ for $l \neq k$ and $C_{ll}(Q) \lesseqgtr 0$ as $\alpha \lesseqgtr 1$. Also, proposition 8.3.2 holds for the Cobb-Douglas form $C(Q) = \prod_{l=1}^{m} Q_l^{\beta_l}$, $\sum_{l=1}^{m} \beta_l = 1$, $0 < \beta_l < 1$, where $C_{lk}(Q) > 0$ for $l \neq k$ and $C_{ll} < 0$.

8.4 The Value Allocation and the Core

The core of the benefit game is defined in the standard way. An imputation vector $y = (y^1, \ldots, y^n)$ is in the *core* of the benefit allocation game (8.3.1) if it satisfies

$$\mu(I)y = v(I), \quad \mu(S)y \geq v(S), \qquad \text{for all coalitions } S \in \Omega.$$

All net benefits are distributed and each coalition receives at least what it can obtain on its own.

Assume that the goods satisfy *complementarity in demand*:[11]

$$U^i(x + z) - U^i(x) \leq U^i(x + y + z) - U^i(x + y) \tag{8.4.1}$$

for all i and $x, y, z \geq 0$ such that $\sum_{l=1}^{m} y_l z_l$. As a preliminary result, the effect of coalition size on the optimal outputs is considered. The proof employs a result from Mirman, Tauman, and Zang (1983a).

PROPOSITION 8.4.1 *Given complementarity in demand for all goods and all consumers, (8.4.1), and given cost complementarity for all goods in production, $q^i(\mu)$ is increasing in the size of the coalition μ.*

The proof is given in the appendix. An immediate corollary of proposition 8.4.1 is that the elasticities ξ^i in proposition 8.3.1 are positive, so that *the average marginal cost prices are positive for all consumer types $i = 1, \ldots, n$.*

It is now shown that the Aumann-Shapley value is in the core of the benefit game given in (8.3.1). The proof uses the fact that there are a finite number of consumer types. The proof shows that the number of consumers of each type have *complementary* effects on total benefits, $B_{ij}(\mu) \geq 0$. This approach has been applied by Mirman and Tauman (1982) and Mirman,

Tauman, and Zang (1983a) in the context of cost and profit allocation within the firm. Note also that the proof requires the sufficient condition (8.3.3) for an interior maximum to hold.

PROPOSITION 8.4.2   *Given complementarity in demand for all goods and all consumers, (8.4.1), and given cost complementarity of all goods in production, the Aumann-Shapley value allocation is in the core.*

Proof   As noted above, $v(I) = B(\mu(I))$. Differentiating $B_i(\mu)$ in (8.3.6) and applying the first-order conditions (8.3.5), for $i \neq j$,

$$B_{ij}(\mu) = -\sum_{k=1}^{m} \sum_{l=1}^{m} C_{lk} \left(\sum_{r=1}^{n} \mu^r q^r \right) q_l^i \left[\sum_{r=1}^{n} \mu^r \frac{\partial q_k^r}{\partial \mu^j} + q_k^j \right], \tag{8.4.2}$$

where $q^i = q^i(\mu)$, for all $i, j = 1, \ldots, n$. By cost complementarity, $C_{lk} \leq 0$ for $l, k = 1, \ldots, m$. By proposition 8.4.1, $\partial q_l^r / \partial \mu^j \geq 0$ for all $r, j = 1, \ldots, n$. Therefore, $B_{ij}(\mu) \geq 0$ for all $i, j = 1, \ldots, n$, which implies that $B_i(\mu)$ is monotonic in μ. Then, by the definition of the Aumann-Shapley value imputation, for any $S \in \Omega, S \neq \emptyset$,

$$\phi(B \circ \mu)(S) = \sum_{i=1}^{n} \mu^i(S) \int_0^1 B_i(t\mu(I)) \, dt$$

$$\geq \sum_{i=1}^{n} \mu^i(S) \int_0^1 B_i(t\mu(S)) \, dt$$

$$= B \circ \mu(S). \quad \text{QED}$$

Thus, the Aumann-Shapley value is in the core of the benefit allocation game. This is a useful result since the value gives an explicit characterization of the allocation that can be used to compute support prices.

   The analysis may be given the following interpretation. Suppose that a regulated utility operates in a large market with n customer classes. Let the firm price its output at marginal cost, $p_k^* = C_k(\sum_{i \in N} q^{i*})$. Then, for each customer class i, choose fixed charges E_i^{i*} as in (8.3.16). Then it follows that these fixed fees combined with marginal cost pricing support an allocation in the core of the cooperative game of net benefit allocation. This implies that no coalition of consumers will have incentive to drop off of the system and recontract with another firm.

   The necessary condition that no group of consumers may subsidize another and the assumption that $C_{lk} \leq 0$ for all l, k have a particularly interesting implication for the value of the fixed fees. Let $E^{i*} = \sum_{k=1}^{n} E_k^{i*}$

denote the total of the fixed fees paid by customer class i. Then

$$0 \leq E^{i*} \leq C\left(\sum_{i \in N} q^{i*}\right) - \sum_{k=1}^{m} C_k(q^{i*})q_k^{i*}.$$

This condition states that the total fixed fees (or subsidies to the firm) paid by a customer class cannot exceed the unattributed portion of production costs, where attributed costs are obtained by valuation of output at marginal cost.

Appendix

Proof of Proposition 8.2.1 Let (q^*, x^*) represent an allocation in the core. Let $Q = \sum_{i \in N} q^{i*}$ and $X = \sum_{i \in N} x^{i*}$ represent total outputs and the total amount of the money commodity. Consider now an exchange economy with total endowments equal to (Q, X) and with consumers $i \in N$ having preferences U^i. Then (q^*, x^*) represents a Pareto optimal allocation of (Q, X) for the exchange economy. Otherwise, one could construct a feasible allocation $(q^{i'}, x^{i'})$ such that $\sum_{i \in N} q^{i'} = Q$ and $\sum_{i \in N} x^{i'} = X$ with $U^i(q^{i'}, x^{i'}) > U^i(q^{i*}, x^{i*})$, which contradicts the definition of a Pareto optimal allocation.

Given the exchange economy with total endowments equal to $Y = (Q, X)$, let y_0^i, $i \in N$, represent initial endowments, where $\sum_{i \in N} y_0^i = Y$. Define the Pareto optimal allocation $y^{i*} = (q^{i*}, x^{i*})$. Then, by the basic efficiency theorem of welfare economics (see, for example Arrow and Hahn, 1971, theorem 4.4, p. 194) applied to a pure exchange economy, there exists a price vector $\bar{p} \in \mathbb{R}_+^{m+1}$ such that $\bar{p} > 0$, and an allocation of initial endowments y_0^i, $i \in N$, such that the Pareto efficient allocation y^{i*}, $i \in N$, is attained as a competitive equilibrium. Let I^i represent the value of the consumer's initial endowment,

$$I^i \equiv \bar{p} y_0^i.$$

Then y^{i*} maximizes U^i on the set $\{y^i : \bar{p} y^i \leq I^i\}$. By nonsatiation, $\bar{p} y^{i*} = I^i$.

By homogeneity of demand and Walras's law, it is possible to normalize the price vector $\bar{p}$ in such a way that $p_{m+1} = 1$ and $p^* \in \mathbb{R}_+^m$ is defined by $p_l^* = \bar{p}_l / \bar{p}_{m+1}$, $l = 1, \ldots, m$. Then, returning to the production economy, define transfers E^{i*} by

$$E^{i*} = I^i / \bar{p}_{m+1} - \omega^i, \qquad i \in N.$$

Thus, transfers fully allocate profits,

$$\sum_{i \in N} E^{i*} = \sum_{i \in N} (I^i/\bar{p}_{m+1} - \omega^i)$$

$$= \sum_{i \in N} p^* q^{i*} + \sum_{i \in N} (x^{i*} - \omega^i)$$

$$= \sum_{i \in N} p^* q^{i*} - C\left(\sum_{i \in N} q^{i*}\right),$$

since $\sum_{i \in N} (\omega^i - x^i) = C(\sum_{i \in N} q^i)$ for all Pareto optimal allocations (q^i, x^i). Thus, (q^{i*}, x^{i*}) maximizes U^i on the budget set given by the constraint

$$p^* q^i + x^i = \omega^i + E^{i*}$$

by individual rationality.   QED

Proof of Proposition 8.3.1   Integrate the marginal benefit equation (8.3.6) and add and subtract the term

$$\int_0^1 \sum_{l=1}^m U_l^i(q^i(t\mu)) \left(\sum_{j=1}^n (\partial q_l^i/\partial \mu^j)\mu^j t\right) dt.$$

Integrate by parts and use (8.3.10). Note that $q^i(0) = 0$ and $U^i(0) = 0$. Then

$$\int_0^1 B_i(t\bar{\mu}) \, dt = U^i(q^{i*}) - \int_0^1 \sum_{l=1}^m C_l \left(\sum_{j=1}^n tq^i(t\bar{\mu})\bar{\mu}^j\right)$$

$$\cdot \left(q_l^i(t\bar{\mu}) + t \sum_{j=1}^n (\partial q_l^i/\partial \mu_j)\bar{\mu}^j \, dt\right).$$

Rearranging terms, it follows that

$$\int_0^1 B_i(t\bar{\mu}) \, dt = U^i(q^{i*}) - \sum_{l=1}^m q_l^{i*} \int_0^1 C_l \left(\sum_{j=1}^n tq^j(t\bar{\mu})\bar{\mu}^j\right)$$

$$\cdot \left(\frac{q_l^i(t\bar{\mu})}{q_l^{i*}} + t \sum_{j=1}^n \frac{\partial q_l^i}{\partial \mu^j} \frac{\bar{\mu}^j}{q_l^{i*}}\right) dt.$$

Now, let ρ^{i*} be given by

$$\rho_l^{i*} = \int_0^1 C_l \left(\sum_{j=1}^n t\bar{\mu}^j q^j(t\bar{\mu})\right) \xi_l^i(t) \, dt,$$

where

$$\xi_l^i(t) \equiv \xi_l^i(t, \bar{\mu}, q^{i*}) = \left(\frac{q_l^i}{q_l^{i*}} + t \sum_{j=1}^n \frac{\partial q_l^i}{\partial \mu^j} \frac{\bar{\mu}^j}{q_l^{i*}}\right)$$

and $q_l^i = q_l^i(t\bar{\mu})$. Note that the weights $\xi_l^i(t)$ are normalized, $\int_0^1 \xi_l^i(t) = 1$.

QED

Proof of Proposition 8.4.1   From the definition of W, the first-order condition $\nabla_{\tilde{q}} W(\tilde{q}, \mu) = 0$ and the envelope theorem,

$$[\nabla_\mu \tilde{q}(\mu)] = -[\nabla_{\tilde{q}\tilde{q}}^2 W(\tilde{q}(\mu), \mu)]^{-1} [\nabla_{\tilde{q}\mu}^2 W(\tilde{q}(\mu), \mu)]^\mathrm{T},$$

where $[\nabla_\mu \tilde{q}(\mu)]$ is an $n \times n \cdot m$ matrix, $\nabla_{\tilde{q}\tilde{q}}^2 W$ is an $n \cdot m \times n \cdot m$ matrix, and $\nabla_{\tilde{q}\mu}^2 W$ is an $n \times n \cdot m$ matrix.

First, consider $[\nabla_{\tilde{q}\mu}^2 W]$. From (8.3.5),

$$\frac{\partial^2 W(\tilde{q}, \mu)}{\partial q_l^i \, \partial \mu^j} = -\mu^i \sum_{k=1}^m C_{lk}\left(\sum_{r=1}^n \mu^r q^r \right) q_k^j \geq 0$$

by cost complementarities for all $i, j = 1, \dots, n, l, k = 1, \dots, m$, and $q^i = q^i(\mu)$. Thus, the matrix $[\nabla_{\tilde{q}\mu}^2 W]$ has all positive elements. Similarly, from (8.3.5),

$$\frac{\partial^2 W(\tilde{q}, \mu)}{\partial q_l^i \, \partial \mu^i} = \mu^i \left[U_{lk}^i(q^i) - C_{lk}\left(\sum_{j=1}^n \mu^j q^j \right) \mu^i \right]$$

for $l \neq k, l, k = 1, \dots, m$, and $\tilde{q} = \tilde{q}(\mu)$, and

$$\frac{\partial^2 W(\tilde{q}, \mu)}{\partial q_l^i \, \partial q_k^j} = -\mu^i \mu^j C_{lk}\left(\sum_{r=1}^n \mu^r q^r \right)$$

for $i \neq j, i, j = 1, \dots, n, l, k = 1, \dots, m$, and $\tilde{q} = \tilde{q}(\mu)$. By demand and cost complementarities, $\partial^2 W(\tilde{q}, \mu)/\partial q_l^i \, \partial q_k^i \geq 0$ for $l \neq k$ and $\partial^2 W(\tilde{q}, \mu)/\partial q_l^i \, \partial q_k^j \geq 0$ for $i \neq j$. Thus, the off-diagonal elements are nonnegative. By condition (8.3.3) and theorem 4.3 in Fiedler and Ptak (employed by Mirman, Tauman, and Zang, 1983a), it follows that $[\nabla_{\tilde{q}\tilde{q}}^2 W]^{-1}$ is a matrix with all nonpositive elements. Therefore, $\partial q^i(\mu)/\partial \mu^j \geq 0$ for all $i, j = 1, \dots, n$.   QED

Notes

1. See Kahn (1970) for an extensive literature survey of the large pre-1970 debate over marginal cost pricing.

2. Silberberg (1980) shows that Hotelling did not correctly prove his result. Hotelling (1938) asserts that "if we start from a system of excise taxes, or any system in which sales are not at marginal costs, ... there is a possible distribution of personal income taxes such that everyone will be better satisfied to change to the system of income taxes with sales at marginal cost."

3. Brown and Heal (1980) examine a nonlinear pricing system with personalized tariffs such that firm production plans are supported in a restricted sense. The result is that any efficient equilibrium may be supported in a restricted sense by a system of marginal cost prices

and two-part tariffs if the efficient equilibrium exists. For an application of the valuation equilibrium approach to public goods, see Mas-Colell (1980b).

4. Thus, if $Q(p)$ is an m-vector of market demands and $C(Q)$ is a multiproduct cost function, the marginal cost price vector p solves $p_l = C_l(Q(p))$, $l = 1, \ldots, m$. Compare with the earlier discussion of market clearing, subsidy-free prices.

5. De V. Graff (1967, p. 154) states, "It seems fairly clear that the conditions which have to be met before it is correct (from a welfare viewpoint) to set price equal to marginal cost in a particular industry are so restrictive that they are unlikely to be satisfied in practice. The survival of the marginal cost pricing principle is probably no more than an indication of the extent to which the majority of professional economists are ignorant of the assumptions required for its validity." De V. Graff emphasizes that the marginal equivalences of the Pareto optimum are necessary but not sufficient for attainment of the welfare frontier and that, in any case, the marginal equivalences must be satisfied simultaneously. The implication of this discussion is that regulators or managers of public enterprises should not necessarily strive for marginal cost pricing in an imperfect world, particularly given the absence of marginal cost pricing in other sectors of the economy.

6. This is pointed out by Guesnerie (1975a, p. 22), who states, "Contrary to what is often implicitly admitted, problems of revenues and problems of management of the public sector cannot be separated, even on a theoretical basis. Even if it is able to lead to economic states compatible with the behavior of other agents, public management of nonconvex firms can guarantee the attainability of (at least) one Pareto optimal state only for 'good' distribution of revenues." The analysis of Guesnerie (1975a) is extended by Brown and Heal (1979).

7. The results in this section are closely related to a paper of Mas-Colell (1980a), who examines a simple one-input–one-output model. Mas-Colell points out that value allocations are applicable even in the presence of increasing returns to scale when competitive allocations fail to exist. However, Mas-Colell notes that the "applicability of the Shapley value theory to some non-classical economic situations such as increasing returns is limited to the transferable utility case." While maintaining the transferable utility hypothesis, this section examines the *multiproduct* cost allocation problem when the goods exhibit demand and cost complementarities. It must be emphasized that increasing returns here is taken to mean an increase in costs proportionally greater than an increase in outputs given efficient input combinations at each output level. This differs from increasing returns to inputs in the production function as appears in Mas-Colell (1980a). See also Ichiishi and Quinzii (1983).

8. Spulber (1986b) studies the benefit allocation problem. The analysis must be distinguished from applications of the Aumann-Shapley value to games of cost allocation by Mirman and Tauman (1982), Billera and Heath (1982), and others. The finite player benefit allocation game is related to work of Mirman, Tauman, and Zang (1983a) on profit allocation within the firm.

9. Formally, let Ω be the Borel sigma algebra of I. Let F be a measure on Ω, $F(\varnothing) = 0$ and $F(I) = 1$. A consumer $s \in I$ has the utility function $U(q(s), s)F(ds)$, where $q(s) \in \mathbb{R}_+^m$ is the vector of goods. To represent the finite number of consumer types, let S^i, $i = 1, \ldots, n$, be a *partition of I* such that

$$U(q(s), s) = U^i(q^i), \qquad s \in S^i.$$

Define the *vector measure* $\mu = (\mu^1, \ldots, \mu^n)$ by $\mu^i(S) \equiv F(S \cap S^i)$, $S \in \Omega$. Clearly $\sum_{i \in N} \mu^i(I) = 1$. Thus, for any coalition $S \in \Omega$, there is associated a unique vector $\mu \in \mathbb{R}_+^n$.

10. For a finite player benefit allocation game similar to (8.3.1), see Sharkey (1982b) and Sorenson, Tschirhart, and Whinston (1978). As in Mas-Colell (1980a), the benefit game (8.3.1) can be obtained from a model of a production economy in which consumer endowments are productive inputs. However, it should again be emphasized that returns to scale are defined here based upon the cost function. Further, the goal of the present paper is a partial equilibrium analysis of benefit allocation within a specific industry.

11. This assumption is used by Sharkey (1982b) as a sufficient condition for nonemptiness of the core in a finite player net benefit game. The condition states that "the incremental gain in utility to buyer i when any output vector z is added to an initial output vector x does not decrease when the initial output vector is increased in a direction y that is orthogonal to z" (Sharkey, 1982b, p. 66). Given twice differentiable utility, complementarity (8.4.1) is equivalent to $U_{lk}^i(q) \geq 0$, for all outputs q and goods $l \neq k$.

9 Franchise Competition

A traditional legal justification for government regulation of public utilities is that the firm must obtain a franchise from the government. Kahn (1970, vol. 1, p. 5) points out that there are "situations in which the very ability of the firm to do business required that it obtain a franchise from the state, which admittedly gave the latter the contractual right to insist on such regulations as it saw fit." The word *franchise*, as it is used here, means a public grant of rights or privileges. These rights or privileges may range from the right to serve the market to the use of public right of way for transmission lines or pipelines. The granting of a public franchise is seen as entailing contractual stipulations, at least implicitly, as a quid pro quo. These contractual stipulations may take the form of government regulation of any and all aspects of the firm's business activities.[1] Thus, the awarding of a limited number of franchises to utility companies is not necessarily a substitute for regulation, as is commonly believed; rather, it forms a legal basis for the application of government regulation.

It has been frequently suggested that the traditional regulation of natural monopoly, which a government franchise entails, can be obviated by properly designing a system whereby firms compete to obtain the franchise.[2] Demsetz (1968) distinguishes the *technological* definition of natural monopoly from the potential for competition for the right to serve the market.[3] Thus, while subadditive production technology suggests the need for a single producer, the number of potential producers may be quite large. This suggests that it may be possible to design a mechanism that will take advantage of competition for the right to serve the market so as to achieve desirable objectives—in particular, elimination of monopoly rents, efficient pricing, and productive efficiency. The problem, of course, is how to design such a mechanism without introducing the high transaction costs and administrative complexity of traditional regulation. This chapter will propose such a mechanism, called *franchise competition*, that can be used to achieve a full range of efficient pricing objectives.

Franchise bidding schemes have been asserted to be efficient means of replacing traditional utility regulation. Demsetz (1968, p. 68) states that "[t]he correct way to view the problem is one of selecting the best type of contract." Williamson (1976, p. 101) responds that the complexity of the contracting process and the high level of "transactional detail" that needs to be specified implies that "one also needs to be instructed on how to proceed." It is easy to criticize actual regulatory procedures on the basis of an idealized competitive process for which the operational details are not specified. It is just as easy to envision the problems that may arise from overly simple bidding schemes. Demsetz (1968, p. 63) suggests that the restraint of the market can be substituted for regulation by awarding the franchise "to that company which seemed to offer the best price-quality package." How to determine the best price-quality package is not specified, and therein lies the rub. Who is to rank the alternatives offered by competing firms? Will the preferences of consumers somehow make the determination, or will the arbitrary choices of a regulatory commission be required?

While competition between firms may improve the performance of regulation, a mechanism that involves choices of quality, prices, and products by a regulator cannot properly be labeled "market directed." Elimination of monopoly rents is not sufficient to guarantee efficient pricing; see Telser (1969, 1971). Even assuming uniform quality of service, it is evident that when multiproduct economies of scope are present, firms will bid price vectors.[4] Ranking price vectors by the government franchising authority, even if the ranking implicitly employs a social welfare function, requires knowledge of consumer preferences or the interposition of regulator's preferences. The "lowest price" or "best price-quality package" is thus no longer meaningful in a general framework.

In this chapter, a *franchise competition* mechanism is proposed in which consumers enter directly into the bargaining process with potential producers. The function of the regulatory authority is to set the "market rules" under which bargaining between consumers and potential producers takes place and to establish criteria for determining winners. It will be shown that the theory of price-setting cooperative games developed in preceding chapters provides a blueprint for the design of franchise competition.

The franchise competition described here is meant to suggest the ideal case in which there are no sunk costs. My purpose is simply to show how a franchise competition can replace price regulation. It is evident that actual franchise contracts will always involve difficulties that are associated with any contract: namely, transaction costs, incorporation of risk, and monitoring of performance. There also exist serious difficulties in recontracting or in the reallocation of franchise contracts that are passed over at present. An important problem occurs when firms invest nonrecoverable or sunk costs to serve a particular market. Demsetz (1968, p. 63) suggests that public ownership of, say, a distribution system for a utility company will avoid the problems of sunk costs. However, construction, maintenance, and operation of a distribution system are often activities involving cost complementarities. It may not be so easy to allocate these activities between different firms.

9.1 Franchise Competition Design

The government agency awarding rights to serve has a number of policy instruments at its disposal. The price mechanism offered by firms may be specified. The conditions for winning the franchise decide the number of firms that will serve the market. This may vary from exclusive monopoly to limited access to the market under various supplier requirements. The agency can require a firm to specify all or specific subsets of the vector of products to the relevant market. The firms may be allowed to serve a subset of consumers, or they may be required to serve all consumers. The firm may be allowed to ration its outputs directly, or it may be required to serve all demands generated at its prices as a "common carrier."

The closest scheme to that which is proposed here is that of Posner (1972a). Posner (1972a, p. 115) suggests a solicitation period at the end of which the franchise would be "awarded to the applicant whose guaranteed receipts, on the basis of subscriber commitments, were largest." This procedure is criticized by Williamson (1976, p. 80) who asks, "Thus, if price-quality package A wins the competition, on Posner's criterion, over price-quality mixes B, C, D, and E, where A is a high price, high quality mode and B through E are all variants on a low price-quality mix, does it follow that package A is socially preferred?" The franchise allocation mechanism proposed here addresses this question. The multiproduct assumption is sufficiently general to allow firms to differ in terms of the prices charged for a set of services of varying quality. The winning price vector is such that the outcome is socially preferred.

Consider an industry with technology $C(\cdot)$ characterized by natural monopoly. Firms are assumed to have equal access to the common technology. There are no entry barriers in the form of product differentiation, patents, or ownership of resources. There is assumed to be no market uncertainty. While production for the market may require sunk costs, there are no sunk costs required to bid for the right to serve the market before entry occurs. Thus, the only entry barriers that will be present will be those established by the government in its design of a franchise allocation mechanism. In this sense, the market satisfies the criteria of a *contestable market* of Baumol, Panzar, and Willig (1982). Further, it is assumed that there are a large number of potential entrants. It is assumed that firms are not able to collude and behave competitively in seeking the franchise.

The firms wish to serve the market for a specified period of time. The vector of goods $(Q_1, \ldots, Q_m)$ may refer simply to differentiated products (peak and off-peak electricity service), to products provided at different dates, or to products provided at different locations. In terms of the franchise allocation itself, I consider a static model with unlimited possibilities for recontracting.

Let the set of consumers, N, $N = \{1, \ldots, n\}$, define the relevant market. Consumers have preferences U^i and endowments ω^i. Let $\theta \subseteq \mathbb{R}^{mn}$ represent the set of output allocations among consumers $q = (q^1, \ldots, q^n)$, $q^i \in \mathbb{R}^m_+$ for all i. Define a price mechanism P as a map that assigns elements in the set of consumers N and the set of output allocations θ to a vector of payments for each consumer i. Let $\mathscr{P}$ represent the set of price mechanisms such that for all $P \in \mathscr{P}$, $P: N \times \theta \to \mathbb{R}^n$. The definition of a price mechanism is sufficiently general to allow discriminatory or personalized pricing. Consumers choose among the contracts offered by firms so as to maximize their indirect utility.

The first task of the government agency is to specify the *price mechanism* to be employed by firms. The following price mechanisms are of special interest:

1. Linear pricing, $p \in \mathbb{R}^m_+$, assigns the payment pq^i to each consumer i purchasing q^i.

2. Two-part pricing (p, E), $p \in \mathbb{R}^m_+$, $E \in \mathbb{R}_+$, assigns payments $pq^i + E$ to each consumer i purchasing q^i.

3. Personalized entry fees with common unit prices, (p, E^i), assign the payment $pq^i + E^i$ to each consumer i purchasing q^i.

Thus, the government agency selects a subset of the set of price mechanisms $\mathscr{P}' \subset \mathscr{P}$ that are available to firms.

Second, assume that firms select the segment of the market they wish to serve by negotiating a *service contract* with a group of consumers $S \subseteq N$. For (P, S) to be a contract, it must be accepted by all consumers $i \in S$.

Definition 9.1.1 A *service contract* (P, S) consisting of a price mechanism $P \in \mathscr{P}$ and a group of consumers $S \subseteq N$, is an offer by a firm to sell the products $Q = (Q_1, \ldots, Q_m)$ for payments $P(i, q^i)$, $i = 1, \ldots, n$, such that all of the demands of the consumers $i \in S$ are met.

The firm agrees to serve all of the demands of its proposed market S if it obtains a franchise. This requirement is similar to the "common carrier" obligation that a firm meet all of the reasonable demands of consumers in its chosen market. This restriction is also present in Posner (1972).[5] It is required that firms receive no subsidies and that they break even.

Definition 9.1.2 A service contract (P, S) is said to be *feasible* if the firm makes nonnegative profits,

$$\sum_{i \in S} P(i, q^i) \geq C\left(\sum_{i \in S} q^i\right),$$

where q^i represents the demand of consumer i given P.

Third, each consumer is allowed to accept *at most one* service contract. The cooperative game described above assumes that consumers cannot split their purchases across firms. Most consumers do obtain each utility service from a single firm (e.g., electricity, natural gas, local telephone, water, cable TV).[6] However, this is probably due to government restriction of entry rather than being a market response to the fixed costs of connection to a distribution system. The requirement that consumers select only one firm is implicit in Posner's bidding scheme (1972a, p. 115) which operates "by beginning the bargaining process with an open season in which all franchise applicants were free to solicit the area's residents for a set period of time. This would not be a poll; the applicants would seek to obtain actual commitments from potential subscribers."

The requirement that consumers not split their purchase of any single good or of different goods is crucial. If a consumer may split his purchases across firms, he may "arbitrage" by purchasing goods from the lowest-cost supplier. This will severely restrict the available contracts that may be offered. While the lowest possible price on a particular good is generally perceived to be a desirable economic objective, this may not be the case when production entails cost complementarities across goods. One may object to the restriction by noting that consumers would generally wish to choose to contract with several firms. For example, in the United States, many consumers are served by several long-distance companies. It is for this reason, however, that enforcement of contracting with a single firm is a binding constraint on consumer behavior. This constraint may be binding regardless of whether or not the pricing mechanism involves fixed entry fees. Note that in public utility markets (electricity, natural gas, water, telecommunications, CATV), it may be desirable to avoid costly duplication of effort or disruption of public rights of way in laying more than one pipeline or cable to a household for a given service.

Finally, *recontracting* is permitted. Implicitly, it is assumed that transaction costs are low. Recontracting is also discussed by Posner (1972a, p. 115), who notes that a majority rule approach may distort consumer preferences and observes that "problems of this sort are resolved in a market by recontracting." Posner suggests that the market may be approximated "by a run-off solicitation campaign or by permitting subscribers to sign up with more than one system—but these may be awkward and expensive." Although recontracting is permitted, it need not take place. If a firm offers a second-best core price p^* to the entire set of consumers, this will block all other offers of prices outside of the core. Ties between two second-best core prices are excluded by the requirement that firms obtain commitments from subscribers. The extent of recontracting required for the competition process to reach a second-best core price may be examined by experimentation. Subscribers may sign up with more than one firm sequentially, not simultaneously. It is the commitment to one firm by subscribers that yields the welfare properties of the second-best core solution.

Winners of the franchise competition are those firms that have successfully contracted to provide service to a group of consumers after recontracting has taken place. Winners of the competition are given the right to serve the market under the terms of their proposed service contracts.

The franchise competition is now defined formally.

Definition 9.1.3   A *franchise competition* has the following characteristics:

a. The government agency selects a class of price mechanisms $\mathscr{P}' \subset \mathscr{P}$.

b. Each firm offers a feasible service contract (P, S) such that $P \in \mathscr{P}'$ and $S \subseteq N$ that is acceptable to all consumers $i \in S$.

c. Consumers are allowed to contract with, at most, one firm.

d. Recontracting is permitted. Consumers only recontract if their well-being is strictly improved.

e. Firms with service contracts $\{(P(j), S(j)\}, j = 1, \ldots, J$, are winners of the competition if no further recontracting occurs.

For completeness, the following definition is needed.

Definition 9.1.4   If the service contracts $\{P(j), S(j)\}$, $j = 1, \ldots, J$, are winners of the franchise competition, they are said to be *equilibrium* service contracts.

Thus, a franchise competition is identified by the list $(\mathscr{P}', C, N, U^i, \omega^i)$ consisting of the permitted price mechanisms $\mathscr{P}'$, the common technology C, the set of consumers N, and the consumer preferences and endowments (U^i, ω^i).

Two important points need to be made. First, it is not true that a single firm will always win simply because the technology is subadditive. It is easy to provide counterexamples in which more than one firm wins the competition. Second, the question of "ties" is not a problem because consumers must choose a single supplier. If two firms offer identical prices and contract with different groups of consumers, subadditivity of costs implies that there exists a service contract yielding nonnegative profits for the two consumer groups combined.

The question of whether one or more firms will win, or if indeed there exists an equilibrium set of contracts such that no recontracting occurs, depends on the price mechanism, consumer demands, and the properties of the common technology. The remaining sections of this chapter examine the following general proposition.

PROPOSITION 9.1.1   *A monopoly contract* (P^*, N) *wins the franchise competition* $(\mathscr{P}', C, N, U^i, \omega^i)$ *if and only if* P^* *is in the core of the second-best game for price mechanisms* $\mathscr{P}'$, *common costs* C, *and the set of consumers* N *with preferences* U^i *and endowments* ω^i.

The intuition for this result may be obtained by comparing the definition of the franchise competition with the definitions of the core of the games studied in chapters 6, 7, and 8.

The theory of franchise competition may be extended by identifying competitions in which more than one firm wins with cooperative games for which the core is empty but where there exists a stable partition of the set of consumers N. This is the concept of the C-stable solution considered for public goods by Guesnerie and Oddou (1979, 1981) and discussed in chapter 6. The franchise competition results obtained in the present chapter apply only to the monopoly case. It is relatively straightforward to extend these results to the case of multiple winners.

9.2 Franchise Competition with Linear Prices

Consider now a franchise competition in which the government agency requires the firms to set linear prices, $p \in \mathbb{R}_+^m$. It is assumed that an unlimited number of potential entrants may offer consumers service contracts. The question that is addressed is, Under what conditions will a single firm win the franchise? Further, the properties of the price vector of the winning contract are of particular interest.

The first result shows that the set of prices that result in a single winner of the franchise competition is identical with the set of prices in the second-best core (see chapter 6).

PROPOSITION 9.2.1   *The pair (p^*, N) is an equilibrium service contract if and only if p^* is in the second-best core.*

Proof   Suppose that (p^*, N) is an equilibrium service contract but is not in the second-best core. Then there exists a set $S \subseteq N$ such that $S \neq \varnothing$ and for some price vector p',

$$p' \sum_{i \in S} q^i(p', \omega^i) - C\left(\sum_{i \in S} q^i(p', \omega^i) \right) \geq 0$$

and

$$V^i(p', \omega^i) \geq V^i(p, \omega^i)$$

for all $i \in S$ and strictly greater for some $i \in S$. But then the contract (p', S) dominates (p^*, N) for the members of S, which contradicts the assertion that (p^*, N) is an equilibrium service contract.

Suppose now that p^* is in the second-best core. Then, by definition of the second-best core, there does not exist $S \subseteq N, S \neq \varnothing$, such that a feasible service contract $(p', S'), S' \subseteq N$, can be constructed that improves the well-being of all consumers $i \in S$. Thus, the contract (p^*, N) is an equilibrium service contract since no recontracting can occur.   QED

Thus, the possible outcomes of the cooperative game with linear pricing and of the franchise competition are identical in terms of output allocations, prices, and the number of producers. The intuitive explanation for this result is simply that free access of potential producers to the franchise competition bids away monopoly rents. Thus, the net result of recontracting with free entry is that price decisions are identical to those when the firms are managed by their customers.

The identity between the core of the cooperative game and the set of equilibrium prices for franchise competition implies that the necessary conditions obtained in chapter 6 apply to the franchise competition. In particular, p^* is a zero-profit price. There does not exist a lower price yielding nonnegative profits for a firm serving any subset of the market. Most important, p^* is a Ramsey-Boiteux price vector. The regulatory authority achieves this price vector without imposing any rate regulation on the firm and without any knowledge whatsoever of consumer preference. Social welfare is maximized in a second-best sense with absolutely no requirement that the regulatory agency consult any measure of social welfare.

Note that the equilibrium price vector p^* is consumer subsidy-free (no group of consumers subsidizes another), but in general it need not be subsidy-free across goods. Compare this to free entry of firms in a contestable market. There, free entry eliminates all subsidies across goods (and thus across consumer groups). But sustainable monopoly prices need not be Ramsey optimal and certainly need not be in the second-best core. This distinction highlights the importance of condition (c) in definition 9.1.3. If consumers can contract with more than one firm, then by purchasing each good from the lowest-cost supplier, they will eliminate all subsidies across goods. Any contract with these cross-subsidies will be dominated for a subset of consumers purchasing a subset of goods.

The existence results obtained for the second best-core also apply to the linear-pricing franchise competition. In particular, given assumption 5.1.1 on consumer preferences and the requirement that consumers devote a fixed proportion of their income to the goods produced by the firm in the relevant market, and also given the weighted cost function $C_k(\cdot)$ in chapter 6, there is a k^*, $0 < k^* < 1$, such that for all k, $k^* \le k \le 1$, there exists at least one equilibrium service contract (p^*, N). Thus, if the technology of firms can be approximately described by an affine cost function, it is meaningful to speak of a monopoly winner of the franchise auction.

9.3   Franchise Competition with Two-Part Tariffs

Equilibria of the franchise competition with two-part tariffs can be identified with points in the second-best core when two-part tariffs are the price mechanism. While price discrimination is commonly associated with monopoly, oligopoly competition with two-part tariffs by firms may easily be imagined; see Calem and Spulber (1984). Further, oligopoly competition with two-part tariffs exists in many markets including computers, transportation, amusement parks, and across markets, such as occurs between electricity and natural gas for home heating.

Note that the use of two-part tariffs (p, E) requires the absence of arbitrage by consumers against the fixed entry fee. This restriction is standard in utility markets where the fixed fee E represents a "connection charge" that applies only to sales to a single residence or business.

The main result is obtained by comparing the definition of the second-best core with two-part pricing (7.2.1) with the franchise competition when the regulatory agency requires a two-part pricing mechanism (p, E).

PROPOSITION 9.3.1   *The pair $((p^*, E^*), N)$ is an equilibrium service contract if and only if (p^*, E^*) is in the second-best core with two-part tariffs.*

The proof follows that for proposition 9.2.1 and will not be repeated here.

The existence of an equilibrium service contract in which a single firm serves the market is implied by proposition 7.2.1. In particular, if the appropriate demand assumptions are satisfied (5.1.1, 7.2.1) and the cost function is sufficiently similar to an affine cost function, there exists at least one equilibrium service contract $((p^*, E^*), N)$.

9.4   Franchise Competition with Personalized Tariffs

The feasibility of designing a franchise competition with personalized tariffs depends upon whether firms have sufficient information about each individual's preferences. It must be emphasized that in the contract negotiation with firms, consumers have an incentive to misrepresent their preferences. Thus, the franchise competition with personalized prices is unlikely to be feasible. The following discussion is meant to be instructive with regard to the design of an optimal pricing policy without explicit consideration of the trade-off between efficient pricing and costly information.

As shown in chapter 8, given the existence of a core allocation in a general nontransferable utility economy, there always exists a price vector p^* and a set of personalized entry fees $(E^{1*}, \dots, E^{n*})$ that support the core allocation. This implies the following result.

PROPOSITION 9.4.1   *The contract $((p^*, E^{1*}, \dots, E^{n*}), N)$ is an equilibrium service contract if and only if $(p^*, E^{1*}, \dots, E^{n*})$ supports a core allocation.*

The proof follows that of proposition 9.2.1. Essentially, the competitive bidding of firms establishes a vector of entry fees $(E^1*, \ldots, E^{n*})$ that effectuate transfers between consumers. As was shown in chapter 8, for the special case of a continuum of agents and transferable utility, the Aumann-Shapley value is in the core and can be supported by marginal cost prices and entry fees based on averages of marginal cost prices. It is evident that the marginal cost price mechanism with personalized tariffs is an equilibrium service contract under the assumptions given in chapter 8. As noted in chapter 8, the tariffs may be applied to customer classes to yield an outcome that is approximately optimal.

The preceding discussion examined the design of a franchise competition for three price mechanisms: second-best linear pricing, second-best two-part tariffs, and optimal pricing with personalized fixed fees. The results obtained demonstrate that various welfare objectives may be achieved for a government agency regulating an industry whose technology has increasing returns to scale without recourse to traditional cost-of-service rate regulation. As emphasized above, the results depend heavily on the assumptions of free access by firms to a known common technology and the absence of transaction costs or demand uncertainty. In this "friction-less" ideal case, it is evident that regulation need not entail maximization of a social welfare function by a regulator. Rather, competitive market forces may be channeled to obtain particular efficient outcomes.

The conclusion that a franchise competition results in a second-best optimum should not necessarily be intepreted to mean that market allocations are superior to regulated regimes. Rather, the franchise competition is suggested as a regulatory instrument. Many current or past regulatory regimes (in electricity, telecommunications, transportation) have been shown to involve subsidies across goods. As emphasized in the contestable markets literature, free entry competition eliminates these cross-subsidies entirely. This may be inconsistent with achieving second-best optimal allocations. The franchise competition provides a *middle ground* in which the restriction that consumers contract with only a single firm may permit subsidies across goods, thus allowing second-best optimal prices to be achieved. Thus, the restriction of contracting in markets with technology that has increasing returns to scale may provide a means of improving productive efficiency. This approach may improve the performance of markets in which the prices, number of firms, production technology, and range of available services are directly regulated.

To illustrate a simple practical application, consider the "equal access" program in the U.S. market for long-distance telecommunications. Under this program, which is being applied under a regional basis, consumers are asked (within a given period of time) to select a single long-distance carrier from the list of carriers that serve their area. The long-distance carriers heavily advertise the type of service offered and their schedule of tariffs on long-distance calls of varying distances and at different times of the day. Under the "equal access" program, the consumer selection of a single carrier allows him to reach the carrier by dialing a single number. At the same time, all other carriers can still be accessed by dialing additional numbers. The result will be that consumers may use more than one carrier if their cost savings justify more than one access charge. The consumers can then arbitrage against differences in rate structures, thus eliminating potential subsidies across goods even where the resulting tariffs may lower consumer welfare. One may conjecture that if consumers were required to select a single carrier for any given period (say, a month at a time), assuming that large returns to scale are present, then this might result in an improvement of the long-run efficiency of rate schedules of firms remaining in the market.

Notes

1. Businesses are "clothed in the public interest" if they "are carried on under the authority of a public grant of privileges which either expressly or impliedly imposes the affirmative duty of rendering a public service demanded by any member of the public. Such are the railroads, other common carriers and public utilities" (*Wolff Packing Company* v. *Kansas*, (1923, 262 U.S. 522, pp. 535–537). This case is quoted in Kahn (1970, vol. 1, p. 5). Two other classes of businesses that are "clothed in the public interest" in *Wolff Packing Company* v. *Kansas* are those occupations that are traditionally regulated ("keepers of inns, cabs, and grist mills") and those businesses for which the owner "by devoting his business to the public use, in effect grants the public an interest in that use and subjects himself to public regulation to the extent of that interest." See Kahn (1970) for additional discussion.

2. An important historical overview and critical evaluation of franchise auctions is given in Schmalensee (1979a). Schmalensee also discusses operating franchise schemes in which the government owns the assets of the utility.

3. Demsetz (1968, p. 57) emphasizes that "the determinants of competition in market negotiations differ from and should not be confused with the determinants of the number of firms from which production will issue after contractual negotiations have been complete."

4. Williamson (1976, p. 75) identifies the following relevant factors in evaluating alternative regulatory mechanisms: "(1) the costs of ascertaining and aggregating consumer preferences through direct solicitation; (2) the efficacy of scalar bidding; (3) the degree to which technology is well developed; (4) demand uncertainty; (5) the degree to which incumbent suppliers acquire idiosyncratic skills; (6) the extent to which specialized, long-lived equipment is involved; and

(7) the susceptibility of the political process to opportunistic representations and the differential proclivity, among modes, to make them." Factors (3)–(7) will be dealt with in later chapters. For the purposes of this chapter, I abstract away from these issues. For the present, my concern is with (1) consumer preferences and (2) relative prices.

5. Posner (1972a, p. 115) states that "to keep the solicitation process honest, each applicant would be required to contract in advance that, in the event he won, he would provide the level of service, and at the rate represented, in his solicitation drive."

6. Note that different firms supply each type of utility (electricity, telephones, etc.). I am simply requiring that an individual consumer be served by one telephone company, one electricity company, etc.

III ADMINISTRATIVE REGULATION OF MARKETS

10 Barriers to Entry 1: Rate Regulation and Bargaining

In the presence of significant *sunk costs*, direct regulation of prices may be required in industries with scale economies that are large relative to the size of the market. In the absence of sunk costs, competition may serve to assure efficient production levels and elimination of some monopoly rents. Further, regulation of entry in the form of a franchise competition may be employed to achieve, indirectly, welfare-optimal pricing objectives. However, many regulated industries, particularly utilities, are characterized by high levels of irreversible, industry-specific investment. In this setting, competitive entry and exit is costly and may fail to yield an efficient industry equilibrium. Even a competition to serve the market, before costs are sunk, is of limited value because a single franchise auction will not serve to guarantee efficient pricing and investment over time.[1]

One solution to the problem of sunk costs is full public ownership and control of utilities. Many U.S. utilities are publicly owned in the sense that they are owned and operated by the local government, or in the case of the Tennessee Valley Authority (TVA) by the federal government, which determines the firm's prices and production decisions and regulates entry. In most other countries, telecommunications, electricity, water, and natural gas are nationalized, that is, owned and managed by the state. For markets in which the government is the principal consumer, such as weapons for national defense, the government in many countries other than the United States is the principal producer as well, owning and operating the defense industry. There is, however, a preference for private or investor ownership of industry in the United States.

A hybrid solution, proposed by Demsetz (1967), is for the local government to own utility plant, equipment, and transmission facilities. By placing ownership in the hands of government, the costly duplication of transmission facilities is avoided. Further, the sunk costs of plant and equipment need not be linked to the entry and exit of firms that operate the utility. Demsetz (1967) proposes that by divorcing ownership and control, repeated franchise auctions may be held, or repeated renegotiation of franchise contracts between the state and the utility managers may be achieved without large entry costs. However, the dependence of this proposal on state rather than private ownership of industrial facilities is questionable. Further, as noted previously in chapter 9, the multidimensional nature of the choice problem facing the auctioneer will complicate the selection of winners. Given multiproduct firms or alternative price-quality options, simple rules for the selection of franchise winners will not be feasible.

Inevitably, the board awarding the franchise will face all of the decisions currently faced by regulators. If fixed term contracts are signed, the franchise board will also face the standard problems of monitoring and enforcement of contract terms. Thus, government ownership of utility capital is not in itself a replacement for government regulation of performance.

This chapter focuses on rate regulation of investor-owned utilities. There are two sets of key issues. The first concerns what prices, output, and quality of service will be chosen and the allocation of risk between consumers and the regulated firm—this set of issues is the focus of the present chapter, which assumes that full information about costs and demand is available. The second set of issues regards monitoring and enforcement of desired firm behavior in the presence of incomplete information about demand and costs—this is addressed in chapter 11.

The principal feature of government utility regulation is the rate hearing. Rate hearings are particular examples of case-by-case adjudication, discussed in chapter 2. Rate hearings are hearings held in public and on the record and are governed by similar rules of due process and administrative procedure. The characteristics of the rule-making and adjudication processes discussed in chapter 2 are particularly applicable to utility rate cases. Thus, rate hearings are mechanisms for gathering information about market demand for utility services and about the utility's costs and technology. The hearing process involves an exchange of information between the market participants and the regulator and also among the market participants themselves. These informational issues are addressed in the next chapter.

The rate-making process involves adversarial interaction between interested parties. I identify the utility's interest with those of its investors who seek to maximize profits. The opposing interests are those of the utility's customers who seek to maximize their gains from trade. The rate hearing may be compared to a court proceeding in which the regulatory commission, within the constraints imposed by its legislative mandate, decides between the competing interests of the utility and its customers. The rate-hearing process may therefore be described as a *bargaining process*. This bargaining process is the focus of the present chapter. The chapter begins with a description of rate hearings and emphasizes the second-best nature of rate bargaining. The bargaining framework is presented in a game theory setting in section 10.2. Bargaining over prices and over admissible utility costs is considered in section 10.3, and bargaining over the allowable rate of return is discussed in section 10.4. The risk-sharing aspects of the utility rate structure are presented in section 10.5.

10.1 Rate Hearings

The discussion of rate regulation presented in this section emphasizes two important institutional aspects. The first topic is the adversarial nature of rate hearings and their characterization as a bargaining process between consumers and the regulated firm. The second topic is the second-best nature of regulatory proceedings. Rate setting is often based on measurement of the utility's costs. Rather than bargaining directly over output or quality of service and total payments, rate hearings generally focus on measurement of cost and demand and dispute the formula used to calculate rates. This indirect approach can lead to efficiency losses.

10.1.1 Rate Hearings as Bargaining

The high level of consumer and firm effort and expenditure devoted to participation in the rate-hearing process provides important evidence that both sides stand to gain by that participation. The effectiveness of consumer and firm presentations in rate hearings has been observed empirically; see Joskow (1972). In this sense, it is reasonable to assert that regulatory commissions are influenced by the debate in rate hearings. The source of consumer and firm bargaining power need not, of course, depend upon the eloquence of their testimony. Rather, the degree of effort expended may signal potential political impacts of various rate decisions and the potential for legislative intervention. Also, the effort devoted to rate hearings may indicate the potential for judicial challenges of regulatory decisions. Whatever the source of these countervailing influences, however, we may interpret the final outcome as reflecting the relative bargaining strength of consumers and firms.

The adversarial nature of regulatory proceedings and the aspect of division of rents from exchange are also in conformity with the view of rate hearings as a negotiation process. Although the decision ultimately falls to the regulatory commission, subject to legislative and judicial oversight, the decision may be seen as a reflection of the positions taken by consumers and the regulated firm. The rates that are chosen involve a trade-off between these competing interests.

If rate hearings do indeed involve negotiation between consumers and firms, does this imply that there is no role for the regulator? Precisely the opposite is true. Given transaction costs, it may not be feasible for consumers to form large coalitions for the purpose of bargaining directly with large-scale firms. Thus, with the high costs of coalition formation, achieving cooperative equilibria of the type discussed in preceding chapters may not be possible. An important role for regulation may simply be the provision of a forum for negotiation of utility rates and service contracts between consumer representatives and firms, much as the legal system provides a forum for the resolution of private contractual disputes.[2] The rate hearing has often been characterized as a cumbersome and costly administrative procedure. However, these costs must be compared with the overall cost and effectiveness of negotiation of utility rates between firms and consumers in the marketplace, see Goldberg (1976).

Given rate hearings as a forum for negotiation between consumers and firms, the regulatory commission performs the important function of establishing rules for the negotiation game and mechanisms for the resolution of conflict. The administrative rules governing rate hearings provide a set of guidelines for the debate. Further, the regulatory commission, as will be noted below, selects the issues that are open to debate. Thus, the proposed rate adjustment may be discussed in terms of admissible expenditures, the allowable rate of return, risk sharing implications, accounting procedures, methods for the measurement of costs, and so on. The regulatory commission's method of calculating rates influences the type of arguments made in the regulatory hearings.

The regulatory commission acts as an arbiter and may select an outcome from the set of admissible rates. Thus, the regulator may choose between competing outcomes, especially if bargaining does not yield an unique solution. The choices made by the regulator may follow some announced rules (see the discussion in section 2.4). Alternatively, the regulator's choices may reflect the preferences of the regulatory bureaucracy, the preferences of the electorate as reflected by the state legislature, or the potential for court challenges by consumers and firms and the possibility of judicial reversal of rate decisions.

One important aspect of the rate structure is that of income redistribution across consumers. For example, Bolton and Meiners (1986) argue that lifeline rates and energy audits serve to redistribute income—the lifeline rate benefiting only those low-income electricity users with high demands, and the energy audits benefiting high-income consumers at the expense of all others. There are also intergenerational transfers through current lower rates and lower investment followed by future higher rates; see Navarro (1983). It is apparent that negotiation over the rate structure and utility investment will generate *coalitions* of residential, commercial, and industrial customers due to income redistribution effects. The issue of cross-subsidies across customer classes was addressed in chapters 3–8. Much remains to be done in studying the public choice aspects of rate regulation. For the purposes of this chapter, I restrict attention to bargaining between a representative consumer and the regulated firm.

10.1.2   Rate Setting

The focus of the present discussion is on regulation by state utility commissions of investor-owned utilities. The state utility commissions regulate electricity, telecommunications, and natural gas. In many states, the commissions also regulate water, sewage, transportation, banks, securities, insurance, and, in some cases, warehouses. The main concern here is the regulation of prices charged by utilities. Generally, price regulation occurs in the context of public rate hearings in which regulated firms, their customers, and other interested parties have the opportunity to express their concerns and perhaps influence the decisions of the utility commission.

Markets for utilities are affected by many other types of regulation and governmental activity not considered here. In particular, public utilities owned by municipalities have rates set by the municipality. At the federal level, the Federal Energy Regulatory commission (FERC) sets rates for interstate wholesale electric power transactions and regulates oil and natural gas pipelines as well. Also, the Securities and Exchange Commission (SEC) and FERC regulate utility mergers and securities transactions. Electric utilities are also subject to regulation from the Environmental Protection Agency (EPA) and the Nuclear Regulatory Commission (NRC). Interstate telephone services are subject to regulation by the Federal Communications Commission (FCC).

As is generally the case with regulatory agencies, state utility commissions have considerable autonomy with respect to the legislative and executive branches of government. The state legislatures delegate regulatory tasks and thus avoid much of the controversy surrounding specific decisions, particularly those involving rate setting. As Gormley (1983, p. 24) observes, "The legislative branch has been especially reluctant to enact clear laws for regulatory agencies which ... impose penalties for which legislators would prefer not to be blamed." Further, Gormley (1983, p. 27) observes that in the case of elected commissioners "electoral accountability manifests itself more in constituent services than in public policy decisions." The primary external effects on agency policymaking and decisions arise from the activities of external pressure groups.[3] There is an increasing degree of participation in rate hearings by consumer, industry, and commercial interest groups and state-sponsored public advocates, as well as the regulated firms themselves. For a sample of 12 states, Gormley (1983, pp. 46–47) lists 72 grass roots advocacy groups that intervened in utility commission hearings in a one-year period between 1978 and 1979.[4] Further, increased intervention by proxy advocates, such as state attorneys general and consumer counsels, has been observed.[5] Finally, utility companies are active in the provision of information to utility commissions and in representations at the rate hearings.[6] The issue of rate regulation under incomplete information is addressed in the next chapter. The large amount of effort expended by public advocates and regulated firms suggests that each has much to gain from participation in the rate-hearing process.

The rate-hearing process does not necessarily set rates directly. Rather, rates are often set *indirectly* through decisions on methods of estimating costs, demand, and rates of return. By influencing decisions on the determinants of the rate structure, consumer, industrial, and commercial interest groups and regulated firms are able to affect the rate schedules ultimately chosen by utility commissions. Generally, the interests of customer groups and the utility are diametrically opposed. In this sense, the rate-hearing process is comparable to a bargaining situation. The customer groups and the utility negotiate on the underlying determinants of the rate structure. The set of outcomes of the bargaining process depends on how rates are set by the utility commission and on what aspects of rate setting are open for discussion, e.g., cost and demand estimates, and rates of return.

The rate structure that is chosen by the regulatory commission has two significant aspects. First, for given output and cost levels, rate levels may be seen as determining the size of transfers between utility customers and the owners or shareholders of the regulated firm. Utility rates must permit the firm to earn nonnegative profits. Further, utility customers must have positive gains from trade if they are to purchase the regulated firm's output. This establishes a range within which rates determine the *distribution of income* between the customers and owners of the regulated firm. Second, the decisions underlying the rate structure may affect the regulated firm's output, input choices, and costs. These decisions determine *allocative efficiency* within the regulated market. The rates that are approved by regulatory commissions may be seen as a compromise between the positions of customer interests and those of the regulated firm. Because of legal or institutional constraints, the market allocations attainable through regulation may be severely limited. Thus, instead of direct bargaining over rate levels, rates are determined indirectly through bargaining over the allowable rate of return or on definitions of capital equipment. The outcomes obtained through regulation may then lead to suboptimal resource allocation or departures from cost minimization.

Another view of the rate regulation process is that utility rates reflect the preferences of regulatory commissioners or their staffs.[7] This view need not be inconsistent with a characterization of rate hearings as a bargaining process. Rather, the regulated outcome may reflect the relative bargaining strengths or effectiveness of utility or customer representatives. These advocates may succeed in part by convincing utility commissioners or members of the commission staff. In this sense, the choices of the commission may be ascribed to the regulatory agency's preferences.

The courts have applied an "end result" test in evaluating utility commission rate decisions. In the Permian Basin Area Rate Cases (390 U.S. 747, 1968), the Supreme Court held that an agency's rate decision should be upheld if it is within a "zone of reasonableness."[8] In evaluating regulatory commission decisions, the Supreme Court in Permian Basin stated that the reviewing court[9] "must determine whether the order may reasonably be expected to maintain financial integrity, attract necessary capital, and fairly compensate investors for the risks they have assumed, and yet provide appropriate protection to the relevant public interest, both existing and foreseeable." The "zone of reasonableness" suggests that while firms must obtain nonnegative profits, utility customers must obtain positive gains from trade. In this sense the "zone of reasonableness" may be compared to the set of "individually rational" exchanges between the utility and its customers.

The regulatory commissions calculate maximum prices based on a complex series of decisions that are often controversial. The pricing policy may be characterized as a *cost-based* pricing method and, as such, does not involve any explicit welfare calculations (see chapter 3). Although the price calculations of regulators have seemingly little to do with welfare maximization, it is possible that the rate-hearing process itself may lead to rates that satisfy some second-best efficiency criteria. In particular, if some weight is given to consumer surplus and to the profits of regulated firms, maximum rates may reflect the marginal benefits of lower rates to consumers and the marginal effects of lower rates on firm profits. The complicated pricing formulas employed by regulators allow for considerable discretion at each step. Thus, consumer or firm interest groups may have significant influence on the rates that are ultimately chosen if they can affect the decisions made in the application of the pricing formula.

The pricing formula essentially involves an estimate of the firm's variable and fixed costs.[10] The firm's *variable costs* (*VC*) include operating expenses, taxes, and depreciation. The firm's fixed costs are estimated by calculating the firm's capital stock referred to as the *rate base* (*RB*). This is the sum of firm investments net of depreciation. The cost of capital for the firm is represented by a chosen *allowable rate of return* (*ROR*). The cost of capital is obtained by taking the product of the regulated firm's rate base and the allowable rate of return on capital. The total cost (*TC*) is then referred to as the firm's *revenue requirement*,

$$TC = VC + ROR \cdot RB. \tag{10.1.1}$$

Rates are then set in such a way that the revenues generated cover the total cost or revenue requirement, *TC*. Given multiple outputs (or multiple customer classes), the rate-setting problem is a multiproduct pricing problem. The relative rates set for multiple products or charged to each customer class are referred to as the *rate structure*. The rate-making process may thus be divided into four steps: (1) calculation of variable costs; (2) calculation of the rate base; (3) selection of the allowable rate of return; and (4) design of the rate structure. Controversy generally attends alternative methods for determining the various elements in the pricing formula. Consider now the scope of decisions available to regulators and the ultimate impact of decisions on rates.

1. In calculation of operating expenses and other *variable costs*, commissions generally consider *historical costs* by selecting a *test year*. Clearly, if the firm's costs vary over time, selection of the test year will lead to varying estimates of variable costs. In an inflationary period, more recent test years will yield greater cost estimates than will earlier test years, assuming that cost estimates are not adjusted to current dollar values.[11] If an attempt

is made to adjust for inflation, the projected future estimates of inflation will have an effect on the cost estimates and thus on the firm's revenue requirement. Beyond the selection of a test year, a number of serious problems exist in the estimation of variable costs from past operating expenses. Changes in relative prices affect the costs of producing a given output. Further, output changes are likely if rates are altered or if consumer demands shift. Consumer demand changes may occur due to changes in prices of substitutes, income, or the size of the firm's customer base. In the case of electricity or natural gas, conservation efforts by consumers may increase demand elasticity. In any case, it is clear that historical variable costs can, at best, only approximate current or future variable cost. The test year can be a future year in which cost estimates are based on projections of customer demand and factor prices. In this case, there is considerable latitude for variation in demand and cost data supplied by customer and utility representatives.

Various arguments in favor of alternative methods of estimating variable cost may be presented by customer and utility representatives. However, their pursuit of self-interest suggests that advocating a particular cost measurement approach will be dictated by the ultimate effect of the approach on rate levels. Thus, in an inflationary period, customer advocates may argue for past test years while utility advocates may argue for more recent or future test years. McCormick (1986) notes that as of 1980 almost all states employ original cost accounting, and attributes this to consumer lobbying and voting efforts.

Given significant changes in particular input prices, utility and customer groups may differ on the method of inclusion of price changes in operating expenditure estimates. With increases in energy or labor costs, customer advocates may favor historical cost measures, delays in cost adjustments, or lags in the regulatory process itself. Because of regulatory lags, utilities may be expected to favor automatic adjustment of variable cost estimates for current input price increases. Fuel costs constitute a large share of the costs of electric utilities. Automatic adjustment clauses that allow rates to reflect increases in fuel costs have been widely employed by regulatory commissions. The use of fuel adjustment clauses, by assuring pass-through of fuel costs, may lead the utility to select a fuel-intensive technology, thus leading to inefficiency.[12] On the effects of automatic fuel adjustment see Kendrick (1975), Joskow and MacAvoy (1975), Trebing (1976c), Gollop and Karlson (1978), Stewart (1982), and Baron and DeBondt (1979, 1981). In the case of labor costs, it has been argued that pass-throughs of labor costs lead to greater wage settlements than would be observed in competitive industries. This suggests that regulators should be involved in the wage bargaining between the utility and its employees or that "unreasonable" wage settlements should not be covered by rate increases. However, empirical verification of excessive wage rates in regulated industries has been mixed.[13]

2. In calculating the rate base, a number of issues are open to debate that have serious consequences for rates. First, there is an important difference between the *historical* (or original) cost of plant construction and purchase of capital equipment and the *replacement* cost. Economists generally argue for replacement costs as the correct measure of market value. The key issue for the market participants, however, is which method leads to higher rates. As observed by Gellhorn and Pierce (1982), regulated firms have argued for reproduction costs in the most recent inflationary period, with consumers arguing for historical costs, while the opposite sides have been taken in periods of falling costs. According to Gellhorn and Pierce (1982), 38 states use original cost to value the rate base and the other states use a weighted average of original and replacement costs referred to as "fair value." Given the "fair value" method, it is apparent that the consumer and firm intervenors will bargain over the relative weights to be used.

Another important issue is what assets of the utility to include in the rate base. A standard requirement that assets be "used and useful" gives the firm incentive to employ all of its assets to assure that the costs of the assets are reflected in its rates. This may result in inefficiencies if there are costs to using all available capacity and production requirements can be met at less than full capacity.

A significant related aspect of rate base measurement concerns the inclusion of the costs of "construction work in progress" (CWIP) in the rate base, as opposed to paying for construction after the asset is put into service. This is achieved through an "allowance for funds used during construction" (AFUDC). Gellhorn and Pierce (1982) state that "[a]s of 1976, 35 states and at least one major federal agency permitted firms to include some portion of CWIP in rate base." Gellhorn and Pierce observe that although the present discounted value of costs is identical in each case, the principal difference lies in the risk that with AFUDC, future rate decisions may disallow the asset as not "prudently acquired." This has been the case with a number of nuclear power plants, the costs of which have been borne by investors. Thus, consumers may be expected to prefer future payment for construction as a means of shifting risk to the utility's investors.

Vertically integrated companies pose complicated problems for rate regulation. The main problem is measurement of the cost of internally produced intermediate goods. This requires an evaluation of whether the internal transfer price of the intermediate good reflects its costs of production. Additional problems arise in determining the capital stock of the vertically integrated firm, particularly if the upstream division sells part of its output in markets that are not regulated. It is then not appropriate to treat the entire capital stock of the integrated firm as the rate base. Furthermore, upstream and downstream productive technologies may be *linked* as defined in chapter 3. Capital goods, in particular, may be public inputs in upstream and downstream production. This precludes full attribution of costs to upstream and downstream divisions and complicates the problem of determining the appropriate rate base.

A case in point is the regulation of telephone rates. The breakup of AT&T was essentially a vertical divestiture separating research (Bell Laboratories), manufacturing (Western Electric), long distance, and local service. Before the divestiture, AT&T strongly maintained that technological interdependences between research, manufacturing, and transmission services created substantial benefits. As Kahn (1971, p. 300) observes in this regard, "Not in petroleum, steel, cement, aluminum, motion pictures, or grocery distribution, in all of which integration has been both widely prevalent and strenuously debated, have its protagonists based their arguments so directly on technological grounds." It would be of some interest to test whether *economies of sequence* as defined in chapter 3 existed before divestiture by comparison with the costs of the nonintegrated postdivestiture firms.

Regulators are concerned that transfer prices are excessive, raising rates for downstream services and in some cases subsidizing upstream production. This problem occurs in such industries as telecommunications, electricity, and natural gas, where production and transmission are provided by a single firm; see, for example, Kahn (1971, p. 290). The transfer pricing test proposed in chapter 3 may be useful in determining an allowable range for internal prices. Let $C(Q)$ be the vertically integrated firm's total costs and let $C^U(X)$ and $C^D(Q; X)$ be estimates of the upstream costs of the intermediate input X and the downstream costs of the final output

Q given the intermediate input X. Then recall that the transfer price ρ of X must take values between average internal and stand alone costs, $[C(Q) - C^D(Q; X)]/X \le \rho \le C^U(X)/X$.

3. The maximum allowed *rate of return* is also an indirect way in which consumers and the regulated firm negotiate rates. The debate over an appropriate rate of return is generally in terms of the rate of return earned in industries with comparable risk, as in the Hope Natural Gas decision. The effects of rate of return regulation have been widely discussed in the context of the Averch Johnson model; see section 10.4. For finance analyses of the selection of rates of return in regulatory hearings, see, for example, Myers (1972), Pettway (1978), and Greenwald (1984).[14] The question of risk sharing and rate regulation are addressed in section 10.5. A variable rate of return is viewed as desirable to allow the regulated utility and its customers to share the risks associated with demand and cost fluctuations.

4. The relative prices for different utility services or charged to different customer classes constitute the utility's rate structure. Given multiple services or discriminatory pricing, various customer groups will present opposing viewpoints. This aspect of rate hearings will lead to the formation of customer coalitions representing, for example, residential, commercial, and industrial electricity customers. In this sense, bargaining over the rate structure may be compared to cooperative pricing games, such as the second-best pricing game discussed in chapter 6. The structure of the game can be modified to include the utility company itself as a player.

An important factor affecting the rate structure is the opportunity for certain customers to contract with alternative suppliers and to *bypass* the regulated utility. Customer classes, such as industrial customers, with the potential to seek new sources of supply will argue for a relaxation of entry regulations and for rates that are competitive with outside offers. Other customer classes, without similar access to competitive suppliers, may experience rate increases as joint costs are shifted to captive customers and rates are reduced to potential bypassers. I return to deregulation and bypass in the concluding chapter.

The choice of rules for allocating nonattributable joint costs affects the relative prices of services offered by utilities. Customer classes can be expected to disagree about cost allocation methods to the extent that their rates are increased. For example, joint fixed costs may be allocated on the basis of fully distributed cost rules, as discussed in chapter 3. Customer classes with, say, a lower share of total output than their share of total attributable cost would prefer a relative output method to a relative attributable cost method. The outcome of bargaining over the rate structure may reflect the political influence of customer classes and the preferences of regulators. This can create rate structures that favor residential customers at the expense of commercial or industrial customers or that favor rural customers at the expense of urban customers. The result may be discriminatory rates, which entail subsidies across utility services or across customer classes. Rate regulation combined with entry restrictions can lead to rate structures that depart significantly from efficient pricing.

The combination of decisions in categories (1)–(4) has been referred to as the "regulatory climate" by financial analysts. It should be emphasized that a dynamic analysis is required to evaluate the effects of regulatory policy on the cost of capital. A number of studies have emphasized that regulatory policies that are proconsumer in the short run may raise the long-term cost of capital for the utility in the long run, thus making consumers worse off. See Dubin and Navarro (1982) for an empirical study and discussion of the effects of the regulatory climate on the cost of capital to electric utilities. For my purposes here, I focus on the *short-run* effects of regulatory policy on static efficiency and on the allocation of economic rents between consumers and the firm.

10.2   The Bargaining Framework

Given the preceding discussion, it appears reasonable, as a first approximation, to approach rate regulation as a cooperative game with two players. One player represents the regulated firm and, broadly speaking, seeks to maximize profits for the firm's owners or dividends for the firm's investors. The other player represents the firm's customers and seeks to maximize consumer welfare. The role of the regulator can be that of an arbiter seeking to find a "reasonable" solution. The bargaining solution may reflect arbitrary criteria for what is a reasonable method of selecting an outcome. Alternatively, the bargaining solution may reflect the regulator's preferences or the relative bargaining strengths of the two players.

Let V represent the consumer's indirect utility. Let Π represent firm profits. Let $S \subset \mathbb{R}^2_+$ represent the feasible set.[15] Let $(\overline{V}, \overline{\Pi})$ represent the opportunity costs of entering the regulated market for the consumer and firm, respectively.[16] Thus, $\bar{V}$ represents the indirect utility of consumers obtained by purchasing substitutes to the regulated firm's output. Profit, $\bar{\Pi}$, represents the returns available to the regulated firm in other markets.

My primary concern is with the set of alternative outcomes (V, Π) that forms the core, contract curve, or efficient set for the bargaining game. An outcome (V, Π) is said to be *efficient* (or on the efficient frontier) if it satisfies three requirements. The outcome must be *feasible*, $(V, \Pi) \in S$. The outcome must be *individually rational*, $V \geq \bar{V}$ and $\Pi \geq \bar{\Pi}$. Finally, the outcome must be *Pareto optimal*, i.e., there does not exist $(V', \Pi') \in S$ such that $(V', \Pi') \geq (V, \Pi)$, $(V', \Pi') \neq (V, \Pi)$. Let $\mathscr{P}(S)$ denote the set of efficient outcomes.

Outcomes (V^*, Π^*) in the efficient set $\mathscr{P}(S)$ may be considered as solutions to the dual problems

$$\max_{(V, \Pi) \in S} V \quad \text{subject to } \Pi \geq \Pi^*, \tag{10.2.1}$$

$$\max_{(V, \Pi) \in S} \Pi \quad \text{subject to } V \geq V^*. \tag{10.2.2}$$

In particular, one may identify two "extreme points" of the efficient set. Assuming that regulation is in the "public interest," the regulated outcome will yield maximum consumer indirect utility $V_{\max}$, where $V_{\max}$ is the solution to

$$\max_{(V, \Pi) \in S} V \quad \text{subject to } \Pi \geq \bar{\Pi}. \tag{10.2.3}$$

Alternatively, if regulators are "captured" by the firms they regulate, the firm obtains monopoly profits $\Pi_{\max}$, which is the solution to

$$\max_{(V, \Pi) \in S} \Pi \quad \text{subject to } V \geq \bar{V}. \tag{10.2.4}$$

Usually, one expects regulated outcomes to take intermediate values in the efficient set. These outcomes correspond to the "zone of reasonableness" discussed previously. It will generally be possible to represent the efficient set or *contract curve* by the relation

$$V = P(\Pi), \tag{10.2.5}$$

where $P: [\bar{\Pi}, \Pi_{\max}] \rightarrow [\bar{V}, V_{\max}]$ and $(V_{\max}, \Pi_{\max})$ represent maximum attainable indirect utilities on the contract curve for the consumer and firm. Given $P(\cdot)$ differentiable, the slope of the efficient frontier is given by

$$\frac{dV}{d\Pi} = P'(\Pi), \tag{10.2.6}$$

for $\Pi \in [\bar{\Pi}, \Pi_{max}]$. This slope denotes the marginal rate of transformation of profits for the regulated firm into consumer indirect utility.

Although the concern here is primarily with the set of efficient outcomes $\mathscr{P}$, particular "bargaining solutions" may be considered. A bargaining solution, f, is assumed to select a specific outcome in S given $(\bar{V}, \bar{\Pi})$, $f(S, \bar{V}, \bar{\Pi}) \in S$. Many alternative solutions have been proposed.[17] I shall focus on the well-known Nash (1950, 1953) bargaining solution. The Nash bargaining solution, f^N, can be shown to be the unique bargaining solution satisfying a set of four axioms; see Nash (1950, 1953), Luce and Raiffa (1957), and Owen (1982).[18] Another approach is suggested by van Damme (1986), who examines the bargaining game in a dynamic, noncooperative setting. The independence of irrelevant alternatives axiom is replaced by a monotonicity axiom due to Roth (1979) and Kihlstrom, Roth, and Schmeidler (1981). Then van Damme (1986) introduces a dynamic bargaining procedure in which players continue bargaining over the set of payoffs that do not exceed previous demands. Van Damme shows the Nash bargaining solution to be the unique subgame perfect equilibrium of a two-stage game in which players choose bargaining solutions in the first stage and chance selects a bargaining game in the second stage. For further discussion of the Nash bargaining solution in dynamic models, see Binmore, Rubinstein, and Wolinsky (1986).

The Nash bargaining solution, $f^N(\cdot)$, is defined as follows:

$$f^N(S, \bar{V}, \bar{\Pi}) = \underset{(V, \Pi) \in S}{\arg \max} (V - \bar{V})(\Pi - \bar{\Pi}). \tag{10.2.7}$$

The Nash solution selects an outcome in the efficient set $\mathscr{P}$. The Nash outcome, (V^*, Π^*), thus solves the maximization problem in Π,

$$\max_{\Pi} (P(\Pi) - \bar{V})(\Pi - \bar{\Pi}). \tag{10.2.8}$$

The solution is then given by

$$P'(\Pi^*) = \frac{-(V^* - \bar{V})}{\Pi^* - \bar{\Pi}}, \tag{10.2.9}$$

where $V^* = P(\Pi^*)$. The right-hand side of (10.2.9) represents relative gains from trade for the consumer and firm. Thus, the Nash bargaining solution equates the marginal rate of transformation of profits into consumer indirect utility to relative gains from trade.

10.3 Bargaining over Rates and Costs

10.3.1 First-Best Pricing

Consider a simple case in which consumers and the regulated firm bargain over output Q and total rate payments R. The representative consumer has utility $U(Q, x)$, where x is a numeraire good. Let ω be the consumer's endowment. Thus, consumer indirect utility is given by $V(Q, R) = U(Q, \omega - R)$. The firm has cost $C(Q)$ and profits defined by $\Pi(Q, R) = R - C(Q)$. Assume that U is concave and increasing in (Q, x) and that $U_{Qx} \geq 0$. Let marginal costs be nondecreasing, $C''(Q) \geq 0$. Let the opportunity costs of trade be given by $\bar{V} = U(0, \omega)$ and $\bar{\Pi} = 0$.

Given R, we may obtain a Pareto optimal output schedule $Q = Q(R)$ from

$$U_Q(Q, \omega - R)/U_x(Q, \omega - R) = C'(Q). \tag{10.3.1}$$

This is the standard marginal cost-pricing result. Thus, the payment R may be in the form of a two-part tariff $R = E + pQ$, with $p = C'(Q)$. The key point of equation (10.3.1) is that output depends on the payment level R due to the income effects of payments on consumer utility. In particular, the optimal output schedule is decreasing in R since my assumptions imply

$$\frac{dQ(R)}{dR} = \frac{U_{Qx}(Q, \omega - R) - C'(Q)U_{xx}(Q, \omega - R)}{U_{QQ}(Q, \omega - R) - C''(Q)U_x(Q, \omega - R) - C'(Q)U_{xQ}(Q, \omega - R)}$$

$$< 0. \tag{10.3.2}$$

See figure 10.3.1. Let R_{min} and R_{max} denote the lowest and highest payment levels in the efficient set, where R_{min} and R_{max} solve[19]

$$R_{min} = C(Q(R_{min})) + \bar{\Pi}, \qquad U(Q(R_{max}), \omega - R_{max}) = \bar{U}. \tag{10.3.3}$$

Thus, $R \in [R_{min}, R_{max}]$ and $Q \in [Q(R_{max}), Q(R_{min})]$.

Let $R(\Pi)$ be defined by $\Pi = R - C(Q(R))$, where $dR(\Pi)/d\Pi = 1/(1 - C'(Q) dQ(R)/dR) > 0$. Then the efficient frontier is given by

$$V = P(\Pi) = U(Q(R(\Pi)), \omega - R(\Pi)). \tag{10.3.4}$$

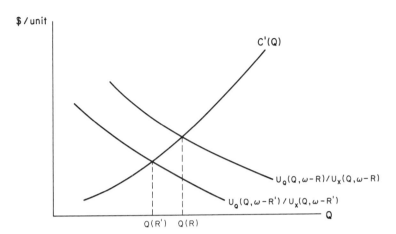

Figure 10.3.1
The output schedule is decreasing in payments, $R' > R$.

By the envelope theorem, the marginal rate of transformation along the efficient frontier is simply

$$P'(\Pi) = -U_x(Q(R(\Pi)), \omega - R(\Pi)). \tag{10.3.5}$$

The efficient frontier is concave since

$$P''(\Pi) = [-U_{xQ}(dQ/dR) + U_{xx}](dR/d\Pi) < 0.$$

Consider the Nash bargaining solution in the first-best case. Given output $Q = Q(R)$ from equation (10.3.1), the revenue R^* solves

$$U_x(Q(R^*), \omega - R^*) = (V^* - \bar{V})/(\Pi^* - \bar{\Pi}), \tag{10.3.6}$$

where $V^* = U(Q(R^*), \omega - R^*)$ and $\Pi^* = R^* - C(Q(R^*))$. The consumer's marginal utility of income is set equal to relative gains from trade for the consumer and firm. The solution is shown in figure 10.3.2. In this case both output and payment levels depend on the bargaining solution.

Consider the special case in which the consumer has a constant marginal utility of income, $U(Q, x) = u(Q) + x$. Then optimal output is unaffected by payment levels, $u'(Q^*) = C'(Q^*)$. Thus the bargaining problem is strictly concerned with setting payment levels. The transformation curve will be linear with a unitary slope. The Nash bargaining solution then simply equates gains from trade for the consumer and regulated firm, $V^* - \bar{V} =$

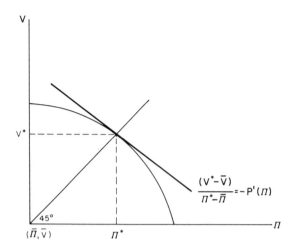

Figure 10.3.2
The Nash bargaining solution.

$\Pi^* - \bar{\Pi}$. Thus, $u(Q^*) + \omega - R^* - \bar{V} = R^* - C(Q^*) - \bar{\Pi}$ and the payment level R^* solves

$$R^* = (1/2)[u(Q^*) + \omega - \bar{V} + C(Q^*) + \bar{\Pi}]. \tag{10.3.7}$$

10.3.2 Second-Best Pricing

Consider now the effects on rate bargaining of restricting payments to linear prices. The second-best pricing problem is obtained. The single-good case is examined first. Demand $Q = Q(p)$ is given by $U_Q(Q, \omega - pQ)/U_x(Q, \omega - pQ) = p$. The price level $p(\Pi)$ is given by the profit equation, $\Pi = pQ(p) - C(Q(p))$. The efficient frontier is given as before,

$$V = P(\Pi) = U(Q(p(\Pi)), \omega - p(\Pi)Q(p(\Pi))). \tag{10.3.8}$$

Applying the envelope condition, the marginal rate of transformation is then

$$P'(\Pi) = -U_x(Q, \omega - pQ)Q\frac{dp(\Pi)}{d\Pi}, \tag{10.3.9}$$

where $Q = Q(p)$ and $p = p(\Pi)$. The price level is increasing in the firm profit level, $dp(\Pi)/d\Pi = 1/[Q(p) + (p - C'(Q(p)))\,\partial Q/\partial p] > 0$ for $p < p_m$, where p_m is the monopoly price. The price level takes values in the interval $[p_{min}, p_{max}]$, where p_{min} solves $\bar{\Pi} = p_{min}Q(p_{min}) - C(Q(p_{min}))$. The maximum price equals $\min\{p_m, \tilde{p}\}$, where $\tilde{p}$ solves $\bar{U} = U(Q(\tilde{p}), \omega - \tilde{p}Q(\tilde{p}))$. The efficient frontier is concave, given concave firm profits.[20]

Consider the Nash bargaining solution to the second-best pricing problem. From (10.2.9), equate the marginal rate of transformation to relative gains from trade,

$$\frac{U_x(Q^*, \omega - p^*Q^*)Q^*}{Q^* + (p - C'(Q^*))\partial Q/\partial p} = \frac{V^* - V}{\Pi^* - \bar{\Pi}}, \tag{10.3.10}$$

where $Q^* = Q(p^*)$, $p^* = p(\Pi^*)$. Rearranging terms in equation (10.3.10) and letting $\eta_D = -(\partial Q(p)/\partial p)(p/Q)$ denote the elasticity of demand give an equation for the relative markup above marginal cost,

$$\frac{p - C'(Q)}{p} = \frac{1}{\eta_D}\left(1 - U_x(Q^*, \omega - p^*Q^*)\frac{(\Pi^* - \bar{\Pi})}{(V^* - \bar{V})}\right). \tag{10.3.11}$$

It is of interest that even in the one good case, the consumer elasticity of demand is a determinant of the firm's relative markup. This is because demand elasticity affects marginal profits, which appears as the denominator in the marginal rate of transformation, $dV/d\Pi$. In addition, recall that in the first-best case, the marginal rate of transformation was U_x. Thus, the term in parentheses on the right of (10.3.11) represents the departure from unity of the ratio of U_x to the relative gains from trade, $(V^* - \bar{V})/(\Pi^* - \bar{\Pi})$. This distortion is due to using linear pricing to achieve both rationing of the good Q and allocation of payments between the consumer and the firm. Let $d = [1 - U_x/((V^* - \bar{V})/(\Pi^* - \bar{\Pi}))]$ represent the distortion factor. Thus, the relative markup given by the Nash bargaining solution equals the distortion factor d times the reciprocal of demand elasticity.

Consider now the multiple-goods version of the second-best-pricing problem. Suppose there are only two regulated goods—say, peak and off-peak electricity. Let prices $p_1 = h_1(\Pi)$, $p_2 = h_2(\Pi)$ solve the familiar second-best Pareto optimality conditions,

$$Q_1(p^*)/Q_2(p^*) = \Pi_1(p^*)/\Pi_2(p^*), \tag{10.3.12}$$

where $\Pi_i(p) = \partial\Pi(p)/\partial p_i$, $i = 1, 2$. From the zero-profit constraint, $\Pi_1(p)h_1'(\Pi) + \Pi_2(p)h_2'(\Pi) = 1$. Thus, the marginal rate of transformation between profits and consumer indirect utility is given by

$$P'(\Pi) = V_1(p)h'_1(\Pi) + V_2(p)h'_2(\Pi)$$

$$= V_2(p)\left[\frac{V_1(p)}{V_2(p)}h'_1(\Pi) + h'_2(\Pi)\right]$$

$$= -U_x(Q, \omega - pQ)Q_2/\Pi_2(p) = -U_x(Q, \omega - pQ)Q_1/\Pi_1(p). \quad (10.3.13)$$

The Nash bargaining solution yields

$$U_x(Q, \omega - pQ)Q_l = [(V^* - \bar{V})/(\Pi^* - \bar{\Pi})]\Pi_l(p), \qquad l = 1, 2. \quad (10.3.14)$$

This is equivalent to second-best pricing if the shadow price on the non-zero-profit condition takes the value $\gamma = (V^* - \bar{V})/(\Pi^* - \bar{\Pi})$ and the constraint is replaced by $\Pi(p) \geq \Pi^*$.

10.3.3   Cost-Based Pricing

Consider now a rate hearing in which rates depend entirely on the definition of total cost adopted by the regulatory authority. Let C_{τ_0} represent total historical costs for the test year τ_0. Suppose that C_{τ_1} represents projected total costs or costs calculated on the basis of replacement values. Assume that due to inflation or changes in relative input prices, historical costs are less than replacement costs, $C_{\tau_0} < C_{\tau_1}$. The regulatory authority follows a "fair value" pricing formula in estimating total costs,

$$C_\lambda = \lambda C_{\tau_0} + (1 - \lambda)C_{\tau_1}, \quad (10.3.15)$$

where λ takes values between zero and one. The issue to be resolved at the rate hearing is the value of the weight λ.

   Given a choice of λ, total revenue must not exceed C_λ. Given inverse demand $p(Q)$, the firm's revenue function equals $R(Q) = p(Q)Q$. Let $C(Q)$ represent actual costs as perceived by the regulated firm. Assume that revenue is concave in Q and costs are convex for output $Q > 0$. Then the firm will choose output to solve the following problem:

$$\max_Q [R(Q) - C(Q)] \qquad \text{subject to } R(Q) \leq C_\lambda. \quad (10.3.16)$$

Let Q^m represent the unconstrained monopoly output. Suppose that the revenue requirement constraint is strictly binding, $C_\lambda \leq R(Q^m)$. Then, if $Q > 0$ solves (10.3.16), it follows that profit is maximized where $R(Q) = C_\lambda$. Thus, output is a function of the cost weight λ, $Q = Q(\lambda)$. Note that output is strictly decreasing in λ, $\partial Q/\partial \lambda = (C_{\tau_0} - C_{\tau_1})/R'(Q)$. The firm's profit as a function of λ is then simply

$$\Pi(\lambda) = C_\lambda - C(Q(\lambda)). \tag{10.3.17}$$

Profits are strictly decreasing in λ, since $\Pi'(\lambda) = (C_{\tau_0} - C_{\tau_1})[(R'(Q) - C'(Q))/R'(Q)]$. The contract curve is defined by

$$V = P(\Pi) = U(Q(\lambda), \omega - R(Q(\lambda))), \tag{10.3.18}$$

where the weight $\lambda = \lambda(\Pi)$ is uniquely associated with each profit level. The slope of the efficient frontier is then positive,

$$P'(\Pi) = -U_x(Q, \omega - R(Q))Qp'(Q)/(R'(Q) - C'(Q)). \tag{10.3.19}$$

But this is just (10.3.9) for the second-best pricing problem. If the marginal rate of transformation is equated to the relative gains from trade, (10.3.10) and (10.3.11) are again obtained. This implies that the relative markup at the bargaining solution is the same as that under second-best pricing. The same analysis may be extended to the multiproduct case. This yields the surprising conclusion that cost-based price regulation is equivalent to Ramsey price regulation. The reason for this is that the linear price reflects bargaining between consumers and the regulated firm over the rents from exchange.

10.4   Bargaining over the Rate of Return

As a basic framework, consider the Averch-Johnson (A-J) model (1962) of rate of return regulation. The Averch-Johnson model has been examined within a large literature; see, in particular, Baumol and Klevorick (1970), Takayama (1969), Zajac (1972), Bailey and Malone (1970), Johnson (1973), and Marino (1979). In this model, the regulator selects a maximum allowable rate of return, s, which it is assumed strictly exceeds the cost of capital, r. Assume also that s is less than or equal to the monopoly rate of return s_m. The firm maximizes profits subject to a rate of return constraint by choosing output and input levels.

Let revenue be given by $R(Q) = Qp(Q)$, where $p(Q)$ is market inverse demand. The firm purchases a single variable input, labor, at competitive wage w. The firm's capital stock or rate base K is purchased at a competitive price r. The utility's production technology is described by a neoclassical production function, $Q = f(K, L)$. Assume that f is twice differentiable, increasing, and concave in capital and labor. Let $f_K \equiv \partial f(K, L)/\partial K$ and $f_L \equiv \partial f(K, L)/\partial L$.

For ease of presentation, suppose also that f is homothetic. The homotheticity assumption implies that there is a *unique* capital-labor ratio K^0/L^0 that equates the marginal rate of technical substitution to the factor price ratio r/w. This restriction allows an examination of the capital-labor bias that is independent of the firm's output level. The homotheticity condition admits CES and Cobb–Douglas-type production functions. These forms are used in empirical studies of regulation by Smithson (1978), Hayashi and Trapani (1976), Courville (1974), Schmalensee (1977), and Baron and Taggart (1977). Spann (1974), Peterson (1975), Boyes (1976), and Giordano (1982) employ more general forms.

The firm's rate of return is defined by revenues net of operating expenses divided by the rate base, $ROR = (R(Q) - wL)/K$. The utility is assumed to maximize profits subject to its production constraint and the maximum rate of return constraint, $ROR \leq s$. Thus, one may define the firm's profit as a function of its maximum allowable rate of return,

$$\Pi(s) = \max_{Q,K,L} R(Q) - wL - rK$$

$$\text{subject to} \quad Q = f(K,L), R(Q) - wL \leq sK. \tag{10.4.1}$$

As is well-known (see Baumol and Klevorick, 1970), the first-order necessary conditions imply

$$R'(Q)f_K(K,L) = r - (\xi/(1 - \xi))(s - r), \tag{10.4.2}$$

$$R'(Q)f_L(K,L) = w, \tag{10.4.3}$$

where ξ is the shadow price on the rate of return constraint. Solving (10.4.2), (10.4.3), and the production and rate of return constraints, yields a solution parameterized by the maximum allowed rate of return s, $Q(s)$, $K(s)$, $L(s)$, $\xi(s)$.

Combining (10.4.2) and (10.4.3), it follows that

$$f_K(K,L)/f_L(K,L) = r/w - (\xi/(1 - \xi))(s - r)/w. \tag{10.4.4}$$

The shadow price ξ is positive and less than one; see Zajac (1972). Thus, by homotheticity, it is immediate that the capital-labor ratio exceeds the cost-minimizing capital-labor ratio. In general, the capital-labor ratio will exceed the cost-minimizing ratio at the regulated firm's output level, although it need not exceed the cost-minimizing ratio at the unregulated profit-maximizing output; see Baumol and Klevorick (1970).

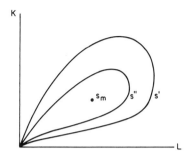

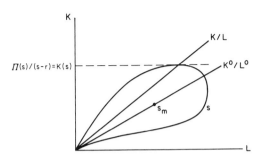

Figure 10.4.1
Lines of iso rate of return.

Figure 10.4.2
The regulated capital-labor ratio K/L is above
the optimum K^0/L^0.

The maximization may be characterized graphically as in Zajac (1970) and Baumol and Klevorick (1970). The regulatory constraint, $ROR \le s$ can be represented in input space using the production function. Suppose that the rate of return constraint is binding, $R(f(K,L)) - wL - sK = 0$. Then two isorate of return lines are given in figure 10.4.1. Suppose that the allowed rate of return s'' exceeds s'. Then, in figure 10.4.1, the isorate of return line for s'' lies "inside" the isorate of return line for s'. The point s_m indicates the monopoly inputs that earn the maximum rate of return s_m.

Substitute from the rate of return constraint into the objective function. Then the firm's profit function is given by $\Pi(s) = (s - r)K(s)$, where $K(s)$ is obtained from the solution to problem (10.4.1). Thus, maximizing profit entails selecting the largest capital stock that strictly satisfies the rate of return constraint; see figure 10.4.2. By homotheticity of f the efficient capital-labor combinations may be represented as a straight line. Note that the profit maximum, s_m, lies on the efficient locus. As shown in figure 10.4.2, the regulated capital-labor ratio K/L exceeds the efficient ratio K^0/L^0.

Differentiating both sides of $\Pi(s) = (s - r)K(s)$ with respect to the allowed rate of return yields

$$\Pi'(s) = K(s) + (s - r)\,dK/ds. \tag{10.4.5}$$

Using the envelope result, $\Pi'(s) = \xi K$, it follows that the effect of the rate of return on capital is

$$dK/ds = -K(1 - \xi)/(s - r). \tag{10.4.6}$$

Thus, the capital stock is *decreasing* in the allowed rate of return, since $0 < \xi < 1$, as noted, and $s > r$ by assumption.

Consider the effect of an increase in the allowable rate of return on the utility's profits,

$$\Pi'(s) = \xi K. \tag{10.4.7}$$

Thus, the marginal effect on profit of increases in the allowable rate of return equals the shadow price on the firm's rate of return constraint times the rate base. If the allowable rate of return is set by choosing profits $s = \Pi^{-1}(\Pi)$, it follows that $\partial s/\partial \Pi = 1/\xi K > 0$.

Assume that isoquants have the standard convex shape; that is, the marginal rate of technical substitution f_K/f_L is decreasing in the capital-labor ratio. The effect of the allowable rate of return on the firm's output and employment levels is in general ambiguous. However, given a diminishing marginal rate of technical substitution, it follows that $f_{LL}/f_L < f_{LK}/f_K$. From the production relation, $dQ/ds = f_K \, dK/ds + f_L \, dL/ds$. Further, from (10.4.3),

$$R''(Q)f_L(f_K \, dK + f_L \, dL) + R'(Q)(f_{LK} \, dK + f_{LL} \, dL) = 0. \tag{10.4.8}$$

Thus, changes in output and capital are related in the following manner:

$$\frac{dQ}{ds} = \left(\frac{R'(Q)(f_K f_{LL} - f_L f_{LK})}{R''(Q)(f_L)^2 + R'(Q)f_{LL}} \right) \frac{dK}{ds}. \tag{10.4.9}$$

The denominator is negative, since R is concave in Q and f is concave in L. Then dQ/ds has the same sign as dK/ds, since by assumption $(f_K f_{LL} - f_L f_{LK}) < 0$; see Baumol and Klevorick (1970) for a similar derivation. Therefore, given a diminishing marginal rate of technical substitution, output is *decreasing* in the allowed rate of return.[21]

Clearly, consumer welfare is reduced by a lower equilibrium output. Thus, consumer welfare is reduced by increases in the allowable rate of return, s, if output is decreasing in s. The rate of return varies in the interval (r, s_m), yielding a direct trade-off between consumer welfare and utility profits.[22] As the rate of return approaches the monopoly level, the regulatory commission may be said to be captured by the utility. As the rate of return falls to the competitive level, regulation may be said to be in the public interest. Of course, given ambiguous effects of the rate of return on output, the trade-off will not always be so direct.

The efficient frontier is easily constructed by noting that equilibrium output depends on the rate of return, $Q = Q(s)$,

$$V = P(\Pi) = U(Q(s), \omega - R(Q(s))), \tag{10.4.10}$$

where $s = s(\Pi) = \Pi^{-1}(\Pi)$. As before, the underlying rate of return takes values in some range $[s_{\min}, s_{\max}]$. Applying the envelope condition yields the marginal rate of transformation,

$$P'(\Pi) = -U_x(Q, \omega - R(Q))Qp'(Q)\frac{\partial Q}{\partial s}\frac{ds}{d\Pi}, \tag{10.4.11}$$

where $Q = Q(s)$ and $s = s(\Pi)$. Note that $ds/d\Pi = 1/\xi K$. Then (10.4.11) reduces to

$$P'(\Pi) = U_\zeta(Q, \omega - R(Q))\frac{\partial Q}{\partial s}\frac{1}{\eta_D \xi K}, \tag{10.4.12}$$

given that $1/\eta_D \equiv Qp'(Q)/p(Q)$. The slope of the efficient frontier equals the marginal utility of output times the fall in output due to raising s over the elasticity of demand times the marginal effect on profits from raising s.

The Nash bargaining solution may be used to calculate the allowable rate of return. In particular, equate the marginal rate of transformation to the ratio of gains from trade,

$$\frac{-U_Q(Q, \omega - R(Q))(\partial Q/\partial s)}{\eta_D \xi K} = \frac{V^* - \bar{V}}{\Pi^* - \bar{\Pi}}, \tag{10.4.13}$$

where $V^* = U(Q, \omega - R(Q))$ and $\Pi^* = R(Q) - C(Q)$. Letting $Q = Q(s)$, equation (10.4.13) may be solved for the allowable rate of return s^*. The marginal benefits to the consumer from a lower rate of return $-U_Q(Q, \omega - R(Q))(\partial Q/\partial s)/\eta_D$ are equal to relative gains from trade, $(V^* - \bar{V})/(\Pi^* - \bar{\Pi})$, times the lower profit for the firm, ξK.

This section has focused on a static analysis. The pricing decisions of the firm have been examined in a dynamic framework in a number of papers. The effects of regulatory lag on pricing when the output price is imperfectly adjusted by regulators is examined by Bailey and Coleman (1971), Baumol and Klevorick (1970), and Davies (1973).[23] The investment decisions of a firm given adjustment costs and irreversibilities is studied in a dynamic setting by El-Hodiri and Takayama (1981)[24] and Spulber and Becker (1983). The effects of constraining the rate of return, while yielding immediate benefits for consumers may reduce welfare in future periods by reducing incentives for investment in future periods. The standard overcapitalization result observed in a static setting may not occur in a dynamic model. Spulber and Becker (1983) consider a two-period model in which the utility experiences either regulatory lag or deregulation in the second period.

In the regulatory lag case, the firm acts as a monopolist in the first (unregulated) period and acts as an Averch-Johnson firm in the second (regulated) period. This leads the firm to desire more capital in the second period, as might be expected from the static A-J model, where a regulated firm employs more capital than an unregulated firm. However, because the firm desires more capital in the second period than in the first, and because of internal adjustment costs, the firm employs more capital in the first period than would be optimal in a single period. This causes the firm to overcapitalize in the first period, leading to a lower than optimal labor-capital ratio. The firm may not overcapitalize in the regulated second period because the marginal costs of adjusting the capital stock offset the incentive to overcapitalize created by the rate of return constraint. Thus, the Averch-Johnson effect is observed *before* regulation but not necessarily afterward. Sufficient conditions are given for the capital bias to increase after regulation.

In the deregulation case considered by Spulber and Becker (1983), the firm wishes to act as a monopolist in the second (unregulated) period and as an Averch-Johnson firm in the first (regulated) period. The rate of return constraint gives the firm an incentive to employ more capital in the first period than in the second period. With reversible investment, conditions are given under which capital stock is reduced in the second period. Due to symmetric adjustment costs, the Averch-Johnson bias is preserved in the unregulated period, although labor-capital rates are lower in the regulated period as in the regulatory lag case. When investment is irreversible, the firm desiring to employ a lower capital stock as a monopolist in the second period is constrained to maintain a constant capital stock. Conditions are given under which the flexible input, labor, is constant, thus implying a constant labor-capital ratio and output.

This analysis suggests that dynamic considerations must exist in the regulatory-bargaining process. In particular, the sequence of allowable rates of return will affect the firm's investment strategy over time. The results obtained by Spulber and Becker (1983) suggest that an empirical test for regulatory bias must involve specification of a dynamic model.

This may partly explain the somewhat contradictory results obtained by a number of empirical papers that are tests of static models. See the empirical studies of Courville (1974), Spann (1974), Peterson (1975), Hayashi and Trapani (1976), Boyes (1976), Smithson (1978), and Giordano (1982). Boyes (1976), in particular, finds a lack of evidence for the A-J effect and suggests that various intertemporal effects may be responsible for this. An interesting question would be whether the A-J effect can be observed when capital is imperfectly flexible and not at an equilibrium level. The effectiveness to the rate of return constraint may then affect the speed of adjustment of the equilibrium capital stock. Nickell (1978) examines the literature on testing investment demand equations when adjustment costs are present. These techniques may be applicable to a test of the A-J hypothesis in a dynamic investment framework.

10.5 Bargaining and Risk Sharing

The market for electricity and other regulated utility services is subject to considerable uncertainty. Regulatory decisions affecting the utility's output, quality of service, and rate structure involve sharing of risk between consumers and the utility. The degree to which risk shifting occurs is of great concern to regulators, consumers, and investors in publicly owned utilities. Traditionally, utilities have been assured a deterministic rate of return, which has caused the risks of supply and demand shocks to be shifted to consumers. With the disallowance of some large-scale expenditures (such as nuclear power plants), increasing reliance on market valuations of electricity, and performance-based compensation, utility regulators have shifted some risks to the utility's owners. In this section, bargaining over rates and output is examined in a stochastic setting.[25] The object of this analysis is to represent the negotiation over risk-sharing arrangements implicit in rate hearings.

The utility's cost function is given by $C(Q, \theta)$, where Q represents output or quality and reliability of service and θ represents an exogenous supply shock. Let θ be distributed by the continuous cumulative distribution function $G(\theta)$. Assume that $C_\theta > 0$, $C_{Q\theta} > 0$ and $C_{QQ} > 0$. The consumers and utility have common beliefs about the probability distribution of shocks θ. The disturbance θ may represent factor price changes, such as oil price increases, wage demands by labor, and capital market costs.

The disturbance θ can also represent technological uncertainty, such as equipment failure.[26] Technological change can also be modeled by the random parameter θ. Finally, the effect of other regulations on costs (such as environmental regulation) may be handled by a random disturbance θ.

Let $\Pi(Q, R, \theta) = R - C(Q, \theta)$ represent firm profits for each realization of the random variable θ. It is assumed that the firm's owners may be risk averse, with concave utility of profits $Z(\Pi)$. Let minimum utility for the firm be given by $\bar{Z} > 0$.

Let consumer indirect utility be as before, $V(Q, R) = U(Q, \omega - R)$. For ease of exposition, ignore demand side shocks for now. Pareto optimal risk sharing is achieved by a complete contingent contract between the utility and consumers, $(Q(\theta), R(\theta))$, which satisfies

$$U_Q(Q(\theta), \omega - R(\theta)) = \lambda Z'(R(\theta) - C(Q(\theta), \theta))C_Q(Q(\theta), \theta), \qquad (10.5.1)$$

$$U_x(Q(\theta), \omega - R(\theta)) = \lambda Z'(R(\theta) - C(Q(\theta), \theta)) \qquad (10.5.2)$$

for all θ. Associated with each Pareto optimum is a weight λ that is constant across all states θ. The Pareto set is defined by values of expected utility, $V^e \equiv EV$, $Z^e \equiv EZ$, for the consumer and firm such that $V^e \geq \bar{V}$ and $Z^e \geq \bar{Z}$. Combining equations (10.5.1) and (10.5.2) yields

$$U_Q(Q(\theta), \omega - R(\theta)) = U_x(Q(\theta), \omega - R(\theta))C_Q(Q(\theta), \theta), \qquad (10.5.3)$$

in each state θ. Compare equation (10.5.3) with (10.3.1) for the deterministic case.

The Pareto frontier is then defined by $V^e \geq \bar{V}$, $Z^e \geq \bar{Z}$ such that

$$V^e \equiv P(Z^e) \equiv \int U(Q(\theta, Z^e), \omega - R(\theta, Z^e)) \, dG(\theta), \qquad (10.5.4)$$

and where (Q, R, λ) solves equations (10.5.1), (10.5.2), and the following condition:

$$Z^e \equiv \int Z(R(\theta, Z^e) - C(Q(\theta, Z^e), \theta)) \, dG(\theta). \qquad (10.5.5)$$

The trade-off along the Pareto frontier is given by

$$P'(Z^e) = \int \left[U_Q \frac{\partial Q}{\partial Z^e} - U_x \frac{\partial R}{\partial Z^e} \right] dG(\theta). \qquad (10.5.6)$$

Substituting from equations (10.5.1) and (10.5.2) into (10.5.6), it follows that

$$P'(Z^e) = \lambda(Z^e) \int \left[Z' \left(C_Q \frac{\partial Q}{\partial Z^e} - \frac{\partial R}{\partial Z^e} \right) \right] dG(\theta). \tag{10.5.7}$$

Differentiating (10.4.4) totally with respect to the firm's utility Z^e gives

$$1 = \int \left[Z' \left(\frac{\partial R}{\partial Z^e} - C_Q \frac{\partial Q}{\partial Z^e} \right) \right] dG(\theta). \tag{10.5.8}$$

Thus, combining equations (10.5.7) and (10.5.8), the slope of the utility possibilities frontier is simply

$$P'(Z^e) = -\lambda(Z^e). \tag{10.5.9}$$

The trade-off between consumer marginal utility and firm marginal benefits is constant across states, so that $P'(Z^e) = -U_Q(Q, \omega - R)/Z'(R - C(Q, \theta))C_Q(Q, \theta) = -U_x(Q, \omega - R)/Z'(R - C(Q, \theta))$ for all θ, where $Q = Q(\theta, Z^e)$, $R = R(\theta, Z^e)$.

The Nash bargaining solution is obtained by the standard maximization,

$$\max_{\{Q(\theta), R(\theta)\}} \left[\int U(Q, \omega - R) \, dG(\theta) - \bar{V} \right] \left[\int Z(R - C(Q, \theta)) \, dG(\theta) - \bar{Z} \right]. \tag{10.5.10}$$

It follows immediately that

$$\frac{U_x(Q^*(\theta), \omega - R^*(\theta))}{Z'(R^*(\theta) - C(Q^*(\theta), \theta))} = \frac{(V^* - \bar{V})}{(Z^* - \bar{Z})} \tag{10.5.11}$$

for all θ, where $V^* = \int U(Q^*(\theta), \omega - R^*(\theta)) \, dG(\theta)$, $Z^* = \int Z(R^*(\theta) - C(Q^*(\theta), \theta)) \, dG(\theta)$ and (Q^*, R^*) satisfies equation (10.5.3) for each θ. Therefore, the relative expected gains from trade $(V^* - \bar{V})/(Z^* - \bar{Z})$ determine the trade-off between marginal utilities for the consumer and firm across states θ.

From (10.5.3), it is apparent that optimal output and rates cannot both be constant across states θ due to the effect of the shocks on marginal costs. Generally, optimal risk sharing will involve both variable rates and variable output. Thus, requiring constant rates in a period in which costs vary entails avoidable welfare losses. Further, changes in costs should also be reflected in variable output or quality of service.

The preceding conclusion also applies even given risk neutrality on the part of the firm, assuming nonseparable consumer utility. Let Z exhibit constant marginal utility. Then, from (10.5.2), the consumer's marginal utility of income must be constant across states, $U_x = \lambda$ for all θ. However, since Q and R cannot both be constant across θ, it follows that Q and R both vary to maintain $U_x = \lambda$. One interpretation of this is that output fluctuations are required for optimal production, while rate fluctuations represent insurance provided by the firm. Still assuming risk neutrality for the firm, suppose that a constant output or a constant quality of service is imposed by the regulator. The result will be a second-best optimum in which rates are also held constant to maintain a constant marginal utility of income for the consumer. In this case the firm absorbs all cost fluctuations as profit fluctuations. The constant output and rates $(\bar{Q}, \bar{R})$ solve

$$U_Q(\bar{Q}, \omega - \bar{R}) = \lambda \int C_Q(\bar{Q}, \theta) \, dG(\theta),$$

and $U_x(\bar{Q}, \omega - \bar{R}) = \lambda$. Conversely, suppose that the regulator requires fixed rates. Then output or quality varies with costs. The output schedule $\tilde{Q}$ and constant rates $\tilde{R}$ will satisfy $U_Q(\tilde{Q}(\theta), \omega - \tilde{R}) = \lambda C_Q(\tilde{Q}(\theta), \theta)$ and $\int U_x(\tilde{Q}(\theta), \omega - \tilde{R}) \, dG(\theta) = \lambda$. Here, the consumer's expected marginal utility of income will vary depending on changes in costs. Given my assumptions on costs, the output level will be strictly decreasing in the cost parameter θ. The output fluctuations will partially offset the effect of the shocks θ on the firm's costs.

Given second-best pricing, optimal risk sharing will lead to variable rates and variable output whether the firm is risk averse or risk neutral. Letting demand $Q(p)$ be given by $U_Q(Q, \omega - pQ)/U_x(Q, \omega - pQ) = p$, the rate $p = p(\theta)$ solves

$$U_x(Q, \omega - pQ) = \lambda Z'(pQ - C(Q, \theta))[p(\partial Q/\partial p) + Q - C_Q(Q, \theta)(\partial Q/\partial p)].$$

Clearly, fixing per unit prices at a constant level will cause all cost fluctuations to be reflected in firm profits. Constant prices will then solve

$$U_x(Q, \omega - pQ) = \lambda \int Z'(pQ - C(Q, \theta))[(p - C_Q(Q, \theta))(\partial Q/\partial p) + Q] \, dG(\theta).$$

It has been common regulatory practice to assure the regulated firm a constant or riskless rate of return.[27] In the simple one-good framework, let the effects of the disturbance θ be confined to variable costs $c(Q, \theta)$. Let r represent the cost of capital and let K represent the rate base; costs are then $C(Q, \theta) = rK + c(Q, \theta)$. A constant rate of return $s > r$ requires that output and rates be such that $R - c(Q, \theta) = sK$ for all θ. Thus, firm profits are constant $\Pi = (s - r)K$. Letting $R = pQ(p)$, it follows that output and rates must vary with every cost shock, $\partial p/\partial \theta = c_\theta(Q, \theta)/(p(\partial Q/\partial p) + Q - c_Q(\partial Q/\partial p))$. Thus, maintaining a riskless rate of return for the firm shifts all risks to the consumer in the form of varying prices. Both the firm and consumer can benefit from risk sharing and a variable rate of return.

A related issue is the pass-through to rates of variable cost increases through automatic fuel cost adjustment clauses. The incentives for input distortions created by second-best regulation with automatic cost pass-throughs are well-known (see the discussion in section 10.1). As shown in Baron and DeBondt (1981), if the random cost parameter is observable, then first-best regulation requires sharing of the risks of variable factor prices between consumers and the regulated firm. Baron and DeBondt observe that imperfect observation of factor costs leads to imperfect adjustment relative to the full information case. Imperfect information results in a distortion of the potential risk-sharing function of fuel cost adjustment clauses.

Consider now the presence of demand shocks. Generally, these can be modeled by letting $U = U(Q, \omega(\mu) - R, \mu)$, where μ is a random variable that affects consumer income, $\omega(\mu)$, and tastes. Demand shocks might also include changes in the price of substitutes or energy conservation efforts. A great amount of attention has been given to utility pricing in the presence of fluctuating demand, particularly in the context of peak load pricing and the choice of capacity to accommodate peak demand. On utility pricing in the presence of uncertain demand, see Boiteux (1951b), Brown and Johnson (1969), Meyer (1975), Sherman and Visscher (1978), and Riordan (1984).

Notes

1. See Williamson's (1976) discussion of sunk costs in the context of cable television franchise awards.

2. See Goldberg (1976) on regulation as an "administered contract."

3. See Gormley (1983) and Fessler (1942).

4. Gormley (1983, p. 34) observes that "the overall level of public participation in public utility proceedings rose sharply in the 1970s, as a wide variety of interest groups intervened on behalf of consumers, the poor, and other underrepresented interests."

5. Gormley (1983, p. 34) finds that "the mid-1970s witnessed a sharp increase in the number of state public advocacy offices, which were empowered to represent consumers in public utility commission proceedings and, in most instances, the courts." Overall, grass roots

advocates or proxy advocates have been actively involved in utility commission hearings in three-fourths of the states according to Gormley (1983, p. 64).

6. Gormley (1983, p. 32) observes that "utility companies dominate the flow of information to public utility commissions" through "legal briefs, statistical compilations, feasibility studies, and customer surveys." Of particular importance in rate setting are forecasts of demand, input supplies, and cost of capital estimates provided by the regulated firm.

7. Gormley (1983) studies the preferences of public utility commissioners and their staffs and states that (p. 128) "on most issues, utilities are more likely to be supported by the staff than by the commissioners, more likely to be supported by the commissioners than by public advocates."

8. See Gellhorn and Pierce (1982, p. 165).

9. The decision in Permian Basin is quoted in Gellhorn and Pierce (1982, p. 166).

10. See, for example, Breyer (1982, chapter 3), Pierce, Allison, and Martin (1980), Gellhorn and Pierce (1982), and Kahn (1970, chapter 2).

11. Some commissions adjust cost estimates for inflation; see Breyer (1982, p. 50).

12. Interfuel substitution in electricity generation is considered in Atkinson and Halvorsen (1976).

13. Ehrenberg (1979) finds that regulation may have led to higher wages in telecommunications. However, Grawe and Kafoglis (1982) suggest this may not be the case in regulated industries, although unionization may be a factor and the extent of unionization itself may be partly dependent on regulation.

14. Greenwald (1984) examines the issue of "fair" rates of return in regulated industries. Greenwald (1984, p. 85) observes that with repeated regulation and imperfectly flexible capital "a regulatory authority can always systematically violate investor expectations (in the short run at least) by pursuing a sufficiently aggressive pricing policy." Greenwald (1984, p. 94) notes that "fairness merely implies that allowed price levels equate the market value of a utility to its rate base."

15. Let S be a nonempty, compact, convex subset of $\mathbb{R}^2_+$.

16. It is assumed that the opportunity costs $(\bar{V}, \bar{\Pi})$ are given. Generally, these allocations are given by the amounts that the two players can assure themselves through noncooperative behavior. Thus, $(\bar{V}, \bar{\Pi})$ generally represents the amounts obtained by maximin strategies.

17. These solutions include the Nash bargaining solution (Nash, 1950, 1953), Kalai and Smorodinsky (1975), and Perles and Maschler (1981). See the survey in Roth (1979).

18. The Nash bargaining solution (Nash, 1950, 1953) is the unique solution satisfying a set of axioms that includes efficiency (feasibility, individual rationality, and Pareto optimality), independence of irrelevant alternatives, independence of linear transformations, and symmetry.

19. Profits are strictly increasing in R,

$$\frac{\partial \Pi(Q(R), R)}{\partial R} = 1 - C'(Q)\frac{dQ(R)}{dR} > 0$$

Consumer utility is strictly decreasing in R,

$$\frac{\partial U(Q(R), \omega - R)}{\partial R} = U_Q(Q, \omega - R)\frac{dQ(R)}{dR} - U_x(Q, \omega - R) < 0.$$

Thus, $R_{\min}$ solves $\Pi(Q(R_{\min}), R_{\min}) = \bar{\Pi}$ and $R_{\max}$ solves $V(Q(R_{\max}), R_{\max}) = \bar{V}$.

20. Let $\Pi(p) = pQ(p) - C(Q(p))$. Then

$$P''(\Pi) = (1/\Pi'(p))^2 [[-U_{xQ} + U_{xx}(pQ'(p) + Q)]Q\Pi'(p)$$

$$- \Pi'(p)U_x + \Pi''(p)U_{xQ}]\frac{dp(\Pi)}{d\Pi}.$$

If $\Pi''(p) < 0$, then $P''(\Pi) < 0$.

21. The effect of regulation on labor demand is ambiguous.

22. Klevorick (1971) considers the rate of return that maximizes social welfare. This is related to our framework, since the Nash bargaining solution may be associated with "welfare weights on consumer indirect utility and firm profits." Note, however, that Klevorick (1971) employs optimal pricing. See also Klevorick (1966).

23. See also the extensive dynamic analysis of Klevorick (1973) concerning operation and research activities of a firm subject to stochastic regulatory reviews.

24. El-Hodiri and Takayama (1981) examine a continuous time model for finite and infinite planning horizons. They first consider the properties of a steady-state solution derived for an infinite horizon problem. They find an A-J effect for the case of a binding regulatory constraint at each instance. Next they consider a finite horizon framework where capital is permitted to change over time. In this framework, the regulatory constraint need not be effective for all time (p. 39). Their main result in this case is that investment cannot be greater for all time along the regulated path as compared with the unregulated path. In an example, they show that if the regulatory constraint is effective for all time, then the terminal stock of capital under regulation exceeds the terminal stock of capital obtained, assuming that regulation is never a binding constraint.

25. For an analysis of bargaining under uncertainty and a comparison of the Nash solution with the Harsanyi and Raiffa-Kalai-Smorodinsky solutions, see Riddell (1981).

26. For a discussion of service reliability and price regulation, see Marchand (1973) and Crew and Kleindorfer (1978).

27. Utility regulation under uncertainty is analyzed by Perrakis (1976), Klevorick (1973), and Meyer (1976). An interesting extension of the study of regulatory distortions under uncertainty would be to allow for imperfectly adjustable capital. Unanticipated demand shifts or changes in regulatory policy would increase the possibility of excess or insufficient capital and therefore increase the firm's costs of adjustment.

11 Barriers to Entry 2: Rate Regulation and Bargaining under Asymmetric Information

Rate regulation, as I have emphasized, involves bargaining between market participants and an exchange of information about consumer demand and firm costs. Regulatory rate hearings provide a means of information gathering and arbitration of bargaining for the administrative regulatory agency. This suggests that rate regulation should be studied using models of bargaining under asymmetric information. This chapter presents a bargaining model in which consumers have private information about demand and firms have private information about costs. The range of bargaining outcomes is studied, and the consequences of asymmetric information for allocative efficiency are examined.

The main virtue of resource allocation by competitive markets is that consumers possess the best information about their individual preferences and firms possess the best information about their respective technologies. The price system transmits information about resource scarcity, and market participants make demand and supply decisions on the basis of individual objectives. A regulatory authority intervening in the allocative mechanism is at a double disadvantage as a consequence of asymmetry of information. First, the regulator is unable to anticipate accurately the effects of regulatory policies, such as price controls, on the resulting consumer demand and firm supply decisions. In addition to uncertainty about the outcome of regulatory actions, the regulator is unable to assess the welfare effects, since he cannot directly observe consumer benefits—or, in some cases, firm profits. Thus, mitigation of monopoly pricing in the presence of barriers to entry and natural monopoly technology may be worthwhile, but measurement of the welfare benefits of regulation is problematic.

It is useful at the outset to distinguish between my approach and that taken in the large literature on regulation under asymmetric information.[1] There are three significant differences. First, the literature emphasizes the interaction between the regulatory agency and the firm, leaving consumers out of the regulatory process. Consumer demand is specified exogenously. Consumer interests are represented by a weighting of consumer surplus in the regulator's objective function. The view is generally taken that the regulatory process is one in which regulators engage in a process of command and control, monitoring the pricing, output, product quality, and information disclosure of firms. In my view, this approach neglects the interposition of utility regulators between the utility and its customers. Recognition that the market for utility services is regulated, rather than the behavior of a given firm, places emphasis on regulatory policies that emerge from a consensus among market participants.

Second, the literature on regulation under asymmetric information usually examines a Stackelberg game with the regulator as a first mover and the regulated firm as a Cournot follower. The regulator is assumed to make a credible commitment to an incentive schedule that induces the regulated firm to reveal its private information regarding costs or demand. The principal agent approach is problematic, as is widely noted, because the regulator's commitment may not be credible. After the firm's costs have been observed, the regulator has an incentive to revise its price or subsidy schedule in light of available information. Similarly, incentive mechanisms that involve determining the probability of auditing the firm on the basis of the firm's cost report are not credible. Threats to audit will not deter misrepresentation of costs if the firm anticipates that the regulator will not carry out a costly audit after costs have been reported. The model of precommitment to incentive schedules by regulators is also not an accurate description of rate regulation. Generally, regulators respond to rate proposals made by firms. Regulatory hearings can involve repeated revisions of rate proposals. Bargaining between market participants is a process of give-and-take rather than take-it-or-leave-it. This has important consequences for the regulated outcome.

Third, the preceding assumption of Stackelberg strategies by regulators determines the allocation of rents at the regulated equilibrium. By precommitment, the regulator is able to exercise monopsony power. The regulator acting in the public interest extracts all rents from the regulated firm up to the information rents that are provided to induce revelations of costs. The efficiency distortions observed in models of regulation result not only from information asymmetry but from the principal agent framework.

The stylized bargaining model presented here explicitly includes consumers as well as the regulated firm in the process of selecting output and prices. Second, a range of outcomes is identified which reflects alternative bargaining procedures. Finally, allocation of rents between the consumer and firm may vary. An important consequence of this is that efficient outcomes need not be ruled out. The main conclusion of the present chapter is that full information efficiency may be achieved if the economic rents from exchange are sufficient to cover information rents for consumers and firms.

The chapter is organized as follows. The basic model and the information structure are set out in section 11.1. Efficient mechanisms are defined in section 11.2 for discrete consumer and firm types. Feasible and efficient mechanisms are examined in section 11.3 for the general case of continuous consumer and firm types. Section 11.4 gives a sufficient condition for the full information optimum to be attainable. Further, two "extreme points" of the set of efficient mechanisms are studied and are shown to correspond to monopsony and monopoly outcomes. The monopsony outcome is compared to principal agent models of regulation.

11.1   Bargaining with Unknown Demand and Supply

This section outlines the bargaining game played by consumers and firms in a regulated industry. It is assumed that the consumers have private information about preferences that is not known by the regulator or the firm. The firm's costs are not fully known by the regulator or the consumer. The consumer and firm bargain over the total output to be produced and over total payments. Bayesian equilibria of the negotiation process are represented as a direct revelation game.[2] In other words, given the negotiation process, there exists a mechanism, consisting of an output and payment function, such that the consumer and firm have incentive to reveal correctly private information about demand and supply, respectively, and to participate in the revelation game. The class of negotiation processes may be quite general, including the exchange of a *series* of offers and counteroffers or negotiation mechanisms with specific rules for conflict resolution. Thus, the direct revelation bargaining game need not simply represent negotiation in which the consumer or the firm must commit to a price or output level. Rather, the underlying negotiation process is left unspecified. Particular outcomes can be the result of relative bargaining ability.

Alternatively, the direct revelation bargaining game may be viewed as a game in which the regulator is a first mover that commits to a direct revelation mechanism. In this context, both the consumer and firm act as followers in their choice of actions, either in terms of output and payments or in terms of announcement of demand and cost parameters. Particular direct revelation mechanisms are then chosen based on the *regulator's* preferences. However, because the consumer and firm are both players, we use the Holmström and Myerson (1983) criterion of *interim incentive efficiency*. Given this criterion, the regulator, as an arbitrator, must independently consider all possible types of consumers and all possible types of firms in choosing a mechanism. Averaging over types to consider expected consumer surplus or expected firm profits may yield a *specific* regulatory objective function. However, I argue that this particular set of welfare weights for individual types greatly restricts the set of feasible mechanisms and need not be imposed a priori.

The consumer purchases a good Q from the regulated firm and a numeraire good Y. The consumer has private information about a preference parameter $\mu \in [0, 1]$. Let consumer utility be given by $U(Q, \mu) + Y$, where $U(Q, \mu)$ has the form

$$U(Q, \mu) = \int_0^Q p(q, \mu) \, dq. \tag{11.1.1}$$

Further, assume that the consumer's marginal willingness to pay for the regulated firm's output, $p(Q, \mu)$, is additively separable in output and the taste parameter,

$$p(Q, \mu) = \alpha(\mu) + \beta(Q). \tag{11.1.2}$$

Let $\alpha(\cdot)$ be a nonnegative, twice continuously differentiable, increasing, and concave function for $\mu \in [0, 1]$. Let $\beta(\cdot)$ be differentiable and decreasing for $Q > 0$. Assume that marginal willingness to pay is always positive for sufficiently small output levels, i.e., there exists $\varepsilon > 0$ such that $\alpha(0) + \beta(Q) > 0$ for $Q \in [0, \varepsilon)$.

The regulated firm has private information about a cost parameter θ that takes values in the interval $[0, 1]$. The regulated firm's cost function $C(Q, \theta)$ has the form[3]

$$C(Q, \theta) = k + \int_0^Q c(q, \theta) \, dq \tag{11.1.3}$$

for $Q > 0$. The cost function is assumed to satisfy $C(0, \theta) = 0$ to indicate that no production costs are incurred unless production takes place. Marginal costs, $c(Q, \theta)$, are assumed to be additively separable in output and the cost parameter,

$$c(Q, \theta) = \gamma(\theta) + \sigma(Q). \tag{11.1.4}$$

Let $\gamma(\cdot)$ be nonnegative, twice continuously differentiable, increasing, and concave for $\theta \in [0, 1]$. Let $\sigma(\cdot)$ be nonnegative, differentiable, and increasing.

The regulator and the firm have common beliefs about the value of the consumer's taste parameter. To clarify the effects of asymmetric information, suppose initially that there is a finite number of possible consumer types, μ_i, $i = 1, \ldots, n$, where $\mu_i \leq \mu_j$ for $i \leq j$. The regulator and the firm beliefs about the likelihood of consumer types are represented by a set of probabilities, $f_i > 0$, $i = 1, \ldots, n$, $\sum_{i=1}^{n} f_i = 1$. The regulator and consumer have common beliefs about the likelihood of particular cost parameter values, θ_l, $l = 1, \ldots, m$, where $\theta_l \leq \theta_k$ for $l \leq k$. The beliefs of the regulator and the consumer are given by $g_l > 0$, $l = 1, \ldots, m$, $\sum_{l=1}^{m} g_l = 1$. In later sections, a continuum of types for the consumer and the firm is examined. The regulator and firm beliefs about the distribution of the consumer's taste parameter are represented by a nonnegative, increasing, and differentiable cumulative probability distribution $F: [0, 1] \rightarrow [0, 1]$, where $F(0) = 0$, $F(1) = 1$, and $dF(\mu) = f(\mu) d\mu$. In the continuum case, the cumulative probability distribution for the firm's cost parameter is given by a non-negative, increasing, and differentiable cumulative probability distribution $G: [0, 1] \rightarrow [0, 1]$, where $G(0) = 0$, $G(1) = 1$, and $dG(\theta) = g(\theta) d\theta$. The distribution functions $F(\cdot)$ and $G(\cdot)$ are common knowledge.

The outcome of the bargaining process involving the consumer, firm, and regulator is an *output*, Q, and a *payment* by the consumer to the firm, R. By standard arguments, the *revelation principle*[4] implies that any negotiation process may be represented as a direct revelation game. In particular, there is a mechanism $(Q(\mu, \theta), R(\mu, \theta))$ that achieves the same outcome as the negotiation process where the consumer and firm have the incentive to reveal correctly the value of their respective demand and cost parameters.

Given the discrete parameter framework, the direct revelation mechanisms are given by $n \times m$ matrices of output and payment pairs, $[Q_{il}, R_{il}]$, $i = 1, \ldots, n$, $l = 1, \ldots, m$, where $Q_{il} \equiv Q(\mu_i, \theta_l)$ and $R_{il} \equiv R(\mu_i, \theta_l)$ represent outputs and payments associated with particular consumer and firm types. The matrix $[Q_{il}, R_{il}]$ may be viewed as a matrix of outcomes associated with n potential moves available to the consumer and m potential moves available to the producer. The moves in the direct revelation game are simply the announcements of parameter values μ_i and θ_l, respectively, where (Q_{il}, R_{il}) is optimal for a consumer of type i conditional on the firm being of type l and vice versa.

Given a mechanism $(Q(\mu, \theta), R(\mu, \theta))$, the consumer's indirect value of reporting a parameter value $\hat{\mu}_j$ given that this true demand parameter value is μ_i is given by

$$V(\mu_i, \hat{\mu}_j) = \sum_{l=1}^{m} [U(Q(\hat{\mu}_j, \theta_l), \mu_i) - R(\hat{\mu}_j, \theta_l)]g_l. \tag{11.1.5}$$

The consumer must take into account the possible values of the firm's cost parameter in choosing the reported value of his demand parameter. The firm's cost parameter report $\hat{\theta}_k$ given the true cost parameter θ_l depends upon the possible values the consumer's demand parameter may take. The firm's indirect profit function is then

$$\Pi(\theta_l, \hat{\theta}_k) = \sum_{i=1}^{n} [R(\mu_i, \hat{\theta}_k) - C(Q(\mu_i, \hat{\theta}_k), \theta_l)]f_i. \tag{11.1.6}$$

It is required that the mechanism (Q, R) be *incentive compatible*; that is, truth-telling is a preferred strategy for all consumer and firm types given truth-telling by the other party,

$$V(\mu_i, \mu_i) \geq V(\mu_i, \hat{\mu}_j) \qquad \text{for all } i, j = 1, \ldots, n,$$
$$\Pi(\theta_l, \theta_l) \geq \Pi(\theta_l, \hat{\theta}_k) \qquad \text{for all } l, k = 1, \ldots, m. \tag{11.1.7}$$

Let $V(\mu_i) \equiv V(\mu_i, Q, R) \equiv V(\mu_i, \mu_i)$, and $\Pi(\theta_l) \equiv \Pi(\theta_l, Q, R) \equiv \Pi(\theta_l, \theta_l)$, where $V(\mu_i)$, $\Pi(\theta_l)$ represent indirect consumer benefits and firm profits with the particular mechanism suppressed. It is assumed that both the consumer and regulated firm must have gains from trade from their transactions in the regulated market. Thus, the mechanism (Q, R) is required to be *individually rational*,

$$V(\mu_i) \geq 0, \quad i = 1, \ldots, n, \qquad \text{and} \qquad \Pi(\theta_l) \geq 0, \quad l = 1, \ldots, m. \tag{11.1.8}$$

Consider the implications of incentive compatibility. From (11.1.7),

$$\sum_{l=1}^{m} Q_{il} g_l(\alpha(\mu_i) - \alpha(\mu_j)) \geq V(\mu_i, \mu_i) - V(\mu_j, \mu_j)$$
$$\geq \sum_{l=1}^{m} Q_{jl} g_l(\alpha(\mu_i) - \alpha(\mu_j)), \qquad i, j = 1, \ldots, n, \tag{11.1.9}$$

$$\sum_{i=1}^{n} Q_{il} f_i(\gamma(\theta_k) - \gamma(\theta_l)) \geq \Pi(\theta_l, \theta_l) - \Pi(\theta_k, \theta_k)$$

$$\geq \sum_{i=1}^{n} Q_{ik} f_i(\gamma(\theta_k) - \gamma(\theta_l)), \qquad l, k = 1, \ldots, m.$$

$$(11.1.10)$$

Equations (11.1.9) and (11.1.10) imply the following monotonicity results.

LEMMA 11.1.1   (a) *Expected output for the consumer,* $\sum_{l=1}^{m} Q_{il} g_l$, *is nondecreasing in the consumer's demand parameter. Expected output for the firm,* $\sum_{i=1}^{n} Q_{il} f_i$, *is nonincreasing in the firm's cost parameter.* (b) *Expected consumer net benefits,* $V(\mu_i)$, *are nondecreasing in the consumer's demand parameter. Expected profits,* $\Pi(\theta_l)$, *are nonincreasing in the firm's cost parameter.*

From (11.1.9), $\mu_i \geq \mu_j$ implies $\sum_{l=1}^{m} Q_{il} g_l \geq \sum_{l=1}^{m} Q_{jl} g_l$ for all $i, j = 1, \ldots, n$. Further, $V(\mu_i, \mu_i) - V(\mu_j, \mu_j) \geq 0$ for $\mu_i \geq \mu_j$, $i, j = 1, \ldots, n$. Similar arguments for the firm follow from (11.1.10).

The incentive compatibility requirement as embodied in (11.1.9) and (11.1.10) allows a restatement of the individual rationality conditions. It is sufficient for individual rationality to be satisfied if gains from trade are obtained by the consumer with the lowest demand parameter value and by the firm with the highest cost parameter value,

$$V(\mu_1) \geq 0, \qquad \Pi(\theta_m) \geq 0. \qquad (11.1.11)$$

Consider the consumer's indifference surfaces over realizations of outputs and payments. For consumer i, there is a trade-off between values of the $2m$ vector $(Q_{i1}, \ldots, Q_{im}, R_{i1}, \ldots, R_{im})$. Consider the indifference curves projected on (Q_{il}, R_{il}) space keeping values of (Q_{ik}, R_{ik}) constant for $l \neq k$. The *marginal rate of substitution* is

$$\left. \frac{dR_{il}}{dQ_{il}} \right|_{V(\mu_i) = \overline{V}_i} = p(Q_{il}, \mu_i).$$

The indifference curve is increasing and concave, since $p(Q, \mu_i)$ is decreasing in Q. Further, the indifference curves are parallel and are lower for greater values of net benefits $\overline{V}_i$. Also, note that consumers with greater values of μ_i have steeper indifference curves,

$$\frac{d}{d\mu_i} \left(\left. \frac{dR_{il}}{dQ_{il}} \right|_{V(\mu_i) = \overline{V}_i} \right) = Q_{il} \alpha'(\mu_i) > 0.$$

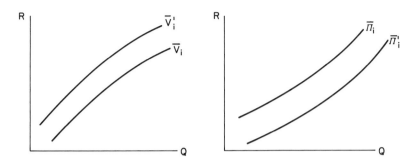

Figure 11.1.1
(Left) Indifference curves, $\bar{V}_i > \bar{V}_i'$. (Right) Isoprofit contours, $\bar{\Pi}_i > \bar{\Pi}_i'$.

Similar analysis of firm isoprofit contours is possible. The firm ranks $2n$ vectors $(Q_{1l}, \ldots, Q_{nl}, R_{1l}, \ldots, R_{nl})$. The *slope of the isoprofit contour* is then equal to marginal cost,

$$\left.\frac{dR_{il}}{dQ_{il}}\right|_{\Pi(\theta_l)=\bar{\Pi}_l} = c(Q_{il}, \theta_l).$$

The isoprofit contour is thus increasing and convex, since $c(Q, \theta_l)$ is increasing in Q. The isoprofit contours are parallel and are higher for greater values of profit $\bar{\Pi}_l$. Firms with greater cost parameters θ_l have steeper isoprofit contours,

$$\frac{d}{d\theta_l}\left(\left.\frac{dR_{il}}{dQ_{il}}\right|_{\Pi(\theta_l)=\bar{\Pi}_l}\right) = Q_{il}\gamma'(\theta_l) > 0.$$

Indifference curves for a consumer and isoprofit contours for a firm are given in figure 11.1.1.

The large number of constraints on the choice of a mechanism resulting from incentive compatibility, $n(n-1) + m(m-1)$, may be reduced somewhat by noting that only *local constraints* are needed. Since indifference curves for the consumer in the space of any particular output and payment pair (Q_{il}, R_{il}) become steeper for higher values of the demand parameter, it suffices that revelation of parameter value μ_i by consumer i dominates revelation of either μ_{i+1} or μ_{i-1}. A similar argument applies to the firm's isoprofit contours. Thus, $2(n-1) + 2(m-1)$ constraints are obtained,

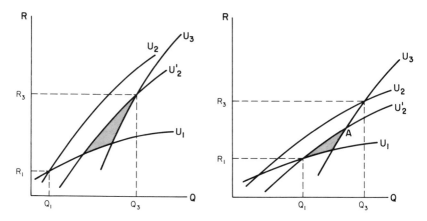

Figure 11.1.2 (left) and 11.1.3 (right)
Local incentive compatibility constraints need not be binding.

$$\sum_{l=1}^{m} [U(Q_{il}, \mu_i) - R_{il}]g_l \geq \sum_{l=1}^{m} [U(Q_{i+1,l}, \mu_i) - R_{i+1,l}]g_l, \quad i = 1, \ldots, n-1,$$

$$\sum_{l=1}^{m} [U(Q_{il}, \mu_i) - R_{il}]g_l \geq \sum_{l=1}^{m} [U(Q_{i-1,l}, \mu_i) - R_{i-1,l}]g_l, \quad i = 2, \ldots, n,$$

$$\sum_{i=1}^{n} [R_{il} - C(Q_{il}, \theta_l)]f_i \geq \sum_{i=1}^{n} [R_{i,l+1} - C(Q_{i,l+1}, \theta_l)]f_i, \quad l = 1, \ldots, m-1,$$

$$\sum_{i=1}^{n} [R_{il} - C(Q_{il}, \theta_l)]f_i \geq \sum_{i=1}^{n} [R_{i,l-1} - C(Q_{i,l-1}, \theta_l)]f_i, \quad l = 2, \ldots, m. \tag{11.1.12}$$

To allow for all possible allocations of rent for mechanisms within the Pareto set, one cannot require any of the local constraints to be binding a priori. The two local constraints restrict the vectors of output and payment pairs to a *set*. Suppose, for example, that there is only one type of firm. The restriction on the pair (Q_2, R_2) resulting from consumer 2's incentive constraints is shown by the shaded areas in figures 11.1.2 and 11.1.3. The shaded areas must lie above the indifference curves for consumer types 1 and 3 to guarantee that they prefer their output payment pairs—respectively, (Q_1, R_1) and (Q_3, R_3)—to consumer 2's output and payment, (Q_2, R_2). The upper and lower constraints *need not be binding* for efficient mechanisms. The two possible cases for the sets that satisfy the local incentive compatibility constraints are shown in figure 11.1.2 and 11.1.3. If all of the local downward constraints are binding, then (Q_2, R_2) must be point A in figure 11.1.3. In general, however, the output payment pair (Q_2, R_2) may take any value in the shaded area in figure 11.1.2 or 11.1.3. Similar feasible sets exist for the firm. The possibility that incentive compatibility constraints are not binding is an interesting consequence of the bilateral monopoly aspect of bargaining. This differs from results in the nonlinear pricing or principal agent literature that employ Stackelberg solution concepts.[5]

11.2 Efficient Mechanisms

Let mechanisms (Q, R) that are incentive compatible and individually rational be referred to as *feasible*. Given that the consumer and firm communicate with each other and with the regulator through rate hearings, the class of mechanisms may be restricted to those that are efficient in the sense of Holmström and Myerson (1983).

Definition 11.2.1 A mechanism (Q, R) is said to be *interim incentive efficient* if it is feasible (incentive compatible and individually rational) and there does not exist another feasible mechanism (Q', R') such that

$$V(\mu_i, Q', R') > V(\mu_i, Q, R) \qquad \text{for all } i = 1, \ldots, n,$$
$$\Pi(\theta_l, Q', R') > \Pi(\theta_l, Q, R) \qquad \text{for all } l = 1, \ldots, m.$$
$$(11.2.1)$$

Let $\mathscr{P}$ represent the set of interim incentive efficient mechanisms (Q, R).

As is standard in games with asymmetric information, the n consumer types and m firm types may each be viewed as separate players, even though there is actually only one consumer and one firm each possessing private information. In this sense, the set of interim incentive efficient mechanisms may be characterized in a manner similar to full information Pareto optima; see, for example, Varian (1978) or my previous characterization of second-best Pareto optimal pricing in chapter 5. The optimal allocation, represented by the feasible mechanism $[Q, R]$, must be chosen in such a way that there is no other allocation $[Q', R']$ such that a consumer of any type (or firm of any type) can be made better off without making any other type of consumer or firm worse off. Thus, a feasible mechanism (Q, R) is interim incentive efficient if and only if it is a Pareto optimal allocation for the economy with consumers $i = 1, \ldots, n$ and firms $j = 1, \ldots, m$, where the preferences of both consumers and firms are considered. This identity is stated formally in the following proposition.

PROPOSITION 11.2.1   *A mechanism (Q^*, R^*) is in the set $\mathscr{P}$ if and only if it solves the following problems for all i,*

$$\max_{Q,R} V(\mu_i, Q, R)$$

subject to

$$V(\mu_j, Q, R) \geq V(\mu_j, Q^*, R^*), \qquad j = 1, \ldots, n, \quad j \neq i,$$

$$\Pi(\theta_k, Q, R) \geq \Pi(\theta_k, Q^*, R^*), \qquad k = 1, \ldots, n,$$

and (11.1.11) *and* (11.1.12), *and solves the following problems for all l:*

$$\max_{Q,R} \Pi(\theta_l, Q, R)$$

subject to

$$V(\mu_j, Q, R) \geq V(\mu_j, Q^*, R^*), \qquad j = 1, \ldots, n,$$

$$\Pi(\theta_k, Q, R) \geq \Pi(\theta_k, Q^*, R^*), \qquad k = 1, \ldots, m, \quad k \neq l,$$

and (11.1.11) *and* (11.1.12).

The problems in proposition 11.2.1 can be solved as Lagrange-Kuhn-Tucker problems.

An examination of the definition of an efficient mechanism shows that the local upper and lower incentive compatibility constraints (11.1.12) need not be binding for efficient mechanisms. Further, the individual rationality constraints (11.1.11), $V(\mu_1) \geq 0$, $\Pi(\theta_m) \geq 0$, need not be binding either. Because of the possibly nonbinding constraints, it follows that the set of efficient mechanisms under incomplete information depends upon minimum net benefit levels for *all types of agents*. It is no longer sufficient, as in the full information case, to vary the reservation utility for the consumer or the reservation profit level for the firm to generate the entire set of Pareto optimal exchanges. The result in proposition 11.2.1 implies that the "contract curve" may be generated only by specifying minimum values for net benefits for *all* consumer and firm types save for one agent type. Then by suitably varying minimum net benefit levels—say, $V(\mu_j, Q^*, R^*)$, $j = 1, \ldots, n, j \neq i$, and $\Pi(\theta_l, Q^*, R^*)$, $l = 1, \ldots, m$—by choosing various mechanisms (Q^*, R^*) in $\mathscr{P}$, the set of efficient contracts may be generated.

It is commonly asserted that Pareto optima in problems of asymmetric information may be obtained by varying one agent's minimum utility level, as in the nonlinear pricing problem. However, incentive compatibility implies that recovery of all efficient allocations requires varying the minimum benefits or opportunity cost for all but one type of agent. The economic intuition is that efficient mechanisms must allow for all feasible allocations of the rents from exchange across all consumer and firm types.

The outcome of the regulatory process is assumed to be a particular mechanism in $\mathscr{P}$. The particular mechanism may be one that maximizes the regulator's preferences over $\mathscr{P}$. The regulator's preferences reflect different weights given to benefits received by consumers and firms in the regulated industry. Alternatively, the regulator may simply be viewed as an arbitrator selecting a mechanism that reflects the relative bargaining power of the consumer and firm. Formally, the two approaches are identical. In particular, it can be shown that given any mechanism (Q^*, R^*) in $\mathscr{P}$, there is a set of weights $(a_1, \ldots, a_n, b_1, \ldots, b_m)$ on the net benefits of consumer types and the profits of firm types such that a regulator maximizing the weighted sum of consumer benefits and firm profits would select (Q^*, R^*) from the set of feasible mechanisms.

To analyze the problem, consider again the incentive compatibility constraints. By the definitions of $V(\mu_i)$ and $\Pi(\theta_l)$, the local constraints (11.1.12) may be written as follows:

$$V(\mu_i) - V(\mu_{i+1})$$

$$\geq \sum_{l=1}^{m} Q_{i+1,l} g_l(\alpha(\mu_i) - \alpha(\mu_{i+1})), \qquad i = 1, \ldots, n-1,$$

$$V(\mu_i) - V(\mu_{i-1})$$

$$\geq \sum_{l=1}^{m} Q_{i-1,l} g_l(\alpha(\mu_i) - \alpha(\mu_{i-1})), \qquad i = 2, \ldots, n,$$

(11.2.2)

$$\Pi(\theta_l) - \Pi(\theta_{l+1})$$

$$\geq \sum_{i=1}^{n} Q_{i,l+1} f_i(\gamma(\theta_{l+1}) - \gamma(\theta_l)), \qquad l = 1, \ldots, m-1,$$

$$\Pi(\theta_l) - \Pi(\theta_{l-1})$$

$$\geq \sum_{i=1}^{n} Q_{i,l-1} f_i(\gamma(\theta_{l-1}) - \gamma(\theta_l)), \qquad l = 2, \ldots, m.$$

Thus, the output and payment pairs (Q_{il}, R_{il}), $i = 1, \ldots, n$, $l = 1, \ldots, m$, must be chosen such that outputs Q_{il}, consumer net benefits $V(\mu_i)$, and firm profits $\Pi(\theta_l)$ satisfy the restrictions in (11.2.2). Note that the additive separability of the consumer marginal willingness to pay and of marginal cost results in constraints (11.2.2) that are linear in output levels Q_{il}.

Given the constraints (11.2.2), the maximization problems in proposition 11.2.1 may be recast in terms of outputs, consumer net benefits, and firm profits, with payments R_{il} implicitly determined. For convenience, define $V_i \equiv V(\mu_i, Q, R)$, $V_i^* \equiv V(\mu_i, Q^*, R^*)$, $\Pi_l \equiv \Pi(\theta_l, Q, R)$, $\Pi_l^* \equiv \Pi(\theta_l, Q^*, R^*)$. Then it follows that the maximization problems in proposition 11.2.1 are *linear programming* problems in Q_{il}, V_i, and Π_l, $i = 1, \ldots, n$, $l = 1, \ldots, m$. This suggests that a regulator with preferences described by a weighted sum of consumer net benefits and firm profits will select any mechanism in $\mathscr{P}$ given an appropriate choice of weights. The proof is given in the appendix.[6]

PROPOSITION 11.2.2   *A mechanism (Q^*, R^*) is in the set $\mathscr{P}$ only if there exist weights $(a_1, \ldots, a_n, b_1, \ldots, b_m)$, where $\sum_{i=1}^n a_i = \sum_{l=1}^m b_l = 1$ such that (Q^*, R^*) maximizes a weighted sum of consumer net benefits and firm profits*

$$\sum_{i=1}^n a_i V(\mu_i, Q, R) + \sum_{l=1}^m b_l \Pi(\theta_l, Q, R)$$

subject to the incentive compatibility constraints (11.1.12) and individual rationality constraints (11.1.11).

Note that the weights a_i and b_l depend only on information about each consumer and firm type; that is, a_i and b_l are indexed by $i = 1, \ldots, n$ and $l = 1, \ldots, m$. Holmström and Myerson (1983) state that the concept of interim incentive efficiency can be represented by an additive weighted social welfare function. Proposition 11.2.2 makes explicit the relationship between choice of weights and the regulator's problem of selecting an efficient mechanism from the set of feasible mechanisms.

Consider a general representation of the regulator's preferences, W: $\mathbb{R}_+^{n+m} \to \mathbb{R}_+$, which depends on values of consumer net benefits and firm profits,

$$W = W(V(\mu_1, Q, R), \ldots, V(\mu_n, Q, R), \Pi(\theta_1, Q, R), \ldots, \Pi(\theta_m, Q, R)),$$

where W is increasing in consumer utility and firm profits. This is not a standard social welfare function in that firm profits are taken into consideration. The regulator treats the possible types of the consumer and firm as if they were different consumers and firms. By the revelation principle, it is possible to restrict the regulator's choice of a mechanism to those that are incentive compatible. Further, it is assumed that both consumers and firms have the freedom to exit from the market so that the individual rationality condition must hold for the regulator's mechanism. The regulator chooses a mechanism (Q^*, R^*) that maximizes the welfare measure W subject to the feasibility constraints (11.1.11) and (11.1.12). Since W is increasing in consumer net benefits and firm profits, the following result is obtained by standard arguments.

PROPOSITION 11.2.3   *A mechanism (Q^*, R^*) chosen by the regulator to maximize W subject to (11.1.11) and (11.1.12) is in the set $\mathscr{P}$.*

The proposition shows the connection between the optimal choices made by a regulator and efficient bargaining solutions.

11.3   Properties of the Bargaining Mechanism

11.3.1   Characterization of Feasible Mechanisms

The bargaining model is now extended to allow for continuous frequency distributions of consumer and firm types. The direct mechanism is defined by $(Q(\mu, \theta), R(\mu, \theta))$, where μ, θ are in the interval $[0, 1]$. For convenience, represent expected output and payments as follows:

$$Q_\mu(\mu) \equiv \int_0^1 Q(\mu, \theta) \, dG(\theta), \qquad Q_\theta(\theta) \equiv \int_0^1 Q(\mu, \theta) \, dF(\mu),$$

$$\tag{11.3.1}$$

$$R_\mu(\mu) \equiv \int_0^1 R(\mu, \theta) \, dG(\theta), \qquad R_\theta(\theta) \equiv \int_0^1 R(\mu, \theta) \, dF(\mu).$$

Proceeding informally, the incentive compatibility restrictions (11.1.9) and (11.1.10) for the continuum case are

$$Q_\mu(\mu_i)(\alpha(\mu_i) - \alpha(\mu_j)) \geq V(\mu_i) - V(\mu_j)$$

$$\geq Q_\mu(\mu_j)(\alpha(\mu_i) - \alpha(\mu_j)), \tag{11.3.2}$$

$$Q_\theta(\theta_l)(\gamma(\theta_k) - \gamma(\theta_l)) \geq \Pi(\theta_l) - \Pi(\theta_k)$$

$$\geq Q_\theta(\theta_k)(\gamma(\theta_k) - \gamma(\theta_l)) \tag{11.3.3}$$

for arbitrary parameter values $\mu_i, \mu_j \in [0, 1]$ and $\theta_l, \theta_k \in [0, 1]$. Taking limits as $\mu_j \to \mu_i$ (respectively, $\theta_k \to \theta_l$) implies for the continuum case that

$$V'(\mu) = Q_\mu(\mu)\alpha'(\mu) \qquad \text{and} \qquad \Pi'(\theta) = -Q_\theta(\theta)\gamma'(\theta). \tag{11.3.4}$$

Integrating the equations in (11.3.4), the indirect value functions for a consumer of type μ and a firm of type θ may written as

$$V(\mu) = V(0) + \int_0^\mu Q_\mu(\tilde{\mu})\alpha'(\tilde{\mu})\,d\tilde{\mu}, \tag{11.3.5}$$

$$\Pi(\theta) = \Pi(1) + \int_\theta^1 Q_\theta(\tilde{\theta})\gamma'(\tilde{\theta})\,d\tilde{\theta}. \tag{11.3.6}$$

When the distributions of μ_i and θ_l are discrete, the incentive compatibility and individual rationality constraints, (11.1.12) and (11.1.11), allow a range of quantity payment pairs to be efficient. In particular, the vector (Q_{il}, R_{il}), $l = 1, \ldots, m$, can be adjusted to alter the net benefits of a consumer of type i and all firms $l = 1, \ldots, m$ without necessarily affecting the ordinal rankings of other consumers, $j \neq i$, over the set of quantity-payment vectors given by the mechanism (Q, R). Thus, there is a range within which (Q_{il}, R_{il}), $l = 1, \ldots, m$, may be varied without affecting the net benefits of other consumers; see figures 11.1.2 and 11.1.3. The argument applies to the outcome for the lowest-demand consumer (Q_{1l}, R_{1l}), $l = 1, \ldots, m$, or for the highest-cost firm (Q_{im}, R_{im}), $i = 1, \ldots, n$. When there exist *continuous* distributions of consumer and firm types, this is no longer true. The upper and lower constraints are binding, (11.3.3), for the limiting case of continuum of types. This implies that the minimum consumer net benefit or the minimum firm profits determine the net benefits received by all agents, given an output schedule $Q(\mu, \theta)$. This insight provides a preliminary characterization of the set of feasible mechanisms. The proof is given in the appendix.

PROPOSITION 11.3.1 *Given continuous distributions of consumer and firm types, for any feasible mechanism (Q, R), the expected payment schedules $R_\mu(\mu)$ and $R_\theta(\theta)$ are uniquely specified given the output schedule $Q(\mu, \theta)$ and either the minimum consumer net benefit $V(0)$ or the minimum firm profit level $\Pi(1)$.*

The indirect value functions in equations (11.3.5) and (11.3.6) may be given the following interpretation. For any given mechanism, $V(0)$ and $\Pi(1)$

represent the returns to joint production for the consumer and firm, respectively. If $V(0) > 0$ or $\Pi(1) > 0$, the consumer or firm earns positive rents from joint production relative to their outside opportunity. The second terms in equations (11.3.5) and (11.3.6), $\int_0^\mu Q_\mu(\tilde{\mu})\alpha'(\tilde{\mu})\,d\tilde{\mu}$ and $\int_\theta^1 Q_\theta(\tilde{\theta})\gamma'(\tilde{\theta})\,d\tilde{\theta}$, represent the rents earned by the consumer of type μ and firm of type θ due to private information. Under certainty, the net benefits of an increase in the demand parameter are $\partial[U(Q,\mu) - C(Q,\theta)]/\partial\mu = Q\alpha'(\mu)$. The consumer with demand parameter μ retains the marginal value of net benefits up to μ. This is required to induce truth-telling by the consumer. The firm of type θ retains the cost reductions due to a reduction of the cost parameter from 1 to θ. One may calculate the *ex ante information rents* for the consumer and firm using integration by parts,

$$A^1(Q) = \int_0^1 \int_0^1 Q(\mu,\theta)\alpha'(\mu)((1 - F(\mu))/f(\mu))\,dF(\mu)\,dG(\theta),$$

$$A^2(Q) = \int_0^1 \int_0^1 Q(\mu,\theta)\gamma'(\theta)(G(\theta)/g(\theta))\,dF(\mu)\,dG(\theta).$$

Further, one may define the *ex ante rents from exchange*,

$$B(Q) \equiv \int_0^1 \int_0^1 [U(Q(\mu,\theta),\mu) - C(Q(\mu,\theta),\theta)]\,dF(\mu)\,dG(\theta).$$

Given these definitions, the set of feasible mechanisms may be further characterized.

If $Q(\mu,\theta)$ is any output schedule, then the payment schedule $R(\mu,\theta)$ is said to *support* $Q(\mu,\theta)$ if the pair $(Q(\mu,\theta), R(\mu,\theta))$ is a feasible mechanism for all consumers μ and all firms θ. Myerson and Satterthwaite (1983, theorem 1) characterize feasible mechanisms for the single-object bargaining problem. Their result is extended to the case of production with generalized utility and cost functions. The proof is given in the appendix.[7]

PROPOSITION 11.3.2 *For any output schedule $Q(\mu,\theta)$, there exists a payment schedule $R(\mu,\theta) \geq 0$ that supports $Q(\mu,\theta)$ if and only if $Q_\mu(\mu)$ is nondecreasing in μ, $Q_\theta(\theta)$ is nonincreasing in θ, and*

$$B(Q) \geq A^1(Q) + A^2(Q). \tag{11.3.7}$$

The feasibility condition (11.3.7) states that ex ante net benefits from exchange must cover the ex ante information rents. This constraint is an important source of the efficiency distortions under asymmetric information. Generally, one can expect output levels to be reduced so that information rents are lowered for the consumer and firm.

11.3.2 Characterization of Efficient Mechanisms

By arguments similar to propositions 11.2.1 and 11.2.2 a feasible mechanism is interim incentive efficient, $(Q, R) \in \mathscr{P}$, if and only if there exists a set of weights $a(\mu)$, $b(\theta)$ such that (Q, R) maximizes

$$\int_0^1 V(\mu, Q, R)\, da(\mu) + \int_0^1 \Pi(\theta, Q, R)\, db(\theta), \qquad (11.3.8)$$

where $a(\mu)$ and $b(\theta)$ are nondecreasing and $a(0) = b(0) = 0$, $a(1) = b(1) = 1$. This generalizes Myerson's (1985) single-object trading problem to allow for production and general consumer and firm objective functions. Substituting for V and Π from (11.3.5) and (11.3.6), (11.3.8) is then

$$\int_0^1 V(\mu, Q, R)\, da(\mu) + \int_0^1 \Pi(\theta, Q, R)\, db(\theta)$$

$$= V(0) + \Pi(1) + \int_0^1 \left[\int_0^\mu Q_\mu(\tilde{\mu}) \alpha'(\tilde{\mu})\, d\tilde{\mu} \right] da(\mu)$$

$$+ \int_0^1 \left[\int_\theta^1 Q_\theta(\tilde{\theta}) \gamma'(\tilde{\theta})\, d\tilde{\theta} \right] db(\theta). \qquad (11.3.9)$$

Substituting for $V(0) + \Pi(1)$ from equation (7) in the appendix and integrating by parts imply

$$\int_0^1 V(\mu, Q, R)\, da(\mu) + \int_0^1 \Pi(\theta, Q, R)\, db(\theta)$$

$$= \int_0^1 \int_0^1 \left[U(Q, \mu) - C(Q, \theta) - Q\frac{\alpha'(\mu)}{f(\mu)}(a(\mu) - F(\mu)) \right.$$

$$\left. + Q\frac{\gamma'(\theta)}{g(\theta)}(b(\theta) - G(\theta)) \right] dF(\mu)\, dG(\theta). \qquad (11.3.10)$$

Let $I(Q, \mu, \theta)$ represent the bracketed terms in (11.3.10), $I(Q, \mu, \theta) \equiv [U(Q, \mu) - C(Q, \theta) - Q\lambda^1(\mu) + Q\lambda^2(\theta)]$, where

$$\lambda^1(\mu) \equiv (\alpha'(\mu)/f(\mu))(a(\mu) - F(\mu)), \qquad \lambda^2(\theta) \equiv (\gamma'(\theta)/g(\theta))(b(\theta) - G(\theta)).$$

The set of efficient mechanisms may then be characterized in a useful way.

PROPOSITION 11.3.3 *The mechanism (Q, R) is in $\mathscr{P}$ if and only if there exist nondecreasing weights, $a(\mu)$, $b(\theta)$, with $a(0) = b(0) = 0$ and $a(1) = b(1) = 1$, such that Q solves*

$$\max_{Q} \int_0^1 \int_0^1 I(Q, \mu, \theta) \, dF(\mu) \, dG(\theta) \tag{11.3.11}$$

subject to $Q_\mu(\mu)$ nondecreasing in μ, $Q_\theta(\theta)$ nonincreasing in θ, and (11.3.7).

Consider first the *unconstrained* pointwise maximum of $\int_0^1 \int_0^1 I(Q, \mu, \theta) \times dF(\mu) \, dG(\theta)$.[8] The unconstrained maximum $\bar{Q}(\mu, \theta)$ is defined by the following conditions. For $\bar{Q}(\mu, \theta) > 0$,

$$p(\bar{Q}, \mu) - c(\bar{Q}, \theta) = \lambda^1(\mu) - \lambda^2(\theta), \tag{11.3.12}$$

and $\bar{Q}(\mu, \theta) = 0$ for

$$p(0, \mu) - c(0, \theta) < \lambda^1(\mu) - \lambda^2(\theta).$$

The unconstrained maximum solution $\bar{Q}(\mu, \theta)$ exists and is unique for any set of weights $(a(\cdot), b(\cdot))$.[9]

Suppose that the distribution functions, $F(\cdot)$ and $G(\cdot)$, and the weights, $a(\cdot)$ and $b(\cdot)$, are chosen in such a way that $(\lambda^1(\mu) - \alpha(\mu))$ is nonincreasing in μ and such that $(\lambda^2(\theta) - \gamma(\theta))$ is nonincreasing in θ. Then the unconstrained maximum $\bar{Q}(\mu, \theta)$ coincides with the efficient solution, $Q^*(\mu, \theta)$. To see this, differentiate (11.3.12) with respect to μ and θ,

$$\frac{\partial \bar{Q}}{\partial \mu} = \frac{\lambda^{1\prime}(\mu) - \alpha'(\mu)}{\beta'(\bar{Q}) - \sigma'(\bar{Q})} \geq 0, \qquad \frac{\partial \bar{Q}}{\partial \mu} = -\frac{(\lambda^{2\prime}(\theta) - \gamma'(\theta))}{\beta'(\bar{Q}) - \sigma'(\bar{Q})} \leq 0. \tag{11.3.13}$$

Thus, the equilibrium output schedule is nondecreasing in the demand parameter μ and nonincreasing in the cost parameter θ. The requirements for incentive compatibility of the output schedule are satisfied. So, the constraints in the regulator's maximization problem (11.3.11) are satisfied.[10]

In general, the efficient solution may involve *pooling* of consumers by demand parameters or of firms by cost parameters.[11] Pooling occurs as a result of the boundary requirements on the maximization problem for the efficient output schedule.[12] These boundary conditions are an expression of incentive compatibility requirements on the bargaining mechanism (Q, R). Thus, feasibility may require output levels to be constant across consumer or firm types. Examples of possible forms of the optimal output schedule in the case of pooling are illustrated in figure 11.3.1.

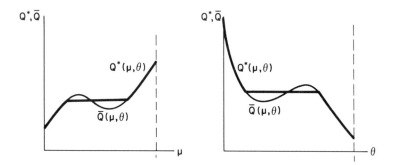

Figure 11.3.1
(Left) Pooling across consumer types. (Right) Pooling across firm types.

11.4 Bargaining Equilibria: Efficiency, Monopoly, and Monopsony

11.4.1 Full Information Efficiency

Due to information asymmetry, there is a trade-off between adjusting the output level to achieve productive efficiency and providing consumers and firms with the incentive to reveal their respective demand and cost characteristics. This trade-off can only be avoided if the rents from exchange are sufficiently large in comparison with information rents. Consumers and firms then can obtain compensation for revealing private information, and outputs can be adjusted optimally so that marginal benefits equal marginal costs.

The first-order necessary conditions for the unconstrained solutions (11.3.12) illustrate the potential inefficiency of production and exchange that is due to asymmetric information. The full information optimum is defined by the output at which supply and demand intersect, $Q^F(\mu, \theta)$, where Q^F solves $p(Q, \mu) = c(Q, \theta)$. The term $\lambda^1(\mu) - \lambda^2(\theta)$ represents the *economic rent* that could be appropriated by the consumer and the firm from a marginal increase in output. If this quantity is nonzero, it drives a *wedge* between the consumer's marginal willingness to pay and the firm's marginal cost. This is shown in figure 11.4.1. The competitive or full information allocation requires that trading continue until all potential rents from the transaction have been obtained; that is, trading continues until $Q = Q^F(\mu, \theta)$. The allocation of the total rents depends on the bargaining power of the consumer and firm.

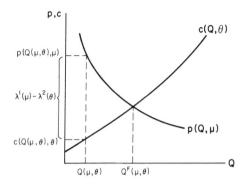

Figure 11.4.1
Inefficiency due to asymmetric information.

It is easily shown that the full information optimum, $Q^F(\mu, \theta)$, is an unconstrained optimum, $\bar{Q}(\mu, \theta)$. In particular, $Q^F(\mu, \theta)$ is nondecreasing in the demand parameter μ, since increases in μ shift demand to the right. Also, $Q^F(\mu, \theta)$ is nonincreasing in θ, since increases in θ shift the marginal cost curve left.[13] Therefore, $Q^F(\mu, \theta)$ satisfies the monotonicity conditions that are necessary and sufficient for incentive compatibility. For $Q^F(\mu, \theta)$ to be a feasible mechanism, it remains only to satisfy the individual rationality conditions. I state this somewhat surprising result formally.

PROPOSITION 11.4.1   *There exist interim incentive mechanisms (Q^*, R^*) that are full information efficient, $Q^*(\mu, \theta) = Q^F(\mu, \theta)$, if and only if*

$$B(Q^F) \geq A^1(Q^F) + A^2(Q^F).$$

The existence of efficient mechanisms that are also full information efficient thus depends on whether constraint (11.3.7) holds at the competitive output levels $Q^F(\mu, \theta)$. In general, this need not hold. The full information efficient allocation may not sustain positive expected gains from trade, so that the mechanism does not satisfy individual rationality. The expected gains from trade must be sufficiently large at the competitive full information output to cover the costs of inducing the consumer and firm to reveal their private information correctly. The relative levels of expected gains from trade and information rents at the full information output depend on the form of utility, costs, and the frequency distributions $F(\mu)$ and $G(\theta)$.[14]

We illustrate the proposition with a useful example. Let utility and cost be quadratic,

$$U(Q, \mu) = (\mu + v_0)Q - (v_1/2)Q^2,$$

$$C(Q, \theta) = (\theta + c_0)Q + (c_1/2)Q^2,$$

where $v_0, v_1, c_0,$ and c_1 are positive parameters. Also, let F and G be uniform distributions on $[0, 1]$. Then $Q^*(\mu, \theta) = Q^F(\mu, \theta) = (1/(v_1 + c_1))(v_0 + \mu - c_0 - \theta)$ satisfies the individual rationality conditions if and only if

$$v_0 - c_0 \geq 1 + 1/\sqrt{2}.$$

This requires calculation of $B(Q^F)$, $A^1(Q^F)$, and $A^2(Q^F)$. Thus, the demand intercept must exceed the supply intercept by at least $1/\sqrt{2}$. This is a way of guaranteeing that gains from trade, measured by the area above marginal cost and below demand, are sufficiently large. For a wide range of parameter values, full information efficiency is attainable. If the rents from exchange are sufficiently large, departures from efficiency need not occur. Inefficiency may still be observed as a consequence of market power. I now turn to consideration of this question.

11.4.2   Monopoly and Nonlinear Pricing

Consider a *two-stage* bargaining game in which the regulated firm can commit itself to some bargaining strategy in the first stage and the consumer must respond in the second stage. This case may be interpreted as representing "capture" of the regulator by an influential firm, since commitment yields monopoly rents. Two results are established. First, the firm's most preferred strategy is to offer the nonlinear monopoly price schedule.[15] Second, this strategy corresponds to an interim incentive efficient mechanism for the direct revelation game. The first result is analogous to Samuelson (1984), who shows that commitment to an offer price is the buyer's preferred strategy in a single-object model. The second result extends Myerson (1985), who shows the efficiency of committing to a price for the single-object model.

By making a take-it-or-leave-it offer, the regulated firm reveals its costs to the consumer. However, the consumer cannot make use of the information if the firm is able to commit itself to the offered nonlinear price schedule. The consumer selects an output and payment pair and thus reveals his demand characteristic to the firm.

A very brief summary of the nonlinear pricing model is given. Given the outlay schedule $P(\cdot)$, the consumer of type μ chooses a demand $Q^D = Q^D(\mu) \geq 0$ to maximize net benefits,

$$V(\mu) = \max_{Q} [U(Q, \mu) - P(Q)]. \tag{11.4.1}$$

Let $Q^D(\mu) = Q^D(\mu, P(\cdot))$. Further, note that $V(\mu) = U(Q^D(\mu), \mu) - P(Q^D(\mu))$. It can be shown that incentive compatibility requires $V'(\mu) = U_\mu(Q^D(\mu), \mu) = \alpha'(\mu)Q^D(\mu)$. The monopolist raises the schedule P until gains from trade are equal to zero for at least the lowest demand consumer, i.e., $V(0) = 0$. Thus, $V(\mu) = \int_0^\mu \alpha'(\tilde{\mu})Q^D(\tilde{\mu}) \, d\tilde{\mu}$. Finally, note that incentive compatibility requires $Q^D(\mu)$ to be nondecreasing in μ.

The firm of type θ chooses the schedule $P(\cdot) = P(\cdot; \theta)$ to maximize expected profits,

$$\Pi(\theta) = \max_{P(\cdot)} \int_0^1 [P(Q^D) - C(Q^D, \theta)] \, dF(\mu), \tag{11.4.2}$$

subject to $Q^D(\mu, P(\cdot))$ from the consumer's problem, the gains from trade condition $V(0) \geq 0$, and $Q^D(\mu)$ nondecreasing in μ. From the consumer's problem (11.4.1), note that

$$P(Q^D(\mu)) = U(Q^D(\mu), \mu) - V(\mu)$$

$$= U(Q^D(\mu), \mu) - \int_0^\mu \alpha'(\tilde{\mu})Q^D(\tilde{\mu}) \, d\tilde{\mu}. \tag{11.4.3}$$

Substituting from (11.4.3) into the firm's problem and integrating by parts yield

$$\Pi(\theta) = \max_{Q^D} \int_0^1 [U(Q^D, \mu) - C(Q^D, \theta)$$

$$- Q^D(\alpha'(\mu)/f(\mu))(1 - F(\mu))] \, dF(\mu), \tag{11.4.4}$$

subject to $Q^D(\mu)$ nondecreasing in μ.

It is easy to show that $\Pi(\theta) \geq 0$ for all θ and that the equilibrium output schedule chosen by a firm of type θ, $Q(\mu, \theta) = Q^D(\mu, P(\cdot; \theta))$ is nondecreasing in θ.

If the firm is able to make commitments, its most preferred strategy will be to offer the consumer a profit maximizing nonlinear price schedule, $P(\cdot)$. The outcome corresponds to an efficient mechanism.

PROPOSITION 11.4.2   *A first and final offer by the firm of a profit-maximizing nonlinear price schedule, $P(\cdot)$, and the corresponding demand schedule, Q, are* *equivalent to an efficient mechanism for the direct revelation bargaining game.*

Compare the control problem associated with (11.4.4) with the maximization problem for efficient mechanisms (11.3.10). Let $b(\theta) = G(\theta)$ for all θ and let $a(\mu) = 1$ for $\mu \in (0, 1]$ and $a(0) = 0$. Then it can be shown that the control problems are identical.

11.4.3 Monopsony and the Baron-Myerson Model

Consider now a two-stage bargaining game in which the consumer can commit to a bargaining strategy in the first stage and the regulated firm must respond in the second stage. This case may be interpreted as the "public interest" model of regulation in which regulators do not give positive weight in their objective functions to the expected profits of firms. Suppose that the consumer or regulator makes a take-it-or-leave-it offer of a nonlinear compensation schedule to the firm. The firm is rewarded on the basis of total output produced, as with piece rate schedules in labor contracts.

The firm of type θ faced with a nonlinear price schedule $P(\cdot)$ chooses to supply $Q^S = Q^S(\theta) \geq 0$ to maximize profits,

$$\Pi(\theta) = \max_{Q} \ [P(Q) - C(Q, \theta)]. \tag{11.4.5}$$

Let $Q^S(\theta) = Q^S(\theta, P(\cdot))$. Let $\Pi(\theta) = P(Q^S(\theta)) - C(Q^S(\theta), \theta)$. By incentive compatibility (and standard envelope theorem arguments), it follows that $\Pi'(\theta) = -C_\theta(Q^S(\theta), \theta) = -\gamma'(\theta)Q^S(\theta)$. The monopsonist or public interest regulator lowers the payment schedule P until gains from trade are equal to zero for at least the highest cost type, i.e., $\Pi(1) = 0$. Thus, $\Pi(\theta) = \int_\theta^1 \gamma'(\tilde{\theta})Q^S(\tilde{\theta}) \, d\tilde{\theta}$. Finally, incentive compatibility requires $Q^S(\theta)$ to be nonincreasing in μ.

The consumer of type μ chooses the compensation schedule $P(\cdot) = P(\cdot ; \mu)$ to maximize his expected net benefits,

$$V(\mu) = \max_{P(\cdot)} \int_0^1 [U(Q^S, \mu) - P(Q^S)] \, dG(\theta), \tag{11.4.6}$$

subject to $Q^S = Q^S(\theta, P(\cdot))$ from the firm's profit maximization problem, the firm's break-even condition $\Pi(1) \geq 0$, and $Q^S(\theta)$ nonincreasing in θ. Substitute for $P(Q^S)$ from the firm's problem, where $P(Q^S(\theta)) = \Pi(\theta) + C(Q^S(\theta), \theta) = \int_\theta^1 \gamma'(\tilde{\theta})Q^S(\tilde{\theta}) \, d\tilde{\theta} + C(Q^S(\theta), \theta)$. After integration by parts,

$$V(\mu) = \max_{Q^S} \int_0^1 [U(Q^S, \mu) - C(Q^S, \theta)$$

$$- Q^S(\gamma'(\theta)/g(\theta))G(\theta)]\, dG(\theta), \tag{11.4.7}$$

subject to $Q^S(\theta)$ nonincreasing in θ. It is easy to show that $V(\mu) \geq 0$ for all μ and the equilibrium supply schedule chosen by the consumer, $Q(\mu, \theta) - Q^S(\theta, P(\cdot; \mu))$, is nondecreasing in μ.

If the consumer is able to make commitments, his most preferred strategy will be to offer the firm a nonlinear compensation schedule, $P(\cdot)$. The outcome corresponds to an efficient mechanism.

PROPOSITION 11.4.3   *A first and final offer by the consumer of a nonlinear price schedule that maximizes net benefits, $P(\cdot)$, and the corresponding supply schedule, Q, are equivalent to an efficient mechanism for the direct revelation bargaining game.*

Compare the control problem for (11.4.7) with (11.3.10). Let $a(\mu) = F(\mu)$ and $b(\theta) = 0$ for $\theta \in [0, 1)$ and $b(1) = 1$. Then it can be shown that the two problems are identical.

It should be apparent that the optimal compensation schedule offered by the consumer is closely related to principal agent models of regulation under asymmetric information. Consider the Baron and Myerson (1982) regulation model. In their model, there is only a single type of consumer whose demand is known to the regulator and the firm. I continue to allow private information on consumer demand, but I suppose that the regulator is only interested in expected consumer surplus. Further in the Baron and Myerson (1982) model it is assumed that the regulator maximizes a weighted sum of expected gains to consumers plus expected profit for the firm weighted by a constant $\bar{b}$, $0 \leq \bar{b} \leq 1$. Thus, to obtain the same objective function in my framework, let the weights $(a(\cdot), b(\cdot))$ be given by

$$a(\mu) = F(\mu) \quad \text{and} \quad b(\theta) = \begin{cases} \bar{b}G(\theta), & \theta \in [0, 1) \\ 1, & \theta = 1. \end{cases}$$

Then (11.3.10) is

$$\int_0^1 V(\mu, Q, R)\, dF(\mu) + \bar{b} \int_0^1 \Pi(\theta, Q, R)\, dG(\theta)$$

$$= \int_0^1 \int_0^1 [U(Q, \mu) - C(Q, \theta) - (1 - \bar{b})Q(\gamma'(\theta)/g(\theta))G(\theta)]\, dG(\theta). \tag{11.4.8}$$

Comparing (11.4.8) with Baron and Myerson (1982), it is easily shown that the solutions to their model and to (11.4.8) are identical for the same cost and utility function specification. Therefore, the Baron and Myerson optimal regulatory policy is a solution to the bargaining problem. Given that $\lambda^2(\theta) - \gamma(\theta) = -[(1 - \bar{b})(\gamma'(\theta)/g(\theta))G(\theta) + \gamma(\theta)]$ is nonincreasing in θ, then for $Q(\mu, \theta) > 0$,

$$p(\mu, \theta) = c(Q, \theta) + (1 - \bar{b})(\gamma'(\theta)/g(\theta))G(\theta).$$

Note that $Q(\mu, \theta) = 0$ for

$$p(0, \mu) - c(0, \theta) < (1 - \bar{b})(\gamma'(\theta)/g(\theta))G(\theta),$$

or if $Q(\mu, \theta) = 0$ is required by constraints on the consumer or firm gains from trade.

As noted by Baron and Myerson (1982), for an example with a specific cost function, the case of equal weights on expected consumer surplus and expected firm profits ($\bar{b} = 1$) eliminates welfare losses and yields the solution proposed by Loeb and Magat (1979) in which consumers compensate firms sufficiently for correct revelation of their marginal costs. In my framework, it was shown that maximization of expected consumer surplus and firm profits is necessary and sufficient for the efficient mechanism to be ex post efficient if equation (11.3.7) is satisfied. If $\bar{b} = 0$, then the Baron and Myerson solution coincides with the first and final offer of a nonlinear price schedule by the consumer.

Baron and Myerson (1982) thus consider the particular set of weights on firm profits, $b(\theta) = \bar{b}G(\theta)$, that involves a rescaling of the cumulative distribution function $G(\theta)$. This is probably a reasonable conjecture about the form of a regulator's preferences. However, the full range of weights cannot be ruled out a priori in characterizing the set of solutions to a *bargaining game*. As Myerson (1984, p. 465) observes, with or without an arbitrator, all types may be significant, "because each player must express a compromise among the preferences of all of his possible types in bargaining, in order to not reveal his true type during the bargaining process." At issue then is the nature of the regulatory process. If regulation is an expression of the regulator's preferences, then a welfare measure based on expected utility and expected costs may be appropriate. If regulation is an "administered contract" involving bargaining, then each potential consumer and firm type should be given weight and the full set of interim incentive efficient mechanisms should be considered.

The preceding analysis of regulation as a bargaining process between consumers and firms shows that a wide range of efficient solutions exists that depends upon the relative weights $(a(\cdot), b(\cdot))$ given to consumer and firm types. The weighting functions $(a(\cdot), b(\cdot))$ determine the form of the output schedule $Q^*(\mu, \theta)$ as a function of the demand and cost parameters. Emphasis on expected consumer surplus and expected firm profits in models of welfare maximization by a regulator may exclude many solutions of interest. The set of efficient solutions includes monopoly nonlinear pricing, monopsony nonlinear compensation schedules, and the Baron and Myerson (1982) regulation model. For particular forms of consumer willingness to pay functions and firm marginal cost functions, the set of interim incentive efficient mechanisms also includes mechanisms that are ex post or full information efficient. The analysis of the set of interim incentive efficient mechanisms presented here shows that bilateral asymmetric information may lead to pooling across consumer types, firm types, or both at Bayesian equilibria of the direct revelation game. This implies that the regulatory process may involve efficiency losses due to incomplete information about either consumer or firm characteristics.

The bargaining analysis of regulation presented here emphasizes the involvement of both consumers and firms in the regulatory process. In addition, it is observed that there can be incomplete information about both the demand and supply sides of the market. Incomplete information about consumers creates difficulties not only in estimating demand but also in assessing the welfare effects of regulation. The bargaining model yields a wide range of potential allocations of economic rent between consumers and the regulated firm. This suggests that additional study of regulatory institutions is required. Dynamic bargaining models may yield insights into the process of information gathering and rate setting by regulatory agencies.

Appendix

Proof of Proposition 11.2.2   Let (Q^*, R^*) be efficient. Then a unique vector of consumer net benefits and firm profits is defined by

$$V_i^* = \sum_{l=1}^{m} [U(Q_{il}^*, \mu_i) - R_{il}^*]g_l, \tag{1}$$

$$\Pi_l^* = \sum_{i=1}^{n} [R_{il}^* - C(Q_{il}^*)]f_i. \tag{2}$$

Then, given (V^*, Π^*, Q^*), the vector R^* is determined by (1) and (2). Thus, the interim efficient allocation is given by (V^*, Π^*, Q^*). Consider the constraints imposed on vectors (V, Π, Q) by the requirements of incentive compatibility and individual rationality. In particular, since the constraints (11.1.11) and (11.2.2) are linear, there exists a matrix of constants B such that (11.1.11) and (11.2.2) are represented by $B(V, \Pi, Q) \geq 0$. Define the set $\mathscr{B}$ for some (V, Π, Q) by

$$\mathscr{B} \equiv \{s \in \mathbb{R}^r : s \leq (V, \Pi, B(V, \Pi, Q)')\}, \tag{3}$$

where $r = n + m + (2n - 1) + (2m - 1)$. Define the set $\mathscr{A}$ by

$$\mathscr{A} \equiv \{s \in \mathbb{R}^r : s > (V^*, \Pi^*, 0)\}. \tag{4}$$

Clearly $\mathscr{A}$ and $\mathscr{B}$ are convex sets. Since (V^*, Π^*) is interim efficient, the sets $\mathscr{A}$ and $\mathscr{B}$ are disjoint. Further, the vector $(V^*, \Pi^*, 0)$ is on the boundary of $\mathscr{A}$. Thus, there exists a separating hyperplane (a, b, h), $a \in \mathbb{R}^n_+$, $b \in \mathbb{R}^m_+$, $h \in \mathbb{R}^{(2n-1+2m-1)}$ such that

$$aV + b\Pi + hB(V, \Pi, Q) \leq aV^* + b\Pi^*. \tag{5}$$

It follows that if $(V, \Pi) = (V^*, \Pi^*)$, then $hB(V, \Pi, Q) \leq 0$. But since $B(V^*, \Pi^*, Q^*) \geq 0$ and $h \geq 0$, it follows that $hB(V, \Pi, Q) = 0$. Thus, a Kuhn-Tucker problem is obtained given constants a and b and Kuhn-Tucker multiplier h,

$$L = aV + b\Pi + hB(V, \Pi, Q). \quad \text{QED} \tag{6}$$

Before proving proposition 11.3.1, the following lemma is established. The proof is similar to the approach taken in Myerson and Satterthwaite (1983, theorem 1) for the single-object bargaining problem.

LEMMA 1 *Given an incentive compatible mechanism (Q, R) and continuous distributions of consumer and firm types,*

$$V(0) + \Pi(1) = \int_0^1 \int_0^1 [U(Q, \mu) - C(Q, \theta) - Q\alpha'(\mu)((1 - F(\mu))/f(\mu))$$

$$- Q\gamma'(\theta)(G(\theta)/g(\theta))] \, dF(\mu) \, dG(\theta), \tag{7}$$

where $Q = Q(\mu, \theta)$.

Proof From (11.3.5) and (11.3.6),

$$V(0) + \Pi(1) = V(\mu) + \Pi(\theta) - \int_0^\mu Q_\mu(\tilde{\mu})\alpha'(\tilde{\mu}) \, d\tilde{\mu} - \int_\theta^1 Q_\theta(\tilde{\theta})\gamma'(\tilde{\theta}) \, d\tilde{\theta} \tag{8}$$

for all μ and θ. From the definition of $V(\mu)$ and $\Pi(\theta)$, taking integrals over μ and θ on both sides, (8) is rewritten as follows:

$$V(0) + \Pi(1) = \int_0^1 \int_0^1 [U(Q(\mu, \theta), \mu) - C(Q(\mu, \theta), \theta)$$

$$- \int_0^\mu Q(\tilde{\mu}, \theta) \alpha'(\tilde{\mu}) d\tilde{\mu}$$

$$- \int_\theta^1 Q(\mu, \tilde{\theta}) \gamma'(\tilde{\theta}) d\tilde{\theta}] dF(\mu) dG(\theta). \tag{9}$$

Integrating eq. (9) by parts yields (7).   QED

Proof of Proposition 11.3.1   Suppose only $Q(\mu, \theta)$ and $V(0)$ are known. From (7), given $Q(\mu, \theta)$, the quantity $V(0) + \Pi(1)$ is determined. Thus, it is sufficient to know $Q(\mu, \theta)$ and $V(0)$ to know $\Pi(1)$. From (11.3.5) and (11.3.6), $V(\mu)$ and $\Pi(\theta)$ are uniquely determined by $Q(\mu, \theta)$, $V(0)$, and $\Pi(1)$. Finally, from the definitions of $V(\mu)$ and $\Pi(\theta)$,

$$R_\mu(\mu) = \int_0^1 U(Q(\mu, \theta), \mu) dG(\theta) - V(\mu),$$

$$R_\theta(\theta) = \int_0^1 C(Q(\mu, \theta), \theta) dF(\mu) - \Pi(\theta). \tag{10}$$

Thus, $R_\mu(\mu)$ and $R_\theta(\theta)$ are uniquely determined by $Q(\mu, \theta)$ and $V(0)$.   QED

Proof of Proposition 11.3.2   Given that R supports Q, i.e., (Q, R) is feasible, it has already been shown that $Q_\mu(\mu)$ is nondecreasing in μ, and $Q_\theta(\theta)$ is nonincreasing in θ. Inequality (11.3.7) follows from lemma 1, $V(0) \geq 0$, and $\Pi(1) \geq 0$.

Now assume that $Q_\mu(\mu)$ is nondecreasing, $Q_\theta(\theta)$ is nonincreasing, and (11.3.7) holds. From the definitions of $V(\mu)$ and $P(\theta)$, Q and R must satisfy

$$V'(\mu) = Q_\mu(\mu)\alpha'(\mu) + \int_0^1 [p(Q(\mu, \theta), \mu)(\partial Q(\mu, \theta)/\partial\mu)] dG(\theta) - (\partial R_\mu(\mu)/\partial\mu),$$
$$\tag{11}$$

$$\Pi'(\theta) = (\partial R_\theta(\theta)/\partial\theta) - Q_\theta(\theta)\gamma'(\theta) - \int_0^1 [c(Q(\mu, \theta), \theta)(\partial Q(\mu, \theta)/\partial\theta)] dF(\mu).$$
$$\tag{12}$$

Further, if the necessary conditions for incentive compatibility, (11.3.4), are satisfied, then (11) and (12) imply that

$$\int_0^1 [p(Q(\mu,\theta),\mu)(\partial Q(\mu,\theta)/\partial\mu)]\, dG(\theta) = \partial R_\mu(\mu)/\partial\mu, \tag{13}$$

$$\int_0^1 [c(Q(\mu,\theta),\theta)(\partial Q(\mu,\theta)/\partial\theta)]\, dF(\mu) = \partial R_\theta(\theta)/\partial\theta. \tag{14}$$

Thus, there are two partial differential equations that may be used to define $R(\mu,\theta)$. Fix the end point $R(0,\theta)$ in such a way that $U(0) = 0$, i.e., $\int_0^1 U(Q(0,\theta),0)\, dG(\theta) = R_\mu(0)$. The following payment schedule is a solution to (13) and (14) given $R_\mu(0)$:

$$R(\mu,\theta) = \int_0^1 \left[\int_0^\mu p(Q(\tilde{\mu},\tilde{\theta}),\tilde{\mu})(\partial Q(\tilde{\mu},\tilde{\theta})/\partial\mu)\, d\tilde{\mu} \right] dG(\tilde{\theta})$$

$$- \int_0^1 \left[\int_\theta^1 c(Q(\tilde{\mu},\tilde{\theta}),\tilde{\theta})(\partial Q(\tilde{\mu},\tilde{\theta})/\partial\theta)\, d\tilde{\theta} \right] dF(\tilde{\mu})$$

$$- \int_0^1 \left[\int_0^1 c(Q(\tilde{\mu},\tilde{\theta}),\tilde{\theta})(\partial Q(\tilde{\mu},\tilde{\theta})/\partial\theta)G(\tilde{\theta})\, d\tilde{\theta} \right] dF(\tilde{\mu})$$

$$+ \int_0^1 U(Q(0,\tilde{\theta}),0)\, dG(\tilde{\theta}). \tag{15}$$

Given $Q_\mu(\mu)$ nondecreasing in μ and $Q_\theta(\theta)$ nonincreasing in θ, it follows that $R(\mu,\theta)$ is nonnegative.

Given R defined by (15), it follows that $\partial R_\mu(\mu)/\partial\mu$ and $\partial R_\theta(\theta)/\partial\theta$ satisfy (13) and (14). Therefore, it follows that

$$\left.\frac{\partial U(\mu,\hat{\mu})}{\partial\hat{\mu}}\right|_{\hat{\mu}=\mu} = 0, \qquad \left.\frac{\partial \Pi(\theta,\hat{\theta})}{\partial\hat{\theta}}\right|_{\hat{\theta}=\theta} = 0,$$

so that (Q,R) is incentive compatible. For (Q,R) incentive compatible, (7) holds by lemma 11.1.1. Thus, given (11.3.7) in the statement of the proposition, $\Pi(1) \geq 0$. Since R is chosen in such a way that $V(0) = 0$, it follows that (Q,R) is individually rational.   QED

Notes

1. Useful surveys and interpretation of the literature on regulation under asymmetric information are given by Baron (1987), Besanko and Sappington (1987), and Caillaud et al. (1985). An early study by Loeb and Magat (1979) proposes a decentralized method of utility regulation in which the regulator awards all consumer surplus to the regulated firm, which

then has the incentive to set a competitive price, as would occur under first-degree price discrimination. Franchise bidding or taxation can reclaim part of the subsidy. The seminal study in a principal agent framework is Baron and Myerson (1982). See also Baron and DeBondt (1981), Sappington (1983), Baron (1984), Baron and Besanko (1984a), and Laffont and Tirole (1986). Riordan (1984) studies the case where a regulated firm has better information about market demand than does a regulator. Extensions of the model of regulation under asymmetric information to a dynamic setting are given in Baron and Besanko (1984b) and Sappington and Sibley (1984).

2. The bargaining game between a representative consumer and firm is studied here using the approach of Myerson (1979, 1985), Myerson and Satterthwaite (1983), and Holmström and Myerson (1984).

3. The results may be generalized to allow fixed costs to depend on the firm's type as well, $k = k(\theta)$.

4. On the revelation principle see Myerson (1979), Dasgupta, Hammond, and Maskin (1979), Gibbard (1973), and Harris and Townsend (1981).

5. For example, in the model of nonlinear pricing by a monopolist, the "local downward" constraints imposed by the requirement of incentive compatibility for the consumer must be strictly binding. This is due to the ability of the price-discriminating monopolist to appropriate all monopoly rents net of the information costs of obtaining consumer self-selection; see Spence (1980) and Maskin and Riley (1984). In Besanko and Spulber (1986), antitrust enforcement is studied in a model in which "local upward" constraints for the firm must be binding.

6. The proof uses standard Kuhn-Tucker and linear programming arguments; see, for example, Intriligator (1971).

7. The proof restricts attention to (piecewise) continuously differentiable functions for ease of presentation.

8. Note that $I(Q, \mu, \theta)$ is twice differentiable (C^2) and strictly concave in Q, $I_{QQ} = \beta'(Q) - \sigma'(Q) < 0$. Recall also that $\alpha(\mu)$ and $\gamma(\theta)$ are C^2 and concave in μ and θ, respectively.

9. Assume that the weights $a(\mu)$ and $b(\theta)$ are piecewise C^1. The cumulative probability distributions $F(\mu)$ and $G(\theta)$ are C^2. Then it can be shown that the unconstrained solution, $\bar{Q}$, is piecewise C^1 in μ and θ.

10. The unconstrained optimal solution allows pooling across consumer types and across firm types, since $\bar{Q}$ may be constant in μ or θ. If $(\lambda^1(\mu) - \alpha(\mu))$ and $(\lambda^2(\theta) - \gamma(\theta))$ are *strictly* decreasing in μ and θ, respectively, then the optimal solution, $Q^*(\mu, \theta)$, is a *separating* equilibrium for μ and θ such that $\bar{Q} > 0$. Further, one may partition $[0, 1] \times [0, 1]$ into two regions, one where $\bar{Q}(\mu, \theta) > 0$ and one where $\bar{Q}(\mu, \theta) = 0$. The region containing (μ, θ) such that $\bar{Q} > 0$ is given by (μ, θ) above the positively sloped line $\mu(\theta)$ given by $\lambda^1(\mu(\theta)) - \alpha(\mu(\theta)) = \lambda^2(\theta) - \gamma(\theta)$. To illustrate this case, suppose that F and G are uniform distributions. Then choose weights $(a(\cdot), b(\cdot))$ such that $a'(\mu) < 2$, $b'(\theta) < 2$, $a(\mu) \geq \mu$, and $b(\theta) \geq \theta$. Then, by concavity of $\alpha(\cdot)$ and $\gamma(\cdot)$, $(\lambda^{1\prime}(\mu) - \alpha'(\mu)) < 0$ and $(\lambda^{2\prime}(\theta) - \gamma'(\theta)) < 0$. Thus, the unique, efficient mechanism for each set of these weights yields a separating equilibrium.

11. Mechanisms that do not distinguish between distinct types of agents are said to *pool* those agents. Mechanisms that distinguish between agents of distinct types by inducing them to reveal their types are said to *separate* those agents. The terms are from the field of insurance. Insurance contracts are said to pool or separate individuals in terms of risk classes.

12. A strong characterization theorem is given in Spulber (1988a). The control problem required to solve the optimization in equation (11.3.11) is not a standard classical control problem due to the presence of two independent variables μ and θ. This problem appears to be quite difficult in general and would require an extension of the maximum principle to the two-parameter case. The problem is further complicated by the presence of the expected value partial differential equations that are the boundary constraints. Fortunately, this

problem can be characterized given the particular characteristics of the bargaining model presented here. The approach involves application and extension of results due to Guesnerie and Laffont (1984) for the one-parameter case.

13. Formally, let $a(\mu) = F(\mu)$ and $b(\theta) = G(\theta)$. Then $\lambda^1(\mu) = \lambda^2(\theta) = 0$, and $Q^F(\mu, \theta) > 0$ solves $p(Q, \mu) = c(Q, \theta)$. For $p(0, \mu) - c(0, \theta) < 0$, $Q(\mu, \theta) = 0$. Clearly, $Q^F(\mu, \theta)$ is nondecreasing in μ and nonincreasing in θ. For $Q > 0$, $\partial Q^F/\partial\mu = -\alpha'(\mu)/(\beta'(Q) - \sigma'(Q))$, and $\partial Q^F/\partial\theta = +\gamma'(\theta)/(\beta'(Q) - \sigma'(Q))$, so that $\partial Q^F/\partial\mu > 0$, $\partial Q^F/\partial\theta < 0$ for $Q^F > 0$.

14. It is interesting to compare the variable quantity model with the single-object bargaining problem of Myerson and Satterthwaite (1983). There, ex post efficiency will not occur unless the support for the buyer's reservation values is everywhere above that of the seller. With variable output, a more robust efficiency result is obtained because the equilibrium output adjusts to reflect values of the demand and cost parameters. For example, high marginal cost is reflected in a low output rather than in a decision not to trade.

15. Nonlinear pricing by a monopoly is studied by Spence (1977c, 1980), Spulber (1981b), Maskin and Riley (1984), and others.

12 Externalities 1: Bargaining

The presence of externalities, such as environmental pollution, is a generally recognized source of market failure. Without proper adjustment of externality levels, market equilibria will not achieve Pareto optimality. Thus, there may be welfare gains from the establishment of social institutions that allow adjustment of pollution levels to reflect the benefits and damages from pollution discharges. The key issue is whether efficiency is enhanced by legal rules alone or whether these must be supplemented by direct administrative regulation.

Administrative regulation of pollution generally involves establishing and enforcing aggregate standards. Independently of how they are enforced, these standards may have significant consequences for the efficient allocation of resources as well as for the distribution of income. The establishment of aggregate standards is therefore an important area in which bargaining and coalition formation take place. The standards that are chosen reflect the negotiation efforts of diverse consumer, labor, and industry interest groups. Section 12.1 examines U.S. environmental regulation in the areas of air and water pollution. The opportunities for bargaining among interest groups in the setting of standards and in their implementation and enforcement are emphasized. Section 12.2 considers the analysis of Coase (1960) and its implications for bargaining in the context of administrative regulation. A model showing how aggregate standards are established is examined in the next chapter.

An alternative to regulation of externalities suggested by Coase (1960) is for private individuals (polluters and victims) to bargain over pollution abatement and compensatory payments. This is a viable alternative to regulation if property rights are well-defined, transactions costs are low, there is a small number of injurers and victims, and the effects of pollution are easily identified. Sections 12.3 and 12.4 examine allocative efficiency when private bargaining is feasible. First, bargaining between a polluting firm and a consumer in a full information setting is considered. The effects of the property rights assignment on the efficient frontier are examined. Then private bargaining is studied under asymmetric information about the benefits of discharging pollution and the damages suffered by receptors. Asymmetric information may prevent private bargaining from reaching socially optimal pollution discharge levels. Regulation of externalities under incomplete information is examined in the next chapter.

12.1 Regulatory Standards and Public Hearings

Environmental regulation is primarily based on standards for *aggregate* externality levels. The aggregate externality standards are distinct from enforcement efforts and policy instruments, which may include effluent taxes, marketable permits, technological requirements, input controls, and effluent quotas. The term "quotas" is used to distinguish discharge or emission limits placed on individual pollution sources, often referred to as standards, from aggregate standards. Aggregate standards are usually specified and enforced by appropriate regulatory agencies. Congressional legislation generally involves broad environmental quality requirements that give considerable flexibility to regulators, primarily the Environmental Protection Agency (EPA), in their interpretation. Under the Clean Air Act Amendments of 1970 and the Federal Water Pollution Control Act Amendments of 1972, Congress specified broad goals for environmental quality. The legislation requires the EPA to set aggregate standards or monitor aggregate standards set by the states. First, the stated goals of this legislation are briefly reviewed, and then the EPA's standard-setting procedures are considered. I shall argue that because the EPA follows administrative procedures, as outlined in chapter 2, the standard-setting process may be viewed as *bargaining* between consumer, industry, and environmental interest groups. The standards are promulgated through the formal rule-making process with public hearings on the record and with presentations by adversarial interest groups.

The 1970 Clean Air Amendments to the 1967 Air Quality Act charged the EPA with setting national ambient air quality standards (NAAQS), particularly for the most common air pollutants: carbon monoxide, hydrocarbons, lead, nitrogen dioxide, ozone, particulates, and sulfur dioxide. The EPA was charged with setting two types of quality standards: primary standards, based on human health protection, and secondary standards, based largely on reducing property damage. In addition, the act itself set technological standards and quotas for auto emissions. Also, the act requires establishment of aggregate emission standards for hazardous air pollutants based on public health considerations. The EPA was also required to set emission quotas called *new source performance standards* (NSPS) for new stationary sources of pollution. Finally, the EPA was charged with setting *control technique guidelines* for pollution control equipment to be used by existing stationary sources.

Within specified regions,[1] state and local regulators are charged with devising State Implementation Plans (SIPs) for implementation of the aggregate standards subject to EPA approval. If the states do not establish implementation plans, the EPA has the authority to establish its own implementation plan, which may involve emissions quotas.[2] Further, the EPA has the authority to set emissions quotas for new stationary sources, hazardous air pollutants, and vehicles.[3] Based on regional air quality, states were required to enforce various technological specifications including "reasonably available control technology" (RACT), "lowest achievable emission rate" (LAER), and "best available control technology" (BACT).

The 1970 Clean Air Act Amendments specify in detail various aspects of the rule-making procedure for establishing aggregate standards. In addition the standard-setting procedure is subject to the Administrative Procedures Act. There are three principal ways in which bargaining enters into the regulations. The first is in the standard-setting process itself. The second is in enforcement, which involves case-by-case adjudication and bargaining between the EPA and the states. The third is bargaining between the EPA or state agency and the polluters after standards have been set.

The standards are set primarily by the EPA and are announced as *rules* in the sense given in chapter 2. The EPA announces a proposed standard. A public hearing is held in which technical experts, concerned consumer and industry representatives, and government officials present their arguments. As Davies and Davies (1975) emphasize, "Extended bargaining may take place between EPA and these groups." Further, interpretation and enforcement of standards is subject to negotiation: "Even where the standards have been established by law, as in the case of the automobile standards, there is considerable leeway in interpretation. The test methods and enforcement procedure may be just as important as the specific numbers established as the standard" (Davies and Davies, 1975). Davies and Davies observe that the rules for setting standards established by the 1970 Clean Air Amendments "themselves may get changed in the course of bargaining over the standards," as occurred in a case involving the Sierra Club.[4] Thus, an important component of rule-making hearings and judicial oversight is interpretation of the legislation.

The 1970 Clean Air Amendments rely on enforcement by the states, particularly through state regulation of emissions. While the State Implementation Plans to achieve national ambient air quality standards are subject to EPA approval, there is considerable room for choice of emissions regulations. The EPA faces significant information costs in evaluating state regulatory programs and all of the regulations therein for all of the states. The approval process allows for extended negotiations between the EPA and state administrators over the effectiveness and design of state plans.

Finally, in implementing the standards, additional bargaining is involved. As noted by Ruff (1981, p. 246), for controls on existing stationary sources,

Unfortunately, the "enforceable" regulations were (and still are) typically little more than starting points for negotiations between the control agency and the individual sources, each of which will argue that: (1) he is in compliance with the regulations; (2) if not, it is because the regulation is unreasonable as a general rule; (3) if not, then the regulation is unreasonable in this specific case; (4) if not, then it is up to the regulatory agency to tell him how he can comply; (5) if forced to take the steps recommended by the regulatory agency, he cannot be held responsible for the results; and (6) he needs more time. The regulatory agency, unable to fight every battle, will define the regulations so that most sources are in compliance or can easily become so and will work out agreements promising future action by the worst violator. These agreements then become the "enforceable regulations" and, if they are not complied with, another round of negotiating begins.

Similar issues arise in regulation of water pollution. Under the 1972 Federal Water Pollution Control Amendments (FWPCA), the EPA was charged with setting standards in the form of limits on effluent discharges and specification of pollution control technology. The FWPCA specifies broad goals for water quality. The act states that its objective is "to restore and maintain the chemical, physical, and biological integrity of the Nation's waters." To achieve this the act specifies the following:

(1) it is the national goal that the discharge of pollutants into the navigable waters be eliminated by 1985;

(2) it is the national goal that wherever attainable, an interim goal of water quality which provides for the protection and propagation of fish, shellfish, and wildlife and provides for recreation in and on the water be achieved by July 1, 1983;

(3) it is the national policy that the discharge of toxic pollutants in toxic amounts be prohibited.

In addition, the act provides for federal construction assistance for publicly owned waste treatment works (POTWs), areawide waste treatment plans, and research and development on technology to reduce water pollution. Although the elimination of discharges was far from being achieved by 1985, the goals stated by the act continue to guide environmental policy.

To achieve the stated objectives the act requires (section 301b(1)) "application of the best practicable control technology" (BPT) to point sources other than POTWs. The act (section 304b1(B)) states that determination of the BPT requires the regulator to consider the "total cost of application of technology in relation to the effluent reduction benefits to be achieved and to take into account the age of equipment and facilities involved, the process employed, the engineering aspects of the application of various types of control techniques, process changes, non-water quality environmental impact (including energy requirements) and such other factors as the Administrator deems appropriate." For new pollution sources and other point sources at a later date, the act (section 301b(2)(A)) requires implementation of the "best available technology economically achievable" (BAT). In addition, the act requires the EPA to specify pretreatment standards for discharges into POTWs and effluent standards for toxic pollutants. The primary regulatory policy instrument of the 1972 FWPCA is a national permit program with accompanying quotas and technological standards for individual point sources. The National Pollutant Discharge Elimination System (NPDES) (section 402a1) involves issuance of pollution discharge permits by the EPA or state administrator after public hearing. This program depends heavily on state administration and enforcement.

The opportunities for bargaining under the 1972 FWPCA are similar to those identified for the 1970 Clean Air Amendments. The 1972 act requires that all effluent limitations, either discharge quotas or technological requirements, be set through the public hearing process (section 302b1). The act specifies that the administrator hold a public hearing "to determine the relationship of the economic and social costs of achieving any such limitation." As with other regulatory programs, the public-hearing process will involve extensive bargaining between opposing interest groups involving consumers, producers, state and local governments, and technical experts. In addition, since much of the enforcement provisions depends upon state implementation, there will be considerable room for negotiation between federal and state officials over the design and approval of state water quality regulations and extensive debate at the state and local levels as well.

Two examples of the effect of bargaining on the interpretation and enforcement of the 1972 FWPCA are significant. One involves a 1976 settlement agreement negotiated between the EPA and a number of environmental interest groups that resulted in guidelines for setting effluent quotas for point sources and pretreatment standards for "65 toxic pollutants from 21 major industrial categories"; see Ruff (1981, p. 254). As Ruff notes, these requirements were incorporated into later legislation, the 1977 FWPCA. Another important case, discussed extensively by Tolchin and Tolchin (1983), involves pretreatment regulations affecting "sixty thousand industrial facilities" (p. 74) discharging effluents to POTWs. Tolchin and Tolchin (1983, p. 75) observe that in setting the pretreatment regulations, EPA held four public hearings and sixteen public meetings between 1977 and 1981 receiving over four hundred public comments.[5]

To summarize, bargaining over externalities may occur at a number of stages in the regulatory process. The setting of aggregate standards for environmental quality by Congress involves lobbying and bargaining between political interest groups. At stake are votes and campaign contributions that may depend on the impact of environmental standards on profits, factor payments, employment, and the distribution of income. Further, the setting of specific standards and regulations by the EPA involves bargaining by consumer and firm interest groups through public hearings. State implementation plans and enforcement procedures create intergovernmental negotiation between state and federal authorities. Finally, at the point of enforcement, individual polluters may have occasion to negotiate with regulatory agencies on the interpretation and applicability of pollution quotas, technological specifications, and additional rules.

12.2   The Coase Theorem

In the presence of external diseconomies, such as environmental pollution, the creators of external damages may be identified as injurers, while the consumers of external damages may be identified as victims. From a legal standpoint, either side of the transaction may possess certain rights. The producer of the externality may have the right to pursue the economic activity that creates the diseconomy as a by-product. Further, the producer may have the right to discharge pollutants into the air, water, or ground. Alternatively, the consumer of the externality may have the right to clean air or water or to be free from the harm caused by air or water pollution. The legal definition of these property rights has profound implications for resulting market equilibria, particularly for those goods that entail pollution as a by-product. The legal definition of rights may also affect the extent of external diseconomies through private negotiation and legal enforcement. Finally, the legal definition of rights provides the framework within which the effectiveness and necessity of government regulation of externality-creating activities can be evaluated.

In "The Problem of Social Cost," Coase (1960) raised a number of issues with great significance for the economic analysis of law and regulation. The principal assertion, which has come to be known as the *Coase theorem* (1960), is the following: "It is necessary to know whether the damaging business is liable or not for damage caused since without the establishment of this initial delimitation of rights there can be no market transactions to transfer and recombine them. But the ultimate result (which maximizes the value of production) is independent of the legal position if the pricing system is assumed to work without cost." The Coase theorem thus emphasizes that while some assignment of legal rights is essential for achieving economic efficiency, the particular allocation of those rights does not affect the efficiency of the market outcome in the absence of transaction costs.[6] Thus, if the victim of pollution has rights, the factory must compensate the victim in excess of marginal damages if the factory wishes to pollute. If the factory has rights, the potential victim must bribe the factory to reduce its pollution. The Coase theorem thus implies that in the absence of transaction costs, the welfare optimum is attainable through market transactions after an assignment of legal rights. This remarkable conclusion subsumes a series of important insights, which are now discussed.

A crucial issue addressed by Coase (1960) is the *reciprocal* nature of the externalities problem. For Coase, the issue is not imply that "*A* inflicts harm on *B*" and should be restrained. The converse is, "To avoid the harm to *B* would inflict harm on *A*." Thus, the degree to which the externality is alleviated requires attention to the trade-off between the values of the externality to the injurer and the victim. The marginal net benefits to the firm discharging pollution as a by-product reflect the market valuation of the firm's output. These benefits must be weighed against the marginal damages of pollution suffered by the victim. This was recognized by Pigou in *The Economics of Welfare* (1920), although Pigou is roundly criticized by Coase for placing the burden of liability on the polluting factory. Pigou emphasizes that the marginal social costs of production be equated to the marginal social benefits. The marginal social costs of production are the sum of marginal private costs for the factory (MPC) and marginal external costs (MEC) of damages to the victim. The marginal social benefits of production represent the marginal private benefits (MPB) to purchasers of the factory's final output Q. Placing the burden of avoiding harm on the factory causes the factory to internalize MEC as part of its marginal costs, so that at the market equilibrium,

$MPC(Q^*) + MEC(Q^*) = MPB(Q^*).$

Alternatively, if we trade off the net benefits of the factory's productive activity with the damages to the victim, we have at the market equilibrium, following Coase,

$MEC(Q^*) = MPB(Q^*) - MPC(Q^*).$

In this sense, the welfare analysis of Coase is identical with that of Pigou.

The emphasis on reciprocity of harm identified by Coase has parallels throughout law. In nuisance law, the creation of externalities as a by-product of an economic activity may be seen as "incompatible uses" of nonexclusive property rights (Posner, 1977, pp. 34–35). Thus, the discharge of pollutants by the factory that affects nearby households may be seen as incompatible uses of proximate properties for industrial and residential purposes. The socially optimal solution involves some combination of reduced pollution and pollution avoidance by homeowners. Similarly, in tort law, liability for accidents has long been viewed in terms of the negligence of the injurer and the possible contributory negligence of the victim. Harm caused by a stranger, such as between a factory discharging chemical pollutants, and a bystander must involve an assessment of the factory's negligence and the contribution of the victim to the accident in choosing to be near the factory contrary to posted health warnings. If the injury is not between strangers, such as that associated with products liability, workplace safety, or breach of contract, the reciprocal aspects of alleviating the harm must also be emphasized. These issues are considered in the discussion of internalities in chapters 14 and 15. In each of these areas of law, property, tort, and contracts, application of the Coase theorem suggests that, without transaction costs, an assignment of legal rights is necessary for private transactions to resolve conflict. However, the specific assignment of rights or liability need not affect the efficiency of the outcome.

The Coase theorem stresses the importance of property rights as a basis for private negotiation. As emphasized in chapter 1, the definition, assignment, and transferability of property rights are an essential prerequisite for market transactions. Coase then recognizes the efficiency of private negotiation in the absence of transaction costs. The efficiency of market transactions is certainly central to welfare economics. Coase's contribution here is to emphasize the applicability of the efficiency result to bargaining over external damages and compensatory payments. Thus, transactions need not be limited to traditional commodities. Rather, negotiation over the extent of the externality and payments to reduce harm (if the factory has rights) or payments for compensation (if the victim has rights) are well-defined.

A significant feature of the analysis of Coase (1960) is the emphasis placed on transaction costs in the comparison of alternative market and administrative approaches to resource allocation. The efficiency of private bargaining in the absence of transaction costs has an important converse when transaction costs are present. Similarly, the neutral effects of the assignment of rights in the absence of transaction costs is no longer valid when negotiation is costly. Consider, first, the efficiency of private bargaining versus public regulation.

The presence of private transaction costs may affect the degree to which private bargaining approaches an efficient outcome. Given large numbers of injurers or victims, costly communication, or asymmetric information about the benefits and costs of externalities, private bargaining may fail to achieve efficiency or may break down altogether. Coase emphasizes that the benefits of government regulation with its coercive powers must be weighed against administrative costs. Thus, the net benefits of a system based on legal assignment of rights with private bargaining must be compared to the net benefits of government regulation. Given both large private and public transaction costs, it should not be surprising that environmental regulation involves a mixture of private bargaining with judicial enforcement and direct administrative intervention.

Assignment of legal rights, given transaction costs, must then depend on the ultimate effect of property rights on the outcome of bargaining. Take an extreme case in which transaction costs are so high that potential injurers and victims are unable to negotiate at all. In particular, transaction costs exceed the gains from trade between injurer and victim; see Woj (1985). This implies that private bargaining cannot take place and the status quo is maintained. Giving the factory an entitlement to discharge pollutants will lead homeowners either to suffer damages directly or to avoid them by moving away. Giving the factory no right to discharge pollutants by giving an entitlement to homeowners, in the form of an injunction against pollution, will lead the factory either to eliminate all pollutants or to shut down. In this extreme example, the two regimes, involving pollution or no pollution, must be compared in determining the assignment of rights. As an intermediate case, the government may specify a maximum level of pollution for the factory, giving the factory the right to pollute up to that level. This situation corresponds to pollution standards imposed in environmental regulation. If the government is charged with setting and enforcing pollution standards, this has the inevitable consequence of reintroducing the administrative apparatus with its attendant costs.

Calabresi and Melamed (1972) emphasize the importance of transaction costs in determining the legal remedy; see also Posner (1977, pp. 48–52). By specifying money damages as the legal remedy, enforced through private suits by homeowners, the factory will have incentive to select an optimal level of pollution—the level that equates the marginal net benefits to the factory of discharging pollutants with the marginal external damages. This assumes, of course, that the judicial costs are not also prohibitive. The legal costs to plaintiffs and defendants and the costs of correctly determining damages must be taken into account when choosing a legal remedy. Note also that public assignment of entitlements may require costly administrative allocation; see chapter 1.

In the control of externalities, must the choice be restricted to private bargaining versus command and control regulation? Surely, the possibility that transaction costs may inhibit private bargaining suggests a role for regulation in mitigating these costs. One possibility is for the regulatory agency to act as an intermediary or broker between potential injurers and victims. In the presence of externalities with many polluters and large numbers of victims, as in the case of air pollution, individual negotiation is ruled out. However, the institution of the regulatory hearing allows *negotiation by proxy*. Representatives of industry and consumer groups, by presenting arguments in the public hearing and by supplying information to the regulatory authority, may indirectly negotiate pollution levels, abatement technology, or effluent charges. The rule-making and adjudicatory hearings of the federal EPA and state environmental regulation agencies may be seen as performing precisely this function. The hearings serve to emphasize the reciprocal nature of environmental regulations through the expressed interests of affected parties. Therefore, the net benefits of pollution to industry are weighed against the external costs of pollution imposed on consumers and firms. The regulatory framework in the United

States does not provide for compensation of victims, although compensation schemes have been implemented abroad.[7] Further, environmental regulation may affect legal action for recovery of damages. In this sense, the U.S. system of administrative regulation contains the basic elements of bargaining over the extent of externalities.

The environmental regulation process may then be likened to bargaining between suppliers of pollution, generally private industry, and receptors of pollution, both consumers and firms. Thus, environmental regulation may be seen as arbitration between participants in the market for pollution, e.g., producers of externalities and potential consumers. In this manner, environmental regulation has a structure that is similar to rate regulation in markets for services of natural monopolies. The regulator participates in the process of choosing output and price vectors for the regulated firms in the form of effluent quotas and effluent charges. The regulator determines the level of transfers, if any, between consumers, firms, and the public sector. Further, regulatory decisions regarding output of externalities and transfer payments have implications for the distribution of income among participants in the regulated market. The basic structure of *private* bargaining over environmental quality is examined in the next two sections. The analysis is extended to *public* bargaining through regulatory intermediaries in the following chapter.

12.3   Private Bargaining and Property Rights

The extent of external diseconomies may be determined by bargaining. Although the bargaining model discussed in this section is interpreted in terms of private negotiation, the view that public regulation of environmental use also involves trading off consumer and firm benefits is emphasized later.

Let V represent the indirect utility for the representative consumer (or victim). Let Π be the profits of the representative firm (or injurer). The Pareto set is defined as in chapter 10. The consumer's utility is given by $V = U(E, \omega + R)$, where U is decreasing and concave in the effluent $E > 0$. The consumer's endowment is given by ω. The term R refers to the transfer from the firm to the consumer. If R is positive, it represents compensation for damages paid by the firm to the consumer. If R is negative, it represents a bribe or incentive to reduce pollution paid by the consumer to the firm.

Let p and r be the prices of outputs q and inputs x. The firm's profits are a function of its effluent level E:

$$\pi(E) = \max_{q,(x_j)} \left[pq - \sum_{j=1}^{m} r_j x_j - F \right],$$

subject to technological constraints $f(x) \geq q$ and $E \geq h(x)$. Assume that profits are concave in E and increasing (decreasing) in E as E is less than (greater than) the pollution level $\bar{E}$, $\pi'(\bar{E}) = 0$. Given a transfer R made to the consumer, the firm's profits are given by $\Pi = \pi(E) - R$.

Suppose first that the *consumer* has property rights; that is, the firm must compensate the consumer for any damages created by the pollution E. In this case, the consumer's minimum utility level is given by $V^C = U(0, \omega)$, the zero-pollution point. The firm's minimum profit level is given by $\Pi^C = \pi(0)$, the profits attainable without pollution. The Pareto frontier is then defined using the effluent payment schedule, $E = E(R)$, which solves

$$-U_E(E, \omega + R)/U_x(E, \omega + R) = \pi'(E). \tag{12.3.1}$$

Profits are strictly decreasing in R, while consumer benefits are increasing in R. The minimum payment solves $U(E(R_{\min}), \omega - R_{\min}) = V^C$. The maximum payment solves $\pi(E(R_{\max})) - R_{\max} = \Pi^C$. Let $V_{\max} = U(E(R_{\max}), \omega + R_{\max})$ and $\Pi_{\max} = \pi(E(R_{\min})) - R_{\min}$. The efficient frontier is defined by

$$V = P(\Pi) = U(E(R(\Pi)), \omega + R(\Pi)), \tag{12.3.2}$$

where Π takes values in $[\Pi^C, \Pi_{\max}]$ and V takes values in $[V^C, V_{\max}]$. The trade-offs along the efficient frontier $V = P(\Pi)$ are then

$$P'(\Pi) = -U_x(E(R(\Pi)), \omega + R(\Pi)). \tag{12.3.3}$$

The point made by the preceding discussion is that the efficient pollution level is not unique. Rather, due to the presence of consumer income effects, there is a range of efficient pollution levels that may result from bargaining between the consumer and firm. The range of efficient pollution levels is determined by the opportunity costs for the consumer and firm and the consumer's income level ω.

Consider now the case where the firm has property rights. The firm is assumed to have the right to discharge any level of effluent E. In this case, the consumer must provide the firm with some compensation R for profits foregone due to inputs devoted to pollution abatement or output reductions required to meet pollution levels. The firm will set a maxi-

mum pollution level of $\bar{E}$ without bargaining. The minimum utility for
the consumer is thus $V^F = U(\bar{E}, \omega)$. The firm's minimum profit level is
$\Pi^F = \pi(\bar{E})$. The efficient frontier is defined by equations (12.3.1) and (12.3.2)
with the payment R less than zero. The consumer's indirect utility takes
values in the interval $[V^F, V_{max}]$, where $V_{max} = P(\Pi^F)$. The firm's profit
takes values in the interval $[\Pi^F, \Pi_{max}]$, where Π_{max} solves $V^F = P(\Pi_{max})$.

Compare the effects of the property rights assignment on the efficient
frontier. First, the location of the efficient frontier is affected by the direction
of payments between consumer and firm. Second, the end points of the
efficient frontier are determined by the effect of the property right assignment on the opportunity costs of not bargaining for the consumer and firm.
The effluent and payment levels achieved by bargaining under the two
property rights regimes depends on the relative bargaining strengths of the
two parties or the method of arbitration. Generally, for the same bargaining
solution, one expects the effluent levels to be greater under the regime
in which the firm has property rights than under the regime in which
the consumer has property rights. The Nash bargaining solution will be
affected by the slope of the efficient frontier and the opportunity costs, as
in figure 12.3.1.

In figure 12.3.1, the equilibrium indirect utility of the consumer is greater

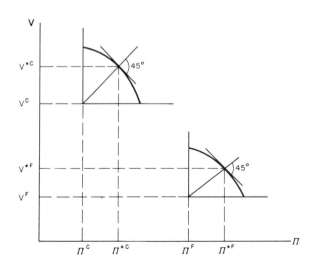

Figure 12.3.1
Effect of property rights assignments on the Nash bargaining solution.

in the regime where the consumer has property rights $V^{*C} > V^{*F}$. Similarly, $\Pi^{*C} < \Pi^{*F}$. The preceding discussion is summarized as follows.

PROPOSITION 12.3.1   (a) *Efficient externality levels are not unique but are defined by an efficient range.* (b) *The efficient range for externalities is sensitive to the assignment of property rights between the consumer and firm and to the consumer's income level.*

Consider now the bargaining problem in the absence of income effects. Let $D(E)$ represent the money value of damages to the consumer. Then consumer benefits are given by $U(E, \omega + R) = \omega + R - D(E)$. In this case, the optimal effluent level E^* is determined independently of transfers, to maximize gains from trade,

$$D'(E^*) = \pi'(E^*). \tag{12.3.4}$$

The role of bargaining is then simply to determine the required transfer. This case corresponds most closely with the standard interpretation of the Coase theorem (1960); see also Turvey (1963). The optimal outcome is represented in figure 12.3.2. If the consumer has property rights, bargaining leads to an increase in effluent level up to E^* from the consumer's desired level of zero in the absence of transfers. Transfers to the consumer $R^C > 0$ must be such that $\pi(E^*) \geq R^C \geq D(E^*)$. If the firm has property rights, bargaining leads to a reduction in effluent levels from the firm's profit-maximizing level $\bar{E}$ down to E^*. Transfers to the firm $R^F > 0$ must be

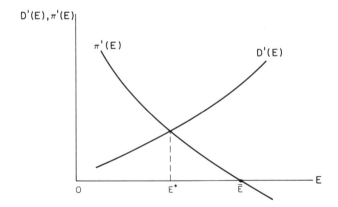

Figure 12.3.2
The socially optimal externality level, E^*.

such that

$$D(\bar{E}) - D(E^*) \geq R^F \geq \pi(\bar{E}) - \pi(E^*). \tag{12.3.5}$$

Thus, bargaining leads to the optimal effluent level independently of the assignment of property rights when consumer income effects are absent.

12.4 Private Bargaining under Asymmetric Information

The problem of bargaining over externality levels and compensatory payments described in the preceding sections may involve asymmetries in information. The damage suffered by the receptor of pollution may not be known to the supplier of the externality. The victim has an incentive to overstate the damages from the externality in order to reduce the externality or alter the size of the compensatory payment. The injurer's net benefits from supplying the externality may also not be known. A firm discharging pollution may have costs of pollution abatement that are unknown to the receptors of pollution. Further, the firm's production costs and revenue function may be unknown to the receptors of pollution, yielding uncertainty about the firm's net benefits from discharging pollution. The firm has incentive to overstate its benefits from discharging pollution to increase the externality and affect the size of the compensatory payment.

The presence of asymmetric information about damages from pollution and benefits obtained by the polluter is an important source of transaction costs. The polluter and victim may incur costs in attempting to learn more about the other party's costs or benefits. The bargaining process itself may be complicated by uncertainty about the other party's net benefits. Finally, asymmetric information may preclude achieving an efficient outcome in terms of the level of pollution even in the absence of consumer income effects.

For ease of presentation, I focus attention only on the case where the consumer has property rights and must be compensated by the firm. The same analysis applies to the case where the firm discharging pollutants has property rights. The outcome of bargaining may differ due to the effect of the property rights assignment on consumer and firm opportunity costs, depending on the solution concept for the bargaining game.

The two parties, a consumer harmed by an externality and a firm that creates the externality, bargain over the level of the externality, E, and the compensation payment to be made to the consumer, R. The consumer suffers damages $D(E, \mu)$, where the parameter $\mu \in [0, 1]$ is distributed according to the cumulative probability distribution $F(\mu)$. The firm earns profits $\pi(E, \theta)$ from a productive activity that generates the externality E as a by-product. The parameter $\theta \in [0, 1]$ is distributed according to the cumulative probability distribution function $G(\theta)$.

Attention is restricted to Bayesian equilibria of bargaining games. By the revelation principle, for any Bayesian equilibrium of any bargaining game, there is an equivalent incentive compatible direct mechanism that always yields the same outcomes when the agents play the truth-telling strategy. Recall from chapter 11 that direct mechanisms are characterized by outcome functions $(E(\mu, \theta), R(\mu, \theta))$ that depend on agent reports of their types to an arbitrator. A direct mechanism is (Bayesian) incentive compatible if truthful reports of agent types are a Bayes-Nash equilibrium. Direct mechanisms that are feasible, that is, individually rational and Bayesian incentive compatible are characterized.

Consider the form $D(E, \mu) = \mu E + \delta(E)$ for the consumer's damage function. The firm's profit has the form $\pi(E, \mu) = \theta E + \eta(E)$. Thus, for higher values of μ, the consumer suffers greater damages. For higher values of θ, the firm's net benefits from discharging pollution are greater. The net benefit to the consumer of type μ from reporting parameter $\hat{\mu}$ to the arbitrator is given by

$$V(\mu, \hat{\mu}) = \int_0^1 [R(\hat{\mu}, \theta) - D(E(\hat{\mu}, \theta), \mu)] \, dF(\theta). \tag{12.4.1}$$

The net benefit to the firm of type θ from reporting parameter $\hat{\theta}$ is given by

$$\Pi(\theta, \hat{\theta}) = \int_0^1 [\pi(E(\mu, \hat{\theta}), \theta) - R(\mu, \hat{\theta})] \, dF(\mu). \tag{12.4.2}$$

Define the following terms to represent expected externality and payment levels:

$$E_\mu(\mu) = \int_0^1 E(\mu, \theta) \, dG(\theta), \qquad E_\theta(\theta) = \int_0^1 E(\mu, \theta) \, dF(\mu),$$

$$R_\mu(\mu) = \int_0^1 R(\mu, \theta) \, dG(\theta), \qquad R_\theta(\theta) = \int_0^1 R(\mu, \theta) \, dF(\mu).$$

Given these preliminaries, analysis of the externalities bargaining problem may be carried out in a manner that is similar to the bargaining problem studied in chapter 11.[8] In particular, proposition 11.3.2 may be applied.

PROPOSITION 12.4.1   *For any externalities schedule $E(\mu, \theta)$, there exists a compensation schedule $R(\mu, \theta) \geq 0$ that supports $E(\mu, \theta)$ if and only if $E_\mu(\mu)$ is nonincreasing in μ, $E_\theta(\theta)$ is nondecreasing in θ, and*

$$\int_0^1 \int_0^1 [\pi(E, \theta) - D(E, \mu) + E[F(\mu)/f(\mu)$$

$$+ (1 - G(\theta))/g(\theta)]]dF(\mu)\,dG(\theta) \geq 0. \tag{12.4.3}$$

Further, it can be shown that a feasible direct mechanism, (E, R), is interim incentive efficient if and only if there exist weights $a(\mu)$, $b(\theta)$ such that (Q, R) maximizes

$$\int_0^1 V(\mu, E, R)\,da(\mu) + \int_0^1 \Pi(\theta, E, R)\,db(\theta), \tag{12.4.4}$$

where $a(\mu)$ and $b(\theta)$ are nondecreasing and $a(0) = b(0) = 0$, $a(1) = b(1) = 1$. By similar arguments, the objective function in (12.4.4) is rewritten as a maximum problem in Q,

$$\int_0^1 \int_0^1 [\pi(E, \theta) - D(E, \mu)$$

$$+ E[(a(\mu) - F(\mu))/f(\mu) - (b(\theta) - G(\theta))/g(\theta)]]dF(\mu)\,dG(\theta). \tag{12.4.5}$$

To focus on the solution unconstrained by boundary conditions, impose the standard monotonicity conditions. Let $[(a(\mu) - F(\mu))/f(\mu) - \mu]$ be monotonically decreasing in μ and let $[(b(\theta) - G(\theta))/g(\theta) - \theta]$ be monotonically decreasing in θ. Then, by arguments similar to those given in chapter 11, for any given set of weights $(a(\mu), b(\theta))$, the unconstrained maximum of equation (12.4.5) yields an interim incentive efficient mechanism, (E^*, R^*), where E^* solves the following equation for (12.4.3) nonbinding,

$$\pi_E(E, \theta) - D_E(E, \mu) = (b(\theta) - G(\theta))/g(\theta) - (a(\mu) - F(\mu))/f(\mu), \tag{12.4.6}$$

and R^* supports E^*. Let $\lambda(\mu, \theta) = (b(\theta) - G(\theta))/g(\theta) - (a(\mu) - F(\mu))/f(\mu)$. By varying the weights, one may generate the set of interim incentive efficient mechanisms.

The solution to (12.4.6) is represented in figure 12.4.1. The presence of

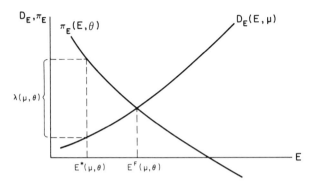

Figure 12.4.1
Inefficiency of the externality level due to asymmetric information.

asymmetric information about the damages to the consumer and net benefits to the firm prevents the optimal adjustment of the externality level E^* to the full information optimum E^F. Thus, under asymmetric information, private bargaining over externalities does not yield the full information optimum. Put differently, the consumer and firm fail to capture the gains from trade in externalities. It should be emphasized that externality levels may be above or below the full information optimum E^F, depending on the relative weights $(a(\mu), b(\theta))$ or the underlying bargaining solution.

The set of interim incentive efficient outcomes may be used to characterize a dual bargaining game involving a price for the externality. Suppose that the bargaining game involves assigning a two-part payment schedule for the firm. The firm must pay a per unit effluent charge t and a lump sum payment P. The proceeds from both the effluent charge and the payment P are given in a lump sum $T = tE + P$ to the consumer. The consumer takes the externality level as a given. The firm chooses the externality level E after the effluent charge t and payment P have been agreed upon. Given that (t, P) is the Bayes-Nash equilibrium of a bargaining game, there is a corresponding direct mechanism $(t(\mu, \theta), P(\mu, \theta))$. If the mechanism (t, P) is an (interim incentive) efficient mechanism, there is a corresponding efficient mechanism (E, R). Define (E, R) by solving

$$\pi_E(E, \theta) = t(\mu, \theta), \tag{12.4.7}$$

$$R = t(\mu, \theta)E + P(\mu, \theta), \tag{12.4.8}$$

for (E, R) as a function of μ and θ given $t(\cdot, \cdot)$ and $P(\cdot, \cdot)$.

The discussion of private negotiation over externalities and payments in this section emphasizes the similarity with bargaining over the quantity and price of private goods. Thus, once a property rights assignment has been made, the negotiation model may be applied. The presence of informational asymmetries causes the same types of departures from the full information optimum in the externalities case as were observed in the private goods case with small numbers of agents. An important issue for environmental regulation is the case of multiple polluters and multiple receptors. In the multiple-receptors case, the public goods nature of externalities complicates the bargaining problem. In the multiple-polluters case, the contribution of each polluter to aggregate externality levels must be identified and externality levels optimally adjusted for each firm. These issues are addressed in the next chapter.

Notes

1. The country was divided into 247 "air basins." These regions were referred to as *air quality control regions*. The regions were divided into two groups, attainment and nonattainment areas, by specific pollutants.

2. See Davies and Davies (1975).

3. See Davies and Davies (1975) for additional discussion.

4. *Sierra Club et al.* v. *Administrator of EPA*, U.S. Court of Appeals for the District of Columbia Circuit, Case No. 72-1528, *Federal Register* 38: 135 (July 16, 1973), pp. 18986–19000.

5. As Tolchin and Tolchin (1983) note, these regulations were temporarily held up by the Office of Management and Budget (OMB) but reinstated following a lawsuit by the National Resources Defense Council (1982). Of interest is the court's decision that the EPA's reasons for postponing the regulations did "not constitute good cause for EPA's failure to comply with the APA"; see Tolchin and Tolchin (1983, p. 79).

6. See also Turvey (1963) and Buchanan and Stubblebine (1962).

7. Anderson et al. (1977, pp. 49–51) state that under the 1973 Law for the Compensation of Pollution-Related Health Damage, Japan uses charges for air and water pollution and toxic waste to finance compensation of victims for health costs. Also, an OECD proposal for charges on airplane noise provides for monetary compensation of victims; Anderson et al. (1977, pp. 82–85).

8. Note that Bayesian incentive compatibility requires

$$V(\mu, \mu) \geq V(\mu, \hat{\mu}) \qquad \text{for all } \mu, \hat{\mu} \in [0, 1],$$

$$\Pi(\theta, \theta) \geq \Pi(\theta, \hat{\theta}) \qquad \text{for all } \theta, \hat{\theta} \in [0, 1].$$

Individual rationality given that the consumer has property rights is defined by $V(\mu, \mu) \geq 0$, $\Pi(\theta, \theta) \geq 0$.

13 Externalities 2: Policy Implementation

Aggregate standards for environmental pollution reflect bargaining both in the design of environmental legislation and in carrying out the legislation. Setting aggregate standards reflects the trade-offs between environmental damages and the costs of pollution abatement. The costs of reducing pollution are reflected in the market equilibrium price and output levels of final products. Bargaining over aggregate standards is examined in section 13.1. The bargaining framework makes explicit the trade-off between production and pollution. Consumers both purchase the final outputs and suffer damages from pollution. In the absence of compensatory transfers between consumers and firms, the bargaining solution differs from the social optimum. To compensate firms for increased pollution abatement, it may be necessary to reduce output levels below their optimal levels. Further, marginal damages may not equal marginal abatement costs. Thus, bargaining over aggregate standards may be expected to yield only second-best environmental quality regulations.

The enforcement of aggregate standards is addressed in sections 13.2 and 13.3. The impact of alternative policy instruments on market structure and allocative efficiency is examined. It is shown that for any given aggregate standard, the regulated social optimum is achieved through Pigouvian effluent taxes and with tradable emissions permits. Then the allocative inefficiency introduced by alternative policy instruments is described. It is shown that quotas, output taxes and entry fees, subsidies, and technological standards create incorrect incentives for market entry, firm scale, and production levels.

An important problem facing regulators in the design of effluent taxes is imperfect information about firm production costs and pollution abatement costs. The design of regulatory mechanisms under asymmetric information is considered in section 13.4. The regulator must estimate abatement costs across firms in setting effluent charges for individual firms where firm technologies are heterogeneous. The costs of regulation then include the costs of inducing firms to reveal private information. The regulated outcome will generally depart from the full information optimum if the net benefits from the product market at optimal output levels do not cover the rents to private information earned by firms. Aggregate output and effluent levels are shown to be lower at the regulated optimum than the full information optimum.

13.1   Second-Best Regulation

The setting of specific standards for ambient air quality or water quality occurs for the most part through bargaining in agency public hearings. Baumol and Oates (1975, pp. 199–201) observe that when environmental quality is a pure, Samuelsonian public good, environmental quality standards will generally represent a compromise between consumers with different valuations of externality levels. Under regulation, one can also expect firms directly to play a role in setting quality standards. The regulatory agency weighs various viewpoints expressed by consumers and firms that are harmed by pollution and by consumers and firms that benefit directly or indirectly by the discharge of pollution.

For bargaining to take place, there must be a quid pro quo. What is traded between polluters and pollutees that can be expressed in economic terms? As noted in the preceding chapter, the pollution debate involves political influence through votes and campaign contributions. Yet there is more at stake than simply the income redistribution inherent in effluent or emissions standards. A trade-off exists between the costs and benefits of pollution reduction. Unlike the case of private bargaining, however, one cannot necessarily implement a system of compensatory transfers to induce some consumers to bear the damages from externalities or to induce others to bear the indirect costs of pollution abatement. If a complete system of transfers could be implemented, then an optimal adjustment of pollution to levels that equate marginal damages from pollution to the marginal costs of abatement might be achieved. Compensatory transfers are unworkable since accurate assessment of damages and benefits from the creation of externalities is not possible and the distribution of transfer payments to all individuals in society involves prohibitive administrative costs.

In the absence of compensatory transfers, consumers and firms harmed by externalities bear the full costs. If effluent standards are mandated by law and enforced by regulatory agencies, the firms subject to these regulations bear the cost of pollution abatement. However, these costs are passed on to the firms' customers through higher prices. Further, firms may also adjust input use, which may have effects on the level of employment. In the sense that consumers are both victims of environmental pollution and customers of firms subject to environmental regulation, consumers perceive a trade-off between improved environmental quality and the prices paid for commodities. These prices reflect the cost of meeting environmental quotas that are imposed on firms. In addition, employees of the firms perceive a trade-off between environmental quality and the wages they receive. Wages reflect the marginal productivity of labor that may be reduced (or, in some cases, increased) by the environmental quotas imposed on firms.

Environmental regulations that reflect the trade-off between externalities and output (or employment) are necessarily *second-best* regulations. In the absence of lump sum transfers, consumers must be compensated for increased pollution by lower product prices. Alternatively, firms are compensated for reduced pollution by increased product prices. In the area of environmental regulation, the notion of second-best policy instruments encompasses all manner of command and control approaches. However, for the purposes of this section, second best is interpreted as bargaining over the extent of the externality in the absence of transfers. This corresponds closely with U.S. environmental regulation in which effluent charges are viewed as exclusively punitive and not compensatory. In the sense that charges contribute to general revenues and are used to reduce taxes or increase government services, they may be seen as transfers. The trade-off to be examined here is between the direct costs of pollution and the benefits created by the economic activity that generates pollution as a by-product. The absence of transfers implies that reducing pollution may cause a departure from optimal effluent and final output levels.

For ease of presentation of the basic issues, I employ a representative consumer and firm. Suppose that consumers purchase the firm's output level Q at price p. The consumer's utility is assumed to be additively separable in output Q, a numeraire good x, and damages from the externality E, $U = U(Q) + x - D(E)$. Let ω be the consumer's income. The representative consumer's indirect utility for goods Q and x is given by

$$B(p) = \max_{Q} \ [U(Q) + \omega - pQ],$$

where $Q = Q(p)$ represents the consumer's demand. The consumer's net benefits in the presence of externalities are then $V(p, E) = B(p) - D(E)$.

Externality levels affect the market price of output through firm decision making. The representative firm's profit is given by $\Pi(p, E) = pQ(p) - C(Q(p), E)$. Let demand be downward sloping, $dQ(p)/dp < 0$. Assume increasing marginal production costs, $C_{QQ} > 0$, and cost complementarity in the production of output and effluents in the relevant range, $C_{QE} < 0$. Consider two alternative market structures.

i. If it is assumed that firms are competitive in the product market, then the equilibrium price $p = p^c(E)$ solves $p = C_Q(Q(p), E)$ for any given E. Then it follows that the market price is *reduced* if the firm is permitted to discharge a greater amount of effluents,

$$\frac{\partial p^c(E)}{\partial E} = \frac{C_{QE}(Q, E)}{1 - C_{QQ}(Q, E) \, dQ/dp}. \tag{13.1.1}$$

ii. If it is assumed that firms have market power, then the equilibrium price $p = p^m(E)$ solves $p \, dQ/dp + Q(p) = C_Q(Q(p), E)$ for any given E. Then, given profits concave in Q, the market price is again reduced if the firm is permitted to discharge a greater amount of effluents,

$$\frac{\partial p^m(E)}{\partial E} = \frac{C_{QE}(Q, E)}{p \, d^2Q/dp^2 + 2 \, dQ/dp - C_{QQ}(Q, E) \, dQ/dp}. \tag{13.1.2}$$

Thus, the effect of regulated effluent standards on prices is dependent on the market power of firms. Let $p = p(E)$ represent a general function associating environmental standards with market prices.

Let consumer and firm opportunity costs be normalized to zero. The set of feasible externality levels, E, is given by E such that $V(E) = V(p(E), E) \geq 0$ and $\Pi(E) = \Pi(p(E), E) \geq 0$. These externality levels define the set of feasible consumer net benefit and firm profit pairs, (V, Π). The set of efficient pairs (V, Π) need not be convex. Using $B'(p) = -Q$, consider first the effect of externality levels on consumer indirect benefits,

$$V'(E) = -Q \, \partial p/\partial E - D'(E). \tag{13.1.3}$$

Consumer marginal net benefits may be increasing or decreasing in externality levels as the effect of increased effluent levels on consumer surplus exceeds or is less than marginal damages, $-Q(\partial p/\partial E) \gtrless D'(E)$. Similarly, for the firm in the competitive case,

$$\Pi'(E) = Q \, \partial p^c/\partial E - C_E(Q, E). \tag{13.1.4}$$

Thus, firm profits are increasing or decreasing in externality levels as the effects on revenues are less than or greater than the cost savings, $(-C_E) \gtrless -Q(\partial p^c/\partial E)$. In the monopoly case, the effect of relaxing effluent standards is unambiguously positive for E such that $C_E < 0$,

$$\Pi'(E) = -C_E(Q, E). \tag{13.1.5}$$

The set of feasible pairs (V, Π) is defined in $V = B(p(E)) - D(E)$, where $E = E(\Pi)$ solves $\Pi = p(E)Q(p(E)) - C(Q(p(E)), E)$ and $V \geq 0$, $\Pi \geq 0$.

Suppose that the efficient frontier is well defined for some range of externality levels. The marginal rate of transformation is then

$$P'(\Pi) = \frac{B'(p) \, \partial p/\partial E - D'(E)}{(\partial p/\partial E)[Q + p \, dQ/dp - C_Q \, dQ/dp] - C_E}. \tag{13.1.6}$$

Note that $B'(p) = -Q(p)$. In the competitive case, the marginal rate of transformation is therefore

$$P'(\Pi) = -[Q \, \partial p^c/\partial E + D'(E)]/[Q \, \partial p^c/\partial E - C_E]. \tag{13.1.7}$$

In the monopoly case, the marginal rate of transformation is simply

$$P'(\Pi) = [Q \, \partial p^m/\partial E + D'(E)]/C_E. \tag{13.1.8}$$

The trade-off along the efficient frontier is given by the marginal net benefits to consumers from stricter pollution controls divided by the marginal losses imposed on firms.

Suppose that the Nash bargaining solution is well-defined,[1] $P'(\Pi^*) = -V^*/\Pi^*$. Rearranging terms, one has for the competitive case

$$D'(E^*) + C_E(Q(p^*), E^*) = (1 - V^*/\Pi^*)[Q(p^*) \, \partial p^c/\partial E - C_E(Q(p^*), E^*)], \tag{13.1.9}$$

where $p^* = p^c(E^*)$, $V^* = B(p^*) - D(E^*)$, and $\Pi^* = \Pi(E^*)$.

Compare the Nash solution with the *socially optimal* effluent level, E^O,

$$D'(E^O) + C_E(Q(p(E^O)), E^O) = 0. \tag{13.1.10}$$

In general, the bargaining solution differs from the social optimum. The reason is that the effect of effluent levels on market prices causes consumers and firms to weigh the net benefits of price changes in addition to the costs of pollution abatement and external damages. The bargaining solution E^* thus involves a departure from the socially optimal effluent level E^O as represented in figure 13.1.1. The negotiated outcome may yield externality levels that are less than or greater than E^O. In addition, the market allocation itself departs from the optimum, $(p(E^O), Q(p(E^O)))$, due to imperfectly set pollution standards.

Thus, "social bargaining" over externalities through the intermediation of a regulatory agency fails to yield a social optimum. The perceived

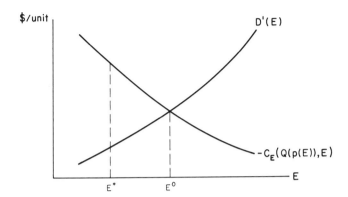

Figure 13.1.1
The Nash bargaining solution E^* and the socially optimal externality E^0.

trade-off is between environmental quality and product prices or output in the absence of lump sum transfers. This obscures the underlying trade-off between environmental damages and abatement costs. Thus, the market allocation of output is made to compensate for regulatory imperfections in the adjustment of externality levels.

The preceding discussion may be easily extended to a multiconsumer setting with multiple types of pollutants. The second-best nature of standards in the absence of transfers becomes apparent when the present analysis is compared to that of second-best pricing under economies of scale given in chapter 5. Let $V^i(E) = B^i(p) - D^i(E)$ represent consumer i's indirect benefits from environmental pollution for the set of consumers $i \in N$. The representative firm assumption is maintained. Various air and water pollutants are represented by $E = (E_1, \ldots, E_L)$. Suppose that the firm's profits satisfy a minimum returns constraint $\Pi(E) \geq \bar{\Pi}$. The firm may be either competitive or a monopolist as before. The minimum profit $\bar{\Pi}$ may be simply a break-even constraint or may be set through bargaining with the firm. Then one may define second-best externality levels. Again, observe that unlike the standard definition of Pareto optimality, the regulated regime gives weight to the level of firm profits.

Definition 13.1.1   An externality vector E^* is *second-best Pareto optimal* if $\Pi(E^*) \geq \bar{\Pi}$ and if there does not exist an externality vector E' such that $\Pi(E') \geq \bar{\Pi}$, $V^i(E') \geq V^i(E^*)$ for all $i \in N$ and $V^i(E') > V^i(E^*)$ for some consumers $i \in N$.

Given definition 13.1.1, one may define weights λ^i, $i \in N$, and γ such that a second-best externality vector E^* solves the following maximization problem,

$$\max_E \left[\sum_{i \in N} \lambda^i V^i(E) + \gamma \Pi(E) \right]. \tag{13.1.11}$$

Thus, the marginal social valuation of externalities is proportional to the firm's marginal profit,

$$\sum_{i \in N} \lambda^i V_l^i(E^*) = -\gamma \Pi_l(E^*), \qquad l = 1, \ldots, L. \tag{13.1.12}$$

Recall that $V_l^i(E) = B^{i'}(p)\,\partial p/\partial E_l - D_l^i(E)$. Note that $B^{i'}(p) = -q^i$, where q^i is consumer i's consumption. For the competitive case $\Pi_l(E) = Q\,\partial p^c/\partial E_l - C_{E_l}$, where $Q = \sum_{i \in N} q^i$ and $\partial p^c/\partial E_l = C_{QE_l}/(1 - C_{QQ}\,dQ/dp)$. Thus, equation (13.1.12) may be rewritten as follows:

$$\sum_{i \in N} \lambda^i D_l^i(E^*) + C_{E_l}(Q, E^*)$$

$$= (1 - \gamma)C_{E_l}(Q, E^*) + \left[\sum_{i \in N} \lambda^i q^i - \gamma Q \right] \frac{(-C_{QE_l})}{1 - C_{QQ}\,dQ/dp}, \quad l = 1, \ldots, L. \tag{13.1.13}$$

The departure of the second-best externality levels E^* from the social optimum is illustrated by equation (13.1.13). The two terms on the right-hand-side drive a wedge between marginal social damages and the costs of pollution abatement to the firm $(-C_{E_l})$. The last term represents the social valuation of a fall in price, $\sum_{i \in N} \lambda^i q^i$, net of the value of the firm's revenue loss from a fall in price, γQ, times the effect of the externality on the competitive price. Observe that if the firm's abatement costs are additively separable, $C_{QE_l} = 0$, the distortion in effluent levels is then due only to the firm's profit constraint.

Taking ratios on the first-order conditions for two types of pollutants l and k gives

$$\frac{\sum_{i \in N} \lambda^i D_l^i(E^*) + \gamma C_{E_l}(Q, E^*)}{\sum_{i \in N} \lambda^i D_k^i(E^*) + \gamma C_{E_k}(Q, E^*)} = \frac{(\partial p^c/\partial E_l)}{(\partial p^c/\partial E_k)}, \tag{13.1.14}$$

for l, $k = 1, \ldots, L$. Thus, the social marginal rate of transformation of externality l to k equals the ratio of price changes due to changes in externality levels.

Compare the preceding discussion to selection of effluent fees, $t = (t_1, \ldots, t_L)$. In the absence of consideration of the income distribution between consumers and firms, it is well-known that effluent fees yield a Pareto optimal allocation of resources in a competitive market. Thus, effluent levels E_l^O are set such that $\sum_{i \in N} \lambda^i D_l^i(E^O) + C_{E_l}(Q, E^O) = 0$ for $l = 1, \ldots, L$. However, the regulator may place various weights on firm profits depending upon the relative bargaining strengths of consumers and firms. The effect of effluent fees on the distribution of income implies that second-best effluent fees will be chosen. In the absence of lump sum transfers, the revenues generated by the effluent taxes will reduce firm profits, and, if considered as a transfer to consumers, the tax revenue will increase consumer income. In selecting second-best optimal effluent fees that take into account the distribution of income, the regulator will then depart from socially optimal levels.

Given effluent fees $t = (t_1, \ldots, t_L)$, the competitive firm will choose output and effluent levels such that

$$p = C_Q(Q(p), E), \tag{13.1.15}$$

$$-t_l = C_{E_l}(Q(p), E), \qquad l = 1, \ldots, L. \tag{13.1.16}$$

We may solve equations (13.1.15) and (13.1.16) for the price and effluent levels as a function of the tax, $p = p(t)$, $E = E(t)$.

Again assuming a representative consumer, the second-best problem is to choose effluent taxes t to maximize the following:

$$[B(p(t)) - D(E(t)) + tE] + \gamma[p(t)Q(p(t)) - C(Q(p), E) - tE]. \tag{13.1.17}$$

The optimality conditions are then calculated using (13.1.15) and (13.1.16),

$$\sum_{k=1}^{L} [D_k(E) - t_k](\partial E_k/\partial t_l) = B'(p)(\partial p/\partial t_l) + E_l + \gamma[Q(\partial p/\partial t_l) - E_l]. \tag{13.1.18}$$

Using $B'(p) = -Q$ and (13.1.16), observe that the marginal net benefits of a tax to consumers equals the marginal cost to firms, $B'(p)(\partial p/\partial t_l) + E_l = -(Q(\partial p/\partial t_l) - E_l)$. The effects of the effluent tax include the effect on payments, $Q(\partial p/\partial t_l)$, due to cost complementarity between output and effluents. Thus, (13.1.18) has the form

$$\sum_{k=1}^{L} (D_k(E) - C_{E_k})(\partial E_k/\partial t_l) = (1 - \gamma)[E_l - Q(\partial p/\partial t_l)]. \tag{13.1.19}$$

Unless $\gamma = 1$, it will not be optimal to set effluent fees equal to marginal social damages, $t_l \neq D_l$.

13.2   Aggregate Standards and Market Structure

Environmental regulation generally involves specification of aggregate standards in the form of maximum upper limits on total production of externalities, $E^* > 0$. Given m firms in an industry, the total of individual externality levels must not exceed the aggregate standards, $\sum_{j=1}^{m} e^j \leq E^*$. Therefore, enforcement of environmental regulations reduces to allocation among competing users of a scarce resource: the rights to discharge externalities. In this sense, regulation of externalities, such as air, water, and solid waste pollution, is formally identical to regulation of extraction of common property resources, such as common pools of oil and gas, fish stocks, water supplies, public grazing land, and the radio spectrum. The regulator's objective is to allocate the rights to the highest value users. Further, the long-run objective of the regulator is to promote an efficient industry structure, with the cost minimizing number and size of firms. The next section examines a number of alternative policy instruments that have been used or proposed for use in environmental regulation: effluent taxes, tradable permits, effluent quotas, output taxes, subsidies, and technological standards. The effects of these instruments on allocative efficiency at the market equilibrium are compared.

13.2.1   Optimal Market Structure

This section describes optimal structure given an aggregate pollution standard. It is assumed that the output market is contestable; i.e., there are no entry barriers and firms produce nondifferentiated output with identical costs. The assumption of identical firms is made to highlight the fact that distortions can be caused by such policy instruments as quotas without firm heterogeneity. Even in a full information, competitive market setting, instruments that do not properly price the scarce resource, E^*, lead to inefficient firm scale and industry size.

Let firm costs be given by

$$C(q, e) = K + V(q, e),$$

where $K > 0$ and V is twice differentiable and convex in (q, e) and increasing in q. Let the private minimum efficient scale be defined by $q_M = q_M(e)$, where $C_q(q_M, e) = C(q_M, e)/q_M$. Assume that $(C_e/q - C_{qe}) \leq 0$. Then the efficient scale is nonincreasing in the externality level, $\partial q_M(e)/\partial e = [C_e(q_M, e)/q_M - C_{qe}(q_M, e)]/C_{qq}(q_M, e) \leq 0$. Let $C_e(q, e) \gtreqless 0$ as $e \lesseqgtr e(q)$ for $e(q) < \infty$, $q > 0$. This reflects the resource costs of generating as well as abating pollution. For $e < e(q)$, it is costly to abate pollution. For $e > e(q)$, creation of excess pollution is costly. In what follows, I ignore the integer problem and treat the number of firms m as a continuous variable. The same results hold with little modification if m is allowed to be small and integer valued. Firms are assumed to behave competitively as price takers.

In the absence of regulation, firms will choose the cost-minimizing level of pollution. The effluent level as a function of the firm's output, $e = e(q)$, solves $V_e(q, e) = 0$. Let inverse demand be given by $p = P(Q)$. Then market equilibrium with free entry, $(\tilde{q}, \tilde{m})$, satisfies the standard zero-profit condition, $P(\tilde{m}\tilde{q})\tilde{q} - C(\tilde{q}, e(\tilde{q})) = 0$, and price equals marginal cost, $P(\tilde{m}\tilde{q}) = C_q(\tilde{q}, e(\tilde{q}))$. So, the unregulated effluent level is $\tilde{e} = e(\tilde{q})$. Note that by convexity of C, the optimum requires uniform allocation of outputs and effluent levels across firms. The social optimum requires *no regulation* if it turns out that at the competitive equilibrium,

$$\tilde{m}e(\tilde{q}) \leq E^*.$$

In this case the aggregate standard is not a binding constraint and rents accruing to the scarce resource of pollution rights E^* are zero. If these rents are positive $\tilde{m}e(\tilde{q}) > E^*$, then regulation is required to achieve the legal standard.

The socially optimal allocation of effluent levels across firms may be obtained by maximizing net surplus,

$$\int_0^{mq} P(Q)\, dQ - mC(q, e),$$

over m, q, and e subject to $E^* \geq me$. Let ξ be the shadow price on the aggregate externality constraint. Then the necessary conditions for optimal allocation of effluents are

$$P(m^*q^*)q^* - C(q^*, e^*) - \gamma^*e^* = 0, \tag{13.2.1}$$

$$P(m^*q^*) - C_q(q^*, e^*) = 0, \tag{13.2.2}$$

$$-C_e(q^*, e^*) - \gamma^* = 0, \tag{13.2.3}$$

$$\gamma^*(E^* - m^*e^*) = 0, \qquad \gamma^* \geq 0. \tag{13.2.4}$$

The solution (m^*, q^*, e^*) is referred to as the regulated social optimum.

Turn now to an analysis of alternative policy instruments. The outcomes will be compared to the unregulated market equilibrium and the regulated social optimum.

13.2.2   Externality Taxes

The approaches generally favored by economists are externality taxes or tradable permits. Externality taxes are also referred to as effluent or emissions charges in the case of water or air pollution and as royalties or in situ prices in the case of natural resources. The optimality of externality taxes in a free entry model is discussed by Baumol and Oates (1975, p. 179), Schulze and D'Arge (1974), and Spulber (1985a). The following result is obtained immediately from (13.2.1)–(13.2.4).

PROPOSITION 13.2.1   *Selection of an externality tax* $t^* = \gamma^*$ *achieves the regulated social optimum.*

By cost minimization, firms select $e^* = E^*/m^*$ in such a way that $-C_e(q^*, e^*) = t^*$. Free entry equates revenues to total costs, $P(m^*q^*)q^* - C(q^*, e^*) - t^*e^* = 0$. The tax provides correct incentives for entry and for production at the efficient scale, where marginal costs equal average costs, $C_q(q^*, e^*) = C(q^*, e^*)/q^* + t^*e^*/q^*$.

13.2.3   Tradable Permits

The regulator may simply issue permits for the discharge of E^* units. The feasibility of this scheme has been widely debated. See Tietenberg (1980, 1985) for extensive literature surveys and policy analysis of trading in licenses for air emissions.[2] The issuance of permits has the important advantage that the regulator need not know the market data on output demand, production cost, and abatement costs. The initial permit price may be set through competitive bidding. The price of permits can then vary with retrading.

The demand for permits $X^D = X^D(\rho)$ priced at ρ is given by $X^D = m(\rho)x^D(\rho)$, where $x^D(\rho)$ and $m(\rho)$ solve

$$P(mq)q - C(q, x) - \rho x = 0, \tag{13.2.5}$$

$$-C_e(q, x) - \rho = 0, \tag{13.2.6}$$

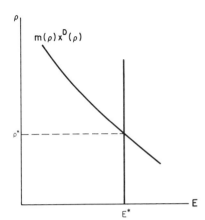

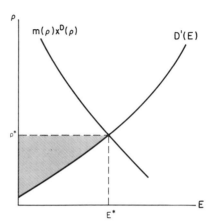

Figure 13.2.1
The market price of permits.

Figure 13.2.2
Economic rents of environmental resources.

for $P(mq) = C_q(q, x)$. Clearly, by issuing exactly E^* permits, equations (13.2.1)–(13.2.4) are exactly satisfied and the permit market clears at $\rho^* = t^*$, $X^D(\rho^*) = E^*$.

PROPOSITION 13.2.2   *Issuance of E^* tradable permits achieves the regulated social optimum.*

The permit market equilibrium is represented in figure 13.2.1.

The demand for permits represents the marginal valuation of environmental services. The rents accruing to permit owners reflect the value of permits and the availability of permits as determined by the aggregate standard. Suppose that the aggregate standard is set equal to the socially optimal pollution level. Then the price of permits will equate the marginal value of environmental services to the marginal damages from pollution,

$$P(m^*q^*)q^*/e^* - c(q^*, e^*)/e^* = \rho^* = D'(m^*e^*). \tag{13.2.7}$$

This is represented in figure 13.2.2. The area under the marginal damage curve is the cost of supplying environmental services. If the permits are auctioned by the government, revenues will equal p^*E^*. The area above the marginal damages curve and below the permit price may be interpreted as the economic rents accruing to environmental resources. This corresponds to the shaded area in figure 13.2.2.

The firm's private marginal costs, exclusive of the cost of permits, equal $C_q(q, e) + C_e(q, e)\, \partial e(q)/\partial q$, where $\partial e(q)/\partial q = -C_{eq}/C_{ee}$. Since marginal abatement costs equal the permit price, $-C_e = \rho^* = D'(m^*e^*)$, and price equals C_q, equation (13.2.7) can be rewritten as

$$C_q(q^*, e^*) + C_e(q^*, e^*)\, \partial e(q^*)/\partial q - C(q^*, e^*)/q^*$$

$$= D'(m^*e^*)e^*/q^* - D'(m^*e^*)\, \partial e(q^*)/\partial q. \qquad (13.2.8)$$

The difference between the firm's marginal and average private costs equal the difference between the firm's average and marginal external costs. This implies the following.

PROPOSITION 13.2.3   *At the market equilibrium with the socially optimal number of tradable permits, if the firm's average damages exceed (are less than) marginal damages, the firm will operate above (below) the private minimum efficient scale.*

The effluent permit system gives firms the incentive to adjust optimally their scale to reflect the difference between average and marginal external costs.

The issuance of tradable emissions permits involves the creation of limited property rights. By establishing property rights to use of the environment (air and water) for specific discharges of pollutants, a market in permits may then be formed. This is a very important case of a regulatory policy instrument that takes advantage of the market allocation mechanism. The permits are allocated to those firms that place the highest value on discharging pollutants. The market achieves the socially optimal output, firm scale, and market structure relative to the aggregate standard.

13.3   Policy Instruments and Allocative Inefficiency

Regulation of environmental pollution has employed a wide variety of policy instruments. As has been shown, optimal externality levels are achieved by pollution taxes or by market allocation of the scarce resource through tradable permits. In practice, regulators favor policy instruments, such as quotas, output taxes, entry fees, subsidies, and technological standards. This preference may be due to lower costs of monitoring and enforcing quotas or technological standards as compared with calculating and implementing taxes. In resource regulation, policymakers also favor quotas, entry restrictions, and technological standards. In fisheries regulation, policymakers employ such instruments as catch quotas, vessel quotas, vessel licenses, restricted areas, limited seasons, and technological restrictions on fishing equipment and vessel length and horsepower; see Spulber (1982) and Clark (1982). As in the case of pollution, these instruments create incentives for inefficient activity, while tradable permits achieve socially optimal resource production and allocation. The allocative inefficiencies that result from alternative policy instruments are now considered.

13.3.1   Quotas

Suppose that the regulator attempts to achieve the aggregate standard E^* by imposition of an across-the-board quota $\bar{e}$. The per firm quota $\bar{e}$ must be calculated in such a way that total industry pollution does not exceed the desired total. If the regulator fails to anticipate correctly the entry or exit of firms, the aggregate standard may not be met. Alternatively, even if the regulator is able to anticipate entry, distortions will occur.

Suppose first that the regulator is able to calculate the industry size that will obtain after the imposition of a per firm quota, $\bar{m}$. Then there is an equilibrium that satisfies the entry condition, $P(\bar{m}\bar{q})\bar{q} - C(\bar{q},\bar{e}) = 0$, and profit maximization, $P(\bar{m}\bar{q}) = C_q(\bar{q},\bar{e})$, and the resource constraint, $\bar{m}\bar{e} = E^*$. Comparing this equilibrium with the regulated social optimum yields the following.

PROPOSITION 13.3.1   *To meet the aggregate standard E^*, per firm quotas must be set below the optimal level, $\bar{e} < e^*$. This results in excessive entry, $\bar{m} > m^*$, and inefficiently low outputs $\bar{q} < q^*$.*

Proof   Suppose $\bar{e} \geq e^*$. Then, since $\bar{m}\bar{e} = m^*e^* = E^*$, $\bar{m} \leq m^*$. Since demand is downward sloping and output and effluent are cost complements,

$$C_q(q^*,e^*) = P(m^*q^*)$$

$$\leq P(\bar{m}\bar{q})$$

$$= C_q(\bar{q},\bar{e})$$

$$\leq C_q(\bar{q},e^*).$$

Since marginal costs are upward sloping, $q^* \leq \bar{q}$. Because $C_q(\bar{q},\bar{e}) - C(\bar{q},\bar{e})/\bar{q} = 0$, $\bar{q}$ is the private minimum efficient scale output level. Thus, given that average costs are U-shaped,

$C_q(q^*, \bar{e}) - C(q^*, \bar{e})/q^* \leq 0.$

By assumption, $C_{qe}(q, e) - C_e(q, e)/q \geq 0$, so that

$C_q(q^*, e^*) - C(q^*, e^*)/q^* \leq 0.$

But since $C_e < 0$, this contradicts (13.2.8). Thus, $\bar{e} < e^*$, $\bar{m} > m^*$, and $\bar{q} < q^*$. QED

Proposition 13.3.1 demonstrates that quotas are inefficient at the long-run industry equilibrium, even given homogeneous firms. The explanation for this result is that the quota confers a valuable property right on the industry. Since the pollution rights are nontransferable, the right to discharge pollutants up to E^* is essentially a free good. This leads to excessive entry, which reduces output per firm at the industry equilibrium below the efficient output level.

If the regulator fails to take into account the entry and exit of firms in the selection of the per firm quota, additional problems exist. If the regulator sets quotas based on the size of the unregulated industry, per firm levels of effluent will be excessively low. Further, exit will occur, leading to total pollution levels less than the aggregate standard. Thus, by not accounting for exit, the regulator places high cost burdens on individual firms and on the industry, since the total pollution levels are not allocated. On the other hand, suppose that the regulator is able to calculate the socially optimal standard e^*. By imposing e^* without the incentives for exit created by a tax or tradable permit system, excessive entry will occur, leading to total pollution in excess of the aggregate standard E^*. Because entry exceeds socially optimal levels, m^*, firms will operate below the efficient scale, q^*. Thus, per firm quotas lead to long-run inefficiency no matter how they are determined. If the quotas achieve the desired aggregate standard, they impose large cost burdens in terms of pollution abatement on individual firms. If quotas are set to allocate the permitted pollution levels in an optimal way, excessive entry results, leading to violation of the legal standards by the industry as a whole.

Given a fixed number of heterogeneous firms, the various policy instruments may involve great variations in private costs across firms. It is well-known that when firms have different technologies due to differences

in production techniques or abatement procedures, all policies that result
in symmetric allocations of externality production across firms are inefficient. Thus, for example, across-the-board quotas are dominated by effluent taxes.[3] Effluent taxes and tradable permits result in equality of
marginal returns from production of externalities across firms. Firms with
relatively higher marginal returns from generation of externalities, due, for
example, to high abatement costs, supply greater shares of the total E^* than
do other firms. A uniform effluent quota involves higher private costs since
firms with high abatement costs are required to perform the same degree
of pollution removal as firms with low abatement costs. In the case of two
firms, let $\pi^j(e^j)$, $j = 1$, 2, represent profits as a function of externality
discharges. If profits are concave in externalities, then the allocation of E^*
that maximizes total profits requires $\pi^{1\prime}(e^{1*}) = \pi^{2\prime}(e^{2*})$ for $e^{1*} + e^{2*} = E^*$.
This may be achieved through a tax t that is equal to $t^* = \pi^{1\prime}(e^{1*}) =
\pi^{2\prime}(e^{2*})$. The solution is represented in figure 13.3.1. An across-the-board
quota of $E^*/2$ requires firm 2 with the high marginal benefits from producing externalities to reduce its externality discharges below the optimal level,
and the opposite occurs from firm 1 (see figure 13.3.1). Clearly, since
$\pi^{2\prime}(E^*/2) > \pi^{1\prime}(E^*/2)$, a redistribution of effluent production levels from
firm 1 to firm 2 will increase aggregate profits without increasing total
effluent production. The issue of firm differences is taken up again in the
discussion of informational asymmetry in the next section.

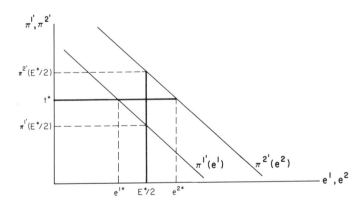

Figure 13.3.1
Effluent taxes yield higher total profits than across-the-board quotas.

13.3.2   Output Taxes and Entry Fees

The efficient rationing of scarce environmental resources requires putting
a price on those resources, as has been emphasized. In some policy discussions, taxing the firms' *output* and the imposition of *entry fees* on firms have
been suggested as ways to curtail the effluent-generating activity. These
indirect means of reducing externalities are meaningful only if output per
firm or the number of firms is proportional to the externality.[4] This will
not generally hold, as input substitution and the scale of individual firms
will affect the costs of achieving pollution levels through indirect means.

Consider, first, the output tax τ. The industry equilibrium (e', q', m') will
solve

$$(P(m'q') - \tau)q' - C(q', e') = 0, \tag{13.3.1}$$

$$(P(m'q') - \tau) = C_q(q', e'), \tag{13.3.2}$$

$$C_e(q', e') = 0. \tag{13.3.3}$$

From equations (13.3.1) and (13.3.2), it follows that firms operate at the
private minimum efficient scale. Thus, output and per firm effluent levels
are exactly equal to those observed at the unregulated market equilibrium
$(e', q') = (\tilde{e}, \tilde{q})$. Thus, the output tax cannot be chosen to achieve the regulated social optimum. The aggregate standard can be met by increasing the
tax until industry size falls to $m' = E^*/\tilde{e}$. To verify the feasibility of this,
note that since (e', q') does not depend on the tax τ, $\partial m'/\partial r = 1/P'(m'q')q' <$
0. The cost of the output tax is then a restriction of entry and a reduction
in total output. Furthermore, firms operate at an inefficient scale and the
per firm effluent level is set at an inefficiently high level, given the per firm
output level since $C_e(q', e') = 0$. To summarize:

PROPOSITION 13.3.2   *The output tax achieves the aggregate standard by
reducing entry and total output. Firms operate at private minimum efficient
scale. Per firm externality levels are the same as at the unregulated market
equilibrium.*

The failure of output taxes is due to the need to control the effluent and
output levels of individual firms. Output taxes provide no incentive for
firms to reduce pollution by abatement measures or input substitution. It
has been suggested that a combination of output taxes and entry fees
provides incentive for firms to operate at an efficient scale and for entry

to result in an efficient industry size.[5] Given an output tax τ and a lump-sum entry free $T > 0$, the industry equilibrium satisfies equations (13.3.2), (13.3.3), and

$$(P(m'q') - \tau)q' - C(q',e') - T = 0. \tag{13.3.4}$$

Combining (13.3.2) and (13.3.4), it is apparent that both output and effluent levels can be controlled by the entry fee T, since $C_q(q',e')q' - C(q',e') = T$. Further, the number of firms at the industry equilibrium can be controlled by adjustment of the output tax. However, because there is no direct control of the firm's externality level, it is generally not possible to adjust the taxes (τ, T) to achieve the regulated social optimum, (e^*, q^*, m^*).

In meeting the aggregate standard, $e'm' = E^*$, the regulator can only hope to achieve either the optimal industry size and per firm effluent level or else the efficient per firm output.

PROPOSITION 13.3.3   (i) *The regulator may choose $\tau > 0$ and T such that $m' = m^*$ and $e' = e^*$. In this case, firms operate with lower outputs than at the optimum, $q' < q^*$. The entry fee satisfies $T \gtreqless 0$ as $q' \gtreqless q_M(e^*)$. (ii) The regulator may choose $\tau > 0$, $T > 0$ such that $q' = q^*$. In this case, per firm effluent levels are inefficiently high, and the industry size is inefficiently low, $e' > e^*$, $m' < m^*$.*

To prove statement (i), note that if $e' = e^*$,

$$-C_e(q',e^*) = 0 < -C_e(q^*,e^*).$$

Since $C_{eq} < 0$, $q' < q^*$. Thus, effluents are controlled indirectly by raising the entry fee, and consequently by reducing output. The industry size m^* is set by adjustment of τ to equal $\tau = P(m^*q') - C_q(q',e^*)$. The output tax τ is positive, since $P(m^*q') > P(m^*q^*) = C_q(q^*,e^*) > C_q(q',e^*)$. If output is driven below minimum efficient scale, $q_M(e^*)$, a subsidy may be required, $T < 0$.

To obtain statement (ii), note that if $q' = q^*$,

$$-C_e(q^*,e') = 0 < -C_e(q^*,e^*).$$

Since $C_{ee} > 0$, $e' > e^*$. Then recall that $C_q(q^*,e^*)q^* - C(q^*,e^*) = te^* > 0$. Since $\partial[C_q q - C]/\partial e \geq 0$, there is a positive entry fee $T \geq te^*$ such that $C_q(q^*,e')q^* - C(q^*,e') = T$. The output tax is positive, since $P(m'q^*) > P(m^*q^*) = C_q(q^*,e^*) > C_q(q^*,e')$.

The output tax and entry fee are certainly second-best instruments. Thus, in meeting the aggregate standard, the welfare-maximizing regulator would be expected to adjust (τ, T) to yield a market equilibrium in which e, q, and m depart from their optimal levels.

13.3.3 Subsidies

Suppose that the regulator offers subsidies per unit of effluent discharged to induce the firm to reduce pollution. Aside from the cost of the subsidy itself, what effect will the subsidy have on efficiency? Let S represent the maximal subsidy per firm. Then, given a marginal subsidy rate s, the offer of a subsidy $(S - se)$ leads the firm to choose an externality level e^s such that

$$-C_e(q, e^s) = s. \qquad (13.3.5)$$

If s is set equal to the Pigouvian tax, then (13.3.5) has the same form as the optimal condition $-C_e(q^*, e^*) = \gamma^*$. However, the subsidy has very different implications for industry equilibrium. The subsidy provides incentives for additional entry. Further, the subsidy creates incentives for firms to operate below private minimum efficient scale at the industry equilibrium, $q < q_M(e^s)$, since q satisfies $C_q(q, e^s)q - C(q, e^s) + (S - se^s) = 0$.

Baumol and Oates (1975) consider the effect of subsidies on the equilibrium of a competitive industry. In the case of no abatement technology, with effluent an increasing function of output, Baumol and Oates (1975, p. 183) show that with a marginal subsidy rate equal to the Pigouvian tax, total output and emission levels will be "not only greater than those that would occur under the tax but even greater than they would be in the absence of either tax or subsidy." Further, in the presence of abatement technology, Baumol and Oates (1975, p. 187) demonstrate that the effect of an increase in the marginal subsidy rate "will be an increase in the polluting output and possibly a decrease in abatement expenditures and a rise in total emissions."

13.3.4 Technological Standards

As emphasized in section 12.1, regulatory enforcement of the Clean Air Act and Water Pollution Control Act Amendments often involves specification of abatement technology. Suppose that the emissions produced at a given output level q depend on an abatement technology $e = h(q, x)$, where x

represents a technological efficiency parameter. Let $h_q \equiv \partial h/\partial q$ and $h_x \equiv \partial h/\partial x$. The emissions discharged can be reduced by increasing the parameter x, $h_x < 0$. The cost of abatement technology of type x is $k(x)$. Let the firm's production cost function be given by $c(q)$, where $c'(q) > 0$, $c''(q) > 0$, and $c(0) \geq 0$. In the present framework, the regulator's choice of abatement technology can be represented by requiring the firm to choose a particular level of the efficiency parameter x.

Let the regulator's choice of an abatement technology standard equal the parameter value $\bar{x}$. In this case, the industry equilibrium is given by

$$P(\overline{mq})\bar{q} - c(\bar{q}) - k(\bar{x}) = 0, \tag{13.3.6}$$

$$P(\overline{mq}) - c'(\bar{q}) = 0, \tag{13.3.7}$$

where effluents discharged by each firm equal $\bar{e} = h(\bar{q}, \bar{x})$. Clearly, an increase in the technology standard reduces effluents generated by a firm for any level of output. Further, the total cost of meeting the standard serves as an entry barrier, and thus reduces industry size for any given per firm output. The technology standard causes the firm to produce above its private minimum efficient scale, since $c'(\bar{q})\bar{q} - c(\bar{q}) = k(\bar{x})$. Increases in $\bar{x}$ raise the firm's equilibrium output, $\partial \bar{q}/\partial \bar{x} = k'(\bar{x})/c''(\bar{q})\bar{q} > 0$, given an upward-sloping marginal cost curve. Thus, it follows from (13.3.7) that a higher technology standard reduces the equilibrium number of firms,

$$\frac{\partial \bar{m}}{\partial \bar{x}} = \frac{-[P'\bar{m} - c''] }{P'\bar{q}} \frac{\partial \bar{q}}{\partial \bar{x}} < 0. \tag{13.3.8}$$

However, since output rises with the technology standard $\bar{x}$, an increase in $\bar{x}$ has an ambiguous effect on effluents discharged by each firm,

$$\frac{\partial \bar{e}}{\partial \bar{x}} = h_q(\bar{q}, \bar{x})\frac{\partial \bar{q}}{\partial \bar{x}} + h_x(\bar{q}, \bar{x}). \tag{13.3.9}$$

Thus, $\partial \bar{e}/\partial \bar{x} \gtreqless 0$ as $h_q \partial \bar{q}/\partial \bar{x} \gtreqless -h_x$. A tightening of technological standards may thus have the paradoxical effect of increasing total pollution if the per firm increase in pollution exceeds the reduction in total pollution due to exit.

Compare the effects of a standard $\bar{x}$ with the optimal allocation of E^*. Choosing market structure and firm size optimally gives

$$P(m^*q^*)q^* - c(q^*) - k(x^*) - \gamma^*h(q^*, x^*) = 0, \tag{13.3.10}$$

$$P(m^*q^*) - c'(q^*) - \gamma^*h_q(q^*, x^*) = 0 \tag{13.3.11}$$

$$-k'(x^*) - \gamma^*h_x(q^*, x^*) = 0, \tag{13.3.12}$$

$$\gamma^*(E^* - m^*e^*) = 0, \qquad \gamma^* \geq 0. \tag{13.3.13}$$

As before, the optimum can be achieved simply by imposing a Pigouvian effluent tax equal to γ^*. Combining (13.3.10) and (13.3.11), it follows that the difference between marginal and average production costs is related to the difference between the average and marginal effect of output on emissions

$$c'(q^*)q^* - c(q^*) - k(x^*) = \gamma^*(h(q^*, x^*) - h_q(q^*, x^*)q^*). \tag{13.3.14}$$

Consider the case of an emissions function that is linear in q, so that $h = h_q q$. Then it follows that by setting the technological standard $\bar{x}$ equal to x^*, from (13.3.6), (13.3.7), and (13.3.14), $\bar{q} = q^*$. Further, $\bar{e} = e^* = h(q^*, x^*)$. However, since price equals marginal private costs, entry will be excessive, $\bar{m} > m^*$, because

$$P(m^*q^*) > c'(q^*) = P(\bar{m}q^*).$$

Thus, the aggregate effluent standard will be exceeded due to entry. Suppose now that $\bar{x} < x^*$. Then, given h linear in q, equations (13.3.6), (13.3.7), and (13.3.14) imply that $\bar{q} < q^*$. Further, if $\partial\bar{e}/\partial\bar{x} < 0$, $\bar{e} > e^*$. It can be shown that $\bar{q} < q^*$ implies that $\bar{m} > m^*$. So, $\bar{m}\bar{e} > m^*e^* = E^*$ and the aggregate standard is violated. Thus, we may state the following.

PROPOSITION 13.3.4 *Suppose that the abatement technology is linear in output and that per firm effluent levels are decreasing in the technological standard. Then meeting the aggregate pollution standard requires setting a technological standard above the optimal level, $\bar{x} > x^*$. This implies that the equilibrium industry size and output per firm will be above the optimal level, $\bar{m} > m^*$, and $\bar{q} > q^*$. Further, per firm levels of effluent will be below the optimal level, $\bar{e} < e^*$.*

In the case of abatement technology that is nonlinear in output, the technological standard required to meet aggregate pollution standards can be expected to diverge even further from the social optimum. The reasons are twofold. First, output levels will not be adjusted optimally by firms.

When the abatement technology standard is imposed, firms may operate at an inefficient output level, since the firm does not bear the marginal external costs of increasing its output. This is not reflected in the market price as in equation (13.3.11). The firm does not directly realize the costs of additional emissions due to increased output. Meeting the abatement technology standard is viewed as an end in itself, not as a means of reducing emissions. Second, incentives for entry are distorted by the scale of individual firms. If abatement costs lead the firm to operate at an inefficient scale and external costs are not reflected in the firm's market price, the industry size will then be inefficient.

A particularly interesting application of technology standards is the creation of differential standards for incumbent firms and new entrants. Generally, new entrants face much stricter technological standards than are imposed on existing sources. Although these differential rates are explained as mechanisms for eliminating increases in pollution damage while assuring the viability of existing firms, they are effectively an entry barrier in the product market. This phenomenon is often observed for all types of regulation and is referred to as a *grandfather* rule. Existing industry interests are more likely to support (or reduce their opposition to) new regulations if they receive monopoly rents as a quid pro quo.

The new source standards may be viewed as a means of controlling entry. In the present framework, where total effluent depends on the number and scale of firms, the effect of entry restrictions may improve the efficiency of technological standards, albeit in an inexact manner. If the firms in the industry behave as Cournot oligopolists, the effect of entry restrictions and standards $\bar{x}$ for existing firms implies that monopoly rents may be earned and price may exceed marginal cost,

$$P(\bar{m}\bar{q})\bar{q} - c(\bar{q}) - k(\bar{x}) > 0, \tag{13.3.15}$$

$$P(\bar{m}\bar{q}) - c'(\bar{q}) = -P'(\bar{m}\bar{q})\bar{q} > 0. \tag{13.3.16}$$

Compare equations (13.3.15) and (13.3.16) with (13.3.10) and (13.3.11). Firm profits at the optimum exceed zero by the external value of effluent discharges $\gamma^* h(q^*, x^*)$. Further, price exceeds marginal costs by the marginal value of effluents generated by additional output, $\gamma^* h_q(q^*, x^*)$. Thus, the dual technology standard reduces entry and leads to a greater output price. In this sense, the general direction of the incentive effects of dual technological constraints promote efficiency. This result is surprising in view of the many problems generally associated with technological standards. It must be emphasized that technological standards are difficult to implement, since they require regulators to obtain complicated technical information. It may be difficult to monitor installation and maintenance of sophisticated abatement equipment. In any case, there is, of course, no regulatory substitute for firm decision making in the selection of the most efficient technology and input mix.

13.4   Environmental Regulation under Asymmetric Information

Regulation of heterogeneous firms poses serious difficulties for the design of environmental standards. These problems are compounded further by the fact that firm differences are often unobservable. Firms may have private information about the costs of production and the costs of pollution abatement. Furthermore, the efforts devoted by firms to the abatement of pollution may be unobservable as well and not easily inferred from cost, output, or technological data. Regulatory authorities attempting to limit pollution thus may face classic problems of adverse selection and moral hazard. The information available to regulators will affect the extent to which the use of pollution standards, technological standards, effluent fees, or other policy instruments achieves regulatory objectives.

The design of optimal regulatory penalties under asymmetric information is studied in this section. The costs of pollution abatement are known only to firms. Abatement costs may differ across firms. The regulator attempts to design a socially optimal, incentive compatible, regulatory mechanism whereby firms' abatement and production levels are adjusted to reflect their cost differences. As was done throughout the discussion of environmental regulation, the trade-off between pollution abatement and consumer welfare in the *final output* market is stressed. The discussion is based on the model in Spulber (1988c).

13.4.1   The Product Market

The consequences of pollution abatement are identified by observing outputs and prices in the competitive output market. In the presence of asymmetric information about firm costs, interaction between environmental regulation and the output market is of particular significance, as output levels are not known when regulations are designed.

A firm to type j has a cost function $C(q^j, e^j, \theta^j)$, where θ^j is a technology parameter that takes values in the interval $[0, 1]$. For ease of presentation, assume that costs have the following *quadratic* form:

$$C(q, e, \theta^j) = (\alpha/2)(e^2 + q^2) - \gamma eq - \theta^j e, \qquad (13.4.1)$$

for $j = 1, \ldots, m$. Thus, marginal production costs are increasing in q. Output and pollution are cost complements, $C_{12} = -\gamma < 0$. Since $C_2 = \alpha e - \gamma q - \theta^j$, increased effluent generation lowers costs if $e \leq (\gamma q + \theta^j)/\alpha$ and raises costs otherwise. To assure convexity of costs in (q, e), assume that $\alpha > \gamma$. Finally, note that $C_3 = -e$. Thus, the costs of reducing pollution (abatement) increase with the technology parameter θ^j.

The cost parameter θ^j represents firm j's private information. For ease of discussion, assume that the beliefs of the regulator and firms about the distribution of the θ^j parameters may be represented by the cumulative distribution functions $F^j(\theta^j), j = 1, \ldots, m$, which are common knowledge. That is, the θ^j parameters are assumed to be independently but not necessarily identically distributed. Let $F(0) = 0$, $F(1) = 1$, $f(\theta) \equiv dF(\theta)/d\theta > 0$. Also, let $F^n(\theta) = \Pi_{i=1}^n F^i(\theta^i)$.

Define firm profits as a function of p, e^j, and θ^j,

$$\pi(p, e^j, \theta^j) \equiv pq(p, e^j) - C(q(p, e^j), e^j, \theta^j), \qquad j = 1, \ldots, m. \qquad (13.4.2)$$

Firms behave competitively, taking the product price p as given. Thus, each firm's marginal cost equals the product price, $p = C_1(q^j, e^j, \theta^j)$,

$$p = \alpha q^j - \gamma e^j, \qquad j = 1, \ldots, m. \qquad (13.4.3)$$

Note that by the form of costs as given in equation (13.4.1), each firm's supply curve does not depend directly on the technology parameter θ^j, so that $q^j = q(p, e^j)$, but the parameter will affect its choice of pollution e^j and so will indirectly determine its market supply. Applying equation (13.4.3) and the envelope theorem, note that $\pi_2(p, e^j, \theta^j) = -C_2 = -\alpha e^j + \gamma q^j + \theta^j$, and $\pi_3(p, e^j, \theta^j) = e^j$.

Now solve for the product market equilibrium using the demand equation,

$$p = P\left(\sum_{i=1}^m q^i\right), \qquad (13.4.4)$$

and the supply equations (13.4.3),

$$q^j = q(p, e^j), \qquad j = 1, \ldots, m. \tag{13.4.5}$$

Price and output can be solved for as functions of any given effluent levels, $p = p(e^1, \ldots, e^m)$, $q^j = q^j(e^1, \ldots, e^m)$, $j = 1, \ldots, m$. Given the quadratic cost function, it follows that total output is *increasing* in the effluents generated by any individual firm. Therefore, any pollution abatement reduces total output and raises the market price. It can also be demonstrated that each firm's market equilibrium output is *increasing* in its *own* effluent level but *decreasing* in the effluent levels of *other* firms, $\partial q^j / \partial e^j > 0$ and $\partial q^j / \partial e^l < 0$, $l \neq j$.

13.4.2   The Regulatory Mechanism

The regulator attempts to control effluent levels e^j, $j = 1, \ldots, m$, through a system of penalties. The regulator must select desired effluent levels in the absence of full information about firm costs and the ultimate consequences of abatement on the product market equilibrium. The m regulated firms send messages, s^j, to the regulator regarding their costs.[6] Based on the messages received, the regulator assigns effluent levels e^j and penalties t^j to each firm,[7]

$$e^j = e^j(s^1, \ldots, s^m), \qquad t^j = t^j(s^1, \ldots, s^m).$$

Since firms do not know each other's private information θ^j, each follows a *Bayes-Nash* strategy in choosing their message. The Bayes-Nash equilibrium strategies $\tilde{s}^j = \tilde{s}^j(\theta^j)$ depend only on each firm's private information.[8]

By standard revelation principle arguments, the regulatory mechanism (e^j, t^j) may be represented by a *direct mechanism* that assigns effluent levels and penalties depending upon that firm's announced parameter value.[9] Thus, the firm's message is a reported parameter value. The direct mechanism is represented as $E^j(\theta^j, \theta^{(j)})$, $T^j(\theta^j, \theta^{(j)})$, $j = 1, \ldots, m$, where $\theta^{(j)} = (\theta^1, \ldots, \theta^{j-1}, \theta^{j+1}, \ldots, \theta^m)$. Firms play a Bayes-Nash game given the direct mechanism. Each firm chooses its parameter report $\hat{\theta}^j$ under the belief that truth-telling is the Bayes-Nash equilibrium strategy for all other firms.

Let $I^n = \times^n[0, 1]$ and $dF^{(j)} = dF^1(\theta^1) \ldots dF^{j-1}(\theta^{j-1}) dF^{j+1}(\theta^{j+1}) \ldots dF^m(\theta^m)$. Firm j's expected effluent level and payments if it announces parameter value θ^j, given that other firms pursue truth-telling strategies, are represented by

$$t^j(\theta^j) \equiv \int_{I^{m-1}} T^j(\theta^j, \theta^{(j)}) \, dF^{(j)},$$

(13.4.6)

$$e^j(\theta^j) \equiv \int_{I^{m-1}} E^j(\theta^j, \theta^{(j)}) \, dF^{(j)}.$$

Each firm takes the market price as given when it announces its parameter value to the regulator. The particular value of the market price is not important in determining firm j's parameter report. Firm j's profit from reporting parameter value $\hat\theta$ given that its true parameter is θ is given by

$$\Pi^j(\theta^j, \hat\theta^j) \equiv \int_{I^{m-1}} \pi(p, E^j(\hat\theta^j, \theta^{(j)}), \theta^j) \, dF^{(j)} - t^j(\hat\theta^j), \quad j = 1, \dots, m. \quad (13.4.7)$$

Incentive compatibility requires $\Pi^j(\theta, \theta) \geq \Pi^j(\theta, \hat\theta)$ for all $\theta, \hat\theta$ in $[0, 1]$. Let $\Pi^j(\theta) \equiv \Pi^j(\theta, \theta)$. *Individual rationality* requires $\Pi^j(\theta) \geq 0$ for all θ in $[0, 1]$, $j = 1, \dots, m$.

The mechanism must also yield an allocation that is *individually rational* for consumers. There must be nonnegative gains from trade for consumers. Gains from trade, $V \geq 0$, are defined to equal gains from consuming output, net of external damages plus effluent taxes paid by firms that are given to consumers as a lump sum payment. Define

$$S\left(\sum_{j=1}^{m} q^j\right) \equiv \int_0^{(\sum_{j=1}^{m} q^j)} P(Q) \, dQ$$

as gross consumers' surplus. Then, net gains from trade for consumers equals

$$V = \int_{I^m} \left[S\left(\sum_{j=1}^{m} q^j\right) - p \sum_{j=1}^{m} q^j - D\left(\sum_{j=1}^{m} E^j\right) + \sum_{j=1}^{m} T^j \right] dF. \quad (13.4.8)$$

A mechanism (E^j, T^j), $j = 1, \dots, m$, is said to be *feasible* if it is incentive compatible for firms and individually rational for both consumers and firms.

The welfare analysis that follows views pollution taxes T^j as pure transfers from consumers to firms, with no welfare effects. Social welfare is defined as consumer surplus, net of damages from pollution and production costs.[10] Since market equilibrium outputs are dependent on effluent levels, write expected net benefits as

$$B(E^1, \ldots, E^m) \equiv \int_{I^m} \left[S\left(\sum_{j=1}^{m} q^j \right) - D\left(\sum_{j=1}^{m} E^j \right) - \sum_{j=1}^{m} C(q^j, E^j, \theta^j) \right] dF.$$
(13.4.9)

To induce truth-telling, the regulator must compensate the firm. Thus, the regulated firm earns rents from private information. Higher values of the parameter θ^j lower total cost but raise the marginal costs of pollution abatement, since $\partial^2 C/\partial e \, \partial \theta < 0$. For truth-telling to be optimal for the firm, requires $\Pi_2^j(\theta, \theta) = 0$, or

$$\int_{I^{m-1}} \pi_2(p, E^j, \theta^j)(\partial E^j/\partial \theta^j) \, dF^{(j)} - \partial t^j(\theta^j)/\partial \theta^j = 0,$$
(13.4.10)

where $\pi_2 = -\alpha E^j + \gamma q^j + \theta^j$. By the envelope theorem, $\Pi^{j'}(\theta) \equiv \Pi_2^j(\theta, \theta) = e^j(\theta)$. By integration,

$$\Pi^j(\theta) = \Pi^j(0) + \int_0^\theta e^j(x) \, dx.$$
(13.4.11)

Since $\Pi^j(\theta^j)$ is nondecreasing in θ^j, individual rationality is satisfied for all firms if $\Pi^j(0) \geq 0, j = 1, \ldots, m$. The profit earned by the firm with the lowest cost parameter represents the minimum return for a regulated firm. Thus, any gains earned by firms with higher cost parameter values may be characterized as returns to their private information, that is, $\Pi^j(\theta^j) - \Pi^j(0) = \int_0^{\theta^j} e^j(x) \, dx$. Taking the expectation of this term, and applying integration by parts, define *ex ante* rents to private information for a type j firm by

$$R^j(E^j) \equiv \int_{I^m} E^j((1 - F^j(\theta^j))/f^j(\theta^j)) \, dF.$$
(13.4.12)

The set of feasible mechanisms[11] is now characterized.

PROPOSITION 13.4.1   *A direct mechanism* $(E^j(\theta^j, \theta^{(j)}), T^j(\theta^j, \theta^{(j)})), j = 1, \ldots, m$, *is feasible if and only if*

$$\partial e^j(\theta^j)/\partial \theta^j \geq 0, \qquad j = 1, \ldots, m,$$
(13.4.13)

$$B(E^1, \ldots, E^m) \geq \sum_{j=1}^{m} R^j(E^j).$$
(13.4.14)

The inequality (13.4.13) is simply a monotonicity condition required to achieve incentive compatibility. The constraint in equation (13.4.14) is primarily due to *individual rationality* requirements. This is a "budget-balancing" condition that has important implications for the attainment of optimal externality levels under asymmetric information. As will be seen, efficiency may not be attained due to the costs of inducing truth-telling.

13.4.3   The Efficient Mechanism

The regulator's objective is to maximize expected social welfare $B(E^1, \ldots, E^m)$. By proposition 13.4.1, the optimal mechanism (E^j, T^j) solves the following problem, $\max_{(E^1, \ldots, E^m)} B(E^1, \ldots, E^m)$ subject to conditions (13.4.13) and (13.4.14). Let η be the multiplier associated with the inequality constraint (13.4.14). The regulator's objective function is then

$$W = (1 + \eta)B(E^1, \ldots, E^m) - \eta \sum_{j=1}^{m} R^j(E^j), \tag{13.4.15}$$

where $\eta(B - \sum R^j) = 0$, $(B - \sum R^j) \geq 0$. The regulator maximizes constrained welfare W subject to the monotonicity constraint (13.4.13). If the monotonicity constraint is nonbinding, then the optimal mechanism is the (pointwise) maximum of W with respect to E^l,

$$(1 + \eta) \sum_{j=1}^{m} \left[\left[P\left(\sum_{j=1}^{m} q^j \right) - C_1(q^j, E^j, \theta^j) \right] (\partial q^j / \partial E^l) \right]$$

$$- (1 + \eta)D'\left(\sum_{j=1}^{m} E^j \right) - (1 + \eta)C_2(q^l, E^l, \theta^l)$$

$$- \eta((1 - F^l(\theta^l))/f^l(\theta^l)) = 0, \qquad l = 1, \ldots, m. \tag{13.4.16}$$

At the market equilibrium, price equals marginal cost for each firm. Also, since $C_2(q^l, E^l, \theta^l) = \alpha E^l - \gamma q^l - \theta^l$, the optimality condition (13.4.16) simplifies to

$$D'\left(\sum_{j=1}^{m} E^j \right) = -\alpha E^l + \gamma q^l + \theta^l - (\eta/(1 + \eta))((1 - F^l(\theta^l))/f^l(\theta^l)),$$

$$l = 1, \ldots, m. \tag{13.4.17}$$

To summarize:[12]

PROPOSITION 13.4.2   *Given the monotonicity condition* (13.4.13), *the optimal mechanism* (E^j, T^j) *satisfies equation* (13.4.17).

The optimal regulatory mechanism, as characterized by equation (13.4.17), is represented in figure 13.4.1. Note that marginal abatement

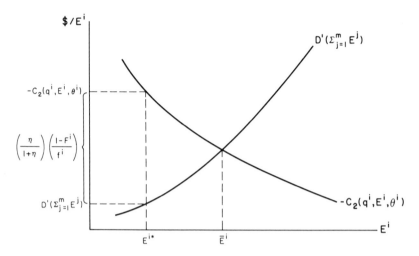

Figure 13.4.1
The optimal regulated effluent level for individual firms, E^{i*}.

costs, $-C_2$, are decreasing in E^i.[13] The costs of inducing truth-telling by firms is a wedge between marginal damages and marginal abatement costs.

It is worthwhile comparing the optimal regulatory mechanism under asymmetric information with the full information optimum. The full information optimal pollution levels $(\bar{E}^1, \ldots, \bar{E}^m)$ equate marginal damages to marginal cost, $D'(\sum_{j=1}^m \bar{E}^j) = -C_2(q^i, \bar{E}^i, \theta^i)$, $i = 1, \ldots, m$. But, since $\partial \bar{E}^i / \partial \theta^i > 0$, it follows that the full information effluent levels are monotonic in the own technology parameter and therefore satisfy the necessary condition for incentive compatibility. This immediately implies the following result.

PROPOSITION 13.4.3   *The full information optimum* $(\bar{E}^1, \ldots, \bar{E}^m)$ *coincides with the asymmetric information equilibrium if and only if the budget-balancing condition* (13.4.14) *is nonbinding at* $(\bar{E}^1, \ldots, \bar{E}^m)$.

In the environmental regulation model of Dasgupta, Hammond, and Maskin (1980), the full information optimum is attainable through dominant strategies but the government's budget does not balance. This budget-balancing problem reappears in our Bayes-Nash framework. Here, however, individual rationality requires the net benefits of production to be sufficiently large to cover the costs of inducing truth-telling by firms. This may happen if net benefits are relatively large. In Spulber (1988a), a quadratic example is given in which total market rent does indeed cover information costs even with bilateral asymmetric information. In general, however, large information costs imply that the budget constraint will be strictly binding.

If the feasibility condition $B \geq \sum_{j=1}^{m} R^j$ is binding and η is nonzero, then marginal damages from environmental pollution, D', are less than marginal abatement costs for firms, $-C_2$, by a positive factor $(\eta/(1+\eta))((1-F^l)/f^l)$. Thus, for any given set of output vectors, $(q^1, \ldots, q^m)$, the optimal effluent level, E^{j*}, is less than the level that equates marginal damages to marginal abatement costs, $\bar{E}^j$. So, *ceteris paribus*, asymmetric information drives a wedge between social and private costs in such a way that per firm pollution levels are *less* than optimal.

If the feasibility condition is nonbinding and $\eta = 0$, then the full information optimum is attained and $D'(\sum_{j=1}^{m} \bar{E}^j) = -C_2(q^l, \bar{E}^l, \theta^l)$, $l = 1, \ldots, m$. Therefore, a key determinant of whether the full information optimum can be achieved is whether the net benefits from production at the full information optimum, $B(\bar{E}^1, \ldots, \bar{E}^m)$, cover the expected information rents earned by firms, $\sum_{j=1}^{m} R^j(\bar{E}^j)$. It is generally likely that the budget-balancing condition will be binding.

The result that, *ceteris paribus*, pollution levels are lower under asymmetric information is counterintuitive. One would expect that, since firms wish to overstate the value of their private information parameter θ to exaggerate abatement costs, effluents would exceed optimal levels. However, higher reports of θ are met with greater taxes, since $\partial t/\partial \theta \geq 0$. Also, higher-$\theta$ firms discharge greater levels of pollutants. To reward higher-θ firms for revealing their private information, the welfare benefits from pollution reduction must be *positive* at the margin, that is, $-D' - C_2 > 0$. Clearly, for firms with the highest θ values, $\theta^l = 1$, $D'(\sum_{j=1}^{m} E^j) = -C_2(q^l, E^l, \theta^l)$, so that $E^{l*} = \bar{E}^{l*}$. For firms with lower θ values, to obtain tax reductions requires marginal damages to be less than marginal abatement costs, so that $E^{l*} < \bar{E}^{l*}$.

Let $(\bar{Q}, \bar{E})$ represent total market output and externality levels under full information and let (Q^*, E^*) represent total market output and externality levels under asymmetric information. Summing both sides of the price equals marginal cost equation, the set of market equilibrium output and effluent levels is given by the function $Q^M(E)$, which solves

$$Q^M(E): \quad mP(Q) = \alpha Q - \gamma E. \tag{13.4.18}$$

Clearly, $\partial Q^M(E)/\partial E = \gamma/(\alpha - mP'(Q)) > 0$. Summing both sides of

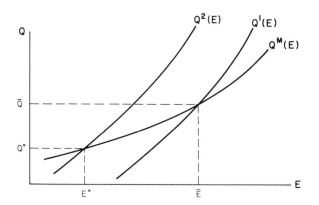

Figure 13.4.2
Total output and effluent under asymmetric information are below optimal levels.

$D'(\sum_{j=1}^{m} e^j) = -C_2$, let $Q^1(E)$ be the set of total outputs for which E is the socially optimal total effluent level under full information,

$$Q^1(E): \quad mD'(E) = -\alpha E + \gamma Q + \sum_{j=1}^{m} \theta^j. \tag{13.4.19}$$

The output and externality $(\bar{Q}, \bar{E})$ at the full information social optimum solve $\bar{Q} = Q^M(\bar{E}) = Q^1(\bar{E})$. Note that $\partial Q^1(E)/\partial E = (mD''(E) + \alpha)/\gamma > \partial Q^M(E)/\partial E$. Now define the set of total outputs for which E is the optimal total effluent level under asymmetric information by summing over both sides of equation (13.4.17),

$$Q^2(E): \quad mD'(E) = -\alpha E + \gamma Q + \sum_{j=1}^{m} \theta^j - (\eta/(1+\eta)) \sum_{j=1}^{m} ((1-F^j)/f^j). \tag{13.4.20}$$

The regulated market-clearing output and externality level (Q^*, E^*) solve $Q^* = Q^M(E^*) = Q^2(E^*)$. The curves Q^M, Q^1, and Q^2 are represented in figure 13.4.2. Comparing the definitions, it follows that output levels under regulation are greater than at the full information optimum for any given externality level, $Q^2(E) \geq Q^1(E)$ for any $(\theta^1, \ldots, \theta^m)$. From figure 13.4.2 the following is obtained.

PROPOSITION 13.4.4   *Total output and effluent levels are lower under asymmetric information than at the full information optimum, $\bar{Q} > Q^*$ and $\bar{E} > E^*$.*

Recall from the optimality condition (13.4.17) that marginal external damages, D', are below marginal abatement costs, $-C_2$, for all firm types $\theta^j < 1$. Each firm's effluent level will be below the level that equates marginal damages to marginal abatement costs, all other things being equal. Finally, since market clearing output levels are increasing in the aggregate externality level, the regulated equilibrium will involve both lowered output and total effluent levels.

The aggregate results do not disaggregate easily due to the heterogeneity of firms. One may state a sufficient condition for individual firms to have lower output and externality levels at the regulated market equilibrium than at the full information social optimum. Let (q^{j*}, e^{j*}), $j = 1, \ldots, m$, represent output and externality levels for firms at the regulated market equilibrium and let $(\bar{q}^j, \bar{e}^j)$ represent corresponding optimal values. The following is proved in Spulber (1988c).

PROPOSITION 13.4.5 *Output and externality levels for any firm $j = 1, \ldots, m$ are lower at the regulated market equilibrium than at the full information social optimum, $q^{j*} < \bar{q}^j$ and $e^{j*} < \bar{e}^j$, if $\sum_{l=1}^{m}((1 - F^l)/f^l)/m \leq ((1 - F^j)/f^j)$.*

To interpret this condition, suppose that all firm parameters are distributed according to the uniform distribution. Then, if the firm's cost parameter, θ^j, is less than or equal to the average across all firms, $\sum_{l=1}^{m}\theta^l/m$, the firm will produce an output and effluent below the full information optimum. Recall that lower-θ^j firms face higher costs. On the other hand, the possibility that firms with high-θ^j-parameter values may have output and effluents greater than or equal to the full information optimum reflects the approximate equality of marginal abatement costs to marginal external damages for those firms.

13.4.4 One-Round Communication

If the regulatory game does not allow an exchange of messages between the regulator and firms, the regulator must design the tax rule before any inference about firm costs can be made. Suppose that the regulator may tax firms on the basis of all observed pollution levels, $T^j = T^j(e^1, \ldots, e^m)$. Actual firm choices of pollution levels will then provide a signal to the regulator about firm costs, as well as determining a firm's tax payments. Firms will choose effluent levels according to a Bayes-Nash strategy. The vector $(\tilde{e}^1, \ldots, \tilde{e}^m)$ will be a Bayes-Nash equilibrium if $\tilde{e}^j(\theta^j)$ solves

$$\pi(p, \tilde{e}^j, \theta^j) - \int_{I^{m-1}} T^j(\tilde{e}^j, \tilde{e}^{(j)}) \, dF^{(j)}$$

$$\geq \pi(p, e^j, \theta^j) - \int_{I^{m-1}} T^j(e^j, \tilde{e}^{(j)}) \, dF^{(j)}. \qquad (13.4.21)$$

This type of regulation game is referred to as "one-round communication" by Dasgupta, Hammond, and Maskin (1980). By the revelation principle, the direct mechanism corresponding to this game has the form $E^j(\theta^j)$, $T^j(\theta^j, \theta^{(j)})$. As before define $t^j(\theta^j) \equiv \int_{I^{m-1}} T^j(\theta^j, \theta^{(j)}) \, dF^{(j)}$. Then the reduced form mechanism $(E^j(\theta^j), t^j(\theta^j))$, $j = 1, \ldots, m$, depends only on each firm's own parameter.

By similar analysis, the optimal direct mechanism for the restricted regulation game can be shown to satisfy

$$\int_{I^{m-1}} D'\left(\sum_{j=1}^m E^j\right) dF^{(l)} = -\alpha E^l + \gamma q^l + \theta^l$$

$$-(\eta/(1+\eta))((1-F^l(\theta^l))/f^l(\theta^l)), \qquad l = 1, \ldots, m. \qquad (13.4.22)$$

One may no longer establish that the full information optimum is attainable by regulation under asymmetric information, since firm effluent levels will not depend on the entire vector of cost parameters. This point is made by Dasgupta, Hammond, and Maskin (1980). In the present framework, note that budget balancing ($\eta = 0$) is no longer sufficient for feasibility of a mechanism corresponding to the full information optimum.

An alternative approach is to recognize the limits of "one-stage communication" and to define a second-best optimum. The *second-best optimum* consists of a competitive equilibrium in the product market, $P(\sum_{j=1}^m q^j) = C_1(q^i, E^i, \theta^i)$, and firm marginal abatement costs equal to expected marginal damages. Thus, $\bar{E}^i(\theta^i)$ solves

$$\int_{I^{m-1}} D'\left(\sum_{j=1}^m E^j(\theta^j)\right) dF^{(j)} = -C_2(q^i, E^i, \theta^i), \qquad i = 1, \ldots, m. \qquad (13.4.23)$$

This immediately implies the following.

PROPOSITION 13.4.6   *Optimal regulation under asymmetric information with one-round communication achieves the second-best optimum, $\bar{E}^1(\theta^1)$, ..., $\bar{E}^m(\theta^m)$, if and only if the budget balancing condition is nonbinding for the mechanism $(\bar{E}^1, \ldots, \bar{E}^m)$.*

The trade-off between output and environmental damages has important implications for regulation under asymmetric information about production costs and pollution abatement costs. Regulated firms earn information rents that depend on the value of their privately observed cost parameter. Firms have incentive to overestimate the costs of abatement in communicating with the regulatory authority. For the regulatory mechanism to be both incentive compatible and individually rational, the expected gains from trade between consumers and firms net of environmental damages must be sufficient to cover the expected information rents that will be earned by firms.

If net gains from trade exceed expected firm information rents at the full information optimum, then the full information optimum is attainable by a direct revelation mechanism. The Bayes-Nash nature of the regulatory game does not eliminate the budget-balancing problem. If the constraint that net gains from trade exceed expected information rents is strictly binding, then the well-known equal marginal cost rule is violated. Marginal costs of pollution abatement are not equal across firms, nor do these equal marginal external damages. The individual rationality restriction implies that both effluent and output levels are lower under asymmetric information.

Notes

1. For the special case where the set of solutions is symmetric, since consumer and firm opportunity costs are zero, $V^* = \Pi^*$ if feasible and the Nash solution coincides with the social optimum in the competitive case. In general, this need not be the case. Any variation in consumer or firm opportunity costs or asymmetries in the feasible set will eliminate this result. Further, in the monopoly case, even if $V^* = \Pi^*$, the Nash solution yields $D'(E^*) + C_E = -Q \, \partial p^m / \partial E$. As might be expected, the presence of market power for the firm distorts the externality level set at the Nash bargaining solution.

2. See also Hahn (1983, 1987), Hahn and Noll (1982), Lyon (1982), and Anderson (1983) on marketable permits.

3. This result is well-known in the externalities literature; see especially Kneese and Bower (1968) and Baumol and Oates (1975, p. 144).

4. Baumol and Oates (1975, p. 45) state that "[i]nputs and outputs that generate smoke are, of course, subject to tax but only in proportion to the smoke they produce." In practice, there may not be a proportional relationship between a firm's final output and its emissions. As Plott (1966) finds, a tax per unit of output may increase a firm's emissions if they are an inferior input. Burrows (1979, footnote 2) notes that the original Pigou analysis refers to "'taxes' on external-cost-generating activities such as petrol duty and motor vehicle license tax." Burrows (1979, p. 495) interprets the Pigouvian tax as being a charge per unit of effluent emission. See also Baumol (1972) on this point.

5. This is suggested by Carlton and Loury (1980, 1986), for example. See Spulber (1985a) for further discussion on the importance of efficient input levels.

6. This model is much more general than the one given by Kwerel (1977), who considers a simple framework in which the regulator minimizes the sum of pollution damages and abatement costs. Firms communicate their entire cost function to the regulator, who then issues a fixed number of pollution licenses. The present model, with product market interaction, requires a more complicated mechanism. The present approach also differs from the environmental regulation model of Dasgupta, Hammond, and Maskin (1980), who use a *dominant strategy* setting.

7. Dasgupta, Hammond, and Maskin (1980) refer to this type of procedure as "two-round communication."

8. Let $(s^1, \ldots, s^m)$ take values in $S = S^1 \times \cdots \times S^m$, where S^j is firm j's message space. Since the market price p is a function of effluent levels, one may write profit as $\pi^j(e, \theta^j)$. Let $s^{(j)} = s^1,$ $\ldots, s^{j-1}, s^{j+1}, \ldots, s^m$. Let $e = (e^1, \ldots, e^m), dF^{(j)} = dF^1 \cdots dF^{j-1} dF^{j+1} \cdots dF^m$ and $I^n = \bigtimes^n [0, 1]$. Then, the Bayes-Nash equilibrium of the regulatory game in messages, $(\tilde{s}^1, \ldots, \tilde{s}^m)$, is defined by $\tilde{s}^j(\theta^j)$ in such a way that

$$\int_{I^{m-1}} [\pi^j(e(\tilde{s}^j, \tilde{s}^{(j)}), \theta^j) - t^j(\tilde{s}^j, \tilde{s}^{(j)})] \, dF^{(j)}$$

$$\geq \int_{I^{m-1}} [\pi^j(e(s^j, \tilde{s}^{(j)}), \theta^j) - t^j(s^j, \tilde{s}^{(j)})] \, dF^{(j)}$$

for all messages s^j in S^j.

9. Define the direct mechanism by $E^j(\theta^j, \theta^{(j)}) = e^j(s^1(\theta^1), \ldots, s^m(\theta^m))$ and $T^j(\theta^j, \theta^{(j)}) = t^j(s^1(\theta^1), \ldots, s^m(\theta^m))$.

10. The problem can be generalized to allow the regulator to give positive weight to firm profits in the social welfare function. However, this does not add to the present discussion.

11. A proof appears in Spulber (1988c). For related derivations see Guesnerie and Laffont (1984) for the one-parameter setting and Myerson and Satterthwaite (1983) and Spulber (1988a) for the multiple-parameter setting. The difference in the present analysis is the emphasis on the comparison of expected welfare with the information rents earned by firms.

12. The proof is given in Spulber (1988c). There it is shown that a simple sufficient condition for monotonicity can be obtained. Define $H^j(\theta^j) \equiv \theta^j - (\eta/(1 + \eta))((1 - F(\theta^1))/f^1(\theta^1))$. Let $h^j(\theta^j) \equiv dH^j(\theta^j)/d\theta^j$. The sufficient monotonicity condition on H^j is just $h^j(\theta^j) \geq 0, j = 1, \ldots,$ m. This monotonicity condition is satisfied by a number of familiar distributions including the uniform, $F^j(\theta) = \theta$, and the exponential, $F^j(\theta) = (1 - e^{-\xi\theta})/(1 - e^{-\xi})$. The monotonicity condition will be shown to guarantee that the optimal mechanism yields a fully separating equilibrium. It is possible to relax the condition by allowing $h^j(\theta^j)$ to change sign a finite number of times; see Guesnerie and Laffont (1984) and also Spulber (1988a). Relaxing the condition in this manner allows pooling across firm types but does not significantly add to the present analysis.

13. This follows since

$$\frac{\partial^2 C(q^i, e^i, \theta^i)}{\partial e^{i2}} = -\alpha + \gamma(\partial q^i/\partial e^i) = -((\alpha^2 - \gamma^2)/\alpha) + (\gamma^2/\alpha)P'/(\alpha - mP').$$

14 Internalities 1: Regulation and Liability

Government regulation of product and labor markets has increased significantly in the areas of safety and health. New regulatory institutions, such as the Consumer Product Safety Commission and the Occupational Safety and Health Administration, have been created to address increased public concern with product quality and workplace safety. The complex of product quality, workplace safety, and environmental regulations, called "social" or "new wave" regulations, is often viewed as a single unit by economists and policymakers. This is because these regulations all focus on health and safety, cut across industry boundaries, pervade almost every purchase or employment decision taken by consumers and firms, and differ from traditional concerns with price, output, and market structure that typify regulation of utilities and transportation.

It is important, however, to distinguish between those regulations that seek to abate externalities and those that are concerned with *internalities* associated with exchange and private contracts. With externalities, such as environmental pollution, regulations seek to mitigate harm to third parties in the absence of contractual relations between victims and injurers. With product quality and workplace safety, contractual relations between victim and injurer are already in existence and often well-defined. Regulation of product quality and workplace safety is superimposed on these contractual relations, which have already adjusted for internalities. Internalities have been mitigated to the extent feasible given available information, the extent of competition, and the effectiveness of legal and other social institutions. For these reasons, regulation of internalities must be evaluated in comparison with market equilibria, taking special care to emphasize alternative legal institutions, such as tort law.

The present chapter begins in section 14.1 with an overview of internalities regulation in the areas of product quality and workplace safety. The major laws and regulatory agencies that are active in these areas are examined. It is discovered that the causes of internalities, namely, costly contingent contracts, moral hazard, and adverse selection, are also the same factors that hinder regulatory solutions. These issues are reexamined in chapter 15. The rest of the chapter examines market equilibrium under full information as a benchmark case. Section 14.2 reviews significant results on the neutrality of alternative legal liability rules in a competitive market. In section 14.3 the effects of imperfect competition on the performance of liability rules are studied. A limited role for regulation is identified if entry barriers are present. Finally, in section 14.4, the functioning of liability rules is studied in the absence of entry barriers. In contestable markets with large scale economies, alternative liability assignments are shown to achieve second-best optimality.

14.1   Product Quality and Workplace Safety

A large class of laws and regulatory activities is directed toward abating the safety and health risks associated with hazardous products and working conditions. These regulations have a significant impact on the effective functioning of product and labor markets and on the form of contractual relations. Parallel issues arise in the seemingly diverse areas of consumer safety and workplace safety, each of which is addressed in an extensive and often distinct literature. This section briefly reviews the related economic literature and identifies the principal regulatory institutions. The similarities in regulatory agendas and problems encountered in these two areas are emphasized.

14.1.1   Product Quality

The study of markets must begin with a definition of commodities. *Commodities* may be defined by their characteristics as in Lancaster (1971, 1979), and these properties may be fixed or variable. Consumers have preferences defined over the set of commodities or their underlying characteristics. *Product quality* generally refers to arbitrary summary measures of product characteristics that are identified as significant. Product quality is often associated with a particular performance criterion, such as *durability* of a consumer investment good (e.g., automobiles and appliances), or such characteristics as likelihood of breakdown, amount of complementary commodities required (e.g., gas mileage), and aesthetic aspects. Quality may be immediately apparent, as with *search* goods, or may require consumption, as with *experience* goods. If product quality does not meet consumer expectations, then consumer benefits from using the good are reduced. It may be necessary to repair the product or purchase a replacement. Two special types of product performance are of great importance because of their potential for catastrophic harm to consumers. One aspect of product performance, referred to as *product safety*, applies to the possibility of consumer injury from a single use of the product. An example of this might be the possibility of an exploding gas tank if an automobile is involved in an accident. The other aspect of product performance, *product health*, applies to the long-term health risks from using the product. This might refer to a drug that failed either to be safe or to be effective. It should be emphasized that product safety and health characteristics apply both to search and experience goods. Consumers may choose to purchase a good with known safety or health risks (such as cigarettes). Practically all purchases of goods, even when information is incomplete, involve some assumption of risk by the consumer.

This section briefly considers regulation of product characteristics, particularly product safety and health. The type of regulatory policies applied to consumer products and pharmaceuticals is critically examined, and an effort is made to determine whether there is a possible role for regulation of product quality in a competitive market. For pharmaceuticals, there is general agreement that the government has a role to play in the dissemination of information and in mandating disclosure. There does not exist a strong consensus on how the government should regulate the testing and marketing of new drugs. In the case of product safety (excluding food and drugs), the case for government intervention is less convincing. Many of the accident risks related to consumer products are apparent to consumers.

One may identify two broad areas of product health and safety regulation: food additives and pharmaceuticals regulated by the Food and Drug Administration (FDA), and other consumer products regulated by the Consumer Product Safety Commission (CPSC). Other agencies in the Department of Agriculture are concerned with quality of food; see chapter 1. In addition, the National Highway Traffic Safety Administration sets standards for automobile safety,[1] and the Federal Aviation Administration regulates air travel safety. For the present purposes, it is sufficient to focus on the FDA and the CPSC.

Food and Drug Administration   Federal regulation of pharmaceuticals in the United States begins with the Pure Food and Drug Act of 1906 and the Food, Drug and Cosmetic Act of 1938. The 1906 act was primarily targeted at deceptive claims for patent medicines sold in interstate commerce. The 1938 act introduced the requirement of "adequate" testing for safety. The intervening period saw the establishment of the Food and Drug Administration (FDA) in 1931, now in the Department of Health and Human Services. Amendments to the Food, Drug and Cosmetic Act established important regulations. Food additives are reviewed for safety under the 1958 amendments. The 1962 Kefauver-Harris Amendments require drugs to be proven effective as well as safe. The 1968 Delayney Amendments require the FDA to ban food additives that are carcinogenic. The 1976 Medical Device Amendments extend the process of premarket testing and approval to medical products, such as heart pacemakers.[2]

The FDA's mission in the market for pharmaceuticals is the control of drug safety and effectiveness through regulation of drug testing and licensing of approved drugs. The FDA also regulates drug labeling and advertising. The FDA establishes general rules for drug testing and obtaining permission to market a drug and reviews the test results on a case-by-case basis. Thus FDA rule making is primarily concerned with test procedures and establishment of criteria for safety and effectiveness of drugs. Extensive adjudication is required to review applications to market new drugs. Manufacturers bear the burden of proving safety and effectiveness of new drugs.

The principal regulatory interaction in the market for pharmaceuticals is between the FDA and manufacturers. The manufacturers conduct drug tests and supply information to the FDA. Consumer interest groups and the medical profession exercise comparatively less direct influence. The main source of public pressure on the FDA is through congressional oversight.[3] FDA decisions are subject to challenges through the courts, although the courts have generally allowed the agency considerable discretion. The regulatory-bargaining model does not apply directly to FDA decision making, although one may readily identify various interest groups representing consumers, doctors, hospitals, and pharmaceutical manufacturers.

The FDA takes a standards-based approach to the regulation of pharmaceuticals. Standards exist both for testing procedures and for marketing approval. Testing standards involve extensive specification of technical requirements for animal and human tests. Review of applications for approval of new drugs applies what are often arbitrary standards that determine whether the clinical tests were conducted properly and whether the drug is safe and effective. The FDA has often been criticized for not taking explicit account of costs and benefits in its regulatory decisions. This is intentional and reflects the agency's interpretation of the relevant legislation. An FDA administrator, Crout (1975), states that "we do not pay attention to the economic consequences of our decisions and the law does not ask us to."[4]

The procedures for testing of drugs prior to marketing approval involve benefits and costs. Increased testing reduces the risks of approving unsafe or ineffective drugs and yields greater information about proper usage. As Grabowski and Vernon (1983) observe, the FDA trades off the risks of approving drugs that are not safe and effective (a type 2 error) against the risks of rejecting a useful drug (a type 1 error). Further, testing is in itself costly and delays the introduction of new drugs. These costs of testing may reduce incentives for research and development of new drugs; see Bailey (1972), Peltzman (1973, 1974), and Grabowski and Vernon (1983). Although these studies precede major innovations in biotechnology, Grabowski and Vernon (1983), in examining the literature on incentives to innovate, observe that marketing lags reduce effective patent life, thus reducing rents from innovation. Finally, since testing costs are nonrecoverable, they create a barrier to market entry in addition to the licensing requirements.

A similar picture of the food additive screening process emerges; see Pape (1982) for a discussion of legislative issues in the regulation of food ingredients. Food additives must undergo extensive tests to show that they are safe and effective. FDA approval of a petition involves both informal rule making and in some cases a formal hearing on the record; see Breyer (1982, chapter 7). Breyer describes the difficulties inherent in estimating the costs and benefits of approving risky products and in determining the distributional effects of these decisions. For both food and drug safety, the FDA faces the task of designing "evidentiary rules governing burdens of proof" (Breyer 1982, p. 153). This often requires a high degree of scientific expertise on the part of the regulatory agency and can in itself create delays in testing and marketing new drugs.

Before considering alternatives to administrative regulation of the market for pharmaceuticals, it is useful to identify the benefits of regulation and proposals for improvement of the current system. Then alternatives that rely on the marketplace and the law of torts are considered.

The present system of regulation by the FDA is a combination of centralized information gathering and licensing of new drugs. The FDA evaluates applications for approval of new drugs, controls clinical testing of drugs, disseminates information about drugs, sets standards for manufacturing of drugs, and imposes labeling and disclosure requirements. These activities require a very high level of scientific and technical expertise. To the extent that centralized information generation and processing is optimal, there are potential benefits from this type of regulation. Given the high costs of properly evaluating the benefits and risks of new drugs, it is desirable to avoid unnecessary duplication of effort. Further, the often noted public good nature of information argues for production and dissemination by a single producer. Several features of the pharmaceutical market reinforce the benefits of centralized evaluation of the properties of drugs. Consumers are not equipped to obtain and evaluate the large amount of scientific information required to determine if a single drug is either safe or effective. The distinction between those drugs available with and without a prescription provides an important signal to consumers. The approval of drugs by the FDA as safe and effective provides an additional signal that is easily understood by consumers. Consumers without medical training have four additional sources of information: physicians, pharmacists, labels, and popular books on the properties of pharmaceuticals. Labels are generally nontechnical and often given very brief descriptions of directions for use and possible side effects. The consumer is not equipped to evaluate the accuracy of the labels and might not benefit from more complicated instructions. As a consequence, labeling and disclosure regulations are of value of consumers. Pharmacists provide very limited information to consumers, usually confined to indicating what nonprescription drugs are available. Pharmacists cannot be expected to evaluate properly the characteristics of pharmaceuticals in the absence of centralized screening and licensing. Physicians are the consumer's principal source of advice about pharmaceuticals. Few physicians have the technical expertise to evaluate basic research on drug safety and effectiveness. Physicians rely in part on drug company representatives and FDA information as well as medical associations for information on new drugs. Since the quality and training of physicians is far from homogeneous, consumers face a difficult problem in evaluating a physician's prescription of a drug—they must first attempt to evaluate the physician. In this setting, independent certification of safety and effectiveness of drugs provides a useful safeguard, even if a patient must obtain a second physician's opinion on whether the drug is safe and effective for that individual's particular medical condition.

Centralized regulation not only involves production of information in the evaluation of new drugs, but also involves a decision as to what level of risks are acceptable. In most cases, economists generally favor placing decisions about risks versus benefits in the hands of individual consumers. Since consumers differ in terms of their valuations of a drug's benefits and attitudes toward risk, there may be welfare losses from imposition of uniform risk levels. However, these costs may be outweighed by the high information costs of evaluating the risks of new drugs. Furthermore, in many cases, a number of alternative drugs and medical procedures are available for a particular condition, so that a patient and physician have a choice of alternative risks and benefits. The combination of the functions of monitoring drug tests and screening risks and benefits may yield additional economies for regulation.

The implementation of FDA policies has been criticized as being overly risk averse and for excessive reliance on internal experts. Grabowski and Vernon (1983) examine a number of major proposals for regulatory reform. These include the following. First is the suggestion that the FDA decentralize its control over clinical trials with greater reliance on private institutions such as research hospitals. Second is the recommendation that the conditions for approval of marketing for a new drug be relaxed, while postmarket monitoring of the drug's performance should be increased. Third is the suggestion that the FDA increase its reliance on the advice of independent experts and on foreign data. Fourth is the reform of FDA administrative rule making to streamline the new drug approval process. This can include creation of a "probably safe and effective" classification and shifting the burden of proof to the FDA for denial of a new drug application (Grabowski and Vernon, 1983, p. 72). Many of the proposed reforms increase the efficiency of the FDA but do not represent fundamental changes in the regulatory process. Grabowski and Vernon (1983, p. 71) observe that "the development of our regulatory institutions has been much more closely bound to a due-process, adversarial, administrative tradition than to a 'consensus of scientific experts' approach." They recommend that the FDA concentrate on certifying and disseminating information rather than on the licensing of new drugs. A problem with this proposal and others, such as postmarket testing, is that the harmful health effects of improperly tested pharmaceuticals may be latent and observable only with a lag in those taking the drug or even in their offspring.

The consequences of complete abolition of the FDA are viewed favorably by Weimer (1982). Weimer emphasizes that private sources of information would replace the FDA, including hospitals, medical associations, and independent testing firms, and proposes a system of private enforcement based on strengthened strict liability laws. This approach, while drawing on the efficiency of the market as a producer of information, would be likely to place a high burden on the courts, creating delays and inefficiencies that might exceed those of the present regulatory system.

Consumer Product Safety Commission   The Consumer Product Safety Commission (CPSC) was established in 1972 as an independent regulatory agency by the Consumer Product Safety Act. Its main tasks are the collection and distribution of information on consumer product hazards and the creation and enforcement of product safety standards. Product standards are announced and implemented through administrative rule-making procedures. Enforcement of standards may result in product recalls, repairs, or outright bans. The CPSC has tended to focus on detailed engineering design requirements rather than on standards for safe performance. This approach has been the subject of criticism.[5]

Unlike pharmaceuticals, most of the consumer products examined by the CPSC involve risks of injury that are quite evident to consumers. The leading causes of injuries include stairs, bicycles, baseballs, and nails; see Viscusi (1984). Thus, there is often little justification for market intervention by the CPSC on grounds of imperfect information. As Viscusi (1984, p. 37) observes, "For all supporting analyses for CPSC standards, the existence of a risk and CPSC's capacity to alter that risk serve as the primary basis for intervention. The presence of any inadequacy in market processes or its importance has not been at the forefront of policy decisions." For an insightful and detailed study of the CPSC see Viscusi (1984).

Since the risks of product failure are well understood for many of the products regulated by the CPSC, it is apparent that most of the safety problems the agency addresses can be handled by the market in the context of products liability law. Warranty agreements and private insurance appear sufficient to provide additional risk-sharing arrangements. Products liability issues are discussed further in the next section.

14.1.2   Workplace Safety

Although workplace health and safety regulations are referred to as part of "new wave" regulations, regulation of factory safety by the states dates back to 1867.[6] The greater part of workplace safety regulation is carried out by the Occupational Safety and Health Administration (OSHA) in the Department of Labor. Established by the Occupational Safety and Health Act of 1970, OSHA represents a major shift of enforcement efforts and standard setting away from the states to the federal government. Regulation of workplace health and safety is comparable to environmental regulation in that regulatory standards are established and enforced with little regard for incentive-based instruments. The important aspect of working conditions that differs from the case of externalities is that workers and management have recourse to direct negotiation of wages and the work environment. Regulation of the workplace is superimposed on a relatively competitive labor market. The present work examines briefly whether administrative safety regulation can be of use in this setting. The focus is on OSHA, although the conclusions reached here apply to other federal and state agencies that regulate workplace safety; see section 2.1. A role for regulation is identified in the provision of information to market participants, particularly in the area of long-term health hazards and occupational disease. It is suggested also that increased reliance on private collective bargaining rather than on administrative regulation may be desirable in unionized industries. A general problem has been excessive concern by OSHA with standards-based regulation of safety in the workplace as compared with OSHA efforts to reduce the risks of occupational disease. Reordering priorities will allow regulatory resources and firm prevention expenditures to be focused on long-term health risks.

Without question, federal workplace safety and health regulation, particularly through OSHA, has opened up new channels of bargaining between workers and management as well as involving various other interest groups in the regulatory process.[7] Through union and other representatives, workers participate extensively in the design and enforcement of regulatory policy. This had been absent under state regulation which primarily involved the state agency and firm management.[8] Unions and management play an important role through lobbying of congressional oversight committees and through direct involvement in OSHA's public hearings on regulatory standards.[9] Extensive public hearings allow oral and written testimony for the record by labor, business, and other interest groups. Workers may participate in standards development and may request evaluation of hazards by the National Institute of Occupational Safety and Health (NIOSH). The OSHA rule-making procedure often includes appointment of an advisory committee composed of labor and industry representatives with public meetings on the record.[10] Since OSHA relies heavily on unions for reports of violations and on management for voluntary compliance, both sides have considerable input into the enforcement process as well.

The standard-setting process reflects past as well as present negotiation. The great majority of OSHA standards were state standards and "consensus" standards created by private institutions, such as the American National Standards Institute and the National Fire Protection Association.[11] OSHA has proceeded more slowly in adopting new standards, in part due to the time required for negotiation of new standards, the controversy they generate, and the difficulty in determining the potential costs and benefits of new rules.

Given that workplace safety and wage compensation are determined in a competitive labor market, what need is there for government intervention in the contractual relations between workers and firms? Does health and safety regulation serve to promote or reduce efficiency in the labor market? One explanation is that OSHA serves to redistribute income. Mendeloff (1979, p. 29) finds that "local unions can use OSHA as a lever to increase their bargaining power," primarily by obtaining wage concessions from not reporting violations to OSHA, but also by achieving safety and health improvements not attainable through collective bargaining. There appears to be a belief that government-imposed regulations will have less significant effects on employment at a particular firm if they are imposed on all firms within an industry or across industries. To examine whether health and safety regulations go beyond redistributive effects, *internalities* in the workplace are now considered.

The first issue that arises is why workers and firms cannot negotiate complete contingent contracts. Ideally, employment contracts should contain not just a risk premium for employment hazards but also, if workers are risk averse, a state contingent payment schedule reflecting potential accidents and harm to the workers. Risk premiums do exist in many contracts in the form of hazard pay and pay scales that depend either explicitly or implicitly on job characteristics.[12] However, the high costs of collective contract negotiation may limit the adjustment of contractual terms. Further, lack of information about the risks of accidents and potential occupational disease make fully contingent contracts costly and in some cases unattainable. Opportunities for worker health insurance are available to workers and management through private insurance. Workers' compensation programs provide medical expenses and coverage of lost income to disabled workers, although evidence suggests that the effectiveness of this coverage has been limited.[13]

An absence of complete contingent contracts and limited insurance coverage for illness and lost wages suggest a need for assignment of liability by a tort system. However, the effectiveness of the tort system is constrained by workers' compensation programs that rule out suits against employers. According to the Office of Technology Assessment (1985), this has caused the "spectacular growth" in "third-party" suits against manufacturers and suppliers of equipment and products used by employees. Thus, in the presence of workers' compensation programs, the tort system fails to provide a suitable replacement for complete contingent contracts. This implies incentives for taking care by workers and their employers will be inadequate.

There is evidence that the workers' compensation system does not provide sufficient incentives to the firm to take care in avoiding accidents. Russell (1974) has found that individual firms' insurance premiums are not fully adjusted for their accident rates and compensation costs. The risk-sharing aspects of workers' compensation are emphasized at the cost of *moral hazard*. Employers may free-ride on workers' compensation by reducing expenditures that might improve worker health and safety. The Office of Technology Assessment (1985) concludes that "changes in the system that lead to a greater proportion of the costs of illnesses and injuries being paid by employers would enhance the prevention incentives of workers' compensation." Imperfect observation of worker and employer care levels has been advanced as an argument for regulation of workplace safety; see, for example, Diamond (1977) and Nichols and Zeckhauser (1977). Rea (1981) argues that moral hazard problems do not apply only to private insurance providers, but extend to a workers' compensation board or a government insurance agency. He observes that mandatory public insurance or government regulation of safety may result in reduced worker safety precautions.[14]

To correct the lack of incentives to take care provided by workers' compensation, Smith (1976) suggests imposition of an "injury tax." Smith (1976) argues that an injury tax is preferable to regulation by health and safety standards, since it would allow flexibility of response by employers, who could choose the least-cost approach to reducing injuries, and since employers could address all injuries rather than physical hazards. Although taxes generally dominate standards in terms of incentives, this proposal seems fundamentally flawed. The harm caused to employees is an *internality*; there should generally be no external social costs. In environmental regulation, the effluent tax reflects the marginal social cost of external damages imposed on society by the firm. If the costs of injury are confined to the worker, the injury tax has the worker and firm taken together paying twice for the same injury. If some compensating variation in wages is present, the employer pays for risks through wages and through the injury tax. Excessive employer care may result, yielding higher prices and, in some cases, lower employment. Workers may respond to risk reduction with reduced care.

The injury tax may be better suited to enforcing safety regulations, since hazards that cause injury are more easily monitored than the long-term health of workers. Furthermore, in the case of occupational disease, prevention is a desirable objective. Bacow (1980, pp. 53–54) observes that the injury tax, besides being politically infeasible, involves high monitoring costs if exposure to hazardous substances is to be taxed. Further, Bacow finds that if the firm is only concerned with expected fines, that is, the probability of injury times the tax, large penalties will be required to induce care, as is the case with the current system of OSHA fines. Implementation of a system of large fines would be constrained, however, by limited liability and regulatory preference for firm viability. Viscusi (1983, p. 160) suggests that penalties linked to health risk levels be imposed in the place of standards but restricts this to situations in which the market- and government-supplied risk information fail to yield efficient risk levels. Penalties do provide a more appealing enforcement system than standards. For most other situations, an improvement in the workers' compensation system, particularly through premiums based on risk or merit-rating,[15] is a more desirable policy.

The *moral hazard* problems associated with workers' compensation are further complicated by *adverse selection problems* in the labor market. Employees lack information about workplace safety and long-term health risks, information that is often available to employers. Employers have incentive to conceal or understate health risks to avoid the wage compensation these risks would require. The interviews conducted by Nelkin and Brown (1984) make it apparent that many workers have little conception of the risks they face in the workplace and no precise understanding of the long-term health implications of exposure to hazardous chemicals. This appears to be an area in which bounded rationality may have disastrous implications. On the other hand, Viscusi (1979) finds evidence that suggest that workers learn about the workplace hazards while on the job. Viscusi (1979, pp. 218–219) finds that within industries "the injury rate is an important determinant of the aggregate quit rate," and that for individual workers "[s]trong quit intention probabilities are more than doubled if the worker views his job as hazardous." Viscusi (1979, 1983) finds support for the hypothesis of compensating wage differentials despite the observation that workers have little information on health hazards before taking the job.

The functioning of the labor market could possibly be improved by government educational programs for workers and disclosure require-ments for employers. There are two problems with government provision of information in this market. This type of information production prom-ises to be costly. The sheer volume of health and safety information in-volved may complicate dissemination and reduce usefulness to workers. Also, there is much that is not known regarding long-term health risks. Additional scientific research must be performed for many industrial hazards and health risks. The high cost of information gathering and the limited scientific knowledge available to regulators and health pro-fessionals is stressed by Lave (1981). Lave (1981) identifies a spectrum of decision frameworks for policymakers in health and safety that vary in terms of the data and analysis required of regulators. Regulatory options include reliance on the market, outright bans of hazardous substances, identifying risk trade-offs from specific regulations, and benefit-cost analysis.

The benefits of care in terms of accident reduction and avoidance of illness are generally unknown. The Congressional Office of Technology Assessment (1985) finds, for example, that educational programs for workers and safety professionals have received little evaluation. The report also finds that information that is available is often inaccessible, such as information provided by NIOSH.

Against this background, it is perhaps not overly surprising that regu-lators have relied on a standards-based approach.[16] This approach has been criticized on a number of grounds. Standards are generally arbitrary and are often applied across the board with little regard for differing costs of care across firms or even across industries. Safety standards are usually engineering requirements that specify firm technology and inputs without focusing on effectiveness or "performance."[17] Standards have focused on employer care and have often neglected personal protective equipment or training of employees. It is generally observed that OSHA has devoted little attention to benefit-cost comparisons in designing or enforcing health and safety standards.[18] It is evident that OSHA should decrease its emphasis on preventing injury through standards-based regulation and focus its efforts on long-term health risks, where information is not as readily available to market participants. Excessive attention to short-term safety and injuries is costly in terms of both regulatory resources and employer compliance. The opportunity costs of this type of policy are undoubtedly a reduction in efforts to abate the long-term risks of occupational disease.

Throughout this book, I have emphasized that regulation is in many ways a bargaining process between market participants. An important suggestion for policy reform in workplace health and safety regulation due to Bacow (1980) accords closely with this view. Bacow recommends increased attention to health and safety in collective bargaining between organized labor and management; see also Bureau of National Affairs (1971). The proposal applies to heavily unionized industries, such as steel and automobiles, since little more than a quarter of U.S. workers are union members. Bacow observes that many OSHA functions are performed better by unions—union health and safety representatives are better at monitoring and enforcing OSHA regulations than infrequent OSHA inspections; some health and safety issues lend themselves to arbitration procedures; and worker care may be improved through union training programs. Bacow (1980, pp. 103–121) proposes a number of measures that OSHA can use to increase the effectiveness of collective bargaining in achieving regulatory objectives. These include the following: "Train health and safety stewards; Exempt workplaces from OSHA inspection; Respond quickly to union complaints; Exempt unions from liability, fund industry morbidity and mortality studies; Expand health-hazard evaluation program; Expand right to refuse hazardous work; Give H & S training to arbitrators; Undertake cost of H & S arbitration, Integrate H & S training into apprenticeship programs." In chapter 2 and elsewhere I have emphasized that regulatory agencies provide a non-market forum for negotiation and arbitration between contending market participants. For unionized industries, a private mechanism is in place for negotiation of health and safety issues in conjunction with pay and benefits. This mechanism may be used to reduce exclusive reliance on government-administered negotiation while taking advantage of the superior information of interested parties. It should be emphasized that the measures taken to enhance collective bargaining will have a side effect. Subsidizing union activities or strengthening their hand in negotiation, will create incentives for increased expansion and formation of unions. Since unions exercise some monopoly power, the policy will certainly entail welfare losses in the absence of countervailing market power of employers. These efficiency costs must be balanced against possible improvements in regulatory effectiveness.

14.2   Liability Rules

Assignment of liability through tort law is an alternative to administrative regulation of product and workplace safety. This section explores the efficiency properties of competitive markets under alternative liability regimes. The neutrality of liability assignment under full information is shown to hold with homogeneous consumers and firms. With heterogeneous agents, due care standards are subject to the same criticisms leveled at regulatory standards.

Tort law is the subject of a large literature in law and economics, which is not reviewed here. The incentive effects of legal rules on the care levels of injurers and victims are studied by McKean (1970), Brown (1973, 1974), Diamond (1973a, b), Green (1976), Hamada (1976), Epple and Raviv (1978), Shavell (1980b), Simon (1981), Landes and Posner (1985), and many others.[19] The discussion in this section is most similar to that of Shavell (1980b).

14.2.1   The Coase Theorem and the Market

The Coase theorem provides an important guide to the incentive effects of assignment of liability. In a *bilateral* negotiation between a potential injurer and victim, the assignment of liability to the injurer (strict liability) or to the victim (no liability) should not affect the efficiency of bargaining over an associated transaction or contract, at least in the absence of transaction costs. This is practically a tautology in that bargaining must yield efficient allocation for the parties if the transaction is voluntary. In the absence of specific institutional constraints, the terms of the contract will reflect the potential costs or benefits implicit in any assignment of liability for damages. The assignment of legal rights may therefore be made arbitrarily.

Does the conclusion that assignment of liability is arbitrary in the absence of transaction costs carry over to a market setting? The analysis of the contractual relation suggests that the market equilibrium may be unaffected by the choice of a liability rule. Furthermore, given the efficient operation of a system of privately enforced, judicially administered rights, the analysis suggests that administrative regulation is unnecessary. Unless regulation also performs efficiently and costs less to administer, it may be undesirable to regulate product quality and safety. We now examine the assignment of legal rights under alternative assumptions. The consequences of alternative legal entitlements are shown to differ considerably. The efficiency of strict liability fails to hold when the care level of victims plays a role in determining the extent of likelihood of harm. The effectiveness of negligence and strict liability with a defense of contributory negligence fails in the presence of heterogeneous consumers and firms. Finally, the effectiveness of no liability depends on efficiency of the market equilibrium and thus requires constant returns to scale.

14.2.2 Liability and Negligence with Homogeneous Consumers and Firms

Consider a product whose possible failure imposes an expected monetary loss on the representative consumer, $L(q, z)$, as a function of the quantity purchased, q, and the care level chosen by the representative producer, z. The form of the loss function is sufficiently general to allow for scale effects of consumption on losses; see Marino (1986). Also, the producer's care level may affect the *amount* and *likelihood* of loss. For example, a given level of damages $l(q, z)$ can occur with probability $\eta(z)$ and the product can function without loss with probability $(1 - \eta(z))$. Let L be increasing and convex in q and decreasing and convex in z. The firm's costs of production, $C = C(q, z)$, are assumed to be increasing and convex in output and care. Firms and consumers are assumed to be risk neutral. Both risk neutrality and risk aversion for consumers are considered. Consumer net benefits are represented by $V = u(q) - L(q, z)$ for the risk neutral case.

The *social optimum* is obtained by maximizing welfare, $W(q, z) \equiv u(q) - L(q, z) - C(q, z)$, over output and the producer's care level. These solve the first-order conditions[20]

$$u'(q^*) - L_q(q^*, z^*) - C_q(q^*, z^*) = 0, \tag{14.2.1}$$

$$-L_z(q^*, z^*) - C_z(q^*, z^*) = 0. \tag{14.2.2}$$

As in a model of externalities, the marginal value of consuming the good net of marginal expected damages equals marginal production costs. The marginal reduction in damages due to the producer taking care is set

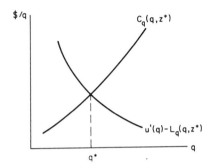

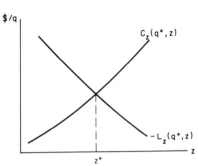

Figure 14.2.1
Socially optimal output q.

Figure 14.2.2
Socially optimal producer care z.

equal to the marginal costs of care. These conditions are illustrated in figures 14.2.1 and 14.2.2.

The Coase theorem has been discussed by many in the context of products liability. In the absence of transaction costs, it is evident that regardless of the assignment of liability for damages, a risk neutral consumer and firm will negotiate an output and care level equal to the socially optimal quantities (q^*, z^*). Further, total payments R will take values in the interval $C(q^*, z^*) \leq R \leq u(q^*) - L(q^*, z^*)$ to assure that the consumer and firm receive gains from trade.

The Coasian bargaining analysis extends to a market setting with a fixed market structure and full information. We review Shavell's (1980b) analysis of this problem. Under strict liability, the firm bears all monetary losses and the market price satisfies $u'(q^*) = p = C_q(q^*, z^*) + L_q(q^*, z^*)$, while firms choose the optimal care level, $-L_z(q^*, z^*) = C_z(q^*, z^*)$. The firm "internalizes" the consumer's damages in its production decisions. An alternative legal regime is negligence with a due care standard equal to z^*. If the firm chooses $z \geq z^*$, it is not liable for any damages faced by the consumer. The firm chooses the minimal care level required, $z = z^*$. The market equilibrium price is lower, reflecting the reduction in consumer willingness to pay due to marginal damages, $u'(q^*) - L_q(q^*, z^*) = p = C_q(q^*, z^*)$, and the optimal output is produced. Finally, in the case of consumer liability, that is, no liability on the part of the producer, competition between firms will cause them to choose a uniform care level equal to the socially optimal level. The argument requires costs to have the form $C(q, z) = c(z)q$. Then consider two market segments, one offering a good of quality z' at price $p' = c(z')$ and another with optimal quality z^* and price $p^* = c(z^*)$. Then, all consumers will shop in the market in which producers choose an optimal care level, since

$$u(q^*) - c(z^*)q^* - L(q^*, z^*) \geq u(q') - c(z')q' - L(q', z'),$$

for all q', z'. Then, it follows that

$$u(q^*) - p^*q^* - L(q^*, z^*) \geq u(q') - p'q' - L(q', z'),$$

where $q^* = q(p^*, z^*)$, $q' = q(p', z')$, and $q(p, z)$ solves $u'(q) - L(q, z) = p$. For general cost functions, the preceding argument may not hold, since the competitive market mechanism need not force producers to select the desired care level. With increasing marginal costs of production for example, multiple products may be offered at varying quality and price levels. The example with constant marginal costs yields an optimal allocation since the price reveals the average costs of care, $c(z) = C/q$, as well as the marginal costs of production, C_q. In the long run, average and marginal costs should tend toward equality, with small firms engaged in free entry competition. The following is widely known; see, for example, Rosen (1974) and Shavell (1980b):

PROPOSITION 14.2.1   *Given full information, the competitive market attains the socially optimal output and product quality level under strict liability, under negligence, and if $C(q, z)/q = C_q(q, z)$, under no liability as well.*

Thus, internalities do not occur in a competitive setting under full information regardless of the legal remedy for harm to consumers resulting from the products they purchase. As long as some assignment of legal rights exists, the market equilibrium price or contract terms adjust to reflect the net expected value of the product, thus leading to a socially optimal outcome.

The care taken by the *consumer* in using the product or by the *worker* in avoiding workplace accidents usually has a significant effect on expected damages from product failure. The degree of caution exercised by a motorist in driving a car or by a patient in following a doctor's instructions for taking a drug may effect the extent and likelihood of harm. Let x be the potential victim's care level. The individual has disutility from taking care, $u_x(q, x) < 0$. The social optimum (q^*, z^*, x^*) is obtained by adding the condition

$$u_x(q^*, x^*) - L_x(q^*, z^*, x^*) = 0 \tag{14.2.3}$$

to equations (14.2.1) and (14.2.2). Where the victim's care plays a significant role, strict liability is no longer an efficient rule, as there are no incentives for the victim to take care. If the injurer and victim *bargain* over output and care levels, then strict liability, or any other assignment of liability, will be efficient. However, in a market setting, it is generally assumed that consumers "shop" across firms but that firms cannot monitor consumer use of their product in advance. Thus, there is an implicit asymmetry of information in the present market model. Consumers have complete information about the firm's care in producing a reliable product. Firms, on the other hand, have no direct mechanism for ensuring compliance with standards of care by consumers. If the rule of strict liability is modified to allow the firm a defense of *contributory negligence*, then the efficiency of strict liability is restored. By establishing a standard of due care equal to x^*, and requiring that consumers meet this standard to recover damages, consumers will select a due care level at x^*, and the market equilibrium will be socially optimal. In fact, care levels (z^*, x^*) constitute a Nash equilibrium. The following result is standard; for additional discussion, see Shavell (1980).

PROPOSITION 14.2.2   *Given full information, the competitive market attains the socially optimal output and product quality level under strict liability with a defense of contributory negligence, under negligence, and if $C(q, z)/q = C_q(q, z)$, under no liability as well. The rule of strict liability does not yield a social optimum since consumers choose not to take care.*

The issue of contributory negligence has important parallels in environmental pollution and nuisance law. If the polluter is assigned liability for damages, there may be incentives for pollutees to become victims by choice even if pollutees are the least-cost avoiders of pollution. Wittman (1980) observes that the common law doctrine of "coming to the nuisance" gives property rights to the party who was there first (either victim or injurer) on the "reasonable" presumption that the new entrant is the least-cost avoider, although this need not always be the case. The object is to establish precedents to promote "efficient behavior in the future"; see Wittman (1980).

A similar issue arises in products liability. We wish to discourage consumers from purchasing unsafe products and workers from working at unsafe jobs if efficiency is better served by their avoiding harm. In the present context, this corresponds to creating incentives for the selection of the optimal level of due care by consumers and workers. If the firm assumes full liability for harm, then as observed above, the victim's care level will be inefficiently low. Wittman (1981) suggests an alternative approach to liability when the care of victims can reduce expected damages, called *marginal cost liability*, which takes the victim's prevention costs x into account.

In the market model, let the firm's costs have the form $C(q, z) = C(q) + z$, and let consumer net benefits have the form $u(q, x) = u(q) - x$. Let $x(q, z)$ represent the victim's care level, which equates the marginal cost of care to the marginal reduction in expected losses,

$$-L_x(q, z, x(q, z)) = 1. \tag{14.2.4}$$

Then, Wittman (1981) defines *strict liability* as requiring the injurer to compensate the victim for both losses $L(q, z, x(q, z))$ *and* "reasonable" avoidance costs $x = x(q, z)$. The firm's profit is then

$$\pi = pq - C(q) - z - L(q, z, x(q, z)) - x(q, z). \tag{14.2.5}$$

From the consumer's problem, $p = u'(q)$. The firm's profit is maximized by choosing output and care such that

$$p - C'(q) - L_q(q, z, x(q, z)) - (L_x(q, z, x(q, z)) - 1)\frac{\partial x(q, z)}{\partial q} = 0, \tag{14.2.6}$$

$$-1 - L_z(q, z, x(q, z)) - (L_x(q, z, x(q, z)) - 1)\frac{\partial x(q, z)}{\partial z} = 0. \tag{14.2.7}$$

Since he is compensated up to $x = x(q, z)$, the consumer will choose exactly this level of care. From the definition of the schedule $x(q, z)$ in equation (14.2.4) and $p = u'(q)$, it is apparent that the social optimum (q^*, x^*, z^*) is attained.

PROPOSITION 14.2.3   *Given full information, the competitive market attains the social optimum under strict liability if the victim's prevention costs are included in damages.*

14.2.3   Negligence with Heterogeneous Consumers and Firms

The strong efficiency properties of alternative forms of liability obtained above are standard in the law and economics literature. The efficiency of negligence and of strict liability with a defense of contributory negligence depend heavily on the notion of due care. The court verifies whether a standard of due care has been met. However, as anyone familiar with the application of arbitrary quotas in other regulatory settings can readily attest, arbitrary standards create inefficient outcomes. When there are differences across firms, it is inefficient to require all firms to supply the same degree of care. For example, social costs may not be minimized by requiring all retail stores to exercise the same degree of caution in terms of lighting, guard rails, stairs, etc. Newer stores might more easily meet a given technological standard than older stores. Similarly, given heterogeneous consumers, it may be undesirable to require the same degree of caution to be exercised by private car drivers and commercial truck drivers.

The crucial issue is whether the due care standard is to be generally applied across-the-board or whether the standard is set for each firm on a case-by-case basis. If the due care standard is set on a case-by-case basis, it is then an *ex post* standard. The court must determine whether a firm showed negligence or a consumer showed contributory negligence after an accident occurs. There are two significant problems with this approach. First, there may be considerable uncertainty on the part of consumers and firms regarding the degree of care expected of them by the legal system. How much care is sufficient to meet their personal due care standard? If due care is to be individually tailored and is to apply ex post, there appears to be no possibility for an individual to determine a priori what standard they must meet. Precedents may not apply to their particular situation, or precedents may be contradictory. The result is that individuals are utterly unable to predict what is due care and may as a result supply inefficiently high or low care levels.

The second problem with case-by-case due care standards is the high information costs imposed on the courts. The court must be able to observe the marginal costs of care of the injurer and marginal damage function of the victim to settle each injury claim. The optimal level of care for each individual must be calculated, and the actual care taken then must be determined and compared. This creates high costs of litigation in comparison with a strict liability rule.

The negligence formula of Judge Learned Hand finds a potential injurer to be negligent if expected costs of care are less than expected damages. Posner's (1986, p. 149) restatement of the Hand formula in marginal terms is that the marginal costs of care should equal the marginal reduction in expected damages at the due care standard. This is just the socially optimal cost minimization rule considered above, $-L_z(q^*, z^*) - C_x(q^*, z^*) = 0$. As Posner (1986, pp. 151–152) observes, however, because of high information costs, courts may apply a "reasonable-man standard" based on average accident avoidance costs. If injurers and victims foresee that reasonable man standards are applied in similar cases, an a priori due care standard then exists that applies across-the-board.

The difficulties associated with across-the-board pollution standards reappear in products liability. Suppose there are two firms with production costs $C^j(q^j, z^j)$, $j = 1, 2$. The money value of damages is just $L(q^j, z^j) = q^j l(z^j)$ for each good. The socially optimal values of $(q^j, z^j), j = 1, 2$, must satisfy

$$u'(q^{1*} + q^{2*}) = l(z^{j*}) + C_q^j(q^{j*}, z^{j*}), \qquad j = 1, 2, \tag{14.2.8}$$

$$-q^{j*} l'(z^{j*}) = C_z^j(q^{j*}, z^{j*}), \qquad j = 1, 2. \tag{14.2.9}$$

Suppose that given q^{j*}, $j = 1, 2$, $C_z^1(q^{1*}, z)/q^{1*}$ exceeds $C_z^2(q^{2*}, z)/q^{2*}$ for all $z > 0$. Then the socially optimal levels of care are given by z^{1*}, z^{2*} in figure 14.2.3. Suppose that a reasonable man standard of care is applied to the industry by the courts that is based on an average of the costs of care. The additional costs of increasing firm 1's care level will outweigh the cost savings to firm 2 from reducing care. Thus, there will be an increase in the total costs of care. Further, the market allocation of output between the two firms will change, reflecting the effect of care on marginal production costs. This will create additional welfare losses.

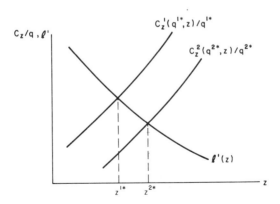

Figure 14.2.3
Optimal care levels with heterogeneous firms.

The analysis is much the same for the case of two consumers, $i = 1, 2$, given the rule of strict liability with a defense of contributory negligence. Consumers may be expected to differ in terms of money value of damages and disutility of taking care, $u^i(q^i) - L^i(q^i, z, x^i), i = 1, 2$. The social optimum is then

$$u^i_{q^i}(q^{i*}, x^{i*}) - L^i(q^{i*}, z^*, x^{i*}) = C_q(q^{1*} + q^{2*}, z^*), \qquad i = 1, 2, \qquad (14.2.10)$$

$$u^i_{x^i}(q^{i*}, x^{i*}) - L^i_{x^i}(q^{i*}, z^*, x^{i*}) = 0, \qquad i = 1, 2, \qquad (14.2.11)$$

$$-L^1_z(q^{1*}, z^*, x^{1*}) - L^2_z(q^{2*}, z^*, x^{2*}) = C_z(q^{1*} + q^{2*}, z^*). \qquad (14.2.12)$$

Imposing a reasonable man standard on consumer behavior will not only distort consumer care levels but will also lead to inefficient allocation of output and inefficient producer care levels as well.

It is reasonable to expect that high costs of obtaining information and the additional costs of litigation will lead courts toward application of reasonable man standards with some adjustments for exceptional cases. The argument given above suggests that inefficiency is a likely consequence of negligence-based liability rules.

14.3 Entry Barriers

It is evident that if market power creates incentives for reduced output supply, a monopolist may not select optimal levels of care in avoiding damage to customers. Suppose that entry barriers, such as sunk costs, exist, and that a single firm chooses output q and care z. A similar situation has been examined in great detail in the literature on product quality.[21] This section applies the analysis of product quality under monopoly to examine the level of care supplied by a monopoly under alternative liability rules.

Under strict liability, the monopolist chooses output and care to maximize profit $\Pi(q, z) = pq - L(q, z) - C(q, z)$,

$$p + q^M(\partial p / \partial q) - L_q(q^M, z^M) - C_q(q^M, z^M) = 0, \qquad (14.3.1)$$

$$-L_z(q^M, z^M) - C_z(q^M, z^M) = 0, \qquad (14.3.2)$$

where $p = u'(q)$. Assume that the second-order conditions for a global maximum hold. The degree of care taken by a monopolist will depend, as is usual in this type of comparative statics analysis, on the cross-effects of care and output on the monopolist's costs. The analysis is quite similar to that of Sheshinski (1976) for product quality; see also Spence (1975).

PROPOSITION 14.3.1   *Under strict liability, the following hold:* (i) *The monopoly output is less than the optimal output,* $q^M < q^*$. (ii) *If* $\partial(L_z/C_z)/\partial q = 0$, $z^M = z^*$. (iii) *If* $\partial(L_z/C_z)/\partial q \neq 0$, *then for* $(L_{zq} + C_{zq}) > 0$, $((L_{zq} + C_{zq}) < 0)$, *the monopolist provides more (less) care than is optimal,* $z^M > z^*(z^M < z^*)$.

To establish proposition 14.3.1, observe first from equations (14.2.2) and (14.3.2) that $W_z(q, z) = \Pi_z(q, z)$. If $\partial(L_z/C_z)/\partial q = 0$, then z^M and z^* are determined independently of q. If $\partial(L_z/C_z)/\partial q \neq 0$, then in the (z, q) quadrant, $W_z = \Pi_z = 0$ is downward (upward) sloping as $(L_{zq} + C_{zq}) > 0$ $((L_{zq} + C_{zq}) < 0)$. Also, $W_q = 0$ and $\Pi_q = 0$ are downward (upward) sloping as $(L_{zq} + C_{zq}) > 0$ $((L_{zq} + C_{zq}) < 0)$. Further, given the second-order conditions for the problems of the social optimum and monopoly, the slope of $W_z = \Pi_z$ is less than (greater than) $W_q = 0$ and $\Pi_q = 0$ as $(L_{zq} + C_{zq}) > 0$ $((L_{zq} + C_{zq}) < 0)$. By standard arguments, $\Pi_q = 0$ lies below $W_q = 0$ for all z. These relations are represented in figures 14.3.1 and 14.3.2.

The lower output supplied by a monopolist reduces the expected damages from product failure. This reduces the monopolist's liability and may lead to more or less than optimal care levels. The fact that a monopolist devotes less care and produces a more hazardous product is not entirely bad since the reduced sales to consumers lower expected accidents. On the other hand, if the monopolist supplies more care than is optimal, this also entails welfare losses since consumers purchase a product that is more reliable but more expensive than is optimal.

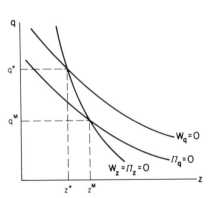

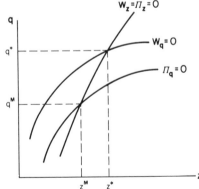

Figure 14.3.1
The monopolist provides excessive care if $(L_{zq} + C_{zq}) > 0$.

Figure 14.3.2
The monopolist provides insufficient care if $(L_{zq} + C_{zq}) < 0$.

It is not difficult to conceive of situations in which there are cost complementarities between output and care. If producing more goods or better quality goods involves a public input, such as management supervision or a common computer facility, then $C_{zq} \leq 0$ might be observed. Assuming as before that $L_{qz} < 0$, then the monopolist supplies *less* care than is optimal. The lower output produced by a monopolist raises the marginal costs of care while reducing the marginal expected damages avoided by increased care. In this case the monopolist reduces his liability by selling fewer goods rather than by producing goods of higher quality.

In the products liability literature, we often find $\partial(L_z/C_z)/\partial q = 0$. For example, Shavell (1980b) assumes $L(q, z) = ql(z)$ and $C(q, z) = qc(z)$, i.e., no scale effects in either the damage or cost functions. Epple and Raviv (1978) consider a special case of this model in which a product may fail with probability ρ and cause a per unit loss l. Care may reduce either the likelihood or severity of loss, $L(q, z) = ql(z)\rho(z)$. We can generalize to allow for scale effects as well, $L(q, z) = q^2 l(z)$ and $C(q, z) = q^2 c(z)$. In all of these problems, producer care is invariant with respect to market structure. However, the analysis in proposition 14.3.1 shows that this invariance is a very special case.

Under negligence, the monopolist equates marginal revenue to marginal cost, $\Pi_q(q, \bar{z}) = 0$, given a due care standard $\bar{z}$, where inverse demand is given by $p(q, z) = u'(q) - L_q(q, z)$. A problem arises regarding the choice of the due care standard. Let $q^M(\bar{z})$ be the monopolist's output as a function of the due care standard, $\Pi_q(q^M(\bar{z}), \bar{z}) = 0$. Assume that the second-order sufficient condition is satisfied for all z, $\Pi_{qq} < 0$. Also, let output and producer care be profit substitutes, $\Pi_{qz} < 0$. Then the monopolist's output is decreasing in the due care standard, $\partial q^M(z)/\partial z = -\Pi_{qz}/\Pi_{qq} < 0$. An excessively stringent care level will further lower the monopoly output level. It is no longer desirable to set a due care standard equal to the unconstrained optimal level z^*. Rather, a constrained due care standard $\bar{z}^M$ must be chosen to maximize social welfare subject to the presence of monopoly power, $W = W(q^M(z), z)$. The constrained due care standard, $\bar{z}^*$, solves

$$W_z(q^M(\bar{z}^*), \bar{z}^*)/W_q(q^M(\bar{z}^*), \bar{z}^*) = -\partial q^M(\bar{z}^*)/\partial z. \tag{14.3.3}$$

The marginal rate of substitution between quality and output for the social welfare measure is set equal to the marginal effect of the due care standard on the monopolist's output. It may be necessary to set the constrained due care standard above or below the social optimum. Sheshinski (1976) discusses a similar situation in the context of product quality regulation.

Finally, under no liability, the monopolist chooses both output and care such that $\Pi_q(q, z) = 0$ and $\Pi_z(q, z) = 0$, where $p(q; z) = u'(q) - L_q(q, z)$. This case parallels the quality literature; see Sheshinski (1976) and others. There it is shown that output and product quality may be greater or less than the social optimum, depending on the form of inverse demand and production cost functions.

14.4   Contestable Markets and Producer Care

The preceding analysis of products liability in the presence of entry barriers demonstrates the effects of monopoly power on product safety. The assignment of liability under tort law affects the distribution of economic rents between injurer and victim and alters incentives for the producer to take care. The monopolist may supply a level of care above or below the socially optimal level, depending on the form of the expected loss function and the production cost function. Consumers are offered a price-quality package that is inferior to the competitive price-quality package even if the monopolist's product is of higher quality.

The imperfect incentives to take care are due to market power, not to production by a single firm. This section reexamines monopoly prices and quality in a contestable market. It is shown that in the absence of entry barriers, potential competition creates incentives for improvements in product quality and safety. Since the sustainable monopoly price is equal to average costs, output levels are second-best optimal. Thus, optimal producer care levels must be redefined relative to second-best output levels. It is shown that in contestable markets with full information about producer care levels, the second-best optimum is attained.

14.4.1   Strict Liability

Assume that production costs $C(q, z)$ exhibit sufficient scale economies for production of the total output by a single firm to be efficient.[22] Let average costs $C(q, z)/q$ be downward sloping in q for all z. Let $Q(p, z)$ represent consumer demand for a product priced at p when the firm's care level is z. Assume as before that there is a representative consumer[23] with net benefits $u(q) - L(q, z)$.

Under *strict liability*, the producer's total costs are $L(q, z) + C(q, z)$.

Suppose that damages plus production costs exhibit output scale effects such that average total cost $(L(q, z) + C(q, z))/q$ falls over an initial range of outputs. Thus, production economies overcome increasing average damages in this range. A sustainable monopoly equilibrium must be defined relative to the liability rule.

Definition 14.4.1   A price, output, and care level (p^*, q^*, z^*) constitutes a *sustainable monopoly equilibrium under strict liability* if for all (p^e, q^e, z^e)

i. $p^* q^* - L(q^*, z^*) - C(q^*, z^*) \geq 0$,

ii. $p^e q^e \leq L(q^e, z^e) + C(q^e, z^e)$, for

iii. $q^e \leq Q(p^e), p^e \leq p^*$.

The definition states that the monopolist must break even. An entrant may choose any output and care level subject to the upper limit on output imposed by market demand. Any price that is lower than the incumbent's yields losses for the new entrant.

Due to the presence of economies of scale, a *second best optimum* such that revenues cover both production costs and the firm's liability for damages must be defined. Thus, choose p, z to maximize $[u(Q(p)) - pQ(p)]$ such that

$$pQ(p) - L(Q(p), z) - C(Q(p), z) \geq 0.$$

For any z, the second-best price satisfies the zero-profit constraint and the second-best care level minimizes total cost,

$$p = (L(Q(p), z) + C(Q(p), z))/Q(p), \tag{14.4.1}$$

$$-L_z(Q(p), z) - C_z(Q(p), z) = 0. \tag{14.4.2}$$

The second-best optimum under strict liability is given by $(\tilde{p}, \tilde{q}, \tilde{z})$, where $\tilde{p}$, $\tilde{z}$ solve (14.4.1) and (14.4.2) and $\tilde{q} = Q(\tilde{p})$. Assume that the second-best optimal output occurs in a region of increasing returns. This is represented in figure 14.4.1.

Begin by comparing the second-best optimum to the unconstrained social optimum defined by equations (14.2.1) and (14.2.2).

PROPOSITION 14.4.1   *Under strict liability, the following hold:*

i. *The second-best output is less than the optimal output,* $\tilde{q} < q^*$.

ii. *As* $(L_{zq} + C_{zq}) > 0$ $((L_{zq} + C_{zq}) < 0)$, *the second-best optimal care level is greater (less) than optimal,* $\tilde{z} > z^*$ $(\tilde{z} < z^*)$.

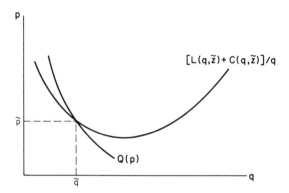

Figure 14.4.1
Sustainable monopoly with strict liability.

It is of interest to note the similarity to the monopoly solution. The proof is also similar to that given for proposition 14.3.1. One may rewrite equations (14.4.1) and (14.4.2) as $u'(\tilde{q}) = L(\tilde{q}, \tilde{z})/\tilde{q} + C(\tilde{q}, \tilde{z})/\tilde{q}$, and $-L_z(\tilde{q}, \tilde{z}) - C_z(\tilde{q}, \tilde{z}) = 0$, respectively. Comparing with equations (14.2.1) and (14.4.2) yields figures analogous to figure 14.3.1.

The crucial issue is the performance of the market relative to the second-best optimum. By standard arguments—see Baumol, Panzar, and Willig (1982)—the sustainable price must be an average cost price; see figure 14.4.1. Furthermore, the firm has incentive to minimize total cost over its care level, since only the firms that use inputs efficiently may remain in the market.

PROPOSITION 14.4.2   *Under strict liability, the sustainable monopoly equilibrium coincides with the second-best optimum* $(\tilde{p}, \tilde{q}, \tilde{z})$.

The result shows that monopoly need not imply a distortion in levels of care other than departures from the optimum due to linear pricing under economies of scale.

14.4.2   Negligence and No Liability

Under the negligence rule, consumers bear all losses from accidents if the firm meets the due care standard, $\bar{z}$. Thus, consumer demand, $Q(p, z)$, maximizes $u(q) - L(q, z)$. The definition of sustainability must be modified accordingly. The representative consumer is said to prefer a price, output, and care level (p', q', z') to another vector (p'', q'', z'') if he obtains greater net benefits, $u(q') - L(q', z') - p'q' > u(q'') - L(q'', z'') - p''q''$, where $q = Q(p, z)$.

Definition 14.4.2   A price, output, and care level (p^*, q^*, z^*) constitutes a *sustainable monopoly equilibrium under the negligence rule* if z^* and z^e are greater than or equal to $\bar{z}$, and

i. $p^*q^* - C(q^*, z^*) \geq 0$,

ii. $p^e q^e \leq C(q^e, z^e)$,

iii. $q^e \leq Q(p^e, z^e)$,

for all (p^e, q^e, z^e) that are preferred by the consumer to (p^*, q^*, z^*) and $q^* = Q(p^*, z^*)$.

The definition allows an entrant to offer consumers a higher-priced but safer product than that offered by the incumbent.

Assume that the due care standard, $\bar{z}$, is set at the second-best optimal level of care. For the problem to be tractable, assume away output scale effects in the damage function, $L(q, z) = ql(z)$. The analysis of the second best must be modified, since consumers suffer damages.

The second-best price and care level must maximize $[u(Q(p, z)) - L(Q(p, z), z) - pQ(p, z)]$ such that $pQ(p, z) - C(Q(p, z), z) \geq 0$. Let γ be the shadow price on the break-even constraint. Note that $u'(q) - L_q(q, z) - p = 0$, so that the first-order conditions reduce to

$$Q = \gamma[(p - C_q)(\partial Q/\partial p) + Q], \tag{14.4.3}$$

$$L_z = \gamma[(p - C_q)(\partial Q/\partial z) - C_z], \tag{14.4.4}$$

$$\gamma[pQ(p, z) - C(Q(p, z), z)] = 0, \qquad \gamma \geq 0. \tag{14.4.5}$$

From equation (14.4.3), $Q > 0$ implies that $\gamma > 0$. So, $p = C(Q(p, z), z)/Q(p, z)$. Note that $\partial Q/\partial p = 1/u''(Q)$ and $\partial Q/\partial z = L_{qz}/u''(Q)$, which implies the following

PROPOSITION 14.4.3   *Given $L(q, z) = ql(z)$, the second-best optimum under negligence and under no liability coincides with the second-best optimum under strict liability, $(\tilde{p}, \tilde{q}, \tilde{z})$.*

Now consider market performance under the negligence rule. It is evident that the only sustainable market equilibrium price equals average cost. Both entrants and incumbents will choose the minimum care level to avoid liability: the due care standard $\bar{z}$. Thus, under negligence with $\bar{z} = \tilde{z}$, the second-best optimum is attained.

Under no liability, definition 14.4.2 applies to the sustainable monopoly if one ignores the due care standard. Then, producer care levels are determined entirely by market forces. For any market equilibrium care level, entry requires $u'(q) - L_q(q, z) = p = C(q, z)/q$. Further, by the definition of sustainable monopoly equilibrium, there cannot be a welfare-improving price-quality package that breaks even. Thus, the market equilibrium (p, q, z) must maximize $u(q) - L(q, z) - pq$ subject to the nonnegative profits constraint, and the second-best optimum is again obtained. To summarize:

PROPOSITION 14.4.4   *Under negligence with a second-best due care level,* $\bar{z} = \tilde{z}$, *and under no liability, the sustainable monopoly equilibrium coincides with the second-best optimum,* $(\tilde{p}, \tilde{q}, \tilde{z})$.

The observation that the incumbent must offer consumers the optimal care level is similar to that of Shavell (1980b) and Rosen (1974) in a perfect competition setting. It seems reasonable to extend the approach to a perfectly contestable market. The second-best optimality of market equilibria under the alternative negligence rules implies that monopoly alone cannot justify regulation of product quality or safety. Product quality and safety are not necessarily determined by market structure. The producer chooses the second-best optimal level of care regardless of the legal liability rule. The threat of competitive entry provides sufficient incentives for the producer to take due care. These results have been obtained in a market with complete information. The market mechanism may not create incentive for firms to take sufficient care if product quality or workplace safety is imperfectly observable. This issue is the subject of the next chapter.

Notes

1. For an evaluation of auto safety regulations, see Peltzman (1975), MacAvoy (1979), and Arnould and Grabowski (1981).

2. For historical background on the Food, Drug and Cosmetic Act, see Peltzman (1974), Quirk (1980), Temin (1981), and Grabowski and Vernon (1983).

3. For a discussion of legislative oversight of the FDA, see Quirk (1980).

4. This passage is quoted in Grabowski and Vernon (1978, p. 287).

5. Detailed CPSC regulations for bicycles and swimming pool slides have been overturned by the courts. Meiners (1982, p. 295) notes that in the case of swimming pools, the CPSC

safety standards were found to be "ill-conceived and not supported by sufficient technical information or economic justifications."

6. Kelman (1980) notes an 1867 Massachusetts law creating a Department of Factory Inspection.

7. Interest groups include private health associations, such as the American Public Health Association (Kelman, 1980, p. 242). See Office of Technology Assessment (1985) and Bartel and Thomas (1985) for further discussion.

8. See Mendeloff (1979) for further discussion of state regulation.

9. Mendeloff (1979) reviews the debates and legislative history underlying the OSH Act.

10. See Kelman (1980, pp. 244–245).

11. According to Smith (1976, pp. 9–10), of the 4,400 interim standards announced by OSHA at its inception, 45% came from the private consensus organizations and the rest were already in place under the Walsh-Healey, Construction Safety and Longshoring Safety Acts. See also Mendeloff (1979, p. 36).

12. Mendeloff (1979, pp. 10–11) discusses the system of "job evaluation" that determines wages based partly on working conditions. He observes that compensating differentials may not clearly reflect risks due to positive correlation between promotion and reduction of risk and due to the observed "stickiness" of risk premiums over time.

13. Mendeloff (1979, p. 11) and Smith (1976, p. 81) note that state workers' compensation (WC) programs replaced less than half of lost wages in 1970.

14. Empirical studies confirm a positive relation between workers' compensation and accidents; see Chelius (1974, 1977) and Butler and Worrall (1983).

15. Viscusi (1980, 1983) provides two important studies of workplace safety. See Viscusi (1980, 1983) for a discussion of workers' compensation insurance and merit rating. Viscusi (1983, pp. 78–79) observes that adverse selection problems in the private insurance market justify mandatory workers' compensation programs, since a voluntary program would primarily attract high risk workers. However, he notes (1983, p. 183) that as workers' compensation programs are administered by the states, they are independent of federal risk regulation.

16. Bacow (1980, pp. 16–17) gives a discussion of the political preference for command and control regulation of health and safety.

17. For case studies of OSHA regulation of the aerospace and chemical industries and the vinyl chloride and cottondust cases, see Northrup et al. (1978). Mendeloff (1979), Viscusi (1983), and others discuss the superiority of performance standards as compared to engineering or design standards.

18. This may be due in large part to the imprecise wording of the OSH Act; see Page (1975).

19. See Landes and Posner (1985) for additional discussion and references. The Landes and Posner paper is in a special issue of the *Journal of Legal Studies* that is devoted to tort law reform.

20. Assume that second-order sufficient conditions for a global maximum hold,

$$u''(q) - L_{qq} - C_{qq} < 0, \qquad -(L_{zz} + C_{zz}) < 0,$$

and

$$-(u'' - L_{qq} - C_{qq})(L_{zz} + C_{zz}) - (L_{zq} + C_{zq})(L_{qz} + C_{qz}) > 0.$$

21. The effects of market power on the performance of products liability rules is studied by Epple and Raviv (1978) and Polinski and Rogerson (1983). Early references on product quality

include Levhari and Peles (1973), Spence (1975), Sheshinski (1976), Kihlstrom and Levhari (1977) and Dixit (1979b). Also note in this regard early literature on product durability—Levhari and Srinivasan (1969), Kleiman and Ophir (1966), Schmalensee (1970), Coase (1972), Swan (1970, 1971, 1980), Seiper and Swan (1972), Parks (1974), Kamien and Schwartz (1974), Gaskins (1974), Stokey (1981), Bulow (1982), and Kahn (1986).

22. See Marino (1986) for an analysis of the perfectly competitive industry.

23. Note that in a multiproduct setting, with cost complementarities across goods, the market may fail to attain the second-best optimum without additional restrictions; see chapter 6. The products liability rules thus may not yield second-best optimal care levels with multiproduct firms. The case of heterogeneous consumers is addressed in Spulber (1988b).

15 Internalities 2: Risk and Asymmetric Information

Public pressure for increased regulation of product quality and workplace safety has coincided with a reevaluation of the two principal social institutions that allocate the risks of injury and losses. Insurance markets have experienced "crises" associated with higher premiums and deductibles and selective, but often temporary, denial of coverage to corporations, services (physicians, schools), and individual consumers. At the same time, tort law reform has been the subject of both public and scholarly debate.[1] This chapter considers regulation of product quality and workplace safety with emphasis on efficient allocation of risk and decision making under asymmetric information. It seeks to determine a potential role for regulation given risk allocation by competitive insurance markets and assignment of liability under tort law. The transmission of information in the market is contrasted with public policy aimed at alleviating internalities.

Internalities have been examined, in chapter 14, in a deterministic, full information setting. The analysis did not identify a potential need for regulation to mitigate internalities in the areas of product quality and workplace safety. Legal liability rules were found sufficient to provide incentives for efficient levels of consumer and producer care. The competitive market generally creates incentives for efficient care levels that compensate for particular allocations of liability. A possible exception to the efficiency of the tort system stems from barriers to entry of producers. Distortions in output levels due to market power in turn lead to inefficient producer care levels. These care levels may be remedied through legal negligence rules or through standards-based regulation. However, public policy directed at reducing the barriers to entry would appear to be a more effective regulatory solution.

If product quality and workplace safety are not easily monitored or if the costs of care are not observable, Calabresi's (1970) suggestion to assign liability to the least-cost avoider of losses cannot be followed. Regulation may perform a useful function as a consequence of inefficiencies arising from costly contract contingencies, moral hazard, or adverse selection. The present chapter examines the underlying sources of internalities and the efficiency of liability rules and private contracts in competitive markets. Section 15.1 considers allocative efficiency under alternative liability rules when consumers are risk averse and purchase products that entail the possibility of losses. Internalities may arise as a consequence of costly contract contingencies, limited liability of producers, and imperfect insurance markets. Section 15.2 examines double moral hazard problems, which may arise in the design of mechanisms to promote consumer and producer care in accident avoidance. Section 15.3 considers double adverse selection problems, which arise when expected losses from product failure depend on unobservable exogenous consumer characteristics and product quality. Section 15.4 studies communication in the marketplace through signaling of private information and disclosure. Regulatory policies are evaluated and compared to market alternatives. The discussion in the present chapter is given in the context of product quality but may be easily extended to a discussion of workplace health and safety issues.

15.1   Risk and Insurance

How well do legal liability rules perform as a mechanism for risk allocation between injurers and victims? This question is of importance in a market where costly contract contingencies prevent optimal risk shifting between consumers and firms. The present section examines producer care and the allocation of risk from uncertain product quality where consumers are risk averse. Market allocations may fail to be efficient if producer liability is limited. The incentive properties of liability rules depend also on the contractual opportunities in private insurance markets. The incentive properties of third-party insurance are considered and are shown to depend on whether premiums reflect expected losses. Producers may be able to avoid taking due care through liability insurance or industry compensation funds. The ways in which product risks are allocated is seen to be an important determinant of product quality and allocative efficiency.

Consumer welfare is affected not only by the expected losses from product failure but also by the risks associated with potential accidents. Consumers are risk averse with concave utility $U(q, y)$ where y is a numeraire commodity and q is a consumption good that entails a random monetary loss L. Losses are observed after the product q is purchased. The consumer's residual income is then used to purchase the numeraire, $y = \omega - pq - L$, where p is the price of good q.[2]

The monetary loss, $L(q, z, \xi)$, depends on the quantity purchased by the consumer, q, the product quality or producer care level, z, and a random shock, ξ. It is assumed that the probability distribution of shocks ξ is known and that the sizes of the shocks are observable after they occur. These are very strong assumptions. There are serious difficulties in practice in estimating the likelihood of losses from product failure or accidents in the workplace. Various products or work-related activities may entail unanticipated or unknown health consequences. Considerable effort and expense may be required to obtain and improve estimates of product or workplace risks. In what follows, the effects of producer care are interpreted as reducing expected losses. A more general model than the present one should include producer and consumer efforts devoted to gathering and interpreting information about product risks. Producer care involves not only reducing product risk but also assessing the likelihood and magnitude of losses and the effectiveness of prevention efforts. In addition, losses may not be fully observable ex post. Health effects related to particular products or the workplace environment may be aggravated by other products and activities and idiosyncratic characteristics of the consumer or worker. The risks of product failure must therefore include uncertainty in ex post estimation of losses.

Losses, $L(q, z, \xi)$, are increasing in q, decreasing in z, and increasing in ξ. The shock ξ is commonly observed and has a cumulative distribution function $H(\cdot)$, $h(\xi) \equiv dH(\xi)/d\xi$, $\xi \in [0, \infty)$. As in the preceding chapter, denote expected losses by $L(q, z) \equiv \int_0^\infty L(q, z, \xi) \, dH(\xi)$.

Firms are risk neutral. Firms must choose their care level, z, before observing the shock ξ. This suggests that it may be desirable to shift the product safety risks from risk averse consumers to the firm. Firm profits are given by $\pi = \int_0^\infty R(\xi) \, dH(\xi) - C(q, z)$, where $R(\xi)$ is a state contingent transfer from consumers to the firm and $C(q, z)$ represents production costs.

The social optimum is presented as a benchmark case. Let social welfare be defined by a weighted sum of expected consumer utility and firm profits,

$$W = \int_0^\infty U(q, \omega - R(\xi) - L(q, z, \xi)) \, dH(\xi)$$

$$+ \gamma \left[\int_0^\infty R(\xi) \, dH(\xi) - C(q, z) \right]. \tag{15.1.1}$$

The first-order necessary conditions for q, z, and $R(\xi)$ that maximize social welfare are as follows:

$$\int_0^\infty [U(q, \omega - R - L) - U_y(q, \omega - R - L)L_q] \, dH(\xi) - \gamma C_q(q, z) = 0, \tag{15.1.2}$$

$$- \int_0^\infty U_y L_z \, dH(\xi) - \gamma C_z(q, z) = 0, \tag{15.1.3}$$

$$- U_y(q, \omega - R - L) h(\xi) + \gamma h(\xi) = 0. \tag{15.1.4}$$

From (15.1.4), the consumer's marginal utility of income is constant across states of the world, $U_y(q, \omega - R(\xi) - L(q, z, \xi)) = \gamma$, since risks are shifted to the firm. Thus, $R(\xi) + L(q, z, \xi) = P^*$ for all ξ, where P^* is a constant. From (15.1.2) and (15.1.3), the social optimum q^*, z^* is defined by

$$U_q(q^*, \omega - P^*)/U_y(q^*, \omega - P^*) - C_q(q^*, z^*) - L_q(q^*, z^*) = 0, \qquad (15.1.5)$$

$$-L_z(q^*, z^*) - C_z(q^*, z^*) = 0. \qquad (15.1.6)$$

Because the consumer is fully insured, the consumer's marginal rate of substitution equals marginal production costs plus marginal expected losses due to output, $C_q + L_q$. The marginal cost of care equals the marginal reduction in expected losses from product failure.

The alternative rules of strict liability and negligence as well as absence of liability (*caveat emptor*) have different implications for risk allocation. For a related analysis of liability rules under uncertainty, see Shavell (1982a). *Strict liability* acts as a complete contingent contract that shifts all risks to the producer. Given a product price p, the profit-maximizing producer chooses output and care such that

$$p = C_q(q, z) + L_q(q, z),$$

$$-L_z(q, z) - C_z(q, z) = 0.$$

The consumer equates his marginal rate of substitution to the product price, $U_q(q, \omega - pq)/U_y(q, \omega - pq) = p$. Thus, $q = q^*$, $z = z^*$, and $pq = P^*$. The competitive market attains the social optimum even with risk averse consumers. The strict liability rule optimally allocates risk without any explicit risk-sharing agreement. See Shavell (1982a) for a similar conclusion..

Consider market exchange when the rule of *negligence* with a due care standard of z^* applies. The firm will choose care just to meet the standard, and the consumer bears all of the risks. This results in a departure from the socially optimal output level. Similarly, if the producer is *not liable* for damages, the consumer must bear all of the risks of product failure. Both output and producer care may fail to be optimal in the absence of explicit risk-sharing arrangements.

In the absence of transaction costs, it should be possible for consumers and firms to negotiate a complete contingent contract such that the risks of damages from product failure are optimally allocated regardless of the assignment of liability for harm. If this is the case, the consumer will purchase full product insurance from the firm. It is easy to establish that the competitive market again yields socially optimal output and care levels. The insurance provided by the seller may be in the form of a guarantee or product warranty; see Heal (1977), Spence (1977b), and Epple and Raviv (1978). Product insurance provides a contingent contract between consumers and firms. If the producer is not liable for damages, the consumer has an incentive to purchase from the producer offering the best price-quality package, including optimal producer care and the best product insurance contract. Under full information, this will result in optimal output and care levels at the market equilibrium. As in the previous chapter, this requires average production costs to be minimized, $C(q, z)/q = C_q(q, z)$.

Contract contingencies are however costly to implement.[3] This may preclude negotiation of complete contingent agreements between the consumer and firm in the form of insurance or warranties. The consumer may not find third-party product insurance. The consumer will then adjust his purchases to reduce the risks of product failure, and the socially optimal output and producer care levels may not be attained. Producers may provide insufficient care, since they bear no risks, or producers may provide excessive care if significant reductions in consumer risk are required to sell the product. Suppose that a product either functions perfectly, with some probability $(1 - \eta)$, or fails completely, with some probability η.[4] There may be a cost to taking even this simple contingency into account. This will be sufficient to create inefficiencies under the negligence rule or in the absence of liability. This would argue for the application of the strict liability rule, although this rule is also subject to limitations.

Legal limits on liability will affect the incentive properties of the strict liability rule, which otherwise requires full coverage of the consumer's losses. The consequences of limited liability have been observed in a number of important class action suits. Two well-known examples are the cases against the asbestos industry and against manufacturers of intrauterine birth control devices. Suppose that for some states of the world, losses exceed the firm's assets, $A > 0$, which are recognized by the court as the firm's maximum liability.[5] How will the market perform with this restriction?

Consider the market equilibrium given limited producer liability. Define $\bar{\xi}(q, z)$ as the critical value of the random parameter at which losses equal the firm's assets, $L(q, z, \bar{\xi}(q, z)) = A$. Then, assuming that the consumer is unable to insure losses either through the insurance market or through contractual arrangement with the firm, consumer expected utility is given by $B(q, z)$,

$$B(q, z) \equiv U(q, \omega - pq)H(\bar{\xi}) + \int_{\underline{\xi}}^{\infty} U(q, y(q, z, \xi))h(\xi)\,d\xi, \tag{15.1.7}$$

where $y(q, z, \xi) \equiv \omega - pq + A - L(q, z, \xi)$. At the market equilibrium price and care level, consumer demand satisfies $B_q(q, z) = 0$,

$$U_q(q, \omega - pq)H(\bar{\xi}) + \int_{\underline{\xi}}^{\infty} [U_q(q, y(q, z, \xi)) - U_y(q, y(q, z, \xi))L_q]h(\xi)\,d\xi$$

$$= p[U_y(q, \omega - pq)H(\bar{\xi}) + \int_{\underline{\xi}}^{\infty} U_y(q, y(q, z, \xi))h(\xi)\,d\xi]. \tag{15.1.8}$$

For $\xi \geq \bar{\xi}$, by hypothesis consumer losses exceed the firm's liability, so that consumption of the numeraire is less than income minus expenditures, $y(q, z, \xi) \leq \omega - pq$. Suppose that the goods q and z are such that $U_{qy} > 0$. Then (15.1.8) implies that

$$U_q(q, \omega - pq)/U_y(q, \omega - pq) > p + \int_{\underline{\xi}}^{\infty} L_q(q, z, \xi)h(\xi)\,d\xi. \tag{15.1.9}$$

Thus, the consumer's marginal rate of substitution between consumption and net expenditures exceeds the price plus marginal expected losses in excess of firm liability.

The firm's expected profits are derived similarly,

$$\Pi(q, z) = pq - C(q, z) - \int_{\underline{\xi}}^{\infty} L(q, z, \xi)h(\xi)\,d\xi - A(1 - H(\bar{\xi})). \tag{15.1.10}$$

From the firm's profit maximization,

$$C_q(q, z) + L_q(q, z) = p + \int_{\underline{\xi}}^{\infty} L_q(q, z, \xi)h(\xi)\,d\xi, \tag{15.1.11}$$

$$-C_z(q, z) - L_z(q, z) = -\int_{\underline{\xi}}^{\infty} L_z(q, z, \xi)h(\xi)\,d\xi. \tag{15.1.12}$$

Let (p', q', z') represent the market equilibrium with limited liability. Expected marginal costs of output exceed the price, $C_q + L_q > p'$, and expected marginal costs of care are positive, $-(C_z + L_z) > 0$. Combining (15.1.9) and (15.1.11), the consumer's marginal rate of substitution evaluated at his net expenditure exceeds the expected marginal cost of output,

$$U_q(q', \omega - p'q')/U_y(q', \omega - p'q') > C_q(q', z') + L_q(q', z').$$

The market equilibrium (p', q', z') clearly departs from the social optimum as defined by (15.1.5) and (15.1.6).

Shavell (1984b) finds that limited liability may argue for safety regulations. If the firm is able to purchase liability insurance, and care is not directly observable at low cost, the firm may not have an incentive to take sufficient care. This issue is addressed in the next section. Shavell (1984b, pp. 369–370) observes that inability to pay for harm is a determinant of safety regulation in areas such as fire prevention, safety of food and drugs, and environmental and health-related damages for which "potential liability could exceed the assets of the firms involved (certainly of their employees), and the deterrent effect of tort law is therefore diluted."

The preceding discussion has established that consumers may face product risks if firms have limited liability. These product risks may not be insured by producers if contingent contracts are costly. Consumers may be able to reduce risks by purchasing insurance against product failure from third parties on competitive insurance markets. In practice, this is generally not possible for most products, although third-party service and warranty arrangements do exist for some major purchases, such as automobiles. If third-party insurance is available, it will generally not reflect the risks associated with specific products, but rather an average risk across a related set of products. This poses serious moral hazard problems, as producers will have little incentive to take care in the absence of either liability for damages or reductions in demand due to product risks. Thus, with third-party insurance, the market equilibrium will fail to yield efficient producer care levels. For now, the issue of producer moral hazard is put aside. Similarly, consumer care (contributory negligence) issues are ignored. These will be addressed in the next section.

Suppose that the consumer is able to obtain fair insurance against product risks.[6] Suppose also that the insurance coverage exactly reflects the expected losses associated with product failure.[7] Then, since consumption will affect the size of the premium, $L(q, z)$, purchases will be adjusted accordingly. Thus, demand, $q = q(p, z)$, solves

$$U_q(q, \omega - pq - L(q, z))/U_y(q, \omega - pq - L(q, z)) = p + L_q(q, z). \qquad (15.1.13)$$

The firm faces no risk and sets output in such a way that marginal cost equals price, $C_q(q, z) = p$. Therefore, the social optimum is attained.

The ability of consumers to obtain third-party insurance depends in part on the extent of competition in the insurance market. Suppose that there exist entry barriers in insurance so that consumers face market insurance that is not actuarily fair. The premium per unit of insurance is *loaded* by a factor $\lambda > 1$, so that the insurance premium equals λL for coverage of losses L. Epple and Raviv (1978) describe this situation in a two-state model. By well-known arguments, the consumer facing loaded premiums will not obtain full insurance.[8] The consumer bear part of the risk of product failure, which implies.

PROPOSITION 15.1.1   *If insurance markets are not competitive, and producers do not provide insurance, the market equilibrium under no liability and under the negligence rule fails to be efficient.*

The legal due care standard should generally not be set at the socially optimal level, z^*, in the case where consumers must self-insure. It may be necessary to require greater than optimal levels of care to reduce consumer risk in the second-best case with imperfect insurance markets.

An important feature of markets in which risks are associated with product quality and workplace safety is liability insurance for producers. Producers insure against potential damage claims that they may face. The important question this raises is what effect such insurance has on the incentives of producers to take care in reducing health and accident risks. It has already been shown that limited liability may reduce producer incentives to take care. If a producer is isolated from the effects of tort liability by liability insurance, this may also eliminate incentives for care. Damage payments compensate victims but have no deterrence effects. Abraham (1986) suggests that insurance pricing may not accurately reflect expected damages that are caused by individual firms and thus do not lead to sufficient care. He notes a move away from "occurrence" coverage, which relies on prediction of future damages, toward "claims-made" coverage, which reflects expected current liability costs as a result of past producer actions. It is evident that in the long run, competitive pressures in insurance markets should lead to premiums that reflect the anticipated damages caused by the individual producer purchasing insurance. This will cause producers to select optimal care levels in anticipation of future insurance costs. In practice, the process of adjusting premiums to individual producer care levels may take a long time. During this period of adjustment, care levels will be nonoptimal. Furthermore, standard moral hazard and adverse selection problems exist. The insurer may be unable to monitor the care level and product quality of individual producers accurately. Risk pooling will affect incentives for producer care.

Similar problems are associated with industry funds in which the fund compensates victims and firms reimburse the fund.[9] The effectiveness of such a fund in promoting efficient producer care depends on accurate reflection of risk in the payments made by individual producers. More serious incentive problems arise in connection with industry funds that are based on fixed contributions by individual firms. If the contributions of firms do not reflect producer care levels and anticipated losses, moral hazard problems will exist. Firms will have incentive to lower care levels and "free ride" on the compensation of victims provided by the fund.[10] The incentives for accident prevention from government-administered funds are even worse. McKean (1970) refers to such funds as "taxpayer liability," and predicts a rise in both the demand and supply of unsafe products, the elimination of liability insurance, and ultimately the imposition of government regulation simply to make the fund workable. McKean observes that the result would be insufficient consumer and producer care accompanied by high administrative and enforcement costs.

The preceding analysis suggests a number of ways in which markets may fail when consumers are risk averse. Limited liability will alter the efficiency properties of strict liability. If transaction costs exist, consumers and producers will not negotiate complete contingent contracts. This implies that under a negligence rule or in the absence of assignment of liability, market equilibria will often fail to be efficient. Imperfect insurance markets will reduce consumer opportunities for self-insurance or lead to partial coverage of the risks of product failure. These market imperfections imply that government regulation may be needed in response to consumer aversion toward the risks from product failure. Government regulation should not take the form of compensation funds that eliminate producer incentives for accident prevention. Regulatory efforts should be directed at promotion of insurance that reflects producer care and the risks of losses. A useful function of government in insurance markets may be to collect and supply information about product or workplace risks that allows insurance contracts to reflect these risks more accurately and that allows consumers and workers to make informed decisions.

15.2   Moral Hazard

The efforts expended by consumers, workers, and firms to reduce injuries and losses from unsafe products or workplaces may not be directly observable. This creates moral hazard problems that may lead to inefficient market allocations. The terms of contracts between consumers and firms cannot be based directly on care levels. If care levels cannot be directly inferred from observed losses, it may not be possible to achieve optimal risk sharing between consumers and firms while simultaneously providing incentives for efficient care levels. Product warranties will not necessarily result in optimal risk sharing and safe product design. Moral hazard problems extend beyond the contractual relationship between buyer and seller. Moral hazard arises in the relationship between an insurer and a firm seeking liability insurance or between firms that jointly manage a compensation fund. The inefficiency of market allocation in the presence of moral hazard is widely recognized.[11] The unobservability of care levels implies that private contracts between consumers and producers or between workers and their employers will not capture all potential gains from trade. Internalities are thus present when unobservable accident prevention efforts affect product quality and workplace safety.

The present discussion focuses on liability rules and the general problem of designing transfers between injurers and victims. The joint interest of the consumer and firm is minimization of the sum of losses from product failure and the cost of care. This objective may not be achieved at the market equilibrium, since each agent has an incentive to shirk in taking care by free riding on the other party's care. A consumer may be negligent in using what he knows to be a safe product; e.g., he may not comply with directions in using pharmaceuticals. A producer may devote less effort in product design if customers are perceived to be careful users; e.g., manufacturing equipment may meet different safety standards than equipment for home use.

Two main problems arise as a result of moral hazard. First, it is shown here that there may not exist *any* transfer payment such that consumer and producer care levels are chosen optimally. This implies that strict liability rules will not assure efficient exchange. Private bargaining in the absence of liability will also not yield efficiency. Second, negligence-contributory negligence rules based on due care standards are not applicable, since compliance with the standards cannot be monitored. These two problems suggest that alternative liability rules may not create incentives for optimal provision of care when monitoring of care is imperfect. This market failure may be remedied in part by government regulation. The design of a system of rewards and penalties to induce consumers and firms to take care is a special case of multiagent moral hazard problems. This section applies this approach to the double moral hazard problem in product markets. The analysis is related to that of Kambhu (1982) and Holmström (1982); see also Mann and Wissink (1983) and Cooper and Ross (1985).

Consider a market with homogeneous consumers and firms. The representative consumer purchases a good q and derives benefits $u(q)$. The consumer takes care at cost x. The firm produces the good at cost $C(q)$ and takes care at cost z. To simplify the discussion, both the consumer and firm are assumed to be risk neutral. Care levels are unobservable, while losses from product failure are observable after an accident occurs.[12] The per unit loss caused by an accident depends on care levels. The loss occurs with probability η, $0 < \eta < 1$, so that expected losses are $L(q, x, z) = \eta q l(x, z)$. The loss function is differentiable, decreasing, and convex in care levels x and z. The analysis can easily be extended by allowing the likelihood of an accident to depend on care levels.

Any ex post transfer mechanism must depend only on the size of losses, since care is unobservable, $T = T(ql)$. Thus, care levels affect transfers only through their effect on losses. The transfer mechanism may result from private negotiation, or it may be imposed by law. The transfer mechanism may represent private insurance provided by the firm, such as a warranty or contingent payment. In addition, the transfer may represent tort liability. If $T(ql) = 0$ for all losses, it is the no liability case. $T(ql) = ql$ represents the strict liability case. As has already been noted, when care levels cannot be observed, no liability will only induce consumers to take care, while strict liability will only induce the firm to take care. It will be shown that inefficiencies of this type extend to all transfer mechanisms. Note that negligence-contributory negligence rules cannot be implemented, since care levels cannot be directly monitored to verify compliance with due care standards.

Consumer and firm net benefits are defined as follows:

$$V(q, x, z, p) = u(q) - pq - x - \eta q l(x, z) + \eta T(ql(x, z)), \tag{15.2.1}$$

$$\pi(q, x, z, p) = pq - C(q) - z - \eta T(ql(x, z)). \tag{15.2.2}$$

Care levels are chosen using noncooperative Nash strategies. Consumers and firms correctly anticipate the market clearing price. The market equilibrium, $(\bar{p}, \bar{q}, \bar{x}, \bar{z})$, is defined by the following conditions:[13]

$$u'(\bar{q}) - \eta l(\bar{x}, \bar{z}) + \eta T'(\bar{q}l(\bar{x}, \bar{z}))l(\bar{x}, \bar{z}) = \bar{p}, \tag{15.2.3}$$

$$\bar{p} = C'(\bar{q}) + \eta T'(\bar{q}l(\bar{x}, \bar{z}))l(\bar{x}, \bar{z}), \tag{15.2.4}$$

$$1 = -\eta \bar{q} l_1(\bar{x}, \bar{z}) + \eta T'(\bar{q}l(\bar{x}, \bar{z}))\bar{q}l_1(\bar{x}, \bar{z}), \tag{15.2.5}$$

$$1 = -\eta T'(\bar{q}l(\bar{x}, \bar{z}))\bar{q}l_2(\bar{x}, \bar{z}). \tag{15.2.6}$$

From (15.2.3) and (15.2.4), $u'(\bar{q}) - C'(\bar{q}) = \eta l(\bar{x}, \bar{z})$.

The socially optimal output and care levels, (q^*, x^*, z^*), satisfy $u'(q^*) - C'(q^*) = \eta l(x^*, z^*)$, where care levels minimize the costs of care plus expected losses, $1 = -\eta q^* l_1(x^*, z^*) = -\eta q^* l_2(x^*, z^*)$. Compare with the market equilibrium. To obtain $1 = -\eta q l_2(x, z)$ requires $T'(ql) = 1$, as is the case under strict liability. But, under strict liability, the consumer does not take care. For $1 = -\eta q l_1(x, z)$, $T'(ql) = 0$ is required as with no liability, but, as in that case, the firm would not take care. Thus

PROPOSITION 15.2.1   *There does not exist a transfer function, $T(ql)$, such that market equilibrium output and care levels, $(\bar{q}, \bar{x}, \bar{z})$, correspond to the social optimum, (q^*, x^*, z^*).*

The inefficiency of transfers is primarily a consequence of their *budget-balancing* property.[14] It is widely recognized as a general proposition that balanced mechanisms do not yield efficient behavior.[15] Implementation via dominant strategy mechanisms fails to be Pareto optimal, since a net surplus is obtained by the government or regulatory authority. The effects of budget balancing on buyer and seller care are noted by Kambhu (1982) and are implicit in Green (1976).

The budget-balancing problem is intrinsic to enforcement of law through damage payments. All assignments of damages through liability rules will yield inefficient care levels, where both parties to a transaction may engage in accident avoidance and where care levels are not observable. Separate incentives are needed to reduce the producer's negligence and the consumer's contributory negligence. One source of inefficiency results from the failure of courts to monitor care levels perfectly. By using observed losses or any other imperfect proxy for assessing care levels, liability rules create incentives for inefficient contracts and suboptimal consumer and producer care.[16]

The main implication of the balancing problem is that private contracts that create incentives for mutually efficient care in product and workplace safety cannot form. Thus, a third party is required to achieve efficient care levels. The role of the third party may be played by the courts, but additional requirements beyond standard liability rules are needed. The courts can transfer less than the total fine to defendants. The incentive effects of this approach on private enforcement are very much at issue. Alternatively, there may be a limited role for a regulator in the establishment of product or workplace safety standards in addition to the judicial enforcement system. Joint public and private enforcement may address the problem of insufficient care.

By decoupling damages or transfer payments, one may provide incentives for efficient care. Let $T^1(ql)$ be the payment received by the consumer or victim and let $T^2(ql)$ be the payment made by the firm or injurer. Consider transfers that yield a net surplus, $T^2(ql) \geq T^1(ql) \geq 0$. Let T^1 and T^2 be step functions of observed monetary losses,

$$T^1(ql) = \begin{cases} d & \text{if } l \leq l(x^*, z^*) \\ 0 & \text{otherwise,} \end{cases} \quad T^2(ql) = \begin{cases} d & \text{if } l \leq l(x^*, z^*) \\ d + z^*/\eta & \text{otherwise,} \end{cases} \quad (15.2.7)$$

for a constant parameter d, $0 \leq d \leq l(x^*, z^*)$.

PROPOSITION 15.2.2 *Given the incentive schedules T^1 and T^2, the market equilibrium corresponds to optimal output and care levels.*

It is verified that (q^*, x^*, z^*) is attained at a market equilibrium, $(\bar{p}, \bar{q}, \bar{x}, \bar{z})$. Let $\bar{p}$ be such that

$$u'(q^*) - \eta l(x^*, z^*) = \bar{p} = C'(q^*).$$

Then, given $\bar{p}$ and $\bar{z} = z^*$, the consumer will obtain a damage payment in the event of an accident only if observed losses do not exceed $l(x^*, z^*)$. The consumer chooses the minimum care level $\bar{x}$ such that $l \leq l(x^*, z^*)$ and $1 = -\eta q l_1(x^*, z^*)$, so that $\bar{x} = x^*$. Consumer demand, $\bar{q}^D$, solves $u'(\bar{q}^D) - \eta l(x^*, z^*) = \bar{p}$. The firm is indifferent between taking no care and care level z^* and so chooses $\bar{z} = z^*$. The firm's supply, $\bar{q}^S$, solves $\bar{p} = C'(\bar{q}^S)$. Thus, $\bar{q}^D = \bar{q}^S = q^*$.

The transfer scheme is similar to a sharing rule in Holmström's (1982) team problem. The problem may be restated along the lines of Mirrlees

(1974) and Holmström (1982) to allow for a more general presentation of uncertain losses as in the preceding section of the chapter, $L = L(x, z, \xi)$, where ξ is a random parameter with cumulative distribution function $H(\xi)$. In this general setting, transfer rules can be devised that share losses between the victim and injurer and that yield approximately optimal care levels. If the consumer and firm have bounded endowments, or limited liability, some government subsidies may be required to approximate the efficient allocation. The problem of mechanism design is further complicated if agents are risk averse. This will prevent attainment of optimal care levels, since the familiar trade-off between risk sharing and incentives for unobservable effort is encountered.

The incentive scheme T^1, T^2 generates no surplus at the market equilibrium. The incentive scheme T^1, T^2 is not analogous to the various liability rules in tort law, since fines and transfers need not balance in equilibrium. Compare this incentive scheme with strict liability combined with the defense of contributory negligence. There, the defendant need not pay damages if the victim is found not to have taken due care. With the present incentive scheme, if the plaintiff's losses are sufficiently large, even as a result of the plaintiff's negligence, the defendant is liable for a damage payment or fine equal to $d + z^*/\eta$. As with the contributory negligence rule, the plaintiff does not receive a damage payment. Conversely, if the victim takes due care but the injurer is negligent, in the sense that losses exceed $l(x^*, z^*)$, the victim will not receive a payment but the injurer will still pay $d + z^*/\eta$. The incentive scheme T^1, T^2 may involve both public and private enforcement. For per unit losses less than or equal to $l(x^*, z^*)$, the amount d constitutes a damage payment by which the injurer compensates the victim. For catastrophic losses, $l > l(x^*, z^*)$, the victim is not compensated and the government collects $d + z^*/\eta$ as a tax or fine. Note, however, that large losses are never observed in equilibrium.

The preceding analysis does not imply that an injury tax is an appropriate remedy. If a proportional injury tax is applied to the firm, the market equilibrium conditions may be altered in an unanticipated way. Suppose that liability for damages is allocated by a fixed share, s, for the consumer and $(1 - s)$ for the firm. Let t be the injury tax per unit of losses ql. The market equilibrium conditions are then

$$u'(q) - C'(q) - (1 + t)\eta l(x, z) = 0, \tag{15.2.8}$$

$$-1 = s\eta q l_1(x, z) = (1 - s + t)\eta q l_2(x, z). \tag{15.2.9}$$

Clearly, no tax can achieve the social optimum, as can be seen by comparing (15.2.8) and (15.2.9) with the optimal conditions. The effects of the tax will be reflected in the consumer's care and will distort the market output level as well.

The presence of unobservable consumer and producer care levels suggests that private insurance arrangements between consumers and producers, or involving third-party insurers, may result in inefficient care and output levels. In addition, tort liability cannot be relied on to induce efficient care when both consumers and producers may exercise precaution in avoiding accidents. The consequences of insufficient care may be quite serious, since costly injuries and losses may result from product failure or workplace accidents. Tragic health consequences may result from prolonged exposure to hazardous products or unsafe working conditions. These might be avoided through precautions that are less costly than the expected value of losses.

The present analysis makes clear that to achieve efficiency requires intervention in the transaction by a third party. Arrow (1968) observes that given moral hazard "nonmarket controls, whether internalized as moral principles or externally imposed, are to some extent essential for efficiency." While government intervention is perhaps necessary for optimal resource allocation, it is not evident that such intervention will be sufficient or even partially successful. The main issue, assuming that regulation of product quality and workplace safety is in the public interest, is what policy instruments should be used to remedy the consequences of moral hazard. One approach stresses the use of taxes to alleviate market failure. Helpman and Laffont (1975) and Greenwald and Stiglitz (1986) examine the effects of moral hazard in a general equilibrium setting. They demonstrate that corrective taxation may yield Pareto improvements in market allocations. Arnott and Stiglitz (1986) characterize optimal taxes that can alleviate moral hazard by taxing complementary or substitute commodities to increase efforts to prevent losses. Such taxes may impose high information requirements on public agencies. Identification of complementary or substitute goods may not be obvious in practice. One industry's complementary good for safety may be another's substitute good.

Government insurance programs may reduce care efforts of consumers and firms, since these programs are also subject to moral hazard. It is certainly clear that publicly provided insurance must reflect a firm's accident record and any available proxies for consumer and firm care levels.

Simple provision of risk-pooling arrangements, or worse, the shifting of risks to the government, will vastly reduce incentives for care and exacerbate moral hazard problems. The choice between public and private insurance programs, administrative costs aside, depends on who has the best information on care levels. In the case of workplace safety, workers or unions may have the best information about employer care levels and employers may be the best observers of employee care. When complex technical issues are involved in monitoring producer care in producing safe goods or in designing a safe workplace, government agencies may have superior information. Government agencies have an advantage over consumers or employees in that they can mandate specific actions by producers to improve product quality or workplace safety. These regulatory standards are often directed at proxies for care, and as noted in the preceding chapter, there may be little impact on the frequency and severity of accidents. Government regulatory standards for product quality or workplace safety may impose high costs on consumers and firms without yielding commensurate reductions in expected losses. Regulatory standards create additional costs in that the contractual arrangements between consumers and firms are constrained. Moreover, if standards are not targeted at care levels, or if monitoring of compliance is imperfect, enforcement of standards is subject to the same problems of moral hazard that affect market transactions. Consumer and firm efforts at accident avoidance may be reduced and efforts may be devoted to avoidance of the government standards themselves. Imperfect monitoring of care levels is complicated by unobservable characteristics of consumers and firms. This is the subject of the next two sections.

15.3   Adverse Selection

The preceding section addressed the problem of *double moral hazard*. Various incentive schemes were examined that induced the consumer and firm to increase their respective care levels in using and manufacturing a product. Care levels were not directly observable, and were thus not explicitly accounted for in the contract between the consumer and firm. However, because of complete information about consumer demand, firm costs, and the form of the expected damages function, each agent was able to make a conjecture about the other agent's equilibrium care level. At the Nash equilibrium, these conjectures were verified.

In the presence of asymmetric information about demand, costs, and the expected losses from product failure, it is no longer possible to adjust consumption and payments to account for agent care levels. Since both agents may possess private information about the cost of care and the likelihood of product failure, one encounters a problem of *double adverse selection*. It is assumed here that consumer and firm care levels are fixed but unknown to the other party. It is shown that efficient allocations will depend on the prior assignment of liability. This is an interesting aspect of product liability under asymmetric information. In general, with full information, efficiency notions are independent of the legal institutions that assign liability.

The present section restricts attention to bargaining between a representative consumer and firm to focus on the effects of asymmetric information on output, care levels, and the allocation of rents.[17] Discussion of issues associated with the equilibria of markets under asymmetric information is deferred to the next section. The contract between the consumer and firm may represent, for example, a contract between a consumer and a building contractor for the construction of a house. The consumer may have private information about the characteristics of the property on which the house will be built, while the contractor may have private information about the durability of building materials, the quality of the architectural design, or the skill level of his employees. Estimation of the expected quality of the house will depend on information supplied by both parties. Alternatively, the contract may be for medical care between a patient and physician. The patient may have private information about his propensity to follow a prescription, his tolerance of particular drugs, or the results of previous treatments. The physician may possess detailed technical knowledge that is unavailable to the patient. The private information known to the patient and physician may bear on the estimated success of the treatment. The model applies to negotiation between a worker and employer over wages and productivity. The worker may have private information about his health, skill level, or past accidents, while the employer may have information about the health consequences of workplace conditions or likelihood of accidents.

A consumer and firm negotiate a contract for the production and delivery of a product that specifies the quantity to be produced and the total payment, R. The product may fail, which will cause expected monetary losses, $L = ql$.[18] The consumer obtains monetary benefits from consumption, $u(q)$, where u is twice differentiable, increasing, and concave. The firm's costs, $C(q)$, are twice differentiable, increasing, and convex for $q > 0$. Legal assignment of liability is represented by a constant parameter s, $0 \leq s \leq 1$, where sL represents the consumer's share of expected losses and $(1 - s)L$ is the firm's share. The parameter may represent no liability ($s = 1$), strict liability ($s = 0$), or comparative negligence ($0 < s < 1$).

The consumer and firm are assumed to be risk neutral so that problems of risk sharing may be ignored, and the focus may be exclusively on the effects of asymmetric information. Under full information, the optimal output, q^F, is such that the marginal benefits of consumption, net of expected losses per unit, equals marginal costs, $u'(q^F) - l = C'(q^F)$. It should be emphasized again that with full information, the optimal output is independent of the allocation of liability between the two parties. Also, given the absence of income effects, the optimal output is independent of the allocation of rents from exchange. As suggested by the related analysis of Coase, bargaining between the two parties will result in the optimal output level regardless of the assignment of liability for damages.

The optimal output must be defined in a different manner if the determination of the optimum is constrained by limits on available information. Consider the *interim incentive efficient* output and payment levels. Bargaining between the consumer and firm over output and payments is also affected by asymmetries in available information. For this reason, the full set of interim incentive efficient output and payment levels is examined.

Expected losses are represented by a function $l = l(u, \theta)$, where the parameters μ and θ represent the private information of the consumer and firm, respectively. The parameter μ represents the consumer's private information about his contributory negligence level, or about exogenous factors that may increase the likelihood of a loss. The parameter θ represents the firm's information about its negligence level or unobservable characteristics of the product. Expected losses are differentiable, increasing, and convex in negligence levels μ and θ. Let $\partial l(\mu, \theta)/\partial \mu = l_1(\mu, \theta) > 0$ and $\partial l(\mu, \theta)/\partial \theta = l_2(u, \theta) > 0$. Also, negligence levels are complements in producing losses, $l_{12} = l_{21} > 0$. The parameters μ and θ take values in the interval $[0, 1]$ and have cumulative probability distribution functions $F(\mu)$ and $G(\theta)$ that are common knowledge. Let $f(\mu) = dF(\mu)$ and $g(\theta) = dG(\theta)$, $F(0) = G(0) = 0$, and $F(1) = G(1) = 1$.

Given shared liability, $0 < s < 1$, the bargaining problem is simply that of determining the output and price of a product of unknown value. For a related discussion of bargaining over the amount (and likelihood) of a pretrial settlement in tort cases, with unobservable negligence and contributory negligence, see Spulber (1985). By now familiar revelation principle arguments, one may represent the bargaining outcome of a direct mechanism $(q(\mu, \theta), R(\mu, \theta))$ for which truth-telling is an equilibrium Bayes-Nash strategy for the two parties. The indirect benefit of reporting parameter value $\hat{\mu}$ by a consumer of type μ is defined by

$$V(\mu, \hat{\mu}) = \int_0^1 [u(q(\hat{\mu}, \theta)) - sq(\hat{\mu}, \theta)l(\mu, \theta) - R(\hat{\mu}, \theta)] \, dG(\theta). \tag{15.3.1}$$

Similarly, for the firm,

$$\Pi(\theta, \hat{\theta}) = \int_0^1 [R(\mu, \hat{\theta}) - C(q(\mu, \hat{\theta})) - (1 - s)q(\mu, \hat{\theta})l(\mu, \theta)] \, dF(\mu). \tag{15.3.2}$$

The mechanism must satisfy incentive compatibility, $V(\mu, \mu) \geq V(\mu, \hat{\mu})$, for all μ, $\hat{\mu}$ in $[0, 1]$, and $\Pi(\theta, \theta) \geq \Pi(\theta, \hat{\theta})$ for all θ, $\hat{\theta}$ in $[0, 1]$. In addition it is required that the consumer and firm obtain gains from trade from the transactions given zero opportunity costs, $V(\mu) \equiv V(\mu, \mu) \geq 0$ and $\Pi(\theta) \equiv \Pi(\theta, \theta) \geq 0$ for all μ, θ in $[0, 1]$.

By arguments given earlier, rewrite the indirect valuations of negligence levels as follows:

$$V(\mu) = V(1) + \int_\mu^1 \int_0^1 sq(\tilde{\mu}, \theta)l_1(\hat{\mu}, \theta) \, dG(\theta) \, d\tilde{\mu}, \tag{15.3.3}$$

$$\Pi(\theta) = \Pi(1) + \int_\theta^1 \int_0^1 (1 - s)q(\mu, \tilde{\theta})l_2(\mu, \tilde{\theta}) \, dF(\mu) \, d\tilde{\theta}. \tag{15.3.4}$$

Since l is increasing in μ and θ, V and Π are decreasing in μ and θ, respectively. Thus, gains from trade or individual rationality is satisfied if $V(1) \geq 0$ and $\Pi(1) \geq 0$.

I begin by characterizing feasible direct mechanisms, that is, mechanisms satisfying incentive compatibility and individual rationality. Information rents are given by $V(\mu) - V(1)$ and $\Pi(\theta) - \Pi(1)$ for the consumer and firm. Define expected information rents for the consumer and firm by $A^1(q) \equiv \int_0^1 V(\mu) \, dF(\mu) - V(1)$ and $A^2(q) \equiv \int_0^1 \Pi(\theta) \, dG(\theta) - \Pi(1)$. Therefore, using integration by parts,

$$A^1(q) = \int_0^1 \int_0^1 sq(\mu, \theta)l_1(\mu, \theta)(F(\mu)/f(\mu)) \, dF(\mu) \, dG(\theta), \tag{15.3.5}$$

$$A^2(q) = \int_0^1 \int_0^1 (1-s)q(\mu,\theta)l_2(\mu,\theta)(G(\theta)/g(\theta))\,dF(\mu)\,dG(\theta). \qquad (15.3.6)$$

Interestingly, the information rents of the consumer and firm are *increasing* in their assigned share of expected losses from product failure.

Define the net benefits from exchange, given the output schedule $q(\mu,\theta)$, by

$$B(q) \equiv \int_0^1 \int_0^1 [u(q(\mu,\theta)) - C(q(\mu,\theta)) - q(\mu,\theta)l(\mu,\theta)]\,dF(\mu)\,dG(\theta).$$
$$\qquad (15.3.7)$$

Arguments given previously (in chapter 11) establish

PROPOSITION 15.3.1   *The mechanism (q, R) is feasible if and only if*

$$\int_0^1 l_1(\mu,\theta)(\partial q(\mu,\theta)/\partial\mu)\,dG(\theta) \le 0, \qquad (15.3.8)$$

$$\int_0^1 l_2(\mu,\theta)(\partial q(\mu,\theta)/\partial\theta)\,dF(\mu) \le 0, \qquad (15.3.9)$$

$$B(q) \ge A^1(q) + A^2(q). \qquad (15.3.10)$$

Conditions (15.3.8) and (15.3.9) are due to incentive compatibility and are similar to monotonicity conditions on the output schedule. These conditions are satisfied, for example, if the output schedule is decreasing in μ and θ. Condition (15.3.10) is due to individual rationality. It states that truth-telling requires the expected rents from exchange to cover the sum of expected information rents for the consumer and firm. This condition is essentially a budget-balancing restriction.

Recall that a direct mechanism (q^*, R^*) is *interim incentive efficient* if and only if there does not exist another feasible mechanism (q', R') such that $V(\mu; q', R') > V(\mu; q^*, R^*)$ for all μ in $[0, 1]$ and $\Pi(\theta; q', R') > \Pi(\theta; q^*, R^*)$ for all θ in $[0, 1]$. The mechanism (q^*, R^*) can be shown to be efficient if and only if there exist nondecreasing weights,[19] $a(\mu)$, $b(\theta)$, with $a(0) = b(0) = 0$ and $a(1) = b(1) = 1$ such that $q \ge 0$ solves

$$\max_q \int_0^1 \int_0^1 I(q,\mu,\theta)\,dF(\mu)\,dG(\theta) \qquad (15.3.11)$$

subject to (15.3.8), (15.3.9), and (15.3.10), where I is defined by

$$I(q,\mu,\theta) \equiv [u(q) - C(q) - ql(\mu,\theta) + sl_1\lambda^1(\mu) + (1-s)l_2\lambda^2(\theta)], \qquad (15.3.12)$$

and where

$$\lambda^1(\mu) \equiv (a(\mu) - F(\mu))/f(\mu), \qquad \lambda^2(\theta) \equiv (b(\theta) - G(\theta))/g(\theta).$$

Our approach follows that of Myerson (1985) for a related problem. Rather than explore the problem in its full generality, for purposes of exposition I restrict attention to mechanisms that maximize the sum of expected consumer and firm net benefits, that is, where the weights are equal to the cumulative distribution functions, $a(\mu) = F(\mu)$ for all μ and $b(\theta) = G(\theta)$ for all θ. Social welfare is therefore equal to $B(q)$. This restriction selects a particular outcome in the bargaining set. However, many of the statements made about this outcome generalize to all allocations in the bargaining set.

The full information efficient output maximizes expected social benefits. Furthermore, note that the full information output is a decreasing function of the negligence parameters,

$$\partial q^F(\mu, \theta)/\partial\mu = l_1(\mu, \theta)/(u''(q^F) - C''(q^F)) < 0,$$
$$\partial q^F(\mu, \theta)/\partial\theta = l_2(\mu, \theta)/(u''(q^F) - C''(q^F)) < 0.$$

(15.3.13)

Therefore, the full information output schedule satisfies the incentive compatibility conditions (15.3.8), (15.3.9). This immediately implies that the full information optimum may be attainable under asymmetric information.

PROPOSITION 15.3.2   *The full information output schedule, $q^F(\mu, \theta)$, corresponds to an interim incentive efficient mechanism if and only if $B(q^F) \geq A^1(q^F) + A^2(q^F)$.*

This result makes clear that budget balancing in private transactions may be the source of inefficiency under asymmetric information. The budget may balance at the full information optimum only if expected rents from exchange are sufficiently large relative to information rents.[20] In this sense, the force of the budget-balancing restriction differs from the moral hazard case since an efficient transfer mechanism is always ruled out by a related budget-balancing condition.

If exchange rents are not sufficient to cover information rents, attaining the full information output may require intervention by a third party, either a government agency or a private broker, to subsidize or tax the transfers. To examine the effects of the budget-balancing condition, (15.3.10), make the standard regularity assumption that hazard rates $f(\mu)/F(\mu)$ and $g(\theta)/G(\theta)$ are nonincreasing in the parameters μ and θ. This is satisfied, for

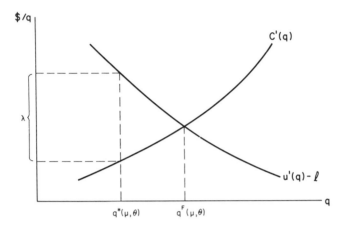

Figure 15.3.1
Interim incentive efficient output $q^*(\mu, \theta)$.

example, by the uniform distribution and the exponential distribution, $F(\mu) = (1 - e^{-h\mu})/(1 - e^{-h})$, for any constant $h > 0$. Let γ be the the the shadow price on the constraint $B(q) \geq A^1(q) + A^2(q)$. I have already considered the case of a nonbinding constraint in proposition 15.3.1. The proof of the following is given in the appendix.

PROPOSITION 15.3.3   *The interim incentive efficient mechanism that maximizes expected net benefits, $q^*(\mu, \theta)$, solves the following conditions:*

$$u'(q^*) - C'(q^*) - l = (\gamma^*/(1 + \gamma^*))[sl_1(F/f) + (1 - s)l_2(G/g)], \quad (15.3.14)$$

$$B(q^*) - A^1(q^*) - A^2(q^*) = 0. \tag{15.3.15}$$

The effects of a binding constraint are shown in figure 15.3.1. Let λ represent the wedge $(\gamma^*/(1 + \gamma^*))[sl_1(F/f) + (1 - s)l_2(G/g)]$. Clearly, output is lowered by the presence of asymmetric information about the potential losses from product failure. The effect of internalities is to create unappropriated gains from trade. These are due to the constraint that the rents from exchange must cover information rents for the consumer and firm.

An important effect of asymmetric information is evident from the characterization of the efficient mechanism given by proposition 15.3.3. *The allocation of liability for losses affects the efficient output level.* This occurs because information rents are dependent on the allocation of liability, as represented by the sharing rule s. Thus, interim incentive efficient mechanisms must take these rents into account if the budget-balancing condition (15.3.10) is strictly binding. This is in contrast to the full information efficient output, $q^F(\mu, \theta)$, which is independent of s.[21] Furthermore, the allocation of liability affects social welfare, relative to any interim incentive efficient mechanism. Write social welfare, W, as a function of the parameter s, noting that q^* and γ^* depend on s,

$$W(s) = B(q^*) + \gamma^*[B(q^*) - A^1(q^*) - A^2(q^*)].\qquad(15.3.16)$$

Differentiate with respect to s, and apply (15.3.14), (15.3.15), and the envelope theorem,

$$W'(s) = \gamma^* \int_0^1 \int_0^1 q^*[l_2(G/g) - l_1(F/f)]\,dF(\mu)\,dG(\theta).\qquad(15.3.17)$$

This implies that relative to a given welfare criterion, there exists an optimal allocation of liability. Suppose, for example, that the distribution functions of agent types are uniform, $F(\mu) = \mu$ and $G(\theta) = \theta$. Let the loss function have the form $l(\mu, \theta) = \mu\theta + \mu$. Then $W'(s) = -\gamma^* \int_0^1 \int_0^1 q^* \mu\,d\mu\,d\theta < 0$ and the optimal rule is strict liability for producers. ($s = 0$). Conversely, if the loss function has the form $l(\mu, \theta) = \mu\theta + \theta$, then $W'(s) = \gamma^* \int_0^1 \int_0^1 q^* \theta\,d\mu\,d\theta > 0$ and the optimal rule is no liability for producers ($s = 1$). Finally, if $l(\mu, \theta) = \mu\theta$, welfare is neutral with regard to the assignment of liability.[22]

The discussion has thus far emphasized the output that maximizes expected net benefits for the consumer and firm. Market transactions may yield a wide range of outcomes. Suppose, for example, that the firm acts as a monopolist. Then, its optimal strategy, if such a commitment is feasible, is to make consumers a first and final offer of a profit-maximizing nonlinear price schedule, $P(q; \theta)$. Consumers are able to infer the product quality parameter, θ, and adjust their purchases accordingly. Consumers reveal their type by self-selection based on the size of their purchase. Consumers differ in terms of their information about product failure, to the extent that they bear those losses,

$$u'(q) - sl(\mu, \theta) = \partial P(q; \theta)/\partial q.\qquad(15.3.18)$$

The monopolist chooses the schedule such that the consumption schedule solves[23]

$$u'(q^m) - C'(q^m) - l(\mu, \theta) = sl_1(\theta)F(\mu)/f(\mu).\qquad(15.3.19)$$

Consider now the second-best assignment of liability given monopoly,

$$W'(s) = \int_0^1 \int_0^1 [u'(q^m) - C'(q^m) - l(\mu, \theta)](\partial q^m/\partial s)\,dF(\mu)\,dG(\theta). \quad (15.3.20)$$

By (15.3.19) the bracketed term is positive, and output is decreasing in s, $\partial q^m/\partial s = l_1(F/f)/(u'' - C'') < 0$. Thus, welfare is decreasing in the liability parameter, and $s = 0$ maximizes welfare.

PROPOSITION 15.3.4   *Given monopoly, strict liability is optimal.*

Shifting all responsibility for losses to the producer eliminates all consumer differences. The producer must then set the standard linear monopoly price where marginal revenue equals marginal cost.

   Asymmetry in available information about consumer and producer care levels implies that private contracts will generally not achieve efficient resource allocation. The preceding analysis establishes that, without additional forms of communication between market participants, liability rules will not be sufficient to guarantee efficiency. This accords with the view, expressed in the literature on product liability and product quality regulation, that imperfectly perceived risks may cause liability rules to perform ineffectively; see particularly Shavell (1984a,b). The problem may be exacerbated if litigation is costly. Simon (1981) analyzes the decision to sue when litigation is costly and product quality is unobservable and shows that litigation costs are an important determinant of the effectiveness of liability rules. However, it is evident that regulatory agencies face similar administrative costs and constraints on available information. The question to be addressed is whether regulatory policies can be designed that alleviate informational constraints and improve market performance. The effectiveness of communication in the marketplace is an important determinant of the role of regulation in the presence of moral hazard and adverse selection. These issues are addressed in the next section.

15.4   Signaling and Disclosure

Market equilibrium allocations may fail to be efficient, given moral hazard and adverse selection. Moral hazard problems may arise if consumers and firms take unobservable actions that affect expected losses from product failure. The extent to which care is taken in reducing the magnitude and likelihood of accidents or product failure may not be sufficient to maximize the joint benefits from exchange. Adverse selection problems may exist, given unobservable characteristics of consumers and of firms and the products they supply. Imperfect sorting of consumers by demand attributes or of firms by cost or product quality may create exchange agreements that fail to capture all available gains from trade. The internalities resulting from costly communication and costly monitoring of economic activities suggest a potential role for government intervention. The purpose of this section is to examine whether regulation can effectively mitigate internalities and to consider what form such regulations should take.

Unregulated markets may be the most efficient mechanism for information transmission. It would be incorrect to conclude that markets fail simply on the basis of imperfect information. The degree to which moral hazard and adverse selection problems affect the efficiency of markets depends on whether alternative sources of information are available regarding consumer and firm actions and characteristics. It must be verified whether these alternative means of communication can alleviate the constraints imposed by costly information. There are many important sources of information in markets.

The main source of market information is, of course, the *price system*, which provides data on consumer marginal rates of substitution, producer marginal costs, and the relative scarcity of goods. At the same time price can be an important signal of product quality (Spence, 1973a) and an important determinant of quality (Stiglitz, 1987). Other means of information transmission in markets include *advertising, contract terms* in addition to price, and *reputation*. I shall briefly review the literature on market signaling.

Government regulation in response to imperfect information may take a variety of forms. Market signaling may be used to enhance regulatory actions, or signaling may be sufficient to obviate any need for government intervention. Regulators may attempt to enhance the performance of the market by promoting efficient disclosure of information. On the other hand, regulators may choose to intervene directly in consumer and producer decisions on the basis of superior information. It is argued that direct intervention in market allocation is generally not desirable if market signaling and disclosure are feasible alternatives.

15.4.1 Signaling and Adverse Selection

As a benchmark, it is useful to identify the relationship between product quality and price in a full information, competitive market setting. Rosen's classic (1974) paper provides such an analysis by considering the hedonic prices of product characteristics. Consumers purchase one unit of a good with J characteristics, $z = (z_1, \ldots, z_J)$. Consumers have income ω and purchase a numeraire y. Consumer utility is given by $U = U(z, y)$. The *hedonic price function* depends on the vector of product characteristics, $p = p(z)$. Let $p_j(z) \equiv dp(z)/\partial z_j$ denote the marginal effect of a product characteristic on the hedonic price. The consumer's problem is to choose the desired characteristics of the heterogeneous good and the quantity of the numeraire good, subject to a nonlinear budget constraint,

$$\max_{z, y} U(z, y) \qquad \text{subject to } p(z) + y = \omega. \tag{15.4.1}$$

The first-order necessary conditions include the budget constraint and the equalization of marginal rates of substitution between attributes and the numeraire to the marginal hedonic price,

$$U_{z_j}(z, y)/U_y(z, y) = p_j(z), \qquad j = 1, \ldots, J. \tag{15.4.2}$$

A continuum of competitive firms may exist. Each firm supplies a single good with a particular mix of attributes. A firm produces q units of a product and has cost $C(z, q)$. A firm maximizes profits, $\pi = p(q)q - C(z, q)$, over output and product attributes,

$$p(z) = C_q(z, q), \tag{15.4.3}$$

$$p_j(z)q = C_{z_j}(z, q), \qquad j = 1, \ldots, J. \tag{15.4.4}$$

The market equilibrium, if it exists, is defined for a given set of consumers with various preferences, and a set of firms with various technologies. The market equilibrium consists of a set of products Z, a hedonic price schedule $p(z)$, and a total output schedule $Q(z)$ for each product z in the set Z.

A simple illustration of the effects of regulation of product quality on social welfare is easily obtained for the case of a single attribute; see Rosen (1974). Suppose that all consumers are identical and all firms have identical U-shaped average costs. Also, let $C(z, q)$ be increasing and convex in z. Let $q(z)$ denote the minimum efficient scale given z; i.e., $q(z)$ solves $\min_q C(z, q)/q$. The market equilibrium price is then

$$p(z) = C_q(z, q(z)) = C(z, q(z))/q(z). \tag{15.4.5}$$

Social welfare is defined by

$$W(z) \equiv U(z, \omega - p(z)). \tag{15.4.6}$$

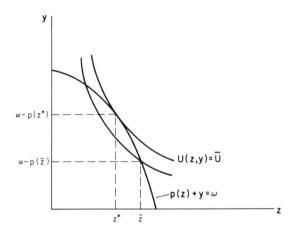

Figure 15.4.1
Welfare loss due to a minimum quality constraint $\bar{z}$.

The market equilibrium quality level is socially optimal and satisfies
$U_z(z^*, \omega - p(z^*))/U_y(z^*, \omega - p(z^*)) = p'(z^*) = C_z(z^*, q(z^*))/q(z^*)$. This is
illustrated in figure 15.4.1. Regulation in the form of a binding quality
constraint, $\bar{z} > z^*$, lowers social welfare; see figure 15.4.1. The social welfare
loss is therefore

$$W(z^*) - W(\bar{z}) = -\int_{z^*}^{\bar{z}} [U_z - U_y p'(z)]\, dz. \tag{15.4.7}$$

This reflects the higher costs of producing better-quality goods, net of the
benefits of consuming them. Given a constant marginal utility of income,
the welfare loss equals $\Delta W = \int_{z^*}^{\bar{z}} p'(z)\, dz - (u(\bar{z}) - u(z^*))$.

If product attributes are not directly observable, it is not evident that the
price of each product will correspond to its quality. The price may no longer
provide an indicator to consumers of the marginal costs of increasing
particular quality attributes. The consumer will not be able to select from
the set of products based on their attributes and the hedonic price function.
The consequences of imperfect observability have been identified in a
variety of models.

Adverse selection and market equilibrium are examined in Akerlof's
well-known (1970) paper on the market for lemons. Akerlof provides an
example of nonexistence of market equilibrium due to adverse selection.[24]
Existence of feasible trading mechanisms can be shown for a simple model

of product quality. Consider negotiation between a buyer and a seller over an object of unknown value. The present discussion applies Myerson and Satterthwaite (1983) and Myerson (1985) to a simple product quality model. Let θ represent the likelihood the product may fail. The value of θ is known only to the seller. The buyer's beliefs are represented by a distribution $G(\theta)$ on $[0, 1]$. The trades between buyer and seller may be represented by a direct mechanism, $(p(\theta), \tau(\theta))$, where p is the expected price of the good and $\tau(\theta)$ is the probability of exchange, $0 \le \tau(\theta) \le 1$. The buyer's benefits of purchasing a product of quality θ are $u - \theta l$, where l is the loss from product failure and $0 < l < u$. The producer's costs are a decreasing function of θ, $c(\theta)$. The net benefits for buyer and seller are then

$$U(p, \tau) = \int_0^1 ((u - \theta l)\tau(\theta) - p(\theta)) \, dG(\theta),\tag{15.4.8}$$

$$\Pi(\theta, p, \tau) = p(\theta) - \tau(\theta)c(\theta).\tag{15.4.9}$$

Feasibility requires that the expected net benefits from exchange exceed the expected information rents,

$$\int_0^1 [u - \theta l - c(\theta)]\tau(\theta) \, dG(\theta)$$

$$\ge -\int_0^1 [(1 - G(\theta))/g(\theta)]c'(\theta)\tau(\theta) \, dG(\theta),\tag{15.4.10}$$

and that $\tau(\theta)$ be nondecreasing in θ. For example, if $G(\theta)$ is uniform and $c(\theta) = 1 - \theta$, this requires

$$\int_0^1 [u - \theta l - 2(1 - \theta)]\tau(\theta) \, d\theta \ge 0.$$

This holds for all $\tau \ge 0$ if $u \ge 2$. If $u < 2$, this holds, for example, if $\tau(\theta) = 1$ for $(2 - u)/(2 - l) \le \theta < 1$ and $\tau(\theta) = 0$ otherwise. Continuing with the example, suppose that the buyer makes a take-it-or-leave-it offer of a price p^* to the seller.[25] The seller of type θ will accept only if $p \ge 1 - \theta$. The buyer therefore maximizes $U = \int_{1-p}^1 (u - \theta l - p) \, d\theta$ over p, $0 \le p \le 1$, For $u \ge 2$, $p^* = 1$. For $u < 2$, $p^* = (u - l)/(2 - l)$. Thus, for $u < 2$, no exchange occurs if the likelihood of product failure is below $\theta^* = 1 - p^* = (2 - u)/(2 - l)$, as required for feasibility.

The potential failure of exchange to take place, even though gains from trade may be positive, illustrates the inefficiency of the market under asymmetric information that was recognized by Akerlof. In the present example, if $u = 3/2$ and $l = 1/2$, gains from trade equal $u - \theta l - c(\theta) = (1 + \theta)/2$, which is positive for all θ. Thus, some products that are safer, but costlier to produce, are not provided as a direct consequence of information constraints.

Wilson (1979, 1980) extends the intuition of the Akerlof framework to examine alternative market mechanisms under adverse selection.[26] Wilson (1979) considers three price-setting conventions: prices set by buyers, by sellers, or by an auctioneer. Buyer and seller reservation prices are proportional to quality, with quality unobservable to buyers. With a Walrasian auctioneer, multiple equilibria may exist with the highest price yielding the greatest social welfare and the highest average product quality, by attracting more higher-product quality sellers into the market. When the buyers set prices, the equilibrium may involve a unique, Walrasian equilibrium price or a distribution of prices and excess supply. Multiple equilibria may occur when the informed parties (sellers) make bids.

Stiglitz (1984) emphasizes that product quality may depend on price at a market equilibrium since "beliefs about quality, about what it is that is being traded, depend (rationally) on price." Stiglitz argues that the reversal of the traditional relationship between price and quality implies that demand curves may not be downward sloping, market equilibria may involve rationing, and price dispersion may exist. This requires a fundamental reevaluation of both descriptive analysis and welfare conclusions based on the traditional supply-and-demand framework. See Stiglitz's surveys (1984, 1987) for additional discussion and references regarding self-selection in capital, labor, and product markets.

The accuracy of consumer information about unobservable product quality will in turn affect the information conveyed by prices. This is confirmed by Wolinsky's (1983) model in which prices are signals of product quality. Consumers obtain information about product quality by observing a product attribute that is jointly distributed with product quality. Product quality is heterogeneous across firms. At a separating market equilibrium, prices reflect quality levels. The markups above marginal cost reflect the accuracy of consumer perceptions of product quality.

The information conveyed by prices has been examined in a number of alternative settings. Nonexistence of rational expectations equilibria is observed in Kreps (1977) and Grossman and Stiglitz (1980). In Cooper and Ross (1984), nonexistence of a rational expectations equilibrium is examined when some consumers are imperfectly informed about product quality. If an equilibrium exists, prices will convey only partial information about product quality. Precommitment by firms is assumed by Salop and Stiglitz (1977) and Chan and Leland (1982). Salop and Stiglitz show that when consumers are imperfectly informed about prices and the cost of purchasing information differs across consumers, the market equilibrium may involve price dispersion. Chan and Leland extend this model by allowing sellers to choose price and product quality and by allowing buyers to purchase both price and quality information. When both types of information are costly, uninformed consumers may pay more and obtain a good of lower quality than informed consumers.

The model of market signaling is due to Spence (1973a,b, 1974) and has been developed by Rothschild and Stiglitz (1976), Wilson (1977), and Riley (1975, 1979). The signaling model is now applied to examine how the market equilibrium with unobservable product quality is modified if firms may provide a signal to consumers (in addition to price). The signal may represent various proxies for product quality, including advertising, sales effort, testing data, product labeling, quality certification, packaging, and design. The consumer's net benefits are not directly affected by the signal[27] and so retain the form $U(p, \theta) = u - \theta l - p$.[28] The signal, t, is costly for the firm. Firm costs, $C(\theta, t)$, are decreasing in the parameter θ and increasing and convex in the signal t. Firm profits are represented by $\Pi(p, \theta, t) = p - C(\theta, t)$, where θ is the producer's private information. Let the marginal cost of signaling be increasing in the likelihood of an accident, $C_{t\theta}(\theta, t) > 0$. The marginal costs of a higher signal will be lower for a higher-quality (lower θ) product. Rothschild and Stiglitz (1976) and Wilson (1977) show that a Nash equilibrium defined by free entry of firms of all types, each supplying a single product, cannot involve pooling across types. Thus, at the market equilibrium, a schedule of prices and signals $(p(\theta), t(\theta))$ must have separate values for firms offering products of varying quality levels. In this sense, one has what may be characterized as a hedonic price schedule of the type examined by Rosen (1974) and discussed previously. On the other hand, as Rothschild and Stiglitz (1976) have shown, the separating equilibrium may fail to exist, as there may always be pooling contracts that dominate Nash equilibrium separating contracts. When separating contracts do exist, they are Pareto efficient in a restricted sense.[29] Ideally, no signals should be required, since signals provide no direct value to buyers and are costly to sellers. However, the market equilibrium, if it exists, is efficient relative to private communication technology as represented by signaling costs.

Advertising serves as the primary direct source of information for consumers about the prices, characteristics and variety of products. Advertising conveys only imperfect information about product quality, since it is often a partial substitute for information that can be obtained only after consumption of the product. Thus, information about product quality is generally obtained by consumers through inference using advertising messages as a proxy for experience of the product. Since consumers must frequently make purchasing decisions on the basis of advertising, it is important to examine the extent to which advertising messages are informative about product quality.[30]

In classic papers, Nelson (1970, 1974) distinguishes between "search" and "experience" goods. Search implies that "inspection must occur prior to purchasing the brand," while experience requires evaluation after purchase (1970, p. 312). Clearly, these activities are not mutually exclusive. Consumers may inspect a set of brands and then, simultaneously or sequentially, purchase a subset of these brands. Search costs include the costs of transportation and the time costs of shopping, while experience entails the purchase price of the product and the opportunity costs of not purchasing other products with different characteristics. Higher-quality brands may be expected to have relatively more repeat purchases than lower-quality brands. Nelson (1974) finds that advertising yields greater returns for such higher-quality experience goods, which in turn implies that advertising has value to consumers as a signal of quality.[31]

The relationship between advertising signals and product quality is important for regulation of product quality. If advertising provides sufficiently accurate information about product characteristics, given the costs of providing such information, regulation of product quality may be unnecessary, since competition and consumer choice will monitor product quality. Thus, the debate over whether the supply of advertising is itself socially optimal is somewhat beside the point for this discussion.[32] Advertising is generally modeled as a quantity that is costly to firms and enters as a parameter in the consumer's net benefits. The standard treatment of advertising as a signal presumes that consumers make inferences regarding product quality based on the amount of advertising expenditures undertaken by the firm. This approach neglects the explicit information content of advertising. Even if some advertising messages may not be credible or may convey only general impressions, other advertising messages signal verifiable information, such as price, location, and observable product characteristics. Product descriptions in advertising may also provide information about unobservable quality.

Advertising as a signal of product quality is examined by Kihlstrom and Riordan (1984) in a model where consumers learn about product quality through experience or producer reputation. If higher-quality producers have higher marginal costs than lower-quality producers, they find that there will not be any (noninformative) advertising in equilibrium. This case, for which repeat purchases are not sufficient for advertising to signal quality, differs from Nelson's (1970, 1974) analyses.[33] The link between advertising and the quality of experience goods identified by Nelson is reexamined by Milgrom and Roberts (1986b) using a market model in which both price and advertising may simultaneously signal product quality.[34] They give sufficient conditions under which a separating sequential equilibrium exists. They find that low-quality firms do not advertise, while high-quality firms only advertise to the extent needed to supplement price signals.

Seller reputation provides another important source of information in markets.[35] Consumers learn about product attributes and seller characteristics from purchases. To attract repeat purchases, producers must produce products of a certain quality and devote effort to maintaining quality over time. The information conveyed by consumer learning may thus provide incentives for firms to take care in production.[36] Shapiro (1982, 1983) considers seller reputation when quality is unobservable. Shapiro (1982) examines moral hazard problems that may arise when a monopolist supplies a good of unobservable quality and consumers form adaptive expectations about the producer's reputation. Quality is shown to be below the full information level. In this model, there are no alternative signals of product quality, such as advertising. Allen (1984) also considers moral hazard problems in a dynamic model of product quality choice. Consumers may make inferences using price and output, if output is observable. The first-best equilibrium may obtain under certain conditions. Allen shows that with warranties, the first-best equilibrium is more likely to obtain.

The market provides a wide variety of signals in addition to price, advertising, and seller reputation. Sellers and their products have many observable characteristics. A seller may be established for a long period of time or signal product quality through location and other attributes of the firm. Products may have apparent attributes that provide information about unobservable ones. See Spence (1977b) on signaling and warranties. Consumers may make some inferences about maintenance or reliability from observation of an automobile before purchase (e.g., number of cylinders, fuel requirements). Products, broadly defined to include contract terms, may have multiple attributes that provide information about quality, including guarantees, warranties, and service agreements. Observation of multiple signals including price and advertising allows consumers to confirm inferences that may not be made as accurately with fewer signals.

Finally, consumers have access to privately supplied information obtained from third parties. Private research organizations, such as testing laboratories, and specialized publications provide comparative information about product characteristics. Publications exist that provide information about pharmaceuticals, restaurants and hotels, automobiles, electronics and computers, investments, and a broad variety of consumer goods. Thus, "experience" goods need not require direct experiences by the consumer. Producers have incentives to supply higher-quality products to maintain their ratings with third parties. A significant amount of information about products is provided through retailers and other middlemen[37] (specialty stores, travel agents, pharmacists, stock brokers). Finally, consumers may seek advice from experienced third parties (lawyers, doctors, mechanics, accountants) in evaluating contract terms or product characteristics. These alternative sources mitigate the free rider problems associated with the public good aspect of information provided by producers. Economies of scale in the production of information may be achieved by centralized information gathering by third parties to market transactions.

15.4.2 Disclosure

In the unregulated market place, the consumer has numerous direct and indirect sources of information. To summarize the preceding discussion these are as follows:

i. search (observation of product characteristics before purchase),

ii. experience (observation of product characteristics after purchase),

iii. prices as signals,

iv. advertising as a signal,

v. seller reputation,

vi. contract terms as signals (warranties, service, observable product characteristics),

vii. retailers and middlemen, and

viii. purchase of information from independent third parties.

Thus, asymmetry in the information possessed initially by consumers and firms need not imply that differences in knowledge persist over time. The market establishes numerous means of communication between traders. Furthermore, competition yields disclosure of information through self-selection. Over the long run, seller reputation effects also promote disclosure. Therefore, consumers are often able to make informed choices on the basis of information provided in the marketplace. Internalities may be a significant feature of only a limited set of transactions.

An interesting analysis of disclosure appears in Jovanovich (1982). He shows that if there are no benefits from false claims, the market may actually provide incentives for overinvestment in disclosure; see also Spence (1973b) and Stiglitz (1975). Matthews and Postlewaite (1985) allow the firm to decide whether or not to test for (exogenous) product quality before deciding whether to disclose private information. They find that if disclosure is mandatory, this "makes claims of ignorance credible" and a firm may wish to avoid becoming informed, so disclosure laws may not be effective without the imposition of additional information-gathering requirements.

Barriers to entry need not justify regulation on the basis of imperfect information. It is not evident that a firm with market power is better placed to exploit its private information about product quality. Grossman (1981a) finds that a monopolist has an incentive to disclose information about product quality voluntarily when there is no moral hazard on the consumer side. See also Grossman and Hart (1980). Grossman considers the case where quality is verifiable ex post and the case where losses, but not the underlying quality level, are observable ex post. In the first case, laws against fraud rule out misrepresentation. The seller can only understate quality, something that would lower revenues of a high-quality producer. Therefore, consumers can infer that a product is of low quality if producers make less than full disclosure. All sellers, except the seller with the lowest quality, will fully disclose their quality. In the second case, where quality is not verifiable, the seller will offer a warranty that fully insures consumers. Grossman assumes costless disclosure and warranties and concludes that not only are mandated warranties and disclosure unnecessary, but that excessive disclosure of irrelevant information in compliance with regulation may interfere with consumer inference of product quality. Milgrom (1981) shows that in a sequential equilibrium, full disclosure will take place. Milgrom and Roberts (1986a) extend this discussion and conclude that (p. 30) "skepticism on the part of the decisionmaker and/or competition among interested parties can result in the emergence of all the relevant information and the selection of an optimal decision." Their analysis suggests that firms often have an incentive to disclose product quality and safety to consumers. Furthermore, the "interested parties" have incentives to make full disclosure in regulatory hearings as well. From this it may be concluded that unobservability of product quality or of producer characteristics can never serve in itself as a justification for regulation or mandated disclosure. Rather, it must be demonstrated that incentives are absent for voluntary private disclosure. This analysis must incorporate the costs of information gathering and disclosure.

To discern a potential role for regulation, it must first be established that the market does not supply consumers with the means to make informed choices and that regulatory agencies can provide such information at less cost than private alternatives. Regulators may choose between two principal policy directions. The first is to attempt to enhance the market's ability to transmit information. Disclosure regulations may rely on the market to determine the nature and amount of information to be produced, or they may entail direct government intervention. Policy actions include

i. removal of legal, contractual, or regulatory restrictions on communication,

ii. standardization of terms used to communicate between market participants,

iii. mandated disclosure of information, and

iv. direct government production and dissemination of information.

The second policy direction is to abandon reliance on disclosure and market competition by directly intervening in transactions between consumers and firms. The wide range of regulatory actions that specify product quality, durability, safety, and other characteristics, or that impose standards on production technology and workplace health and safety, ultimately reflects the choice to bypass market decision making. Such regulations are often justified on the basis of imperfect information. Thus, direct regulation of product quality and disclosure regulations may be viewed as policy options representing opposing views of the market allocation mechanism.

The removal of barriers to entry in the market for information should certainly be a goal for regulatory policy. Elimination of entry barriers allows market participants to make decisions regarding the quantity of information to be supplied. Competition will generally assure that information is produced and transmitted in an efficient manner. For example, removing some restrictions on advertising promotes competition among suppliers and can improve the information available to consumers. If barriers to communication are the result of regulatory policy, this should be a relatively simple problem to remedy. Regulators should not restrict market signaling. Ordover and Weiss (1981) suggest that by prohibiting exculpatory clauses in contracts, under a regime of strict liability, price discrimination between careful and careless consumers through consumer signaling can be blocked. They argue informally that the resulting equilibrium will be Pareto superior to a separating market equilibrium. However, their policy may restrict communication and may lead to Pareto inferior-pooling equilibria or exclusion of customer classes from the market.

The costs of preparing and communicating information may limit the information available to consumers. By establishing standard disclosure rules and terms, regulators may reduce the private costs of establishing standards. In this regulators provide a "unit of account" that allows producers to transmit summary information and allows consumers to make comparisons between different products. This may reduce the costs of search and of decision making while promoting competition among producers in terms of product quality. The danger of this is that producers compete to improve their performance in terms of the summary measure (miles per gallon for cars, energy usage for appliances) while neglecting other features that are desired by consumers but less easily identified or described. The focal point established by government standards may divert attention from important product characteristics. Labeling of food contents, for example (vitamins, cholesterol, sugar), many create standardized products with undesirable features for some consumers (e.g., artificial sweeteners).

A number of alternative regulatory responses to imperfect information are considered by Beales, Craswell, and Salop (1981a,b). These include removing government and private restrictions on information exchange, regulation of advertising, and establishing a common metric so that product information is comparable. They recommend (1981b, p. 413) direct regulation of information rather than remedies that address "the effect of imperfect information" (e.g., contract terms, prices, product characteristics). They propose a "market information policy" based on cost-benefit analysis,[38] which, of course, requires government agencies to collect the information on product quality required to estimate costs and benefits.

Mandated disclosure of information may be desirable in markets where competition cannot be relied upon to induce revelation. However, such regulations are subject to all of the problems that attend command-and-control regulation and standard setting. These regulations are costly to design and enforce, and they presume highly informed regulators. There may be high costs of information gathering and distribution imposed on firms. These costs are ultimately borne by consumers, who may have desired different types of information than those mandated by regulators. Disclosure regulations may yield benefits in terms of informed consumer decisions about the product and increased competition among suppliers.

The desirability of disclosure provisions in securities regulation has been widely questioned.[39] In a critical study of the Securities and Exchange Commission (SEC), Stigler (1964b) finds the performance of the SEC to be at variance with its purpose. Stigler (1964b) states that the general view of the purpose of securities regulation is "to increase the portion of truth in the world and to prevent or punish fraud." On the other hand, Beaver (1980, p. 324) observes that if the private costs of reaching and enforcing agreements to disclose information are high, then "the SEC may have a comparative advantage in effectively eliminating private search for information."[40] It is possible that the high costs of preparing and interpreting information about corporations may create high transaction costs. These costs will determine the degree of disclosure observed in the marketplace. The welfare gains from improvements in disclosure must be balanced against the costs of creating and enforcing securities regulations.[41]

Regulation is applied directly to advertising, particularly by the FTC. The FTC has acted against deceptive advertising in a wide variety of consumer product industries. Craswell (1985, p. 660) argues that deceptive advertising should be viewed as "potentially dangerous products" with risks of damage and costs of mitigating damages. He proposes an application of the negligence standard of Judge Learned Hand: "An ad would be deemed deceptive if and only if the advertiser failed to take some precaution that would have reduced the net injury caused by the ad." This departs from the traditional view of deceptive advertising as per se illegal and costless to avoid.[42] Craswell emphasizes the difficulties encountered in measuring injuries to customers from incorrectly informed purchase decisions.[43] The costs of reducing deception may include a lowering of the information content of ads, the costs of increasing product quality to match that implied by the ad, and the costs of research to substantiate advertising claims. Craswell (1985, p. 722) stresses that the producer need not obtain benefits from deliberate fraud, but rather faces costs of reducing misperceptions created by advertising.

Finally, it should be noted that governments engage in significant information production. It has been frequently observed that information is a public good and as such constitutes an entirely appropriate activity for governments. Government-sponsored research in the areas of health and safety in products and the workplace may yield substantial net benefits. Traditional caveats about the difficulty of optimally supplying public goods of course apply here.

Regulation of product quality has been analyzed in an asymmetric information setting; see particularly Baron (1981), Shavell (1984b),[44] and Besanko, Donnenfeld, and White (1987).[45] These analyses, and the many regulatory models that incorporate asymmetric information are important as an antidote to the traditional view of regulation as a command-and-control mechanism in which the regulator may achieve optimal outcomes constrained only by the policy instruments at his disposal. The limited information available to regulators causes them to surrender some information rents to firms in order to elicit truth-telling. Optimal regulatory policy will then allow departures from full information optimal pricing and product quality. A recognition that regulators may operate under incomplete information has an additional implication. It serves to counteract the view that welfare-enhancing product quality standards can be designed and implemented simply as a result of the superior information possessed by regulators. Asymmetric information in the marketplace may be expected to reappear in the interaction between regulators and market participants.

The principal conclusion to be drawn from the preceding discussion is that asymmetric information may not be sufficient to cause internalities. While moral hazard problems may be caused by the unobservability of actions, such as producer care, there may exist competitive forces that mitigate these effects. Similarly, although adverse selection problems may arise as a result of unobservable characteristics, such as product quality, there may exist market incentives such that consumers and producers communicate private information. Communication may take the form of indirect signals, through price, advertising, observable product charac-teristics, and producer reputation. Communication may involve voluntary direct disclosure of private information. Therefore, asymmetric information is not a sufficient justification for regulation. Rather, it must first be demon-strated that internalities, unappropriated costs or benefits of individual transactions, are present. Second, it must be shown that public intervention can mitigate these internalities in a more effective manner than competitive markets. Third, it must be verified that the information gathering and disclosure by regulators is more effective or less costly than private com-munication. Finally, government disclosure policies that ultimately rely on competitive markets for resource allocation must take precedence, where feasible, over direct government regulation of product quality and workplace safety.

Appendix

Proof of proposition 15.3.3   To verify that the mechanism $q^*(\mu, \theta)$ that solves (15.3.14) and (15.3.15) satisfies the incentive compatibility constraints (15.3.8) and (15.3.9), it is sufficient to differentiate partially the first-order condition (15.3.14) with respect to μ and θ,

$$\partial q^*(\mu, \theta)/\partial \mu = \{l_1 + (\gamma/(1 + \gamma))[sl_{11}(F/f) + sl_1 \partial(F/f)/\partial \mu$$

$$+ (1 - s)l_{21}(G/g)]\}/(u'' - C''),$$

$$\partial q^*(\mu, \theta)/\partial \theta = \{l_2 + (\gamma/(1 + \gamma))[sl_{12}(F/f) + (1 - s)l_{22}(G/g)$$

$$+ (1 - s)l_2 \partial(G/g)/\partial \theta]\}/(u'' - C'').$$

Clearly, q^* is decreasing in μ and θ, since $l_2 > 0$, $l_{11} > 0$, $l_{22} > 0$, $l_{12} > 0$, and $\partial(F/f)/\partial \mu > 0$, $\partial(G/g)/\partial \theta > 0$.   QED

Notes

1. See, for example, the special issue of the *Journal of Legal Studies*, volume 14, December 1985, titled "Critical Issues in Tort Law Reform: A Search for Principles."

2. Negative values of the numeraire are allowed. Alternatively, losses may be small relative to residual income. In a more general setting, nonmonetary losses could directly affect consumer well-being to represent "pain and suffering" or disutility from inconvenience.

3. See Dye (1985) on labor contracts for which costs depend on the number of contingencies.

4. Let $L(q, z, \xi) = l(q, z)$ for all $\xi \leq \tilde{\xi}$ and let $L(q, z, \xi) = 0$ for all $\xi > \tilde{\xi}$, given some constant $\tilde{\xi} > 0$. Then the loss occurs with a constant probability $\eta = G(\tilde{\xi})$ and no loss occurs with probability $(1 - \eta)$.

5. Limited liability is considered by Shavell (1984a), who shows that in a simple model with risk neutral parties, care is less than first best but increasing in harm below the level of assets. Shavell shows that it may be possible to improve matters by jointly applying a regulatory standard in the presence of strict liability.

6. This, of course, requires a competitive insurance market and assumes no costs of administering or writing insurance contracts. As is well-known, if such costs exist, consumers do not fully insure and a deductible is present in the equilibrium policy. In this case, consumers bear some risk, and we again have a departure from the social optimum in the product market.

7. Insurance premiums that reflect *estimated risks* are said to be *feature rated*, while those that reflect *historical losses* of an individual product or activity are said to be *experience rated*; see, for example, Abraham (1986, p. 46). An example of feature rating in automobile service agreements is if a higher premium is charged for a more expensive car.

8. The consumer chooses a policy by selecting the percentage of losses, s, to be covered by insurance, $0 \leq s \leq 1$. Coverage s is chosen to maximize

$$\int_0^\infty U(q, \omega - pq - s\lambda L(q, z) - (1 - s)L(q, z, \xi)) \, dH(\xi).$$

Choosing s optimally, yields

$$\left[\int_0^\infty U_y L(q, z, \xi) h(\xi) \, d\xi / L(q, z) \int_0^\infty U_y h(\xi) \, d\xi \right] = \lambda > 1,$$

where $U_y = U_y(q, \omega - pq - s\lambda L(q, z) - (1 - s)L(q, z, \xi))$. Therefore, $s < 1$ and coverage is not full.

9. Abraham (1986, p. 52) refers to these as "subrogation funds" and observes that actual funds are a mixture of subrogation and nonsubrogation aspects. Under subrogation, "the fund acquires the victim's rights against that party (to the extent of payment out of the fund) once the fund has paid the victim" (Abraham, 1986, p. 53).

10. Abraham (1986, p. 45) concludes that "the deterrent effects of special compensation funds, even when linked with surrogate regulation by the insurance industry, cannot effectively replace direct governmental regulation of environmental hazards."

11. See Arrow (1965, 1968), Kihlstrom and Pauly (1971), Spence and Zeckhauser (1971), Pauly (1968, 1974), and Zeckhauser (1970). Pauly (1974) shows that the competitive equilibrium of an insurance market with moral hazard involves excessive insurance and insufficient accident prevention as compared to the full information social optimum.

12. The incentive schemes discussed in this section are based on losses observed ex post, since ex ante actions to reduce expected losses are not observable. Wittman (1977) observes that

the choice of regulation of ex ante inputs versus ex post actions, such as tort liability, is in part a function of available information and monitoring costs.

13. The equilibrium may be represented formally as a Nash equilibrium with three players: a consumer, a firm, and a Walrasian auctioneer. The consumer and firm choose output and care levels as a best response to the equilibrium price and the other party's care level,

$$V(\bar{q}^D, \bar{x}, \bar{z}, \bar{p}) \geq V(q^D, x, \bar{z}, \bar{p}) \qquad \text{for all } q^D, x,$$

$$\Pi(\bar{q}^S, \bar{x}, \bar{z}, \bar{p}) \geq \Pi(q^S, \bar{x}, z, \bar{p}) \qquad \text{for all } q^S, z.$$

The Walrasian auctioneer selects a price $\bar{p}$ such that the market clears at $\bar{p}, \bar{q}^D = \bar{q}^S = \bar{q}$.

14. The free rider problem within partnerships and labor-managed firms is attributed to the absence of a monitor by Alchian and Demsetz (1972). Holmström (1982, p. 327) observes that the 'free rider problem is not solely the consequence of the unobservability of actions, but equally the consequence of imposing budget balancing.'

15. The Groves (1973, 1976) mechanism provides a solution to the free rider problem but does not yield a balanced budget. See also Groves and Loeb (1975), Groves and Ledyard (1977a,b), Green and Laffont (1977), d'Aspremont and Gérard-Varet (1979), and Holmström (1982).

16. A related question is how to achieve optimal private enforcement of law. Landes and Posner (1975) note that public enforcement costs can be lowered by raising fines and lowering the probability of detection while maintaining efficient levels of deterrence. However, a fine in excess of damages will stimulate excessive private enforcement efforts. What may be needed is a separation between fines paid by the injurer and payments to enforcers. *Decoupling* of fines and damage payments also plays a role in private enforcement of antitrust law; see chapter 19.

17. The moral hazard model of the preceding section and the adverse selection models in the present section may be combined. It may be assumed that care yields disutility for consumers but that the cost of care for consumers is private information. The costs of care for firms may also be unobservable. Then bargaining between the consumer and firm over output and payments will reveal information about the costs of care. Adjustment of care levels will be inefficient, reflecting imperfect monitoring of care as well as unobservable costs of care.

18. As noted previously, the absence of scale effects on expected losses is standard in the products quality literature; see, for example, Epple and Raviv (1978) and Shavell (1980b).

19. A mechanism is interim incentive efficient if and only if it maximizes

$$\int_0^1 V(\mu)\,da(\mu) + \int_0^1 \Pi(\theta)\,db(\theta)$$

subject to (15.3.8)–(15.3.10). Again, note that this approach is due to Myerson (1985).

20. As in chapter 11, simple examples under which exchange rents are sufficient to cover information rents may be given.

21. The comparative static effects of the liability parameter s are indeterminate and somewhat complicated, since s affects the first-order condition for output and, indirectly, the budget balancing condition as well: (15.3.14) and (15.3.15).

22. Alternative forms of the loss functions may yield interior values for s.

23. Given the regularity conditions on the hazard rate, (f/F), if follows that q is monotonically decreasing in μ, so that incentive compatibility is satisfied. There may be the problem of an "informed principal" on the producer side. For present purposes, it is assumed that conditions are satisfied such that $P(q; \theta)$ represents the firm's preferred strategy.

24. Nonexistence in the "market for lemons" is due largely to the multiplicative nature of the example given by Akerlof (1970). For existence examples, see Myerson (1985).

25. See Myerson (1985) and Chatterjee and Samuelson (1983) for discussion of this strategy in bargaining over the price of an indivisible object.

26. See Greenwald (1986) for an extension to the labor market.

27. Dependence of benefits on the signal may be included in various ways. For example, the size of the loss can be a function of some observable quality level, $l = l(t)$.

28. The model may be generalized to allow risk aversion. Let $u(\cdot)$ be the utility of net income and let ω be the consumer's income. Then expected utility is defined as follows: $U(p, \theta) = (1 - \theta)u(\omega - p) + \theta u(\omega - p - l)$.

29. Riley (1985) gives a sufficient condition for the existence of a separating market equilibrium. In the present framework, suppose that θ can take only three possible values, $\{\theta_0, \theta_1, \theta_2\}$, where $\theta_0 > u/l > \theta_1 > \theta_2$. Then, in equilibrium, only products of type θ_1 and θ_2 are sold. The separating equilibrium exists if the marginal cost of signaling product quality $C_t(\theta, t)$ increases sufficiently rapidly in θ (compared to the relative proportions of firms of type 1 to types 1 and 2 combined).

30. The extent to which advertising is informative is discussed by Telser (1964) and Ferguson (1974); see also Schmalensee (1972).

31. Schmalensee (1978b) considers a model in which consumers are unable to distinguish the relation between advertising and product quality and finds that low-quality producers may advertise at the market equilibrium.

32. For example, Dixit and Norman (1978) show that advertising is excessive whether judged by pre- or postadvertising tests when advertising reduces demand elasticity. Advertising is sometimes viewed as insufficient because of its public good nature; see Spence (1975). Spulber (1984b) shows that nonlinear pricing by a monopolist allows the firm to recover advertising outlays by assessing consumers' marginal valuation of advertising. Kotowitz and Mathewson (1979a) compare advertising with dissemination of information by consumers through demonstration effects using a diffusion model. They conclude that monopolists do not produce excessive information. Elsewhere, Kotowitz and Mathewson (1979b) find that, given adaptive expectations, advertising may contain misleading information in the short run and that the monopolist substitutes advertising for product quality although the welfare effects of such substitution are ambiguous.

33. Advertising does function as a signal, and multiple advertising equilibria are observed under different cost assumptions by Kihlstrom and Riordan (1984).

34. This represents multidimensional signaling, examined by Wilson (1985) and others.

35. See Kreps and Wilson (1982) for a general discussion of reputation and strategy in games with imperfect information.

36. Klein and Leffler (1981) examine a deterministic market model in which consumers observe a brand's product quality after purchase. Producers offering higher-quality goods charge a price premium, which acts as a quality indicator. Firms may still "cheat" by offering high-priced, low-quality goods if the current returns from doing so outweigh future losses from a bad reputation. See also Schmalensee (1978b) and Smallwood and Conlisk (1979) on product quality selection and seller reputation.

37. See the discussion of incentives for provision of information and vertical restraints in chapter 16.

38. See Schmalensee (1981a) for a comment on this "market information policy." He compares market information policy to antitrust policy circa 1911 in terms of the absence of well-defined economic and legal standards to be applied in forming legal judgments and regulatory policy.

Schmalensee suggests the need for development of economic analysis of market information that will act as an "analogue to industrial organization economics."

39. A number of papers in the debate over the SEC are reprinted in Posner and Scott (1980).

40. Beaver (1980, p. 324) notes that private search may lead to excessive production of information, while the public good aspects of information may lead to insufficient disclosure. The predominance of either effect will influence production of information by the market.

41. Beaver (1980, p. 321) notes that there are direct and indirect costs of disclosure as well as costs of regulation: "The direct costs of disclosure include the costs of the production, certification, dissemination, processing and interpretation of disclosures.... The indirect costs include the adverse effects of disclosure on competitive advantage ... and legal liability .... The costs of regulation include the costs involved in the development, compliance, enforcement and litigation of disclosure regulations."

42. Schmalensee (1981b) states that "there is apparently only one consensus per se offense in the market information area: making false claims is to market information as price-fixing is to antitrust law."

43. Craswell (1985) observes that the injuries to competitors caused by deceptive advertising may be transitory and suggests that remedies are best left to the competitive market.

44. Shavell (1984b) provides a model in which regulation of care levels is imposed under incomplete information about producer costs of care. He compares liability with safety regulation and concludes that they may be used jointly, with regulation providing a minimum standard and liability providing additional incentives for care for firms with higher expected losses. Shavell does not consider the possibility that the market may regulate product quality through signaling or other means of transmitting information to consumers.

45. Besanko, Donnenfeld, and White (1987) consider the possibility of regulating a discriminating monopolist who offers an array of goods of varying quality levels. The source of imperfect information in their model is the presence of two consumer classes who are induced to purchase products of differing quality. They show that an optimally chosen quality standard may lessen pricing distortions. A price ceiling has ambiguous welfare effects but does affect the distribution of income across consumer types.

IV ANTITRUST: EFFICIENCY AND COMPETITION

16 Antitrust Law and Regulation

Antitrust enforcement is generally portrayed as the promotion or protection of competition through restraint of anticompetitive behavior by large firms. Antitrust involves much more than interaction between enforcement agencies and particular firms, however. Antitrust is a complex administrative regulatory mechanism that extensively intervenes in *market allocation*, affecting prices, output, product variety, and innovation, not just the size of firms. This chapter examines the characteristics of antitrust law and enforcement and emphasizes the close connection with the forms of administrative regulation of markets studied thus far.

The antitrust laws and agencies are discussed in section 16.1. The antitrust agencies are seen to have legislative, judicial, and executive functions, as do administrative regulatory agencies. The agencies engage in information collection and also act as policymakers. They engage in *bargaining* with industry through consent decrees, merger requirements, and rule making. The decisions made by the antitrust agencies have important consequences for almost all market actions of firms, including pricing, product characteristics, asset ownership, mergers, research and development, and market entry. Thus, antitrust law and enforcement is one of the major regulatory forces.

The antitrust statutes were developed in response to various political pressures and reflect a variety of social objectives from protecting small business to limiting the size of firms. Some lawyers and economists have chosen to interpret the objective of the antitrust statutes as the achievement of economic efficiency rather than the promotion of competition. This position is taken, for example, by Bork (1978). Without necessarily endorsing the notion of antitrust as a form of regulation in the "public interest," the present work examines antitrust as a remedy for market failure. Sections 16.2, 16.3, and 16.4 consider the antitrust laws as attempts to cope with perceived barriers to entry, externalities, and internalities. These categories of market failure prove to be useful not only in identifying areas in which antitrust can improve the efficient operation of the market but also in discovering areas in which antitrust enforcement is directed at nonexistent market failure and therefore *interferes* with efficient market operation.

The discussion in section 16.2 emphasizes antitrust action against collusion to fix prices. In the absence of entry barriers, e.g., sunk costs, collusion generally will either be unprofitable or will invite competitive entry. Section 16.3 examines anticompetitive practices. Many antitrust cases allege harm done to rivals' ability to compete in a manner suggestive of externalities. My analysis of this issue concludes that many exclusionary practices, such as predatory pricing, are either unprofitable or do not reduce competition. Exclusionary practices that operate through the market entail costs for the firm engaging in them and so do not properly constitute externalities. Thus, antitrust action against these practices may in many cases be detrimental to competition. The role of internalities in antitrust is addressed in section 16.4. The actions (by the FTC) directed at improvement of contract terms and consumer protection may be a useful response to internalities caused by costly contract contingencies or imperfect information in the market. Antitrust actions against vertical restraints may, however, reduce the effectiveness of market responses to internalities.

16.1   Statutes and Administrative Agencies

16.1.1   The Statutes

The principal antitrust statutes are the Sherman Act (1890), the Clayton Act (1914), and the Federal Trade Commission (FTC) Act (1914). The FTC Act is discussed below along with the FTC. Important later amendments of the Clayton Act are the Robinson-Patman Act (1936) and the Celler-Kefauver Act (1950). The purpose here is to give a brief summary of the major statutes and a discussion of the economic aspects of enforcement. The extensive case law and legal and economic analyses of antitrust policy, which have been ably discussed elsewhere, are not reviewed.

The Sherman Act forbids both collusion and individual firm attempts to obtain monopoly power. Section 1 declares illegal "every contract, combination in the form of trust or otherwise, or conspiracy, in restraint of trade or commerce." Section 2 addresses the act of monopolizing and "attempts to monopolize." Although Senator Sherman characterized the act as a "remedial statute to enforce by civil process ... the common law against monopolies" (Thorelli 1955, p. 181), it represents a significant departure from common law both in its scope and enforcement implications. The development and origins of the Sherman Act are set out by Thorelli (1955) and Letwin (1965).

The Clayton Act is aimed at a number of practices where "the effect" of the practice "may be substantially to lessen competition or tend to create a monopoly in any line of commerce." The practices declared illegal under this condition include price discrimination (section 2), tying and exclusive dealing (section 3), mergers between competitors (section 7), and interlocking directorates (section 8). Section 4 of the Clayton Act provides for trebling of damages in private suits (supplanting section 7 of the Sherman Act).

The Robinson-Patman Act (amending section 2 of the Clayton Act) forbids price discrimination that lessens competition. The act allows for price discrimination due to cost differentials in production and delivery[1] and due to meeting the competition "in good faith." The Celler-Kefauver Act (amending section 7 of the Clayton Act) includes horizontal, vertical, and conglomerate mergers (through acquisition of a firm's stock or assets) that would substantially "lessen competition" or "create a monopoly."

These rather general and basic antitrust rules provide the foundation for wide application and considerable extensions by the antitrust enforcement agencies. Through policy decisions, case selection, settlement agreements, and announced guidelines, the antitrust agencies have broadened the scope and added detail to antitrust law. The full complexity of antitrust law is contained in a century of American case law.

16.1.2 The Agencies

Antitrust Division The Antitrust Division (AD) of the Department of Justice (DOJ) is charged with enforcement of the Sherman Act and the Clayton Act through investigation and in some cases prosecution in federal court. In many ways, the AD resembles other regulatory agencies, particularly those situated in cabinet level departments of the executive branch. Of importance is the considerable latitude given the AD in case selection by its mandate and the statutes it enforces. The AD engages in extensive information gathering through reception of public complaints and antitrust investigations. The AD is involved in rule making through announcement of antitrust guidelines and policies. The AD also engages in adjudication, particularly in negotiating settlements or consent decrees.

It is important to address the issue of whether the AD is properly considered as a regulatory agency. A key observation due to Weaver (1977, p. 5) is that the antitrust statutes do not determine "whether the enforcement relationship between government and business will be a purely adversary one or will include elements of bargaining and cooperation." Since a majority of (noncriminal) antitrust cases are settled by consent decree,[2] it may be argued that bargaining plays a significant role in antitrust, just as was observed in the case of rate hearings, environmental standards enforcement, and other areas of regulation. Weaver (1977, p. 26) argues that by making the AD a prosecutor, Congress did not follow "the already available model of the regulatory commission but the device of the courts and the common law." Thus, interpretation of the law in particular cases remains the task of the judiciary. However, in the selection of cases and in the internal allocation of enforcement effort, it is evident that the AD makes antitrust policy.

The AD and the FTC have taken on traditional regulatory roles, particularly in their enforcement of merger rules. The approval of mergers often involves extensive bargaining between the DOJ, other regulatory agencies, and the parties to the merger. The DOJ has in many cases required specific divestitures or other actions by potential merger partners as a precondition for the merger to be allowed. This differs from the simple decision as to whether or not to approve a specific merger. The specific requirements imposed by the DOJ may have a significant impact on market structure and the individual characteristics of firms after the merger takes place. In some cases, the merger requirements are identical to traditional regulatory rule making and adjudication. A case in point is the 1986 acquisition of Eastern Airlines by Texas Air Corporation. The DOJ and the Department of Transportation spelled out specific requirements for the merger, including the number of airport landing slots that would have to be sold to competitors, a regulatory task formerly associated with the Civil Aeronautics Board.[3] Railroad mergers involve complicated agreements to sell trackage rights to competitors and to not abandon portions of track. Oil company mergers involve divestiture of retail outlets or refining capacity. These merger requirements are a form of entry and investment regulation.

Federal Trade Commission   The Federal Trade Commission (FTC) was established under the FTC Act. The initial mandate (under section 5 of the FTC Act) was to prevent "unfair methods of competition" and "unfair or deceptive acts or practices in or affecting commerce." Thus, the FTC is involved both in the promotion of competition and in consumer protection. In the promotion of competition, the activities of the FTC are comparable to the Antitrust Division of the DOJ. In consumer protection, the mission of the FTC is perhaps better compared to regulatory agencies, such as the Consumer Product Safety Commission and the Securities and Exchange

Commission. An important debate within the FTC is between law enforcement in response to complaints and planning of case selection to achieve broader objectives in particular industries.[4]

The FTC, like the Antitrust Division of the DOJ, has many of the characteristics of other administrative regulatory agencies.[5] The FTC has considerable discretion in its selection of cases, and thus acts as a policymaker in antitrust.[6] The FTC gathers information both through public complaints and through investigations. While the FTC is subject to executive, legislative, and judicial oversight, FTC decision making and case selection does not closely involve public interest groups.[7] Congressional oversight and intervention has been limited as well, with some widely noted exceptions. FTC powers with regard to antitrust enforcement include investigation, prosecution, and administrative adjudication under the FTC Act (section 5) and the Clayton Act (sections 2, 3, 7, and 8).[8]

In the 1970s, the FTC's powers increased, particularly under the Magnuson-Moss Warranty-FTC Improvements Act of 1975 (hereafter the Magnuson-Moss Act)—which conferred broad rule-making powers and increased enforcement authority in consumer protection. The act establishes regulations and disclosure requirements for consumer product warranties, but relies heavily on FTC rule making to determine interpretation and enforcement.[9] Under the act, the FTC may make Trade Regulation Rules. The formal public rule-making procedures follow the Administrative Procedures Act[10] as well as additional requirements including statements by the FTC on the "unfairness" of the acts to which the rule applies and the "economic effects of the rule."[11] The first Trade Regulation Rule under the FTC Improvements Act attempted to remove restraints on advertising of eyeglasses by industry associations and may be viewed as a type of deregulation. In promulgating the rule, the FTC emphasized the importance of the market in the allocation of goods and dissemination of information.[12]

Additional FTC powers stem from a large array of special statutes.[13] These include the power to seek injunctions and premerger notification procedures.[14] Special statutes apply to particular industries, such as textiles, cigarettes, and consumer loans.

The preceding discussion sets out the antitrust laws and the two major agencies charged with their enforcement. There is no question that the antitrust laws, as is the case with other forms of market regulation, reflect a variety of policy objectives, many of which conflict with economic efficiency. These include promotion of small business, reducing the political power of large firms, consumer protection, and targeted assistance and penalties directed at specific firms or industries. If cost gains from consolidation of production outweigh welfare losses from monopoly, promotion of competition by antitrust may conflict with the public interest. Recognizing this, nevertheless the rest of this chapter is devoted to a welfare analysis of antitrust policies. If antitrust policy has a role to play in improving the efficiency of the market, it must address market failure. Antitrust policies are classified by the market failures they are meant to address: barriers to entry, externalities, and internalities. This provides useful criteria for the evaluation of antitrust policy.

16.2   Barriers to Entry: Collusion

16.2.1   Enforcement and Barriers to Entry

The exercise of monopoly power requires the presence of barriers to entry of new competitors. Accordingly, acts such as collusion and horizontal mergers necessitate entry barriers to increase the market power of the firms involved. This economic analysis of competition has a bearing on the effectiveness and desirability of antitrust enforcement. Of particular relevance are the Sherman Act restrictions on collusion and monopolization and the Clayton Act restrictions on mergers. These are addressed in turn.

Posner (1976a) makes an important and useful suggestion of a two-stage economic approach to enforcement of the Sherman Act as it applies to collusion: "The first would involve identifying those markets in which conditions are propitious for the emergence of collusion; the second determining whether collusive pricing in fact exists in such a market" (1976a, p. 55). As Posner notes, the first stage allows efficient allocation of scarce enforcement,[15] and the second stage allows "ambiguous conduct" to be evaluated.[16] This two-stage approach appears to be applicable to the design of optimal enforcement policy and guides the present discussion.

Of the factors that allow or facilitate collusion, the present work is most interested in those factors that render collusion "effective" in generating *market power* for firms and in yielding *monopoly profits*. Although price fixing is per se illegal, the scarcity of enforcement resources suggests that effective price fixing might be the most desirable focus of enforcement efforts.

The principal determinant of the effectiveness of collusion is the existence of barriers to entry in the sense of Stigler.[17] As discussed in chapter 1, one may eliminate product differentiation, absolute cost advantages, and economies of scale as entry barriers. The principal entry barrier is due to sunk costs. Delays and the time needed to establish a plant or to learn about market conditions certainly impede entry. These entry costs may be viewed as a form of sunk costs. In the absence of sunk costs, collusive pricing will attract new entry. Even if market concentration is high, and a few firms succeed in raising prices, this will serve to provide incentives for new firms to be established, which then sell at prices below those of the cartel. Even if economies of scale are large, it is observed from the contestable markets literature that large-scale entrants may undercut the prices set by established firms if these firms earn above-normal profits. This suggests that antitrust enforcement efforts should be confined to those industries where sunk costs remove at least some significant share of expected returns to entry.

Two other entry barriers should be mentioned in addition to sunk costs. The first results from product or process innovations protected by patents. Although many innovations may be copied or competed against by rivals offering close substitutes, it remains possible for firms to obtain some monopoly rents from patents. However, these rents constitute a return to innovation and are meant to provide incentives for research and development. Thus, eliminating these monopoly rents through antitrust enforcement may go against the purpose of the patent. A firm that acquires monopoly through licensing of a patent from an inventor or through patenting its own innovations is therefore not to be treated in the same manner as a firm acquiring monopoly power through the erection of less desirable entry barriers. The second type of entry barrier is that resulting from exclusive ownership of natural resource inputs. It appears unlikely that a firm can achieve exclusive ownership of a natural resource. Furthermore, if the resource ownership rights are purchased, the purchase price will absorb all monopoly rents. If the firm acquires the resources through discovery, the resource rents constitute a return to exploration in a manner similar to patent protection for innovative activity.

Antitrust responses to the perceived problem of market concentration include divestiture and prevention of mergers. The notion of potential entry is not new to these areas of antitrust enforcement. However, the argument of "potential competition" has been used to block mergers[18] and joint ventures.[19] The courts have applied the potential competition doctrine as a means of ruling out acquisitions or joint ventures involving a firm that the court has identified as a potential entrant. This approach is fundamentally different from the contestable markets view, which focuses on the characteristics of the market, (e.g., low entry barriers) rather than identifying specific potential competitors. Traditionally, models of competitive entry have been founded on the presumption that where profit incentives for entry exist, entry will take place. One or more firms will attempt to enter the market.[20] Whether the entrant is newly formed or already established in another industry or geographic area need not be important for the analysis of entry.

A common view in antitrust policy discussions, as expressed, for example, by Reynolds and Reeves (1976), is that "elimination of one of a few objectively qualified potential entrants by leading firm acquisition will injure competition and increase oligopolistic behavior in the market." They suggest study of the Standard Industrial Classification (SIC) Census categories to identify "sources of entrants." This approach seems flawed in that entrants need not be easily identifiable. Further, why would a change in ownership of a firm necessarily alter market behavior? The presence of oligopolistic behavior depends on such factors as entry barriers rather than ownership. If a potential entrant chooses to acquire an established firm, the profit opportunities for de novo entry are unchanged. If the newly acquired firm were to raise prices, the opportunities for entry would, if anything, be enhanced. This suggests that antitrust protection of specific potential entrants is unwarranted.

16.2.2   Cartel Stability

Even in the presence of entry barriers, collusion may be impracticable due to the costs of coordinating price or output decisions and the incentives for cartel members to deviate from cartel pricing agreements. As shown by d'Aspremont et al. (1983), cartels are not stable if the market has many small firms. Then individual firms have incentive to cheat by increasing output to where marginal cost equals price, since no firm individually affects the price. They show, however, that with large firms there is always an incentive for at least one firm to restrict its output, so that there always exists a stable cartel comprising some members of the industry.

Collusion in a market with m sellers of a homogeneous good generally takes the form of output reductions to raise the market price. The optimal collusive output given $m^1 < m$ firms in the cartel depends on the competitive reaction of the competitive fringe, that is, the $m - m^1$ firms in the market that elect not to join the cartel. In addition, the nature of competition in the market between the cartel and the fringe will have a significant impact on cartel behavior. Whether the cartel and the fringe pursue price or quantity setting strategies or pursue nonprice competition through advertising, product differentiation, or research and development is an important consideration.

The cartel stability analysis of d'Aspremont et al. (1983) is carried out in a model in which the cartel commits itself to defending a price. In their setting, the fringe firms take the cartel-set price as given and choose output by setting their marginal cost equal to the price. Thus, $Q^F(p) = \sum_{j=m^1+1}^{m} q^j(p)$ is the supply of the fringe, where $q^j(p)$ solves $p = C'(q^j)$. The cartel or "dominant firm" chooses p to maximize profits per firm for cartel members,

$$\pi^D(m^1) = \max_p p \left[\frac{D(p) - Q^F(p)}{m^1} \right] - C \left[\frac{D(p) - Q^F(p)}{m^1} \right]. \tag{16.2.1}$$

The model is in the tradition of models in which a dominant firm sets the price and a competitive fringe acts as a price taker. The analysis is recast in a Cournot-Nash setting.

Let the market structure m be fixed. Let firms $q^j, j = 1, \ldots, m^1$, be cartel members. The cartel may pursue a price or quantity strategy. Consider first a quantity strategy. Then assume that the $m - m^1$ competitive fringe firms set quantities as well. Then the market equilibrium is a Cournot-Nash type equilibrium, $q^{j*}, j = 1, \ldots, m$, where the cartel acts as a single player. The cartel chooses $q^j, j = 1, \ldots, m^1$, to maximize profits, where $p = P(Q)$ is market inverse demand,

$$\Pi(q^1, \ldots, q^{m^1}, q^{m^1+1*}, \ldots, q^{m*})$$

$$= P \left[\sum_{j=1}^{m^1} q^j + \sum_{j=m^1+1}^{m} q^{j*} \right] \sum_{j=1}^{m^1} q^j - \sum_{j=1}^{m^1} C(q^j). \tag{16.2.2}$$

The fringe firms each choose $q^i, i = m^1 + 1, \ldots, m$, to maximize profits taking all other outputs as given,

$$\Pi(q^i, q^*/q^i) = P \left[\sum_{j \neq i}^{m} q^{j*} + q^i \right] q^i - C(q^i). \tag{16.2.3}$$

Let marginal costs be increasing. Assume that there are no side payments and that all firms in the cartel are active and produce a positive and equal output, q^{1*}. Then, from the first-order conditions for the cartel and fringe,

$$-P'\left[\sum_{j=1}^{m} q^{j*}\right]m^1 q^{1*} + C'(q^{1*}) = P\left[\sum_{j=1}^{m} q^{j*}\right]$$

$$= -P'\left[\sum_{j=1}^{m} q^{j*}\right]q^{j*} + C'(q^{j*}), \quad (16.2.4)$$

for j in the fringe, $j = m^1 + 1, \ldots, m$. From equation (16.2.4) follows

PROPOSITION 16.2.1   *The output of each firm in the competitive fringe is larger than that of a firm in the cartel.*

The members of the cartel restrict their output for the good of the cartel. This reduction of output benefits the firms in the competitive fringe as well. It is evident that marginal revenue for firms in the cartel exceeds zero, since demand is downward sloping,

$$P\left[\sum_{j=1}^{m} q^{j*}\right] + P'\left[\sum_{j=1}^{m} q^{j*}\right]q^{1*} - C'(q^{1*})$$

$$> P\left[\sum_{j=1}^{m} q^{j*}\right] + P'\left[\sum_{j=1}^{m} q^{j*}\right]m^1 q^{1*} - C'(q^{1*}) = 0.$$

Therefore, it is apparent that cartel members would have an incentive to raise their output if all other firms were to keep theirs constant. In addition, the following holds.

PROPOSITION 16.2.2   *The profit of each firm in the competitive fringe is greater than that of a firm in the cartel.*

Let $\pi^C(m^1)$ and $\pi^F(m^1)$ represent the profits of a firm in a cartel and a firm in the competitive fringe, respectively, when m^1 firms are colluding. The profit functions are shown in figure 16.2.1. Clearly, the profits of firms both within and outside the cartel increase with cartel membership. By proposition 16.2.2, the line showing profits for a firm in the fringe lies above that for a firm in the cartel. Then m^{1*} represents a stable cartel size, since no fringe firm has incentive to join the cartel, $\pi^C(m^{1*} + 1) < \pi^F(m^{1*})$, and no cartel member has incentive to cheat, $\pi^F(m^{1*} - 1) < \pi^C(m^{1*})$. As shown by

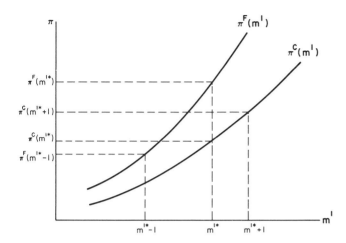

Figure 16.2.1
The cartel with m^{1*} firms is stable.

d'Aspremont et al. (1983), there is always a stable cartel of at least one firm (and, of course, at most involving all firms in the industry).

A persuasive argument can be made against long-run cartel stability or the effectiveness of monopolization. Entry barriers may be effective only temporarily. Bottlenecks may be circumvented by innovative competitors. With changing cost and demand conditions, new entrants may find it worthwhile to sink costs. The higher profits earned by a competitive fringe firm as compared to a cartel member create incentives for entry.

Critics of antitrust policy against collusion and monopolization have stressed that long-run market forces eliminate monopoly rents and market power. Armentano (1982, p. 67), for example, argues that Standard Oil had dramatically lost market share (from 34% of oil production in 1898 to 11% in 1906) when the federal suit was filed in 1906. At issue is the length of time the competitive process requires to eliminate price fixing. Proponents of antitrust might respond that while competition may prevail in the long run, antitrust enforcement is concerned with reducing social welfare losses in the intervening period before prices are reduced. Further, antitrust enforcement seeks to provide deterrence against future collusion and monopolization even if the social welfare losses are temporary and subject to mitigation by competition. Against this argument must be weighed the slow response time of antitrust prosecution and the length of antitrust trials. This suggests that reliance on the market for remedies may not yield significantly greater delays. The high administrative and legal costs of antitrust enforcement are also to be considered. These factors indicate the desirability of restricting antitrust enforcement to activities that achieve deterrence of collusion at the least cost.

16.3 Externalities: Exclusion

A large segment of antitrust law and enforcement is directed at exclusionary practices. These include predatory pricing, tying agreements, exclusive dealing, and price discrimination. These are actions taken by individual firms that are said to harm rivals or to prevent new entry.[21] Despite extensive economic and legal attention to exclusionary practices, it is my contention that the anticompetitive effects of these practices are often illusory and thus do not call for enforcement efforts.

To identify predatory pricing or innovation as anticompetitive practices appears incorrect on its face. The effects of these actions on a firm's rivals are transmitted through market prices; thus, the full costs of the actions are incurred by the firm taking the action. The literature on exclusionary practices resurrects, in a new form, the old canard of *pecuniary externalities*. These are actions by a firm that affect third parties through the market— for example, when expansion by a firm leads to bidding up of input prices.[22] Because they operate through the market, the costs and benefits of pecuniary externalities are fully internalized. A case for public intervention cannot be made on the basis of social welfare arguments.

A competitive firm seeks to increase profits through lowering its costs relative to those of its rivals or raising demand relative to that faced by its rivals. Thus, profit maximization provides incentives for new products and process innovation as well as other productive activities. *All* pricing or supply actions taken by a firm have some effect on its actual or potential rivals by altering the market equilibrium and by changing the conditions for future entry. Antitrust law enforcement efforts are, it seems, concerned with any action that might improve a firm's market share or deter potential entry. Therefore, at one time or another, antitrust enforcement has examined almost all aspects of competitive pricing and supply behavior.[23] For the student of antitrust, this state of affairs inevitably leads to confusion, since it becomes difficult to separate competitive acts from those that imply monopolization of a market or exclusion of entrants, if indeed such a distinction has any meaning.

Accordingly, this section attempts to provide a classification scheme that distinguishes competitive behavior from exclusionary acts. The exercise is a useful one, since it appears that very few acts are properly exclusionary. In other words, very few market actions should raise antitrust concerns. If the hypothesis is maintained that antitrust enforcement should seek to protect and promote competition, the identification of behavior that is anticompetitive is desired.

The only acts of an individual firm that can impede competition are those acts that directly impair a rival's ability to compete. Thus, I argue for per se legality of almost all competitive market activities, such as price cutting, innovation, and product differentiation. I attempt to identify those few exclusionary practices that are properly outside the market.[24] There may be short-term gains from antitrust action where bottlenecks or essential facilities are involved.

The discussion is divided into actions taken by an established firm that lowers a rival's *revenue* relative to its own and actions that raise a rival's *costs*[25] relative to its own. An established firm faces competition from other established firms and potential entrants. Both of these sources of competition are considered in analyzing competitive externalities. The analysis seeks to determine which competitive actions are simply pecuniary externalities and which actions are externalities in the sense of being exclusionary.

16.3.1 Predatory Pricing

The principal manner of lowering a rival's revenue is by undercutting his price and bidding away customers. If this practice eventually leads to market power for the firm that originally cut its price, predatory pricing is often said to have occurred. A problem that arises in analyzing predatory pricing is the plethora of alternative definitions.[26] A general definition is proposed. Then a characterization of the role of predatory pricing in a competitive setting is sought. It is found that predatory strategies are neither feasible nor even desirable for an established firm.[27] Further, predation is difficult to distinguish from normal competitive behavior in theory or in practice. Finally, alternative proposed remedies for predatory pricing are evaluated, and it is shown that they implicitly involve antitrust enforcement in a form of market regulation.

Predatory pricing must be defined in a dynamic setting. In period one, prices are lowered by an established firm (presumably relative to prices in some preceding period zero). This has the assumed effect of causing the exit of established rival firms or deterring potential entrants. In period two, prices are raised by the established firm to obtain profits due to increased market power resulting from reduced competition or discouraged entrants. Since firms are profit maximizers, it must be that any reduction in prices from lower profits in period one is recovered by the (expected present value of) profits earned in period two.[28]

Definition 16.3.1   Predatory pricing is a price or supply decision taken by an established firm that lowers a rival's or potential entrant's revenue in the current period and that raises the established firm's revenue in a future period.

It should be emphasized that defining predatory pricing does not guarantee that firms will choose to pursue such a policy, nor that it is a cause for antitrust intervention in markets.

An essential requirement for predatory pricing to create market power for an established firm is the presence of entry barriers.[29] Otherwise, even if an incumbent is successful in driving away competitors, other firms may enter in their place or the competitors themselves may return. Even with entry lags, the benefits of causing rival exit are limited by the profits that can be earned before entry occurs. If the firm's price deters entry in the absence of entry barriers, the firm may not be expected to be earning monopoly rents. At the same time, entry barriers in the form of sunk costs are exit barriers as well. A rival with significant sunk costs but low variable costs may also have incentive to remain in the market.[30]

Even if entry barriers are present, it is not evident that predatory pricing strategies maximize profits for an established firm. In terms of entry deterrence, neither an excess capacity strategy nor a high constant output (limit pricing) is a credible threat if firms choose outputs in the postentry equilibrium.[31] If firms compete as Bertrand price setters, it is not clear how a predatory pricing strategy will be optimal against established rivals. Suppose that the rival is at least as efficient as the predator. Then the losses from pricing below cost are higher for the predator than for the victim. The strategy is thus unlikely to be successful. Arguments to the contrary rely on such factors as imperfect capital markets that allow the predator to cover larger losses for a longer period of time than the victim. It does not seem reasonable to apply antitrust enforcement to prevent certain competitive practices if the underlying problem is capital market imperfections. If the rival firm is less efficient than the incumbent firm, there appears to be no reason for government intervention to protect the less efficient firm. If the incumbent earns higher profits after the exit of a less efficient rival, these profits are rents accruing to the firm's effort to lower its costs below those of its rivals.

Building a reputation for being "tough" provides an important instance where predation may be an optimal strategy for a monopolist, as is demonstrated by Kreps and Wilson (1982) and Milgrom and Roberts (1982).[32] These models show that it may be rational for a monopolist to fight an entrant to deter potential entrants. The monopolist may sustain losses in the short run if the long-run effects of reputation are sufficiently valuable. The key element in building a reputation is the asymmetry in information possessed by the incumbent and potential entrants. Kreps and Wilson (1982) assume that the entrant has imperfect information about the incumbent's payoffs. Milgrom and Roberts (1982) allows entrants to be uncertain about the incumbent's overall strategy even if the incumbent finds entry deterrence unprofitable in any given market. These models apply to a monopolist facing sequential entry of a series of rivals over time. They also apply to a multimarket monopolist facing entry in individual markets.

There are a number of ways in which markets may eliminate the benefits from demonstrating "toughness." If the incumbent is a multimarket monopolist, it may successfully combat single-market entrants, but an entrant may successfully enter in several markets at once by also being a multimarket (or multiproduct) firm. This possibility, or coordinated entry by firms in each market, is suggested by Easterbrook (1981, p. 288), who observes that "the threat of predation, far from preventing entry, simply increases its scale." Similarly, in a dynamic setting, an entrant may commit itself to multiperiod production through captial investment. Finally, Easterbrook (1981) has emphasized the importance of long-term *contracts* between potential entrants and customers as a way of mitigating the risks faced by entrants. If customers anticipate future price increases by an incumbent, they have incentive to enter into long-term contracts with an entrant.[33]

The most telling criticism of antitrust action against predatory pricing is the difficulty in distinguishing predatory price reductions from normal competitive price cuts. This point is forcefully brought out by a case study of competition between supermarkets and low-cost warehouse stores by Craswell and Fratrik (1985). After the entry of a warehouse store, super-market chains reduce prices in stores located near the warehouse, a practice called "zone pricing." Warehouses have filed private antitrust suits claiming that these price cuts are predatory. As Craswell and Fratrik emphasize, new entry increases capacity in the local market, and the increased capacity drives down prices as expected in a competitive market. Excess capacity in the market results in exit of some firms after a "shake out" period, followed by price increases that reflect the readjustment in capacity. Established firms may exit if they are less efficient than the warehouse, but the new entrant may exit if he miscalculated his costs. Thus, Craswell and Fratrik (1985) conclude that while the pattern of falling and then rising prices combined with exit of the entrant fits the predatory pricing story, what has in fact occurred is dynamic adjustment of prices and capacity in a competitive market.

Introduction of *new products* has been characterized as predatory.[34] Ordover and Willig (1981, pp.25–26) find prima facie evidence of such predation if new product revenues "fail to exceed the incremental costs of its production plus the reduction in net revenues caused by the diversion of sales from the preexisting products of the innovator." In addition, the product must be profitable after a rival's exit. This notion is the dual of predatory pricing. Cutting the price on an existing product is similar to introducing a higher-quality product at a given price. The same objections raised against the profitability of predatory pricing apply here. If the predator is less efficient in terms of R&D productivity, com-petitive innovation will not be a viable strategy. If the predator is a more efficient innovator, new product innovation is a socially desirable strategy. Innovation may be useful in building a reputation for "toughness," through the introduction of "fighting" models. However, rivals may commit themselves to long-term R&D programs, or several rivals may engage in joint R&D ventures that render reputation strategies unprofitable. Cus-tomers concerned about the viability of products sold by a rival can enter into long-term supply contracts. Finally, and most important, it is difficult to distinguish predation from normal new product innovation. New prod-ucts may encounter initial losses, particularly if the innovator miscalculated the products' appeal to customers. Even if a new product is successful, it must often displace older substitute products. The rise of new products and displacement of old products is part of the normal product cycle in competitive markets.[35]

16.3.2   Remedies for Predatory Pricing

Many of the tests for predatory pricing and proposed legal remedies are closely related to traditional forms of price regulation. This further confirms our assertion that antitrust policy is a form of administrative regulation.

(a) Cost-Based Tests for Predatory Pricing   Various authors have proposed that prices below some measure of an established firm's costs should be prohibited or should serve as evidence of predatory pricing. The best-known proposal is that of Areeda and Turner (1975), which would set a price floor equal to *average variable costs*, as a proxy for *short-run marginal costs*. Joskow and Klevorick (1979) suggest that a higher price floor, equal to *average total costs*, is a more appropriate measure of long-run marginal cost in a competitive market, "including a normal rate of return on capital invested"; see also Williamson (1977). Posner (1976a, p. 190) discusses pricing below *long-run marginal costs*, or "average balance-sheet costs," as a "tolerable proxy." He defines long-run marginal costs as the "additional cost that the producer will incur after his existing plant has worn out and must be replaced." Cost-based tests have found wide application in judicial decisions.[36]

These cost-based tests, perhaps combined with evidence of the firm's intent to exclude rivals, are to be enforced by antitrust authorities and the courts. The notion of requiring a firm to choose its price based on some measure of its costs is surprisingly similar to *cost-based price regulation*. The antitrust enforcement agencies are placed in the position of eliciting cost information from firms and of developing estimates of the firms' cost functions. Many of the traditional problems of regulation under asymmetric information can be expected to arise. The analysis of cost data puts antitrust authorities in a complicated technical realm with all the attendant issues usually faced by utility regulators, e.g., measurement of fixed and variable costs, tax and depreciation allowances, and estimation of rates of return. The antitrust enforcers must carry out this task for *any* industry suspected of predatory pricing, not just on a repeated basis for a small group of firms as in utility regulation. The information and computation costs of these policies appear prohibitive.

Many of the problems associated with cost-based price regulation discussed in chapter 3 would be encountered in antitrust enforcement of this predatory-pricing rule. To assure that a firm covers its costs, when these are fully attributable to each good the firm provides, requires prices to equal or exceed average total costs. Compare this to the Ramsey rule, for separable cost functions, which requires prices to equal average costs exactly. Should antitrust attempt to enforce Ramsey pricing? For a multiproduct firm, antitrust concern with predatory pricing against an entrant would require measurement of the average variable costs or average total cost of each product. This is particularly the case if a multiproduct firm faces entry by a firm supplying only a subset of products or confined to a geographic regional market. If the multiproduct firm were to drop its prices on those products also offered by the entrant, the antitrust authorities would be faced with the problem of attributing the incumbent firm's overhead costs to its various products. But, this again places the antitrust authorities and the courts in the position of utility regulators determining fully distributed cost-pricing policies. This does not seem to be an appropriate task for antitrust enforcement.

(b) Profit-Based Tests for Predatory Pricing   A standard closely related to cost-based tests for predatory pricing, but significant in its policy implications is the requirement that an established firm's reaction to entry satisfy *profit* criteria. Ordover and Willig (1981, p. 9) identify predation "if a practice would be unprofitable without the exit it causes, but profitable with the exit." This antitrust policy would require the antitrust authority to engage in regulation designed to assure established firms a desired *rate-of-return*.

Maintaining a minimum rate-of-return for the established firm requires projection of expected discounted returns by the antitrust authorities and the courts. This not only involves current and future cost and sales data but requires calculation of alternative scenarios with and without continued viability of the entrant.[37] Ordover and Willig suggest that implementation may be simplified through cost-based price floors. They suggest that "avoidable capital costs should always be included in the calculation of price floors." This would introduce the complexities and procedures associated with rate-of-return regulation into antitrust policy. Finally, they propose price floors for multiproduct firms that would take into account average incremental costs and cross-elasticity effects on the established firm's other goods. The calculation of multiproduct price floors again introduces the complexities of fully distributed cost price regulation into antitrust enforcement.

(c) Output and Price Standards for Predatory Pricing   Policies for controlling predatory pricing have been proposed that apply dynamic standards to the established firm's pricing or output decisions.[38] These proposals further involve antitrust authorities and the courts in monitoring industry behavior *over time* much like utility commissions oversee the activities of regulated firms.

An *output* standard, proposed by Williamson (1977, 1979), would require an established firm to not increase output in the face of new entry for some given period, e.g., a year or eighteen months. The goal is to require monopolists to produce at a high entry-deterring output before the threat of entry appears; that is, the legal rule is meant to lead to limit pricing.

A *price* standard, proposed by Baumol (1979b), allows the established firm to cut prices in the face of entry but does not permit the firm to raise prices later in the event that the entrant leaves the market. Baumol (1979b, p. 5) observes that such a "quasi-permanent pricing arrangement does not raise a protective umbrella over the entrant," as do cost-based tests of predatory pricing or output standards. The pricing behavior induced by this standard is also comparable to stationary limit pricing, at least after entry occurs.

The price and output standards, by establishing an ongoing enforcement and monitoring function in antitrust, have the character of regulatory policies.[39] An output standard might need to be readjusted for changes in market demand or in the firm's input costs. A price standard might need to be readjusted to maintain rates-of-return or to account for inflation, demand shifts, or input price changes. It is not difficult to imagine the equivalent of rate hearings in which firms petition for output or price changes, and in which arguments are raised over the appropriate test year, measures of costs, inflation rates, rates of return, etc.

To sum up the preceding discussion, it appears that predatory pricing, if ineffective against equally efficient rivals, is a self-imposed penalty.[40] In this sense, predatory pricing does not constitute a credible threat. Here the analogy between the exclusionary practice of predatory pricing and pecuniary externalities is especially appropriate. Because the costs of price cutting are *internal* to the predator, it cannot be said that harm to rivals from a lower price is a proper externality. *There has been no market failure.* Thus, there is no basis for regulatory intervention.

16.3.3   Tying

Tying refers to the practice of *product bundling* by a firm that requires its customers to purchase more than one commodity. Tie-ins may be achieved through packaging, lease agreements, or the design of systems whose components cannot be supplied by rivals.[41] There is an extensive case law involving tying, which is illegal under the Clayton Act (section 3) if competition is impaired.[42] Antitrust law views tying as an exclusionary device whereby a firm with market power in a particular good bundles the good with another good that is sold in a competitive market, foreclosing rivals from access to that market.

Almost all goods represent product bundles. A car is a bundle involving an auto body, tires, engine parts, etc. This type of bundling may be viewed as a form of vertical integration.[43] It is generally accepted that a monopolist of a particular good does not increase monopoly rents by tying it to a complementary good.[44] Monopoly rents may be obtained by selecting the profit-maximizing price for the monopolized good. If cost complementarities exist, the monopolist in good A may undercut the competitive price of stand-alone producers of good B without tying. Producers of good B have incentive to become multiproduct producers and enter the market for good A as well. In the rare circumstance where good B is only purchased to be used with good A, and new entry into the market for A cannot take place, tying may exclude firms from market B. However, since the monopolist cannot increase monopoly rents by selling both goods, the elimination of competition in market B need not lower social welfare.

16.3.4   Bottlenecks

There may be ways for a firm to obtain monopoly power by vertically integrating into downstream or upstream markets if these markets are characterized by significant barriers to entry. The monopoly rents will accrue in general to those firms already in the monopolized market, so that the firm seeking to vertically integrate will have to pay monopoly rents to enter. Alternatively, achieving exclusionary contracts with upstream suppliers or downstream customers also will require payment of monopoly rents.

The possibility of a downstream firm excluding its rivals by purchasing exclusionary rights from input suppliers has been raised by Krattenmaker and Salop (1986). They argue that a firm that is able to purchase all available inputs would exclude its rivals and earn monopoly rents downstream. Because of these potential monopoly rents, the firm that is intent on being a monopolist can then outbid its competitive rivals, who "stand to gain only the more-competitive, nonexclusion price and profit levels, if they are not excluded."[45] This argument is flawed because as inputs become scarce, their cost is bid up by other downstream firms seeking to remain in the market. The profits of remaining firms are likely to rise if some other downstream firms are successfully excluded.[46] This would allow the remaining firms to raise their bids. Thus, it is unlikely that exclusion can be achieved by a firm contracting in a competitive upstream or downstream market.

It may be the case that a firm with upstream or downstream monopoly power wishes to integrate vertically. One may then characterize the downstream market as a demand bottleneck and the upstream market as a supply bottleneck. A brief analysis of these bottlenecks is now given.

Demand Bottlenecks   Suppose that an established firm is able to lower the demand curve faced by potential rivals through actions that do not involve reducing its own price or increasing its supply. This requires reducing the rivals' access to their customers. This includes exclusionary acts directed at retailers or wholesalers who carry a rival's products. Another example might be control of a retail network involving an "essential facility." This is a bottleneck on the demand side of the market. This is the alleged effect of the airlines' computer reservation systems (see de Silva et al., 1987). It might be possible for the airline that owns the system to deny rivals equal access by biasing the manner in which other airlines' schedules are displayed.[47] Another example is ownership of transmission facilities by an electric utility. Other suppliers may not have equal access to the utility's customers over the utility's transmission lines.

It may be argued that the problem of essential facilities will never be observed. If a firm's rivals wish to serve the market, they have the incentive to construct an alternate set of transmission lines or retail facilities. However, if construction of retail facilities entails sunk costs, the costs of marketing or transporting the product may constitute an entry barrier. If rivals do find it profitable to establish independent marketing facilities, there may be construction delays. During the construction period, the established firm may obtain monopoly rents.

It is now shown how even a partial restriction of rivals' access to market demand can serve as an entry barrier and yield monopoly profits to the established firm in an otherwise contestable market. Let x represent the established firm's investment in its essential facility. Let $Q(p, x)$ represent the portion of market demand available to rivals given the market price p and the essential facility x. Assume that increases in x shift the rivals' demand curve, $Q(p, x)$, to the left. Further, the rivals' demand is less than market demand, $Q(p)$,

$$Q(p, x) \leq Q(p).$$

Rivals' average costs are $AC^2(q)$. The incumbent's average costs are $AC^1(q, x) = C^1(q, x)/q$. Suppose that the incumbent's average costs are higher than a potential entrant's costs, since the incumbent must operate the essential facility. Then, if the revenue gains from lowering rivals' demand outweigh the additional costs, the essential facility may be a barrier to entry.

In figure 16.3.1, the price p^m is a monopoly price sustainable against entry that yields positive profits for the incumbent. Profits equal

$$\pi^m(x) = p^m q^m - C^1(q^m, x), \tag{16.3.1}$$

where p^m is determined by the intersection of the potential entrant's de-

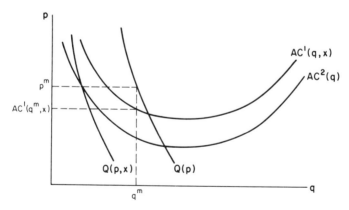

Figure 16.3.1
Lowering rivals' demand to sustain a monopoly.

mand and average cost,

$$p^m = AC^2(Q(p^m, x)), \tag{16.3.2}$$

and $q^m = Q(p^m)$ is the output sold by the incumbent monopolist.

Given the possibility of earning positive profits for some value of x, one may characterize the profit maximizing level of the entry barrier for the incumbent. Maximizing the incumbent's profit, $\pi^m(x)$, gives

$$(p^m - C_1^1(q^m, x)) \partial q^m / \partial x + q^m \partial p^m / \partial x - C_2^1(q^m, x) = 0. \tag{16.3.3}$$

From equations (16.3.2), (16.3.3), and $q^m = Q(p^m)$, one may calculate the incumbent's markup over marginal cost,

$$\frac{p^m - C_1^1(q^m, x^m)}{p^m} = \frac{1}{\eta_D(p^m)} \left[1 - \frac{C_2^1(q^m, x^m)/x^m}{AC^{2'}(Q(p^m, x^m)) \partial Q/\partial x} \right], \tag{16.3.4}$$

where $\eta_D(p^m) = -Q'(p^m)p^m/q^m$ is elasticity of market demand. The value of x that solves equation (16.3.4), x^m, is the size of the entry barrier that will be chosen by the incumbent.

Supply Bottlenecks   Salop and Scheffman (1983) present a model in which a "dominant" firm sets prices and is able to choose a strategic parameter that raises the cost function (and lowers the supply) of a competitive fringe. This causes some of the firms in the competitive fringe to exit and shifts the dominant firm's residual demand to the right. They interpret the strategy of raising rivals' costs as a technological choice by the dominant firm that calls for some costly technological response from fringe firms.[48] This section recasts the Salop and Scheffman (1983) analysis in a model of a market that is contestable in other respects.

Assume that the incumbent firm owns an essential upstream facility and that entry barriers exist in the upstream market. This yields a cost advantage for the incumbent firm that can be used as an entry barrier downstream. The cost advantage is thus immediately translated into monopoly rents for the incumbent. Let $AC^j(q, z) = C^j(q, z)/q$ represent average costs, where $j = 1$ for the incumbent and $j = 2$ for potential entrants. Let z represent the technology parameter. Increases in z raise costs for both the incumbent and potential entrants but yield a cost advantage for the incumbent,

$$AC^1(q, z) < AC^2(q, z).$$

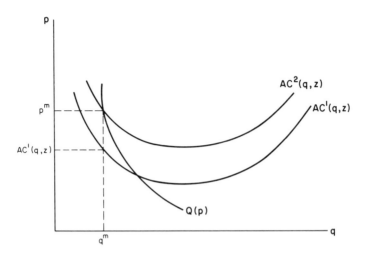

Figure 16.3.2
Raising rivals' costs to sustain a monopoly.

The case of a vertical shift up of entrant's average costs is shown in figure
16.3.2. The incumbent is able to deter entry by setting the price p^m in such
a way that entry at any lower price is unprofitable. The price p^m is a
sustainable monopoly price and at output $q^m = Q(p^m)$ yields profits for the
incumbent equal to

$$\pi^m(z) = p^m Q(p^m) - C^1(Q(p^m), z),   \tag{16.3.5}$$

where p^m solves $p^m = AC^2(Q(p^m), z)$. The effect of increasing the strategic
parameter z on the sustainable monopoly price is

$$\frac{\partial p^m}{\partial z} = \frac{AC_2^2(Q(p^m), z)}{1 - AC_1^2(Q(p^m), z)Q'(p^m)}.   \tag{16.3.6}$$

Thus, the incumbent's profits are maximized by setting z^m in such a way
that a modified monopoly pricing rule is satisfied,

$$\frac{p^m - C_1^1(q^m, z^m)}{p^m} = \frac{1}{\eta_D(p^m)}\left[1 - \frac{C_2^1(q^m, z^m)(1 - AC_1^2(q^m, z^m)Q'(p^m))}{q^m AC_2^2(q^m, z^m)}\right].   \tag{16.3.7}$$

For the incumbent firm to exclude firms from an otherwise contestable
downstream market, it must have control over an essential facility or input

upstream. However, the monopoly rents obtained are those accruing to the essential facility upstream. The preceding analysis serves only to establish the extent to which the firm will invest in upstream facilities.

16.4 Internalities: Vertical Restraints and Unfair Practices

Vertical restraints and vertical integration may be viewed as contractual responses by firms to the problem of internalities in interfirm transactions. Antitrust enforcement and the courts have opposed vertical controls in the past although there is now increased tolerance of vertical restraints. In some cases, these policies may preclude contractual arrangements that increase productive efficiency, particularly in the presence of *economies of sequence*. At the same time, antitrust enforcement by the FTC may play a positive role in mitigating the costs of internalities in transactions between consumers and firms.

16.4.1 Vertical Restraints and Vertical Integration

Transactions between firms are generally viewed as *vertical* interaction; the firm selling outputs is the *upstream* firm, and the firm buying outputs is the *downstream* firm. Like other economic transactions, those between firms are subject to *internalities*; that is, costs or benefits accruing to the firms may not be fully accounted for in the terms of exchange. Purchase agreements may involve costly contingencies, moral hazard, and adverse selection problems. Firms have developed a wide range of formal and informal contractual responses to internalities. These vertical transactions have generated considerable attention in the antitrust literature and extensive antitrust enforcement concern. The purpose of the present discussion is to identify a common framework for analysis of diverse forms of vertical transactions.

Vertical restraints are often viewed as regulations imposed by upstream firms on those downstream. However, in many cases, the restraints are the result of mutually beneficial agreements between suppliers and their customers. A downstream firm, with alternative sources of supply, may find that the benefits of purchasing a supplier's product outweigh the costs of purchasing a tied good or of maintaining resale prices above some minimum level. Similarly, vertical mergers may be hostile takeovers or agreements to achieve the benefits of joint production. Thus, vertical con-

Table 16.4.1
Range of vertical contracts

Direct sales
Fixed price
Price discrimination
Lump sum entry fees
Quantity-dependent price schedules
Royalties
Vertical restraints
Resale price maintenance
Exclusive territories
Exclusive dealing
Tying
Output forcing
Contractual restraints
Contingent contracts
Licensing
Franchise agreements
Vertical integration
Ownership and internal control

trols might be more properly identified as alternative forms of vertical contracts.

A broad spectrum of vertical contracts may be identified. These range from least-restrictive fixed price transactions to the most restrictive, full vertical integration. These options are listed in table 16.4.1. If the upstream firm has market power, it may capture rents through various forms of price discrimination: lump sum entry fees, quantity-dependent pricing, and royalties. Downstream behavior may be altered through such vertical restraints as resale price maintenance, exclusive territories, exclusive dealing, tying, and output forcing. Note that resale price maintenance and exclusive territories apply primarily to retail or wholesale reselling of a manufactured product. The other restraints apply to this case and to inputs in general. Contractual restraints may be exercised through the terms of contingent contracts, licensing, and franchise agreements.

The following discussion presupposes that the upstream firm has market power. Thus, it is implicitly required that there be some type of entry barrier in the upstream market (e.g., significant sunk costs, patents, resource ownership, government regulation). Otherwise, one might expect the upstream output to be supplied at a fixed price. It should again be emphasized that monopoly in the upstream market need not be evidence of entry barriers. The upstream market may be perfectly contestable, with the upstream firm holding its position by virtue of economies of scale and sustainable prices. The downstream market is usually viewed as competitive or monopolistically competitive.[49] The vertical control problem is frequently characterized as a means by which the upstream firm can enhance and capture monopoly rents. However, there may be efficiency benefits from vertical contracts. Williamson (1975, p. 115) makes the important observation that antitrust enforcement should restrict its attention to problems of monopoly, while in competitive industries "the maintained hypothesis ought to be that vertical integration has been undertaken for the purpose of economizing on transactions costs." Williamson (1975, pp. 115–116) allows that vertical integration can raise entry barriers in concentrated industries but suggests that antitrust problems are otherwise unlikely. It should be noted that even in industries in which upstream market power is present, there may be efficiency gains from vertical integration. These efficiency gains may outweigh any welfare losses that might result from monopoly price or output decisions. In practice, it may be hard to distinguish between vertical contracts that serve to enhance efficiency and those that lower consumer welfare.

It is necessary to examine which actions of the downstream firm are of interest to the upstream firm. Clearly, since the upstream firm wishes to maximize profits from the sale of its output, it is directly concerned with the amount of output demanded and the payment received. Indirectly, the upstream firm is concerned with the net returns obtained downstream, since these are the source of the upstream firm's revenues. Thus, the upstream firm is interested in the effects of the downstream firm's actions on the latter's profits and on the profits of other downstream firms. Three classes of relevant actions of the downstream firm may be identified: price, effort, and input substitution.

The *price* charged by the downstream firm for its output is significant if the upstream firm sells to several competing downstream firms. If the upstream firm has market power, it may increase its profits by enforcing collusion downstream. The effect of price competition across downstream firms is referred to as a *horizontal pecuniary externality* by Mathewson and Winter (1984). These effects may be viewed as *internalities*, since the upstream firm is concerned about the reduced revenues from its other downstream customers. The prices set by a particular downstream firm thus may indirectly impose losses in revenue on the upstream firm. These losses can be mitigated, potentially, by negotiation between the upstream and downstream firms. Another important aspect of downstream pricing behavior is the issue of *free riding* raised in Telser's (1960) classic paper. Telser observes that downstream retailers may provide costly sales services, such as information about the product. If customers can obtain information from one retailer but then purchase the good from another retailer offering lower prices but no sales services, there are opportunities for discount retailers to "free ride" on those providing services. The market equilibrium would then involve no supply of these public good services and possibly reduced consumer welfare. Resale price maintenance or exclusive territories are seen by Telser as means of preserving competition in the provision of retail services.

Downstream firm *effort* includes not only sales services[50] but also warranties, advertising, supply of complementary products (e.g., system components, spare parts, computer software), research and development, and productive efficiency. The provision of incentives for productive efficiency and innovation by downstream firms raises classic agency issues. Additional problems arise through the effects of downstream marketing efforts on the demand of other downstream firms. The role of resale price maintenance and exclusive territories in reducing these cross-effects on demand has been analyzed in important work by Mathewson and Winter (1983), Rey and Tirole (1986), Perry and Groff (1985), and Perry and Porter (1986).

Finally, the problem of capturing rents and avoiding *input substitution* has been extensively examined by an ongoing literature on vertical integration.[51] The problem addressed is how the upstream monopolist can capture monopoly rents through alternative tax instruments in addition to input price markups, particularly lump sum charges and output royalties. Of central importance are downstream firm technology and market structure.[52] These issues are relatively straightforward and need not be considered further here.

It is well-known that vertical integration is a mechanism for resolving some of the agency problems present in market transactions; see Arrow (1975) and Williamson (1975). Improvements in monitoring performance and control may be achieved within a firm. The agency aspects of vertical restraints have also been recognized; see Rey and Tirole (1986). The presence of multiple downstream firms makes the vertical integration and vertical restraints problem similar to that of a principal dealing with multiple agents or a supervisor coordinating the members of a team.

It is now examined how internalities can arise in vertical relations between firms.[53] Consider first the case of *costly contract contingencies*. Suppose that the downstream firm is risk averse and faces either cost or demand uncertainty. If other insurance options are not available, the optimal purchase contract with an upstream supplier involves risk sharing through complete contingent contracts. For example, a downstream firm holding inventories faced with random demand has incentive to enter into risk-sharing arrangements with suppliers that may take the form of contingent payments, consignment agreements, and pooling of inventories or financial risks across retailers; see Spulber (1985b). Assuring supplies of inputs or sharing risk have been identified as explanations of vertical integration.[54] Complete contingent contracts for risk sharing in vertical transactions may be costly.[55] At the same time, antitrust enforcement may preclude vertical integration by firms. This may lead upstream firms to seek other means of mitigating the effects of downstream risk.

It has already been noted that the common law of contracts and torts provides some forms of risk sharing. For example, the upstream firm may obtain expectation damages if the downstream firm does not take delivery on goods purchased under a contract. There are other contingencies, related to random demand and costs downstream, that may require contractual responses.

Rey and Tirole (1986) make the interesting observation that the upstream firm's objective of increasing monopoly rents is complicated by the risk-sharing properties of vertical restraints.[56] They find that resale price maintenance shifts demand risks to the upstream firm if the profit margin is constant (although sales and profits vary). If costs are subject to shocks, then resale price maintenance shifts risks onto retailers. Rey and Tirole note further that while exclusive territories makes good use of decentralized information about individual retailers, its risk-sharing properties are limited. They find that in the absence of vertical restraints, downstream competition functions as a "tournament." In some cases, franchise fees yield greater profits than are obtained under vertical restraints.

Finally note that *moral hazard* and *adverse selection* problems may easily arise in vertical relations between firms. It may be costly to monitor the sales or productive effort of downstream firms. The form of vertical contracts may represent attempts to provide incentives for increased effort levels. The downstream firm may have a cost advantage in gathering information about consumer demand. The downstream firm may possess private information about costs. Vertical contracts may reflect incentives for the downstream firm to reveal demand and cost information.

The courts have been generally strict with vertical restraints. While a "rule of reason" approach has been applied to exclusive territories,[57] resale price maintenance remains illegal per se.[58] This suggests that firms may seek alternative means of reducing internalities in vertical transactions by franchise agreements and by vertical integration. Vertical integration can be achieved through internal expansion or vertical merger.

Restrictions on vertical mergers have been reduced somewhat by the 1982 DOJ Merger Guidelines.[59] The guidelines replace concentration ratios used in the 1968 DOJ guidelines with Herfindahl measures of concentration. The guidelines reflect a shift of concern away from the perceived problem of foreclosure of markets by the denial of access to customers or suppliers. Rather, the guidelines specify three broad bases for challenging vertical mergers. The first is "elimination of specific potential entrants." The merger will not be challenged unless the Herfindahl measure of concentration in the market of the acquired firm is above 1,800,[60] or if the acquired firm has a market share above 5% (or more likely above 20%).[61] The second basis for challenge is the effect of the vertical merger on barriers to entry. The guidelines are concerned with mergers that increase the difficulty of entry by requiring a new firm to enter both the upstream and downstream markets. This may be due to higher cost of capital or insufficient economies of scale for the new entrant. Finally, the guidelines worry about vertical integration as a means of facilitating collusion (if the upstream market has a Herfindahl measure of concentration above 1,800). The 1982 DOJ Merger Guidelines do not consider the defense of "specific efficiencies" for mergers subject to challenge. This suggests that such factors as economies of sequence and mitigation of internalities in vertical transactions have a small role in the defense of vertical mergers.

It is not evident that vertical contracts in themselves should cause antitrust intervention. It is not apparent that "elimination of potential entrants" need be of serious concern unless entry barriers exist already. It is also questionable whether economies of sequence achieved from vertical integration can raise entry barriers.[62] This type of argument appears to be a revival of Bain's identification of economies of scale and absolute cost advantage as entry barriers. An efficiency gain from a vertical merger requires new or existing firms to be more efficient by also integrating vertically. This is a desirable result of competition, and does not represent an impediment to entry of rivals who are equally or more efficient. It is not apparent why facilitation of collusion should prevent a vertical merger. Price fixing is already illegal. The vertical merger may legitimately raise antitrust interest in collusion after the merger has taken place, but the merger itself need not cause collusive behavior. Finally, vertical integration may indeed yield monopoly rents in the presence of entry barriers. The welfare losses from monopoly supply decisions must then be balanced against the welfare gains from increased productive efficiency. A similar observation applies to vertical restraints and other vertical contracts.

16.4.2   Unfair Practices

The FTC plays an important role in consumer product markets by regulating such things as contract terms, product warranties, and advertising. FTC interests include "unfair trade practices" and "deceptive acts and practices."[63] FTC activities may serve to reduce the allocative effects of internalities for certain products. What should be noted is that under the general category of antitrust, market regulations are again discovered. These regulations go beyond the common view of antitrust as being directed at promotion of competition.

The presence of asymmetric information about product characteristics or contract terms, perhaps combined with unequal bargaining ability or market power, may lead to inefficiency in bargaining between consumers and firms. Improperly understood contract terms may result in consumers not obtaining gains from trade. These problems are addressed by the common law of contracts and the Uniform Commercial Code, which are directed at "unconscionable" contract terms. Under the Uniform Commercial Code, the courts may refuse to enforce contracts with clauses that are not clearly presented to or not fully understood by one of the parties. This may include some standardized "adhesion" contracts in which consumers cannot bargain over particular contract terms but are presented with the contract on a "take-it-or-leave-it" basis. The FTC has proposed rules regarding adhesion contracts, for example, with regard to creditors' remedies.[64]

Elements of risk sharing, moral hazard, and asymmetric information underlie product warranties. Product warranties are regulated by the FTC under the Magnuson-Moss Warranty Act, which supplements common law and the Uniform Commercial Code. The act requires disclosure of warranty terms, sets standards for "full" and "limited" warranties, and provides for informal dispute resolution.[65] FTC rules provide extremely specific requirements for disclosure of warranty provisions; see Priest (1981, p. 250).

A possible consequence of asymmetric information available to buyers and sellers is misrepresentation of product characteristics and contractual terms. This type of internality is addressed by the common law of fraud. Antitrust law has been interpreted as providing a supplement to common law in this area. In particular, section 5 of the FTC Act, against "unfair or deceptive acts or practices," is applied by the FTC to "deceptive" or "unsubstantiated" advertising. There is some evidence that FTC advertising regulation may create inefficiencies in advertising;[66] see also chapter 15.

Notes

1. The Robinson-Patman Act permits price "differentials which make only due allowance for differences in the cost of manufacture, sale, or delivery resulting from the differing methods or quantities in which such commodities are to such purchasers sold or delivered."

2. See Posner (1976a) on out-of-court settlement in antitrust.

3. See, for example, Nash (1986). Nash quotes a former FTC official who says of antitrust enforcement, "The fix-it policy turns the Justice Department from a prosecutor into a regulator."

4. See Katzman (1980, pp. 27–35) on the debate within the FTC between "reactive" and "proactive" approaches to prosecution.

5. According to the American Bar Association (ABA, 1981b, p. 1) the FTC is "possessed of a combination of adjudicatory, rule-making, fact-finding, advisory and reporting powers." See also Katzman (1980) on the FTC.

6. Indeed, the history of the creation of the FTC suggests that congressional intent was for an administrative agency to spell out rules of conduct. This reflected some distrust of judicial procedure, which was partly a reaction to the "rule of reason" interpretation of the Sherman Act applied in the Standard Oil case; see ABA (1981a) for the historical background of section 5 of the FTC Act.

7. See Katzman (1980) for discussion of FTC interaction with Congress.

8. See ABA (1981b, p. 14). An analysis of FTC enforcement procedures and the role of section 5 of the FTC Act are given in ABA (1981a,b).

9. See Priest, pp. 246–275 in Clarkson and Muris (1981) for an extended discussion of the Magnuson-Moss Warranty Act.

10. See the discussion in chapter 2.

11. See Ellis in Clarkson and Muris (1981, p. 162).

12. Ibid, p. 166. The advertising provisions were rendered moot by court decisions.

13. Early special statutes include the Wool Products Labeling Act (1940), the Fur Products Labeling Act (1951), the Textile Fiber Products Identification Act (1958), the Fair Package and Labeling Act (1966), the Federal Cigarette Labeling and Advertising Act (1966), and the Truth in Lending Act (1968). These statutes are discussed by Muris, pp. 13–17 in Clarkson and Muris (1981). Muris also lists the Fair Credit Reporting Act (1971), the Fair Credit Billing Act amendment (1975) to the Truth in Lending Act, the Equal Credit Opportunity Act (1975), the Consumer Leasing Act (1976), the Fair Debt Collection Practices Act (1977), and the Energy Policy and Conservation Act (1975).

14. The power to seek injunctions comes from the Alaska Pipeline Act (1973). Premerger notification procedures are established by the Hart-Scott-Rodino Antitrust Improvements Act (1976), which amends the Clayton Act.

15. Posner (1976a, pp. 55–62) lists twelve conditions "favorable to collusion": "(1) Market concentrated on the selling side; (2) No fringe of small sellers; (3) Inelastic demand at competitive price; (4) Entry takes a long time; (5) Many customers; (6) Standard product; (7) The principal firms sell at the same level in the chain of distribution; (8) Price competition more important than other forms of competition; (9) High ratio of fixed to variable costs; (10) Demand static or declining over time; (11) Sealed bidding; (12) The industry's antitrust 'record'." This list of conditions is of independent interest, since it implicitly presents testable hypotheses about the determinants of collusion.

16. Posner (1976a, pp. 62–71) lists twelve types of "evidence of collusive behavior": "(1) Fixed relative market shares; (2) Price discrimination; (3) Exchanges of price information; (4) Regional price variations; (5) Identical bids; (6) Price, output and capacity changes at the formation of the cartel; (7) Industry-wide resale price maintenance; (8) Declining market shares of leaders; (9) Amplitude and fluctuation of price changes; (10) Demand elasticity at market price; (11) Level and pattern of profits; (12) Basing-point pricing."

17. Posner (1976, p. 59) notes barriers to entry in the sense of Stigler in connection with the category "Entry takes a long time." See the discussion of barriers to entry in chapter 1.

18. In the 1922 case of *Alcoa* v. *FTC*, a merger was denied that was seen as preventing future competition. See Steiner (1957) on this case and for a defense of the potential competition doctrine in conglomerate merger policy.

19. The well-known 1964 *United States* v. *Penn-Olin Chemical Company* case ruled out a joint venture as reducing potential entry.

20. Posner (1976a, pp. 122–124) criticizes the potential competition doctrine and observes that "the elimination of an individual potential competitor can be expected to have no competitive significance at all, since there are presumably a number of other equally potential competitors" (1976a, p. 123).

21. Posner (1976a, p. 28) defines an exclusionary practice as occurring when a firm "trades a part of its monopoly profits, at least temporarily, for a large market share, by making it unprofitable for other sellers to compete with it."

22. The distinction between "pecuniary" and "technical" externalities is due to Viner (1931); see Scitovsky (1954). Technical externalities, such as environmental pollution, are transmitted outside the market. The notion of pecuniary externalities was used to explain increases or decreases in an input price due to increased demand for the input, depending upon whether the industry supplying the inputs had increasing or decreasing average costs.

23. Thus, product innovation, advertising, building a reputation for quality, and price reductions are competitive practices that have been identified by some as creating barriers to entry.

24. One may identify acts with directly verifiable consequences that may operate outside the market. The classic example is planting a bomb in a rival's factory. Blowing up of rivals' plants was alleged in the 1976 *United States* vs. *Empire Gas Corp.* case. These types of activities

appear rare and anyway constitute criminal activity. The issue of access to essential facilities is discussed later.

25. The notion of raising rivals' costs is due to Williamson (1968), Gilbert (1981), Salop (1981), Salop and Scheffman (1983), and others.

26. Contributions to the predatory pricing literature include McGee (1958, 1980), Telser (1966), Areeda and Turner (1975), Williamson (1977, 1979), Schmalensee (1979b), Joskow and Klevorick (1979), Baumol (1979b), Easterbrook (1981), Brodley and Hay (1981), Ordover and Willig (1981), Salop (1981), Zerbe and Cooper (1982), Hay (1982), Vawter and Zuch (1982), Craswell and Fratrik (1985), and Beckenstein and Gabel (1986). Calvani and Lynch (1983) provide an introductory survey. Empirical tests of predatory pricing and predatory location conducted by Von Hohenbalken and West (1984, 1986) find evidence of this type of behavior.

27. Important critical analyses of predation are given in McGee (1958, 1980), Bork (1978), and Easterbrook (1981).

28. Joskow and Klevorick (1979, p. 219) define predatory pricing as "a reduction of price in the short run so as to drive competing firms out of the market or to discourage entry of new firms in an effort to gain larger profits via higher prices in the long run than would have been earned if the price reduction had not occurred."

29. This observation supports Joskow and Klevorick (1979, p. 230), who emphasize large capital requirements and transferability of assets among the factors increasing the possible profitability of limit pricing. They recommend a "two-tier" legal rule for determining the presence of predatory pricing: first, market structure characteristics and incumbent's market power are examined; and second, an array of cost-based tests are proposed.

30. See Bork (1978) and McGee (1980) on this point.

31. See section 17.5 for a demonstration of this assertion.

32. See also Rosenthal (1981). The models of Rosenthal (1981), Kreps and Wilson (1982), and Milgrom and Roberts (1982) address Selten's (1978) chain store paradox. Selten shows that predation to build a reputation does not occur in a perfect information model.

33. See Easterbrook (1981) for extensive discussion of long-term contracts as a counterstrategy to predatory pricing.

34. Ordover and Willig (1981) discuss "predation through substitute product innovation."

35. The notion of predatory product innovation is closely related to the view that "brand proliferation" can be an exclusionary device, blocking the entry of new firms. This was alleged by the FTC in its 1972 case against ready-to-eat cereal manufacturers. Schmalensee (1978) argues that threatening not to reposition brands is an entry barrier. This is evaluated further in the next chapter.

36. See Calvani and Lynch (1983) for judicial applications of cost-based tests.

37. See Ordover and Willig (1981, pp. 13–14).

38. A rule-of-reason approach proposed by Scherer (1976) would imply even greater involvement of antitrust authorities and the courts in the regulation of markets.

39. Baumol (1979b, p. 7) anticipates this criticism but finds the similarity with regulation "deceptive." He states that price adjustments permitted by the courts to account for cost changes or demand shifts need only be "similar in order of magnitude." It is, however, easy to envision the establishment of specific demand and cost guidelines should such a price standard be put into practice.

40. As Easterbrook (1981, p. 268) observes, "It would be foolish to devote additional resources to preventing conduct that penalizes itself."

41. For an extensive discussion of systems design, see Ordover and Willig (1981). They view the introduction of systems whose components are incompatible with those of rivals as a form of predatory product innovation.

42. See Armentano (1982, chapter 7) for a critical review of the principal cases brought against tying.

43. See Blair and Kaserman (1978a).

44. See, for example, Posner (1976a, pp. 171–184). He discusses in detail tying for the purpose of price discrimination. See also Bowman (1957), Turner (1958), and Singer (1963).

45. Krattenmaker and Salop (1986, p. 111).

46. Krattenmaker and Salop (1986) dismiss the possibility that the last upstream firms to sell inputs to the downstream monopolist will hold out for higher prices. They suggest that a predator can commit to purchasing all rights at a fixed price.

47. See the *Review of Airline Deregulation and Sunset of the Civil Aeronautics Board (Airline Computer Reservations Systems)*, 1983 hearings of the House of Representatives Committee on Public Works and Transportation, Subcommittee on Aviation. The hearing resulted in rules against "biased" computer reservation systems.

48. Salop and Scheffman (1983) include these among exclusionary strategies: product quality and advertising expenditure, bidding up the price of scarce inputs, nonprice vertical restraints (exclusive dealing and territorial restraints), and costly governmental regulations due to costly rent-seeking political activities by the dominant firm. These do not appear to be useful exclusionary devices. The present analysis requires ownership of an essential input upstream.

49. It is possible for the roles to be reversed, with the downstream firm as a monopolist and the upstream market as competitive. Most of the subsequent discussion can be rephrased in terms of downstream restraints placed on upstream suppliers. See the discussion in the preceding section on "raising rivals' costs."

50. The Spence (1975) model of quality selection by a monopolist is applied to a welfare analysis of vertical restraints by Comanor (1985) and Scherer (1983), who suggest that market power upstream may lead to inefficient product quality or service downstream.

51. See Blair and Kaserman (1983) for a comprehensive survey; see especially Warren-Boulton (1974) and Westfield (1981). See also Dixit (1983) and Gallini and Winter (1983).

52. It might appear that the problem of input substitution is not applicable to resale of a manufactured good. If the downstream firm resells the product, the technology appears to resemble a *fixed proportions* technology, with each unit purchased from the manufacturer resold downstream. This need not be so in practice. Most retailers carry many goods. The retailer chooses a product mix just as a downstream producer would choose an input mix. Even if the retailer purchases from only one manufacturer, there may be a product line that allows the retailer to vary the proportions of each good to keep in stock. Finally, the retailer offers a mix of products and retail services. Thus, even a single product combined with retail services need not satisfy the traditional fixed proportions model.

53. In what follows, for ease of discussion, it is generally assumed that the downstream firm is subject to direct risk, that some action of the downstream firm is unobservable, or that the downstream firm possesses private information not available to the upstream firm. Clearly, the same may be said of the upstream firm or about both firms simultaneously, transactions being, of course, symmetric in nature.

54. For general analyses of incentives for vertical integration, see particularly Arrow (1975), Bernhardt (1977), Warren-Boulton (1978), Blair and Kaserman (1978b, 1983), Carlton (1979), and Perry (1982).

55. Williamson (1975, p. 83) mentions the transaction costs of writing complete contingent contracts as a reason for vertical integration.

56. In a deterministic setting, Bork (1965, 1966a) observes that resale price maintenance and exclusive territories are interchangeable.

57. In *Continental T.V.* v. *GTE Sylvania* (1977), the Supreme Court recognized the possible role of vertical restraints in promoting distribution efficiency. For a discussion of later applications of Sylvania, see Rill (1983).

58. *Monsato* v. *Spray Rite Service Corp.* (1984) reaffirmed resale price maintenance as a per se illegal form of price fixing. For overviews of case history prior to 1983, see Halverson (1983) and Campbell and Ware (1983).

59. Williamson (1983, p. 616) observes that while the 1968 vertical Merger Guidelines reflected concern with technological efficiency, the 1982 guidelines reflect "transaction cost economies," to some extent.

60. A Herfindahl index of below 1,800 is met by 6 firms of equal size $H = .1667$ but not by 5 of equal size $H = .2000$.

61. In evaluating the 1982 Merger Guidelines, Ordover and Willig (1983) note that "structural criteria for assessing merger effects, such as the concentration ratios and the market shares pertinent to the merging firms, are even less adequate as predictors of the anticompetitive effects of vertical mergers than they are in the case of horizontal mergers."

62. Ordover and Willig (1983) suggest, however, that a vertical merger may deter entry "by increasing the sunk portion of the requisite investment" or by removing "an efficient source of supply of the needed input or an efficient distributor." They add that a vertical merger may not have these effects unless the secondary market is concentrated and the vertically integrating firm has market power. But see the earlier discussion of lowering rivals' demand and raising rivals' cost in section 16.3.

63. The chairman of the Federal Trade Commission at that time, James C. Miller III, recommended legislative definition of "unfairness." Miller defines an unfair act or practice as one "causing substantial injury to consumers which they could not otherwise have avoided, and where there are not offsetting benefits"; see Kauper et al. (1983).

64. Peterson (1981) examines empirical studies on the effects of regulation on the availability of consumer credit in relation to the proposed FTC Trade Regulation Rule on creditors' remedies.

65. Priest (1981) evaluates Magnuson-Moss. Empirical analyses of consumer warranties by Priest (1981) "suggest that the Act has had only a limited influence on the level of warranty protection."

66. See Grady (1981) for discussion and criticism of the 1972 Pfizer case and the doctrine of unsubstantiated advertising. Grady (1981, p. 244) finds that the FTC and the courts have failed "to preserve in some way the common-law distinction between fact and opinion in FTC advertising law."

17 Antitrust and Competition

A significant factor in antitrust rulings and government enforcement activities is the measurement of market structure based on the number and size of competing firms. This is true for both monopolization and merger cases. A direct association often is drawn between industrial concentration, a high percentage of sales made by a small number of firms, and the economic efficiency of the market equilibrium. The causal link between market structure and the welfare properties and performance of an industry is the hallmark of traditional industrial organization; this link is associated particularly with Bain (1956, 1959). Because the structure-performance link plays such an important role in antitrust law and policy, it is imperative that the theoretical underpinnings of this relation be examined.

The present chapter considers the implications of competition for the structure-performance connection. The debates on this issue in the industrial organization literature are briefly reviewed and measures of concentration are identified in section 17.1. Then four classes of competition are studied. In each case, the competitive model is examined for a fixed market structure and for the free entry case. This approach allows the discussion to control for the effects of entry barriers and of potential entry. In section 17.2, Cournot quantity competition is studied. Sections 17.3 and 17.4 look at Bertrand price competition for the homogeneous products and differentiated products cases, respectively. In section 17.5, simple two-stage dynamic capacity choice models are considered. In the first model, due to Kreps and Scheinkman (1983), two firms choose capacity in the first stage and prices in the second. In the second model, due to Spulber (1981a), a monopolist chooses capacity in the first stage, given the expectation of entry in the second stage. The focus of the discussion throughout is on observed price and quantity levels. The analysis establishes that the competitive strategies and behavior of firms is a crucial determinant of the efficiency of market equilibrium.

17.1 Market Structure and Industrial Performance

17.1.1 The Structure-Performance Debate

Antitrust legislation around the turn of the century reflected a public concern with the effects of industrial concentration both on economic efficiency[1] and on the political power of trusts.[2] The concern among economists about the political effects of monopoly continues to the present. Adams

(1986, p. 405) emphasizes that in his view "[s]ince all power tends to develop into a government in itself, industrial power should be decentralized." Attention by economists to the connections between market structure and efficiency comes later than the main antitrust laws. The study of the links between concentration and efficiency is generally associated with Mason (1939, 1949), Bain (1956, 1959), and more recently Scherer (1980).[3] Scherer (1980, pp. 4–5) lists demand and technology under "basic conditions" and lists under the category of market structure: the number of sellers and buyers, product differentiation, entry barriers, cost functions, vertical integration, and presence of conglomerate firms. Under conduct, Scherer lists pricing behavior, product strategy, advertising, R&D and investment. Finally, Scherer broadly defines performance to include "production and allocative efficiency, progress, full employment and equity." Scherer states that a primary focus is on a causal flow from market structure and/or basic conditions to conduct and performance.[4]

The notion that there are *causal* links between the number and size of firms on the one hand and the economic efficiency of an industry on the other has been challenged, notably by the theory of contestable markets of Baumol, Panzar, and Willig (1982) and others. The model of competition in contestable markets emphasizes *price competition* with homogeneous goods, and in this sense the intellectual predecessor is the model of Bertrand (1883). The theory of contestable markets gives a significant role to potential competition from entry of new firms. This aspect of the contestable markets model has predecessors, notably in the Chicago School in the writings of J. B. Clark (1901) and with J. M. Clark (1912, pp. 121–122): "Size, then, need not in itself make a monopoly. Conceivably a corporation might make all the goods of a given class and yet be held in check, for a time at least, and prevented from doing its worst by merely potential competitors." Further, Clark and Clark (1912, p. 124) provide a clear statement of the effects of potential entry: "If new competition is sure to spring up in case new prices are raised, they will not be raised beyond a moderate limit. They will continue to be held down by a *possible* producing agent, and not merely by those competitors that are present and acting." This insight, of course, falls short of the well-developed theoretical framework of contestable markets analysis. The contestable markets model has met with criticism from Weitzman (1983), Brock (1983), and others. A principal objection is to the assumption of negligible sunk costs. At the same time, contestability has led to a large and growing literature that extends, develops, and tests the theory. See also Spence (1983), Baumol, Panzar, and Willig (1983), Bailey and Baumol (1984), and Baumol and Willig (1986) for further discussion. It is evident that contestability theory has led to a major reevaluation within the field of industrial organization of the links between market structure and performance.

In interpreting the antitrust statutes, the courts have generally accepted large market shares as an indicator of market power. The classic example is the Alcoa case, in which Judge Learned Hand stated that a 33% share of sales did not indicate monopoly, a 64% share was open to question, while a 90% share certainly indicated the presence of monopoly. In merger cases, market share data play a major role in discussions about the competitive effects of the merger. Through its guidelines for horizontal and vertical mergers, the antitrust division of the Department of Justice endorses measures of concentration as an indicator of market power. However, the challenges to the emphasis on concentration in antitrust law and its enforcement have become increasingly frequent and have met with success in the courts and influencing public policy; see Bailey and Baumol (1984).

Is the reliance on measures of concentration in antitrust enforcement and adjudication warranted? Does absolute size indicate that a firm has market power? Does relative size, e.g., a large share of sales, indicate the presence of market power? Finally, does concentration of industry sales in the hands of a few firms indicate monopoly power and economic inefficiency? The present section examines the case against monopoly and briefly describes measures of concentration. The implications of the nature of competition for the structure-performance connection are stated in terms of price- versus quantity-setting competition between firms. The issues raised are then addressed at length in subsequent sections of the chapter. It is shown that the traditional structure-performance link is generally not supported with either Cournot quantity competition or Bertrand price competition.

17.1.2 The Monopoly Question

Costs Why should production of a good or a set of goods be concentrated in the hands of a single firm or a small number of firms? The answer depends on the properties of the production technology and the form of the cost function given prices for inputs. The key question is that of subadditivity (see definition 3.1.6). A *natural monopoly* is said to exist if a single firm produces an output at less cost than could be achieved by dividing that output among two or more firms; see Baumol, Panzar, and Willig (1982). Similarly, a *natural oligopoly* could be defined if a small

number of firms producing a given total output minimizes industry costs.
If production of a given output is least costly when undertaken by one or
a few firms, then a concentrated industry is required to achieve an efficient
allocation of resources. The notion of subadditivity subsumes that of economies of scope. If multioutput production is efficient, then, *ceteris paribus*,
efficiency in resource allocation requires concentration of production across
goods in the hands of one or a few firms.

The presence of subadditive costs at feasible outputs for a given market
demand suggests that alternative market structures must be evaluated in
terms of their total costs. Thus, the marginal costs to the industry of
adding an additional firm are important in assessing the cost-minimizing
industry structure. In the evaluation of horizontal merger proposals, the
joint costs of the merged entity must be compared with the costs of separate
production by the potential partners. If the merger involves rationalization
of production through elimination of redundant facilities or adoption of
new techniques that yield returns to scale, then the cost savings should be
(and generally are) a factor in evaluating the social welfare consequences
of the merger.

Welfare   The case against market power is that a restriction of output,
below the point where marginal social willingness to pay equals marginal
production cost, yields avoidable welfare losses. The "deadweight welfare
losses" equal the traditional monopoly welfare triangles, which do not
require further examination here. The triangles are *abd* and *bcd* in figure
17.1.1, where Q^m is the monopoly output and p^m, p^c are the monopoly
and competitive prices, respectively.

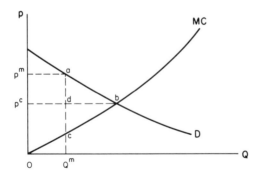

Figure 17.1.1
Deadweight welfare loss from monopoly.

The case against market power is extended by Posner (1976a), who argues that monopoly rents must also be included. These rents are $p^m ac0$ net of fixed costs of production. Posner (1976a) argues that if monopoly rents can only be obtained through government-created barriers to entry, then all potential rents from monopoly power will be dissipated by competition between firms for the exclusive government franchise or other regulations that restrict entry. In other words, firms will spend up to the potential rents in lobbying, legal cost, and political campaign contributions, as is suggested by the rent-seeking literature; see section 2.3. While perhaps appealing as a politically based theory of market entry, the dissipation of monopoly profits through lobbying does not necessarily apply to all entry barriers, which may include patents or exclusive access to natural resources.

How accurate is the implicit behavioral theory of monopoly embodied in the finding that a profit-maximizing monopolist sets output such that marginal revenue equals marginal cost? This assumes that the monopolist charges a single price for each unit sold. Linear pricing is, however, not a profit-maximizing strategy for a firm protected from competition by entry barriers. A protected monopoly can increase profits by price discrimination. The monopolist able to practice first-degree price discrimination will increase output to the point where marginal social benefits exactly equal marginal production costs, thus eliminating any deadweight welfare losses. The extent to which the monopolist may practice price discrimination is, of course, limited by consumer arbitrage opportunities and legal restrictions; see chapter 19. However, it is safe to say that some form of price discrimination is often feasible through quantity discounts, entry fees, coupons, product bundling, geographic pricing, market segmentation, etc. Thus, the welfare losses, even from unrestricted monopoly, are in themselves likely to be mitigated or perhaps negligible. This is not to say that monopoly rents are eliminated. However, if distributional considerations are an issue, then the distinction between equity and efficiency must be emphasized.[5] The efficiency of price discrimination, while frequently discussed, has not been given sufficient emphasis in the evaluation of welfare losses from monopoly. Because price discrimination increases profits, it is to be expected that a monopolist will employ discriminatory sales practices. On this basis, predictions of economic inefficiency due to monopoly, even in the presence of entry barriers, are unlikely to hold.

Measures of Concentration   A vast literature exists on descriptive measures of industrial concentration. See Scherer (1980) and Jacquemin and de Jong (1977) for surveys. The most frequently used measure, the *concentration ratio*, is simply the combined market share of the largest 4, 8, 20, or 50 firms in the industry. The Herfindahl measure of concentration is the sum of squared market shares, $H = \sum_{j=1}^{m} (S^j)^2$, where $\sum_{j=1}^{m} S^j = 1$. The use of this measure was announced by the DOJ for use in merger guidelines in 1981.[6] For an industry with m firms of equal size, $H = 1/m$. In what follows, this measure is emphasized, since the focus is on symmetric equilibria.

A growing literature examines concentration measures with explicit attention to firm *behavior*. Important work includes Lerner's (1933–1934) well-known index of monopoly power and Saving (1970), which shows how concentration ratios for firms in a price leadership model can be related to the Lerner index. Stigler (1964a) and Cowling and Waterson (1976) examine the Herfindahl index within an oligopoly model; see also Donsimoni, Geroski, and Jacquemin (1984).

Axiomatic treatments of income inequality appear in many studies. Application of the axiomatic approach to measuring industrial concentration and the extent of market power is performed by Encaoua and Jacquemin (1980). For a noncooperative Cournot-Nash model, Encaoua and Jacquemin show that an arithmetic average of Lerner indices across firms equals the Herfindahl index multiplied by the reciprocal of demand elasticity.[7] An axiomatic approach to measuring market power within a game theoretic setting analogous to the Shapley axioms is provided by d'Aspremont and Jacquemin (1985). The measure of power within a simple game is then used to measure the power to monopolize. Finally, Dansby and Willig (1979), derive industry performance gradient indices that "measure the rate of potential improvement in the performance of an industry." The indices reduce to transformations of familiar concentration measures (the concentration ratio, Herfindahl index, and Lerner index).

The preceding discussion suggests that the traditional concentration measures are good predictors of market power and the efficiency of industry equilibrium. However, as will be shown in the following sections, the predictive power of these measures depends crucially on whether products are homogeneous or differentiated, whether entry barriers exist, and whether firms compete with prices or quantities. Entry of firms may lower prices, particularly with Cournot quantity competition. However, these welfare benefits tend to be outweighed by cost increases due to lower output per firm. Thus, it is found that concentration measures may not function well as indicators of welfare or as a guide to public policy.

17.2   Cournot Quantity Competition

17.2.1   Quantity Competition with Fixed Market Structure

In this section, it is shown that the traditional view that market structure determines the efficiency of the equilibrium is not generally confirmed by the Cournot (1838) model. Attention is confined to symmetric equilibria.

In what follows, assume that market demand $D(p)$ is continuously differentiable, single valued, and downward sloping. Let market inverse demand $F(Q)$ be twice continuously differentiable and decreasing on $(0, \infty)$. Let costs be twice continuously differentiable on $(0, \infty)$, with $C(0) = 0$. Unless otherwise indicated, average costs AC are strictly U-shaped with minimum at $MES > 0$. Assume that there exists $Q^* > 0$ such that $F(Q) \gtreqless AC(MES)$ as $Q \lesseqgtr Q^*$. The Cournot-Nash equilibrium with m firms, $q^{j*} = q^{j*}(m), j = 1, \ldots, m$, satisfies the standard first-order conditions,

$$F\left(\sum_{j \neq i}^{m} q^{j*} + q^i \right) + F'\left(\sum_{j \neq i}^{m} q^{j*} + q^i \right) q^i - C'(q^i) = 0. \tag{17.2.1}$$

Let $q^{j*}(m) = q^*(m)$ for $j = 1, \ldots, m$. Seade (1980a) presents two conditions that are necessary and sufficient for *stability* of the Cournot equilibrium,

$$F'(q) < C''(q), \tag{17.2.2}$$

$$F''(mq)mq + F'(mq)(m + 1) - C''(q) < 0. \tag{17.2.3}$$

Assume that these conditions are satisfied. Then the second-order conditions for the firms' problems hold,

$$F''q^i + 2F' - C'' < F''q^i + F' + (F' - C'')/m < 0.$$

The first inequality follows from (17.2.2) and the second from (17.2.3).

Stability is sufficient for reduced market concentration to increase total output. This result is obtained by Seade (1980b) and also by Frank (1965), Okuguchi (1973), and Ruffin (1971).

PROPOSITION 17.2.1 (Seade)   *Given profitable entry and stability, entry increases total production.*

From equation (17.2.1), letting $Q(m) = mq^*(m)$,

$$\frac{\partial Q(m)}{\partial m} = \frac{q(F'(mq^*) - C''(q^*))}{F''(mq^*)mq^* + F'(mq^*)(m + 1) - C''(q^*)}. \tag{17.2.4}$$

Then $\partial Q(m)/\partial m > 0$ follows immediately from (17.2.2) and (17.2.3).

Increasing entry reduces the output and profits of each firm; see Seade (1980b) for additional discussion.

PROPOSITION 17.2.2   *Given stability, entry reduces profits per firm and, if $F''q + F' < 0$, entry reduces output per firm.*

Differentiating equation (17.2.1) with respect to m gives

$$\frac{\partial q(m)}{\partial m} = \frac{F''(mq^*)(q^*)^2 + F'(mq^*)q^*}{F''(mq^*)mq^* + F'(mq^*)(m + 1) - C''(q^*)}. \tag{17.2.5}$$

By the stability condition (17.2.3), the denominator is positive and $F''q + F' < 0$ by assumption. Profits are $\pi(m) = F(mq^*(m))q^*(m) - C(q^*(m))$. Rearranging terms, the effect of entry on profits is simply

$$\pi'(m) = (F(mq^*(m)) - C'(q^*(m)))(\partial q^*(m)/\partial m) + F'(mq^*(m))\,\partial Q(m)/\partial m. \tag{17.2.6}$$

Thus, $\pi'(m) < 0$, from (17.2.1)–(17.2.5).

Since entry increases total output, reduced market concentration increases consumer surplus. Welfare considerations must depend on producer surplus as well, and hence on costs. Since entry reduces the output of each firm, they may operate at an inefficient scale with excess capacity. Let welfare be defined as a function of market structure,

$$W(m) = \int_0^{Q(m)} F(x)\,dx - mC(q^*(m)). \tag{17.2.7}$$

Then one can examine the link between the index of concentration $1/m$ and welfare for the Cournot-Nash equilibrium. Using the definition of profits per firm, $\pi(m)$ and the equilibrium condition (17.2.1), it follows that

$$W'(m) = \pi(m) - F'(mq^*(m))mq^*(m)\,\partial q^*(m)/\partial m. \tag{17.2.8}$$

The first term is nonnegative, while the second term is positive. Thus, the effect of entry on welfare is generally ambiguous.

Given *barriers to entry*, profits per firm may be relatively high. Then additional entry may increase welfare. Let $\chi_q \equiv (\partial q/\partial m)(m/q)$ and $\chi_Q \equiv (\partial Q/\partial m)(m/Q)$ represent *elasticity with respect to entry* of per firm output and aggregate output, respectively. Note that $\chi_Q = 1 + \chi_q$, $\chi_Q \geq 0$, and $\chi_q \leq 0$. Let $S \equiv (C'(q)q - C(q))/q^2$ be the slope of the average cost curve. Then a necessary and sufficient condition for reduced market concentration to increase welfare is obtained.

PROPOSITION 17.2.3   *Entry increases welfare if and only if*

$$\pi(m) > q^2 S \chi_q / \chi_Q. \tag{17.2.9}$$

Proof From equation (17.2.8) and the Cournot-Nash equilibrium condition (17.2.1),

$$W'(m) = \pi(m)(1 + \chi_q) - (C'q - C)\chi_q. \tag{17.2.10}$$

Substituting using S yields (17.2.9)   QED

The proposition indicates that for entry to improve welfare, profits must be large relative to increases in average costs due to reduced output per firm. Otherwise, loss of scale economies will eliminate the welfare benefits of lower prices. A positive association between reduced market concentration and welfare can only be established given consideration of profits per firm, output elasticities, and the form of the production function. Since high firm profits require the presence of entry barriers such as sunk costs, reduced concentration may only be desirable in the presence of entry barriers. Thus, public policy directed at concentration may be misplaced if consideration is not given to firm technology and the costs of entry.

In fact, as entry occurs, the term $(q^2 S \chi_q / \chi_Q)$ will dominate profits and welfare will fall. The free entry equilibrium has been shown to lead to excessive entry by von Weizsäcker (1980a,b), M. K. Perry (1984), and Mankiw and Whinston (1986). Noting that $W'(m) < \pi(m)$ from equation (17.2.8), Mankiw and Whinston observe that, since the second-best optimal market structure m° satisfies $W'(m^\circ) = 0$ and the free entry market structure satisfies $\pi(m^*) = 0$, $m^* > m^\circ$.

PROPOSITION 17.2.4   *At a Cournot-Nash equilibrium with free entry, market concentration is less than the social optimum.*

Mankiw and Whinston (1986) show that if one restricts attention to integer numbered firms, and M^* is the market equilibrium and M° the optimum market structure, then $M^* \geq (M^\circ - 1)$. So, at the free entry market equilibrium, market structure may be less than optimal by at most one firm. A direct proof of this result is now given. Let $\lfloor x \rfloor$ be the largest integer less than or equal to x and $\lceil x \rceil$ the smallest integer greater than or equal to x. Then, $\lfloor m^* \rfloor = M^*$ and $\lfloor m^\circ \rfloor \leq M^\circ \leq \lceil m^\circ \rceil$. Since $m^* \geq m^\circ$, it follows immediately that $M^* \geq (M^\circ - 1)$. This result implies that at a free entry equilibrium with several viable firms, concentration is unlikely to be a problem.

17.2.2 Quantity Competition with Entry

Proposition 17.2.3 confirms the standard connection drawn between welfare and concentration in the presence of significant entry barriers. A Cournot-Nash equilibrium with free entry is now considered. Firms have identical technologies and face no costs of entry. The analysis of Novshek (1980a) shows that as the scale of firms becomes small relative to the size of the market, the market equilibrium approaches the competitive equilibrium.[8]

Rescale costs following Novshek (1980a), as in chapter 4 in the present work. An α-size firm corresponding to $C(\cdot)$ has the cost function $C_\alpha(q) \equiv \alpha C(q/\alpha)$. Normalize costs in such a way that the size of the firm equals one, $MES(C) = 1$. Thus, $MES(C_\alpha) = \alpha$. Similarly, rescale market inverse demand in such a way that $F_\beta(Q) = F(Q/\beta)$. Normalize inverse demand in such a way that $F(1) = AC_{min}$. Thus, $F_\beta(\beta) = AC_{min}$. β is referred to as the *size of the market*, since it represents market demand at the minimum average cost price. The market is denoted by (α, C, β, F). The equilibrium concept of a Cournot-Nash equilibrium with free entry stated by Novshek requires outputs of incumbent firms to be a Cournot equilibrium. Further, at the equilibrium firms make nonnegative profits and there are no incentives for additional entry of firms.

Definition 17.2.1 (Novshek)   Given the market (α, C, β, F), a *Cournot-Nash equilibrium with free entry* is a set of positive outputs q^{j*}, $j = 1, \ldots, m$, such that

i. q^{i*} maximizes profits $F_\beta(\sum_{j \neq i}^{m} q^{j*} + q^i)q^i - C_\alpha(q^i)$ for all $q^i \in [0, \infty)$, and
ii. $F_\beta(\sum_{j=1}^{m} q^{j*} + q) - C_\alpha(q) \leq 0$ for all $q \in [0, \infty]$.

The set of all Cournot-Nash market equilibria with free entry is denoted by $E(\alpha, C, \beta, F)$.

Novshek (1980a) proves an important existence result. He shows that there exists some $\zeta > 0$ such that for all α, $\beta \in (0, \infty)$ with $\alpha/\beta \leq \zeta$, the set

$E(\alpha, C, \beta, F)$ is nonempty. In addition, Novshek (1980a) shows that given small firm scale as compared with the size of the market, the Cournot-Nash equilibrium with free entry is approximately competitive. His result and its proof are paraphrased here.

PROPOSITION 17.2.5 (Novshek)   *For all equilibria in $E(\alpha, C, \beta, F)$ with market structure m^* and total output $Q^* = \sum_{j=1}^{m*} q^{j*}$, $Q^* \in [\beta - \alpha, \beta]$.*

Proof Let $q^1, \ldots, q^m$ be any Cournot-Nash equilibrium output vector and $X = \sum_{j=1}^{m} q^j$. Then, if $X > \beta$, $q^j > 0$ for some j and market price $F(X) \le AC_{\min}$. So, the firm producing $q^j > 0$ has negative profits, which contradicts the definition of the Cournot-Nash equilibrium and $C_\alpha(0) = 0$. If $X < \beta - \alpha$, then by producing at minimum efficient scale an entrant earns profit $[F_\beta(X + \alpha) - AC_\alpha(\alpha)]\alpha$. But, since $X + \alpha < \beta$, price exceeds average costs, which is contrary to the free entry condition.   QED

The significance of this result is that a market equilibrium with small firms relative to market size is approximately competitive with the assumption that firms behave as price takers. The result further confirms the traditional view that small firms are required for efficient performance. Next, the case of large firms is considered.

The definition of Cournot-Nash equilibrium is related to the concept of quantity sustainability of Brock and Scheinkman (1983); see definition 4.4.1. A price and quantity pair is quantity sustainable if it yields nonnegative profits for the monopolist and there are no entry opportunities. If firms are *large* relative to the size of the market, the *profit-maximizing* monopoly output is a Cournot-Nash equilibrium and therefore quantity sustainable. Let costs be given by $C(q) = K + V(q)$, where $K > 0$, $V''(q) > 0$.

PROPOSITION 17.2.6   *There exist ζ_0, ζ_1, $\zeta_1 \ge \zeta_0 > 0$ such that for all α, $\beta \in (0, \alpha), \zeta_0 \le \alpha/\beta \le \zeta_1$, the profit-maximizing monopoly output is a Cournot-Nash equilibrium with free entry.*

To prove Proposition 17.2.6, define revenue $R_\beta(q) \equiv F_\beta(q)q$. By assumption, revenue is concave. Further, the residual revenue function $R_\beta(q, q^m) \equiv F_\beta(q^m + q)q$ is everywhere below $R_\beta(q)$ for $q^m > 0$ except at $q = 0$. Since costs are convex, there is a range of α/β such that the profit-maximizing monopoly output is positive and there are no incentives for entry; see figure 17.2.1. This result formally establishes the well-known case of *blockaded entry* of Bain (1956). Thus, if firms set outputs, a positive profit

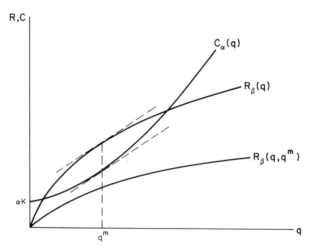

Figure 17.2.1
The profit-maximizing monopoly output is quantity sustainable against entry.

monopoly is sustainable. As observed in chapter 4, the conditions for sustainability of monopoly are far less stringent when firms compete by choosing output levels than when firms set prices. It is evident that a positive profit monopoly is not price sustainable. Therefore, the question of whether the presence of only a single firm producing in the market indicates monopoly power depends on firm behavior. An argument against the notion of quantity sustainability is that price competition allows the entrant to achieve positive profits and that the market will exhaust all profitable opportunities. However, the strategies of price and quantity setting by firms depend on such factors as the timing of price and production decisions and the form of contracts made between incumbent firms and consumers.

17.3 Bertrand Price Competition

17.3.1 Price Competition with a Fixed Market Structure

In simple models of imperfect competition, much is left unspecified. Comparing models in which firms choose output with those in which firms choose prices, significant omissions exist in both. In Cournot quantity models, the market price adjusts to clear the market. Firms sell the entire amount they choose to supply, while the proverbial auctioneer, which sets the equilibrium price, is implicit. In Bertrand price models, the problem of introducing an auctioneer is solved by letting firms adjust prices. However, an equally objectionable assumption is implicit. An unspecified mechanism by which consumer demands are distributed across firms is assumed to operate. In homogeneous output models, the allocation of consumer demand across firms may play a significant role in determining the market equilibrium.

Consider the Bertrand duopoly with identical firms having linear marginal costs and a capacity constraint,

$$C(q) = \begin{cases} cq, & q \le k \\ \infty, & k < q. \end{cases} \qquad (17.3.1)$$

Let market demand $Q(p)$ be downward sloping. Suppose first that either firm can profitably serve the entire market, $Q(c) \le k$. Then a standard assumption at this stage is to assume that the firm with the lowest price captures all of the market, while firms *split the market evenly* if $p_1 = p_2$; see, for example, Shubik (1959, 1980). The market equilibrium occurs where $p_1 = p_2 = c$. Either firm would make a loss by cutting its price and would lose all sales by raising its price.

The Bertrand duopoly model provides more than simply a challenge to the Cournot model. The result raises a fundamental question about the connection between market structure and the degree of market power possessed by firms. The duopoly market may certainly be characterized as having a high degree of concentration. However, a competitive equilibrium is observed. Thus, given sufficient capacity to serve the market, and the absence of collusion, a price war will yield the competitive outcome. This occurs without the traditional prerequisites for competition: price-taking behavior and large numbers of firms. This result creates a significant objection to antitrust action to promote competition based solely on measures of market concentration.

Consider the Bertrand model with the following cost function:

$$C(q) = \begin{cases} F + cq, & q \le k \\ \infty, & k < q. \end{cases} \qquad (17.3.2)$$

The equilibrium is affected by whether F represents fixed or sunk costs. Suppose first that costs F are *sunk*; that is, F represents irreversible investment and both firms are already committed to the market. Then capital costs will not affect current decisions, and one will again observe both prices equal to marginal cost c and firms will incur losses equal to their sunk costs. Although this outcome is inconsistent with perfect foresight, it is quite likely to occur given market uncertainty or unforeseen regulatory policy changes. In industries with large sunk costs, such as railroads, losses from price competition may be observed. Suppose now that F represents fixed costs. In that case, a firm may avoid sustaining a loss by setting its output equal to zero. If both firms must announce prices, a Bertrand equilibrium fails to exist. Let $\tilde{p}$ be the smallest price that equals average cost, $\tilde{p} = F/Q(\tilde{p}) + c$. Prices will never be below $\tilde{p}$. If both firms choose $p_1 = p_2 = \tilde{p}$, then they divide the market between them and they make a loss. If either firm sets a price above $\tilde{p}$, the best response is to undercut slightly, steal the market, and make a profit. Thus, an equilibrium in prices fails to exist.

Suppose in the preceding case that if a firm chooses not to produce, it is not required to announce a price. Alternatively, one firm may be allowed to sell all of its output first in the event of a tie in prices. In either case, there exists an equilibrium in which a single firm produces the entire output demanded at price $\tilde{p}$. This equilibrium is equivalent to the sustainable monopoly price in the entry model of Baumol, Panzar, and Willig (1982), already discussed in chapter 4. Observe again that the relation between observed market concentration and performance is again challenged. The market appears to be a monopoly, yet the producer makes zero profit, price equals average cost, and the least-cost allocation of production across firms occurs.

Consider a further modification of the duopoly model due to Edgeworth (1925); see also Shubik (1959) and Grossman (1981b). Suppose that the capacity constraint is such that a single firm can no longer profitably serve the market, while both firms can with excess capacity. In the constant marginal cost case, let $k < Q(c) < 2k$. Then a Bertrand equilibrium no longer exists. If firm 1 sets price at marginal cost, the best response of the other firm is a higher price to maximize profit, given the residual demand $Q(p) - k$ for $p > c$. Thus, $p_1 = p_2 = c$ cannot be a Nash equilibrium. Let both firms choose a price above marginal cost, $p_1 = p_2 > c$. Then each firm has excess capacity and it is profitable for one firm to undercut its price slightly. Thus, there is no Nash equilibrium with prices above marginal cost. There is thus no Nash equilibrium. There are two widely noted aspects of this nonexistence failure. First, it is apparent that there is a discontinuity in the Bertrand model; a small price cut below that of the other firm leads to a large discrete shift of demand to the discounter. Second, the capacity constraint of Edgeworth may be generalized to increasing average costs. Sharkey (1982a, p. 169) shows that if the industry is a natural monopoly, then there is no Bertrand-Nash equilibrium in prices. He observes that with U-shaped average cost, no equilibrium exists, whether demand cuts average cost to the right or left of minimum efficient scale. Thus, the Bertrand price announcement model is generally inconclusive for analyzing the effects of concentration on performance for a fixed market structure and homogeneous products.

The next two subsections examine competitive entry when incumbents and entrants set prices. As seen above, there are existence problems with the Bertrand equilibrium, given either binding capacity constraints or U-shaped average cost curves. To remedy this problem, turn to two alternative equilibrium concepts. The first is the *contestable markets* model of Baumol, Panzar, and Willig (1982). In this model, incumbent firms commit to a price and sell the market-clearing output. Entrants may only enter by undercutting the established price. Entrants may restrict their sales so as to be less than market-clearing amounts. Entry will only occur if it is profitable. It will be seen that existence issues also arise for this model if average costs are U-shaped. The other model examined is that of Nash equilibria with supply schedules of Grossman (1981b). Firms announce quantities they will supply at various prices. An *auctioneer* selects the equilibrium market price. It is shown that an "approximate competitive equilibrium" exists under some conditions.

17.3.2   Contestable Markets

The concept of sustainable monopoly prices in contestable markets was discussed previously in chapter 4. There it was noted that when the size of firms is sufficiently large relative to market demand, a sustainable monopoly price exists equal to the lowest market-clearing average cost price. This result has important implications for antitrust analysis of market structure as well as for assessing the desirability of regulation. These issues are taken up in chapter 20. For now the focus will be on the contestable markets model as a foundation for discussion of the link between industry structure and performance.

When market demand at the minimum average cost price exceeds the minimum efficient scale of a firm, the existence of a sustainable industry structure at a single market price requires special cost restrictions. Suppose

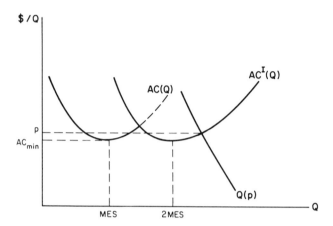

Figure 17.3.1
There is no sustainable multiple-firm equilibrium.

the market is still characterized by natural monopoly but demand is in the region of decreasing returns to scale; then a sustainable monopoly price fails to exist. This is discussed in Baumol, Panzar, and Willig (1982)—to be abbreviated BPW—and is basic to the results in chapter 4. Absence of sustainability is an important issue, which is discussed further in the concluding chapter (chapter 20). For now, the issue is whether a meaningful industry equilibrium exists. In general, with market demand sufficiently large to support two or more firms, there is no clearly defined equilibrium. Consider figure 17.3.1 (based on figure 2.3.3 in BPW). The only possible sustainable industry configuration is a duopoly with total output at the zero-profit price $p = AC^I(Q)$, $Q = Q(p)$, where $AC^I(Q)$ is average minimized industry costs. As BPW (p. 32) note, the multifirm sustainability requirement $p = AC = MC$ cannot be satisfied unless demand intersects AC^I at an integer multiple of minimum efficient scale. BPW (p. 32) state that otherwise "a profitable entry plan must exist; for example, $p^e = AC(MES) < p$ and $q^e = MES < Q(p^e)$. Thus, no sustainable equilibrium exists. Since a fortuitous intersection between the demand curve and a point of minimum industry AC would seem unlikely, *a priori*, it would appear that the prospects for existence of equilibrium in perfectly contestable markets are rather poor" (notation is modified). They present remedies for the existence problem; see BPW (chapter 11). For the single-product case, the solution

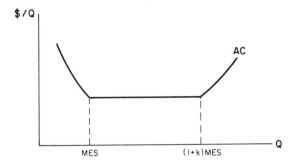

Figure 17.3.2
The flat-bottomed average cost curve.

lies in the flat-bottomed average cost curve, as shown in figure 17.3.2. Then BPW prove the following result (restated):

PROPOSITION 17.3.1 (BPW)   *Let firm average costs have a flat bottom (from MES to* $(1 + k)MES$). *Let industry output* Q^{I} *satisfy*

$$Q^{\mathrm{I}} = Q(p^*), \qquad p^* = AC_{\min}.$$

Then (Q^{I}, p^*) *is a sustainable industry equilibrium if*

$$Q^{\mathrm{I}} \le \bar{m}(1 + k)MES,$$

where $\bar{m}$ *is the largest integer not greater than* Q^{I}/MES.

The idea of the proposition is that with flat-bottomed average costs for individual firms, the *industry* average-minimized cost function will have flat segments equal to minimum average costs. Then, if market demand cuts the industry average cost in one of these flat segments, a sustainable market equilibrium exists with a finite number of firms and price equal to minimum average costs.

From the preceding discussion, it is apparent that under some conditions a zero-profit equilibrium is attained by competitive entry into contestable markets. The key issue is whether market demand occurs in the right output range and the size of the flat bottom of firm average cost curves. BPW (p. 33) observe that the flat-bottomed average cost curve is supported by empirical evidence, on which see Bain (1954). Scherer (1980, chapter 4) finds that minimum efficient scale is determined by unit costs at the plant level but that a region of relatively constant average costs may be achieved through decentralization and multiple divisions. At $(1 + k)MES$, managerial diseconomies are said to raise average costs. Thus, the applicability of the result that the industry equilibrium attains the minimum average cost price depends on an empirical verification of the necessary cost conditions on a case-by-case basis. If these conditions are applicable, we have an important case of efficient industry performance that is independent of market structure.

17.3.3 Free Entry and Competition with Supply Schedules

There is an alternative equilibrium that yields an "approximately competitive" outcome due to Grossman (1981b)—the Nash equilibrium in supply functions. The following discussion is based on Grossman (1981b). Let firms have identical, convex costs given by $C(q) = K + V(q)$, $V''(q) > 0$ for $q > 0$ and $C(0) = 0$.

Definition 17.3.1 A *supply function* for firm i, $q^i(p)$, is a mapping that states how much the firm is willing to supply at various market prices p.

The notion of a supply function is predicated on the requirement that a single price obtains at the market equilibrium. The market-clearing price is selected by an auctioneer represented by a price function $P(\bar{q})$ where $\bar{q}$ is the vector of firm supply schedules. Let $Q^s(p)$ represent an aggregate supply function. Let $D(p)$ be market demand.

Definition 17.3.2 A *market-clearing price function* $P(\bar{q})$ is defined by $P(\bar{q}) = \inf\{p : \text{there exists } Q^s(p) \in \sum \bar{q}^i(p) \text{ satisfying } Q^s(p) \geq D(p)\}$.

Thus, the auctioneer chooses the "smallest price such that supply is larger than demand," but the analysis can also be carried through for "the largest price such that supply is less than demand" (Grossman, 1981b). A feasible supply correspondence is defined as follows.

Definition 17.3.3 The supply correspondence $q^i(\cdot)$: $\mathbb{R}_+ \to$ subsets of $\mathbb{R}_+$ is *feasible* for firm i if

a. $q^i(\cdot)$ is upper semicontinuous and for all $p \geq 0$, $q^i(p)$ is nonempty,

b. $pq^i - C(q^i) \geq 0$ for all $q^i \in q^i(p)$, and

c. $pq - C(q) = pq' - C(q')$ for all $q, q' \in q^i(p)$.

One can now define a market equilibrium in supply schedules.

Definition 17.3.4   The vector of supply schedules $\bar{q}*$ is a *Nash equilibrium in supply schedules* if, for each i, q^{i*} maximizes

$$\Pi^i(\bar{q}*/q^i) = P(\bar{q}*/q^i)q^i(P(\bar{q}*/q^i)) - C(q^i(P(\bar{q}*/q^i))), \qquad (17.3.3)$$

over all feasible supply functions $q^i(\cdot)$.

The approximate competitiveness of a supply schedule equilibrium is now examined. Define the least and the most a firm can produce at price p, $y(p)$ and $Y(p)$, respectively,

$$y(p) = \min\{q : C(q)/q \leq p\}, \qquad Y(p) = \max\{q : C(q)/q \leq p\}.$$

Note that $y(p_{MES}) = Y(p_{MES})$, where $p_{MES} = AC_{\min} = AC(MES)$. Then define an *approximately competitive equilibrium* (m^c, q^c, p^c) by an integer m^c, output per firm $q^c > 0$, and market price p^c, which satisfy

$$m^c MES \leq D(p_{MES}), \qquad (17.3.4)$$

$$(m^c + 1)MES > D(p_{MES}), \qquad (17.3.5)$$

$$D(C'(q^c)) = m^c q^c, \qquad p^c = C'(q^c). \qquad (17.3.6)$$

At this equilibrium, price equals marginal costs, firms make positive profits, and yet there are no incentives for entry. Grossman (1981b, theorem 3) provides sufficient conditions for the existence of a Nash equilibrium in supply schedules that is approximately competitive.

PROPOSITION 17.3.2 (Grossman)   *Let the number of potential entrants equal or exceed $m^c + 1$. Suppose $y(p) \geq D(p) - m^c \min\{q^c, Y(p)\}$ for all $p \geq p_{MES}$. Then there is a Nash equilibrium $\bar{q}*$ such that $m^c q^c \in \sum q^{i*}(p^c)$.*

This result gets around the existence problems observed for the Bertrand equilibrium with U-shaped average cost curves. However, the existence problems noted for sustainability are present here as well. Consider the following example given by Grossman (1981b, p. 168). A monopoly equilibrium, $m^c = 1$, can be attained by setting $q^1(p) = \min\{q^c, Y(p)\}$. This implies that the supply schedule has the form

$$q^1(p) = \begin{cases} 0 & \text{if } p < p_{MES} \\ AC^{-1}(p) & \text{if } p_{MES} \leq p \leq AC(q^c) \\ q^c & \text{if } AC(q^c) \leq p; \end{cases} \qquad (17.3.7)$$

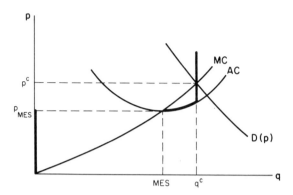

Figure 17.3.3
The monopoly supply schedule.

see figure 17.3.3. In other words, for a price below minimum average cost, zero output is supplied by the feasibility requirement. For a price in between minimum average costs and $AC(q^c)$, the supply schedule follows the average cost curve. For a price above $AC(q^c)$, the firm supplies the fixed quantity q^c and the supply curve is vertical. Is this a sustainable equilibrium? Not necessarily. For example, an entrant can set $p^e - p_{MES}$, $q^e = MES$, thus undercutting p^c, and enter if

$$MES < D(p_{MES}) - q^c,$$

that is, if the size of the firm is less than the size of the market net of the "approximately competitive" output. This is what is ruled out by the assumption in the proposition. One again encounters the hypothesis of entry deterrence by incumbent firms that threaten to maintain a high (constant) post entry output at the Nash equilibrium.

Observe also that the equilibrium reintroduces a link between structure and performance. Although price equals marginal cost, the price is then in excess of average costs. Furthermore, firms operate with insufficient capacity i.e., *above minimum efficient scale*. It follows that as the size of the market increases, relative to the size of the firm, the approximately competitive equilibrium price will approach the minimum average cost price. Let $\alpha = MES(C_\alpha)$ and $\beta = D_\beta(p_{MES})$ as before.

PROPOSITION 17.3.3   *Let $Q^c = m^c q^c$. Then $Q^c \in [\beta - \alpha, \beta]$.*

Proof We have $Q^c \leq \beta$, since price must exceed minimum average cost by feasibility. From equation (17.3.5), $m^c \alpha > \beta - \alpha$. But, since each firm operates above minimum average cost, $q^c > \alpha$. Thus, $m^c q^c > \beta - \alpha$. QED

Thus, as the size of the market gets large relative to the size of the firm, the Nash equilibrium in supply schedules, (m^c, q^c, p^c), approaches the competitive equilibrium.

17.4 Price Competition with Differentiated Products

17.4.1 Differentiated Products and a Fixed Market Structure

The connections between market structure and performance in the presence of price competition were examined for the case of homogeneous goods in the preceding section. These conclusions are altered substantially when product differentiation is introduced. The effects of product differentiation on monopolistic competition have been recognized at least since Hotelling (1929) and Chamberlin (1956). As Hotelling (1929) found, the price war observed by Bertrand may fail to occur, since slightly undercutting a rival's price will only attract a share of the rival's sales. Thus, the link between structure and performance observed in the Cournot quantity model reappears to some degree in a price-setting model with differentiated products.

For ease of exposition, product differentiation is represented within a spatial setting. In particular, it is assumed that the product market is a unit circle. Each consumer has a most preferred product l^* located on the circle. Consumers purchase a single brand l^j located in the brand space. The number of units of brand j purchased by a consumer is given by q^j. A consumer's utility is assumed to depend on the number of units purchased and the (Euclidean) distance between his most preferred good and the characteristics of the brand purchases,

$$U = U(q^j, |l^* - l^j|);$$

see figure 17.4.1. Thus, if a consumer's most preferred good is at distance r from brand j, one may write $U = U(q^j, r)$. Let consumers be uniformly distributed around the circle with density A.

Horstmann and Slivinski (1985) give necessary and sufficient conditions under which a product set and a set of preference orderings on that product set can be represented as a circular product market. These necessary and

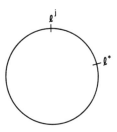

Figure 17.4.1
Distance between brand j and the
consumer's most preferred product l^*.

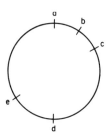

Figure 17.4.2
If the consumer at b is indifferent between
a and c, he is indifferent between e and d.

sufficient conditions are as follows (stated for unit density). First, for every consumer there is exactly one other consumer with an opposite preference ordering. This rules out the single-peakedness condition that is often used in social choice and is necessary for the linear market representation. Second, let consumers a and d have opposite preferences and let c and e have opposite preferences. Then, if a consumer at b is indifferent between goods at a and c, he is also indifferent between goods at e and d; see figure 17.4.2.

In general, demand for each brand j will be a function of the entire vector of prices, $Q^j = Q^j(p_1, \ldots, p_m)$, if there are m brands. For ease of presentation, restrict preferences to the form $U(q^j, r) = u(q^j) - tq^jr$. Then t represents the per unit cost of product differences between brand j and the consumer's most preferred good.

Attention is restricted to symmetric equilibria with m firms. Since firms are evenly located in the brand space, each pair of firms divides a market of length $1/m$ between them. Observe that market structure m is identical to product variety. Alternatively, the Herfindahl measure of concentration $(1/m)$ directly measures the degree of product differentiation by measuring the total market area of each firm at a symmetric equilibrium. Assume that there are a sufficient number of firms such that their potential markets overlap and firms compete with rivals supplying neighboring brands. Assume that there is a Bertrand-Nash equilibrium in prices $p_j, j = 1, \ldots, m$. In addition, assume that no firm undercuts the delivered price of another firm at the other firm's location.[9] Then the one-sided market radius for any firm x satisfies $0 < x < 1/m$. The one-sided market radius of firm i, x_i, between brands i and $i + 1$ equates delivered prices,

$$p_i + tx_i = p_{i+1} + t(1/m - x_i), \tag{17.4.1}$$

as in the Hotelling (1929) model. Thus, x_i is given by

$$x_i = (1/2t)(p_{i+1} - p_i + t/m), \qquad i = 1, \ldots, m, \tag{17.4.2}$$

where $p_{m+1} = p_1$.

Let firms have affine cost functions $C(Q) = K + cQ$. The market demand faced by each firm i is

$$Q^i(p_{i-1}, p_i, p_{i+1}) = A \int_0^{x_i} q(p_i + tr) \, dr$$

$$+ A \int_0^{(1/m - (x_{i-1}))} q(p_i + tr) \, dr, \qquad i = 1, \ldots, m, \quad (17.4.3)$$

with $x_0 = x_m$. The firms choose prices to maximize profits, taking other firms' prices as given,

$$\pi^i(p_{i-1}, p_i, p_{i+1}) = p_i Q^i(p_{i-1}, p_i, p_{i+1})$$

$$- C(Q^i(p_{i-1}, p_i, p_{i+1})), \qquad i = 1, \ldots, m, \tag{17.4.4}$$

where $p_0 = p_m$ and $p_{m+1} = p_1$. The first-order conditions resemble the Cournot equilibrium conditions for output-setting firms,

$$(p_i - c) \partial Q^i(p_{i-1}, p_i, p_{i+1})/\partial p_i + Q^i(p_{i-1}, p_i, p_{i+1}) = 0. \tag{17.4.5}$$

At a symmetric equilibrium $p_i = p$ for all i, $x_i = 1/2m$, and

$$\partial Q^i(p_{i-1}, p_i, p_{i+1})/\partial p_i = 2A \int_0^{1/2m} q'(p_i + tr) \, dr - Aq(p_i + t/2m)/t. \quad (17.4.6)$$

Combining (17.4.5) and (17.4.6), at the symmetric equilibrium[10]

$$(p - c) = \frac{-2 \int_0^{1/2m} q(p + tr) \, dr}{2 \int_0^{1/2m} q'(p + tr) \, dr - q(p + t/2m)/t}$$

$$= \frac{2t \int_0^{1/2m} q(p + tr) \, dr}{2q(p) - q(p + t/2m)}. \tag{17.4.7}$$

Observe that firms choose a *positive markup* as a consequence of the cost of product substitution.

The effect of product differentiation on the equilibrium markup is now considered for small costs of product substitution.

PROPOSITION 17.4.1 $\lim_{t \to 0}(p - c) = 0$.

The result follows from (17.4.7), since the numerator goes to zero and the denominator goes to $q(p)$ as t goes to zero. The implication of proposition 17.4.1 is that the degree of market power obtained by each firm depends on the cost to consumers of purchasing a substitute brand from a rival firm. In the limit, the Bertrand equilibrium is observed, with market structure having little effect on profits and prices. Thus, as the costs of substitution become small, the competitive outcome with price equal to marginal cost is approximated despite price setting by firms and a relatively concentrated market structure.[11]

17.4.2   Prices versus Quantities with Differentiated Products

It is evident that the Nash equilibrium with price-setting firms closely resembles the Nash noncooperative equilibrium with output-setting firms when products are differentiated. In the Bertrand (Cournot) case, each firm adjusts its price (output) so as to set its marginal revenue equal to marginal cost, taking the other firms' prices (outputs) as given. However, the equilibria are quite different both in terms of observed prices and quantities and in terms of the profitability of pursuing a Bertrand or Cournot strategy for individual firms.

Consider a simple linear demand duopoly model discussed in Dixit (1979a) and Singh and Vives (1984). Consumer benefits are given by

$$U(q_1, q_2) = \alpha_1 q_1 + \alpha_2 q_2 - (\beta_1 q_1^2 + 2\gamma q_1 q_2 + \beta_2 q_2^2)/2,$$

where $\beta_1 \beta_2 - \gamma^2 > 0$ and $\alpha_i \beta_j - \alpha_j \gamma > 0$ for $i \neq j$, $i = 1, 2$. The goods are substitutes, independent or complements as $\gamma \gtrless 0$. The Bertrand and Cournot equilibria are easily calculated; see Singh and Vives (1984). Inverse demands are

$$p_1 = \alpha_1 - \beta_1 q_1 - \gamma q_2,$$

$$p_2 = \alpha_2 - \gamma q_2 - \beta_2 q_2.$$

Demands are

$$q_1 = a_1 - b_1 p_1 + c p_2,$$

$$q_2 = a_2 - c p_1 - b_2 p_2,$$

where $\delta = \beta_1 \beta_2 - \gamma^2$, $a_i = (\alpha_i \beta_j - \alpha_j \gamma)/\delta$, and $b_i = \beta_j/\delta$ for $i \neq j$, $i = 1, 2$, and $c = \gamma/\delta$. Thus, the Bertrand and Cournot equilibria are as follows:

$$
\text{Bertrand}
\begin{cases}
p_1^B = \dfrac{2a_1 b_2 + a_2 c}{4b_1 b_2 - c^2}, & q_1^B = b_1 p_1^B, \\[3ex]
p_2^B = \dfrac{2a_2 b_1 + a_1 c}{4b_1 b_2 - c^2}, & q_2^B = b_2 p_2^B;
\end{cases}
$$

$$
\text{Cournot}
\begin{cases}
p_1^c = \beta_1 q_1^c, & q_1^c = \dfrac{2\alpha_1 \beta_2 - \alpha_2 \gamma}{4\beta_1 \beta_2 - \gamma^2}, \\[3ex]
p_2^c = \beta_2 q_2^c, & q_2^c = \dfrac{2\alpha_2 \beta_1 - \alpha_1 \gamma}{4\beta_1 \beta_2 - \gamma^2}.
\end{cases}
$$

As Singh and Vives (1984) point out, the Cournot competition with substitute goods is the dual of the Bertrand competition with complements (and vice versa). There are additional implications for welfare and profits in the linear demand case.

PROPOSITION 17.4.2 (Singh and Vives)   *Consumer surplus and total surplus are larger in Bertrand than in Cournot competition, except when goods are independent, in which case they are equal. Profits are larger, equal, or smaller in Cournot than in Bertrand competition, according to whether the goods are substitutes, independent, or complements.*

In addition, a two-stage game is considered in which firms may choose a *price contract* by commiting to a price with variable quantity in the second period or a *quantity contract* with variable price in the second period.

PROPOSITION 17.4.3 (Singh and Vives)   *In the two-stage game, it is a dominant strategy for firm i to choose the quantity (price) contract if the goods are substitutes (complements).*

Additional results are given by Singh and Vives (1984) for the general demand case, and a useful graphic presentation appears in Cheng (1985).

   The implications of the static analysis for antitrust are of course limited by the dynamic nature of actual competition. However, the preceding results suggest that in considering the effects of market structure on efficiency, the following issues must be addressed:

1. Do firms make commitments to price contracts or quantity contracts?

2. Are competing products substitutes or complements?

The efficiency of Bertrand price competition implies that price competition moderates the welfare effects of market concentration. Thus, given price competition, performance predictions implicitly based on Cournot analysis must be moderated. In addition, given only information about whether competing goods are substitutes (or complements), the analysis allows a prediction of which equilibrium will be observed. The quantity model remains a good predictor for markets in which firms produce substitutes.

17.4.3 Differentiated Products and Entry

As shown in the preceding section, differentiated products implies that positive markups persist even in the presence of price competition. It is therefore natural to ask as in the discussion of the Cournot equilibrium how entry of firms affects prices and profits. In addition, the effects of fixed costs on product variety and market structure at the free entry market equilibrium are considered.

Consider an example with a circular market of unit circumference, linear transport costs, t, marginal production costs equal to zero, and linear consumer demand, $q(p) = a - bp$. Then, for a given market structure m, equilibrium prices are given by

$$p = (1/2)[(a/b + 3t/2m) - ((a/b - t/2m)^2 + 3t^2/m^2)^{1/2}],$$

from equation (17.4.7). Comparative statics on transport costs and market structure yield the following:

$$\frac{\partial p}{\partial t} = \frac{2a/b - t/m - 3p}{2m(a/b + 3t/2m - 2p)}, \tag{17.4.8}$$

$$\frac{\partial p}{\partial m} = \frac{-2ta/b - 11t^2/m + 6tp}{4m^2(a/b + 3t/2m - 2p)}. \tag{17.4.9}$$

It can be shown that the price is increasing in transport costs (or the degree of product differentiation) and decreasing in the number of firms if t/m is sufficiently small relative to a/b. Otherwise, with high transport costs there is a crowding out effect and demand is lowered, thus lowering the price. With very few firms, there are high transport costs. Thus, initially, a greater number of firms, by reducing transport costs, allows prices to rise. As the number of firms becomes large, the price eventually falls, since the effects of increased competition and lower transport costs reinforce each other.

Let firms have fixed cost K and allow free entry. Novshek (1980b) establishes the following result.

PROPOSITION 17.4.4 (Novshek)   *At the competitive equilibrium with free entry,*

i. *There exists a level of fixed costs K^* such that for all $K \in (0, K^*]$, the set of market equilibria is nonempty.*

ii. *If K_s is a sequence of fixed costs such that $K_s \to 0$ and for each s, p(s) is the maximum delivered price paid by any consumer in any market equilibrium, given fixed costs K_s, then $m(s) \to 0$.*

The result establishes that for the pricing model with free entry, price approaches marginal cost as firm fixed costs become small.

To illustrate the differentiated products model with entry, let each consumer purchase a single unit of the good with reservation price a. Then at a symmetric equilibrium, from equation (17.4.7),

$$p - c = t/m. \tag{17.4.10}$$

Clearly, price is increasing in t and falling in m. For demand to be positive at the boundary of each firm's market area requires $a \geq p + t/2m$. Thus, we require $(2/3)(a - c) \geq t/m$. Again, with t/m sufficiently small relative to the consumer's reservation value, the competitive equilibrium is well-defined[12]

The equilibrium market structure m^* is the largest integer such that

$$(p - c)/m^* \geq K. \tag{17.4.11}$$

Then, since $p - c = t/m^*$, m^* is bounded above,

$$m^* \leq (t/K)^{1/2}. \tag{17.4.12}$$

For example, given $K = 1$ and $t = 20$, four firms enter the market, as five firms cannot operate profitably.

Compare the market equilibrium variety with the social optimum. Welfare with market structure m is

$$W = 2m \int_0^{1/2m} (a - c - tr)\,dr - mK$$

$$= a - c - t/4m - mK.$$

Therefore, a socially optimal (integer) market structure is either the largest integer m° such that $m^\circ \leq (1/2)(t/K)^{1/2}$ or $m^\circ + 1$. It is evident that the socially optimal market structure is more concentrated than the free entry structure. For example, with $K = 1$ and $t = 20$, $m^o = 2 < m^* = 4$. Thus, there is excessive variety under monopolistic competition. This result is not robust to changes in the representation of differentiated products; see Salop (1979), Lancaster (1975), Spence (1976), and Dixit and Stiglitz (1977).

The model of entry with differentiated products presented here has been used by Schmalensee (1978a) to examine the antitrust case filed by the Federal Trade Commission (FTC) against the four largest makers of ready-to-eat breakfast cereal: Kellogg, General Mills, General Foods, and Quaker Oats. The complaint charged violation of section 5 of the FTC Act alleging that brand proliferation created a barrier to entry in the cereal market. Schmalensee (1978a, p. 314) argues that "if the established firms can crowd economic space with brands *before* the threat of entry appears ... the entry-deterring threat is that the brands will be not be moved if entry occurs. Since repositioning brands is assumed to involve substantial costs, such a threat is quite credible." Schmalensee finds that in the period 1950–1972, the cereal market was highly concentrated, with significant advertising outlays, new brand introduction, and only limited price competition. He concludes that proposed relief, including divestiture and trademark licensing, would alter the structure of the cereal industry and would be "likely to facilitate entry and to increase price competition."

The key assumption that supports brand proliferation as an entry barrier is the high cost of moving brands, that is, the sunk cost of entering a new brand and the cost of exiting an established one.[13] As Judd (1985) observes, if exit costs are low, the multiproduct monopolist will accommodate entry by withdrawing from particular brands. Unless exit costs are high, the threat to maintain sales of a brand in the face of entry cannot be made credible. The creation and abandonment of many brands by cereal manufacturers suggests that the costs of withdrawing brands may be quite low. This suggests that brand proliferation in itself may not constitute a barrier to entry in the cereal industry.

17.4.4   Geographic Pricing and the Relevant Market

An important issue associated with defining the relevant market for antitrust cases is the extent to which geographic distance between competitors should be considered. The antitrust literature on geographic delineation of markets includes Elzinga and Hogarty (1973), Horowitz (1981), Stigler and Sherwin (1983), and Scheffman and Spiller (1985). Scheffman and Spiller (1985) contrast the economic definition of a market with that specified by the 1982 and 1984 DOJ merger guidelines, which they refer to as an *antitrust market*. In particular, the 1982 revision of the 1984 merger guidelines states, "Formally, a market is defined as a product or group of products and a geographic area in which it is sold such that a hypothetical, profit maximizing firm, not subject to price regulation, that was the only present and future seller of those products in that area would impose a 'small but significant and nontransitory' increase in price above prevailing or likely future levels." [14]

The guidelines further emphasize that the *market* defined for the purpose of antitrust refers to the smallest relevant geographic area such that firms have market power. By contrast, Scheffman and Spiller (1985) observe that an *economic market* refers to an area in which delivered prices are approximately equal. [15]

Consider the differentiated products model as a geographic model with transport costs t per unit of the good transported over a unit distance. Delivered prices for goods i and $i + 1$, at distance r from location i, differ as follows:

$$\Delta p = |(p_i + tr) - (p_{i+1} + t(1/m - r))| = 2t|r - x_i|, \tag{17.4.13}$$

where x_i is the market boundary defined by equation (17.4.1). The wedge between delivered prices depends on the distance from the market boundary and the size of transport costs t. In equilibrium, it was seen that F.O.B. (Freight on Board) mill prices were equal, $p_i = p^*$ for all i and with symmetric location $x_i = 1/2m$ for all i, so that $\Delta p = 2t|r - 1/2m|$. Thus, at firm i's location, the wedge exactly equals $\Delta p = t/m$. In a less concentrated market, i.e., with additional entry, the wedge between delivered prices is reduced.

The geographic pricing model allows an evaluation of a number of methods used to define market areas in antitrust cases. The elasticity of residual demand is an important aspect of measures of market concentration. The well-known Lerner index allows an inference of the firm's relative markup, $(p - MC)/p$, from the reciprocal of demand elasticity. This provides an indirect measure of market power. It is often suggested that cross-price elasticities of demand provide a useful means of establishing market boundaries. In *United States* v. *du Pont* (1956), Justice Reed states that in evaluating the *relevant market* for cellophane in the presence of substitute packaging materials "[w]hat is called for is an appraisal of the 'cross-elasticity' of demand in the trade."[16] Scheffman and Spiller (1985) suggest the use of demand elasticities in a geographic setting where the entire area between firm locations is seen as an economic market. Residual demand elasticities are also discussed in the 1982 and 1984 DOJ Merger Guidelines.

In the geographic pricing model above, the elasticity of demand faced by firm i, $\eta_i = -(p_i/Q^i)(dQ^i/dp_i)$, is obtained from equation (17.4.7) at the symmetric equilibrium,

$$\eta_i = \frac{p_i(2q(p_i) - q(p_i + t/2m))}{2t \int_0^{1/2m} q(p_i + tr)\, dr}. \tag{17.4.14}$$

Then it is easy to calculate a lower bound for demand elasticity,

$$\eta_i \geq p_i \frac{m}{t}\left[1 + \frac{q(p_i) - q(p_i + t/2m)}{q(p_i)}\right]$$

$$\geq cm/t. \tag{17.4.15}$$

Thus, as transport costs become small (or as the number of firms becomes large), the firm's residual demand becomes infinitely elastic, as in the perfectly competitive model. Thus, the opportunities for exercising market power for a firm are reduced by either lower transport costs or closer competitors.

A frequently applied method of delineating geographic markets, proposed by Elzinga and Hogarty (1973), defines an economic market as exhibiting cross-shipments of goods. However, in the market equilibrium of the geographic-pricing model, firm market boundaries do not overlap. As Scheffman and Spiller (1985) observe, shipment tests would then fail to define the economic market, since the two market areas would always appear separate, and thus *understate* the size of economic markets. Empirical tests defining economic markets on the basis of the correlated price movements of Horowitz (1981) and Stigler and Sherwin (1983) perform better since, in equilibrium in the spatial model, adjacent prices are equal.[17] Note, however, that the entire product space is linked in equilibrium. This suggests that prices may be correlated over a very broad area through interregional links. Even though firm i does not compete directly with firm $i + 2$, their prices are correlated through competition with the firm in between them at $i + 1$. Thus, correlated price tests may *overstate* the size of economic markets.

17.5   Capacity Competition

This section examines two dynamic competitive models in which commitments to capacity are made in the first period. It begins with a fixed market structure model, due to Kreps and Scheinkman (1983). Two duopolists engage in a two-stage competition. They choose outputs in the first stage and prices in the second stage. The equilibrium is shown to be a Cournot outcome. The second model, which examines capacity choice when entry occurs, is that of Spulber (1981a). An incumbent firm chooses capacity in the first period and produces in both periods. The entrant chooses both output and capacity in the second period only.

17.5.1   Capacity Competition with a Fixed Market Structure

In Kreps and Scheinkman (1983), two firms simultaneously build capacity k^j at cost $b(k^j)$, $j = 1, 2$. Let $b(k^j)$ be twice differentiable and convex for $k > 0$, with $b(0) = 0$ and $b'(0) > 0$.

In the second stage, firms simultaneously announce prices p_j, $j = 1, 2$. Let $D(p)$ be market demand. Let market inverse demand, $p(\cdot)$, be strictly positive on $(0, Q)$, twice continuously differentiable, decreasing, and concave. For $q \geq Q$, $p(q) = 0$. Price announcements are in the interval $[0, p(0)]$. If $p_1 < p_2$, firm 1 sells output

$$q^1 = \min\{k^1, D(p_1)\},$$

and firm 2 sells

$$q^2 = \min\{k^2, \max\{0, D(p_2) - k^1\}\}.$$

The converse holds for $p_2 < p_1$. If $p_1 = p_2$, then

$$q^j = \min\left\{k^j, \frac{D(p^j)}{2} + \max\left\{0, \frac{D(p^j)}{2} - x_j\right\}\right\}, \qquad j = 1, 2.$$

As noted by Kreps and Scheinkman, "Customers buy first from the cheapest supplier and income effects are absent." Let the static Cournot game with simultaneous choice of outputs and cost functions $b(q^j), j = 1, 2$, be defined by $q^1 = q^2 = q^*(b)$. Then the following subgame perfect Nash equilibrium is obtained.

PROPOSITION 17.5.1 (Kreps-Scheinkman)   *In the two-stage game, there is a unique equilibrium outcome, namely, the Cournot outcome:* $q^1 = q^2 = q^*(b)$, *and* $p_1 = p_2 = p(2q^*(b))$.

Essentially, given capacity levels equal to $q*$, Bertrand price competition drives the market clearing price to the level where both firms produce at full capacity. There are no gains to cutting prices, since each firm is constrained by capacity. There are gains to raising prices if, given that the rival sells at full capacity, a firm can increase profits by selling less output (than at full capacity) and at a higher price than $p(k^1 + k^2)$. This case is ruled out by the initial capacity choices of the firms.

The importance of this result cannot be overemphasized. The equilibrium suggests that even with price competition, the presence of sunk costs in the form of capacity precommitments results in a Cournot outcome. Therefore, the link between market structure and efficient performance predicted by the Cournot model is again observed in the presence of capacity precommitments. The result depends, of course, on capacity not being variable in the second stage. The applicability of the model's conclusions depends on the extent to which investment decisions are irreversible and market-specific.

17.5.2   Capacity Competition and Entry

Suppose now that the postentry game is Cournot-Nash. Further, let the incumbent produce output before and after entry but assume that the entrant is confined to production in the second period. This model is based on Spulber (1981a) and is used to evaluate two behavioral assumptions frequently made in industrial organization: that an established firm deters entry either by a constant high output (the Sylos Postulate) or by high excess capacity (the Excess Capacity Hypothesis).[18]

The *Sylos Postulate*—see Bain (1956), Sylos-Labini (1969), and Modigliani (1958)—asserts not only that potential entrants expect established firms to maintain their output constant as entry occurs, but that established firms keep output constant at a level that deters entry *whether or not it is profitable to do so.* Called a "welcome major breakthrough on the oligopoly front" by Modigliani (1958), the Sylos Postulate underlies many papers in the large theoretical and empirical literature on limit pricing.[19] Yet the Sylos Postulate ignores both the strategic interaction between firms and the dynamic aspects of entry.[20] For example, Gaskins (1971) and Kamien and Schwartz (1971) assume that entry is a function of the current market price.

The *Excess Capacity Hypothesis*, which allows the established firm to freely vary its output, was proposed as an alternative to the Sylos Postulate by Pashigian (1968) and Wenders (1971a) and extended by Spence (1977a) and Dixit (1979a).[21] Spence assumes that potential entrants base their entry decision on the capacity of the established firm, and he then constrains the established firm to choose capacity at or above the entry-deterring level *whether or not it is profitable to do so.* Thus the Excess Capacity Hypothesis also ignores the strategic interaction between firms and the dynamic aspects of entry. In particular, it fails to recognize that the established firm's choice of costly capacity involves a trade-off between pre- and post-entry requirements.

Let firm 1 be the established firm and firm 2 the potential entrant. Let q_1^1, q_2^1 denote the established firm's output in the first and second periods, and let q^2 denote the entrant's output in the second period. Each firm purchases capacity k^1, k^2 at market price z. The variable costs of producing output in each period are identical and given by $c(\cdot)$. The variable cost function $c(\cdot)$ is assumed to be differentiable, increasing, and convex. Let $c(0) = 0$. The market inverse demand $p(\cdot)$ is stationary, differentiable, decreasing, and concave.

Since the entrant produces for only a single period, its output and capacity choice will be identical. The entrant's problem is to choose its output q^2 to maximize its profits net of capacity costs, given the second-period output of the established firm q_2^1. The established firm begins the second period with a fixed plant capacity chosen when it entered the market in the first period. Thus, the established firm must choose its output q_2^1 subject to its capacity constraint $q_2^1 \leq k^1$ and taking the entrant's output q^2 as given. Therefore, given the established firm's capacity k^1, it can be shown that there exists a *capacity-constrained Cournot-Nash equilibrium* (q_2^{1*}, q^{2*}), where the outputs of the established firm and the entrant solve

$$\max_{q_2^1}[p(q_2^1 + q^{2*})q_2^1 - c(q_2^1)] \qquad (17.5.1)$$

subject to $q_2^1 \leq k^1$,

$$\max_{q^2}[p(q_2^{1*} + q^2)q^2 - c(q^2) - zq^2]. \qquad (17.5.2)$$

Consider the postentry game where the capacity constraint on the established firm $(q_2^1 \leq k^1)$ is *not* present. Let $q_2^1 = \gamma^1(q^2)$ and $q^2 = \gamma^2(q_2^1)$ represent the Cournot reaction functions for the established firm and entrant, respectively, in the *unconstrained* postentry game. Let $M^1 = \gamma^1(0)$ and $M^2 = \gamma^2(0)$ be the *unconstrained monopoly outputs* and let (Q^1, Q^2)

be the *entry-blocking intercepts*, where $\gamma^1(Q^2) = 0$ and $\gamma^2(Q^1) = 0$. These reaction curves may be discontinuous due to a positive minimum average cost.

In the capacity-constrained postentry game, the established firm's reaction curve is truncated by capacity k^1. Unless the entry-blocking output Q^1 is less than the short-run monopoly output of the established firm M^1, there is no possibility of the established firm deterring entry in the Cournot-Nash case. Even if $Q^1 < M^1$, the established firm may *still* not find it worthwhile to deter entry when capacity is costly and may choose $k^1 < Q^1$. Entry will be deterred if the monopolist's capacity level without threat of entry k_m equals or exceeds Q^1. This capacity investment condition may be interpreted as Bain's case of "blockaded entry" (see Bain 1956, pp. 21–22; see also Dixit, 1979a). This case will only be observed if the incumbent has a cost advantage and cannot occur with the identical technologies considered here.

Let (N^1, N^2) represent the unconstrained Cournot-Nash equilibrium. If capacity k^1 is chosen to be greater than or equal to N^1, then (N^1, N^2) will be the postentry equilibrium; see figure 17.5.1. When capacity is strictly less than N^1, there is a capacity-constrained Cournot-Nash equilibrium at $(k^1, \gamma^2(k^1))$; see figure 17.5.2.

Given that the established firm behaves competitively as outlined above, the Cournot-Nash equilibrium implicitly defines the value of capacity in the second period $V^N(k)$, given by

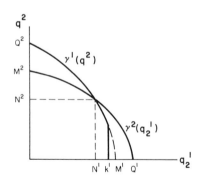

Figure 17.5.1
Unconstrained Cournot-Nash equilibrium, $k^1 \geq N^1$.

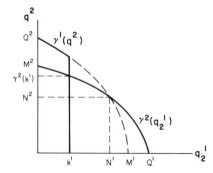

Figure 17.5.2
Capacity-constrained Cournot-Nash equilibrium, $k^1 < N^1$.

$$V^N(k^1) = \begin{cases} p(N^1 + N^2)N^1 - c(N^1) & \text{if } k^1 \geq N^1 \\ p(k^1 + q^2)k^1 - c(k^1) & \text{if } k^1 \leq N^1, \end{cases} \qquad (17.5.3)$$

where $q^2 = \gamma^2(k^1)$ *is taken as given by the established firm.* Note that $V^N(k^1)$ is differentiable in k^1 and is strictly concave for $k^1 \leq N^1$. Also, for $k^1 \geq N^1$, $V^{N\prime}(k^1) = 0$.

Before entry, the established firm wishes to choose output q_1^1 and capacity k^1 to maximize the present discounted value of profits. Given the implicit value of capacity defined in (17.5.3), the backward induction approach of dynamic programming may be employed. The established firm's problem is then

$$\max_{q,k} \left[\pi(q) - k + \frac{1}{1+r} V^N(k) \right] \qquad (17.5.4)$$

subject to $q \leq k$.

The Kuhn-Tucker first-order necessary conditions for the problem are

$$\pi'(q_1^{1*}) = \eta, \qquad (17.5.5)$$

$$\eta + \frac{1}{1+r} V^{N\prime}(k^{1*}) = z, \qquad (17.5.6)$$

$$\eta(k^{1*} - q_1^{1*}) = 0, \qquad \eta \geq 0. \qquad (17.5.7)$$

Let $q_2^{1*} = \min\{k^{1*}, N^1\}$ and $q^{2*} = \gamma^2(q_2^{1*})$. Then it can be shown that $(q_1^{1*}, q_2^{1*}, k^{1*}, q^{2*})$ is a subgame perfect Nash equilibrium for the two-period entry game. From equations (17.5.5)–(17.5.7) it is easy to demonstrate the following.[22]

PROPOSITION 17.5.2   *At the Nash equilibrium* $(q_1^{1*}, q_2^{1*}, k^{1*}, q^{2*})$, *the incumbent operates at full capacity before entry. Capacity is strictly less than the monopoly output,* M^1. *Capacity is greater than, equal to, or less than* N^1 *as* $\pi'(N^1)$ *is greater than, equal to, or less than z.*

The proposition shows that *holding excess capacity is inconsistent with a post entry Cournot-Nash equilibrium. Further, if the short-run net marginal return from producing at the Cournot-Nash output before entry does not exceed the cost of capacity, then output will be kept constant in the face of entry.* In other words, when capacity is relatively expensive, the established firm will produce at full capacity in each period at or below the Cournot-

Nash output. In this case, capacity satisfies the optimality condition,

$$\pi'(k) + \frac{1}{1+r} V^{N'}(k) = z. \tag{17.5.8}$$

If the net marginal returns to producing at the Cournot-Nash output in the first period exceed the cost of capacity, the firm will initially produce at a higher level than the Cournot-Nash equilibrium. Therefore, *when capacity is relatively inexpensive, the established firm will contract its output in the face of entry, thus contradicting the Sylos Postulate.* Then the firm will operate at full capacity in the first period and carry excess capacity in the second. In this case, capacity satisfies $\pi'(k) = z$.

Thus, it is evident that entry deterrence by threats of a price war (excess capacity) or limit pricing (a high constant output) is unlikely to occur. Antitrust action based on these behavioral assumptions is therefore inconsistent.

Notes

1. See the discussion of Bork (1966b) on the Sherman Act.

2. See, for example, the discussion of Weaver (1977) on Senator Sherman's concern about the political power of trusts. At the same time Weaver (1977, p. 20) quotes a speech by Sherman noting public worry about economic inequality stemming from "the concentration of vast combinations of capital to control production and trade and to break down competition." Adams (1986, p. 395) observes that at the time of its passage the Sherman Act was "[h]eralded as a *magna carta* of economic freedom."

3. The empirical work of Berle and Means (1932) on concentration and market power should be noted. See also Weiss (1974) for a valuable survey of empirical tests of the concentration-profit relationship.

4. Scherer notes (1980, p. 6) that a major difference between his work and that of Bain is Scherer's emphasis on firm conduct and its links with performance.

5. Indeed, all sorts of considerations attend criticism of monopoly in addition to the economic efficiency criterion. Adams (1986, pp. 397–402) lists, in addition to resource misallocation, charging consumers high prices, restriction of economic opportunity, delay of technological progress, impeding stabilization policy, and threatening free political institutions as consequences of monopoly.

6. *Wall Street Journal*, November 16, 1981.

7. Encaoua and Jacquemin (1980) also relate the Lerner index to the concentration ratio and entropy measures. In addition, they study the price leadership model for the fixed market structure case and for the dynamic case with threat of entry.

8. The efficiency properties of Cournot equilibria where firm size is small relative to the market are studied by Gabszewicz and Vial (1972), Fraysse and Moreaux (1981), Guesnerie and Hart (1982), Novshek and Sonnenschein (1978), Dasgupta and Ushio (1981), and Ushio (1983, 1985). Ushio (1985) presents necessary and sufficient conditions under which Cournot equilibria in large markets are approximately efficient. In Ushio (1985), Cournot equilibria are said to be *approximately efficient* if per capita welfare loss converges to zero as the number

of times the economy is replicated becomes large. For additional references on monopolistic competition, see Hart (1979, 1983, 1985), McManus (1964), and Roberts (1980).

9. This is based on the modified conjectural variation model of Eaton (1972, 1976) and Novshek (1980b).

10. Note that with large fixed costs, existence can again become a problem as transport costs approach zero. See Novshek (1980b) for an existence result.

11. See Gabszewicz and Thisse (1980) for a related result.

12. For a similar competitive equilibrium and comparative statics with a continuum of firms, see, for example, Salop (1979). Salop also considers a monopoly equilibrium in which market areas do not overlap and a kinked equilibrium in which markets just touch. Salop treats the number of firms as a continuous parameter rather than as an integer.

13. See Eaton and Wooders (1985) for an entry model in a differentiated products setting in which entrants incur sunk costs. West (1981a,b) suggests that spatial preemption may be observed using data on Vancouver, BC, supermarket competition.

14. This passage is quoted in Scheffman and Spiller (1985).

15. Scheffman and Spiller (1985) quote Marshall (1920, p. 324) for the definition of a market as an area where "prices of the same good tend to equality with due allowance for transportation costs." They find the "antitrust market" specified in the DOJ guidelines to be a more appropriate definition, since "the universe specified by the antitrust market is more closely related to the question at issue: are prices likely to rise because of the merger."

16. See 351. U.S. 377, *United States* v. *E. J. du Pont de Nemours and Co.* See Scherer (1980, pp. 534–535) for a discussion of the case.

17. This issue is also discussed in Scheffman and Spiller (1985).

18. The dynamic aspects of capacity and imperfect competition are discussed extensively by Harrod (1952), Hicks (1954), and Hahn (1955), who emphasize the Marshallian distinction between the short and long periods. Hicks and Hahn distinguish between a *closed period* when a monopolist completes construction of his plant and begins producing output and an *open period* when competitors have had time to construct similar plants and also begin supplying output. Arguing that potential entrants "take account not of the actual profits of existing producers but of the profits they themselves could earn if they entered" (p. 239), Hahn finds that, given a downward-sloping demand curve, the established firm may hold excess capacity after entry takes place. Similar results are obtained by Kamien and Schwartz (1972), who examine dynamic capacity investment when the threat of entry is a random function of price. Kamien and Schwartz find that the relative effects of preentry versus postentry profit on the plant size chosen by a monopolist depend upon the rate of interest and on the riskiness of rival entry, but as in Harrod, Hicks, and Hahn, they do not specify the strategy of the potential entrant or the postentry response of the established firm. The present analysis is closely related to the static analysis of Dixit (1980).

19. For a discussion and additional references, see Osborne (1964), Bhagwati (1970), Scherer (1980, pp. 243–252), and Needham (1978, chapter 7).

20. The point made here is quite different from that made by Fisher (1959) and Modigliani (1959), who find that Cournot and Sylos behavior simply imply different *outcomes* in a market model. The problem lies in finding a specification of the rules of the postentry game in which a constant output is a rational strategy for the established firm. Employing alternative ad hoc assumptions concerning the behavior of entrants, Pashigian (1968) and Wenders (1971b) find that an established firm may vary its output over time as a profit-maximizing response to entry. In a *static* model, Dixit (1980) examines a Nash equilibrium in the postentry game and an equilibrium where the *entrant* is a Stackelberg leader and finds that the excess capacity strategy will not be employed.

21. When fixed costs are present, Dixit (1979a) finds that the Excess Capacity Hypothesis allows the established firm to block entrants who could not be effectively deterred with a conventional limit-pricing strategy.

22. A similar result is obtained by Dixit (1980, p. 100) in a static framework. The special case where excess capacity is held *after* entry is noted by Hahn (1955) and Kamien and Schwartz (1972). See also Spulber (1985c).

18 Antitrust and Price Discrimination

Antitrust enforcement against price discrimination is concerned with the welfare consequences for a firm's customers, the effects of discrimination on horizontal competition, and the possible vertical restraints that may be associated with price discrimination by upstream firms. The competitive and welfare effects of price discrimination generally do not justify such antitrust concern. Antitrust restrictions on price discrimination are often an unnecessary form of price regulation that may serve to lower consumer welfare and exclude consumers and some firms from the marketplace.

The competitive and welfare effects of price discrimination are considered in this chapter. Section 18.1 briefly reviews the antitrust restrictions on price discrimination and outlines the welfare aspects. In sections 18.2 and 18.3, a model of nonlinear pricing with differentiated products is considered. The welfare aspects of quantity based pricing are considered for the multiproduct monopoly case and the free entry competition case. Finally, section 18.4 considers multiple price supply schedules in a contestable market. Price discrimination need not be an indicator of entry barriers and is consistent with competition.

18.1 Price Discrimination, Competition, and Welfare

The antitrust statutes and enforcement efforts address price discrimination itself and its effects on competition. The present chapter considers whether public policy against price discrimination is worthwhile from the point of view of social welfare. It also considers in a preliminary way the effects of price competition on a firm's rivals and the effects of upstream price discrimination on downstream competition. After a review of the antitrust statutes, price discrimination is defined and its welfare consequences are considered.

The Clayton Act is directed at price discrimination that may "lessen competition" in a broadly defined sense. This may be interpreted to include selective discounts offered to customers that affect the sales of competitors; this is known as *primary-line* price discrimination. The act may also rule out selective discounts that are offered by upstream firms to some downstream firms but not to the latter's downstream rivals. This is known as *secondary-line* price discrimination.[1] The Clayton Act does not prevent price discrimination "on account of differences in the grade, quality or quantity of the commodity sold, or that makes only due allowance for differences in the cost of selling or transportation, or discrimination in price in the same or different communities made in good faith to meet competition." This passage has raised many questions about the legal defense of price discrimination based on production or transport costs or the requirements of competition. Significantly, the act was interpreted as permitting quantity discounts.[2]

The 1936 Robinson-Patman Act restricted the defenses of price discrimination based on costs and on meeting competition. Furthermore, the act involves the Federal Trade Commission (FTC) in the regulation of price differences based on production costs or quantity sold. The Robinson-Patman Act spells out what amounts to price regulation: "The Federal Trade Commission may, after due investigation and hearing to all interested parties, fix and establish quantity limits, and revise the same as it finds necessary, as to particular commodities or classes of commodities, where it finds that available purchasers in greater quantities were so few as to render differentials on account thereof unjustly discriminatory or promotive of monopoly in any line of commerce." FTC enforcement efforts have varied since the act was passed, with substantial displacement of public enforcement by private enforcement.[3] The act in many ways is anticompetitive in that it may discourage selective price discounts in the pursuit of competition.[4] This includes so-called predatory pricing, which has already been discussed in the preceding chapter. In addition, the act sought to eliminate discounts offered by suppliers to downstream competitors, particularly different prices charged to chain stores versus single stores. Posner (1976b, p. 26) calls the act the "high-water mark of the anti-chain-store movement" of the 1930s.[5]

What is price discrimination? Price discrimination refers to a broad class of firm pricing policies that depart in any way from a uniform per unit price for each unit of output sold. To present a definition requires a specific market setting. Three principal types of assumptions are needed to describe the market. First, one needs to establish *how consumers differ*. Consumers may differ in terms of *preferences*, $U^i(q^i)$, where q^i is a vector of goods purchased by consumer i and U^i is consumer i's utility. Differences in tastes across consumers reflect not only ranking of simple commodity bundles but also differences in attitudes toward risks, rate of time preference, aversion to effort, and so on. Consumer preferences may in some cases be represented by $U^i(q^i) = U(q^i, \mu^i)$ where μ^i is a vector of parameters. Consumers may differ in terms of their *endowments*. This includes not only an initial endowment of goods ω^i, or shares of ownership of firms. Endowments may include consumer ability, geographic location, and information about other market participants.

Second, one needs to determine the *information* available to firms regarding consumer differences. A firm may have complete information about the preferences and endowments of each consumer it serves. The firm may have information only about the frequency distribution of preferences and endowments, say (μ^i, ω^i), across a population of consumers. The firm may possess only aggregate measures of consumer demand, such as is represented by the traditional aggregate market demand function. A firm may have only imperfect information about aggregate demand. Finally, if consumers and firms behave strategically, it is important to specify what is common knowledge and what is known about each other's available information.

Third, one needs to specify *consumer arbitrage opportunities* or the transactions technology. Can a consumer store goods, thus arbitraging over time? Can consumers transport goods across geographic markets? Can consumers exchange goods to take advantage of price differences or quantity discounts? Specification of arbitrage opportunities requires assumptions regarding transferability of ownership of goods, transaction costs, and available information about arbitrage possibilities.

To complete the definition of the market setting requires specification of firm costs and the set of firms that are competing to serve the market. In addition, legal constraints on available pricing policies may restrict firm choices. By varying assumptions on consumer differences, information held by firms, and consumer arbitrage opportunities, one may obtain an almost unlimited number of pricing policies.

Given complete information about each consumer, no consumer arbitrage opportunities, and absence of competition from other firms, the firm is able to price its goods in such a way that the consumer obtains no gains from trade. This is the case of first-degree price discrimination.[6] With costly consumer arbitrage opportunities, price discrimination across consumers under complete information is limited by the costs of exchange between consumers.

With information about the frequency distribution of consumer characteristics, but incomplete information about the attributes of any particular consumer, the firm may offer payment schedules to consumers that depend on the quantity or quality of goods purchased. An instance of this is nonlinear or quantity-dependent pricing. Such pricing may discriminate

across individual consumers by inducing them to reveal their characteristics by the size or quality of their purchase. The incomplete information
about individual characteristics yields information rents for consumers and
prevents the firm from capturing all potential gains from trade. This is
an instance of second-degree price discrimination.

If the firm's information is of an aggregate nature but the firm may
distinguish between groups of consumers, the firm may practice third-
degree price discrimination, charging different constant per unit prices in
each submarket. Such price differences are limited by the cost of consumer
arbitrage across markets, differences in demand elasticity, and the extent
of competition in each submarket. This type of price discrimination is
a special case of profit-maximizing pricing decisions for multiproduct
monopoly. Suppose that a monopolist produces two goods with interdependent demands, $p_j = p_j(q_1, q_2), j = 1, 2$, and joint costs $C(q_1, q_2)$. The
monopolist's profit-maximizing outputs solve

$$p_j + \sum_{i=1}^{2} (\partial p_i/\partial q_j)q_i = C_j(q_1, q_2), \qquad j = 1, 2.$$

The ratio of relative markups is then

$$\frac{(p_1 - C_1)/p_1}{(p_2 - C_2)/p_2} = \frac{1/\eta_1 - (\partial p_2/\partial q_1)q_2/p_1}{1/\eta_2 - (\partial p_1/\partial q_2)q_1/p_2},$$

where elasticity of demand is defined as $\eta_j = -1/(\partial p_j/\partial q_j)(q_j/p_j), j = 1, 2$.
It is thus unlikely that relative markups will be equal for a monopolist.
This is equivalent to the standard definition of price discrimination, which
specifies that the ratio of prices for two goods does not equal the ratio
of marginal costs.[7] This type of price discrimination includes geographic
price discrimination, discrimination across time periods (peak versus off-
peak pricing), and pricing of a product line. Note, however, that monopoly
price discrimination of this type is impossible to distinguish in practice from
break-even pricing by a multiproduct firm where price ratios do not equal
marginal cost ratios. In fact, second-best Pareto optimal prices need not
equal marginal cost ratios, as seen in chapter 5.

As should be apparent from the preceding discussion, price discrimination
is a widespread phenomenon. Indeed, some form of price discrimination is
present in the market for almost every commodity, with the exception of
standardized commodities traded on established spot or futures markets
with many traders. Price discrimination is a significant aspect of product

pricing and is carried out through product line pricing, product bundling, coupons and quantity discounts, prices based on consumer characteristics (age, location, income, etc.), individual bargaining, and so on.[8] An immediate implication of the pervasive practice of price discrimination is that it is for the most part de facto legal. Reducing price discrimination through antitrust enforcement or regulation would be impractical even if such a policy were desirable in some way. Thus, enforcement efforts are inevitably selective and often arbitrary. Next it is considered whether there are social welfare losses from price discrimination.

Price discrimination generally increases profits for a monopoly. One view of such profits is that they constitute a deadweight welfare loss. Posner (1976a) suggests that the additional profits earned through price discrimination are dissipated through the rent-seeking expenditures of firms seeking to obtain government protection from competition. However, additional profits from price discrimination may be used in many other ways that enhance social welfare. Incremental profits may cover the costs of research and development of new products or production processes, leading to increased innovation. Also, incremental profits may cover the costs of establishing brands, leading to increased product variety. In addition, increased profits from price discrimination may cover fixed costs of production and entry costs, thereby increasing entry and competition.

The effect of monopoly price discrimination on social welfare is now examined for a simple model with uniform purchases across consumers. A consumer purchases a unit of the good if its price is not above that consumer's reservation price. Let $p(q)$ represent market inverse demand.[9] Suppose that the monopolist is able to practice third-degree price discrimination by selling q_1 units at price $p_1 = p(q_1)$ and q_2 units at price $p_2 = p(q_1 + q_2)$. Given costs $C(q)$, the monopolist's profit maximization problem is

$$\max_{q_1, q_2}[p(q_1)q_1 + p(q_1 + q_2)q_2 - C(q_1 + q_2)]. \qquad (18.1.1)$$

The first-order conditions are

$$p'(q_1)q_1 + p(q_1) + p'(q_1 + q_2)q_2 = C'(q_1 + q_2), \qquad (18.1.2)$$

$$p'(q_1 + q_2)q_2 + p(q_1 + q_2) = C'(q_1 + q_2). \qquad (18.1.3)$$

In figure 18.1.1, outputs under third-degree price discrimination are compared with the standard monopoly solution. The monopoly marginal

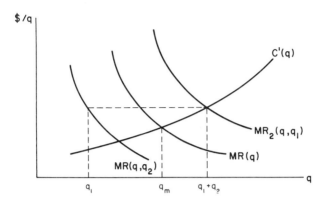

Figure 18.1.1
Third-degree price discrimination raises total output.

revenue is $MR(q) = p'(q)q + p(q)$. The marginal revenue for the high-priced output, for any given q_2, given on the left-hand side of (18.1.2), is

$$MR_1(q; q_2) = p'(q)q + p(q) + p'(q + q_2)q_2.$$

Similarly, for any q_1, the marginal revenue for the total output under third-degree price discrimination is

$$MR_2(q; q_1) = p'(q)(q - q_1) + p(q).$$

Clearly, for $q_1 > 0$, $q_2 > 0$,

$$MR_1(q; q_2) < MR(q) < MR_2(q; q_1).$$

Thus, total output under third-degree price discrimination is higher than the monopoly output. Note also that the high-priced output is below the monopoly level; see figure 18.1.1. Thus, $p_1 > p_m > p_2$. By increasing output, third-degree price discrimination raises social welfare in the reservation price model.[10]

With a general representation of demand in segmented markets, third-degree price discrimination need not increase welfare. Extending the analyses of Pigou (1932) and Robinson (1933), Schmalensee (1981b) and Varian (1985) show that a *necessary* condition for social welfare to increase under third-degree price discrimination, as compared with uniform pricing by a monopoly, is for total *output to increase*. It is easy to construct examples with multiple independent markets where output rises or falls, thus ruling out welfare gains in some cases. For example, given linear demands, Schmalensee (1981b) shows that total output remains constant and social welfare declines when third-degree price discrimination occurs. However, if there are two markets and consumers in one market are excluded by the monopoly price (given a bounded marginal willingness to pay), price discrimination increases welfare if that market is served at the lower discriminatory price; see Varian (1985).

Turn now to secondary line price discrimination carried out by upstream firms selling to retail or wholesale firms or downstream manufacturers. Does price discrimination restrict downstream competition? Price discrimination may create an entry barrier if discounts are given to incumbents but not to new entrants. Then, additional charges for inputs represent a cost to entrants that need not be incurred by incumbents. It is not apparent what an upstream firm would gain by this form of discrimination; see the discussion on vertical restraints in chapter 16. Price discrimination may affect the relative costs of competitors. If firms have different production technologies or produce differentiated commodities, their input demand functions will differ as well. Then upstream firms may increase profits by taking into account variations in elasticities of demand across downstream firms.

Suppose that an upstream supplier is a monopolist and sells an essential input x to two types of downstream firms: chain stores and single-store firms, $j = 1, 2$. The downstream firms sell different but competing services, q_1, q_2, and have different costs. Given free entry downstream, the equilibrium prices for q_1 and q_2 will depend on the price charged for the input x. Then, in equilibrium, the input demands of the two types of firms will depend on the input prices (w_1, w_2) charged to both types,

$$x_j = x_j(w_1, w_2), \qquad j = 1, 2.$$

It may be that with a uniform input price, one type of store is unable to compete and must exit.[11] If the upstream firm charges a discriminatory price, both types of downstream firms may remain in the market. This will enhance both competition and product diversity. The issue of product variety is considered further in the following sections.

It is concluded from the preceding discussion that antitrust action against price discrimination is generally not worthwhile. Because price discrimination is common and intrinsic to most markets, enforcement efforts would be arbitrary and prohibitively costly. In practice, it is difficult to distinguish discriminatory prices from break-even or even second-best optimal pricing by multiproduct firms. Price discrimination in the form of predatory pricing, first-line price discrimination, is unlikely to impede competition, as discussed in the preceding chapter. Additional discussion of competition is given in sections 18.2 and 18.3. Finally, secondary-line price discrimination need not impede downstream competition. Robinson-Patman Act enforcement may serve to reduce competition in many cases. Reductions in federal enforcement efforts against price discrimination have unfortunately been matched by increases in private antitrust action; see Posner (1976b). Repeal of laws against price discrimination appears to be desirable.

18.2   Competitive Price Discrimination with Differentiated Products

Price discrimination has generally been studied in a monopoly setting. The discussion has focused on the capture of consumer surplus by a single seller; see Pigou (1920). However, price discrimination, in its wide variety of forms, is often observed in competitive markets. Quantity discounts, for example, are not necessarily associated with monopoly. Spulber (1979) gives a model of noncooperative equilibrium with price discrimination by firms in which firms sell differentiated products. Nonlinear pricing is analyzed in alternative competitive settings with entry by Spulber (1984a, 1987a). A Bertrand-Nash equilibrium in nonlinear pricing with multiple products is considered by Gal-Or (1981). Monopolistic competition and price discrimination are addressed by Katz (1984), Borenstein (1985), Coyte and Lindsey (1986), and Holmes (1986). Panzar and Postlewaite (1984) study the sustainability of nonlinear price schedules, as noted previously. Oren, Smith, and Wilson (1983) present alternative Cournot-type models of competition in which nonlinear price schedules are adjusted in terms of revenues generated or output sold.

The product market or brand space is represented by a unit circle as in section 17.4. Consumers have a most preferred good and these goods are uniformly distributed around the product market with density A. Consumer utility is represented by $U(q^j, r) \equiv \int_0^{q^j} u(q', r) \, dq'$, where q^j is the quantity of brand j purchased and r is the distance between the consumer's most preferred good and brand j. The consumer's marginal willingness to pay is positive, strictly decreasing and concave in q and r. Output and product quality are complements, $u_{qr} \leq 0$, so marginal willingness to pay

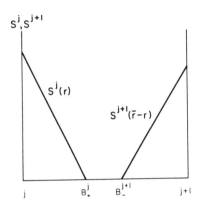

Figure 18.2.1
Local monopoly.

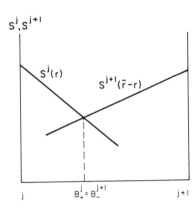

Figure 18.2.2
Competition.

satisfies the noncrossing property. The following discussion is based on Spulber (1987a).

The differentiated products model is used to study the Nash equilibrium pricing policies of single-product firms. Let l^j, $j = 1, \ldots, m$, denote the brands of m firms located on the circular product space. A consumer at distance r from brand j obtains consumer surplus from purchasing brand j,

$$S^j(r) \equiv \max_{q^j}[U(q^j, r) - P^j(q^j)]. \tag{18.2.1}$$

It is easy to show that $S^j(r)$ is nonincreasing in r. Let $\bar{r}$ denote the distance between brand j and the nearest brand, $j + 1$. If the brands are sufficiently differentiated for any given pricing policies P^j, P^{j+1}, then each firm is a local monopolist. If the brands are sufficiently close, then the firms divide the market between them. Let B_+^j and B_-^{j+1} represent the respective market boundaries for the two goods. Then the monopoly and competitive cases are represented in figures 18.2.1 and 18.2.2.

The equilibrium considered here is a Bertrand-Nash equilibrium in price schedules with free entry and exit of firms. Firm strategies consist of a location in brand space l^j and a price schedule $P^j(\cdot)$. Assume also that a modified zero conjectural variation restriction holds to rule out price schedules that undercut that of a rival firm for consumers whose most preferred good is the rival's brand.[12] Thus, it is required that $S^j(\bar{r}) < S^{j+1}(0)$ and $S^j(0) > S^{j+1}(\bar{r})$ if $\bar{r}$ is the distance between brands j and $j + 1$. The market equilibrium then consists of firms m^* and strategies (l^{j*}, P^{j*}),

$j = 1, \ldots, m^*$, such that (i) given (l^{j*}, P^{j*}), $j \neq i$, firm i chooses (l^i, P^i) to maximize profits $i = 1, \ldots, m^*$; (ii) all firms in the market earn nonnegative profits; and (iii) any additional entrant earns negative profits. Attention is restricted to symmetric equilibria in price schedules. Without loss of generality assume symmetric location in brand space.

It can be shown following Spulber (1987a) that the demand schedule is the same as under monopoly nonlinear pricing. Consumer demand $q(r)$ solves $u(q, r) + u_r(q, r)r - c = 0$, for $q(r) > 0$. Firms compete for the market by varying the height of their outlay schedules. For ease of presentation, the local monopoly equilibrium is not considered. The unconstrained monopoly market boundary can be shown to equal $B^m = \min\{1/2, \tilde{B}^m\}$, which solves

$$\int_0^{q(\tilde{B}^m)} u(x, \tilde{B}^m) \, dx - cq(\tilde{B}^m) = -\tilde{B}^m \int_0^{q(\tilde{B}^m)} u_r(x, \tilde{B}^m) \, dx. \tag{18.2.2}$$

It can be shown that with m firms such that $m > \max\{1, 1/2\tilde{B}^m\}$, there is a unique symmetric competitive equilibrium with market boundaries equal to $B^c = 1/2m$. Assume that this condition is satisfied.

Suppose that all firms but one choose the outlay schedule $\bar{P}(q)$. Define $\bar{S}(r) = U(q(r), r) - \bar{P}(q)$. The remaining firm chooses the outlay schedule $P(q)$ such that at its market boundary, B, $S(r) \geq \bar{S}(1/m - B)$. For any given boundary, $B < 1/m$, the firm will increase its outlay schedule until the marginal consumer is exactly indifferent between the two nearest brands, $S(B) = \bar{S}(1/m - B)$. The firm implicitly chooses the height of its outlay schedule by choosing its market boundary. Profit is given by

$$\pi(B) = 2A \int_0^B [U(q(r), r) + U_r(q(r), r)r - cq(r)] \, dr - 2AB\bar{S}(1/m - B). \tag{18.2.3}$$

The competitive market boundary B then solves $\pi'(B) = 0$,

$$U(q(B), B) + U_r(q(B), B)B - cq(B) - \bar{S}(1/m - B) + B\bar{S}'(1/m - B) = 0. \tag{18.2.4}$$

Since $P(q(B)) = U(q(B), B) - S(B) = U(q(B), B) - \bar{S}(1/m - B)$,

$$P(q(B)) = -U_r(q(B), B)B + cq(B) - B\bar{S}'(1/m - B). \tag{18.2.5}$$

From the consumer's problem $\bar{S}'(r) = U_r(q(r), r)$. By symmetry, $B = 1/2m$ at the equilibrium. Thus, using the demand schedule $q(r)$, at the market boundary,

$$P(q(1/2m)) = -(1/m)U_r(q(1/2m), 1/2m) + cq(1/2m). \tag{18.2.6}$$

PROPOSITION 18.2.1 *At the competitive equilibrium, the nonlinear price schedules are given by*

$$P(q) = \int_0^{q(1/2m)} [c - (1/m)u_r(x, 1/2m)]\, dx + \int_{q(1/2m)}^q u(x, r(x))\, dx$$

for $q \geq q(1/2m)$, $r(x) = \min\{r : q(r) = x\}$.

Note that the presence of competition changes the constant portion of the total outlay schedule.

Consider now a quadratic example where $u(q, r) = \alpha - \beta q - tr$ and marginal costs equal zero. For a given market structure m, welfare is equal to $W(m) = (A\alpha/2\beta)(\alpha - t/2m) - mF$. Compare this to a fixed price Cournot-Nash equilibrium. There, welfare equals

$$W^{CN}(m) = (A\alpha/2\beta)[(\alpha - t/2m) + t^2/12m^2 - p^2] - mF.$$

The Cournot-Nash equilibrium price equals (see Novshek, 1980)

$$p = \alpha/2 + (3/4)(t/m) - (1/2)[\alpha^2 - \alpha t/m + (13/4)t^2/m^2]^{1/2}.$$

The following result obtains:

PROPOSITION 18.2.2 *Given quadratic utility, social welfare is greater under Nash equilibrium nonlinear pricing than at the linear-pricing Cournot-Nash equilibrium.*

The quadratic example suggests that in a competitive setting, price discrimination may increase social welfare.

In the quadratic case with nonlinear pricing, profits per firm as a function of market structure m are

$$\pi(m) = (At/\beta m^2)[\alpha - (5/6)(t/m)] - F,$$

for the zero marginal cost case. For sufficiently large m, profits are decreasing in m.[13] Then free entry market structure satisfies $\pi(m) \geq F$ and $\pi(m + 1) < F$. Therefore, as fixed cost per capita, F/A, falls, equilibrium market structure rises.

Compare the equilibrium profit under nonlinear pricing with the Cournot-Nash linear pricing equilibrium. Profits (as calculated in Novshek, 1980b) are

$\pi^{CN}(m) = (At/\beta m^2)[\alpha/8 - (25/16)(t/m) + (7/8)[\alpha^2 - \alpha t/m + 13t^2/4m^2]^{1/2}]$.

Comparing the nonlinear and linear pricing equilibria, it can be shown that $\pi(m) \geq \pi^{CN}(m)$ for m sufficiently large ($m \geq 5$). This implies that for sufficiently small fixed cost per capita, price discrimination through nonlinear pricing yields greater product variety. This may reduce social welfare due to the fixed cost of establishing brands, F. These losses may be balanced by the welfare gains from increased product variety.

18.3   Monopoly Price Discrimination with Differentiated Products

The effects of price discrimination by a multiproduct monopolist on output, profit, product variety, and social welfare are now considered. The section examines a monopolist selling a range of substitute products in a circular product market. Quantity discounts are shown to increase output, profit, product variety, and social welfare relative to third-degree price discrimination and standard linear monopoly pricing. The analysis suggests that restriction of price discrimination may worsen the welfare impacts of barriers to entry.

The monopolist faces no competition due to barriers to entry. The monopolist sells m products, which are assumed to be uniformly located in the brand space. The cost of establishing a brand is $F > 0$. The monopolist has marginal production costs $c > 0$ for each brand. The monopolist must choose both a pricing policy and product variety. Begin with a fixed number of products. Given the symmetric nature of the problem, it follows that the monopolist will sell a brand j to consumers whose most preferred good is within distance $R = 1/2m$ from brand j. Thus, consumers differ in a systematic way, as in the nonlinear pricing model described in section 7.4. Suppose that consumers do not resell the goods after a purchase. Also, assume that the monopolist cannot identify a consumer's most preferred good a priori. Then the monopolist's profit-maximizing pricing policy is a nonlinear price schedule for each brand j. The monopolist chooses $q(r)$ to maximize

$$2A \int_0^{1/2m} [U(q,r) - cq + U_r(q,r)r]\, dr, \qquad (18.3.1)$$

subject to $q(r)$ nonincreasing in r; see equation (11.4.4). It follows from our assumptions that for $q > 0$, $q(r)$ decreasing in r solves

$$u(q,r) - c + u_r(q,r)r = 0. \tag{18.3.2}$$

Let $r(q) \equiv \min\{r : q(r) = q\}$.

PROPOSITION 18.3.1   *The monopolist chooses the nonlinear price schedule given by*

$$P(q) = \int_0^q u(x, r(x))\, dx. \tag{18.3.3}$$

Given a market radius $R = 1/2m$, the monopolist will raise the nonlinear price schedule until the consumer at the market boundary obtains zero consumer surplus, $P(q(R), R) = U(q(R), R)$. So, equation (18.3.3) can be written with the market boundary made explicit,

$$P(q, R) = \int_0^{q(R)} u(x, r(x))\, dx + \int_{q(R)}^q u(x, r(x))\, dx$$

$$= U(q(R), R) + \int_{q(R)}^q u(x, r(x))\, dx, \tag{18.3.4}$$

for $q \geq q(R)$. Differentiating $P(q, R)$, one may characterize the effect of the market radius on the total outlay schedule,

$$P_R(q, R) = U_r(q(R), R), \tag{18.3.5}$$

for $q \geq q(R)$. Thus, increasing the market radius reduces the outlay schedule by the marginal effect of product quality on the marginal consumer.

Next consider the monopolist's choice of product quality. Given m brands, total profit equals

$$\pi(m) = m\left[2A \int_0^{1/2m} [P(q(r), 1/2m) - cq(r)]\, dr - F \right], \tag{18.3.6}$$

where $R = 1/2m$ is the market radius for each brand. The profit-maximizing number of brands solves $\pi'(m) = 0$, so from (18.3.6),

$$2A \int_0^{1/2m} [P(q(r)), 1/2m) - cq(r)]\, dr - F$$

$$= (1/2m)[2A[P(q(1/2m), 1/2m) - cq(1/2m)]]$$

$$+ 2A \int_0^{1/2m} P_R(q(r), 1/2m)\, dr. \tag{18.3.7}$$

Table 18.3.1
Multiplant monopoly

	Nonlinear pricing	Third-degree price discrimination
Total output	$Q^N = (A/\beta)[\alpha - c - t/2m^N]$	$Q^D = (A/2\beta)[\alpha - c - t/4m^D]$
Profit	$\pi^N = (A/2\beta)[\alpha - c - t/m^N]$	$\pi^D = (A/4\beta)[\alpha - c - t/2m^D]$
Number of brands	$(\alpha - c)2t(1/2m^N)^2$ $\quad - (8/3)t^2(1/2m^N)^3 = \beta F/A$	$(1/2)(\alpha - c)t(1/2m^D)^2$ $\quad - (1/3)t^2(1/2m^D)^3 = \beta F/A$
Social welfare	$W^N = (A/2\beta)[(\alpha - c)^2$ $\quad - 3(\alpha - c)t/2m^N$ $\quad + (8/3)t^2(1/2m^N)^2]$	$W^D = (A/8\beta)[3(\alpha - c)^2$ $\quad - 5(\alpha - c)t/2m^D$ $\quad + (7/3)t^2(1/2m^D)^3]$

Substituting in (18.3.7) for P using (18.3.3) and (18.3.5) yields

$$2A \int_0^{1/2m} \left[\int_0^{q(r)} u(x, r(x))\, dx - cq(r) \right] dr - F$$

$$= (1/2m)[2A[U(q(1/2m), 1/2m) - cq(1/2m)]$$

$$+ 2A(1/2m)U_r(q(1/2m), 1/2m)]. \tag{18.3.8}$$

The incremental revenues due to increasing the number of brands are set equal to the marginal revenues lost from reducing the market for each brand. It can be shown that the purchase of the marginal consumer will always be positive; see Spulber (1984a).

In the following discussion, restrict attention to *quadratic* consumer utility, where marginal willingness to pay has the form $u(q, r) = \alpha - \beta q - tr$. Then output, profit, the number of brands, and social welfare are given in table 18.3.1, where the superscript N denotes nonlinear pricing. Assume that output of each brand can be summed in terms of some comparable units.

Begin by comparing the nonlinear pricing equilibrium with the social optimum. At the social optimum, each consumer pays the marginal cost per unit purchased, $u(q, r) = c$, so that demand equals $q^*(r) = (1/\beta)(\alpha - c - tr)$. The social optimum can be supported by first-degree price discrimination to cover the costs of establishing brands. The socially optimal number of brands, m^*, maximizes social welfare, $W(m)$,

$$W(m) = m \left[2A \int_0^{1/2m} [U(q^*(r), r) - cq^*(r)]\, dr - F \right]. \tag{18.3.9}$$

For the quadratic case, m^* solves

$$(\alpha - c)t(1/2m^*)^2 - (2/3)t^2(1/2m^*)^3 = \beta F/A, \qquad (18.3.10)$$

and optimal total output equals $Q^* = (A/\beta)[(\alpha - c) - t/4m^*]$. Comparing the nonlinear pricing monopoly equilibrium with the social optimum gives the following:

PROPOSITION 18.3.2 *Given quadratic utility, the multiproduct nonlinear-pricing monopolist supplies greater product variety than is socially optimal, $m^N > m^*$. Total output and output per brand are smaller than the socially optimal quantities, $Q^N < Q^*$, $Q^N/m^N < Q^*/m^*$.*

It is to be expected that the monopolist supplies less output than is socially optimal. Also, the excessive variety observed under nonlinear pricing is in part due to the assumption that products are substitutes for consumers. It is of interest to compare nonlinear pricing with other forms of price discrimination and with linear-pricing monopoly to assess the welfare effects of price discrimination.

Nonlinear-pricing policies, such as quantity discounts, constitute *second-degree* price discrimination. Consumers at distance r from a particular brand j pay a two-part tariff consisting of a *per unit price* above marginal cost, equal to

$$p(r) = c - u_r(q(r), r)r, \qquad (18.3.11)$$

and a *fixed fee*, equal to

$$E(r) = P(q(r)) - p(r)q(r), \qquad (18.3.12)$$

which is less than consumer surplus. Note that a consumer whose most preferred good has exactly the characteristics of brand j pays a per unit price equal to marginal cost. Given quantity discounts, it follows that a consumer whose most preferred good is farther from a brand pays higher per unit prices but lower fixed fees, $\partial E(r)/\partial r = -(\partial p(r)/\partial r)q(r) < 0$.

If the monopolist had full information about each consumer, it could practice third-degree price discrimination by charging each consumer a *linear* per unit price, ρ^D. Since the consumer sets marginal willingness to pay equal to the price, $u(q, r) = \rho^D$, the profit-maximizing schedule of prices needed to achieve third-degree price discrimination equates marginal revenue to marginal cost for each consumer type,

$u(q,r) + u_q(q,r)q = c.$ (18.3.13)

So, $\rho^D(r) = c - u_q(q^D(r), r)q$, where $q^D(r)$ solves equation (18.3.13). Total output, profit, the number of brands, and social welfare are shown in table 18.3.1 for the quadratic case. The superscript D indicates third-degree price discrimination.

PROPOSITION 18.3.3 *Given quadratic utility and multiproduct monopoly, it follows that total output, output of each brand, profit, product variety, and social welfare are greater under nonlinear pricing than under third-degree price discrimination.*

In fact, the nonlinear-pricing monopolist supplies exactly twice the number of products as the third-degree price-discriminating firm. Total output and profit are also doubled under nonlinear pricing. Interestingly, the output of each brand and profits per brand are equal under the two pricing policies. It can be shown that product variety is insufficient under third-degree price discrimination. Thus, increased variety under nonlinear pricing is one aspect of the higher welfare observed.

It is well-known that third-degree price discrimination improves consumer welfare as compared to standard nondiscriminatory monopoly pricing. With a variable number of products, the following result is standard.[14]

PROPOSITION 18.3.4 *Given quadratic utility and multiproduct monopoly, it follows that total output, output of each brand, profit, product variety, and social welfare are greater under third-degree price discrimination than under linear monopoly pricing.*

The two preceding propositions immediately imply the following interesting corollary.

COROLLARY 18.3.1 *Given quadratic utility and multiproduct monopoly, it follows that total output, output per brand, profit, product variety, and social welfare are greater under nonlinear pricing than under linear pricing.*

These results suggest that allowing price discrimination lessens the welfare losses due to barriers to entry. Therefore, the possibility of antitrust action against price discrimination in the presence of entry barriers may serve to reduce output, product variety, and social welfare. The results also demonstrate that some forms of price discrimination are preferable to others. Quantity discounts increase output and product variety and yield greater welfare as compared to third-degree discrimination. Thus, if restrictions against monopoly price discrimination are to be partially eased, quantity discounts would be a desirable permissible policy. Since such discounts are already widespread in the form of coupons, product bundling by package sizes, and tiered pricing, relaxed enforcement may have anticipated the welfare benefits of nonlinear pricing.

18.4   Sustainable Multiple-Price Schedules

18.4.1   Equilibrium Monopoly Supply Schedules

The contestable markets model of Baumol, Panzar, and Willig (1982) considers linear, nondiscriminatory prices. As shown in chapter 4 in the present work, the sustainable price must yield zero profits for the incumbent firm. Of particular importance for regulation, natural monopoly is a necessary but not sufficient condition for the existence of a sustainable monopoly price. It is of interest to examine whether these conditions are altered by the possibility of price discrimination by incumbent firms and new entrants. This issue is of interest for antitrust because of the connection between competition and price discrimination in the antitrust statutes. The questions to be addressed are whether price discrimination is feasible in a contestable market and whether discrimination can impede competition or act as an entry barrier. If price discrimination is feasible in a contestable market, it must then be determined whether incumbent firms may obtain positive profits. Also, it is examined whether the necessary and sufficient conditions on cost functions required by sustainability are altered by price discrimination.

These issues are examined using the model of Motty Perry (1984), who shows that some forms of price discrimination are indeed feasible in a market with free entry. He shows further that a monopolist may deter entry and still manage to earn positive profits. Further, natural monopoly (subadditive costs) is sufficient but not necessary for the existence of a sustainable monopoly. Perry's model is extended here in a straightforward way to show the existence of a sustainable multiple-firm industry equilibrium and to characterize the sustainable market structure.

Consider a contestable market in which firms produce a single homogeneous output q. All firms have access to identical technology, represented by a cost function $C(q)$. Market demand is $D(p)$ and inverse demand is $F(q)$.

The cost function $C(q)$ is continuously differentiable and nondecreasing on $(0, \infty)$. Average costs $AC(q) \equiv C(q)/q$ are strictly U-shaped with minimum at $q^* \in (0, \infty)$, $AC(q^*) \in (0, \infty)$. Let $\lim_{q \to 0} AC(q) = \infty$. So, costs exhibit subadditivity over some range.

Market demand is continuously differentiable on $(0, \infty)$ and downward sloping, $\partial D(p)/\partial p < 0$, $\partial F(q)/\partial q < 0$. There is assumed to exist $x^* \in (0, \infty)$ such that $F(x) \gtreqless AC(q^*)$ as $x \lesseqgtr x^*$. Define $p^* = AC(q^*)$. Generally, it is assumed that each consumer purchases only one unit of the good and aggregate demand reflects the distribution of consumer reservation prices.

The price discrimination model of Motty Perry (1984) assumes that the incumbent commits to a multiple-price supply strategy. This strategy is credible if one assumes that the incumbent is unable to alter the strategy in reaction to entry. The incumbent sells some units of output at a relatively low price and other units at higher prices. A number of alternative market characterizations may be given. If consumer arbitrage is permitted, the monopolist may still price discriminate by selling lower-priced units of output first and then selling higher-priced units. The monopolist may choose to sell q_1 units at price p_1 and q_2 units at price p_2, $p_2 > p_1$, where $q_1 + q_2 = D(p_2)$. Consumers reallocate the goods until only those with reservation prices above p_2 purchase the good[15]; see figure 18.4.1.

A multiple price schedule or "supply schedule" $s(p)$ is an offer to supply $s(p)$ units at price p *or less* (Perry, 1984). A *supply schedule* is a mapping from prices to outputs that is *nondecreasing* and *continuous from the right*.

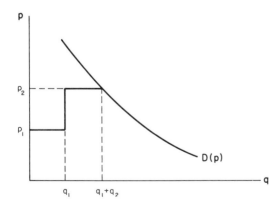

Figure 18.4.1
Multiple-price supply strategy.

The supply schedule generally appears as a step function as in figure 18.4.1. The firm may choose to offer outputs at multiple prices. A natural interpretation of the two-price supply schedule is that the manufacturer offers output to retailers at a "wholesale" price p_1 and also sells output directly at price p_2. Thus, q_1 represents sales by independent retailers.[16] Retailers earn net revenues $(p_2 - p_1)q_1$ from which they may recover their costs. The output q_2 represents direct retail sales by the manufacturer.

Another interpretation of the model is for the firm to set the price of the good at p_2 and issue q_1 coupons that may be redeemed for a refund of $(p_2 - p_1)$ per unit purchased. The coupons would be issued without charge, but retrading in coupons would result in a price of $(p_2 - p_1)$ per coupon. Finally, the firm can simply announce that it will increase the price after q_1 units have been purchased. This is similar to announcements that discounts are available "while supplies last" or for the "first one hundred customers."

The incumbent firm offers a supply schedule $s^0(p)$ and the potential entrant offers $s^1(p)$. Following Motty Perry (1984), define the *residual demand* for potential entrants,

$$D^1(p) = \max\{0, D(p) - s^0(p)\}. \tag{18.4.1}$$

This framework requires that the incumbent's output offer is sold before the entrant's output. This gives the incumbent an important advantage somewhat equivalent to the Sylos Postulate discussed in the preceding chapter. By committing to a sufficiently large output, the established firm is able to shift the entrant's residual demand to the point where entry is unprofitable. The model is much more general than the limit quantity setting. The combined strategy of multiple prices and quantity rationing allows the incumbent to deter entry by a low limit price and to obtain additional revenue by the higher price strategy.

The definition of sustainability in Baumol, Panzar, and Willig (1982) restricts the incumbent to a single-price strategy. Perry (1984) observes that the sustainability framework is based on Bertrand conjectures, which may be represented by the following supply strategy for the incumbent:

$$s^0(p) = \begin{cases} 0, & p < p^0 \\ D(p^0), & p \geq p^0, \end{cases}$$

where $D(p)$ is market demand. Thus, the residual demand faced by the entrant is

$$D^1(p) = \begin{cases} D(p), & p < p^0 \\ 0, & p \geq p^0. \end{cases}$$

The following definitions are from Motty Perry (1984). The *equilibrium price* if there is no entry, $P^e(s^0)$, is defined by

$$p_0^e = P^e(s^0) \equiv \min\{p : s^0(p) \geq D(p)\}, \tag{18.4.2}$$

so that the incumbent's sales equal $Y^0(s^0) = D(p_0^e)$. If entry takes place, the equilibrium price is

$$p_{01}^e = P^e(s^0, s^1) \equiv \min\{p : s^0(p) + s^1(p) \geq D(p)\}. \tag{18.4.3}$$

If entry occurs, the incumbent's and entrant's sales are

$$Y^0 = s^0(p_{01}^e), \qquad Y^1 = s^1(p_{01}^e) = D^1(p_{01}^e),$$

where $s^0(p_{01}^e) = s^1(p_{01}^e) = D(p_{01}^e)$.[17] Following Perry, one may calculate the *profits* of the incumbent and entrant,

$$\pi^0(s^0) = \int_0^{Y^0(s^0)} \psi^0(y)\,dy - C(Y^0(s^0)),$$
$$\pi^1(s^0, s^1) = \int_0^{Y^1(s^0, s^1)} \psi^1(y)\,dy - C(Y^1(s^0, s^1)), \tag{18.4.4}$$

where $\psi^0(y) = s^{0-1}(y)$ and $\psi^1(y) = s^{1-1}(y)$. Now define sustainability for multiple-price schedules.

Definition 18.4.1 (Perry) s^0 *is a sustainable supply function if* $\pi^0(s^0) \geq 0$ *and if* $\pi^1(s^0, s^1) < 0$ *for all supply functions* s^1.

Sustainability is achievable if the cost function is subadditive in the relevant range.

PROPOSITION 18.4.1 (Perry)   *There exists a sustainable supply function* $s^0(p)$ *for the incumbent.*

Perry's discussion proceeds in two stages. First, he shows the existence of a *zero-profit* supply schedule that deters entry,

$$s^0(p) = \begin{cases} 0, & p < p^* \\ q^*, & p^* \leq p < F(q^* + \bar{q}) \\ q^* + \bar{q}, & F(q^* + \bar{q}) \leq p. \end{cases} \tag{18.4.5}$$

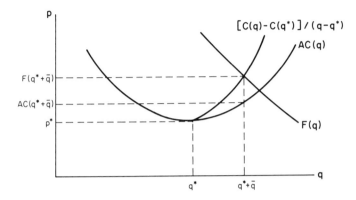

Figure 18.4.2
The incumbent's sustainable zero-profit supply schedule.

This supply strategy involves selling output up to minimum efficient scale at price p^* and output $\bar{q}$ at the market-clearing price. If demand intersects the decreasing portion of average cost, then $\bar{q} = 0$ and one has the standard sustainability of a single price. If demand intersects average cost at an output above minimum efficient scale, then $\bar{q} > 0$ as in figure 18.4.2. In this case, the higher-price output $\bar{q}$ is chosen such that its *average incremental cost equals the market-clearing price*,

$$[C(q^* + \bar{q}) - C(q^*)]/\bar{q} = F(q^* + \bar{q}), \tag{18.4.6}$$

so that the incumbent earns zero profit. The entrant's residual demand will be

$$D^1(p) = \begin{cases} D(p), & p < p^* \\ D(p) - q^*, & p^* \leq p < F(q^* + \bar{q}) \\ 0, & F(q^* + \bar{q}) \leq p, \end{cases} \tag{18.4.7}$$

which is represented by the discontinuous shaded curve in figure 18.4.3. Clearly, no multiple-price strategy is feasible for the entrant.

The next step in Motty Perry's analysis is to select the profit-maximizing entry-deterring supply schedule. This is essentially the "minimum amount needed at each price p to keep the entrant's residual demand at price p or less to the left of his average costs curve" (1984, p. 258). Since the incumbent is at least guaranteed zero profits, the optimal strategy may yield *positive* profits. This implies that potential entry may not be sufficient to eliminate

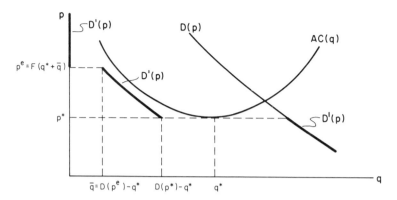

Figure 18.4.3
The entrant's residual demand.

monopoly profits. Further, it shows that natural monopoly is sufficient for sustainability of monopoly. Because the incumbent earns positive profit, it may be possible to deter entry even if market demand is such that equilibrium output is outside the range of outputs for which cost sub-additivity holds. Furthermore, the incumbent may prevail even with cost advantages for the potential entrants.

These results have a number of significant implications. They establish the possibility of price discrimination in a contestable market. Positive profits for the incumbent imply that costless potential entry may not be sufficient to eliminate monopoly rents. Survival of the incumbent subject to the threat of entry need not indicate that the incumbent has greater technical efficiency than the entrant. The competitive market cannot be relied on to achieve average cost pricing. One possible conclusion from these results is that price discrimination impedes competition and acts as a barrier to entry even in a contestable market. This would seem to suggest that if entry barriers were present, price discrimination would create even more severe restrictions on competition. The implications of the model appear to justify antitrust action against price discrimination to promote competition. This policy, however, would follow from an incorrect inference about the model of competition with supply schedules. The model contains a hidden entry barrier. The assumption that the incumbent is able to commit to a supply schedule combined with the requirement that the incumbent's output is sold first gives the incumbent an important *first-*

mover advantage. This permits an effective entry-deterring multiple-price strategy.

The welfare implications of the existence of sustainable positive profit supply schedules are of interest for antitrust policy. The welfare losses from monopoly are not clear-cut. The monopolist is able to earn positive profit only if the size of the market (demand at the minimum average cost price) is greater than the size of the firm (minimum efficient scale). The positive profits earned by the incumbent may be seen as compensation for production above minimum efficient scale.[18] If the monopolist's profit is close to zero, then price is approximately equal to incremental cost of output produced in excess of minimum efficient scale.[19] So, output will generally be *below* the level at which demand intersects marginal cost. The extent of the departure from the socially efficient output level will depend on the ease with which entry may be deterred. With higher fixed costs relative to a given demand, the monopolist is able to deter entry with relatively lower sales at low prices. However, the output distortion must be balanced against the efficiency gains from production by a natural monopoly.[20]

The preceding analysis of monopoly multiple-price supply schedules may yield insight into the concept of the "price squeeze," and its close relative, "raising rivals' costs." For a price squeeze to take place requires a firm with market power upstream to sell wholesale to nonvertically integrated downstream firms and to compete directly with downstream firms by selling retail as well. A price squeeze is then said to exist if the wholesale price charged to downstream firms is intended to exclude them from the market. By "foreclosing" competition downstream, the vertically integrated firm is said to "extend" its monopoly power to the downstream market.[21] The price squeeze may be simply the result of sustainable multiple-price schedules.

The "price squeeze" concept is an integral part of antitrust restriction of vertical mergers. The merger between retailers and manufacturers is seen as anticompetitive if nonintegrated retailers may be foreclosed in the market due to high wholesale prices that do not allow them to cover their costs at the market-clearing retail price. The price squeeze was initially defined by Judge Learned Hand in the 1945 *Alcoa* decision.[22] Hand devised a "transfer price test" that determines whether the integrated firm can profitably sell the good on the retail market if it must pay an internal transfer price equal to the price charged to downstream competitors. If the integrated firm cannot supply the good at the transfer price, a price squeeze is alleged to have occurred.[23] The doctrine of vertical integration to extend monopoly power is not consistent for reasons given in the discussion in section 16.4. What is of interest is to explain the difference between wholesale and retail pricing in the absence of entry barriers either upstream or downstream.

Such an explanation is provided by the monopoly equilibrium supply schedule. The incumbent monopolist offering wholesale and retail prices will choose the schedule $((p_1, q_1), (p_2, q_2))$ to maximize profits while excluding entry. Such a schedule exists by the preceding discussion if the incumbent's output is sold first. This analysis explains the price difference between wholesale and retail. If the incumbent does not have a cost advantage in retail distribution, it is reasonable to expect that the price difference allows recovery of retail cost, thus ruling out price squeeze arguments. What is explained is why the incumbent would offer a discount on the first q_1 units, rather than selling all units at the market-clearing price, p_2. The discount is a response to the competitive pressure of potential entry upstream. This does not suggest that antitrust concern with the wholesale-retail price difference is warranted.[24] Manufacturers generally offer wholesale discounts to compensate wholesalers for marketing services. Such discounts are not distinguishable in practice from multiple-price supply schedules that deter additional entry.

18.4.2 Equilibrium Industry Supply Schedules

Motty Perry's analysis is now extended to demonstrate the existence of sustainable *industry* equilibria with multiple-price schedules.

Define the optimal industry cost function for m firms as follows:

$$C^I(q, m) \equiv \min_{q_i, i=1,\dots,m} \sum_{i=1}^{m} C(q_i). \tag{18.4.8}$$

By choosing the cost minimizing market structure, $m(q)$,

$$m(q) \equiv \arg \min_{m} C^I(q, m), \tag{18.4.9}$$

one may define the efficient industry cost function,

$$C^I(q) = C^I(q, m(q)). \tag{18.4.10}$$

See Baumol, Panzar, and Willig (1982, p. 99) for a similar derivation. As is well-known, the industry average cost will have a scallop shape; see

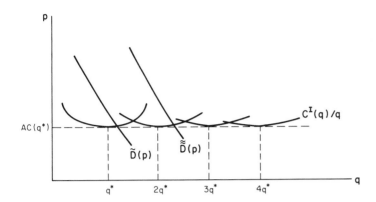

Figure 18.4.4
The industry average cost curve.

Baumol, Panzar, and Willig (1982, p. 32), who give a diagram similar to figure 18.4.4. If market demand is $\tilde{D}(p)$, then the optimal industry structure is a natural monopoly. If the market demand is $\tilde{\tilde{D}}(p)$, the industry is a natural duopoly, and so on.

Given this cost-setting, one may establish the following.

PROPOSITION 18.4.2   *There exists a zero profit industry supply schedule $s^I(p)$ such that the optimal industry structure is sustainable.*

The proof follows that of the earlier proposition of Motty Perry (1984). A zero-profit schedule is obtained using the efficient industry cost function. Let k be the smallest integer such that at the total output equal to $k + 1$ times minimum efficient scale, the price is below the minimum average cost price, $F((k + 1)q^*) < p^*$. Then one can find $\bar{q}$ such that the industry can break even by selling kq^* at price p^* and $\bar{q} \geq 0$ at price $F(kq^* + \bar{q})$, i.e.,

$$p^*kq^* + F(kq^* + \bar{q})\bar{q} = C^I(kq^* + \bar{q}).$$

It can be shown that such an industry supply schedule does not permit entry at a nonnegative profit.

The size of the sustainable industry is $\bar{m} = m(kq^* + \bar{q})$. It follows that $\bar{m}$ equals either k or $k + 1$.[25] Baumol, Panzar, and Willig (1982, pp. 140–141) show the following.

LEMMA   *If C is strictly convex on $(0, 2q^*)$, then the cost-minimizing output allocation has all firms produce equal amounts. The optimal number of* *firms for output q is m' if $AC(q/m') \leq AC(q/(m' + 1))$ and $m' + 1$ if $AC(q/m') \geq AC(q/(m' + 1))$.*

Assume that costs have the convex form

$$C(q) = K + V(q), \qquad K > 0, \qquad \text{and} \qquad V''(q) > 0.$$

Then equal division of output minimizes industry costs and the following individual firm supply schedules sustain the *industry* equilibrium.

PROPOSITION 18.4.3   (i) *The supply schedules defined by*

$$s^i(p) = \begin{cases} 0, & p < p^* \\[2ex] kq^*/\bar{m}, & p^* \leq p < p^e\left(\sum_{i=1}^{m} s^i\right) \\[2ex] (kq^* + \bar{q})/\bar{m}, & p^e\left(\sum_{i=1}^{m} s^i\right) \leq p, \end{cases} \qquad (18.4.11)$$

for $i = 1, \ldots, \bar{m}$, yield zero profit for each firm and sustain the optimal industry structure $\bar{m}$.

(ii) *The sustainable industry structure has $\bar{m} = k$ ($\bar{m} = k + 1$) firms as*

$$AC(q^* + \bar{q}/k) \leq (\geq) AC((kq^* + \bar{q})/(k + 1)).$$

This result eliminates problems that arise in demonstrating the existence of sustainable industry configurations with linear pricing.[26] Multiple-price schedules allow sustainability and cost recovery whether firms produce above or below minimum efficient scale. If firms produce *above* minimum efficient scale, the optimal industry size is $\bar{m} = k$. Then the zero-profit market equilibrium price is equal to the average incremental cost of producing above minimum efficient scale for each firm. Thus, the market-clearing price equals

$$F(kq^* + \bar{q}) = [C(q^* + \bar{q}/k) - C(q^*)]/(\bar{q}/k). \qquad (18.4.12)$$

This is similar to the case shown in figure 18.4.2. If firms produce *below* minimum efficient scale, the optimal industry size is $\bar{m} = k + 1$. Then the zero-profit market equilibrium price is also above average cost, so firms can recover the costs of sales below average cost,

$$F(kq^* + \bar{q}) = [C((kq^* + \bar{q})/(k + 1)) - (k/(k + 1))C(q^*)]/(\bar{q}/(k + 1)). \qquad (18.4.13)$$

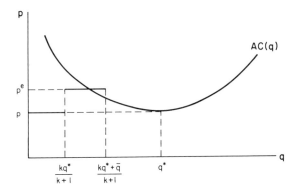

Figure 18.4.5
The market-clearing, sustainable industry price if firms operate below *MES*.

The sustainable, zero-profit market equilibrium price, if firms operate below minimum efficient scale, is shown in figure 18.4.5.

The sustainable industry structure may allow firms to earn positive profits, as in the natural monopoly case. It is to be reemphasized that this need not lead to the conclusion that multiple-price schedules should raise antitrust concerns. The profits earned by high-priced sales are partially used to compensate for sales at prices below average cost. The loss in consumer surplus from sustainable pricing policies may be balanced by welfare gains from industry cost efficiency; that is, production by a few large firms may be due to subadditive costs for each firm at the equilibrium output. The principal conclusion to be drawn from the preceding analysis is that price discrimination through multiple-price schedules should not be taken as evidence of monopolization and exclusion of competitors. Further, the presence of discriminatory multiple-price schedules and of positive profits of incumbents does not indicate that entry barriers are present. Rather, multiple prices and profits are consistent with a sustainable equilibrium in a contestable market.

Notes

1. See Posner (1976b).

2. Posner (1976b, p. 25) cites the (1936) case of *Goodyear Tire and Rubber Co.* v. *FTC*.

3. See Posner (1976b, pp. 30–33) and Rowe (1962).

4. In his introduction to Posner (1976b), Yale Brozen observes that the Robinson-Patman Act was introduced to restore provisions of the National Industry Recovery Act that promoted cartelization and downward price rigidity.

5. See also Rowe (1962).

6. The categories of first-, second-, and third-degree price discrimination are due to Pigou (1920) and are discussed fully in any industrial organization text. See Phlips (1983) for additional discussion of the many types of price discrimination. Phlips divides his discussion into price discrimination based on differences in location, time, income, and product quality. See also the classic discussion of Machlup (1955).

7. See, for example, Davidson (1955), Steiner (1957), and Stigler (1966, p. 209).

8. Machlup (1955) lists many standard techniques. See Phlips (1983) for a useful overview of price discrimination.

9. Such a model is studied by Varian (1985). Varian does not consider the effects of costs on the reservation price model.

10. This is shown by Varian (1985). Chiang and Spatt (1982) provide an extensive welfare analysis of price discrimination.

11. For example, let firm 2 have costs $C^2(q) = F_2 + a_2 wq^2$, with minimum efficient scale at $q = \sqrt{F_2/wa_2}$ and minimum average cost $AC_{min} = 2\sqrt{F_2 wa_2}$. The firm will exit if $p_2 \leq 2\sqrt{F_2 wa_2}$. Thus, if $w \geq (p/2)^2/F_2 a_2$, the cost of the input will cause the firm to exit.

12. See Novshek (1980b) and Eaton (1972, 1976).

13. For $m > (5/4(t/\alpha))$, $\pi'(m) < 0$. Note that $q(1/2m) > 0$ requires $m > t/\alpha$.

14. See Norman (1981) for a comparable result in a spatial setting.

15. There are a number of alternative rationing schemes that may be used. Motty Perry (1984) discusses a scheme in which those with the lowest willingness to pay obtain the good and resale is not permitted. A different rationing scheme exists in the market for airline tickets, since the tickets are nontransferable and any consumer can purchase a ticket priced below his reservation value. Airlines generally offer multiple fares (e.g., economy coach, business, and first class). Let $((p_1, q_1), (p_2, q_2))$ be a two-price supply schedule with $p_1 < p_2$. Then, if quantity is rationed for the low fare, $q_1 < D(p_1)$, all q_1 units are sold. Since anyone with reservation price above p_1 can purchase the good, $q_1/D(p_1)$ is the likelihood that a person with reservation price $p \geq p_1$ will have purchased a unit of q_1. So, $(1 - q_1/D(p_1))$ is the expected proportion of consumers with price above p_1 that lack a low-priced ticket. So, residual demand given (p_1, q_1) is given by the discontinuous function

$$D(p;(p_1,q_1)) = \begin{cases} (1 - q_1/D(p_1))D(p), & p_1 \leq p \\ D(p), & 0 \leq p < p_1. \end{cases}$$

Then (p_2, q_2) clears the market if $q_2 = D(p_2;(p_1,q_1))$, for $p_2 > p_1$.

16. I thank Wayne Shafer for this interpretation.

17. In general, the incumbent's sales are then

$$Y^0(s^0, s^1) = \min\left\{ D(p_{01}^e) - \sup_{p < p_{01}^e} s^1(p), s^0(p_{01}^e) \right\}$$

and the entrant's sales are equal to the residual $Y^1(s^0, s^1) = D(p_{01}^e) - Y^0(s^0, s^1)$; see Motty Perry (1984).

18. Note that a competitive firm producing above minimum efficient scale also earns positive profit. Suppose that the firm is a price taker and sets its marginal cost equal to price. If price

is above minimum average cost, the competitive firm earns zero profits. Additional entry does not take place if an additional firm would drive prices below minimum average cost.

19. Given increasing marginal cost, note that average incremental cost is below marginal cost,

$$[C(q^* + \bar{q}) - C(q^*)]/\bar{q} < C'(q^* + \bar{q}).$$

20. If the firm is not a natural monopoly and is still able to deter entry, this can raise concern about welfare losses from inefficient production as well. This need not call for antitrust enforcement, since in practice it is quite difficult to verify whether the firm's output is within the natural monopoly range.

21. See Joskow (1985a) for an extensive discussion of the antitrust application of the price squeeze concept in the electric power industry.

22. See Joskow (1985a, pp. 186–187) for a discussion of the price squeeze in the *Alcoa* decision.

23. This is different from the transfer price test proposed in chapter 3, which rules out vertical cross-subsidization. The transfer price test of Judge Learned Hand requires that the vertically integrated firm's revenue exceed its cost of downstream production, with the internally produced input valued at the price charged to downstream rivals.

24. An alternative view of the wholesale-retail price difference is given by M. K. Perry (1978, 1980), who considers multiple downstream markets with varying demand elasticities. Vertical integration into retailing provides a means of third-degree price discrimination.

25. See Ginsberg (1974), Baumol and Fischer (1978), and Baumol, Panzar, and Willig (1982) for a general discussion of the cost-minimizing number of firms.

26. Baumol, Panzar, and Willig (1982) resolve existence problems for the industry by assuming flat-bottomed average cost curves.

19 Antitrust Enforcement

Promotion of competition through antitrust enforcement has been portrayed as an alternative to classical administrative regulation.[1] Bork (1978, p. 420), however, identifies a trend in antitrust away from "the ideal of free markets to that of regulated markets."[2] Antitrust enforcement has itself become a form of administrative regulation, where the enforcement agencies create antitrust policy through such actions as selective enforcement, merger guidelines, and direct negotiation with market participants. The present chapter examines the process of antitrust enforcement and emphasizes the many similarities to other forms of regulation.

Antitrust enforcement is in many ways similar to other forms of law enforcement. Efficient enforcement requires deterrence through an optimal combination of penalties and enforcement expenditures. A model of law enforcement is applied to antitrust action against price fixing in section 19.1. It is shown that the objectives of the antitrust agency depend in a critical way on the type of strategic interaction between the agency and a cartel. The model of public enforcement is extended to the case of asymmetric information in sections 19.2 and 19.3 using the model of Besanko and Spulber (1986). The presence of incomplete information about firm costs makes it difficult to distinguish between high-cost competitive firms and low-cost collusive firms on the basis of observed market price. It is shown that optimal antitrust policy takes the form of policies used in models of price regulation under asymmetric information.

Antitrust enforcement is carried out both by public agencies and by the customers and competitors of antitrust law violators. Section 19.4 presents a model of private antitrust enforcement that extends that of Baker (1985). It is shown that market equilibrium under private enforcement may be ineffective unless decoupling of penalties and compensation is implemented. The chapter concludes with a brief comparison of public and private enforcement.

19.1 The Enforcement Process

19.1.1 Antitrust Policy

As with other forms of market regulation, antitrust enforcement involves both direct and indirect interaction between the administrative agency and buyers and sellers. Direct interaction occurs through lodging of complaints to agencies regarding alleged violations of antitrust law, discussion of guidelines, and negotiation of consent decrees. Indirect interaction occurs through attempts by consumers and firms to alter antitrust law and policy through legislative, administrative, and judicial channels.

Much has been written on the indirect determinants of antitrust law and policy. Extensive historical analyses of the antitrust statutes have been performed that examine legislative decision making.[3] There exist theories of the origins of antitrust enforcement that parallel those on the origins of regulation. For example, Reich (1980) characterizes antitrust enforcement as an "industry" with consumers and firms as buyers and government agencies and the antitrust bar as sellers.[4] The legislative and bureaucratic theories of the origins of regulation discussed previously in chapter 2 can be applied equally to antitrust enforcement. In what follows attention is focused only on the direct interaction between antitrust authorities and market participants.

As emphasized previously, antitrust law and enforcement reflects a wide variety of policy goals. These include preserving small firms in an industry, emphasized by Judge Learned Hand in the 1945 *Alcoa* case, and protection of "small dealers and worthy men," which concerned Judge Rufus W. Peckham in the 1897 *Trans-Missouri Freight* case.[5] Bork (1978, p. 51) states that the "only legitimate goal of American antitrust law is the maximization of consumer welfare" and defines *competition* as "any state of affairs in which consumer welfare cannot be enhanced by judicial decree." This approach suggests that policy goals contrary to consumer welfare enhancement, such as protection of small competitors, are inconsistent with antitrust law. Further, intervention in competitive markets by the courts or enforcement agencies is unwarranted. The courts have increasingly come to view the goal of antitrust as promoting competition rather than protecting competitors.

The courts are important policymakers in antitrust through their interpretation of the statutes, particularly with regard to defining exclusionary practices and the nature of competition. In many ways, the courts have avoided taking on the task of market regulation. The per se illegality of cartels allows the courts to avoid tests of legality based on "reasonable price" or "reasonable profit."[6] A clear difference between the courts and administrative agencies lies in arbitration between consumers and producers. Unlike bargaining between consumers and producers in public rate hearings, the courts have no basis upon which to decide prices.[7] Similarly, in merger cases, the courts have no criteria for arbitrating between the

interests of consumers who favor an efficient merger and rival producers
who oppose it.[8] Bork (1978, p. 81) recommends consumer welfare maximization as an exclusive goal to give a consistent "fair warning" to market
participants and to keep policy decisions in Congress. Antitrust should
therefore be concerned with economic efficiency, not with issues of equity
and income distribution.

The first issue to be addressed is the objective of the antitrust enforcement
agencies. An empirical study of the DOJ by Long et al. (1973, p. 361)
suggests that welfare losses or excess profits "appear to play a minor role
in explaining antitrust activity." Hay and Kelley (1974) find that in DOJ
price-fixing cases, greater attention is paid to proving illegality than to the
performance of the industry. Efforts have been made at the FTC to allocate
antitrust resources to maximize welfare, according to Mann and Meehan
(1974). However, in his study of FTC enforcement activities, Liebeler (1981)
observes that FTC industry wide cases (such as petroleum, automobiles,
and breakfast cereals) reflected a failed attempt by the FTC to *plan* its
activities and to apply cost-benefit analysis to the process of case selection.
The case selection method at the FTC, as characterized by Liebeler (1981),
is based on the supposed benefits of reduced industry market share concentration without explicit consideration of the public and private costs
of enforcement, and with little accompanying economic analysis.[9]

The goals of antitrust enforcement are partly reflected in the application
of penalties for violations of law. Easterbrook (1981, p. 319) states that
deterrence is "the first, and probably the only, goal of antitrust penalties."
Penalties associated with public enforcement take the form of fines, jail
sentences and "structural relief" or divestiture.[10] Penalties associated with
private enforcement are generally fines equal to treble damages, generally
three times the overcharges due to the antitrust violation.[11] These penalties
have the goal of providing an incentive for private enforcement activity
against offenders and thus ultimately are also directed at deterrence.

In practice, fines in the form of civil penalties have tended to be small
in price-fixing cases. Posner (1976a) finds that average fines per case rose
from $20,000 in 1900–1919 to only $40,000 in the period 1950–1959 and
$131,000 in the period 1960–1969. In the latter period, average fines were
0.21% of the cartel's total sales (Posner, 1976a, p. 32). The maximum fine
set by the Sherman Act was $5,000, which was raised to $50,000 in 1955
and to $1 million for corporations in 1974; see Posner (1976a, p. 32). Block
et al. (1981) show that average criminal fines as a percentage of sales for

16 cases in the bread industry between 1957 and 1976 were .31%. In the period 1971–1976, civil damages for price fixing in the bread industry ranged from .41% to 19.68% of annual sales, with an average of 2.8%. This suggests that fines will often represent a small proportion of profits.

Antitrust enforcement may be studied by applying the approach taken in the economic literature on crime and punishment; see especially Becker (1968), Stigler (1970), Becker and Stigler (1974), and Landes and Posner (1975). In this analysis there is a trade-off between the social benefits of deterring crime and the costs of detection, prosecution, and punishment of offenders. The optimal enforcement framework has been applied to antitrust by Landes and Posner (1979a), Lee (1980a), Schwartz (1980), Landes (1983), Sarris (1984), and others. In what follows, a simple model of public antitrust enforcement is proposed that allows the identification of many of the significant issues.

19.1.2   A Public Enforcement Model

Suppose that the firms in an industry engage in collusion to fix prices. Suppose that there are n identical firms all of whom are potential colluders.[12] Each firm has a constant returns-to-scale technology, with marginal production costs c. The industry has limited liability equal to $A > 0$. Total industry output is q and market inverse demand is represented by $P(q)$. Industry profits are represented by $\pi(q) = (P(q) - c)q$. The profit function is assumed to be twice differentiable and strictly concave with a unique interior maximum at the monopoly output q^m. Let q^c denote the competitive output, $P(q^c) = c$.

The cartel faces a *probability of detection* $\alpha(q, k)$, which depends on its output, q, and government antitrust enforcement expenditure, k.[13] Assume that $\alpha(q^c, k) = 0$ at the competitive output. The probability of detection is decreasing in the cartel output or equivalently, it is increasing in the cartel's markup above marginal cost, and the probability of detection is increasing in government enforcement costs. Let $\partial\alpha(q, k)/\partial q = \alpha_q(q, k)$ and $\partial\alpha(q, k)/\partial k = \alpha_k(q, k)$. Further, let $\alpha(q, k)$ be twice differentiable, convex in industry output, and concave in enforcement effort, i.e., $\alpha_{qq} > 0$, $\alpha_{kk} < 0$. Increases in industry output lower the marginal effect of enforcement efforts on the likelihood of detection, $\alpha_{qk}(q, k) < 0$. Alternatively, one may say that the cartel price and antitrust enforcement costs are complements in the detection of price fixing.

The cartel faces a penalty for price fixing F. Increases in the penalty have a deterrent effect on price fixing. This allows the antitrust authority to achieve the same level of deterrence at lower cost. Lowering enforcement costs k lowers the probability of detection of cartel activities. It is thus possible to substitute higher fines for enforcement costs to achieve the same expected fine $\alpha(q,k)F$. The optimal fine in the present framework is then set equal to the cartel's maximum liability, $F = A$. The trade-off between fines and the probability of detection is observed in most deterrence models; see Becker (1968), Polinsky and Shavell (1979), and Landsberger and Meilijson (1982).

The antitrust authorities have been observed to pursue various, often conflicting goals. As shall be seen, alternative specifications of the strategic game played by the cartel and the antitrust authority will significantly change the objective of the antitrust authority. This section considers three variations of the enforcement game. In one game, the antitrust authority moves first by committing itself to an enforcement level. The cartel selects its markup taking the enforcement level as given. The antitrust authority takes advantage of its first-mover status by anticipating the reaction of the cartel. The model is similar to that of Lee (1980a).[14] In another game, the cartel moves first by committing itself to a collusive output. The antitrust authority responds with a particular level of enforcement. In this game, the cartel considers the effect of its collusive output on the enforcement response. Finally, the last game considered is a Nash noncooperative game in which the equilibrium strategies of the cartel and the antitrust authority are best responses to each other.

The Antitrust Authority as First Mover   The antitrust authority is assumed to move first by making a binding commitment. This commitment is in the form of antitrust effort or enforcement costs, k. Such a cost is incurred before the cartel's price is observed and is therefore *sunk*. Further, if a cartel is detected, the antitrust authority must incur *fixed* legal costs of prosecution, $K > 0$. Assume that such costs are unavoidable if the cartel has been successfully identified.[15] It is reasonable to suppose that prosecution costs are less than industry liability, $K < A$. In the second stage of the game, the cartel observes enforcement costs k and is able to calculate expected penalties $\alpha(q,k)A$. Given the authority's choice of enforcement costs k in the first period, the cartel decides whether or not to collude and chooses the industy output level, q.

The equilibrium in this simple model is based on the assumption that the antitrust authority can make an irreversible investment in enforcement, k, and a commitment to incur fixed enforcement costs, K. Were such commitments ruled out, the equilibrium of the two-stage game would not be subgame perfect. In particular, the announcement of an intent to incur enforcement and prosecution costs would not necessarily be a credible threat and the deterrence effect of such announcements would be lost. Having deterred price fixing, the antitrust authority would have an incentive to reduce its enforcement efforts ex post. Anticipating this, the cartel would not be deterred by ex ante announcements of enforcement efforts.[16] This issue will be examined shortly by allowing the cartel to move first.

The antitrust authority is assumed to maximize consumer welfare net of enforcement costs. Consumer surplus is given by $\int_0^q P(x)\,dx - P(q)q$. The fines imposed on firms, A, may be considered by the antitrust authority as compensation of victims. The penalties may occur through private suits for treble damages, which in many cases follow successful government prosecution of collusion. The antitrust authority is thus assumed to *include* assessed penalties net of prosecution costs in its measure of the benefits of successful enforcement.[17] The antitrust authority's objective function is as follows:

$$W(q,k) = \int_0^q P(x)\,dx - P(q)q + \alpha(q,k)(A - K) - k. \tag{19.1.1}$$

Therefore, the antitrust authority views both compensation of victims and deterrence as desirable objectives.

Given that the antitrust authority moves first, one must begin by analyzing the cartel's response in the second-stage game. The cartel chooses output to maximize profit $\pi(q)$ net of expected penalties, given enforcement k,

$$\Pi(q,k) = \pi(q) - \alpha(q,k)A. \tag{19.1.2}$$

Thus, marginal profit equals the effect on output of the expected fine, $\pi'(\tilde{q}) = \alpha_q A$. Since $\alpha_q < 0$, output takes values between the competitive and collusive levels, $q^m \leq q \leq q^c$. If $\pi(\tilde{q}) > \alpha(\tilde{q},k)A$, the cartel chooses to collude. The effect of antitrust enforcement is then to *moderate* the cartel markup,

$$\frac{P - c}{P} = \frac{1}{\eta_D} + \alpha_q(q,k)\frac{A}{P}, \tag{19.1.3}$$

where $\eta_D = -P/(P'(q)q)$ is the elasticity of demand. Thus, the cartel's relative markup is *less* than the full *monopoly* markup $1/\eta_D$. If $\pi(\tilde{q}) \leq \alpha(\tilde{q}, k)A$, the cartel is fully competitive, since collusion yields negative expected profits. Assume that at the competitive output, elasticity of demand is large relative to the effect of output on the probability of detection, so that $\pi'(q^c) - \alpha_q(q^c, k)A < 0$ for all k. Since $\pi(q^c) - \alpha(q^c, k)A = 0$, it follows that the cartel output is defined by $q(k) < q^c$, where the cartel reaction curve $q(k)$ is defined by (19.1.3).

The effect of enforcement on the cartel's output is obtained by implicitly differentiating $\pi'(q) = \alpha_q(q, k)A$,

$$\frac{\partial q}{\partial k} = \frac{\alpha_{qk}(q, k)A}{\pi''(q) - \alpha_{qq}(q, k)A} > 0. \tag{19.1.4}$$

Since $\alpha_{qk} < 0$ and the second-order condition for the cartel's problem is satisfied, it follows that the cartel's output is *increasing* in antitrust enforcement efforts.

Consider now the antitrust authority's commitment to enforcement in the first-stage game. Enforcement k is chosen to maximize $W(q, k)$, given the cartel reaction function $q = q(k)$. Thus, the equilibrium strategies k^*, $q^* = q(k^*)$ satisfy

$$[-P'(q^*)q^* + \alpha_q(q^*, k^*)(A - K)] \, \partial q/\partial k + \alpha_k(q^*, k^*)(A - K) = 1. \tag{19.1.5}$$

From the cartel's problem, rewrite (19.1.5),

$$[P(q^*) - c - \alpha_q(q^*, k^*)K] \, \partial q/\partial k + \alpha_k(q^*, k^*)(A - K) = 1. \tag{19.1.6}$$

Observe that $\alpha_k(q^*, k^*)(A - K) < 1$ from $A > K$, $P(q) - c > 0$, $\alpha_q < 0$, and $\partial q/\partial k > 0$. This will be seen to contrast with the alternative enforcement games. The main conclusion from (19.1.6) is that the antitrust authority considers the effect of enforcement costs on output and thus on the cartel markup net of expected prosecution costs, $[P(q^*) - c - \alpha_q k]$. This captures the social welfare effects. In addition, the authority considers the direct marginal benefits of enforcement, $\alpha_k(A - K)$. The sum of these marginal benefits is set equal to the marginal cost of enforcement.

The equilibrium markup can be obtained from (19.1.6),

$$P(q^*) - c = \alpha_q(q^*, k^*)K + [1 - \alpha_k(q^*, k^*)(A - K)]/(\partial q/\partial k). \tag{19.1.7}$$

The markup under optimal enforcement with commitment depends on enforcement costs, potential penalties, and the marginal likelihood of successful prosecution.

The Cartel as First Mover   If the antitrust authority cannot credibly commit itself to a particular enforcement strategy, how will the enforcement equilibrium be altered? To study this possibility, a simple game is posited in which the cartel chooses output q in the first-stage game. In the second-stage game, the antitrust authority responds by choosing enforcement costs k. Reinganum and Wilde (1986) argue that such an approach is warranted since criminal sanctions and allocation of effort to apprehension must be selected "after the crime has been committed" to assure a subgame perfect equilibrium. The decision to prosecute and the selection of antitrust penalties in actual cases often occurs long after antitrust activity has been detected; see Reinganum (1987). The antitrust agencies need not prosecute every case, due to limited resources and various policy considerations. Assessment of antitrust penalties is subject to judicial discretion. For the present purposes, it will be sufficient to examine the effects of choosing enforcement efforts ex post. For ease of exposition, the assumption is maintained that fines are set at the maximum level and that detection of price fixing is followed by prosecution.

In the second stage of the enforcement game, the antitrust authority takes the cartel's output as given. Thus, its enforcement problem is determined by the trade-off between expected compensation net of prosecution costs and the costs of enforcement efforts k. Even if the antitrust authority has $W(q, k)$ as its objective function, it behaves exactly as if it were maximizing expected net fines minus enforcement costs,

$$\alpha(q, k)(A - K) - k,$$

since q is fixed in the first period. This may explain why the enforcement agencies (particularly attorneys) are so concerned with the probability of detection of illegal activities or the likelihood of winning a case, the size of the award, and the expected costs of prosecution and enforcement. Because cartel price-fixing activity has already occurred, it is rational to ignore its social welfare effects and focus on the expected compensation and legal costs. The social welfare losses from price fixing are correctly perceived to be *sunk costs*, so that enforcement efforts depend on specific aspects of the case.

The antitrust authority's reaction function, $k = k(q)$, is given by

$$\alpha_k(q, k)(A - K) = 1. \tag{19.1.8}$$

Compare this with the ex ante enforcement choice in (19.1.6). There, marginal expected compensation net of prosecution costs was less than one. The slope of the authority's reaction function is

$$\frac{\partial k(q)}{\partial q} = -\frac{\alpha_{kk}(q, k)}{\alpha_{kq}(q, k)} < 0. \tag{19.1.9}$$

So, the enforcement reaction function is *downward sloping*. An increase in cartel output *lowers* enforcement efforts by lowering the marginal product of enforcement, $\alpha_{kq} < 0$. Compare this with the previous game, where the authority moves first. There, greater enforcement effort *increases* cartel output by raising the likelihood of detection.

In the first stage of the ex post enforcement game, the cartel maximizes profit net of expected fines, $\Pi(q, k)$, taking into account the antitrust authority's reaction, $k = k(q)$. Thus, there is an equilibrium $q^*, k^* = k(q^*)$, such that

$$\pi'(q^*) - \alpha_q(q^*, k^*)A = \alpha_k(q^*, k^*)A\, \partial k(q^*)/\partial q. \tag{19.1.10}$$

Thus, $\pi'(q^*) < 0$ and $q^m < q^* < q^c$. The reaction of the antitrust authority serves the purpose of deterrence. By having antitrust agencies committed to winning cases ex post, collusive price fixing is reduced ex ante. Note, further, that marginal profit, $\pi'(q)$, is less than the marginal expected fine, $\alpha_q A$, in equilibrium. This is due to the cartel's additional output increment required by the reaction of the antitrust authority.

The Antitrust Authority and the Cartel Move Simultaneously Suppose that the antitrust authority and the cartel must choose their strategies under incomplete information about the other's strategy. In this case, the equilibrium enforcement effort and cartel output may be viewed as best responses to the other player's equilibrium move. Such a situation is described as a Nash equilibrium, q^*, k^*, defined by

$$\Pi(q^*, k^*) \geq \Pi(q, k^*) \qquad \text{for all } q \geq 0,$$
$$W(q^*, k^*) \geq W(q^*, k) \qquad \text{for all } k \geq 0. \tag{19.1.11}$$

The equilibrium is given by the reaction functions $k^* = k(q^*)$ and $q^* = q(k^*)$, which solve (19.1.3) and (19.1.8), that is,

$$\pi'(q^*) = \alpha_q(q^*, k^*)A,$$

$$\alpha_k(q^*, k^*)(A - K) = 1.$$
(19.1.12)

Note that the antitrust authority again does not explicitly consider consumer welfare at a Nash equilibrium, since it has no direct control over the cartel's output. However, the enforcement effort devoted to obtaining compensation still has a deterrent effect on collusion to fix prices. The framework of enforcement with simultaneous moves may provide a more accurate description of agency-cartel interaction.

The effort devoted to detection and prosecution of price fixing or other antitrust violations need not be observable. This makes commitments to antitrust enforcement difficult to verify. Further, as was noted, announcements of enforcement are not credible. If deterrence is achieved through threats of enforcement, the antitrust authority does not necessarily have an incentive to follow through with investigation and prosecution of those antitrust violations that do occur. Antitrust enforcement is costly and does not yield welfare benefits after violations have occurred unless the antitrust authority wishes to build a reputation for toughness to achieve future deterrence in a given market or across markets.

Law enforcement models following the path-breaking approach of Becker (1968) have emphasized the normative aspects of enforcement policy. A positive framework for law enforcement is proposed by Besanko and Spulber (1987). Law enforcement can be viewed as having legislative, executive, and judicial stages. At the first stage, the legislature establishes laws, guidelines, or standards of behavior. The legislature also specifies the range of penalties to be applied for violations of law. The legislature makes a commitment to law enforcement by delegating its authority to an enforcement agency. At the executive stage, an enforcement authority, such as an administrative agency, chooses its enforcement effort in response to incentives established by the legislature. Enforcement effort is of course chosen without complete information about illegal activities. Finally, after apprehension of accused offenders, penalties are applied in the judicial stage. This general description of the enforcement process applies to antitrust as well. The antitrust agencies respond to incentives created by legislative and judicial oversight. Penalties are chosen exogenously by statute and applied by the courts. Precommitment to antitrust enforcement can take the form of merger guidelines or announcements of proscribed behavior. The next two sections present an analysis of optimal enforcement under asymmetric information in which the antitrust authority is able to make credible commitments to enforcement. Additional research is needed to describe antitrust policy in the absence of such commitment opportunities.

19.2   Public Enforcement under Asymmetric Information

One of the principal problems in formulating antitrust policy is lack of information regarding the relevant economic data on firm costs, consumer demand, prices actually charged, market shares, and formal or informal coordination activities. For concreteness, the present work's focus is on the situation where costs are known to firms but not to the antitrust authority. Since the antitrust policy maker has difficulty assessing the degree of firm markups over marginal cost, the extent of welfare losses due to collusion must be inferred from observable data. Even more important, the antitrust authority may not be able to distinguish a priori between a competitive price that is high due to high marginal costs and a collusive price that represents a significant markup over low marginal cost. It is assumed that firm costs and the occurrence of price fixing may be discovered by costly legal action. The design of antitrust policy must then depend upon the antitrust authority's subjective beliefs about costs and other available information—in this case, the observed market price.

In the present model, due to Besanko and Spulber (1986), the antitrust policy is to announce to the firms in an industry a commitment to legal action with a probability that depends upon the observed cartel output or market price.[18] If legal action is taken and firms are found to have colluded to fix prices, a fine is paid. This probability may represent intensity of enforcement expenditures and the resulting likelihood of detection or simply the proportion of firms that face prosecution for various levels of enforcement effort. Announcement of the antitrust policy has both a quantitative and a qualitative effect. The quantitative effect is that existing cartels may choose to lower their markups to reduce the risk of prosecution. The qualitative effect is that firms may choose not to collude at all and thus set prices competitively. The two effects are significantly different because of the per se illegality of price fixing. While there are welfare gains from lower markups, the cartel still faces a fine if caught. Given the null hypothesis that firms are competitive, the authority faces the risk of (1) a type 1 error, prosecution of firms that are then found to be competitive, or (2) a type 2 error, a decision not to prosecute firms that are colluding.

As in the previous section, consider an industry with n identical firms. Total industry output is denoted by q and market (inverse) demand by $P(q)$. Each firm is assumed to have a constant returns to scale technology, where the marginal cost θ_i is known to the firms but unknown to the antitrust authority. Marginal costs can be either low or high, $\theta_i \in \{\theta_1, \theta_2\}$, $\theta_2 > \theta_1$. Low costs occur with probability $\gamma > 0$, and high costs with probability $(1 - \gamma) > 0$. The results of the model are easily extended to m cost types. Firms have combined limited liability equal to $A > 0$. This could represent industry assets, for example. Industry profits are described by the reduced form profit function $\pi(q, \theta_i) = P(q)q - \theta_i q$. The profit function is assumed to be a twice continuously differentiable and strictly concave function of q with a unique interior maximum in q for each θ_i.

The antitrust authority and the industry play a two-stage game. In the first stage, the antitrust authority commits itself to a schedule of *probabilities of suit*, $0 \leq \beta(q) \leq 1$, based on observed industry output.[19] In the second stage, firms choose whether or not to collude. If *collusion* occurs, the industry forms a cartel that chooses output q. Ideally, the cartel would like to set the fully collusive (i.e., monopoly) output q_i^m, where $\pi_1(q_i^m, \theta_i) = P'(q_i^m)q_i^m + P(q_i^m) - \theta_i = 0$. However, because the probability of a suit depends on the output produced by the cartel, the cartel might find it optimal to set collusively an output less than the monopoly output. If the firms decide not to collude, Bertrand-Nash competition between firms takes place, prices fall to the marginal cost, and each firm has an equal share of industry output. The *competitive equilibrium* output, q_i^c, satisfies $P(q_i^c) = \theta_i, i = 1, 2$. Clearly, $q_1^c > q_2^c$ and $\pi(q_i^c, \theta_i) = 0, i = 1, 2$. The industry will collude if collusion yields positive profits (net of expected penalties from price fixing). The industry prefers to be competitive if collusion yields zero expected profits.

If the industry is sued for price fixing, it is assumed that the courts are able to observe costs and to determine perfectly whether or not price fixing has occurred. Since price fixing is required in the present model to lower output below the competitive level, a positive markup above marginal cost may be seen as prima facie evidence of collusion. The game is shown in figure 19.2.1. Note that precommitment by the antitrust authority is essential. Because litigation is costly, the antitrust authority would not wish to

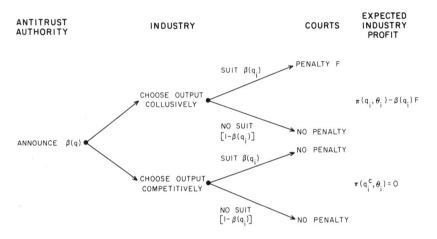

Figure 19.2.1
Commitment to antitrust enforcement.

carry out its threat to sue. In the absence of a credible commitment to sue, however, firms would anticipate that they would not be sued, and the deterrence effects of antitrust policy would be lost.

Because the antitrust authority can precommit to a policy, it will be able to "figure out" the possible equilibrium outputs that might arise in response to any arbitrary policy $\beta(q)$. Since there are only two types of firms and two possible modes of industry behavior (collusive or competitive), only four different levels of output could possibly arise in equilibrium. Therefore, by standard Revelation Principle arguments, there is no loss in generality from considering only four points on the schedule $\beta(q)$: (β_i, q_i), $i = 1, 2$, and (β_i^c, q_i^c), $i = 1, 2$.[20] The output q_i denotes the optimal collusive output for an industry with marginal cost θ_i, and $\beta_i = \beta(q_i)$ is the probability of a suit when q_i is produced. The probability $\beta_i^c = \beta(q_i^c)$ is the probability that the industry is sued when the competitive output q_i^c is produced. Let B represent the schedule $\{(q_1, \beta_1); (q_2, \beta_2); (q_1^c, \beta_1^c); (q_2^c, \beta_2^c)\}$. This framework is easily generalized to m cost types. What makes this problem interesting and unique is that while the cartel output is generally monotonic in cost, $q_1 \geq q_2$, as is the competitive output, the low-cost cartel's output may be greater than, equal to, or less than the high-cost firm's competitive output, $q_1 \gtrless q_2^c$. The antitrust authority's problem thus does not lend itself to simple methods of sorting or pooling the cartel by unknown cost types. The behavior of the cartel must be identified as well. The antitrust authority must distinguish a high-cost competitive industry from a low-cost collusive one.

As before, the effectiveness of enforcement is maximized by reducing the probability of action while raising the fine to its maximum, $F = A$. Potential liability is assumed to be *large* relative to current profits, $A > \pi(q_i^m, \theta_i)$, $i = 1, 2$. The framework is general enough to account for both criminal penalties and large civil penalties (treble damages). Because fines may be large, the antitrust authority can, if it so desires, induce competitive behavior by threatening to sue with a sufficiently high probability.

The antitrust authority wishes to maximize expected social welfare net of prosecution or *enforcement costs* $K > 0$. Consumer benefits are measured by $V(q) = \int_0^q P(x)\,dx$. Fines are treated as pure transfers between firms and customers. Antitrust enforcement costs are assumed not to exceed industry liability, $K < A$. Since only the case in which the antitrust authority can make commitments is being studied, the value to consumers of receiving compensatory payments need not be considered. Including such payments will not alter the equilibrium strategies for this case. The ex ante costs of detection (k in the previous section) are zero. The only costs of raising the probability of suit β are the ex post prosecution or enforcement costs K.

If firms' costs are known, optimal antitrust policy is easy to describe. The cartel "indifference curves" in (β, q) are obtained simply by dividing the isoprofit contours by industry liability, $\beta = (\pi(q_i, \theta_i) - \Pi)/A$. Thus, the antitrust authority need only set the probability of suit, $\beta(q)$, such that $\beta(q) \geq \pi(q_i, \theta_i)/A$ for $0 \leq q < q_i^c$ and $\beta(q) = 0$ for $q \geq q_i^c$, as shown in figure 19.2.2. Since collusion yields zero expected profits for all outputs below q_i^c, no collusion takes place. The socially optimal output is achieved and legal costs are never incurred by the authority. A simple version of this policy is to set $\beta(q) = 1$ for $q < q_i^c$ and $\beta(q) = 0$ otherwise, since raising β is costless ex ante.

With asymmetric information about firm costs, this policy may no longer be optimal. Setting a cutoff output, i.e., an output below which $\beta(q) = 1$ and above which $\beta(q) = 0$ just below q_2^c, will only deter high-cost firms from colluding. Low-cost firms will collude by setting $q_1 = \max\{q_2^c, q_1^m\}$. If the cutoff output is set just below q_1^c, the antitrust authority will be required to sue noncollusive high-cost firms with probability one. As will be demonstrated in the following section, the additional enforcement costs incurred under this strategy will generally exceed the additional welfare generated by deterring collusion. The analysis that follows will examine

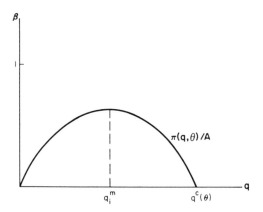

Figure 19.2.2
The cartel's zero-profit contour.

how the antitrust authority will design a self-selection mechanism that reduces the probability of suing high-cost firms while moderating the low-cost firms' price-fixing activities.

Given the schedule of outputs and probabilities of suit B, Besanko and Spulber (1986) identify three classes of *self-selection* constraints required for the schedule to be properly defined. One type of constraint states that if an industry of type i forms a cartel, it will not choose the collusive output of a different type of cartel. This is referred to as self-selection by *cost*,

$$\pi(q_i, \theta_i) - \beta_i A \geq \pi(q_j, \theta_i) - \beta_j A, \qquad i \neq j, \quad i, j = 1, 2. \tag{19.2.1}$$

Another type of constraint states that if any industry of type i forms a cartel, it will not choose the competitive output of a different type of industry; this is referred to as self-selection by *behavior*,

$$\pi(q_i, \theta_i) - \beta_i A \geq \pi(q_j^c, \theta_i) - \beta_j^c A, \qquad i \neq j, \quad i, j = 1, 2. \tag{19.2.2}$$

The final type of self-selection constraint requires the industry to compete if and only if it is profitable to do so. This again involves self-selection by cost and behavior. Since no fine is imposed if the industry is competitive, these are essentially *individual rationality* conditions. Thus, competition (q_i^c, β_i^c) is chosen by a type i industry if and only if

$$\max\{\pi(q_i, \theta_i) - \beta_i A, \pi(q_j, \theta_i) - \beta_j A, \pi(q_j^c, \theta_i) - \beta_j^c A\}$$

$$\leq 0 = \pi(q_i^c, \theta_i), \qquad i \neq j, \quad i, j = 1, 2. \tag{19.2.3}$$

I begin with a monotonicity result that follows from the self-selection conditions. One can rule out a particular configuration of behavior across industry types.

PROPOSITION 19.2.1   *It is never the case that low-cost firms behave competitively while high-cost firms collude.*

Proof   Suppose the converse is true. Then from (19.2.3), $\pi(q_2, \theta_1) - \beta_2 A \leq 0$. Collusion by high-cost firms and (19.2.1)–(19.2.3) require $\pi(q_2, \theta_2) - \beta_2 A > 0$. But, by the definition of π,

$$\pi(q_2, \theta_2) - \beta_2 A = \pi(q_2, \theta_1) - \beta_2 A - q_2(\theta_2 - \theta_1), \tag{19.2.4}$$

which implies $\pi(q_2, \theta_2) - \beta_2 A < 0$ and yields a contradiction.   QED

There are three possible behavior patterns that are not ruled out by proposition 19.2.1:

I. fully competitive equilibrium (neither type colludes),

II. partially competitive equilibrium (low-cost firms collude, high-cost firms compete), and

III. collusive equilibrium (both types collude).

The competitive equilibrium policy I can be interpreted as a policy of law enforcement "at all costs." Because price fixing is per se illegal, it might appear that all possible violations should be prosecuted. However, the presence of enforcement costs implies that complete enforcement of competition is never optimal, unlike the full information case just described. Under asymmetric information, the antitrust authority is always willing to tolerate a "little" collusion by low-cost firms in order to economize on the costs of enforcement, thus ruling out policy I.

To achieve the competitive equilibrium, the antitrust authority can simply set $\beta_1 = \beta_2 = 1$. Then the collusive outputs q_1, q_2 are irrelevant and can be specified arbitrarily. How are β_1^c and β_2^c chosen? For the low-cost industry to forgo collusion, individual rationality implies

$$\pi(q_2^c, \theta_1) - \beta_2^c A \leq 0. \tag{19.2.5}$$

Since $\pi(q_1^c, \theta_2) < 0$, it is never necessary to set a positive β_1^c.[21] Because suits are costly, it follows that it is optimal to set β_1^c equal to zero. Further, to minimize enforcement costs, the antitrust authority will choose the lowest probability of suit that deters low-cost firms from representing themselves as competitive high-cost firms. Thus, β_2^c will be chosen so that (19.2.5) is satisfied as an equality, i.e.,

$$\tilde{\beta}_2^c \equiv \pi(q_2^c, \theta_1)/A = (\theta_2 - \theta_1)q_2^c/A. \tag{19.2.6}$$

To demonstrate that an antitrust policy that induces a fully competitive equilibrium is never optimal, compare the antitrust policy characterized above with a particular policy that induces a (type II) partially competitive equilibrium. It can be shown that a policy that allows a small degree of collusion among low-cost firms while maintaining incentives for high-cost firms to compete always strictly dominates the competitive equilibrium policy in terms of social welfare.

PROPOSITION 19.2.2 *Under asymmetric information, the optimal antitrust policy will always allow low-cost firms to collude and to produce an output strictly less than the perfectly competitive output q_1^c.*

Proof Let low-cost firms collude without penalty; i.e., set $q_1 < q_1^c$ and $\beta_1 = 0$. At the same time, adjust β_2^c in such a way that the self-selection constraint $\pi(q_1, \theta_1) \geq \pi(q_2^c, \theta_1) - \beta_2^c A$ is exactly satisfied. This defines a schedule

$$\beta_2^c(q_1) = [\pi(q_2^c, \theta_1) - \pi(q_1, \theta_1)]/A = \tilde{\beta}_2^c - \pi(q_1, \theta_1)/A. \tag{19.2.7}$$

Given the policy $\{(q_1, \beta_1), (q_2^c, \beta_2^c(q_1))\}$ with $\beta_1 = 0$, expected social welfare is written as a function of q_1, $q_1 < q_1^c$,

$$W(q_1) = \gamma[V(q_1) - \theta_1 q_1] + (1 - \gamma)[V(q_2^c) - \theta_2 q_2^c] - (1 - \gamma)K\beta_2^c(q_1). \tag{19.2.8}$$

It should be apparent that a corner solution $q_1 = q_1^c$ will yield the competitive equilibrium policy. Differentiate the welfare function and evaluate at q_1^c. Since $V'(q_1^c) = P(q_1^c) = \theta_1$, it follows that

$$(dW(q_1)/dq_1)|_{q_1 = q_1^c} = (1 - \gamma)(K/A)\pi_1(q_1^c, \theta_1). \tag{19.2.9}$$

But $\pi_1(q_1^c, \theta_1) = P'(q_1^c)q_1^c < 0$, so that $(dW(q_1)/dq_1)|_{q_1=q_1^c} < 0$. Thus, a policy $\{(q_1, \beta_1), (q_2^c, \beta_2^c)\}$ with $q_1 \in (q_1^c - \varepsilon, q_1^c)$, $\beta_1 = 0$, and $\beta_2^c = \beta_2^c(q_1)$ always strictly dominates the perfectly competitive policy $\{(q_1^c, \beta_1 = 0), (q_2^c, \tilde{\beta}_2^c)\}$.

QED

To interpret this result, observe that the antitrust authority can achieve the fully competitive equilibrium only by threatening to sue with positive probability an industry that charges the perfectly competitive price (θ_2) for a high-cost industry. This policy is necessary in order to deter a low-cost industry from collusively setting this price. The expected costs of carrying out this policy depend on q_1 and are given by $[1 - \gamma] K \beta_2^c(q_1)$. As demonstrated in the proof of proposition 19.2.2, these enforcement costs decrease as q_1 decreases. Intuitively, if the antitrust authority allows a "little collusion" to go unpunished (q_1 slightly below q_1^c, and $\beta_1 = 0$), it can deter "more serious" collusion (low-cost firms charging θ_2) at a lower expected enforcement cost. Of course, allowing a "little collusion" has a deleterious effect on social welfare. However, because q_1^c maximizes the sum of consumers' and producers' surplus, this welfare loss is approximately zero in a neighborhood of q_1^c.

Proposition 19.2.2 rules out the fully competitive equilibrium. This leaves the partially competitive equilibrium and the collusive equilibrium. Both equilibria are characterized in the next section. The equilibrium that is actually observed depends on the relative likelihood of low- or high-cost firms.

19.3 Market Equilibrium with Public Enforcement

19.3.1 Characterization of Optimal Policy

Suppose that the antitrust authority wishes to achieve a *partially competitive equilibrium* (II). The announced antitrust policy in the form of the schedule of outputs and probabilities is such that high-cost firms choose to compete, $q_2 = q_2^c$, and low-cost firms collude, $q_1 \leq q_1^c$. To deter high-cost firms from colluding, the individual rationality conditions (19.2.3) require

$$\max\{\pi(q_2, \theta_2) - \beta_2 A, \pi(q_1, \theta_2) - \beta_1 A, \pi(q_1^c, \theta_2) - \beta_1^c A\} \leq 0. \tag{19.3.1}$$

For low-cost firms to collude, (19.2.1)–(19.2.3) require

$$\pi(q_1, \theta_1) - \beta_1 A \geq \max\{\pi(q_2, \theta_1) - \beta_2 A, \pi(q_2^c, \theta_1) - \beta_2^c A, 0\}. \tag{19.3.2}$$

Consider first equation (19.3.1). Since $\pi(q_1^c, \theta_2) < 0$, it follows that $\pi(q_1^c, \theta_2) - \beta_1^c A < 0$ for all $\beta_1^c \geq 0$. Since the decisions of both types are unaffected by β_1^c, let $\beta_1^c = 0$. Further, since (q_2, β_2) is not chosen, let $\beta_2 = 1$. Then, since $\pi(q, \theta_i) < A$, $i = 1, 2$, for all q, neither type's decision is affected by an arbitrary choice of q_2, say $q_2 \leq \min\{q_1, q_2^c\}$.

It will be shown below that $\pi(q_2^c, \theta_1) - \beta_2^c A \geq 0$. Thus, the effective constraints reduce to

$$\pi(q_1, \theta_2) - \beta_1 A \leq 0, \tag{19.3.1'}$$

$$\pi(q_1, \theta_1) - \beta_1 A \geq \pi(q_2^c, \theta_1) - \beta_2^c A. \tag{19.3.2'}$$

The antitrust authority's problem is then to choose q_1, β_1, and β_2^c to maximize welfare $W(q_1, \beta_1, \beta_2^c)$ subject to (19.3.1'), (19.3.2'), and $0 \leq \beta_1 \leq 1$, $0 \leq \beta_2^c \leq 1$, where

$$W(q_1, \beta_1, \beta_2^c) = \gamma[V(q_1) - \theta_1 q_1 - K\beta_1] + (1 - \gamma)[V(q_2^c) - \theta_2 q_2 - K\beta_2^c]. \tag{19.3.3}$$

In general, given $K > 0$, the constraints $\beta_1 \leq 1$ and $\beta_2^c \leq 1$ will not bind and can thus be ignored in characterizing the optimal solution.

Besanko and Spulber (1986) show that if the antitrust authority wants to achieve a *partially competitive equilibrium*, then the optimal antitrust policy has the following features:

i. $\beta_1 = 0$;

ii. $\beta_2^c = [\pi(q_2^c, \theta_1) - \pi(q_1, \theta_1)]/A$; \hfill (19.3.4)

iii. $q_1 = \max\{\tilde{q}_1, \hat{q}_1\}$, where $\tilde{q}_1$ is determined by the condition

$$\gamma[P(\tilde{q}_1) - \theta_1] + [1 - \gamma](K/A)[P(\tilde{q}_1) + P'(\tilde{q}_1)\tilde{q}_1 - \theta_1] = 0, \tag{19.3.5}$$

and $\hat{q}_1 = \sup\{q : \pi(q, \theta_1) = \pi(q_2^c, \theta_1)\}$; and

iv. $q_1^m < q_1 < q_1^c$.

The output equation (19.3.5) shows the equilibrium optimal markup for the collusive low-cost cartel.

Suppose that both high- and low-cost industries are *collusive*, given the optimal policy. Without loss of generality, one may set $\beta_1^c = 0$ and choose β_2^c such that $\pi(q_1, \theta_1) - \beta_1 A = \pi(q_2^c, \theta_1) - \beta_2^c A$. Then, given individual rationality, the behavioral self-selection constraints (19.2.2) are satisfied. Further, since by (19.2.1) $\pi(q_1, \theta_1) - \beta_1 A \geq \pi(q_2, \theta_1) - \beta_2 A > \pi(q_2, \theta_2) - \beta_2 A$, one need consider the individual rationality condition only for the high-cost firm, i.e., $\pi(q_2, \theta_2) - \beta_2 A > 0$. If this inequality is not satisfied, the partially competitive case holds.

Of the two constraints—given in (19.2.1)—that ensure self-selection by cost, only the "downward" constraint will be binding. In characterizing the optimal policy, only

$$\pi(q_1, \theta_1) - \beta_1 A \geq \pi(q_2, \theta_1) - \beta_2 A \qquad (19.3.6)$$

will be considered, and the slackness of the constraint

$$\pi(q_2, \theta_2) - \beta_2 A \geq \pi(q_1, \theta_2) - \beta_1 A \qquad (19.3.7)$$

will be verified later. For future use, note that when (19.3.6) holds as an equality, (19.3.7) is equivalent to a standard monotonicity requirement,[22]

$$q_2 \leq q_1. \qquad (19.3.8)$$

The antitrust authority's problem is then to maximize $W(q_1, \beta_1, q_2, \beta_2)$ subject to (19.3.6) and $0 \leq \beta_1 \leq 1, 0 \leq \beta_2 \leq 1$, where

$$W(q_1, \beta_1, q_2, \beta_2)$$
$$= \gamma[V(q_1) - \theta_1 q_1 - K\beta_1] + (1 - \gamma)[V(q_2) - \theta_2 q_2 - K\beta_2]. \quad (19.3.9)$$

Take $\pi(q_2, \theta_2) - \beta_2 A > 0$ as a given. Further, ignore the constraints $\beta_1 \leq 1$, $\beta_2 \leq 1$ as before and show that they are satisfied by the optimal unconstrained solution. The Kuhn-Tucker expression is then

$$L = W(q_1, \beta_1, q_2, \beta_2) + \mu[(\pi(q_1, \theta_1) - \beta_1 A) - (\pi(q_2, \theta_1) - \beta_2 A)]$$
$$+ r\beta_1 + \xi\beta_2. \qquad (19.3.10)$$

Besanko and Spulber (1986) show that if the antitrust authority wants to achieve a *collusive equilibrium*, then the optimal antitrust policy has the following features:[23]

i. $\beta_1 = 0$;

ii. $\beta_2 = [\pi(q_2, \theta_1) - \pi(q_1, \theta_1)]/A$; $\qquad (19.3.11)$

iii. $q_1 = \tilde{q}_1$, where $\tilde{q}_1$ is defined as in (19.3.5), which is restated for convenience—

$$\gamma[P(\tilde{q}_1) - \theta_1] + [1 - \gamma](K/A)[P(\tilde{q}_1) + P'(\tilde{q}_1)\tilde{q}_1 - \theta_1] = 0$$

(note that $q_1^m < \tilde{q}_1 < q_1^c$); and

iv. $q_2 = \tilde{q}_2$, where $\tilde{q}_2$ is determined by

$$[P(\tilde{q}_2) - \theta_2] = [P(\tilde{q}_2) + P'(\tilde{q}_2)\tilde{q}_2 - \theta_1](K/A), \qquad (19.3.12)$$

and $\tilde{q}_2 < q_1^m$.

The key point to observe about the equilibrium is the resulting markups above marginal cost chosen by each type of cartel. In the *collusive equilibrium*, both the low- and high-cost industry relative markups satisfy Ramsey-pricing type equations at the collusive equilibrium. From (19.3.5) and (19.3.12),

$$\frac{P(\tilde{q}_1) - \theta_1}{P(\tilde{q}_1)} = \frac{(1 - \gamma)K/A}{\gamma + (1 - \gamma)K/A} \frac{1}{\eta(\tilde{q}_1)}, \tag{19.3.13}$$

$$\frac{P(\tilde{q}_2) - \theta_2}{P(\tilde{q}_2)} = \frac{1}{1 - K/A} \left[\frac{-1}{\eta(\tilde{q}_2)} + \frac{\theta_2 - \theta_1}{P(\tilde{q}_2)} \right], \tag{19.3.14}$$

where $\eta(q) = -1/(P'(q)q/P(q))$ is market demand elasticity. These conditions clearly show how antitrust policy serves to moderate the size of markups by collusive firms. In the *partially competitive equilibrium*, the high-cost cartel behaves competitively and the low-cost cartel chooses a markup as in the first condition, (19.3.13).

19.3.2   Comparative Statics

The optimal antitrust policy depends parametrically on enforcement costs, industry liability, production costs, market demand, and the likelihood of low- and high-cost industries. The focus here is on the collusive equilibrium, which is given by equations (19.3.11), (19.3.5), and (19.3.12). The results for $\tilde{q}_1$ apply to the partially competitive equilibrium as well. Proofs of comparative statics results are omitted for brevity.

Enforcement costs and industry liability (fines) have opposite effects on the market equilibrium.

PROPOSITION 19.3.1   (i) *Both low-cost and high-cost industry outputs are decreasing in K and increasing in A, $\partial \tilde{q}_i / \partial K < 0$, $\partial \tilde{q}_i / \partial A > 0$, i = 1, 2.* (ii) *The likelihood of suit is decreasing in K and increasing in A, $\partial \beta_2 / \partial K < 0$, $\partial \beta_2 / \partial A > 0$.*

Higher enforcement costs allow collusion to increase for all industry types and reduce enforcement efforts.

Penalties have tended to be small in price-fixing cases. The proposition suggests that cartels will respond to lower fines by reducing output levels, while enforcement efforts will decline as well. Note that if fines are bounded below monopoly profits for high-cost firms, then the antitrust authority cannot induce these firms to compete. Thus, low fines or high enforcement costs rule out the partially competitive equilibrium. This suggests that an observed absence of price fixing may be due to other factors that inhibit collusion.

A greater likelihood of low-cost firms improves expected welfare. The output of the low-cost industry increases, as does the enforcement probability.

PROPOSITION 19.3.2 (i) *Low-cost industry output is increasing in* γ, *while high-cost industry output is constant,* $\partial \tilde{q}_1 / \partial \gamma > 0$, $\partial \tilde{q}_2 / \partial \gamma = 0$. (ii) *The likelihood of suit is increasing in* γ, $\partial \beta_2 / \partial \gamma > 0$.

Production costs are now considered.

PROPOSITION 19.3.3 (i) *The output of the low-cost industry is decreasing in* θ_1 *and constant in* θ_2, $\partial \tilde{q}_1 / \partial \theta_1 < 0$, $\partial \tilde{q}_1 / \partial \theta_2 = 0$. (ii) *The output of the high-cost industry is decreasing in* θ_2 *and increasing in* θ_1, $\partial \tilde{q}_2 / \partial \theta_2 < 0$, $\partial \tilde{q}_2 / \partial \theta_1 > 0$. (iii) *The enforcement probability is decreasing in* θ_2, $\partial \beta_2 / \partial \theta_2 < 0$. *The effect of* θ_1 *on* β *is ambiguous.*

Of particular interest is the result that an increase in the costs of low-cost firms requires higher output from high-cost firms. Also note that if high-cost firms' costs rise, the antitrust authority reduces its enforcement efforts.

An important consideration in antitrust analysis is the use of market demand elasticity as an indicator of the monopoly power of firms in the industry. The reciprocal of demand elasticity, known as the Lerner index, is used to infer markups above marginal cost. Equations (19.3.13) and (19.3.14) allow us to apply this approach to the market equilibrium with optimal antitrust enforcement. For ease of presentation, let demand elasticity be constant in the relevant range.

PROPOSITION 19.3.4 *The low-cost industry output is increasing in demand elasticity and the high-cost industry output is decreasing in demand elasticity,* $\partial q_1 / \partial \eta > 0$, $\partial q_2 / \partial \eta < 0$. *The effects of demand elasticity on the probability of suit* β_2 *are ambiguous.*

It is apparent from (19.3.13) and (19.3.14) that relative markups are decreasing in η for the low-cost industry and increasing in η for the high-cost industry. Thus, in the presence of antitrust policy of the type considered here, the Lerner index is a good predictor of market power for the low-cost industry but not for the high-cost industry.

19.3.3   Competition versus Collusion

The question that now arises is why the antitrust authority would allow low-cost firms to collude. Any observed output less than q_2^c represents price fixing by either the low- or high-cost industry. Why does the antitrust authority not threaten to prosecute with probability one whenever $q < q_2^c$ is observed? The answer lies in the value of the probability of a suit at β_2^c. This threat is required to deter the low-cost industry from colluding and choosing output q_2^c. However, it may be costly to deter low-cost firms from choosing q_2^c. By allowing high-cost firms to collude at $q_2 < q_2^c$, the enforcement efforts needed to deter low-cost firms from selecting this output are lower. From $\beta_2 = (\pi(q_2, \theta_1) - \pi(q_1, \theta_1))/A$, note that raising q_2 without lowering q_1 requires *raising* β_2. This is because $\pi_1(q_2, \theta_1) > 0$, since $q_2 < q_1^m$. To raise q_1 as well also requires β_2 because $\pi_1(q_1, \theta_1) < 0$, since $q_1 > q_1^m$. This analysis shows how the present enforcement problem differs from standard principal agent models in which compliance by the highest- or lowest-cost agent may be assured.

When will the antitrust authority induce the collusive equilibrium, and when will it induce the partially competitive equilibrium? To answer these questions, notice that the collusive equilibrium is the solution to

$$\max W(q_1, \beta_1, q_2, \beta_2)$$

$$\text{subject to} \qquad \pi(q_1, \theta_1) - \beta_1 A \geq \pi(q_2, \theta_1) - \beta_2 A, \quad 0 \leq \beta_i \leq 1, \quad i = 1, 2.$$
$$(19.3.15)$$

The partially competitive equilibrium is the solution to the above problem with the additional constraints $q_2 = q_2^c$ and $\pi(q_1, \theta_2) - \beta_1 A \leq 0$. Therefore, expected social welfare is always higher under the collusive equilibrium. Thus, *whenever it is feasible to do so*, the antitrust authority will always structure the antitrust policy to achieve the collusive equilibrium. The collusive equilibrium is feasible if the high-cost industry earns positive profits from collusion, i.e., if $\pi(q_2, \theta_2) - \beta_2 A > 0$. Using the expression for β_2 from (19.3.11) and some straightforward algebra, this inequality can be shown to be equivalent to[24]

$$[P(\tilde{q}_1) - \theta_1]\tilde{q}_1 > [\theta_2 - \theta_1]\tilde{q}_2. \tag{19.3.16}$$

A sufficient condition for equation (19.3.16) to hold is $\tilde{q}_1 < q_2^c$. However, this is also a necessary condition for the partially competitive equilibrium to be fully pooling.

A further characterization of the collusive and partially competitive equilibria may be obtained in terms of the likelihood, γ, that the industry consists of low-cost firms.

PROPOSITION 19.3.5   *There exists $\gamma^* < 1$ such that the optimal policy is partially competitive for all γ such that $\gamma^* \leq \gamma < 1$.*

Proof   Equation (19.3.16) may be rewritten as $\phi(\gamma) = \pi(\tilde{q}_1, \theta_1) - (\theta_2 - \theta_1)\tilde{q}_2 > 0$. In proposition 19.3.2 it is shown that $\partial\tilde{q}_1/\partial\gamma > 0$ and $\partial\tilde{q}_2/\partial\gamma = 0$ at the collusive equilibrium. Since $\pi_1(\tilde{q}_1, \theta_1) < 0$ at the collusive equilibrium and since $\tilde{q}_1$ approaches q_1^c continuously as γ goes to 1, it follows that there exists $\gamma^* < 1$ such that $\phi(\gamma) \leq 0$ for all γ such that $\gamma^* \leq \gamma < 1$. This violates the necessary condition for collusive equilibrium.   QED

The result is plausible since a higher proportion of low-cost firms reduces the expected enforcement costs for prosecution of high-cost firms and raises the benefits of inducing low-cost firms to compete.

A strategic model of antitrust enforcement has been examined that studies the effect of asymmetric information on equilibrium firm behavior and on optimal antitrust policy. High-cost firms may be induced to avoid price fixing and behave competitively, although in general it is optimal to allow low-cost firms to engage in price fixing. Even if high-cost firms behave competitively, the equilibrium price choices of firms subject to optimal antitrust enforcement will nonetheless be monotonically increasing in the firms' marginal costs. The framework of the analysis differs in a significant way from principal agent type models of optimal regulation. The distinction lies in the effects of antitrust policy on both industry *performance* (prices and profits) and industry *conduct* (competition versus collusion).

The analysis of optimal enforcement under asymmetric information further confirms the connection made between antitrust and regulation. First, much like a central planner, the antitrust authority allocates scarce resources to monitoring productive behavior under incomplete information. Second, although starting from a different framework, antitrust enforcement is seen to have incentive effects on firm behavior *in equilibrium* similar to those observed in the large literature on regulation of a monopolist with unknown costs; see, for example, the work of Baron and Myerson (1982). In this literature, the regulator designs a mechanism (setting prices, inputs, or subsidies) such that firms have incentive to reveal their costs correctly. The antitrust authority is limited to the threat of prosecution and imposition of a fine if collusion is observed. However, given the optimal schedule of probabilities of bringing suit, the antitrust authority is able to infer the costs of firms based on the price they choose to set, as in the regulation models. Due to the asymmetry in information, it is not necessarily optimal for enforcement to cause all types of firms to set prices competitively. Some level of monopoly markup is traded off against enforcement expenditures. Monopoly markups are shown to satisfy Ramsey-pricing type rules. Given sufficiently large fines, the highest-cost firms may be induced to set price competitively. Thus, the main implication of the analysis is that the informational requirements of antitrust and the characteristics of the market equilibrium are comparable to those of cost of service regulation. This provides a caveat to the common belief that markets policed by antitrust involve lower transaction costs for government agencies than does traditional price regulation.

19.4   Market Equilibrium with Private Enforcement

The antitrust laws provide for private enforcement through damage awards. Private antitrust suits may be brought by a firm's customers or by its competitors. For buyers of a good, damage awards reduce the costs of purchasing the good, thus altering demand. The welfare consequences of alternative enforcement rules must then take into consideration the resulting market equilibria. We focus on overcharges by firms charged with monopolization or by firms charged with collusion to fix prices. For a firm's competitors, filing antitrust suits may not only yield increased revenues but may constitute a competitive strategy. Alternative enforcement rules may then affect market equilibria by altering the behavior of competing firms. Rivals may seek damages based on losses due to alleged exclusionary practices.[25] The present work considers only enforcement by consumers. It is emphasized that elimination of private enforcement may be desirable in the case of consumers, unless damage awards based on multiples of overcharges can be altered. The elimination of enforcement by rival firms may be desirable under more general circumstances.[26]

The damages imposed on consumers resulting from price fixing by a cartel are calculated with respect to a *reference price* $\bar{p}$. Any difference between the *actual* price, p, and the *reference* price, $\bar{p}$, is assumed to represent damages to consumers *per unit purchased*. The reference price may equal or exceed marginal cost, or it may represent alternative methods of estimating the competitive price as applied by the courts.[27] Let t be the *damage multiple*. Then, if the consumer, after purchasing output q, successfully obtains a legal settlement for price fixing, total damages equal $t(p - \bar{p})q$.

The representative consumer's value of the good is $V(q) = \int_0^q P(x)\,dx$, where $P(x)$ is the consumer's marginal willingness to pay. The consumer may be uncertain about the outcome of a trial, even if he is certain about the formation of a cartel. Let α represent the probability that the consumer will win his case against the cartel. Assume that this estimate of the likelihood of the plaintiff winning is shared by the firms in the cartel. The consumer then has incentive to purchase more at any given price than he would in the absence of a potential damage award. The expected damage award serves to lower the marginal cost of purchasing the good from the cartel.

Given the cartel price p, the consumer chooses demand, $q = Q(p)$, to solve the following maximization problem:

$$\max_q [V(q) + \alpha t(p - \bar{p})q - pq].$$ (19.4.1)

The consumer demand is determined by the following equation:

$$P(q) = p - \alpha t(p - \bar{p}).$$ (19.4.2)

Thus, the consumer marginal willingness to pay is driven below the market price, p.

Given constant marginal costs, the cartel has profits π,

$$\pi(q) = (p - c)q - \alpha t(p - \bar{p})q.$$ (19.4.3)

For ease of exposition, I ignore the possibility of a competitive fringe.[28] If the reference price equals marginal cost, collusion only takes place if the expected damage multiple, αt, is less than one, assuming that price above marginal cost is prima facie evidence of price fixing. With the reference price strictly above marginal cost, but below the unconstrained monopoly price, some collusion to raise price above $\bar{p}$ will always be desirable for the cartel. The cartel output solves

$$(1 + \alpha t)p - c + \alpha t\bar{p} + (1 - \alpha t)q\,\partial p/\partial q = 0,$$ (19.4.4)

where the slope of the consumer inverse demand curve equals from equation

(19.4.2),

$$\partial p/\partial q = (1/(1 - \alpha t))P'(q). \tag{19.4.5}$$

Baker (1985) obtains the result that when buyers are fully informed "no cartels are deterred, regardless of the damage rule" and "all cartels choose the monopoly output." In the present setting, substituting from equations (19.4.2) and (19.4.5) into (19.4.4), it follows that the cartel chooses the monopoly output, q^m, where $P(q^m) + q^m P'(q^m) - c = 0$. The equilibrium price adjusts to compensate for the damage award, $p = (1/(1 - \alpha t))(P(q^m) - \alpha t \bar{p})$. The cartel earns full monopoly profits, since $\pi(q^m) = (p - c)q^m - \alpha t(p - \bar{p})q^m = (P(q^m) - c)q^m$.

The invariance of the monopoly outcome to damage awards reflects both full information on the part of consumers and firms and the absence of transaction costs. Such costs are to be expected in the present context. Suppose that the consumer faces legal costs of bringing suit, $K > 0$. There may also be contingent fees both as a lump sum and as a percentage of the damage payment; see Elzinga and Breit (1976, pp. 72–77). It is assumed here that the damage multiple is adjusted to reflect any proportional contingent charges. Suppose also that the plaintiff's costs K are paid by the defendant if the plaintiff wins the suit (by section 4 of the Clayton Act). Then the consumer chooses to sue only if expected damages exceed expected legal costs,

$$\alpha t(p - \bar{p})Q(p) > (1 - \alpha)K,$$

where $Q(p)$ solves equation (19.4.2) with $p > \bar{p}$. If the consumer chooses not to sue, demand, $q(p)$, solves $P''(q) = p$. The cartel compares its profits with and without consumer suit. If the cartel chooses its price p, $\bar{p} \le p \le \tilde{p}$, where

$$\alpha t(\tilde{p} - \bar{p})q(\tilde{p}) = (1 - \alpha)K,$$

the consumer will not sue for damages, and cartel profits will equal $\pi = (p - c)q(p)$. Otherwise, if the cartel chooses a price above $\tilde{p}$, profits equal $\pi = (P(q^m) - c)q^m - \alpha K$. If $\tilde{p}$ is above p^m or sufficiently close to $p^m = P(q^m)$, the cartel will never face suits. If $\tilde{p}$ is significantly less than $p^m = P(q^m)$, the cartel may choose to risk a lawsuit if profits net of expected damage payments are sufficiently large.

Another form of friction may arise if the firm has limited liability, that is, damage payments are bounded above by $A > 0$, which may represent assets.[29] The firm anticipates a damage payment equal to $t(p - \bar{p})q$ or A, whichever is smaller. The consumer only takes damages into account at the margin if his purchase is less than $\tilde{q} = A/t(p - \bar{p})$. Above $\tilde{q}$, the consumer would obtain all of the firm's assets in the event of a successful suit.

Three cases may be identified depending on the size of *liability* given inverse demand, P, the reference price, $\bar{p}$, the damage multiple, t, and the probability of detection. Suppose that the cartel's liability level is *high*.

$$\frac{t}{1 - \alpha t}(P(q^m) - \bar{p})q^m \leq A. \tag{19.4.6}$$

Then the equilibrium described above is unaffected, since the liability constraint is not binding. Thus, $p = (1/(1 - \alpha t))(P(q^m) - \alpha t \bar{p})$, and the damage payment $t(p - \bar{p})q^m$ never exceeds A by equation (19.4.6). The cartel chooses the monopoly output, q^m, and earns monopoly profit.

Suppose that the cartel has an *intermediate* level of liability,

$$t(P(q^m) - \bar{p})q^m \leq A < \frac{t}{1 - \alpha t}(P(q^m) - \bar{p})q^m. \tag{19.4.7}$$

In this case, the liability constraint is strictly binding, and output is set at the lowest level above q^m such that damages do not exceed liability.[30] So, output $\tilde{q}$ and price solve equation (19.4.2) and

$$t(p - \bar{p})\tilde{q} = A. \tag{19.4.8}$$

Thus, output $\tilde{q}$ solves

$$\frac{t}{1 - \alpha t}(P(\tilde{q}) - \bar{p})\tilde{q} = A. \tag{19.4.9}$$

The firm earns profit $\pi = (\bar{p} - c)\tilde{q} + A(1 - \alpha t)/t$.

Finally, suppose that the cartel has a *low* level of liability,

$$A \leq t(P(q^m) - \bar{p})q^m. \tag{19.4.10}$$

Then the cartel may choose the monopoly output. Consumers expect to obtain damages at most equal to liability A if their suit is successful. So, at the margin, consumers ignore the effect of their purchases on the size of the damage settlement. The market-clearing price is the monopoly price, $p^m = P(q^m)$, and the firm earns monopoly profits net of expected liability,

$\pi = \pi^m - \alpha A$. The preceding discussion is summarized by the following proposition.

PROPOSITION 19.4.1   (i) *With high liability, the cartel chooses output q^m, price $p = (1/(1 - \alpha t))(P(q^m) - \alpha t \bar{p})$, and earns monopoly profits.* (ii) *With an intermediate liability level, the cartel chooses output $\tilde{q} > q^m$, price $p = (1/(1 - \alpha t))(P(\tilde{q}) - \alpha t \bar{p})$, and earns profit $\pi = (\bar{p} - c)\tilde{q} + A(1 - \alpha t)/t$.* (iii) *With low liability, the cartel chooses output q^m, price $p^m = P(q^m)$, and earns monopoly profits net of expected liability $\pi = \pi^m - \alpha A$.*

The private enforcement of antitrust does not improve allocative efficiency for either high or low liability levels. Some improvement may occur in the intermediate liability case, although this case is unlikely to be of much importance if the damage multiple times the probability of a successful suit is close to unity.

The selection of the monopoly output by the cartel depends in part on agreement between consumer and firm estimates of the likelihood of a successful suit. Baker (1985) considers the case of difference between consumer and firm estimates of α, α^c, α^f, which may result from government enforcement activities not directly observed by the consumer but anticipated by the cartel. Given different estimates of the likelihood of a successful suit, the consumer chooses output such that $P(q) = p(1 - \alpha^c t) + \alpha^c t \bar{p}$. Solving the firm's maximization problem for the equilibrium output—in equation (19.4.4)—gives

$$P(q) + qP'(q) - c = (t/(1 - \alpha^f t))(\bar{p} - c)(\alpha^c - \alpha^f). \qquad (19.4.11)$$

Thus, the cartel's output is greater than, equal to, or less than the monopoly output as $\alpha^c \gtreqless \alpha^f$, for $\bar{p} > c$.[31] If the firm has a higher estimate of the likelihood of a suit being successful than does the consumer, allocative efficiency is improved by private enforcement.

The probability of detection of cartel activity may depend on the size of the markup above the cartel's marginal cost. This may be determined endogenously through government enforcement activities, as in the public enforcement model studied in sections 19.2 and 19.3. To examine the effects of a variable probability of suit on private enforcement, take $\alpha(p)$ as an increasing function of price. The cartel then chooses output to maximize profit, $\pi = (p - c)q - \alpha(p)t(p - \bar{p})q$, where price solves $p = (1/(1 - \alpha(p)t))(P(q) - \alpha(p)t\bar{p})$. As before, substituting for p into the profit function gives $\pi = P(q)q - cq$, thus eliminating the probability of detection from the profit function. The markup above the monopoly price without treble damages, $P(q^m)$, is sufficient to compensate for the additional demand created by treble damages, and the cartel chooses the monopoly output. The increased markup exactly compensates for the effect of the cartel's price on the expected damage payment. Thus, treble damages and a variable detection probability have no effect on market efficiency. This differs markedly from Block, Nold, and Sidak (1981), who find that a variable probability of detection causes cartels to moderate their markup. Although they posit proportional antitrust damages, their model ignores the feedback effects of these damages on consumer demand.[32]

Schwartz (1980) and Polinsky (1986) argue for "decoupling" antitrust damages, rather than "detrebling." Decoupling would allow the fine paid by price fixers to differ from the compensation paid to the cartel's customers. Polinsky (1986) observes that when private enforcers receive fines, private enforcement efforts may not be optimal, since it may be desirable to raise damages for deterrence while reducing enforcement costs. He also states that decoupling may require the government to subsidize rather than tax the cartel damage payments. In the present framework, an optimal *tax* can be used to reduce the cartel price at the market equilibrium.

To decouple damages, let $t^c(p - \bar{p})q$ represent the share of damages received by consumers, and let t^f be the damage multiplier used to calculate the cartel's fine, $t^f > t^c$. The government obtains the difference $(t^f - t^c)(p - \bar{p})q$ in the form of a tax. The market price is then $p = (1/(1 - \alpha t^c))(P(q) - \alpha t^c \bar{p})$, and cartel profits equal $\pi(q) = (p - c)q - \alpha t^f(p - \bar{p})q$. So, profits are equal to

$$\pi(q) = \frac{1 - \alpha t^f}{1 - \alpha t^c}\left[P(q) - c + \frac{\alpha(t^f - t^c)(\bar{p} - c)}{1 - \alpha t^f} \right]q. \tag{19.4.12}$$

Decoupling implies that the cartel will moderate its markup, since the profit-maximizing cartel output, $\bar{q}$, solves

$$P(\bar{q}) + P'(\bar{q})\bar{q} - c = -\alpha(t^f - t^c)(\bar{p} - c)/(1 - \alpha t^f). \tag{19.4.13}$$

Decoupling thus reduces markups as long as the reference price exceeds marginal cost, and the cartel price exceeds the reference price. Thus, decoupling increases the effectiveness of private antitrust enforcement.

The preceding analysis allows us to identify a difference between the private and social incentives to bring an antitrust suit. The principal difference is that private suits are meant to recover damages, or some multiple of damages, in the form of transfers of monopoly rents to the firm. This differs considerably from socially optimal antitrust enforcement, which ignores transfers of rents from exchange but is concerned with the maximization of total rents. Thus, socially optimal antitrust enforcement involves bringing suit to eliminate the deadweight welfare loss due to monopoly. With constant marginal cost, this is just the traditional welfare triangle equal to the loss in consumer surplus due to the cartel pricing above marginal cost. The difference between the social and private incentives to bring suit implies that private suits may be excessive if rent transfers are larger than deadweight welfare losses. In fact, the differences between public and private incentives are exacerbated by the feedback effect of damage payments on consumer demand. Private suits do not lead to any change in net transfers and do not eliminate or reduce deadweight welfare losses from monopoly, at least without decoupling of damage payments. Public incentives to bring suit, if based on deadweight welfare losses, are unaffected by damage payments and serve to mitigate cartel markups and thus reduce welfare losses.

The public incentives to bring suit are based on deadweight welfare losses only if the antitrust agency is able to precommit to an enforcement program. One must posit alternative objectives for the antitrust agency if it makes enforcement decisions after the cartel price is observed. The same is required at a Nash equilibrium where the antitrust agency and the cartel chose their strategies without observing the other's move. The alternative objectives for the antitrust authority may include law enforcement per se or the provision of relief for the customers of a monopoly. In this case, the antitrust authority trades off the costs of enforcement against the expected benefits of successful prosecution. Winning the case may be more important ex post than deterrence. Of course, deterrence remains a consideration if the enforcement game is repeated and the antitrust agency wishes to establish a reputation for toughness in enforcing the law.

An additional difference between public and private incentives to sue is suggested by Shavell (1982b) in the context of accident prevention but applies to the antitrust area as well. First, private parties consider only their own legal costs of suit. Social welfare maximization may require the antitrust authority to take into account the potential legal costs not only of consumers but also those of the cartel. Second, and perhaps more important, there may be "externalities" from a public suit, such as the establishment of precedents that affect "the behavior of potential defendants generally" (Shavell, 1982b, p. 334).[33]

The issue remains whether the combination of public and private enforcement of antitrust law is efficient. The preceding analysis has demonstrated that collusive pricing is generally not deterred at a market equilibrium with private enforcement, since consumer demand is affected by the damage payment. This suggests that private enforcement of antitrust at best is unnecessary, and at worst distorts relative prices and involves significant legal costs. Public enforcement of antitrust law has also met with its share of criticism. Posner (1976a, p. 6) extensively discusses "the high price that society has paid for the failure of the antitrust enforcement system to develop a genuinely economic approach to the problem of collusive pricing." The motivation and objectives of the antitrust enforcement agencies have been widely questioned. This does not necessarily imply that the dual system of public and private law enforcement is at fault. Parallel systems of law enforcement have benefits in other areas. The regulatory efforts of the Environmental Protection Agency in mitigating externalities are supplemented by the potential for private suits against polluters. Private tort actions complement the agencies that regulate product and workplace safety (FDA, CPSC, and OSHA). The contract rules established by the Securities and Exchange Commission and the Federal Trade Commission may serve to enhance market efficiency.

These parallel enforcement efforts suggest that a similar division of enforcement tasks between the public and private sectors may be desirable. The role of the antitrust agencies should be to establish general rules or guidelines regarding what constitutes an antitrust violation, particularly in the areas of price fixing and unfair trade practices. The agencies can perform a useful role in information gathering and collection of consumer complaints. Direct public enforcement may be useful in deterring price fixing or fraud in the early stages before significant damage has occurred. Public enforcement should, however, avoid constant fine tuning of policy and attempts at market regulation as has occurred in extended negotiation over specific mergers. At the same time, private enforcement has advantages in that market participants have better information regarding the terms of transactions and the characteristics of sellers. Decoupling of damages may provide a partial solution to improving the effectiveness of private enforcement. Schwartz (1980) recommends decoupling as a means of creating optimal incentives for private enforcement and of imposing the optimal penalties required for deterrence. Broad guidelines and greater precision in defining antitrust rules by public agencies may also provide business with clear signals as to what actions are permissible and may improve customer awareness of potential antitrust violations.

Notes

1. See, for example, the discussion in Breyer (1982, pp. 156–161).

2. Bork (1978, pp. 418–419) identifies additional trends in antitrust "away from political decision by democratic processes toward political choice by courts," greater concern "with group welfare rather than general welfare," and "movement away from the ideal of liberty and reward according to merit toward an ideal of equality of outcome and reward according to status."

3. See Thorelli (1955) and Letwin (1965).

4. Such an analysis is reminiscent of Stigler's (1971) analysis of the supply and demand for government regulation.

5. See Bork (1978, pp. 51–52).

6. See Bork (1978, pp. 73–79).

7. Bork (1978, p. 80) notes that if the court attempts "to arbitrate a price between the competitive and the monopolistic, it will find that there are no criteria whatever to guide its decision."

8. Ibid., p. 80.

9. See Liebeler (1981, pp. 67–68). He states further on p. 72 that "I am able to state without equivocation that the FTC lacks the theory, the data, and the incentive to conduct cost/benefit estimates of its industry wide cases." Liebeler also discusses the FTC approach to vertical relations between firms, which he finds to be based on "outmoded and erroneous concepts of the economics of vertical arrangements" (p. 90). He notes further that in a number of horizontal merger cases, productive efficiency gains have been cited as reasons to deny the merger (p. 95).

10. See Posner (1976a), Elzinga and Breit (1976), Breit and Elzinga (1985), Block and Sidak (1980), and Block, Nold, and Sidak (1981) on antitrust penalties.

11. See Breit and Elzinga (1985) and Easterbrook (1985) for appraisals of the treble-damage remedy.

12. It is assumed for convenience that the cartel serves the entire market. The problem is easily adapted to allow a competitive fringe with supply $S(p)$. Then, given the market demand $D(p)$, the cartel's derived demand is $Q(p) \equiv D(p) - S(p)$.

13. Block, Nold, and Sidak (1981) posit an exogenous probability of detection; see also Feinberg (1984). In the present model, the probability of detection depends on antitrust effort k and is therefore endogenous.

14. The antitrust authority is a Stackelberg leader and the cartel acts as a Cournot follower. This game is similar to the one given by Lee (1980a), who assumes that an antitrust agency acts as a leader and the cartel reacts to antitrust spending. There is no random detection in the model. The formulation of the present model also differs from Lee's in that output in his model is a direct function of antitrust enforcement expenditures and "cartel enforcement expenditures." Lee considers a Cournot-Nash type equilibrium and also mentions an earlier

version of his model in which the cartel moves first. The principal differences are that the analysis given here allows the cartel to choose its collusive output level, the antitrust authority has a general objective function, and detection is random.

15. Of course, prosecution costs can be mitigated by out-of-court settlement negotiation. The cost k is meant to suggest the high expected cost of antitrust trials.

16. The absence of a perfect equilibrium has been noted in related models of regulation—see Baron and Myerson (1982) and Baron and Besanko (1984a)—and in the tax compliance model of Reinganum and Wilde (1984).

17. Normally, welfare measures in such a model would take the fine as a pure transfer between firms and consumers. However, such a transfer may be part of the antitrust authority's objective function. The antitrust agency may view compensation paid to victims in subsequent private suits as a net social benefit. Even penalties that are not paid as compensation may appear to antitrust authorities as a benefit in terms of punishment of offenders. (In sections 19.2 and 19.3 the penalties are taken as a pure transfer.)

18. The policy of commitment to a probability of legal action is similar to an extensive literature on random audits. Recently, random audits have been studied in a setting with incomplete information in the income tax literature by Reinganum and Wilde (1984) and in regulation of firms with unknown costs by Baron and Besanko (1984a). In Baron and Besanko (1984a), the optimal audit policy to assure compliance with a regulatory scheme is to audit with probability zero if the firm reports a cost parameter below a threshold level and to audit with probability one otherwise. The optimality of a zero-one probability schedule in Baron and Besanko (1984a) is due to the price-subsidy schedule imposed on the firm that induces truthful reporting of costs. A general approach to costly state verification is given by Townsend (1979). The present model goes beyond tax audit models because here the firms take action by choosing prices and deciding whether or not to collude. In tax models, agents merely make an income report.

19. An equivalent presentation of the model can be given in which the probability of a suit depends on the cartel price, as was noted in the previous section.

20. See Besanko and Spulber (1986) for a discussion of the global properties of the schedule $\beta(q)$ that *implements* the equilibrium outcomes.

21. Observe that since

$$\pi(q_1^c, \theta_2) = \pi(q_1^c, \theta_1) - (\theta_2 - \theta_1)q_1^c = -(\theta_2 - \theta_1)q_1^c,$$

$\pi(q_1^c, \theta_2) - \beta_1^c A < 0$ for all $\beta_1^c \geq 0$.

22. From (19.2.1), it follows by standard arguments that

$$\pi(q_1, \theta_1) - \pi(q_1, \theta_2) \geq [(\pi(q_1, \theta_1) - \beta_1 A) - (\pi(q_2, \theta_2) - \beta_2 A)]$$

$$\geq \pi(q_2, \theta_1) - \pi(q_2, \theta_2).$$

So, $(\theta_2 - \theta_1)q_1 \geq (\theta_2 - \theta_1)q_2$, or $q_1 \geq q_2$. Thus, (19.3.7) implies (19.3.8). To prove that (19.3.8) implies (19.3.7) when (19.3.6) is binding, note that

$$[\pi(q_2, \theta_2) - \beta_2 A] - [\pi(q_1, \theta_2) - \beta_1 A] = [\pi(q_2, \theta_2) - \pi(q_1, \theta_2)] + [\pi(q_1, \theta_1) - \pi(q_2, \theta_1)]$$

$$= (\theta_2 - \theta_1)(q_1 - q_2) \geq 0.$$

23. Observe in addition that sufficient conditions for a unique interior maximum are satisfied. These conditions reduce to

$$P'(q_1) + ((1 - \gamma)/\gamma)(K/A)(P'(q_1) + P(q_1)q_1) < 0,$$

$$P'(q_2) - (K/A)(P'(q_2) + P(q_2)q_2) < 0.$$

24. Note that

$$\pi(\tilde{q}_2, \theta_2) - \beta_2 A = \pi(\tilde{q}_2, \theta_2) - [\pi(\tilde{q}_2, \theta_1) - \pi(\tilde{q}_1, \theta_1)]A^{-1}A$$

$$= \pi(\tilde{q}_1, \theta_1) - [\pi(\tilde{q}_2, \theta_1) - \pi(\tilde{q}_2, \theta_2)]$$

$$= \{[P(\tilde{q}_1) - \theta_1]\tilde{q}_1 - [\theta_2 - \theta_1]\tilde{q}_2\}.$$

25. Elzinga and Breit (1976, p. 70) identify damage awards to rivals as based on "loss of sales or profits owing to such anticompetitive exclusionary techniques as boycotts, foreclosures, tying arrangements, and the like."

26. See the important analysis of Baumol and Ordover (1985) on this issue. The Supreme Court in the 1986 decision *Cargill Inc.* v. *Monfort of Colorado* (No. 85-473) has restricted suits by competitors seeking to block proposed mergers.

27. Elzinga and Breit (1976, p. 70) identify three techniques of estimating damages imposed by the courts: the "before-and-after" method, the "yardstick" approach, and expert testimony. The "before-and-after" method uses the difference between prices before and after formation of the cartel. The "yardstick" approach employs the price paid by a customer comparable to that paid by the plaintiff. Finally, expert testimony may be used to assess financial damages. In each case, it is apparent that a comparison price level can be constructed.

28. See the cartel model analyzed in section 16.2.

29. Spiller (1986) analyzes the problem of when to file suit in a dynamic model with fixed repeat purchases. He finds that with limited liability, the consumer will postpone suing and continue to make purchases from the cartel until total damages (net of court costs) exactly equal the assets of the cartel. With a low probability of detection, consumers may postpone their suit indefinitely.

30. Suppose that the cartel were to choose output so as to increase damages above the liability constraint. Then the consumer would ignore the effect of his purchases on damages at the margin. The market price would be $p^m = P(q^m)$ and damages would equal $t(P(q^m) - \bar{p})q^m < A$. But this contradicts the previous statement that damages lie above liability.

31. Baker (1985) finds that the cartel chooses the monopoly output when $\alpha^f \neq \alpha^c$ for an assumption that corresponds to $\bar{p} = c$ in the present framework.

32. Block, Nold, and Sidak (1981) test their model on regional bread markets. Their empirical results confirm the assertion that DOJ enforcement efforts reduce markups. The present observation that private enforcement efforts have little effect on the market equilibrium output raises questions about the conclusions drawn from the Block, Nold, and Sidak (1981) analysis. Possible explanations for the observed effects of DOJ enforcement are that criminal, not civil, penalties are the deterrent and that consumers are imperfectly informed about enforcement efforts when consumption decisions are made.

33. See also Landes and Posner (1979b).

V CONCLUSION

20 Regulatory Policy

The preceding discussion has been primarily concerned with general models that are applicable to a wide range of industries and policy issues. To spell out the implications of the models for specific industries would require a detailed examination of the unique product characteristics, market demand patterns, and firm technology that distinguish each industry. Such a study is clearly desirable but lies beyond the scope of this book. One can, however, identify a number of policy conclusions that follow from the analysis. This will suggest a number of additional policy issues that call for future study.

Section 20.1 reviews the discussion of pricing under increasing returns to scale (chapters 3–9) and of rate regulation (chapters 10 and 11). The effects of natural monopoly and sunk cost in regulated industries are emphasized. This leads to a reexamination, in section 20.2, of the effects of bargaining on investment strategies when costs are nonrecoverable and transaction-specific. Section 20.3 looks at deregulation of prices and entry in industries where established firms have not yet fully amortized capital costs incurred under regulation. Section 20.4 examines the convergence of administrative regulation and antitrust. Antitrust policy has taken on traditional regulatory objectives and procedures, while some regulatory agencies are undertaking the promotion of competition.

20.1 Rate Regulation

Regulation of prices and entry is generally associated with a particular combination of two cost conditions. These are, first, significant *sunk costs*, which create barriers to entry, and second, significant *cost subadditivity*, which implies that the market is best served by a monopoly. These cost conditions are actually *market* conditions, since sunk costs must be significant relative to market rents and cost subadditivity must exist within the range of outputs for which average revenues exceed average costs. The existence of sunk costs suggests that competition or potential entry may not be effective in ensuring efficient pricing and product quality. Further, the risks associated with high sunk costs may result in underinvestment. Finally, high sunk costs imply that duplication of irreversible investment in production and distribution facilities may be undesirable. Price regulation may be needed to assure efficient pricing while providing adequate returns for investors. Further, entry restrictions may be required to avoid excessive investment in sunk costs. Subadditivity of costs suggests that entry should be restricted to obtain efficient production by a natural monopoly. This appears to imply the need for price regulation, since the beneficial effects of competition are restricted by regulation of entry. Such is the case for rate and entry regulation, with its apparently contradictory premises. This section examines the basis for regulation if one or the other cost condition does not apply. Sections 20.2 and 20.3 inquire further into the nature of sunk costs and their relation to rate and entry regulation.

Suppose that sunk costs are *minimal* but that costs are subadditive. This was the basic framework for chapters 3–9. A range of pricing options for policymakers was identified there, and the best means to achieve the associated social welfare goals were discussed. Let us briefly review the discussion.

Underlying subadditive costs, public inputs or "joint and common costs" are often found. This is true whether one is considering a single-product firm with economies of scale or a multiproduct firm with cost complementarities due to common inputs or fixed overhead. These types of common inputs are widespread in the utilities sector due to the high costs of transmission facilities, e.g., power lines, telephone lines, oil and natural gas pipelines, and associated transmission equipment. In addition, production facilities may have technologies that involve substantial fixed costs, such as electric generators. The key problem that has traditionally been emphasized is that with single-product or multiple-product economies of scale, prices equal to marginal cost will not yield revenues sufficient to cover the firm's costs. Without the possibility of achieving efficient pricing and maintaining a viable firm in the absence of government subsidies, a wide range of pricing options is available. Selection of these pricing options is a problem for policymakers.

The problem is how to set prices across customer classes and across products. One approach is to follow various *rules of thumb* that have long been in use by regulators in the transportation and utilities sector. These are *cost-based pricing* rules that assign joint and common costs across customer classes or across products on the basis of the proportion of total revenues, total output, or attributable costs that can be identified for each service or product. Other pricing rules that involve a two-part price, a quantity-dependent service charge and a capacity-dependent fixed charge, assign fixed costs to the two charges on the basis of arbitrary or customary proportions. Such pricing rules have little basis in terms of either economic analysis or specific policy objectives. Their only advantage seems to be administrative convenience and ease of computation. This suggests that such pricing rules should be abandoned where possible. If specific income transfers in the form of cross-subsidies are to be imbedded in pricing rules, then the policy objective should perhaps be stated explicitly.

A more appropriate policy objective might be to set prices that eliminate subsidies across product bundles. Such prices do not necessarily provide restrictive guidelines on the allocation of fixed costs. As shown in chapter 3, if attributable costs are properly allocated, almost any allocation of joint costs across products will yield subsidy-free prices. Subsidy-free prices for a product bundle yield revenues below the stand-alone costs of producing that product bundle. Thus, a significant advantage of subsidy-free prices is that they do not create incentives for any group of customers to cease purchasing from the regulated firm and transfer those purchases to another producer. The departure of customers is undesirable, given subadditive cost technology. The cost of common inputs must then be spread over a smaller customer base. Alternatively, the benefits of any existing cost complementarities will be reduced by the fall in demand. The reduction in demand may then result in higher prices for remaining customers, and may even entail loss of financial viability for the regulated firm. These issues are addressed further in section 20.3.

If policymakers have concluded that subsidy-free prices are desirable, and if one maintains the assumption that sunk costs are minimal, this suggests that rate and entry regulation are entirely *unnecessary*. This is the principal policy conclusion obtained from the contestable markets literature. If subsidies across product bundles are present, profit incentives for new entry at lower prices exist. Due to the threat of potential entry, a necessary condition for monopoly prices to be sustainable in a contestable market is for those prices to support the cost function. That is, prices must be subsidy-free across all product bundles smaller than the market-clearing output. Sufficient cost and demand conditions for the existence of sustainable prices were presented in chapter 4.

An important caveat to the benefits of contestability is the possibility that a contestable market equilibrium may not exist even if costs are subadditive. A solution to this problem is multiple price supply schedules. With more general price options, natural monopoly or cost subadditivity is sufficient to guarantee the existence of a sustainable monopoly equilibrium. The cost of this approach is abandonment of uniform prices and the likelihood of positive profits for the incumbent monopoly. There is an interesting policy trade-off here. To assure the cost benefits from subadditivity, at uniform prices with limited firm profits, regulation of prices and entry may be required. The cost benefits may also be achieved without regulation by allowing multiple price supply schedules and positive firm profits. Deregulation avoids the high public and private administrative costs of regulation while securing the many benefits of market competition. Thus, neither subsidy-free pricing nor achieving the benefits of natural monopoly production can provide any reasonable justification for regulation of prices or entry.

Subsidy-free prices may entail welfare costs, as they often rule out Ramsey prices. If the market demand of a customer class is highly inelastic relative to other customer classes, it may be that Ramsey prices are sufficiently increased for products purchased by that customer class so that they are not subsidy-free across all product bundles. Alternatively, Ramsey prices may not be sustainable at a market equilibrium, as noted by Sharkey (1981) and Spulber (1984c). Therefore, market equilibrium prices, while subsidy-free, may yield lower social welfare than under Ramsey pricing. If social welfare maximization is a policy objective, some form of policy intervention may be desirable to assure welfare optimal pricing.

Two points should be noted about welfare optimal pricing. Second-best Pareto optimal prices may be quite difficult to calculate. Such prices reflect social welfare weighting of individual consumer indirect utilities, in addition to calculation of consumer demand functions and the regulated firm's cost function. This significantly complicates the standard rules of thumb associated with Ramsey prices. Basing relative markups above marginal costs on the reciprocal of demand elasticities involves a number of heroic assumptions, including the assumptions that compensatory payments may be made, that consumer surplus is an accurate measure of indirect benefits (or that income effects are negligible), and that demands are independent across goods. Prices that maximize net consumer surplus need not be second-best Pareto optimal. This suggests that Pareto improvement over market pricing may not necessarily be achieved by the imposition of regulation due to the complexity of the pricing problem. The ever present administrative costs of regulation must thus be traded off against potential welfare improvements from second-best pricing policies.

The possibility of customers seeking alternative suppliers raises an additional issue associated with second-best Pareto optimal pricing. Chapter 6 introduced the notion of the second-best core. Prices in the second-best core are such that there is no group of consumers that can be made better off by prices that allocate the products and cover the stand-alone costs of production. Such prices are a possibly empty subset of the set of second-best Pareto optimal prices. Second-best core prices represent a restriction of the notion of subsidy-freeness. Prices in the second-best core are such that no group of customers subsidizes the purchases of another group. However, for a price to be subsidy-free across customer groups does not guarantee that it is a second-best optimal price. The importance of selecting prices in the second-best core is based on the entry problem discussed earlier. If a price is not in the second-best core, there exist profit incentives for a new supplier to enter the market and serve a group of customers at welfare-improving prices. Prices may be higher in some components, and lower in others, as compared with the prevailing prices. As noted previously, entry is not desirable since the benefits of subadditive costs are then reduced and production is organized inefficiently. Prices to those customers still served by the incumbent may increase to reflect the reduction in the customer base.

To achieve second-best pricing, particularly with the second-best core property, does not require imposition of price regulation. The franchise competition, described in chapter 9, demonstrates that in the absence of significant sunk costs, competition between firms can be used to obtain these prices. It was shown that regulatory intervention can be limited to the design of the franchise competition by defining service contract obligations, by specifying the pricing policy to be used, e.g., linear prices, and by designating the winner of the franchise. A natural monopoly may win the franchise if and only if it offers universal service at prices in the second-best core. Clearly, such a competition depends on relatively low costs of contracting and on the feasibility of recontracting. The benefits are the efficiency gains obtained from competition to serve the market and the elimination of the regulator's role in price setting.

The welfare gains that can be achieved from second-best pricing can be further enhanced by second-best price discrimination across customer classes and across product bundles through two-part and multipart pricing. These types of pricing policies further increase the information requirements and complexity of the task imposed on regulators. It is even less likely that multipart tariffs or nonlinear prices can be selected that approach theoretically optimal specifications. Nonetheless, in many cases, quantity discounts can be devised that yield Pareto improvements over linear price schedules. By establishing a franchise competition, and by allowing more general pricing policies, such as two-part pricing, regulators may achieve welfare improvements through market competition, without becoming directly involved in price setting. Thus, without the sunk cost problem, regulators may rely on a market mechanism for price setting.

It should be emphasized that the market conditions associated with sunk costs and natural monopoly need not be permanent. The natural monopoly characteristics of a regulated firm's technology may be eliminated through demand shifts or technological change. If the firm has a U-shaped average cost curve, the range of outputs over which costs are subadditive is bounded. Suppose that a significant rightward shift in market demand occurs. Cost minimization then requires that the market be served by two or more firms. Similarly, technological change may lower average cost as well as reducing the minimum efficient scale. Again, cost minimization may require that two or more firms serve the market. Regulators may respond to these market changes by allowing new entry. If competition is then feasible, deregulation of prices may be more desirable than an extension of regulation to new entrants.

The need to sink costs is also affected by demand and technological changes. Outward shifts in market demand may make the industry more "contestable" by making sunk costs a smaller proportion of total revenue. Technological change may reduce the need for irreversible capital investment. This is precisely the type of technological change that is occurring in telecommunications. Here is a brief illustration of the effects of technological change on sunk costs in this industry. A telephone system supplies transmission capacity, Q, using inputs of lines, L, and switches, S. For the purpose of this discussion, the technology may be represented by

$$Q = F(L, S),$$

where F is a neoclassical production function. The two inputs are fundamentally different in nature. Lines represent sunk costs in terms of the transmission lines themselves and the costs of installation and obtaining the right-of-way. Although switches involve capital investment, some types of switches are easily transferred to alternative customers or alternative locations. The private branch exchange (PBX), for example, represents zero sunk costs, since it is privately owned, and it is easily resold and transferred to other uses. Thus, PBX systems do not represent transaction-specific investments.

Two principal types of technological changes have occurred. First, there has been a significant reduction in the price of switches, which are operated by computers, relative to that of lines.[1] Thus, for any output level, the cost-minimizing input mix involves more switches and fewer lines; see Huber (1987). The cost of lines has remained relatively stable, so that the sunk cost associated with any given output level has fallen. The second form of technological change has been in terms of the increasing productivity of lines and switches. This implies an absolute fall in the number of lines and switches required to provide a given capacity level. A PBX allows a reduction in the number of lines connecting an enterprise with multiple internal telephones to a central office. The PBX switches all internal communication while allowing telephone users to share external lines. Fiber optic cables greatly increase the capacity of the transmission network. At the same time, two transmission technologies, microwave systems and satellite transmission systems, may replace lines altogether in specific applications. Both systems require initial investments by the transmission supplier. However, such investments are not transaction-specific. Customers can switch suppliers, so that competition is feasible. Firms and customers thus are not bound by transaction-specific sunk costs, as is the case with line-based systems. As with PBXs, microwave transmitters and satellite earth stations are privately owned and can be resold or transferred to alternative uses. An important by-product of the potential decrease in the importance of lines in transmission is mitigation of the bottleneck created by the established facilities of local telecommunications firms. Such facilities may no longer be essential, since there are alternative ways to "bypass" them. Intermodal competition from fiber optics, microwave systems, and satellite communication serves to reduce the need for rate regulation of the local telephone exchange monopoly.

If sunk costs become less significant due to growth in demand or due to technological change, changes in regulatory policy may be called for. The regulatory agency may no longer need to restrict entry if the problems associated with duplication of facilities and the risks of large-scale irreversible investment are no longer central, it may become desirable to lift entry restrictions. Competition from new entrants obviates the need for traditional forms of cost-based price regulation. Franchise competition and complete deregulation may be desirable alternatives. Competition from industries supplying substitute goods, such as intermodal competition in transportation, also eliminates the premise for cost-based price regulation. The regulatory agency may achieve its policy objectives by active promotion of competitive entry. The feasibility of such a policy is now evaluated.

20.2 Sunk Costs

Regulation of industries exhibiting sunk costs and natural monopoly has traditionally involved bargaining over the rate structure as well as bargaining over underlying estimates of operating costs, capital expenditures, rates of return, and market demand; see chapter 10. The regulatory process involves explicit attention to the investment decisions of regulated firms to determine whether costs are "prudently incurred" and whether capital equipment remains "used and useful." Rates are set to assure the regulated firm a compensatory rate of return on its rate base or capital stock. The regulatory contract is often justified as a means of mitigating the risks of making large irreversible investments that are faced by regulated utilities. Customers of utilities gain from such commitments, since efficient levels of investment yield lower costs of service. There is an incentive to honor commitments regarding compensatory rates of return to assure that regulated firms will undertake future investment and that they will maintain their existing capital equipment. In practice, honoring commitments to investors in regulated utilities keeps down future borrowing costs by reducing investor risk.

Perhaps the most important aspect of the regulatory bargain is the ability of regulators, customers, and the regulated firm to make commitments both to pricing policies and to irreversible investments. A serious problem in long-term contractual relations is the possibility that either party will take advantage of the other party's contract-specific investments. After irreversible investments have been made by a party to a contract, the costs of such investments are said to be nonrecoverable, or *sunk*. Future decisions cannot be based on these costs, since future actions cannot mitigate past expenditures. To suppose otherwise is to succumb to the "fallacy of sunk costs." Thus, the party that has not made irreversible commitments has an incentive to call for renegotiation of contractual agreements made before sunk costs were incurred. In anticipation of the possible effects of contract renegotiation, the parties to a contract may have an incentive to select inefficient levels of investment.

If contractual commitments are not binding, the contract will not guarantee a return on irreversible investment. It is equivalent to observe that the contract is effectively not based on irreversible actions undertaken by the parties in the contract formation stage. This is precisely the sense in which the actions of an agent are "unobservable" in the principal-agent literature. Thus, the investment decisions made by parties to a nonbinding contract are subject to classic *moral hazard* effects.

The problem of strategic contract renegotiation is widely recognized in regulatory policy debates; see Peacock and Rowley (1972), Schmalensee (1979a), Joskow (1985b, 1987), and Joskow and Schmalensee (1986). The possibility of "reneging" on promises associated with franchise contracts is emphasized by Williamson (1976). Williamson (1976, p. 91) views regulation as a "highly incomplete form of long-term contracting" that assures the supplier a fair rate of return with "adaptation to changing circumstances." Williamson observes the advantages possessed by cable television (CATV) operators in contract renegotiation.

CATV operators are able to "buy in" by low bids and then take advantage of the regulator's sunk costs that are incurred in selecting a firm for the franchise award. Williamson identifies such behavior as *opportunism*, "self-interest seeking with guile" (1985, p. 47). Zupan (1987a,b) conducts empirical work that confirms the significant advantages of incumbency in contract renewal. However, his findings dispute the assertion that CATV operators are able to extract rents from renegotiation. Rather, it is the cities that award franchises that are able to take monopolistic advantage of the investment commitments of the cable operators.

The general problem of "holdup" in contracts has been discussed by Klein, Crawford, and Alchian (1978).[2] Shavell (1980a) examines contract-specific investment under alternative breach of contract remedies. In contract law, such investment is referred to as *reliance*. Rogerson (1984), in a similar setting, emphasizes the possibility that contract renegotiation may reduce incentives for breach. The analysis of Shavell (1980a) and Rogerson (1984) identifies moral hazard as the source of nonoptimal reliance investment. Spulber (1986c) extends the contracts model to allow for interdependent contracts with multiple buyers or sellers. This corresponds to the case of a firm with multiple-input suppliers or subcontractors. Government procurement often involves multiple sources. Ex post competition for sellers mitigates the appropriability of rents from contract renegotiation. This serves to increase the benefits of the buyer's investment made in anticipation of contract performance. Ex post competition thus enforces contract performance. By allowing the buyer to earn a return on fixed investment, competition creates incentives for efficient investment that improves the net benefits available under the contract; see Spulber (1986c).

The effect of commitment on investment has been studied by Grout (1984) and Hart and Holmström (1986). Suppose that the firm will supply one unit of output with production costs, $c(k)$, being a function of initial capital investment, k. Let c be a decreasing, twice-differentiable, convex, and bounded function of k. The buyer's value of the good is given by $v > 0$. Suppose that investment k is irreversible and contract-specific. Then, once costs k have been sunk, but before production costs $c(k)$ have been incurred, the contract price must cover the firm's costs without exceeding the buyer's reservation value,

$$v \geq p \geq c(k).$$

Suppose, following Grout (1984), that renegotiation allocates rents ex post according to the Nash bargaining solution. Then the price equals

$$p^* = (v + c(k))/2. \tag{20.2.1}$$

This corresponds to the discussion of negotiation of rates in chapter 10. The firm maximizes profits, given by

$$\pi(k) = -k + p - c(k) = -k + v/2 - c(k)/2, \tag{20.2.2}$$

where k represents investment costs in future value terms. Profit maximization yields an investment k such that

$$-c'(\overline{k}) = 2. \tag{20.2.3}$$

This is the *moral hazard* effect since underinvestment occurs, $\overline{k} < k^*$, where k^* is the cost-minimizing investment level, $-c'(k^*) = 1$. Both parties are worse off, since the total rents from exchange are reduced by under-investment.

If the regulator and the firm were able to commit to a fixed price contract, the firm would ignore the effects of its investment on the price and capital investment would be at the optimal, cost-minimizing level, k^*.

Suppose that the regulator and firm are able to commit to a *rate of return* on capital, $s > 1$. What will be the resulting price and investment level? Given investment k, the price must be such that the rate of return constraint is satisfied,

$$(p - c(k))/k \leq s,$$

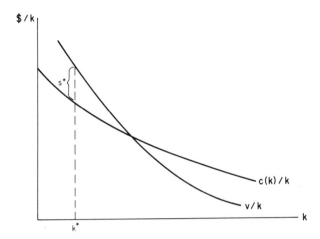

Figure 20.2.1
The optimal investment k^* and corresponding rate of return s^*.

and price does not exceed the market reservation price, $p \leq v$. If $(v - c(k))/k \leq s$, the price will be raised by the seller to its maximum level v. Otherwise, $p = c(k) + sk$. Suppose that $(v - c(k))/k > s$; then the firm's ex ante profit is

$$\pi(k) = -k + p - c(k) = k(s - 1).$$

The firm has incentive to raise investment k as high as possible without violating the rate-of-return constraint. Raising k lowers the rate of return $(p - c(k))/k$ for any given p; see figure 20.2.1. Thus, k will be increased at least until $(v - c(k))/k \leq s$. So, the price will equal the market reservation level and the regulated firm obtains monopoly rents, given any level of investment k.

The effect of rate-of-return regulation on investment depends on the size of the permitted rate-of-return. Let $s^* = (v - c(k^*))/k^*$ be the rate-of-return at the optimal investment level. Then suppose $s > s^*$. The firm will increase its investment to the efficient level k^* that maximizes rents from exchange. The rate-of-return constraint will not be binding. Suppose that $s < s^*$. Then the regulated firm will be required to choose an investment level, $\tilde{k}$, above the efficient level to satisfy the rate-of-return constraint,[3] where $\tilde{k}$ solves $(v - c(\tilde{k}))/\tilde{k} = s$. This is a variant of the standard Averch-Johnson effect.[4] To summarize the discussion:

PROPOSITION 20.2.1   *If the regulator and firm commit to a rate-of-return*
s > 1, the firm will choose an efficient investment level, $\tilde{k} = k^*$, if the rate-
of-return constraint is nonbinding, $s \geq s^*$. If the rate-of-return constraint is
binding, $s < s^*$, the firm will overinvest, $\tilde{k} > k^*$.

The excess investment result is eliminated if there is ex post bargaining
over the rate-of-return s. The rate-of-return constraint implies that the
price equals $p = c(k) + sk$. The Nash bargaining solution yields an allowable rate-of-return equal to half of the market rents per unit of capital
$s = (v - c(k))/2k$. Thus, ex ante profits are

$$\pi(k) = -k + p - c(k) = k(s - 1) = -k + (v - c(k))/2.$$

The firm will underinvest by choosing $\overline{k}$ as before.

Thus, absence of commitment leads to underinvestment, while precommitment to a binding rate-of-return leads to overinvestment. One
common solution to the inefficiency of investment is direct bargaining over
investment levels before investment is undertaken, particularly for major
projects, such as new power plants. This mitigates the investment problem
to the extent that binding commitments on future compensation may be
made. Selection of efficient investment levels is complicated by asymmetric
information about the costs of the regulated firm and future market demand.
Regulated firms may have incentive to overstate both the cost of new
investment and the saving in operating costs such new investment will
generate. The information rents earned by regulated firms may distort
estimates of marginal cost; see chapter 11. Information rents have the
additional effect of increasing the expected returns to capital investment.
Information rents, while not necessarily eliminating underinvestment, serve
to increase investment relative to the full information case, when binding
commitments to future prices are not feasible. This will not generally
alleviate the underinvestment problem; see Tirole (1986). Under asymmetric information, direct supervision of investment and other aspects of
contractual performance are not sufficient to avoid inefficient outcomes
completely.

Concern has been expressed that renegotiation on the part of regulators
can yield monopoly rents for customers and discourage investment by
regulated firms. At the same time, there is a concern that regulated firms
may extract monopoly rents from the market in which they are the sole
owners of specific production and distribution facilities. Are there ways in

which regulators can avoid exclusive dependence on price regulation after sunk costs have been incurred? Joskow and Schmalensee (1983, pp. 20–21) observe that competition is feasible even in the presence of large sunk costs in electric power generation and distribution. They point out that large industrial customers may relocate in different service areas and that customers at the fringe of service areas can switch suppliers. The immobility of utility facilities may thus be alleviated by customer mobility.[5]

It may not be necessary to regulate prices at all in an industry with large sunk costs if the industry faces competition from another industry that is contestable. Bailey and Baumol (1984) observe that the 1976 Railroad Revitalization and Reform Act and the 1980 Staggers Rail Act deregulated pricing in areas with effective competition from other carriers or other modes of transportation, particularly trucks. The issue of deregulation and competition is taken up in the next section.

Another approach to reducing the monopoly rents earned on existing facilities is to require "equal access." This issue arises in a wide variety of industries but generally occurs where transportation or transmission systems are involved. Thus, a rival railroad wishes to obtain "trackage rights" to another railroad's track. Natural gas or oil producers and customers request "contract carriage" over a natural gas or oil pipeline. In electricity, utilities and customers negotiate over access to transmission facilities and services, known as "wheeling." In telecommunications, customers and long-distance companies seek access to the transmission network of the local exchange carrier. Access to the distribution network may increase upstream competition among suppliers. However, the problem of pricing access to transmission facilities is not addressed by requirements that service be supplied without discrimination. The price of access will be sufficient to ration the use of the facilities. If no other transmission facilities are available, the owner of the facility may extract monopoly rents. Users of the system will complain that the transmission network is an "essential facility" or "bottleneck" and will seek rate regulation. If rate regulation is imposed, rates must be set to compensate the owner of the transmission network to encourage maintenance and to provide incentives for future investment.[6] If rates are set in such a way that the owner of the transmission network covers operating expenses, including the opportunity costs of using network capacity, and is able to recover capital costs, it will then be unnecessary to mandate equal access.

Sunk costs are not sufficient in themselves to require price and entry regulation. Large sunk costs are present in many competitive markets. Significant sunk costs are incurred by firms in capital intensive industries (automobiles, steel) and R&D intensive industries (chemicals, computers). Although sunk costs per firm are large, multiple firms serve the market and competitive entry and exit occurs. Most economists would concur that market performance appears to approximate the competitive ideal in terms of innovation, product variety, and prices approaching marginal cost. So, sunk costs need not preclude or prevent competition, even though they are identified as a barrier to entry. Sunk costs need not entail long-term contractual arrangements, as evidenced by the market examples given above. Thus, sunk costs, without natural monopoly, cannot justify regulation, although their absence should indicate that rate regulation is superfluous.

This suggests that sunk costs in themselves may be neither a barrier to entry nor a prerequisite for regulation. Particular attributes of the technology associated with sunk costs may be the source of the problem. Distribution systems based on transmission lines or pipelines involve transaction-specific investments that are both irreversible and costly to duplicate. These investments link a particular supplier to a particular customer. It is the symmetric tie that binds that creates bottlenecks and confers monopoly power on the supplier. At the same time, the irreversible investment confers monopoly power on the customer who has incentive to take advantage of the supplier's capital commitment. Regulation of prices and entry attempts to protect the interests of both parties by reducing the customer's opportunities for contract renegotiation and the supplier's opportunities for monopoly pricing. Reliance on administrative agencies for this type of intermediation must stem from the perception that private bargaining cannot address the contractual issues.

This leads to the conclusion that *internalities*, rather than sunk costs, form the basis for rate and entry regulation. Large transaction costs may complicate private negotiation associated with the establishment of an extensive transmission network. The high cost of writing complete contingent contracts may make private contracting impractical. The presence of risk associated with fluctuating demand, varying input prices, and technological change may not permit irreversible investment in the absence of contractual assurances of future revenue. Significant moral hazard problems may be associated with monitoring contractual performance in the absence of market competition. Furthermore, moral hazard problems will lead to excessive or insufficient transaction-specific investments when such investments cannot be observed or explicitly incorporated in contract terms. Asymmetric information about consumer demand or firm costs may cause private bargaining to yield inefficient output levels or cause negotiations to break off completely even if there are potential gains from trade. Therefore, it should not be surprising if costly contract contingencies, moral hazard, and asymmetric information are a feature of administrative regulation. It is perhaps the presence of internalities in private bargaining, associated with transaction-specific sunk costs, that has led to the imposition of regulation in that market.

20.3 Deregulation and Entry

As has been noted, rate regulation is associated with the conjunction of *sunk costs* and *cost subadditivity*. If demand shifts and technological changes reduce the significance of sunk costs, deregulation of prices and entry is generally desirable, at least in the long run. This section addresses the issue of bypass of established production and transmission facilities. It considers whether policymakers should fully deregulate the industry or allow a transition period with partially controlled entry.

If regulators decide to allow price competition and entry into a previously regulated industry, there is often a difficult intermediate period during which established firms have not recovered their capital costs. Investments may have been made contingent on particular regulatory commitments and may not be fully amortized. In such instances, regulated firms will often ask for a continuation of regulation, particularly in the form of protection from new entry. Regulated firms may claim they are at a disadvantage vis-à-vis potential entrants, since they must recover past capital expenditures. This is a problem not faced by entrants who have the flexibility to tailor investments so as to target specific customers. Furthermore, entrants may take advantage of technological change embodied in new capital equipment.

At the same time, entrants may complain that they are at a disadvantage, since the incumbent has the benefit of an established capital stock and R&D experience accumulated over a long regulated period. Entrants may claim that the incumbent has benefited from its earnings during the regulated period to acquire a competitive advantage. Further, entrants may wish to achieve access to the incumbent's production and distribution facilities without having to incur sunk costs themselves. Entrants may request a continuation of regulation to remove the incumbent's competitive advantages, and to create a "level playing field," effectively providing regulatory protection for new entrants.

To address these deregulation issues, it is important to examine the effect of new entry or bypass on industry costs. The desirability of entry is assessed in terms of cost minimization, given that the incumbent has acquired a significant but nonrecoverable capital stock. Then an attempt is made to determine whether the incumbent is able to recover sunk costs if entry restrictions are lifted.

Consider a formal representation of sunk capital costs in a simple dynamic setting without uncertainty. Capital may be inflexible due to adjustment costs or irreversibility. Let (q, k, l) represent the firm's output, capital, and labor, respectively. Production technology is given by $q = F(k, l)$. The firm faces internal costs of capital adjustment, $I(k - k_0)$, where k_0 denotes the firm's initial capital stock, $I(0) = 0$. Investment is said to be *irreversible*, given that it does not depreciate, if the constraint $k \geq k_0$ is imposed. The following discussion can be generalized to incorporate capital depreciation. Let r represent the cost of capital and let w be the wage rate. One may define operating and investment costs, exclusive of sunk costs, as follows:

$$C(q, k_0) = \min_{k,l} [r(k - k_0) + wl + I(k - k_0)] \tag{20.3.1}$$

subject to $F(k, l) - q \geq 0$, $k - k_0 \geq 0$, and $l \geq 0$. Sunk costs equal rk_0. Note that $C(0, k_0) = 0$. Becker and Spulber (1984) derive several useful properties of the cost function $C(q, k_0)$.[7] Let $k^* = k(q)$ and $l^* = l(q)$ solve (20.3.1). Then

$$C_k(q, k_0) = \begin{cases} -I'(k^* - k_0) - r, & k_0 \leq k^* \\ -wF_1(k^*, l^*)/F_2(k^*, l^*), & k_0 \geq k^* \end{cases} \tag{20.3.2}$$

The function $k(q)$ is increasing in q and $-C_k(q, k_0) \lesseqgtr r$ as $k_0 \gtreqless k(q)$, where $-C_k(q, k^*) = r$. Further, $C_q > 0$, $C_{qq} > 0$, $C_{kk} > 0$, and $C_{qk} = C_{kq} < 0$. Note that $q(k) = k^{-1}(k)$ is the long-run minimum efficient scale.

The first issue to be addressed is whether new entry is desirable if the entrant has the same technology as the incumbent. The entrant has the advantage of avoiding adjustment costs as well as irreversibility of investment. The entrant is able to adjust optimally the capital stock, given the desired output level, $k^* = k(q)$. Entry lowers costs only if the total costs of entry are less than the incumbent's operating costs,

$$C(q, k_0) > C(q, k^*(q)) + rk^*(q). \tag{20.3.3}$$

There are two cases. Suppose that the optimal capital stock for output q exceeds the installed base, $k^* \geq k_0$. Then, using (20.3.2), (20.3.3), and $C_{kk} > 0$, entry will lower costs only if

$$[r + I'(k^* - k_0)](k^* - k_0) > rk^*. \tag{20.3.4}$$

This condition states that the marginal cost of investment times new investment for the incumbent must exceed the total investment costs for the new entrant. This requires that the marginal adjustment costs of investment times investment, $I'(k^* - k_0)(k^* - k_0)$, exceed the entire replacement cost of installed base, rk_0. Such a situation is unlikely, since internal costs of adjustment are likely to be small in comparison to the large value of installed base.

The other case is if a lower capital base is optimal, $k^* < k_0$. Then, by the mean value theorem, (20.3.3) is equivalent to

$$C_k(q, z)k_0 > (C_k(q, z) + r)k^* > 0,$$

for some z such that $k^* \leq z \leq k_0$. But, since $C_k(q, k) < 0$, this yields a contradiction. Thus, even though a smaller utility may be desirable, perhaps due to shrinking demand, it is generally not desirable to replace existing capital by an entirely new facility.

Should entry be permitted to take place if only a *portion* of total output is shifted to the entrant? The cost test in (20.3.3) is extended in a straightforward way. *De novo* entry reduces total production costs if and only if

$$C(q' + q'', k_0) > C(q', k_0) + C(q'', k^*) + rk^*, \tag{20.3.5}$$

where $k^* = k(q'')$. Subtracting $C(q'', k_0)$, from both sides,

$$[C(q' + q'', k_0) - C(q', k_0) - C(q'', k_0)]$$
$$> -[C(q'', k_0) - C(q'', k^*) - rk^*]. \tag{20.3.6}$$

The term on the left-hand side of (20.3.6) is the standard test for subadditivity, while the term on the right-hand side is just the test for new investment discussed previously. If only a portion of output is to be supplied by the new entrant, it is reasonable to expect that the entrant's capital investment will be less than installed base, $k^* < k_0$, so that the test for cost reducing entry requires more than subadditivity. The difference between total cost $C(q' + q'', k_0)$ and the sum of stand-alone costs must exceed the net costs of new investment, $[rk^* + C(q'',k^*) - C(q'',k_0)]$. One may conclude that even partial replacement of an incumbent regulated firm with significant installed capital base requires a more stringent test than natural monopoly.

Suppose that the entrant also has an installed capital base. Let k^A and k^B denote the capital stock for incumbent and entrant, respectively. Then transferring output q' from the incumbent to the entrant, assuming that $q + q'$ and q'' are their respective initial outputs, reduces costs if and only if

$$C(q + q', k_0^A) + C(q'', k_0^B) > C(q, k_0^A) + C(q' + q'', k_0^B). \qquad (20.3.7)$$

This requires incremental costs for the incumbent to exceed incremental costs for the entrant,

$$IC(q'; q, k_0^A) > IC(q'; q'', k_0^B), \qquad (20.3.8)$$

where $IC(q'; q, k) \equiv C(q + q', k) - C(q, k)$. Suppose that each firm's installed capital is appropriate for its initial output, i.e., $k_0^A = k(q + q')$ and $k_0^B = k(q'')$. Further, suppose that the incumbent's initial output is larger than that of the entrant, $q + q' \geq q''$, so that $k_0^A \geq k_0^B$. Subtract $IC(q'; q'', k_0^A)$ from both sides of (20.3.8). By the mean value theorem, the cost test for entry requires

$$IC(q'; q, k_0^A) - IC(q'; q'', k_0^A) > [-\partial IC(q'; q'', k)/\partial k](k_0^A - k_0^B), \qquad (20.3.9)$$

for some k such that $k_0^B \leq k \leq k_0^A$. Note that $\partial IC/\partial k < 0$, since output and capital are cost complements, $C_{kq} < 0$. Thus, at the initial capital stock, the incremental costs of producing q' with an initial output of q must *exceed* the incremental costs of q' with an initial output of q''. If $q'' \geq q$, the cost test is not satisfied, since marginal costs are increasing and $IC(q'; q, k_0^A) \leq IC(q'; q'', k_0^A)$. The test requires that the entrant's initial output q'' be strictly less than the incumbent's postentry output q. This implies that the incumbent will be required to make a substantial capital outlay to accommodate the increase in output.[8] This test is thus more stringent than a marginal cost test.

Finally, if the entrant has a different, presumably superior, technology, the cost test requires incremental cost to be reduced, $IC^A(q'; q, k_0^A) > IC^B(q'; q'', k_0^B)$. The efficiency gains from new technology must outweigh the additional capital outlays required for new entry.

The preceding discussion has established a number of cost tests to determine the desirability of unrestricted entry when an existing capital stock remains productive. This analysis raises the question of whether entry restrictions are needed. It has been noted, following Stigler, that the need to sink costs can be a barrier to new entry and that costs already sunk provide a competitive advantage to the incumbent. The various cost tests presented here confirm that this is indeed so. An incumbent may deter entry even of a more efficient entrant if the entrant cannot cover both production costs and the costs of entry. On the other hand, an entrant that has sufficiently low operating costs may effectively challenge an incumbent by committing capital resources to the market and driving out the incumbent. Such entry and exit decisions occur frequently in competitive markets, and deregulated industries need not behave differently.

Proceed under the assumption that the incumbent has a cost advantage over entrants due to its existing capital. By amortizing this capital, the incumbent is able to price competitively. This would seem to suggest that complete deregulation of entry is desirable and that entry will only take place if entrants increase productive efficiency. There are, however, several conditions under which one may observe inefficient entry. The main problem stems from the existing rate structure of the regulated firm. If the rate structure involves *cross-subsidies*, then profit incentives exist for entry into those submarkets or goods providing the cross-subsidy. This type of "cream-skimming" entry may occur even if it is inefficient in terms of total production costs. Thus, the incumbent may have sufficient cost complementarities such that it is the least-cost producer for those submarkets. Further, the entrant's capital investment may duplicate existing facilities. Regulatory policymakers then must determine whether they wish to protect the existing rate structure. The presence of cross-subsidies may reflect income redistribution policies pursued by regulators. In that case, efficiency considerations would suggest removal of rate regulation rather than the continuation of entry regulation. There will, of course, be distributional consequences for those customers who experience rate increases. It is important to recall that cross-subsidies may reflect Ramsey pricing. In this case, flexible rate regulation that allows the incumbent to compete with new entrants may result in prices that are Pareto inferior to existing rates.

Another way in which inefficient entry may occur is if the incumbent is unable to make binding contractual commitments, since its decisions are subject to regulatory approval. An entrant who is not subject to such regulation may be able to attract customers through supply agreements that promise reduced risk in terms of future prices or quality of service.

Again, an objection may be raised that such inefficient entry could not occur if the incumbent were able to compete without regulatory constraints. It should be noted in response that the constraints placed on the incumbent may be due to alternative regulatory goals, e.g., universal service, or to existing institutional restrictions on the regulator's actions. Given these restrictions, it may be desirable to regulate entry during a transition period until constraints on the incumbent's ability to compete may be removed. During the transition period, the regulators, rather than the competitive market, must determine whether the additional entrant will lower total operating costs and whether additional capital expenditures are desirable. The fact that an entrant wishes to invest need not in itself reflect the efficiency of the investment but rather restrictions on the incumbent's ability to compete.

One objection to open entry is raised by those who feel that a regulatory bargain or social contract was involved when the irreversible investments were incurred. It is emphasized that an "overhang" of sunk costs creates the need for a regulatory transition period to address equity considerations associated with the preceding regulated regime.[9] Egan and Weisman (1986) propose an *exit tax* for customers (toll service carriers or industrial customers) seeking to bypass the established local telecommunications network. They characterize the local network as a public good and suggest that customers who bypass the system should pay compensation for the sunk cost "burden" shifted to users remaining on the system. This policy falls victim to the sunk costs fallacy by its emphasis on the burdens of irreversible investment. Consider the implications of the proposed exit or bypass tax. The exit tax would be set equal to the total costs of the local network *after* bypass minus the attributed costs of serving all other users *before* bypass. Thus, the Egan and Weisman tax depends not only on costs but on the *rate structure* before bypass. Suppose that there are two groups of users, purchasing output vectors q^1 and q^2, respectively. Suppose that user group 2 seeks to bypass the local network. The *rate structure* R^1, R^2 is assumed to cover total costs (here including costs of capital),

$$R^1 + R^2 = C(q^1 + q^2).$$ (20.3.10)

The exit tax to user group 2, T, is calculated as follows:

$$T \equiv C(q^1) - R^1.$$ (20.3.11)

Suppose for purposes of illustration that the bypass technology is equally efficient. Then bypass will occur if and only if user group 2's stand-alone costs plus the exit tax are less than revenues,

$$C(q^2) + T < R^2. \tag{20.3.12}$$

But, substituting for the tax and revenue, (20.3.12) is simply $C(q^1) + C(q^2) < C(q^1 + q^2)$. This is just the reverse of the standard test for natural monopoly. Thus, bypass will occur if and only if the local network is not a natural monopoly. This is a reasonable cost test, except that capital costs of the established firm are included. However, the exit tax involves more than a cost efficiency requirement.

The exit tax can be restated in terms of attributed costs to user group 2 minus the incremental costs of serving user group 2, $T = R^2 - IC^2$, where $IC^2 \equiv C(q^1 + q^2) - C(q^1)$. Thus, the exit tax is positive if and only if the costs attributed to the bypassing customer exceed incremental costs. If user group 2 is paying a subsidy, which is at least equal to the excess of attributed costs over incremental costs, $S = R^2 - C(q^2)$, the tax is then

$$T = S + [C(q^1) + C(q^2) - C(q^1 + q^2)], \tag{20.3.13}$$

where the term in square brackets equals the gains from joint production. Thus, the exit tax requires the potential bypasses to pay the cross-subsidy plus all economies of joint production. This clearly perpetuates cross-subsidies, since the bypasser must remain on the system even if he is paying a cross-subsidy. Furthermore, if regulators must rely on the local network firm for cost estimates, these can be strategically manipulated to understate the incremental costs of serving the potential bypasser. This narrows the difference between attributed costs (possibly overstated as well) and the exit tax, further reducing the net returns to bypass. These considerations make the exit tax an undesirable policy instrument.

Regulating entry for the purpose of maintaining existing cross-subsidies is generally not a desirable policy. The misallocation of resources that price distortions entail has been widely noted. Further, entry should not be blocked simply for the purpose of covering sunk investment that has not yet been fully amortized. If demand growth and technological change have reduced the need to sink costs or have created competitive options, then entry restrictions should be lifted. The cost tests for entry proposed here are applicable under a specific set of circumstances. If the regulatory authority perceives a need for the continued viability of the regulated industry, but that industry is unable to compete effectively due to institutional or government restrictions, unrestricted entry may not improve market efficiency. Such a situation may easily arise when there are jurisdictional conflicts among regulatory agencies. These are noted in the next section. The benefits of entry, including survival of low-cost producers and efficient pricing, may not be achieved if the incumbent must satisfy regulations not imposed on entrants. Costly duplication of capital facilities may occur. Loss of economies of scope may create welfare losses for the remaining customers served by the incumbent firm. Thus, deregulation does not merely require competitive opportunities for entrants; it also requires an equal lifting of restrictions placed on established firms.

20.4   Regulation Meets Antitrust

Regulation and antitrust represent alternative responses to perceived market failure. Regulation refers to general rules and specific actions imposed by administrative agencies on consumers, firms, and the market allocation mechanism. These regulatory actions are the product of an administrative process involving bargaining between market participants and indirect interaction through legislative, executive, and judicial intervention. Regulation often has the effect of restricting competition. By contrast, antitrust is generally viewed as action by the antitrust agencies and the courts to promote competition through enforcement of antitrust law. A disturbing trend may be observed in which these traditional roles are being reversed. Without speculating on the causes or future consequences of such a trend, the previous discussion of regulation and antitrust policy is reviewed briefly in this context. I conclude with some general observations on the purpose of government intervention in markets.

In deregulating prices and entry in some industries, notably transportation and telecommunication, regulators have become actively involved in the promotion of competition. This raises concern that regulators will attempt to influence the nature and direction of competition by interfering in the allocation mechanism. Actions may be taken to achieve policy goals with respect to market structure, innovation, and product quality and variety in the name of increased competition. By "leveling the playing field" in the name of deregulation, regulators may engage in a form of industrial policy, picking anticipated "winners" and protecting new entrants. The resulting industry may be less efficient not only in comparison to an industry with unrestricted entry but even in comparison to the previously regulated industry.

Part of the problem stems from the transition period discussed in the preceding section. There is a danger that a regulatory agency may impose still more regulations on the industry during the transition period before deregulation. Regulators may be tempted to spell out detailed conditions under which previously regulated firms can enter new markets. By reviewing applications for entry during the transition period, regulators may create additional rules and precedents that will play a significant role in determining future industry structure. Indeed, the "transition period" may be extended indefinitely as regulators attempt to plan the course of competition in the newly deregulated industry.

Perhaps coincidentally, antitrust enforcement has become involved in the complex oversight of industry conduct. The present discussion has already observed how the antitrust enforcement agencies have acquired many of the characteristics and procedures of other administrative regulatory agencies, including broad rule-making powers and increased enforcement authority (see chapter 16). In addition, it found that formulation of antitrust policy in the presence of barriers to entry, externalities, and internalities may take the form of traditional regulatory policies. For example, proposed tests for predatory pricing were considered, and their similarity with cost-based or rate-of-return forms of rate regulation were demonstrated. Sullivan (1983, pp. 632–633) argues that antitrust "is not merely regulation" because "antitrust is law and not free-form policy." However, he recognizes that the 1982 Merger Guidelines "suggest the terms of debate for future merger cases" and in so doing change "the options of all who deal with antitrust" (p. 643).

The discussion in the present work noted the existence of market regulations, information gathering, and direct enforcement, particularly in FTC regulation of unfair practices. In the overview of optimal enforcement models in chapter 19, it was shown that optimal antitrust policies against price fixing yield Ramsey type pricing rules. Antitrust policy under asymmetric information may have many of the characteristics of principal-agent type models of rate regulation under asymmetric information. Through strategic case selection and enforcement efforts, antitrust agencies not only create antitrust policy but impose additional rules and guidelines on the behavior of market participants.

The courts have also become involved in administrative regulation. Consider the illustrative example of telecommunications. The Department of Justice brought action against AT&T both in 1956 and 1974 under the Sherman Act. The 1956 case involved monopolization of the telephone equipment market by AT&T's manufacturing division, Western Electric. The case was settled by a negotiated consent decree. The second case, which went to trial in 1981, alleged monopolization of telephone equipment as well as long-distance service. The case resulted in a revised version of the 1956 consent decree known as the "Modified Final Judgment" (MFJ). The principal effect was divestiture by AT&T of its local Bell Operating Companies (BOCs), effective in 1984. The BOCs were required to provide "equal access" to the local network to all long-distance carriers, while they were restricted in their direct participation in other "lines of business," particularly long distance, equipment manufacturing, and information services.

The Federal District Court (District of Columbia), hereafter referred to as the Court, received extensive written and oral public comments on the notice of the proposed settlement.[10] The Court's opinion was issued following the Antitrust Procedures and Penalties Act. The DOJ published notice of the proposed settlement and a "Competitive Impact Statement" in the *Federal Register*.[11] The Court applied a "public interest standard" in its decision to restrict *temporarily* rather than permanently the entry of BOCs into other lines of business. It recognized that future technological change would eliminate the BOCs' "ability to leverage their monopoly power into competitive markets."[12] The principal point to be made is that the MFJ established a complex regulatory apparatus both in the implementation of the consent decree and in the review process for BOC entry into other lines of business. This effectively placed the Court and the DOJ in the regulation business. At the same time, the Federal Communications Commission, the traditional regulator of the industry, began to play a greater role in the promotion of competition, a traditional antitrust objective.[13]

The AT&T divestiture and organization of the seven regional BOCs involved extensive communication between the DOJ, the Court, and AT&T in a manner suggestive of bargaining between administrative agencies and regulated firms. The extensive public commentary involved appears very similar in nature to public comments in response to a notice of proposed rule making or adjudication for regulatory agencies. The bargaining and information-gathering aspects common to regulatory hearings are certainly present in implementation of the consent decree.

The consent decree established equal access procedures. The DOJ monitored the technological aspects of assuring equal access and the rate at which the BOCs met the established schedule and reported back to the Court.[14] The DOJ and the Court were thus in the position of creating and enforcing *common carrier* regulations placed on BOCs. The DOJ and Court oversaw case-by-case bargaining between the BOCs and their customers (notably MCI) over the technological conversions of switching equipment required for equal access. This is again similar to regulatory intervention in market decisions regarding technology and contractual agreements.

At the same time, an administrative agency, the FCC, has been involved in the equal access process. The FCC has actively promoted entry of long-distance competitors to AT&T through consumer balloting; see the discussion in chapter 9. Further, the FCC extended equal access to certain other non-BOC local exchange carriers.[15] Here, the FCC has assisted in the transformation of long distance into a competitive market. While it has continued to intervene in rate setting, the FCC has actively pursued deregulation and the promotion of entry. In attempting to reduce any competitive advantages that might be held by AT&T or the regional BOCs, the FCC adopted rules specifying "structural separation" between these companies and subsidiaries supplying telecommunications equipment.[16] Needless to say, structural relief is a well-known antitrust remedy for monopolization. The FCC further required disclosure of technical information and nondiscriminatory access of AT&T competitors to BOC services.[17] Elimination of discriminatory or exclusive dealing is also a traditional antitrust concern.

Finally, in establishing a temporary line of business restrictions, the Court set up not only a triennial review process but a complex waiver application process. The Department of Justice (1987, p. 25) observes that due to the over 150 requests received between 1984 and 1987 "administration of the process has placed significant demands on the resources of the Department and the Court."[18] In its review of the line of business restriction, the Court has been primarily concerned with (i) preventing cross-subsidization between the BOCs' regulated and competitive activities and (ii) preventing discriminatory pricing or exclusive dealing by the BOCs and their subsidiaries involved in long distance, equipment manufacturing, and information services while (iii) maintaining "universal service." The involvement of the courts and the Department of Justice reflects developments in the antitrust statutes, particularly the 1974 Antitrust Procedures and Penalties Act (PL93-528) and later amendments, hereafter designated the Antitrust Act. The 1974 act seeks to extend standard administrative procedures to antitrust consent decrees, which are the outcome of most antitrust complaints brought by the Department of Justice. The Antitrust Act is intended to address a long-standing congressional concern with its own and public participation in out-of-court settlement of antitrust complaints. A 1959 report of the House Antitrust Subcommittee stated, "The consent decree practice has established an orbit in the twilight zone between established rules of administrative law and judicial procedures."[19] The provisions of the 1974 Antitrust Act are closely related to formal adjudication procedures under the Administrative Procedures Act (APA); see chapter 2.[20] The DOJ, in proposing a consent judgment, is required to file a "competitive impact statement." The statement informs the public of the following (paraphrasing the act): (i) the nature and purpose of the consent decree proceeding, (ii) the alleged violation of antitrust law, (iii) the proposed consent judgment and anticipated competitive impact, and (iv) remedies available to potential private plaintiffs. The Antitrust Act mandates a minimum period of time for public comments to the DOJ. In addition, the Antitrust Act allows the court (i) to take testimony of government officials or expert witnesses, (ii) to appoint consultants or experts, (iii) to authorize participation in a proceeding before the court of interested persons or agencies, and (iv) to review objections filed with the DOJ and the responses made by it.

Clearly, judicial review of consent decrees may take on the characteristics of an extended set of full-blown regulatory hearings. The primary characteristics of regulatory hearings, as already discussed in chapter 2, are bargaining between interested parties and the gathering and exchange of information. Just such concerns are reflected in the Antitrust Act, which seeks to give the court discretion in negotiation, as with independent regulatory agencies, and the ability to gather information.[21] The court is placed in the position of weighing a variety of positions and comments by interested parties.

The court is asked by the Antitrust Act to consider the "competitive impact" of the consent decree and its effect on the "public benefit." Just as the separation of powers and delegation doctrines have been raised with regard to the powers of administrative agencies, the same issues arise in connection with the Antitrust Act. The act requires the courts to oversee the prosecutorial decisions of the DOJ. Thus, the courts become involved in matters of regulation and antitrust policy.[22]

Although specific instances suggest that antitrust policymaking and judicial decisions may play roles traditionally associated with regulation, the major changes in antitrust law and enforcement suggest a loosening of antitrust restrictions. Merger rules and enforcement efforts have allowed a merger wave in the 1980s. There is increased recognition of the effects of competition and potential entry on the efficiency of market allocations. This has led to reduced reliance on market structure data as a basis for determining economic performance of an industry. Awareness of competition in international markets has led to a greater willingness to accept domestic monopoly on the part of antitrust policymakers. The market power of domestic producers is limited by the potential entry of other domestic producers or by international trade. Also, larger multiproduct domestic producers may be able to compete effectively abroad by taking advantage of economies of scale and economies of scope.

Many proposals have been offered for reform of regulation and antitrust. The analysis in preceding chapters suggests that regulatory reforms should be consistent with antitrust reforms. In the absence of market failure, government intervention is not only redundant but can also interfere with allocative efficiency. In areas where deregulation is desirable, it is important for antitrust policy not to take over regulatory tasks. Similarly, promotion of competition by regulatory agencies should not extend to enforcement of antitrust law by those agencies.

In the absence of entry barriers, consistent changes in regulation and antitrust policy may be feasible. In those markets with the potential for new entry or competition from producers of substitute goods, price and entry regulations are not desirable. At the same time, antitrust scrutiny of price fixing or the prevention of mergers will no longer be required in those markets. In the area of regulation, concern over "excessive competition" has generally been discredited. Consistency requires that parallel notions in antitrust, e.g., predatory pricing, should no longer serve as a basis for antitrust enforcement. Consistency is required in other areas of policymaking. For example, antitrust concern with domestic monopoly may be due to the protection of that monopoly by tariff barriers or import quotas. Consistency would suggest that elimination of government-created entry barriers would provide a better solution than antitrust policies that attempt to remedy the market failure attributed to those entry barriers. Absence of consistency in regulation may be due to conflicting jurisdictions. For example, state regulators may restrict the ability of local utilities to compete effectively. This may require federal intervention to supervise prices and entry during a transition to deregulation. Noll (1985) has identified just such a "jurisdictional war" in the telephone industry, where federal deregulation by the FCC has met with resistance from state regulators. Similar conflicts with state regulators have arisen over federal deregulation efforts by the Federal Energy Regulatory Commission (FERC) in natural gas and electricity. These conflicts suggest that second-best regulation of prices and entry may be the result of partial deregulation.

In the area of environmental regulation, reforms can enhance economic efficiency by further increasing the use of market incentives. Air and water pollution can be controlled through marketable emissions licenses that allocate permission to discharge pollutants to the highest-value users. In some areas, such as toxic wastes, a combination of taxes and standards may be desirable, given health risks and administrative costs. In general, incentive-based policy instruments improve allocative efficiency, when compared with emissions quotas, output or input controls, or technological standards.

Regulation may play a role that is complementary to common law in mitigating internalities. Reliance on market incentives is particularly important in this area. In assuring product quality or workplace safety, provision of information to consumers is more likely to promote efficiency than direct regulation. If direct regulation is to be imposed, second-best performance standards are better than complex technological standards. In enhancing market information, reliance on market signaling is more likely to lead to efficient levels of information production than mandated disclosure. Competition in the provision of information will be increased by general rules, e.g., standardized labeling, rather than by costly government intervention to produce its own information e.g., through factory inspectors or government product testing.

One view of regulation would indicate that notions of regulatory reform are beside the point. Since consumers and firms can form contracts or reach various agreements beyond the control of particular regulations, it can be argued that regulation has no effect on economic efficiency. The only costs of regulation would be those involved in adjusting to changes in regulatory policy. Stigler and Friedland (1962) ask whether regulation makes "any difference in the behavior of an industry." They state further that "no degree of care in analyzing the regulations, or even their administration, will tell us whether they rubber-stamp or slightly heckle the state of affairs or substantially alter it." Stigler and Friedland study electric utilities and conclude that regulation is "incapable of forcing the utility to operate at a specified combination of output, price, and cost." The fact that regulation does not have the desired effect does not necessarily imply that it has no effect. Adapting to regulation may create unexpected inefficiency in resource allocation. In this sense, regulatory and antitrust reform continue to be desirable.

Another argument against analysis of the economic welfare effects of regulation as a basis for reform is that regulations are political in nature and thus are not designed to satisfy efficiency considerations. It is true that regulations reflect a wide variety of government policies directed at increasing productivity or investment, causing more rapid technological change, reducing unemployment, or increasing competition in international trade. However, as this work has emphasized, particular regulatory actions are often the outcome of bargaining between market participants. Public input into regulatory policy occurs through public hearing and legislative and executive oversight of administrative agencies. Regulations that enhance allocative efficiency are often in the interest of market participants. Given a limited set of policy instruments, pursuit of income reallocation may indeed occur at the cost of economic efficiency. With a sufficiently broad range of policy instruments, it may be possible to select those that interfere least with the market or that rely on the market allocation mechanism to achieve policy objectives. Regulations will take on new forms as new policy objectives arise or as technological changes are associated with the creation of new industries or new avenues of competition. It is incumbent on policymakers to consider the economic consequences of alternative policies. Normative economic analysis of regulation remains of interest as policy debates generate a never ending supply of economic problems and misconceptions and untested policy instruments.

Regulation is most likely to be effective when it defines property rights and when it establishes general rules for assignment of liability and for contract enforcement. Such rules are most likely to enhance allocative efficiency in markets where externalities or internalities may be mitigated by government mediation. Regulation is least likely to be effective when it promulgates many specific restrictions aimed at achieving short-run policy objectives. Antitrust policy is more likely to enhance efficiency when it promotes competition through enforcement of general rules on collusion, mergers, or unfair trade practices. Antitrust will generally impede competition if it becomes involved in the management of specific industries or negotiation of the terms of specific mergers. In this, I have returned to Hayek's distinction between market rules generally applied and specific government actions. The problem faced in regulatory and antitrust policy is the determination of what constitutes general rules that allow markets to operate efficiently. Attempts to intervene directly in market allocations in response to bargaining over short-term policy objectives should be avoided. The task of efficient regulation is negotiation over the establishment and enforcement of general market rules.

Notes

1. The technological changes in telecommunications are extensively examined in a controversial report prepared for the DOJ by Huber (1987).

2. The problem of holdup can be alleviated by reputation effects; see Klein and Leffler (1981), Lewis (1986), and Zupan (1987b).

3. This follows since equilibrium investment is a decreasing function of s for $s \leq s^*$.

4. That contract rules can create Averch-Johnson input distortions was conjectured by Goldberg (1976).

5. Joskow and Schmalensee (1983) also note the presence of "yardstick" competition in which regulators compare the performance of other regulated firms. This is a problematic approach if the average industry performance is inefficient. It differs fundamentally from competition in that if other firms are efficient, i.e., provide a desirable standard of performance, they do not earn any rewards from their superior performance. "Yardstick competition" makes sense only if the firms are part of the same tournament and thus compete directly for particular rewards.

6. Bailey and Baumol (1984, p. 127) caution that access rates must not be set so low that they subsidize a firm's competitors and do not compensate the owner of the facilities, eventually driving the owner out of business.

7. We make standard neoclassical assumptions. Let F be twice continuously differentiable for $(k, l) \neq 0$, increasing, strictly concave, and homothetic, with normal inputs, $F_{12} = F_{21} > 0$. Let I be twice continuously differentiable and convex, $I(k - k_0) > 0$ for $k \neq k_0$, $I'(k - k_0) \gtrless 0$ as $k \gtrless k_0$. In Becker and Spulber (1984), the cost function $C(q, k_0) + rk_0$ is studied.

8. Suppose that the output to be transferred to the entrant is small. Let q' approach zero in (20.3.8), so that the cost is just

$$C_1(q, k(q)) > C_1(q'', k(q'')).$$

Since C is convex and $-C_2(q, k(q)) = r$, $\partial C_1(q, k(q))/\partial q = (1/C_{22})[C_{11}C_{22} - C_{12}C_{21}] > 0$.

The cost test inequality holds if and only if $q > q''$. With $q' > 0$, the effect of q' on $k^A = k(q' + q)$ must be taken into account.

9. See, for example, Meyer and Tye (1985) and Egan and Weisman (1986).

10. The Court received 600 comments on the proposed settlement and many briefs from over 100 organizations and oral arguments from representatives of 18 organizations; see Department of Justice (1987, p. 12).

11. Ibid. (1987, p. 12).

12. Ibid. (1987, p. 16).

13. It should be noted that state regulatory commissions have continued to restrict entry and competition in local exchange markets in at least 33 states; see Huber (1987).

14. See Department of Justice (1987, p. 20).

15. Ibid. (1987, p. 23).

16. See the amendment of section 64.702 of the Commission's Rules and Regulations (Second Computer Inquiry), FCC.

17. See Department of Justice (1987, pp. 26–31) for an extensive discussion of the FCC Computer II and Computer III decisions and associated rules and orders.

18. Ibid. (1987, p. 25).

19. This passage is quoted in the legislative history of the 1974 act; see U.S. Code (1974, p. 6537).

20. The procedural aspects of the 1974 Antitrust Act amend section 5 of the Clayton Act.

21. The House Antitrust Committee quotes approvingly from Senate Report No. 933-298: "The Committee recognizes that the court must have broad discretion to accommodate a balancing of interest. On the one hand, the court must obtain the necessary information to make its determination that the proposed consent decree is in the public interest. On the other hand, it must preserve the consent decree as a viable settlement option," U.S. Code (1974, pp. 6538–6539).

22. A similar point is made by Hutchinson, who observes that "[w]hen a court reviews the exercise of prosecutorial discretion, it will find itself in a thicket of administrative considerations" and "it does not follow that the federal courts, limited by the Constitution to deciding judicial questions, are the appropriate reviewing agencies" (U.S. Code, 1974, p. 6545).

References

ABA Antitrust Section, 1981a, *The FTC as an Antitrust Enforcement Agency: The Role of Section 5 of the FTC Act in Antitrust Law*, Monograph No. 5, 1.

ABA Antitrust Section, 1981b, *The FTC as an Antitrust Enforcement Agency: Its Structure, Powers and Procedures*, Monograph No. 5, 2.

Abraham, K. S., 1986, *Distributing Risk: Insurance, Legal Thoery, and Public Policy*, New Haven: Yale University Press.

Adams, W. A., 1986, *The Structure of American Industry*, 7th ed. New York: Macmillan.

Adelman, M., 1964, "Efficiency of Resource Use in Crude Petroleum," *Southern Economic Journal*, 31, October, pp. 101–122.

Akerlof, G., 1970, "The Market for Lemons: Qualitative Uncertainty and the Market Mechanism," *Quarterly Journal of Economics*, 84, August, pp. 488–500.

Alchian, A., and H. Demsetz, 1972, "Production, Information Costs, and Economic Organization," *American Economic Review*, 62, December, pp. 777–795.

Allais, M., 1948, "Le Problème de la Coordination des Transport et la Théorie Economique," *Revue d'Economie Politique*, 58, pp. 212–271.

Allen, F., 1984, "Reputation and Product Quality," *Rand Journal of Economics*, 15, Autumn, pp. 311–327.

Anderson, F. R., A. V. Kneese, P. D. Reed, R. B. Stevenson, and S. Taylor, 1977, *Environmental Improvement through Economic Incentives*, Baltimore: Johns Hopkins University Press.

Anderson, T. L., 1983, *Water Rights*, San Francisco: Pacific Institute for Public Policy Research.

Aranson, P. H. 1982, "Pollution Control: The Case for Competition," in *Instead of Regulation: Alternatives to Federal Regulatory Agencies*, R. W. Poole, Jr., ed., Lexington, MA: D.C. Heath, pp. 339–393.

Aranson, P. H., E. Gellhorn, and G. Robinson, 1982, "A Theory of Legislative Delegation," *Cornell Law Review*, 68, November, pp. 1–67.

Areeda, P., and D. Turner, 1975, "Predatory Pricing and Related Practices under Section 2 of the Sherman Act," *Harvard Law Review*, 88, February, pp. 697–733.

Armentano, D. T., 1982, *Antitrust and Monopoly: Anatomy of a Policy Failure*, New York: Wiley.

Arnott, R., and J. E. Stiglitz, 1986, "Moral Hazard and Optimal Commodity Taxation," *Journal of Public Economics*, 29, February, pp. 1–24.

Arnould, R. J., and H. G. Grabowski, 1981, "Auto Safety Regulation: An Analysis of Market Failure," *Bell Journal of Economics*, 12, Spring, pp. 27–48.

Arrow, K. J., 1951, "An Extension of the Basic Theorems of Classical Welfare Economics," in *Proceedings of the Second Berkeley Symposium on Mathematical Statistics and Probability*, J. Neyman, ed., Los Angeles: University of California Press, pp. 507–532.

Arrow, K. J., 1963, "Uncertainty and the Welfare Economics of Medical Care," *American Economic Review*, 53, December, pp. 941–973.

Arrow, K. J., 1965, *Aspects of the Theory of Risk Bearing*, Helsinki: Yrjo Johnassonin Säätio.

Arrow, K. J., 1968, "The Economics of Moral Hazard: Further Comment," *American Economic Review*, 58, June, pp. 537–539.

Arrow, K. J., 1975, "Vertical Integration and Communication," *Bell Journal of Economics*, 6, Spring, pp. 173–183.

Arrow, K. J., and G. Debreu, 1954, "Existence of an Equilibrium for a Competitive Economy," *Econometrica*, 22, July, pp. 265–290.

Arrow, K. J., and F. Hahn, 1971, *General Competitive Analysis*, San Francisco: Holden Day.

Asch, P., 1975, "The Determinants and Effects of Antitrust Policy," *Journal of Law and Economics*, 18, October, pp. 575–581.

Asch, P., and R. Seneca, 1985, *Government and the Marketplace*, Chicago: Dryden Press.

Atkinson, A. B., and J. E. Stiglitz, 1976, "The Design of Tax Structure: Direct versus Indirect Taxation, *Journal of Public Economics*, 6., July/August, pp. 55–75.

Atkinson, A. B., and J. E. Stiglitz, 1980, *Lectures on Public Economics*, New York: McGraw-Hill.

Atkinson, S. E., and R. Halvorsen, 1976, "Interfuel Substitution in Steam Electric Power Generation," *Journal of Political Economy*, 84, October, pp. 959–978.

Aumann, R. J., 1964, "Markets with a Continuum of Traders," *Econometrica*, 32, January, pp. 39–50.

Aumann, R. J., 1975, "Values of Markets with a Continuum of Traders," *Econometrica*, 43., July, pp. 611–646.

Aumann, R. J., and L. S. Shapley 1974, *Values of Non-Atomic Games*, Princeton: Princeton University Press.

Averch, H., and L. L. Johnson, 1962, "Behavior of the Firm under Regulatory Constraint," *American Economic Review*, 52, December, pp. 1053–1069.

Bacow, L. S., 1980, *Bargaining for Job Safety and Health*, Cambridge, MA: MIT Press.

Bailey, E. E., 1973, *Economic Theory of Regulatory Constraint*, Lexington, MA: Lexington Books.

Bailey, E. E., and W. J. Baumol, 1984, "Deregulation and the Theory of Contestable Markets," *Yale Journal on Regulation*, 1, pp. 111–137.

Bailey, E. E., and R. D. Coleman, 1971, "The Effect of Lagged Regulation in an Averch-Johnson Model," *Bell Journal of Economics and Management Science*, Spring, pp. 278–292.

Bailey, E. E., and J. C. Malone, 1970, "Resource Allocation and the Regulated Firm," *Bell Journal Of Economics*, 1, Spring, pp. 129–142.

Bailey, E. E., and J. C. Panzar, Jr., 1981, "The Contestability of Airline Markets during Transition to Deregulation," *Journal of Law and Contemporary Problems*, 44, Winter, pp. 125–145.

Bailey, E. E., D. R. Graham, and D. P. Kaplan, 1985, *Deregulating the Airlines*, Cambridge, MA: MIT Press.

Bailey, M. N., 1972, "Research and Development Costs and Returns: The U.S. Pharmaceutical Industry," *Journal of Political Economy*, January/February, pp. 70–85.

Bain, J. S., 1954, "Economies of Scale, Concentration and Entry," *American Economic Review*, 44, March, pp. 15–39.

Bain, J. S., 1956, *Barriers to New Competition*, Cambridge, MA: Harvard University Press.

Bain, J. S., 1959, *Industrial Organization*, New York: Wiley.

Bain, J. S., 1968, *Industrial Organization*, 2nd ed., New York: Wiley.

Baker, J. B., 1985, *The Effect of Private Antitrust Damage Remedies on Resource Allocation*, Stanford Law School, Working Paper, October.

Baron, D. P., 1981, "Price Regulation, Product Quality, and Asymmetric Information," *American Economic Review*, 71, March, pp. 212–220.

Baron, D. P., 1984, "Regulatory Strategies under Asymmetric Information," in *Bayesian Models in Economic Theory*, M. Boyer and R. E. Kihlstrom, eds., Amsterdam: North-Holland, pp. 155–180.

Baron, D. P., 1985, "Noncooperative Regulation of a Nonlocalized Externality," *Rand Journal of Economics*, 16, Winter, pp. 553–568.

Baron, D. P., 1987, "Design of Regulatory Mechanisms and Institutions," in *Handbook of Industrial Organization*, R. Schmalensee and R. Willig, eds., Amsterdam: North-Holland.

Baron, D. P., and D. Besanko, 1984a, "Regulation, Asymmetric Information and Auditing," *Rand Journal of Economics*, 15, Winter, pp. 447–470.

Baron, D. P., and D. Besanko, 1984b, "Regulation and Information in a Continuing Relationship," *Information Economics and Policy*, 1, 1984, pp. 247–302.

Baron, D. P., and R. R. DeBondt, 1979, "Fuel Adjustment Mechanisms and Economic Efficiency," *Journal of Industrial Economics*, 27, March, pp. 243–261.

Baron, D. P., and R. R. DeBondt, 1981, "On the Design of Regulatory Price Adjustment Mechanisms," *Journal of Economic Theory*, 24, February, pp. 70–94.

Baron, D. P., and R. B. Myerson, 1982, "Regulating a Monopolist with Unknown Cost," *Econometrica*, 50, July, pp. 911–930.

Baron, D. P., and R. A. Taggart, Jr., 1977, "A Model of Regulation under Uncertainty and a Test of Regulatory Bias," *Bell Journal of Economics and Management Science*, Spring, pp. 151–167.

Bartel, A. P., and L. G. Thomas, 1985, "Direct and Indirect Effects of Regulation: A New Look at OSHA's Impact," *Journal of Law and Economics*, 28, April, pp. 1–26.

Bator, F. M., 1958, "The Anatomy of Market Failure," *Quarterly Journal of Economics*, 72, August, pp. 351–379.

Baumol, W. J., 1972, "On Taxation and the Control of Externalities," *American Economic Review*, 62, June, pp. 307–332.

Baumol, W. J., 1977, "On the Proper Cost Tests for Natural Monopoly in a Multiproduct Industry," *American Economic Review*, 67, December, pp. 809–822.

Baumol, W. J., 1979a, "Quasi-Optimality: The Price We Must Pay for a Price System," *Journal of Political Economy*, 87, June, pp. 578–599.

Baumol, W. J., 1979b, "Quasi Permanence of Price Reduction: A Policy for Prevention of Predatory Pricing," *Yale Law Journal*, 89, November, pp. 1–26.

Baumol, W. J., 1986, *Superfairness*, Cambridge, MA: MIT Press.

Baumol, W. J., and D. F. Bradford, 1970, "Optimal Departures from Marginal Cost Pricing," *American Economic Review*, 60, June, pp. 265–283.

Baumol, W. J., and D. Fischer, 1978, "Cost-Minimizing Number of Firms and Determination of Industry Structure," *Quarterly Journal of Economics*, 92, August, pp. 439–467.

Baumol, W. J., and A. K. Klevorick, 1970, "Input Choices and Rate-of-Return Regulation: An Overview of the Discussion," *Bell Journal of Economics and Management Science*, Autumn, pp. 162–190.

Baumol, W. J., and W. E. Oates, 1975, *The Theory of Environmental Policy: Externalities, Public Outlays and The Quality of Life*, Englewood Cliffs, NJ: Prentice-Hall.

Baumol, W. J., and W. E. Oates, 1979, *Economics, Environmental Policy, and the Quality of Life*, Englewood Cliffs, NJ: Prentice-Hall.

Baumol, W. J., and J. A. Ordover, 1977, "On the Optimality of Public-Goods Pricing with Exclusion Devices," *Kyklos*, Fasc. 1, 30, pp. 5–21.

Baumol, W. J., and J. A. Ordover, 1985, "Use of Antitrust to Subvert Competition," *Journal of Law and Economics*, 28, May, pp. 246–266.

Baumol, W. J., and R. D. Willig, 1981, "Fixed Cost, Sunk Cost, Entry Barriers and Sustainability of Monopoly, *Quarterly Journal of Economics*, 95, August, pp. 405–431.

Baumol, W. J., and R. D. Willig, 1986, *Contestability: Developments since the Book*, R. R. #86-01, C. V. Starr Center for Applied Economics, New York University, January.

Baumol, W. J., E. E. Bailey, and R. D. Willig, 1977, "Weak Invisible Hand Theorems on the Sustainability of Prices in a Multiproduct Natural Monopoly," *American Economic Review*, 67, June, pp. 350–365.

Baumol, W. J., J. C. Panzar, and R. D. Willig, 1982, *Contestable Markets and the Theory of Industry Structure*, New York: Harcourt Brace Jovanovich.

Baumol, W. J., J. C. Panzar, and R. D. Willig, 1983, "Contestable Markets: An Uprising in the Theory of Industry Structure: Reply," *American Economic Review*, 73, June, pp. 491–496.

Beales, H., R. Craswell, and S. Salop, 1981a, "The Efficient Regulation of Consumer Information," *Journal of Law and Economics*, 24, December, pp. 491–539.

Beales, H., R. Craswell, and S. Salop, 1981b, "Information Remedies for Consumer Protection," *American Economic Review Papers and Proceedings*, 71, May, pp. 410–413.

Beaver, W. H., 1980, *The Nature of Mandated Disclosure, Report of the Advisory Committee on Corporate Disclosure to the SEC*, 95th Congress, 1st Session, 618–656 (House Comm., Print 95-29, 1977) reprinted in *Economics of Corporation Law and Securities Regulation*, Posner, R. A. and K. E. Scott, eds. (Boston: Little, Brown and Co.), pp. 317–342.

Beckenstein, A. R., and H. L. Gabel, 1986, "Predation Rules: An Economic and Behavioral Analysis," *Antitrust Bulletin*, 31, Spring, pp. 29–49.

Becker, G. S., 1968, "Crime and Punishment: An Economic Approach," *Journal of Political Economy*, 76, March–April, pp. 169–217.

Becker, G. S., 1983, "A Theory of Competition among Pressure Groups for Political Influence," *Quarterly Journal of Economics*, 98, August, pp. 371–400.

Becker, G. S., and G. J. Stigler, 1974, "Law Enforcement Malfeasance, and Compensation of Enforcers," *Journal of Legal Studies*, 3, January, pp. 1–18.

Becker, R. A., and D. F. Spulber, 1984, "The Cost Function Given Imperfectly Flexible Capital," *Economics Letters*, 16, pp. 197–204.

Berglas, E., 1976, "On The Theory of Clubs," *American Economic Review*, 66, May, pp. 116–121.

Berglas, E., 1981, "The Market Provision of Club Goods Once Again," *Journal of Public Economics*, 15, June, pp. 389–393.

Berle, A. A., and G. Means, 1932, *The Modern Corporation and Private Property*, New York: Macmillan.

Bernhardt, I., 1977, "Vertical Integration and Demand Variability," *Journal of Industrial Economics*, 25, March pp. 213–229.

Bertrand, J., 1883, "Theorie Mathématique de la Richesse Sociale," *Journal des Savants*, pp. 499–508.

Besanko, D., and D. M. Sappington, 1987, *Designing Regulatory Policy with Limited Information*, Chur, Switzerland: Harwood Academic Publishers.

Besanko, D., and D. F. Spulber, 1986, *Optimal Antitrust Enforcement under Asymmetric Information*, Department of Economics, University of Southern California.

Besanko, D., and D. F. Spulber, 1987, *Enforcement of Law and Noncooperative Behavior*, School of Business, Indiana University.

Besanko, D., S. Donnenfeld, and L. J. White, 1987, "Monopoly and Quality Distortion: Effects and Remedies," *Quarterly Journal of Economics*, 102, November, pp. 743–768.

Bhagwati, J. N., 1970, "Oligopoly Theory Entry Prevention and Growth," *Oxford Economic Papers*, 22, November, pp. 297–310.

Billera, L. J., and D. C. Heath, 1982, "Allocation of Shared Costs: A Set of Axioms Yielding a Unique Procedure," *Mathematics of Operations Research*, 7, February, pp. 32–39.

Binmore, K., A. Rubinstein, and A. Wolinsky, 1986, "The Nash Bargaining Solution in Economic Modelling," *Rand Journal of Economics*, 17, Summer, pp. 176–188.

Blair, R. D., and D. L. Kaserman, 1978a, "Vertical Integration, Tying and Antitrust Policy," *American Economic Review*, 68, June, pp. 397–402.

Blair, R. D., and D. L. Kaserman, 1978b, "Uncertainty and the Incentive for Vertical Integration," *Southern Economic Journal*, 45, July, pp. 266–272.

Blair, R. D., and D. L. Kaserman, 1983, *Law and Economics of Vertical Integration and Control*, New York: Academic Press.

Block, M. K., and J. G. Sidak, 1980, "The Cost of Antitrust Deterrence: Why Not Hang a Price Fixer Now and Then?" *Georgetown Law Journal*, 68, June, pp. 1131–1139.

Block, M. K., F. C. Nold, and J. G. Sidak, 1981, "The Deterrent Effect of Antitrust Enforcement," *Journal of Political Economy*, 89, June, pp. 429–445.

Boiteux, M., 1949, "La Tarification des Demandes en Pointe: Application de la Théorie de la Vente au Cout Marginal," *Revue Générale de l'Electricité*, 58, pp. 321–340, translated as "Peak Load Pricing," *Journal of Business*, 33, April, 1960, pp. 157–179.

Boiteux, M., 1951a, "Le 'Revenue Distribuable' et les Pertes Economiques," *Econometrica*, 19, April, pp. 112–133.

Boiteux, M., 1951b, "La Tarification au Cout Marginal et les Demandes Aléatoires," *Cahiers du Seminaire d'Econmetrie*, 1, pp. 56–69.

Boiteux, M., 1956, "Sur la gestion des Monopoles Publics astreints à l'Equilibre Budgétaire," *Econometrica*, 24, January, 22–40, translated as "On the Management of Public Monopolies Subject to Budget Constraints," *Journal of Economic Theory*, 1971, 3, September, pp. 219–240.

Bolton, D. C. J., and R. E. Meiners, 1986, "The Politicization of the Electric Utility Industry," in *Electric Power: Deregulation and the Public Interest*, J. C. Moorhouse, ed., San Francisco: Pacific Research Institute, pp. 249–277.

Bonbright, J. C., 1961, *Principles of Public Utility Rates*, New York: Columbia University Press.

Borenstein, S., 1985, "Price Discrimination in Free-Entry Markets," *Rand Journal of Economics*, 16, Autumn, pp. 380–397.

Bork, R. 1965, "The Rule of Reason and the Per Se Concept; Price Fixing and Market Division: I," *Yale Law Journal*, 74, Winter, pp. 775–847.

Bork, R., 1966a, "The Rule of Reason and the Per Se Concept; Price Fixing and Market Division: II," *Yale Law Journal*, 75, January, pp. 373–475.

Bork, R., 1966b, "Legislative Intent and the Policy of the Sherman Act," *Journal of Law and Economics*, 9, October, pp. 7–48.

Bork, R., 1978, *The Antitrust Paradox: A Policy at War with Itself*, New York: Basic Books.

Bös, D., and G. Tillman, 1983, "Cost-Axiomatic Regulatory Pricing," *Journal of Public Economics*, 22, November, pp. 243–256.

Bös, D., and G. Tillman, 1984, "Cost-Axiomatic versus Welfare-Maximizing Marginal Cost Pricing," in *The Performance of Public Enterprises*, M. Marchand, P. Pestieau, and H. Tulkens, eds., Amsterdam: Elsevier Science Publishers, North-Holland, pp. 101–117.

Bowman, W. S., Jr., 1957, "Tying Arrangements and the Leverage Problem," *Yale Law Journal*, 67, November, pp. 19–36.

Boyes, W. J., 1976, "An Empirical Examination of the Averch-Johnson Effect," *Economic Inquiry*, XIV, March, pp. 25–35.

Braeutigam, R. R., 1979, "Optimal Pricing with Intermodal Competition," *American Economic Review*, 69, March, pp. 38–49.

Braeutigam, R. R., 1980, "An Analysis of Fully Distributed Costs Pricing in Regulated Industries," *Bell Journal of Economics*, 11, Spring, pp. 182–196.

Braeutigam, R. R., 1984, "Socially Optimal Pricing with Rivalry and Economies of Scale," *Rand Journal of Economics*, 15, Spring, pp. 127–134.

Breit, W., and K. G. Elzinga, 1985, "Private Antitrust Enforcement: The New Learning," *Journal of Law and Economics*, 28, May, pp. 405–444.

Breyer, S., 1982, *Regulation and Its Reform*, Cambridge, MA: Harvard University Press.

Breyer, S., and R. Stewart, 1979, *Administrative Law and the Regulatory Process*, Boston: Little-Brown.

Brock, G. W., 1975, *The U.S. Computer Industry: A Study of Market Power*, Cambridge, MA: Ballinger.

Brock, W. A., 1983, "Contestable Markets and the Theory of Industry Structure: A Review Article," *Journal of Political Economy*, 91, December, pp. 1055–1066.

Brock, W. A., and J. A. Scheinkman, 1983, "Free Entry and the Sustainability of Natural Monopoly: Bertrand Revisited by Cournot," in *Breaking Up Bell: Essays in Industrial Organization and Regulation*, D. S. Evans, ed., New York: North-Holland, pp. 231–252.

Brodley, J. F., and G. A. Hay, 1981, "Predatory Pricing: Competing Economic Theories and the Evolution of Legal Standards," *Cornell Law Review*, 66, April, pp. 738–803.

Brown, D. J., and G. Heal, 1979, "Equity, Efficiency and Increasing Returns," *Review of Economic Studies*, 46, October, pp. 571–585.

Brown, D. J., and G. Heal, 1980, "Two-Part Tariffs, Marginal Cost Pricing and Increasing Returns in a General Equilibrium Model," *Journal of Public Economics*, 13, February, pp. 25–49.

Brown, G., Jr., and M. B. Johnson, 1969, "Public Utility Output and Pricing under Risk," *American Economic Review*, 59, March, pp. 119–128.

Brown, J. P., 1973, "Toward an Economic Theory of Liability," *Journal of Legal Studies*, 2, June, pp. 323–349.

Brown, J. P., 1974, "Product Liability: The Case of an Asset with Random Life," *American Economic Review*, 64, March, pp. 149–161.

Buchanan, J. M., 1965, "An Economic Theory of Clubs," *Econometrica*, 32, February, pp. 1–14.

Buchanan, J. M., 1967, "Cooperation and Conflict in Public Goods Interaction," *Western Economic Journal*, 5, March pp. 109–121.

Buchanan, J. M., and W. C. Stubblebine, 1962, "Externality," *Economica*, 29, November, pp. 371–384.

Bulow, J., 1982, "Durable-Good Monopolists," *Journal of Political Economy*, 90, April, pp. 314–332.

Bureau of National Affairs, 1971, *OSHA and the Unions: Bargaining for Job Safety and Health*, Washington, D.C.

Burrows, P. B. 1977, "Pollution Control with Variable Production Processes," *Journal of Public Economics*, 8, December, pp. 357–367.

Butler, R. J., and J. D. Worrall, 1983, "Workers' Compensation: Benefit and Injury Claims Rates in the Seventies," *Review of Economics and Statistics*, 65, November, pp. 580–589.

Calabresi, G., 1970, *The Costs of Accidents: A Legal and Economic Analysis*, New Haven: Yale University Press.

Calabresi, G., and A. D. Melamed, 1972, "Property Rules, Liability Rules and Inalienability: One View of the Cathedral," *Harvard Law Review*, 85, April, pp. 1089–1128.

Calem, P. S., and D. F. Spulber, 1984, "Multiproduct Two-Part Tariffs," *International Journal of Industrial Organization*, 2. pp. 105–115.

Caillaud, B., R. Guesnerie, P. Rey, and J. Tirole, 1985, "The Normative Economics of Government Intervention in Production," Technical Report 473, Institute for Mathematical Studies in the Social Sciences, Stanford University.

Calvani, T., and J. M. Lynch, 1983, "Predatory Pricing under the Robinson-Patman and Sherman Acts: An Introduction," *Antitrust Law Journal*, 51, Summer, pp. 375–400.

Campbell, T. J., and C. J. Ware, 1983, "Russell Stover and the Vertical Agreement Puzzle," *Antitrust Law Journal*, 52, pp. 83–93.

Carlton, D. W., 1979, "Vertical Integration in Competitive markets under Uncertainty," *Journal of Industrial Economics*, 27, March, pp. 189–209.

Carlton, D. W., and G. C. Loury, 1980, "The Limitations of Pigouvian Taxes as a Long-Run Remedy for Externalities," *Quarterly Journal of Economics*, 95, November, pp. 559–566.

Carlton, D. W., and G. C. Loury, 1986, "The Limitations of Pigouvian Taxes as a Long-Run Remedy for Externalities: An Extension of Results," *Quarterly Journal of Economics*, 101, August, pp. 631–634.

Chadwick, E., 1859, "Results of Different Principles of Legislation and Administration in Europe; of Competition for the Field, as Compared with Competition within the Field, of Service," *Journal of the Royal Statistical Society*, 22, Series A, September, pp. 381–420.

Chamberlin, E. H., 1956, *The Theory of Monopolistic Competition*, 7th ed., Cambridge, MA: Harvard University Press.

Chan, Y.-S., and H. E. Leland, 1982, "Prices and Qualities in Markets with Costly Information," *Review of Economic Studies*, 49, October, pp. 499–516.

Chatterjee, K., and W. Samuelson, 1983, "Bargaining under Incomplete Information," *Operations Research*, 31, September–October, pp. 835–851.

Chelius, J. R., 1974, "The Control of Industrial Accidents: Economics Theory and Empirical Evidence," *Law and Contemporary Problems*, 38, Summer/Autumn, pp. 700–729.

Chelius, J. R., 1977, "Workplace Safety and Health: The Role of Workers' Compensation," Washington, D.C.: American Enterprise Institute.

Chenery, H. B., 1953, "Process and Production Functions from Engineering Data," Chapter 8 in W. Leontief, ed., *Studies in the Structure of the American Economy*, New York: Oxford University Press, pp. 297–325.

Cheng, L., 1985, "Comparing Bertrand and Cournot Equilibria: A Geometric Approach," *Rand Journal of Economics*, 16, Spring, pp. 146–152.

Cheung, S. N. S., 1970, "The Structure of a Contract and the Theory of a Non-Exclusive Resource," *Journal of Law and Economics*, 13, April, pp. 49–70.

Chiang, R., and C. S. Spatt, 1982, "Imperfect Price Discrimination and Welfare," *Review of Economic Studies*, 49, pp. 155–181.

Chubb, J. E., 1983, *Interest Groups and the Bureaucracy*, Stanford: Stanford University Press.

Clark, C. W., 1982, "Models of Fishery Regulation," in L. J. Mirman and D. F. Spulber, eds., *Essays in the Economics of Renewable Resources*, Amsterdam: North-Holland, pp. 273–287.

Clark, J. B., 1901, *The Control of Trusts: An Argument in Favor of Curbing the Power of Monopoly by a Natural Method*, New York: Macmillan.

Clark, J. B., and J. M. Clark, 1912, *The Control of Trusts*, New York: Macmillan.

Clarkson, K. W., and T. J. Muris, eds., 1981, *The Federal Trade Commission since 1970: Economic Regulation and Bureaucratic Behavior*, Cambridge; Cambridge University Press.

Coase, R. H., 1937, "The Nature of the Firm," *Economica*, 4, November, pp. 386–405.

Coase, R. H., 1946, "The Marginal Cost Controversy," *Economica*, 13, pp. 169–182.

Coase, R. H., 1947, "The Marginal Cost Controversy: Some Further Comments," *Economica*, 14, May, pp. 150–153.

Coase, R. H., 1959, "The Federal Communications Commission," *Journal of Law and Economics*, 2, October, pp. 1–40.

Coase, R. H., 1960, "The Problem of Social Cost," *Journal of Law and Economics*, 3, October, pp. 1–44.

Coase, R. H., 1972, "Durability and Monopoly," *Journal of Law and Economics*, 15, April, pp. 143–149.

Comanor, W. S., 1985, "Vertical Price-Fixing, Vertical Market Restrictions, and the New Antitrust Policy," *Harvard Law Review*, 98, pp. 983–1102.

Cooper, R., and T. W. Ross, 1984, "Prices, Product Qualities and Asymmetric Information: The Competitive Case," *Review of Economic Studies*, 51, April, pp. 197–207.

Cooper, R., and T. W. Ross, 1985, "Product Warranties and Double Moral Hazard," *Rand Journal of Economics*, 16, Spring, pp. 103–113.

Cooter, R., 1985, "Unity in Torts, Contracts and Property: The Model of Precaution," *California Law Review*, 73, January, pp. 1–51.

Cornes, R., and T. Sandler, 1986, *The Theory of Externalities, Public Goods and Club Goods*, Cambridge: Cambridge University Press.

Cournot, A., 1838, *Recherches sur les Principes Mathématiques de la Théorie des Richess*, Paris.

Courville, L., 1974, "Regulation and Efficiency in the Electric Utility Industry," *Bell Journal of Economics and Management Science*, Spring, pp. 53–74.

Cowling, K., and M. Waterson, 1976, "Price-Cost Margins and Market Structure," *Economica*, 43, August, pp. 267–274.

Coyte, P. C., and C. R. Lindsey, 1986, "Spatial Monopoly and Spatial Monopolistic Competition with Two-Part Pricing," University of Alberta, Economics Department, May.

Craswell, R., 1985, "Interpreting Deceptive Advertising," *Boston University Law Review*, 65, July, pp. 658–732.

Craswell, R., and M. R. Fratrik, 1985, "Predatory Pricing Theory Applied: The Case of Supermarkets vs. Warehouse Stores," *Case Western Reserve Law Review*, 36, pp. 1–49.

Crew, M. A., and P. R. Kleindorfer, 1978, "Reliability and Public Utility Pricing," *American Economic Review*, 68, March, pp. 31–40.

Crew, M. A., and P. R. Kleindorfer, 1979, *Public Utility Economics*, New York: St. Martins Press.

Crout, J. R., 1975, Discussion, in R. B. Helms, ed., *Drug Development and Marketing*, Washington, pp. 196–197.

Dales, J. H., 1968, *Pollution, Property and Prices*, Toronto: University of Toronto Press.

Danø, S., 1966, *Industrial Production Models: A Theoretical Study*, New York: Springer-Verlag.

Dansby, R. E., and R. D. Willig, 1979, "Industry Performance Gradient Indexes," *American Economic Review*, 69, June, pp. 249–260.

Dasgupta, P., and Y. Ushio, 1981, "On the Rate of Convergence of Oligopoly Equilibria in Large Markets: An Example," *Economics Letters*, 8, pp. 13–17.

Dasgupta, P., S. Hammond, and E. Maskin, 1979, "The Implementation of Social Choice Rules: Some General Results on Incentive Compatibility," *Review of Economic Studies*, 46, April, pp. 185–216.

Dasgupta, P., S. Hammond, and E. Maskin, 1980, "On Imperfect Information and Optimal Pollution Control," *Review of Economic Studies*, 47, October, pp. 857–860.

d'Aspremont, C., and L.-A. Gérard-Varet, 1979, "Incentives and Incomplete Information," *Journal of Public Economics*, 11, February, pp. 25–45.

d'Aspremont, C., and A. Jacquemin, 1985, "Measuring the Power to Monopolize: A Simple-Game-Theoretic Approach," *European Economic Review*, 27, February, pp. 57–74.

d'Aspremont, C., A. Jacquemin, J. J. Gabzewicz, and J. A. Weymark, 1983, "On the Stability of Collusive Price Leadership," *Canadian Journal of Economics*, 16, February, pp. 17–25.

Davidson, R. K., 1955, *Price Discrimination in Selling Gas and Electricity*, Baltimore: Johns Hopkins Press.

Davies, J. C., III, and B. S. Davies, 1975, *The Politics of Pollution*, Indianapolis: Bobbs-Merrill.

Davis, E. G., 1973, "A Dynamic Model of the Regulated Firm with a Price Adjustment Mechanism," *Bell Journal of Economics and Mangagement Science*, Spring, pp. 270–282.

Davis, O., M. Dempster, and A. Wildavsky, 1966, "A Theory of the Budget Process," *American Political Science Review*, 60, September, pp. 529–547.

Debreu, G., 1959, *Theory of Value*, New Haven: Yale University Press.

Debreu, G., and H. Scarf, 1963, "A Limit Theorem on the Core of an Economy," *International Economic Review*, 4, September, pp. 235–246.

Demsetz, H., 1967, "Toward a Theory of Property Rights," *American Economic Review*, 57, May, pp. 347–359.

Demsetz, H., 1968, "Why Regulate Utilities?" *Journal of Law and Economics*, 11, April, pp. 55–65.

Demsetz, H., 1973, "Joint Supply and Price Discrimination," *Journal of Law and Economics*, 16, pp. 389–415.

Department of Justice (1987), *Report and Recommendations of the United States Concerning the Line of Business Restrictions Imposed on the Bell Operating Companies by the Modification of Final Judgment, U.S. v. Western Electric Co. and AT&T Co.*

Derthick, M., and P. J. Quirk, 1985, *The Politics of Deregulation*, Washington, D.C.: Brookings Institution.

de Silva, H., M. Koehn, P. MacAvoy, and D. F. Spulber 1987, "The Effects of Airline-Owned Computer Reservation Systems on the Performance of the Airline Market," mimeo.

de V. Graff, J., 1967, *Theoretical Welfare Economics*, Cambridge: Cambridge University Press.

Diamond, P. A., 1973a, "Single Activity Accidents," *Journal of Legal Studies*, 3, pp. 107–164.

Diamond, P. A., 1973b, "Accident Law and Resource Allocation," *Bell Journal of Economics*, 5, Autumn, pp. 366–406.

Diamond, P. A., 1975, "A Many-Person Ramsey Tax Rule," *Journal of Public Economics*, 4, August, pp. 227–244.

Diamond, P. A., 1977, "Insurance Theoretic Aspects of Workers' Compensation," in A. S. Blinder and P. Friedman, eds., *Natural Resources, Uncertainty, and General Equilibrium Systems*, New York: Academic Press, pp. 67–89.

Diamond, P. A., and J. A. Mirrlees, 1971a, "Optimal Taxation and Public Production, I: Production Efficiency," *American Economic Review*, 61, March pp. 8–27.

Diamond, P. A., and J. A. Mirrlees, 1971b, "Optimal Taxation and Public Production, II: Tax Rules," *American Economic Review*, 61, June pp. 261–278.

Diewert, W. E., 1973, "Functional Forms for Profit and Transformation Functions," *Journal of Economic Theory*, 6, June, pp. 284–316.

Dixit, A. K., 1970, "On the Optimum Structure of Commodity Taxes," *American Economic Review*, 66, June, pp. 295–301.

Dixit, A. K., 1979a, "A Model of Duopoly Suggesting a Theory of Entry Barriers," *Bell Journal of Economics*, 10, Spring, pp. 20–32.

Dixit, A. K., 1979b, "Quality and Quantity Competition," *Review of Economic Studies*, 46, October, pp. 587–600.

Dixit, A. K., 1980, "The Role of Investment in Entry-Deterrence," *Economics Journal*, 90, March, pp. 95–106.

Dixit, A. K., 1983, "Vertical Integration in a Monopolistically Competitive Industry," *International Journal of Industrial Organization*, 1, September, pp. 63–78.

Dixit, A. K., and V. Norman, 1978, "Advertising and Welfare," *Bell Journal of Economics*, 9, Spring, pp. 1–17.

Dixit, A. K., and J. E. Stiglitz, 1977, "Monopolistic Competition and Optimum Product Diversity," *American Economic Review*, 67, June, pp. 297–308.

Donsimoni, M. P., P. Geroski, and A. Jacquemin, 1984, "Concentration Indices and Market Power: Two Views," *Journal of Industrial Economics*, 4, June, pp. 419–434.

Douglas, G. W., and J. C. Miller, III, 1974, *Economic Deregulation of Domestic Air Transport: Theory and Policy*, Washington, D.C.: Brookings Institution.

Downs, A., 1957, *An Economic Theory of Democracy*, New York: Harper and Row.

Dubin, J. A., and P. Navarro, 1982, "Regulatory Climate and the Cost of Capital," in *Regulatory Reform and Public Utilities*, A. Crew, ed., Lexington, MA: Lexington Books, pp. 141–166.

Dupuit, J., 1969, "On the Measurement of the Utility of Public Works," in *Readings in Welfare Economics*, K. J. Arrow and T. Scitovsky, eds., Homewood: Irwin, pp. 255–283.

Dye, R. A., 1985, "Costly Contract Contingencies," *International Economic Review*, 26, February, pp. 233–250.

Easterbrook, F. H., 1981, "Predatory Strategies and Counterstrategies," *University of Chicago Law Review*, 48, Spring, pp. 263–337.

Easterbrook, F. H. 1985, "Detrebling Antitrust Damages," *Journal of Law and Economics*, 28, May, pp. 445–468.

Eaton, B. C., 1972, "Spatial Competition Revisited," *Canadian Journal of Economics*, pp. 268–278.

Eaton, B. C., 1976, "Free Entry in One Dimensional Models: Pure Profits and Multiple Equilibria," *Journal of Regional Science*, 16, April, pp. 21–33.

Eaton, B. C., and M. H. Wooders, 1985, "Sophisticated Entry in a Model of Spatial Competition," *Rand Journal of Economics*, 16, Summer, pp. 282–297.

Eckel, C. C., 1985, "A General Model of Customer-Class Pricing," *Economics Letters*, 17, pp. 285–289.

Eckel, C. C., and T. Vermaelen, 1986, "Internal Regulation: The Effects of Government Ownership on the Value of the Firm," *Journal of Law and Economics*, October.

Eckel, C. C., and A. R. Vining, 1985, "Elements of a Theory of Mixed Enterprises," *Scottish Journal of Political Economy*, 32, February, pp. 82–93.

Edelman, M., 1967, *The Symbolic Uses of Politics*, Urbana: University of Illinois Press.

Edgeworth, F. Y., 1881, *Mathematical Psychics*, London: Kegan Paul.

Edgeworth, F. Y., 1925, "The Pure Theory of Monopoly" in *Edgeworth, F. Y., Papers Relating to Political Economy*, 1, London: Macmillan.

Egan, B. L., and D. L. Weisman, 1986, "The U.S. Telecommunications Industry in Transition," *Telecommunications Policy*, June, pp. 164–176.

Ehrenberg, R. G., 1979, *The Regulatory Process and Labor Earnings*, New York: Academic Press.

Ekelund, R. B., and J. R. Hulett, 1973, "Joint Supply, The Taussig-Pigou Controversy and the Competitive Provision of Public Goods," *Journal of Law and Economics*, 16, October, pp. 369–387.

El-Hodiri, M., and A. Takayama, 1981, "Dynamic Behavior of the Firm with Adjustment Costs under Regulatory Constraint," *Journal of Economic Dynamics and Control*, 3, February, pp. 29–41.

Elzinga, K. G., and W. Breit, 1976, *The Antitrust Penalties: A Study in Law and Economics*, New Haven: Yale University Press.

Elzinga, K. G., and T. Hogarty, 1973, "The Problem of Geographic Market Delineation in Antimerger Suits," *Antitrust Bulletin*, pp. 45–81.

Encaoua, D., and A. Jacquemin, 1980, "Degree of Monopoly, Indices of Concentration and Threat of Entry," *International Economic Review*, 21, February, pp. 87–105.

Epple, D., and A. Raviv, 1978, "Product Safety: Liability Rules, Market Structure and Imperfect Information," *American Economic Review*, 68, March, pp. 80–95.

Epstein, R. A., 1980, *Modern Products Liability Law*, Westport: Quorum Books.

Epstein, R. A., 1985, "Products Liability as an Insurance Market," *Journal of Legal Studies*, 14, December, pp. 645–669.

Faulhaber, G. R., 1975, "Cross-Subsidization: Pricing in Public Enterprises," *American Economic Review*, 65, December, pp. 966–977.

Faulhaber, G. R., and S. B. Levinson, 1981, "Subsidy-Free Prices and Anonymous Equity," *American Economic Review*, 71, December, pp. 1083–1091.

Faulhaber, G. R., and J. C. Panzar, 1977, *Optimal Two-Part Tariffs with Self-Selection*, Economic Discussion Paper 74, Murray Hill, NJ: Bell Laboratories.

Feinberg, R. M., 1984, "Strategic and Deterrent Pricing Responses to Antitrust Investigations," *International Journal of Industrial Organization*, 2, pp. 75–84.

Feldstein, M. S., 1972a, "Distributional Equity and the Optimal Structure of Public Prices," *American Economic Review*, 62, March, pp. 32–36.

Feldstein, M. S., 1972b, "Equity and Efficiency in Public Sector Pricing: The Optimal Two-Part Tariff," *Quarterly Journal of Economics*, 86, May, pp. 175–187.

Ferguson, J., 1974, *Advertising and Competition: Theory, Measurement, Fact*, Cambridge, MA: Ballinger.

Fessler, J., 1942, *The Independence of State Regulatory Agencies*, Chicago: Public Administration System.

Fiedler, M., and V. Pták, 1962, "On Matrices with Non-Positive Off-Diagonal Elements and Positive Principal Minors," *Czechoslovak Mathematical Journal*, 12, pp. 382–400.

Fiorina, M. P., 1982, "Legislative Choice of Regulatory Forms: Legal Process or Administrative Process," *Public Choice*, 39, pp. 33–66.

Fiorina, M. P., 1986, "Legislator Uncertainty, Legislative Control, and the Delegation of Legislative Power," *Journal of Law, Economics, and Organization*, 2, Spring, pp. 33–51.

Fiorina, M. P., and R. G. Noll, 1978, "Voters, Bureaucrats and Legislators: A Rational Choice Perspective on the Growth of Bureaucracy," *Journal of Public Economics*, 9, April, pp. 239–254.

Fisher, F. M., 1959, "New Developments on the Oligopoly Front," *Journal of Political Economy*, 67, August, pp. 410–413.

Fleming, J. M., 1953, "Optimal Production with Fixed Profits," *Economica*, 20, August, pp. 215–236.

Frank, C. R., 1965, "Entry in a Cournot Market," *Review of Economic Studies*, 32, July, pp. 245–250.

Fraysse, J., and M. Moreaux, 1981, "Cournot Equilibrium under Increasing Returns," *Economics Letters*, 8, pp. 217–220.

Friedlaender, A. F., 1969, *The Dilemma of Freight Transport Regulation*, Washington, D.C.: Brookings Institution.

Friedlaender, A. F., and R. H. Spady, 1981, *Freight Transport Regulation: Equity, Efficiency, and Competition in the Rail and Trucking Industries*, Cambridge, MA: MIT Press.

Friedman, D., 1984, "Efficient Institutions for the Private Enforcement of Law," *Journal of Legal Studies*, 13, June, pp. 379–397.

Friedman, J. W., 1977, *Oligopoly and the Theory of Games*, Amsterdam: North-Holland.

Friedman, J. W., 1986, *Game Theory with Applications to Economics*, New York: Oxford University Press.

Frisch, R., 1939, "The Dupuit Taxation Theorem," *Econometrica*, 7, April, pp. 145–150.

Frisch, R., 1965, *Theory of Production*, Dordrecht: Reidel.

Gabor, A., 1955, "A Note on Block Tariffs," *Review of Economic Studies*, 23, pp. 32–41.

Gabszewicz, J. J., and J.-F. Thisse, 1980, "Entry (and Exit) in a Differentiated Industry," *Journal of Economic Theory*, 22, April, pp. 327–338.

Gabszewicz, J. J., and J. P. Vial, 1972, "Oligopoly 'à la Cournot' in General Equilibrium Analysis," *Journal of Economic Theory*, 4, June, pp. 381–400.

Gallini, N., and R. A. Winter, 1983, "On Vertical Control in Monopolistic Competition," *International Journal of Industrial Organization*, 1, September, pp. 275–286.

Gal-Or, E., 1981, "Nonlinear Pricing-Oligopoly Case," University of Pittsburgh, Graduate School of Business, WP-425.

Gaskins, D. W., 1971, "Dynamic Limit Pricing: Optimal Pricing under Threat of Entry," *Journal of Economic Theory*, 3, September, pp. 306–322.

Gaskins, D. W., 1974, "Alcoa Revisited: The Welfare Implications of a Secondhand Market," *Journal of Economic Theory*, 7, March, pp. 254–271.

Gellhorn, E., and B. B. Boyer, 1981, *Administrative Law and Process*, St. Paul: West Publishing Co.

Gellhorn, E., and R. J. Pierce, Jr., 1982, *Regulated Industries*, St. Paul: West Publishing Co.

Gibbard, A., 1973, "Manipulation of Voting Schemes: A General Result," *Econometrica*, 41, July, pp. 587–602.

Gilbert, R., 1981, "Patents, Sleeping Patents and Entry Deterrence," in *Strategy, Predation and Antitrust Analysis*, S. C. Salop, ed., Federal Trade Commission Report, pp. 205–270.

Ginsberg, W., 1974, "The Multiplant Firm with Increasing Returns to Scale," *Journal of Economic Theory*, 9, November, pp. 283–292.

Giordano, J., 1982, *Regulation-Induced Capital Bias in the U.S. Electric Utility Industry, 1964–1977*, Ph.D. dissertation, Indiana University, Bloomington.

Goldberg, V. P., 1976, "Regulation and Administered Contracts," *Bell Journal of Economics*, 7, Autumn, pp. 426–448.

Gollop, F. M., and S. H. Karlson, 1978, "The Impact of the Fuel Adjustment Mechanism on Economic Efficiency," *Review of Economics and Statistics*, 60, November, pp. 574–584.

Gormley, W. T., Jr., 1983, *The Politics of Public Utility Regulation*, Pittsburgh: University of Pittsburgh Press.

Grabowski, H. G., and J. M. Vernon, 1978, "Consumer Product Safety Regulation," *American Economic Review, Papers and Proceedings*, 68, May, pp. 284–289.

Grabowski, H. G., and J. M. Vernon, 1983, *The Regulation of Pharmaceuticals: Balancing the Benefits and Risks*, Washington, D.C.: American Enterprise Institute.

Grady, M. F., 1981, "Regulating Information: Advertising Overview," in *The Federal Trade Commission since 1970: Economic Regulation and Bureaucratic Behavior*, K. W. Clarkson and T. J. Muris, eds., Cambridge, UK: Cambridge University Press, pp. 222–245.

Grawe, O., and M. Kafoglis, 1982, "Regulation and Relative Wages and Earnings," in *Regulatory Reform and Public Utilities*, M. A. Crew, ed., Lexington, MA: Lexington Books, pp. 213–243.

Green, J., 1976, "On the Optimal Structure of Liability Laws," *Bell Journal of Economics*, 7, Autumn, pp. 553–574.

Green, J., and J.-J. Laffont, 1977, "Characterization of Satisfactory Mechanisms for the Revelation of Preferences for Public Goods," *Econometrica*, 45, March, pp. 427–438.

Greenwald, B. C., 1984, "Rate Base Selection and the Structure of Regulation," *Rand Journal of Economics*, 15, Spring, pp. 85–95.

Greenwald, B. C., 1986, "Adverse Selection in the Labor Market," *Review of Economic Studies*, 53, July, pp. 229–264.

Greenwald, B. C., and J. E. Stiglitz, 1986, "Externalities in Economies with Imperfect Information and Incomplete Markets," *Quarterly Journal of Economics*, 101, May, pp. 229–264.

Grossman, S., 1981a, "The Informational Role of Warranties and Private Disclosure about Product Quality," *Journal of Law and Economics*, 24, December, pp. 461–489.

Grossman, S., 1981b, "Nash Equilibrium and the Industrial Organization of Markets with Large Fixed Costs," *Econometrica*, 49, September, pp. 1149–1172.

Grossman, S., and O. D. Hart, 1980, "Disclosure Laws and Takeover Bids," *Journal of Finance, Papers and Proceedings*, 35, May, pp. 323–333.

Grossman, S., and J. Stiglitz, 1980, "On the Impossibility of Informationally Efficient Markets," *American Economic Review*, 70, June, pp. 393–408.

Grout, P. A., 1984, "Investment and Wages in the Absence of Binding Contract: A Nash Bargaining Approach," *Econometrica*, 52, March pp. 449–460.

Groves, T., 1973, "Incentives in Teams," *Econometrica*, 41, July, pp. 617–631.

Groves, T., 1976, "Information, Incentives, and the Internalization of Production Externalities," in S. Lin, ed., *Theory and Measurement of Economic Externalities*, Boston: Academic Press, pp. 65–83.

Groves, T., and J. O. Ledyard, 1977a, "Optimal Allocation of Public Goods: A Solution to the Free Rider Problem," *Econometrica*, May 45, pp. 65–83.

Groves, T., and J. O. Ledyard, 1977b, "Some Limitations of Demand Revealing Processes," *Public Choice*, 29, Spring, pp. 107–124.

Groves, T., and M. Loeb, 1975, "Incentives and Public Inputs," *Journal of Public Economics*, 4, August, pp. 211–226.

Guesnerie, R., 1975a, "Pareto Optimality in Non-Convex Economics," *Econometrica*, 43, January, pp. 1–29.

Guesnerie, R., 1975b, "Production of the Public Sector and Taxation in a Simple Second Best Model," *Journal of Economic Theory*, 10, April, pp. 127–156.

Guesnerie, R., 1979, "General Statements on Second Best Pareto Optimality," *Journal of Mathematical Economics*, 6, July, pp. 169–194.

Guesnerie, R., 1980, "Second-best Pricing Rules in the Boiteux Tradition," *Journal of Public Economics*, 13, February, pp. 51–80.

Guesnerie, R., and O. D. Hart, 1982, "Welfare Losses due to Imperfect Competition: Asymptotic Results for Cournot-Nash Equilibria with Free Entry," London School of Economics.

Guesnerie, R., and J.-J. Laffont, 1984, "A Complete Solution to a Class of Principal-Agent Problems with an Application to the Control of a Self-Managed Firm," *Journal of Public Economics*, 25, December, pp. 329–369.

Guesnerie, R., and C. Oddou, 1979, "On Economic Games Which Are Not Necessarily Superadditive: Solution Concepts and Application to a Local Public Good Problem with Few Agents," *Economics Letters*, 3, pp. 301–306.

Guesnerie, R., and C. Oddou, 1981, "Second Best Taxation as a Game," *Journal of Economic Theory*, 25, August, pp. 67–91.

Hadley, A. T., 1886, *Railroad Transportation*, New York: G. P. Putnam's Sons.

Hahn, F. H., 1955, "Excess Capacity and Imperfect Competition," *Oxford Economic Papers*, 7, October, pp. 229–240.

Hahn, R. W., 1983, "Designing Markets in Transferable Property Rights: A Practitioner's Guide," in *Buying a Better Environment: Cost Effective Regulation through Permit Trading*, E. F. Joeres and M. H. David, eds., Madison, Wisconsin: University of Wisconsin Press, pp. 83–97.

Hahn, R. W., 1984, "Market Power and Transferable Property Rights," *Quarterly Journal of Economics*, 99, pp. 753–765.

Hahn, R. W., and R. G. Noll, 1982, "Designing a Market for Tradable Emissions Permits," in *Reform of Environmental Regulation*, W. A. Magat, ed., Cambridge, MA: Ballinger.

Hall, R. E., 1973, "The Specification of Technology with Several Kinds of Output," *Journal of Political Economy*, 81, August, pp. 878–892.

Halverson, J. T., 1983, "An Overview of the Legal and Economic Issues Regarding Vertical Arrangements," *Antitrust Law Journal*, 52, pp. 49–82.

Hamada, K., 1976, "Liability Rules and Income Distribution in Product Liability," *American Economic Review*, 66, March, pp. 228–234.

Hanoch, G., 1970, "Homotheticity in Joint Production," *Journal of Economic Theory*, 2, December, pp. 423–426.

Harrington, J. T., and B. A. Frick, 1983, "Opportunities for Public Participation in Administrative Rulemaking," *Natural Resources Lawyer*, 15, No. 3, pp. 537–567.

Harris, M., and R. M. Townsend, 1981, "Resource Allocation under Asymmetric Information," *Econometrica*, 49, January, pp. 33–64.

Harrod, R. F., 1952, "Theory of Imperfect Competition Revised," in *Economic Essays*, London: Macmillan, pp. 139–157.

Hart, O. D., 1979, "Monopolistic Competition in a Large Economy with Differentiated Commodities, *Review of Economic Studies*, 46, January, pp. 1–30.

Hart, O. D., 1983, "Monopolistic Competition in the Spirit of Chamberlin: Special Results," *Economic Journal*.

Hart, O. D., 1985, "Monopolistic Competition in the Spirit of Chamberlin: A General Model," *Review of Economic Studies*, 52, October, pp. 529–546.

Hart, O. D., and B. Holmström, 1986, "The Theory of Contracts," in T. Bewley ed., *Advances in Economic Theory 1985*, New York: Cambridge University Press.

Hay, G. A., 1982, "The Economics of Predatory Pricing," *Antitrust Law Journal*, 51, May, pp. 361–374.

Hay, G. A., and D. Kelley, 1974, "An Empirical Survey of Price Fixing Conspiracies," *Journal of Law and Economics*, 17, April, pp. 13–38.

Hayashi, P. M., and J. M. Trapani, 1976, "Rate of Return Regulation and the Regulated Firm's Choice of Capital-Labor Ratio: Further Empirical Evidence on the Averch-Johnson Model," *Southern Economic Journal*, 42, pp. 384–398.

Hayek, F. A., 1960, *The Consitution of Liberty*, Chicago: University of Chicago Press.

Hayek, F. A., 1973, *Law, Legislation and Liberty, vol. 1: Rules and Order; vol. 2: The Mirage of Social Justice, vol. 3: The Political Order of a Free People*, Chicago: University of Chicago Press.

Hazlett, T., 1985, "The Curious Evolution of Natural Monopoly Theory," in *Unnatural Monopolies: The Case for Deregulating Public Utilities*, R. W. Poole, Jr., ed., Lexington, MA: D. C. Heath, pp. 1–25.

Heal, G. M., 1976, "Do Bad Products Drive out Good?" *Quarterly Journal of Economics*, August, pp. 489–502.

Heal, G. M., 1977, "Guarantees and Risk-Sharing," *Review of Economic Studies*, 44, pp. 549–560.

Heffron, F. A. [with N. McFeeley], 1983, *The Administrative Regulatory Process*, New York: Longman.

Helpman, E., and J.-J. Laffont, 1975, "On Moral Hazard in General Equilibrium Theory," *Journal of Economic Theory*, 10, February, pp. 8–23.

Hicks, J. R., 1954, "The Process of Imperfect Competition," *Oxford Economic Papers*, 6, February, pp. 41–54.

Hildenbrand, W., 1979, *Core and Equilibria in a Large Economy*, Princeton: Princeton University Press.

Hirschleifer, J., 1958, "Peak Loads and Efficient Pricing: Comment," *Quarterly Journal of Economics*, 72, August, pp. 451–462.

Holmes, T. J., 1986, "The Effects of Imperfect Price Discrimination in a Bertrand Oligopoly," University of Wisconsin, February.

Holmström, B., 1979, "Moral Hazard and Observability," *Bell Journal of Economics*, 10, Spring, pp. 74–91.

Holmström, B., 1982, "Moral Hazard in Teams," *Bell Journal of Economics*, 13, Autumn, pp. 324–340.

Holmström, B., and R. B. Myerson, 1983, "Efficient and Durable Decision Rules with Incomplete Information," *Econometrica*, 51, November, pp. 1799–1819.

Horowitz, I., 1981, "Market Definition in Antitrust Analysis: A Regression-Based Approach," *Southern Economic Journal*, 48, pp. 1–16.

Horstmann, J., and A. Slivinski, 1985, "Location Models as Models of Product Choice," *Journal of Economic Theory*, 36, August, pp. 367–386.

Hotelling, H., 1929, "Stability in Competition," *Economic Journal*, 39, March, pp. 41–57.

Hotelling, H., 1938, "The General Welfare in Relation to the Problems of Taxation and of Railway and Utility Rates," *Econometrica*, 6, July, pp. 242–269.

Houthakker, H. S., 1951, "Electricity Tariffs in Theory and Practice," *Economic Journal*, 61, March, pp. 1–25.

Huber, P. W., 1987, *The Geodesic Network: 1987 Report on Competition in the Telephone Industry*, Antitrust Division, U.S. Department of Justice, January.

Ichiishi, T., and M. Quinzii, 1983, "Decentralization of the Core of a Production Economy with Increasing Returns," *International Economic Review*, 24, June, pp. 397–412.

Intriligator, M. D., 1971, *Mathematical Optimization and Economic Theory*, Englewood Cliffs, NJ: Prentice-Hall.

Jacquemin, A., and H. de Jong, 1977, *European Industrial Organization*, New York: Wiley.

Johnson, L. L., 1973, "Behavior of the Firm under Regulatory Constraint: A Reassessment," *American Economic Review*, 63, May, pp. 90–97.

Joskow, P. L., 1972, "The Determination of the Allowed Rate of Return in a Formal Regulatory Hearing," *Bell Journal of Economics*, 3, Autumn, pp. 632–644.

Joskow, P. L., 1974, "Inflation and Environmental Concern: Structural Change in the Process of Public Utility Price Regulation," *Journal of Law and Economics*, 17, October, pp. 291–327.

Joskow, P. L., 1985a, "Mixing Regulatory and Antitrust Policies in the Electric Power Industry: The Price Squeeze and Retail Market Competition," in *Antitrust and Regulation: Essays in Memory of John J. McGowan*, F. M. Fisher, ed., Cambridge, MA: MIT Press, pp. 173–239.

Joskow, P. L., 1985b, "Vertical Integration and Long-Term Contracts: The Case of Coal-Burning Electric Generating Plants," *Journal of Law, Economics and Organization*, Spring, 1, pp. 33–80.

Joskow, P. L., 1987, "Contract Duration and Relationship-Specific Investments: Empirical Evidence from Coal Markets," *American Economic Review*, 77, March pp. 168–185.

Joskow, P. L., and A. K. Klevorick, 1979, "A Framework for Analysing Predatory Pricing," *Yale Law Journal*, 89, December, pp. 213–270.

Joskow, P. L., and P. W. MacAvoy, 1975, "Regulation and the Financial Condition of the Electric Power Companies," *American Economic Review*, 65, May, pp. 295–301.

Joskow, P. L., and R. G. Noll, 1981, "Regulation in Theory and Practice: An Overview," in *Studies in Public Regulation*, Gary Fromm, ed., Cambridge, MA: MIT Press, pp. 1–65.

Joskow, P. L., and R. Schmalensee, 1983, *Markets for Power: An Analysis of Electrical Utility Deregulation*, Cambridge, MA: MIT Press.

Joskow, P. L., and R. Schmalensee, 1986, "Incentive Regulation for Electric Utilities," *Yale Journal on Regulation*, Fall, 4, pp. 1–49.

Jovanovic, B., 1982, "Truthful Disclosure of Information", *Bell Journal of Economics*, 13, Spring, pp. 36–44.

Judd, K. L., 1985, "Credible Spatial Preemption," *Rand Journal of Economics*, 16, Summer, pp. 153–166.

Kahn, A. E., 1970, *The Economics of Regulation: Principles and Institutions*, 1, New York: Wiley.

Kahn, A. E., 1971, *The Economics of Regulation: Principles and Institutions*, 2, New York: Wiley.

Kahn, C., 1986, "The Durable Goods Monopolist and Consistency with Increasing Costs," *Econometrica*, 54, March, pp. 275–294.

Kalai, E., and M. Smorodinsky, 1975, "Other Solutions to Nash's Bargaining Problem," *Econometrica*, 43, May, pp. 513–518.

Kalt, J. P., 1981, *The Economics and Politics of Oil Price Regulation*, Cambridge, MA: MIT Press.

Kalt, J. P., and M. A. Zupan, 1984, "Capture and Ideology in the Economic Theory of Politics," *American Economic Review*, 74, June, pp. 279–300.

Kalt, J. P., and M. A. Zupan, 1986, *The Apparent Ideological Behavior of Legislators: Testing for Principal-Agent Slack in Political Institutions*, Harvard University Working Paper.

Kambhu, J., 1982, "Optimal Product Quality under Asymmetric Information and Moral Hazard," *Bell Journal of Economics*, 13, Autumn, pp. 483–492.

Kamien, M. I., and N. L. Schwartz, 1971, "Limit Pricing and Uncertain Entry," *Econometrica*, 39, May, pp. 441–454.

Kamien, M. I., and N. L. Schwartz, 1972, "Uncertain Entry and Excess Capacity," *American Economic Review*, 62, December, pp. 918–927.

Kamien, M. I., and N. L. Schwartz, 1974, "Product Durability under Monopoly and Competition," *Econometrica*, 42, March, pp. 289–302.

Katz, M. L., 1984, "Price Discrimination and Monopolistic Competition," *Econometrica*, 52, November, pp. 1453–1472.

Katzmann, R. A., 1980, *Regulatory Bureaucracy: The Federal Trade Commission and Antitrust Policy*, Cambridge, MA: MIT Press.

Kau, J. B., and P. H. Rubin, 1979, "Self-Interest, Ideology and Logrolling in Congressional Voting," *Journal of Law and Economics*, 22, October, pp. 365–384.

Kauper, T. E., C. B. Renfrew, I. Scher, and R. A. Whiting, 1983, "Interview with James C. Miller, III, Chairman, Federal Trade Commission," *Antitrust Law Journal*, 52, pp. 3–22.

Keeler, T. E., 1983, *Railroads, Freight and Public Policy*, Washington, D.C.: Brookings Institution.

Kelman, S., 1980, "Occupational Safety and Health Administration," in *The Politics of Regulation*, J. Q. Wilson, ed., New York: Basic Books, pp. 236–266.

Kendrick, J. W., 1975, "Efficiency Incentives and Cost Factors in Public Utility Automatic Revenue Adjustment Clauses," *Bell Journal of Economics*, 6, Spring, pp. 299–313.

Kihlstrom, R. E., and D. Levhari, 1977, "Quality, Regulation and Efficiency," *Kyklos*, 30, Fasc. 2, pp. 214–234.

Kihlstrom, R. E., and M. V. Pauly, 1971, "The Role of Insurance in the Allocation of Risk," *American Economic Review, Papers and Proceedings*, 61, May, pp. 371–379.

Kihlstrom, R. E., and M. H. Riordan, 1984, "Advertising as a Signal," *Journal of Political Economy*, 92, June, pp. 427–450.

Kihlstrom R. E., A. E. Roth, and D. Schmeidler, 1981, "Risk Aversion and Solutions to Nash's Bargaining Problem," in *Game Theory and Mathematical Economics*, O. Moeschlin and D. Pallaschke, eds., Amsterdam: North-Holland, pp. 65–71.

Kleiman, E., and T. Ophir, 1966, "The Durability of Durable Goods," *Review of Economic Studies*, 33, April, pp. 165–178.

Klein, B., and K. B. Leffler, 1981, "The Role of Market Forces in Assuring Contractual Performance," *Journal of Political Economy*, 89, August, pp. 615–641.

Klein, B., R. Crawford, and A. Alchian, 1978, "Vertical Integration, Appropriable Rents, and the Competitive Contracting Process," *Journal of Law and Economics*, October, 21, pp. 297–326.

Klevorick, A. K., 1966, "The Graduated Fair Return: A Regulatory Proposal," *American Economic Review*, 56, June, pp. 577–584.

Klevorick, A. K., 1971, "The 'Optimal' Fair Rate of Return," *Bell Journal of Economics*, 2, Spring, pp. 122–153.

Klevorick, A. K., 1973, "The Behavior of a Firm Subject to Stochastic Regulatory Review," *Bell Journal of Economics and Management Science*, Spring, pp. 57–88.

Kneese, A. V., and B. T. Bower, 1968, *Managing Water Quality: Economics, Technology, Institutions*, Baltimore: Johns Hopkins University Press.

Koehn, M. F., 1979, *Bankruptcy Risk in Financial Depository Intermediaries*, Lexington, MA: Heath-Lexington.

Kotowitz, Y., and F. Mathewson, 1979a, "Informative Advertising and Welfare," *American Economic Review*, 69, June, pp. 284–294.

Kotowitz, Y., and F. Mathewson, 1979b, "Advertising, Consumer Information and Product Quality," *Bell Journal of Economics*, 10, Autumn, pp. 566–588.

Krattenmaker, T. G., and S. C. Salop, 1986, "Competition and Cooperation in the Market for Exclusionary Rights," *American Economic Review, Papers and Proceedings*, 76, May, pp. 109–113.

Kreps, D. M., 1977, "A Note on 'Fulfilled Expectations' Equilibria," *Journal of Economic Theory*, 14, February, pp. 32–43.

Kreps, D. M., and J. A. Scheinkman, 1983, "Quantity Precommitment and Bertrand Competition Yield Cournot Outcomes," *Bell Journal of Economics*, 14, Autumn, pp. 326–337.

Kreps, D. M., and R. Wilson, 1982, "Reputation and Imperfect Information," *Journal of Economic Theory*, 27, August, pp. 253–279.

Krueger, A. O., 1974, "The Political Economy of the Rent Seeking Society," *American Economic Review*, 64, June, pp. 291–303.

Krupnick, A. J., W. A. Magat, and W. Harrington, 1983, "Revealed Rules for Regulatory Decisions: An Empirical Analysis of EPA Rulemaking Behavior," in *An International Comparison in Implementing Pollution Laws*, P. B. Downing and K. I. Hanf, eds., Amsterdam: Kluwer-Nijhoff, pp. 63–84.

Kwerel, E., 1977, "To Tell the Truth: Imperfect Information and Optimal Pollution Control," *Review of Economic Studies*, 44, October, pp. 595–601.

Laffont, J.-J., and J. Tirole, 1986, "Using Cost Observation to Regulate Firms," *Journal of Political Economy*, 94, pp. 614–641.

Lancaster, K., 1971, *Consumer Demand: A New Approach*, New York: Columbia University Press.

Lancaster, K., 1975, "Socially Optimal Product Differentiation," *American Economic Review*, 65, September, pp. 567–585.

Lancaster, K., 1979, *Variety, Equity, and Efficiency*, New York: Columbia University Press.

Landes, W. M., 1983, "Optimal Sanctions for Antitrust Violations," *University of Chicago Law Review*, 50, Spring, pp. 652–678.

Landes, W. M., and R. A. Posner, 1975, "The Private Enforcement of Law," *Journal of Legal Studies*, 4, January, pp. 1–46.

Landes, W. M., and R. A. Posner, 1979a, "Should Indirect Purchasers Have Standing to Sue under the Antitrust Laws? An Economic Analysis of the Rule of Illinois Brick," *University of Chicago Law Review*, 46, Spring, pp. 603–635.

Landes, W. M., and R. A. Posner, 1979b, "Adjudication as a Private Good," *Journal of Legal Studies*, 8, March, pp. 235–284.

Landes, W. M., and R. A. Posner, 1985, "A Positive Economic Analysis of Products Liability," *Journal of Legal Studies*, 14, December, pp. 535–568.

Landsberger, M., and J. Meilijson, 1982, "Incentive Generating State Dependent Penalty System," *Journal of Public Economics*, 19, December, pp. 333–352.

Lave, L. B. 1981, *The Strategy of Social Regulation: Decision Frameworks for Policy*, Washington D. C.: The Brookings Institution.

Lee, L. W., 1980a, "Some Models of Antitrust Enforcement," *Southern Economic Journal*, 47, July, pp. 147–155.

Lee, L. W., 1980b, "A Theory of Just Regulation," *American Economic Review*, 70, December, pp. 848–862.

Lerner, A. P., 1933–34, "The Concept of Monopoly and the Measurement of Monopoly Power," *The Review of Economic Studies*, 1, pp. 157–175.

Lerner, A. P., 1970, "On Optimal Taxes with an Untaxable Sector," *American Economic Review*, 60, June, pp. 284–294.

Letwin, W., 1965, *Law and Economic Policy in America: The Evolution of the Sherman Antitrust Act*, New York: Random House.

Levhari, D., and Y. Peles, 1973, "Market Structure, Quality and Durability," *Bell Journal of Economics*, 4, Spring, pp. 235–248.

Levhari, D., and T. N. Srinivasan, 1969, "Durability of Consumption Goods: Competition versus Monopoly," *American Economic Review*, 59, March, pp. 102–107.

Lewis, T. R., 1986, "Reputation and Contractual Performance in Long-Term Projects," *Rand Journal of Economics*, Summer, 17, pp. 141–157.

Libecap, G. D., and S. N. Wiggins, 1984, "Contractual Responses to the Common Pool: Prorationing of Crude Oil Production," *American Economic Review*, 74, March, pp. 87–98.

Libecap, G. D., and S. N. Wiggins, 1985, "The Influence of Private Contractual Failure on Regulation: The Case of Oil Field Unitization," *Journal of Political Economy*, 93, August, pp. 690–714.

Liebeler, W. J., 1981, "Bureau of Competition: Antitrust Enforcement Activities," in *The Federal Trade Commission Since 1970: Economic Regulation and Bureaucratic Behavior*, K. W. Clarkson and T. J. Muris, eds., Cambridge: Cambridge University Press, pp. 65–97.

Littlechild, S. C., 1970, "A Game-Theoretic Approach to Public Utility Pricing," *Western Economic Journal*, 2, June, pp. 162–166.

Littlechild, S. C., 1975a, "Common Costs, Fixed Charges, Clubs and Games," *Review of Economic Studies*, 43, January, pp. 117–124.

Littlechild, S. C., 1975b, "Two-Part Tariffs and Consumption Externalities," *Bell Journal of Economics*, 6, Autumn, pp. 661–670.

Loeb, M., and W. A. Magat, 1979, "A Decentralized Method for Utility Regulation," *Journal of Law and Economics*, 22, October, pp. 399–404.

Long, W. F., R. Schramm, and R. Tollison, 1973, "The Economic Determinants of Antitrust Activity," *Journal of Law and Economics*, October, 16, pp. 351–364.

Lowi, T. J., 1969, *The End of Liberalism: Ideology, Policy and the Crisis of Public Authority*, New York: Norton.

Lowry, E. D., 1973, "Justification for Regulation: The Case for Natural Monopoly," *Public Utilities Fortnightly*, 92, November, pp. 17–23.

Luce, R., and H. Raiffa, 1957, *Games and Decisions*, New York: Wiley.

Lyon, R. M., 1982, "Auctions and Alternative Procedures for Allocating Pollution Rights," *Land Economics*, 58, February, pp. 16–32.

MacAvoy, P. W., 1965, *The Economic Effects of Regulation: The Trunk-Line Railroad Cartels and the Interstate Commerce Commission before 1900*, Cambridge, MA: MIT Press.

MacAvoy, P. W., 1979, *The Regulated Industries and the Economy*, New York: Norton.

MacAvoy, P. W., 1983, *Energy Policy: An Economic Analysis*, New York: Norton.

MacAvoy, P. W., and R. Noll, 1973, "Relative Prices on Regulated Transactions of the Natural Gas Pipelines," *Bell Journal of Economics*, 4, Spring pp. 212–234.

MacAvoy, P. W., and R. S. Pindyck, 1975, *The Economics of the Natural Gas Shortage (1960–1980)*, New York: Elsevier.

MacAvoy, P. W., and J. W. Snow, eds., 1977a, *Railroad Revitalization and Regulatory Reform*, Washington, D.C.: American Enterprise Institute.

MacAvoy, P. W., and J. W. Snow, eds., 1977b, *Regulation of Entry and Pricing in Truck Transportation*, Washington, D.C.: American Enterprise Institute.

MacAvoy, P. W., and J. W. Snow, eds., 1977c, *Regulation of Passenger Fares and Competition among the Airlines*, Washington, D.C.: American Enterprise Institute.

McCormick, R. E., 1986, "Inflation, Regulation and Financial Adequacy," in *Electric Power: Deregulation and the Public Interest*, J. C. Moorhouse, ed., San Franciso: Pacific Research Institute, pp. 135–161.

McFadden, D., 1975, "The Revealed Preferences of a Government Bureaucracy: Theory," *Bell Journal of Economics*, 6, Autumn, pp. 401–416.

McFadden, D., 1976, "The Revealed Preferences of Government Bureaucracy: Empirical Evidence," *Bell Journal of Economics*, 7, Spring, pp. 55–72.

McGee, J. S., 1958, "Predatory Price Cutting: The Standard Oil (N.J.) Case," *Journal of Law and Economics*, 1, October, pp. 137–169.

McGee, J. S., 1980, "Predatory Pricing Revisited," *Journal of Law and Economics*, 23, October, pp. 289–330.

Machlup, F., 1955, "Characteristics and Types of Price Discrimination," in *Business Concentration and Price Policy*, National Bureau of Economic Research, Princeton: Princeton University Press, pp. 400–423.

McKean, R. N., 1970, "Products Liability: Implications of Some Changing Property Rights," *Quarterly Journal of Economics*, 84, November, pp. 611–626.

McKie, J. W., 1970, "Regulation and the Free Market: The Problem of Boundaries," *Bell Journal of Economics*, 1, Spring, pp. 6–26.

McManus, M., 1964, "Equilibrium Numbers and Size in Cournot Oligopoly," *Yorkshire Bulletin of Economic and Social Resources*, 16, November, pp. 68–75.

Magat, W. A., and E. Estomin, 1981, *The Behavior of Regulatory Agencies in Attacking Regulatory Problems*, A. Fergusen, ed., Cambridge, MA: Ballinger, pp. 95–116.

Magat, W. A., A. J. Krupnick, and W. Harrington, 1986, *Rules in the Making: A Statistical Analysis of Agency Behavior*, Washington, D.C.: Resources for the Future.

Mankiw, N. G., and M. D. Whinston, 1986, "Free Entry and Social Inefficiency," *Rand Journal of Economics*, 17, Spring, pp. 48–58.

Mann, D., and J. Wissink, 1983, "Inside vs. Outside Production: A Contracting Approach to Vertical Integration," mimeo, University of Pennsylvania, April.

Mann, H. M., and J. W. Meehan, Jr., 1974, "Policy Planning for Antitrust Activities: Present Status and Future Prospects," in James A. Dalton and Stanford L. Levin, *The Antitrust Dilemma*, Boston: Heath, pp. 15–26.

Manne, A., 1952, "Multiple-Purpose Public Enterprises—Criteria for Pricing," *Economica*, 19, August, pp. 322–326.

March, J. G., and H. A. Simon, 1958, *Organizations*, New York: Wiley.

Marchand, M. G., 1973, "The Economic Principles of Telephone Rates under a Budgetary Constraint," *Review of Economic Studies*, 40, October, pp. 507–515.

Marino, A. M. 1979, "Capacity Choice under Regulation in a Variable Load Pricing Model with Diverse Technology," *Southern Economic Journal*, 45, January, pp. 858–866.

Marino, A. M., 1986, "Market Liability and Scale Effects," University of Southern California, School of Business Working Paper.

Marshall, A., 1920, *Principles of Economics*, Book V, London: Macmillan.

Mas-Colell, A., 1977, "Competition and Value Allocations of Large Exchange Economies," *Journal of Economic Theory*, 14, April, pp. 419–438.

Mas-Colell, A., 1980a, "Remarks on the Game-Theoretic Analysis of a Simple Distribution of Surplus Problem," *International Journal of Game Theory*, 9, pp. 125–140.

Mas-Colell, A., 1980b, "Efficiency and Decentralization in the Pure Theory of Public Goods," *Quarterly Journal of Economics*, 94, June, pp. 625–641.

Mas-Colell, A., 1982, "Perfect Competition and the Core," *Review of Economics Studies*, 49, January, pp. 15–30.

Maskin, E., and J. Riley, 1984, "Monopoly with Incomplete Information," *Rand Journal of Economics*, 15, Summer, pp. 171–196.

Mason, E. S., 1939, "Price and Production Policies of Large-Scale Enterprise," *American Economic Review*, Supplement, 29, March, pp. 61–74.

Mason, E. S., 1949, "The Current State of the Monopoly Problem in the United States," *Harvard Law Review*, 62, June, pp. 1265–1285.

Mathewson, G. F., and R. A. Winter, 1983, "The Incentives for Resale Price Maintenence under Imperfect Information," *Economic Inquiry*, 21, July, pp. 337–348.

Mathewson, G. F., and R. A. Winter, 1984, "An Economic Theory of Vertical Restraints," *Rand Journal of Economics*, 15, Spring, pp. 27–38.

Matthews, S., and J. Moore, 1984, "Monopoly Provision of Product Quality and Warranties," January, Northwestern University Discussion Paper No. 585.

Matthews, S., and A. Postlewaite, 1985, "Quality Testing and Disclosure," *Rand Journal of Economics*, 16, Autumn, pp. 328–340.

Meier, K. J., 1985, *Regulation: Politics, Bureaucracy, and Economics*, New York: St. Martins Press.

Meiners, R. E., 1982, "What to Do about Hazardous Products," in *Instead of Regulation: Alternatives to Federal Regulatory Agencies*, R. W. Poole, Jr., ed., Lexington, MA: D. C. Heath, pp. 285–309.

Mendeloff, J., 1979, *Regulating Safety: An Economic and Political Analysis of Occupational Safety and Health Policy*, Cambridge, MA: MIT Press.

Meyer, J. R., and C. V. Oster, Jr., 1981, *Airline Deregulation: The Early Experience*, Boston: Auburn House.

Meyer, J. R., and W. B. Tye, 1985, "The Regulatory Transition," *American Economic Review, Papers and Proceedings*, 75, May, pp. 46–51.

Meyer, R. A., 1975, "Monopoly Pricing and Capacity Choice under Uncertainty," *American Economic Review*, 65, June, pp. 326–337.

Meyer, R. A., 1976, "Capital Structure and the Behavior of the Regulated Firm under Uncertainty," *Southern Economic Journal*, 42, April, pp. 600–609.

Milgrom, P., 1981, "Good News and Bad News: Representation Theorems and Applications," *Bell Journal of Economics*, 12, Autumn, pp. 380–391.

Milgrom, P., and J. Roberts, 1982, "Predation, Reputation, and Entry Deterrence," *Journal of Economic Theory*, 27, August, pp. 280–312.

Milgrom, P., and J. Roberts, 1986a, "Relying on the Information of Interested Parties," *Rand Journal of Economics*, 17, Spring, pp. 18–32.

Milgrom, P., and J. Roberts, 1986b, "Price and Advertising Signals of Product Quality," *Journal of Political Economy*, 94, August, pp. 796–821.

Mill, J. S., 1848, *Principles of Political Economy*, reprinted, 1961, New York: Augustus M. Kelly.

Mirman, L. J., and Y. Tauman, 1982, "Demand Compatible Equitable Cost Sharing Prices," *Mathematics of Operations Research*, 7, February, pp. 40–56.

Mirman, L. J., D. Samet, and Y. Tauman, 1983, "An Axiomatic Approach to the Allocation of a Fixed Cost through Prices," *Bell Journal of Economics*, 14, Spring, pp. 139–151.

Mirman, L. J., Y. Tauman, and I. Zang, 1983a, "Merging and the Construction of an Imputation in the Core." Department of Economics, University of Illinois.

Mirman, L. J., Y. Tauman, and I. Zang, 1983b, *Ramsey Prices, Average Cost Prices and Price Sustainability*, Department of Economics, University of Illinois.

Mirman, L. J., Y. Tauman, and I. Zang, 1985, "Supportability, Sustainability and Subsidy Free Prices," *Rand Journal of Economics*, 16, Spring, pp. 114–126.

Mirrlees, J. A., 1971, "An Exploration in the Theory of Optimal Income Taxation," *Review of Economic Studies*, 38, April, pp. 175–208.

Mirrlees, J. A., 1974, "Notes on Welfare Economics, Information and Uncertainty," in Balch, McFadden, and Wu, eds., *Essays in Economic Behavior under Uncertainty*, Amsterdam: North-Holland, pp. 243–258.

Mirrlees, J. A., 1975, "Optimal Taxation in a Two Class Economy," *Journal of Public Economics*, 4, February, pp. 27–34.

Mirrlees, J. A., 1976, "Optimal Tax Theory: A Synthesis," *Journal of Public Economics*, 6, November, pp. 327–358.

Mishan, E. J., 1971, "The Postwar Literature on Externalities: An Interpretive Essay," *Journal of Economic Literature*, 9, March, pp. 1–28.

Mitchell, B. M., 1978, "Optimal Pricing of Local Telephone Service," *American Economic Review*, 68, September, pp. 517–537.

Mitnick, B. M., 1980, *The Political Economy of Regulation*, New York: Columbia University Press.

Modigliani, F., 1958, "New Developments on the Oligopoly Front," *Journal of Political Economy*, 66, June, pp. 215–232.

Modigliani, F., 1959, "New Developments on the Oligopoly Front: Reply," *Journal of Political Economy*, 67, August, pp. 418–419.

Moe, T. M., 1982, "Regulatory Performance and Presidential Administration," *American Journal of Political Science*, 26, pp. 197–224.

Moorhouse, J. C., 1986, *Electric Power: Deregulation and the Public Interest*, San Francisco: Pacific Research Institute.

Mussa, M., and S. Rosen, 1978, "Monopoly and Product Quality," *Journal of Economic Theory*, 18, pp. 310–317.

Myers, S. C., 1972, "The Application of Finance to Public Utility Rate Cases," *Bell Journal of Economics*, 3, Spring, pp. 58–97.

Myerson, R. B., 1979, "Incentive Compatibility and the Bargaining Problem," *Econometrica*, 47, January, pp. 61–73.

Myerson, R. B., 1984, "Two-person Bargaining Problems with Incomplete Information," *Econometrica*, 52, March, pp. 461–487.

Myerson, R. B., 1985, "Analysis of Two Bargaining Problems with Incomplete Information," in *Game-Theoretic Models of Bargaining*, A. E. Roth, ed., Cambridge: Cambridge University Press, pp. 115–148.

Myerson, R. B., and M. A. Satterthwaite, 1983, "Efficient Mechanisms for Bilateral Trading," *Journal of Economic Theory*, 29, April, pp. 265–281.

Nash, J. F., Jr., 1950, "The Bargaining Problem," *Econometrica*, 18, April, pp. 155–162.

Nash, J. F., Jr., 1951, "Non-cooperative Games," *Annals of Mathematics*, 45, pp. 286–295.

Nash, J. F., Jr., 1953, "Two-Person Cooperative Games," *Econometrica*, 21, January, pp. 128–140.

Nash, N. C., 1986, "U.S.'s 'Fix-It' Antitrust Policy," *New York Times*, September 16, p. 34.

Navarro, P., 1983, "Save Now, Freeze Later," *Regulation*, 7, September–October, pp. 31–36.

Needham, D., 1978, *The Economics of Industrial Structure, Conduct and Performance*, New York: St. Martin's Press.

Needham, D., 1983, *The Economics and Politics of Regulation: A Behavioral Approach*, Boston: Little, Brown.

Nelkin, D., and M. S. Brown, 1984, *Workers at Risk: Voices from the Workplace*, Chicago: University of Chicago Press.

Nelson, P., 1970, "Information and Consumer Behavior," *Journal of Political Economy*, 78, March/April, pp. 311–329.

Nelson, P., 1974, "Advertising as Information," *Journal of Political Economy*, 82, July/August, pp. 729–754.

Ng, Y.-K., 1974, "Economic Theory of Clubs: Pareto Optimality Conditions," *Economica*, 40, August, pp. 308–321.

Ng, Y.-K., and W. Weisser, 1974, "Optimal Pricing with a Budget Constraint—the Case of the Two-part Tariff," *Review of Economic Studies*, 41, July, pp. 337–345.

Nichols, A. L., and R. Zeckhauser, 1977, "Government Comes to the Workplace: An Assessment, of OSHA," *Public Interest*, 49, Fall, pp. 39–69.

Nickell, S. J., 1978, *The Industrial Decisions of Firms*, Cambridge: Cambridge University Press.

Niskanen, W., 1971, *Bureaucracy and Representative Government*, Chicago: Aldine-Atherton.

Niskanen, W., 1975, "Bureaucrats and Politicians," *Journal of Law and Economics*, 18, December, pp. 617–643.

Noll, R. G., 1971, *Reforming Regulation: An Evaluation of the Ash Council Proposals*, Washington, D.C.: Brookings Institution.

Noll, R. G., 1985, "'Let Them Make Toll Calls': A State Regulator's Lament," *American Economic Review Papers and Proceedings*, 75, May, pp. 52–56.

Noll, R. G., and B. M. Owen, 1983, *The Political Economy of Deregulation: Interest Groups in the Regulatory Process*, Washington, D.C.: American Enterprise Institute.

Norman, G., 1981, "Spatial Competition and Spatial Price Discrimination," *Review of Economic Studies*, 48, January, pp. 97–111.

Northrup, H. R., R. L. Rowan, and C. R. Perry, 1978, *The Impact of OSHA*, Philadelphia: University of Pennsylvania.

Novshek, W., 1980a, "Cournot Equilibrium with Free Entry," *Review of Economic Studies*, 47, April, pp. 473–486.

Novshek, W., 1980b, "Equilibrium in Simple Spatial (or Differentiated) Product Models," *Journal of Economic Theory*, 22, April, pp. 313–326.

Novshek, W., and H. Sonnenschein, 1978, "Cournot and Walras Equilibrium" *Journal of Economic Theory*, 19, December, pp. 223–266.

Office of Technology Assessment, 1985, United States Congress, *Preventing Illness and Injury in the Workplace*.

Oi, W. Y., 1971, "A Disneyland Dilemma: Two Part Tariffs for a Mickey Mouse Monopoly," *Quarterly Journal of Economics*, 85, February, pp. 77–90.

Oi, W. Y., 1973, "The Economics of Product Safety," *Bell Journal of Economics*, 4, Spring, pp. 3–28.

Okuguchi, K., 1973, "Quasi-Competitiveness and Cournot Oligopoly," *Review of Economic Studies*, 40, January, pp. 145–148.

Ordover, J. A., and A. Weiss, 1981, "Information and the Law: Evaluating Legal Restrictions on Competitive Contracts," *American Economic Review, Papers and Proceedings*, 71, May, pp. 399–404.

Ordover, J. A., and R. D. Willig, 1981, "An Economic Definition of Predation: Pricing and Product Innovation," *Yale Law Journal*, November, pp. 8–53.

Ordover, J. A., and R. D. Willig, 1983, "The 1982 Department of Justice Merger Guidelines: An Economic Assessment," *California Law Review*, 71, March, pp. 535–574.

Oren, S. S., S. A. Smith, and R. B. Wilson, 1983, "Competitive Nonlinear Tariffs," *Journal of Economic Theory*, 29, April, pp. 49–71.

Osborne, D. K., 1964, "The Role of Entry in Oligopoly Theory," *Journal of Political Economy*, 72, August, pp. 396–402.

Osborne, D. K., 1973, "On the Rationality of Limit Pricing," *Journal of Industrial Economics*, 22, September, pp. 71–80.

Owen, B. M., and R. R. Braeutigam, 1978, *The Regulation Game: Strategic Use of the Administrative Process*, Cambridge, MA: Ballinger.

Owen, G., 1982, *Game Theory*, 2nd ed., New York: Academic Press.

Page, J., 1975, "Toward Meaningful Protection of Worker Health and Safety," *Stanford Law Review*, 27, May, pp. 1345–1360.

Panzar, J. C., 1976, "A Neoclassical Approach to Peak Load Pricing," *Bell Journal of Economics*, 7, Autumn, pp. 521–530.

Panzar, J. C., and A. W. Postlewaite, 1984, *Sustainable Outlay Schedules*, Northwestern University, Center for Mathematical Studies, Discussion Paper No. 626S.

Panzar, J. C., and R. D. Willig, 1977, "Free Entry and the Sustainability of Natural Monopoly," *Bell Journal of Economics*, 8, Spring, pp. 1–22.

Pape, S. M., 1982, "Legislative Issues in Food Safety Regulation," in *Social Regulation: Strategies for Reform*, E. Bardach and R. A. Kagan, eds., San Francisco: Institute for Contemporary Studies, pp. 159–176.

Parks, R., 1974, "The Demand and Supply of Durable Goods and Durability," *American Economic Review*, 64, March, pp. 37–55.

Pashigian, P., 1968, "Limit Price and the Market Share of the Leading Firm," *Journal of Industrial Economics*, 16, July, pp. 165–177.

Pauly, M. V., 1967, "Clubs, Commonality and the Core: An Integration of Game Theory and the Theory of Public Goods," *Economica*, 34, August, pp. 314–324.

Pauly, M. V., 1968, "The Economics of Moral Hazard: Comment," *American Economic Review*, 58, June, pp. 531–536.

Pauly, M. V., 1974, "Overinsurance and Public Provision of Insurance: The Roles of Moral Hazard and Adverse Selection," *Quarterly Journal of Economics*, 88, February, pp. 44–62.

Peacock, A. T., and C. K. Rowley, 1972, "Welfare Economics and the Public Regulation of Natural Monopoly," *Journal of Public Economics*, 1, August, pp. 227–244.

Peltzman, S., 1971, "Pricing in Public and Private Enterprises: Electric Utilites in the United States," *Journal of Law and Economics*, 14, April, pp. 109–148.

Peltzman, S., 1973, "An Evaluation of Consumer Protection Legislation: The 1962 Drug Amendments," *Journal of Political Economy*, 81, September/October, pp. 1049–1091.

Peltzman, S., 1974, *Regulation of Pharmaceutical Innovation: The 1962 Amendments*, Washington, D.C.: American Enterprise Institute.

Peltzman, S., 1975, "The Effects of Automobile Safety Regulations," *Journal of Political Economy*, 83, August, pp. 677–725.

Peltzman, S., 1976, "Toward a More General Theory of Regulation," *Journal of Law and Economics*, 19, August, pp. 211–240.

Perles, M. A., and M. Maschler, 1980, *The Super-Additive Solution for the Nash Bargaining Game*, Report No. 1/80, Institute for Advanced Studies, The Hebrew University of Jerusalem.

Perrakis, S., 1976, "Rate of Return Regulation of a Monopoly Firm with Random Demand," *International Economic Review*, 17, February, pp. 149–161.

Perry, M. K., 1978, "Price Discrimination and Forward Integration," *Bell Journal of Economics*, 9, Spring, pp. 209–217.

Perry, M. K., 1980, "Forward Integration by Alcoa, 1880–1930," *Journal of Industrial Economics*, 29, September, pp. 37–53.

Perry, M. K., 1982, "Vertical Integration by Competitive Firms: Uncertainty and Diversification," *Southern Economic Journal*, 49, July, pp. 201–208.

Perry, M. K., 1984, "Scale Economies, Imperfect Competition and Public Policy," *Journal of Industrial Economics*, 32, March, pp. 313–330.

Perry, M. K., and R. H. Groff, 1985, "Resale Price Maintenance and Forward Integration into a Monopolistically Competitive Industry," *Quarterly Journal of Economics*, 100, November, pp. 1293–1311.

Perry, M. K., and R. H. Porter, 1986, "Resale Price Maintenance and Exclusive Territories in the Presence of Retail Service Externalities," *Bell Communications Research*, mimeo, May.

Perry, Motty, 1984, "Sustainable Positive Profit Multiple-Price Strategies in Contestable Markets," *Journal of Economic Theory*, 32, April, pp. 246–265.

Peterson, H. C., 1975, "An Empirical Test of Regulatory Effects," *Bell Journal of Economics and Management Science*, Spring, pp. 111–126.

Peterson, R. L., 1981, "Rewriting Consumer Contracts: Creditor's Remedies," in *The Federal Trade Commission since 1970: Economic Regulation and Bureaucratic Behavior*, K. W. Clarkson and T. J. Muris, eds., Cambridge: Cambridge University Press, pp. 184–203.

Pettway, R. H., 1978, "On the Use of Beta in Regulatory Proceedings: An Empirical Examination," *Bell Journal of Economics*, 9, Spring, pp. 239–248.

Phillips, C. F., Jr., 1969, *The Economics of Regulation: Theory and Practice in the Transportation and Public Utility Industries*, rev. ed., Homewood, IL: Irwin.

Phlips, L., 1983, *The Economics of Price Discrimination*, Cambridge: Cambridge University Press.

Pierce, R. J., G. Allison, and P. Martin, 1980, *Economic Regulation: Energy, Transportation and Utilities*, Charlottesville: Macmillan.

Pigou, A. C., 1920, *The Economics of Welfare*, London: Macmillan.

Pigou, A. C., 1932, *The Economics of Imperfect Competition*, London: Macmillan.

Plott, C. R., 1966, "Externalities and Corrective Taxes," *Economica*, 33, February, pp. 84–87.

Polinsky, A. M., 1980, "Private versus Public Enforcement of Fines," *Journal of Legal Studies*, 9, January, pp. 105–127.

Polinsky, A. M., 1986, "Detrebling versus Decoupling Antitrust Damages: Lessons from the Theory of Enforcement," *Georgetown Law Journal*, 74, April, pp. 1231–1236.

Polinsky, A. M., and W. P. Rogerson, 1983, "Products Liability, Consumer Misperceptions and Market Power," *Bell Journal of Economics*, 14, Autumn, pp. 581–589.

Polinsky, A. M., and S. Shavell, 1979, "The Optimal Tradeoff between the Probability and Magnitude of Fines," *American Economic Review*, 69, December, pp. 880–891.

Posner, R. A., 1971, "Taxation by Regulation," *Bell Journal of Economics*, 2, Spring, pp. 22–50.

Posner, R. A., 1972a, "The Appropriate Scope of Regulation in the Cable Television Industry," *Bell Journal of Economics*, 3, Spring, pp. 98–129.

Posner, R. A., 1972b, "The Behavior of Administrative Agencies, 1," *Journal of Legal Studies*, 1, June, pp. 305–347.

Posner, R. A., 1974, "Theories of Economic Regulation," *Bell Journal*, 5, Autumn, pp. 335–358.

Posner, R. A., 1975, "The Social Costs of Monopoly and Regulation," *Journal of Political Economy*, 83, August, pp. 807–827.

Posner, R. A., 1976a, *Antitrust Law: An Economic Perspective*, Chicago: University of Chicago Press.

Posner, R. A., 1976b, *The Robinson-Patman Act: Federal Regulation of Price Differences*, Washington, D.C.: American Enterprise Institute.

Posner, R. A., 1977, *Economic Analysis of Law*, Boston: Little, Brown.

Posner, R. A., 1986, *Economic Analysis of Law*, 3rd ed., Boston: Little, Brown.

Posner, R. A., and K. E. Scott, eds., 1980, *Economics of Corporation Law and Securities Regulation*, Boston: Little, Brown.

President's Committee on Administrative Management, 1937, *Report of the Committee with Studies of Administrative Management in the Federal Government*, Louis Brownlow, Chairman, 74th Congress, 2nd Session, Washington, D.C.: U.S. Government Printing Office.

Priest, G. L., 1977, "The Common Law Processes and the Selection of Efficient Rules," *Journal of Legal Studies*, 6, January, pp. 65–82.

Priest, G. L., 1981, "Special Statutes: The Structure and Operation of the Magnuson-Moss Warranty Act," in *The Federal Trade Commission since 1970: Economic Regulation and Bureaucratic Behavior*, K. W. Clarkson and T. J. Muris, eds., Cambridge: Cambridge University Press, pp. 246–275.

Quirk, P. J., 1980, "Food and Drug Administration," in *The Politics of Regulation*, J. Q. Wilson, ed., New York: Basic Books, pp. 191–235.

Radner, R., 1968, "Competitive Equilibrium under Uncertainty," *Econometrica*, 36, January, pp. 31–58.

Ramsey, F. P., 1927, "A Contribution to the Theory of Taxation," *Economic Journal*, 37, March, pp. 47–61.

Rea, S. A., Jr., 1981, "Workmen's Compensation and Occupational Safety under Imperfect Information," *American Economic Review*, 71, March, pp. 80–93.

Reagan, M. D., 1987, *Regulation: The Politics of Policy*, Boston: Little, Brown.

Rees, R., 1968, "Second-Best Rules for Public Enterprise Pricing," *Economica*, 35, August, pp. 260–273.

Reich, R. B., 1980, "The Antitrust Industry," *Georgetown Law Journal*, 68, June, pp. 1053–1073.

Reinganum, J. F., 1987, "Plea Bargaining and Prosecutorial Discretion," California Institute of Technology, Working Paper.

Reinganum, J. F., and L. L. Wilde, 1984, "The Economics of Income Taxation: Compliance in a Principle-Agent Framework," *Journal of Public Economics*.

Reinganum, J. F., and L. L. Wilde, 1986, *Credibility and Law Enforcement*, California Institute of Technology, mimeo.

Rey, P., and J. Tirole, 1986, "The Logic of Vertical Restraints," *American Economic Review*, 76, December, pp. 921–939.

Reynolds, R. J., and B. A. Reeves, 1976, "The Economics of Potential Competition," in *Essays in Industrial Organization in Honor of Joe S. Bain*, R. T. Masson and P. D. Qualls, eds., Cambridge, MA: Ballinger.

Riddell, W. C., 1981, "Bargaining under Uncertainty," *American Economic Review*, 71, September, pp. 579–590.

Riley, J. G., 1975, "Competitive Signalling," *Journal of Economic Theory*, 10, April, pp. 174–186.

Riley, J. G., 1979, "Informational Equilibrium," *Econometrica*, 47, March, pp. 331–358.

Riley, J. G., 1985, "Competition with Hidden Knowledge," *Journal of Political Economy*, 93, October, pp. 958–976.

Rill, J. F., 1983, "Non-Price Vertical Restraints since Sylvania: Market Conditions and Dual Distribution," *Antitrust Law Journal*, 52, pp. 95–109.

Riordan, M. H., 1984, "On Delegating Price Authority to a Regulated Firm," *Rand Journal of Economics*, 15, Spring, pp. 108–115.

Ripley, R., and G. Franklin, 1986, *Policy Implementation and Bureaucracy*, 2nd ed., Chicago: Dorsey Press.

Roberts, K., 1979, "Welfare Considerations of Nonlinear Pricing," *Economic Journal*, 89, March, pp. 66–83.

Roberts, K., 1980, "The Limit Points of Monopolistic Competition," *Journal of Economic Theory*, 22, April, pp. 256–287.

Robinson, J., 1933, *Economics of Imperfect Competition*, London: Macmillan.

Rockafellar, R. T., 1970, *Convex Analysis*, Princeton: Princeton University Press.

Rogerson, W. P., 1984, "Efficient Reliance and Damage Measures for Breach of Contract," *Bell Journal of Economics*, 15, Spring, pp. 39–53.

Romer, T., and H. Rosenthal, 1985, *Modern Political Economy and the Study of Regulation*, Carnegie-Mellon University, Graduate School of Industrial Administration, Working Paper.

Rosen, S., 1974, "Hedonic Prices and Implicit Markets: Product Differentiation in Pure Competition," *Journal of Political Economy*, 82, January/February, pp. 34–55.

Rosenthal, R. W., 1976, "Lindahl's Solution and Values for a Public-Goods Example," *Journal of Mathematical Economics*, 3, March, pp. 37–41.

Rosenthal, R. W., 1981, "Games of Perfect Information, Predatory Pricing, and the Chain-Store Paradox," *Journal of Economic Theory*, 25, August, pp. 92–100.

Roth, A. E., 1979, *Axiomatic Models of Bargaining: Lecture Notes in Economics and Mathematics Systems*, Berlin: Springer-Verlag.

Rothschild, M., 1973, "Models of Market Organization with Imperfect Information: A Survey," *Journal of Political Economy*, 81, November/December, pp. 1283–1308.

Rothschild, M., and J. E. Stiglitz, 1976, "Equilibrium in Competitive Insurance Markets: An Essay on the Economics of Imperfect Information," *Quarterly Journal of Economics*, 90, November, pp. 629–649.

Rowe, F. M., 1962, *Price Discrimination under the Robinson-Patman Act*, Boston: Little, Brown.

Rubin, P. H., 1977, "Why Is the Common Law Efficient?" *Journal of Legal Studies*, 6, January, pp. 51–63.

Rubin, P. H., 1982, "Common Law and Statute Law," *Journal of Legal Studies*, 11, June, pp. 205–224.

Rubinstein, A., 1982, "Perfect Equilibrium in a Bargaining Model," *Econometrica*, 50, January, pp. 97–108.

Rubinstein, A., 1987, "A Sequential Strategic Theory of Bargaining," in T. Bewley, ed., *Advances in Economic Theory, 5th World Congress*, Cambridge: Cambridge University Press, pp. 197–224.

Ruff, L. E., 1981, "Federal Environmental Regulation," in *Case Studies in Regulation: Revolution and Reform*, L. W. Weiss and M. W. Klass, eds., Boston: Little, Brown, pp. 235–261.

Ruffin, R., 1971, "Cournot Oligopoly and Competitive Behavior," *Review of Economic Studies*, 38, October, pp. 493–502.

Russell, L., 1974, "Safety Incentives in Workmen's Compensation Insurance," *Journal of Human Resources*, 9, Summer, pp. 361–375.

Salop, S. C., 1979, "Monopolistic Competition with Outside Goods," *Bell Journal of Economics*, 10, Spring, pp. 141–156.

Salop, S. C., 1981, *Introduction in Strategy, Predation and Antitrust Analysis*, S. C. Salop, ed., Federal Trade Commission Report.

Salop, S. C., and D. T. Scheffman, 1983, "Raising Rivals' Costs," *American Economic Review, Papers and Proceedings*, 73, May, pp. 267–271.

Salop, S. C., and J. E. Stiglitz, 1977, "Bargains and Ripoffs: A Model of Monopolistically Competitive Price Dispersion," *Review of Economic Studies*, 44, October, pp. 493–510.

Samet, D., and Y. Tauman, 1982, "The Determination of Marginal-Cost Prices under a Set of Axioms," *Econometrica*, 50, July, pp. 895–910.

Samuelson, P. A., 1951, "Theory of Optimal Taxation," unpublished, prepared for U.S. Treasury.

Samuelson, P. A., 1960, "Harold Hotelling as Mathematical Economist," *American Statistician*, 14, June, pp. 21–25.

Samuelson, P. A., 1966, "The Fundamental Singularity Theorem for Non-joint Production," *International Economic Review*, 7, pp. 34–41.

Samuelson, W., 1984, "Bargaining under Asymmetric Information," *Econometrica*, 52, July, pp. 995–1005.

Sandler, T., and J. T. Tschirhart, 1980, "The Economic Theory of Clubs: An Evaluation Survey," *Journal of Economic Literature*, 18, pp. 1481–1521.

Sappington, D. M., 1983, "Optimal Regulation of a Multiproduct Monopoly with Unknown Technological Capabilities," *Bell Journal of Economics*, 14, Autumn, pp. 453–463.

Sappington, D. M., and D. S. Sibley, 1984, *Regulatory Incentives Schemes Using Historic Cost Data*, Bell Communications Research Working Paper, December.

Sarris, V., 1984, *The Efficiency of Private Antitrust Enforcement: The "Illinois Brick" Decision*, New York: Garland Publishing.

Saving, T., 1970, "Concentration Ratios and the Degree of Monopoly," *International Economic Review*, 11, February, pp. 139–145.

Scarf, H. E. [with T. Hansen], 1973, *The Computation of Economic Equilibria*, New Haven: Yale University Press.

Scheffman, D. T., and P. T. Spiller, 1985, "Geographic Market Definition under the DOJ Merger Guidelines," mimeo, Federal Trade Commission.

Scherer, F. M., 1976, "Predatory Pricing and the Sherman Act: A Comment," *Harvard Law Review*, 89, March, pp. 869–890.

Scherer, F. M., 1980, *Industrial Market Structure and Economic Performance*, 2nd ed., Chicago: Rand McNally.

Scherer, F. M., 1983, "The Economics of Vertical Restraints," *Antitrust Law Journal*, 52, pp. 687–718.

Schmalensee, R., 1970, "Regulation and the Durability of Goods," *Bell Journal of Economics*, 1, Spring, pp. 54–64.

Schmalensee, R., 1972, *The Economics of Advertising*, Amsterdam: North-Holland.

Schmalensee, R., 1977, "Valuing Changes in Regulated Firms' Input Prices," *Southern Economic Journal*, 43, pp. 1346–1351.

Schmalensee, R., 1978a, "Entry Deterrence in the Ready-to-Eat Breakfast Cereal Industry," *Bell Journal of Economics*, 9, Autumn, pp. 305–327.

Schmalensee, R., 1978b, "A Model of Advertising and Product Quality," *Journal of Political Economy*, 86, June, pp. 485–503.

Schmalensee, R., 1979a, *The Control of Natural Monopolies*, Lexington, MA: Heath-Lexington.

Schmalensee, R. 1979b, "On the Use of Economic Models in Antitrust: The Realemon Case," *University of Pennsylvania Law Review*, 127, April, pp. 994–1050.

Schmalensee, R., 1981a, "Comments on Beales, Craswell and Salop," *Journal of Law and Economics*, 24, December, pp. 541–544.

Schmalensee, R., 1981b, "Monopolistic Two-Part Pricing Arrangements," *Bell Journal of Economics*, 12, Autumn, pp. 445–466.

Schmalensee, R., 1981c, "Output and Welfare Implications of Monopolistic Third-Degree Price Discrimination," *American Economic Review*, 71, March, pp. 242–247.

Schubert, G., 1960, *The Public Interest*, Glencoe, IL: Free Press.

Schulze, W., and R. C. D'Arge, 1974, "The Coase Proposition, Informational Constraints and Long-Run Equilibrium," *American Economic Review*, 64, September, pp. 763–772.

Schwartz, A., and L. L. Wilde, 1979, "Intervening in Markets on the Basis of Imperfect Information: A Legal and Economic Analysis," *University of Pennsylvania Law Review*, 127, January, pp. 630–682.

Schwartz, M., and R. J. Reynolds, 1983, "Contestable Markets: An Uprising in the Theory of Industry Structure: Comment," *American Economic Review*, 73, June, pp. 488–490.

Schwartz, W. F., 1980, "An Overview of the Economics of Antitrust Enforcement," *Georgetown Law Journal*, 68, June, pp. 1075–1102.

Scitovsky, T., 1954, "Two Concepts of External Economies," *Journal of Political Economy*, 62, April, pp. 143–151.

Scotchmer, S., 1985a, "Two-Tier Pricing of Shared Facilities in a Free-Entry Equilibrium," *Rand Journal of Economics*, 16, Winter, pp. 456–472.

Scotchmer, S., 1985b, "Profit-Maximizing Clubs," *Journal of Public Economics*, 27, June, pp. 25–45.

Seade, J., 1980a, "The Stability of Cournot Revisited," *Journal of Economic Theory*, 23, August, pp. 15–27.

Seade, J., 1980b, "On the Effects of Entry," *Econometrica*, 48, March, pp. 479–490.

Seiper, E., and P. L. Swan, 1972, "Monopoly and Competition in the Market for Durable Goods," *Review of Economic Studies*, 40, July, pp. 333–351.

Selten, R., 1978, "The Chain-Store Paradox," *Theory and Decision*, 9, pp. 127–159.

Shapiro, C., 1982, "Consumer Information, Product Quality, and Seller Reputation," *Bell Journal of Economics*, 13, Spring, pp. 20–35.

Shapiro, C., 1983, "Premiums for High Quality Products as Returns to Reputations," *Quarterly Journal of Economics*, 98, November, pp. 659–679.

Shapley, L. S., 1953, "A Value for *N*-Person Games," in *Contributions to the Theory of Games*, vol. II, A. W. Kuhn and A. W. Tucker, eds., Princeton: Princeton University Press, pp. 307–317.

Shapley, L. S., 1971, "Cores of Convex Games," *International Journal of Game Theory*, 1, pp. 11–26.

Sharkey, W. W., 1979, "Existence of a Core When There Are Increasing Returns," *Econometrica*, 47, July, pp. 869–876.

Sharkey, W. W., 1981, "Existence of Sustainable Prices of Natural Monopoly Outputs," *Bell Journal of Economics*, 12, Spring, pp. 144–154.

Sharkey, W. W., 1982a, *The Theory of Natural Monopoly*, Cambridge: Cambridge University Press.

Sharkey, W. W., 1982b, "Suggestions for a Game-Theoretic Approach to Public Utility Pricing and Cost Allocation," *Bell Journal of Economics*, 13, Spring, pp. 57–68.

Sharkey, W. W., 1986, "A Theory of Bureaucratic Regulation," Bell Communications Research Working Paper.

Sharkey, W. W., and L. G. Telser, 1978, "Supportable Cost Functions for the Multiproduct Firm," *Journal of Economic Theory*, 18, June, pp. 23–37.

Shavell, S. 1979a, "Risk Sharing and Incentives in the Principal and Agent Relationship," *Bell Journal of Economics*, 10, Spring, pp. 55–73.

Shavell, S. 1979b, "On Moral Hazard and Insurance," *Quarterly Journal of Economics*, 93, November, pp. 541–562.

Shavell, S., 1980a, "Damage Measures for Breach of Contract," *Bell Journal of Economics*, 11, Autumn, pp. 466–490.

Shavell, S., 1980b, "Strict Liability versus Negligence," *Journal of Legal Studies*, 9, January, pp. 1–25.

Shavell, S., 1982a, "On Liability and Insurance," *Bell Journal of Economics*, 13, Spring, pp. 120–132.

Shavell, S., 1982b, "The Social versus the Private Incentive to Bring Suit in a Costly Legal System," *Journal of Legal Studies*, 11, June, pp. 333–339.

Shavell, S., 1984a, "Liability for Harm versus Regulation of Safety," *Journal of Legal Studies*, 13, June, pp. 357–374.

Shavell, S., 1984b, "A Model of the Optimal Use of Liability and Safety Regulation," *Rand Journal of Economics*, 15, Summer, pp. 271–280.

Shepherd, W. G., 1984, "'Contestability' vs. Competition," *American Economic Review*, 74, September, pp. 572–587.

Shepherd, W. G., and C. Wilcox, 1979, *Public Policies toward Business*, 6th ed., Homewood, IL: Irwin.

Shepsle, K. A., 1982, "*The Politics of Regulation* by J. Q. Wilson," book review, *Journal of Political Economy*, 90, February, pp. 216–221.

Sherman, R., and M. Visscher, 1978, "Second Best Pricing with Stochastic Demand," *American Economic Review*, 68, March, 41–53.

Sheshinski, E., 1976, "Price, Quality and Quantity Regulation in Monopoly Situations," *Economica*, 43, May, pp. 127–137.

Shubik, M., 1959, *Strategy and Market Structure*, New York: Wiley.

Shubik, M., 1980, *Market Structure and Behavior*, Cambridge, MA: Harvard University Press.

Shubik, M., 1982, *Game Theory in the Social Sciences: Concepts and Solutions*, Cambridge, MA: MIT Press.

Shubik, M., 1984, *A Game-Theoretic Approach to Political Economy*, Cambridge, MA: MIT Press.

Silberberg, E., 1980, "Harold Hotelling and Marginal Cost Pricing," *American Economic Review*, 70, December, pp. 1054–1057.

Simon, H. A., 1957, *Models of Man*, New York: Wiley.

Simon, H. A., 1972, "Theories of Bounded Rationality," in C. McGuire and R. Radner, eds., *Decision and Organization*, Amsterdam: North-Holland, pp. 161–176.

Simon, M. J., 1981, "Imperfect Information, Costly Litigation and Product Quality," *Bell Journal of Economics*, 12, Spring, pp. 171–184.

Singer, E., 1963, "Market Power and Tying Arrangements," *Antitrust Bulletin*, 8, July/August, pp. 653–657.

Singh, N., and X. Vives, 1984, "Price and Quantity Competition in a Differentiated Duopoly," *Rand Journal of Economics*, 15, Winter pp. 546–554.

Smallwood, D., and J. Conlisk, 1979, "Product Quality in Markets Where Consumers Are Imperfectly Informed," *Quarterly Journal of Economics*, 93, February, pp. 1–23.

Smith, R. S., 1976, *The Occupational Safety and Health Act: Its Goals and Achievements*, Washington, D.C.: American Enterprise Institute.

Smithson, C.W., 1978, "The Degree of Regulation and the Monopoly Firm: Further Empirical Evidence," *Southern Economic Journal*, 44, January, pp. 568–580.

Sorensen, J., J. Tschirhart, and A. Whinston, 1978, "A Theory of Pricing under Decreasing Costs," *American Economic Review*, 68, September, pp. 614–624.

Spann, R. M., 1974, "Rate of Return Regulation and Efficiency in Production: An Empirical Test of the Averch-Johnson Thesis," *Bell Journal of Economics*, 5, Spring, pp. 38–52.

Spence, A. M., 1973a, *Market Signalling: Information Transfer in Hiring and Related Processes*, Cambridge, MA: Harvard University Press.

Spence, A. M., 1973b, "Job Market Signalling," *Quarterly Journal of Economics*, 87, August, pp. 355–379.

Spence, A. M., 1974, "Competitive and Optimal Responses to Signals," *Journal of Economic Theory*, 7, March, pp. 296–332.

Spence, A. M., 1975, "Monopoly, Quality and Regulation," *Bell Journal of Economics*, 6, Autumn, pp. 417–429.

Spence, A. M., 1976, "Product Selection, Fixed Costs and Monopolistic Competition," *Review of Economic Studies*, 43, June, pp. 217–235.

Spence, A. M., 1977a, "Entry Investment and Oligopolistic Pricing," *Bell Journal of Economics*, 8, Autumn, pp. 534–544.

Spence, A. M., 1977b, "Consumer Misperceptions, Product Failure and Producer Liability," *Review of Economic Studies*, 44, October, pp. 561–572.

Spence, A. M., 1977c, "Nonlinear Prices and Welfare," *Journal of Public Economics*, 8, August, pp. 1–18.

Spence, A. M., 1979, "Investment Strategy and Growth in a New Market," *Bell Journal of Economics*, 10, Spring, pp. 1–19.

Spence, A. M., 1980, "Multiproduct Quantity-Dependent Prices and Profitability Constraints," *Review of Economic Studies*, 47, October, pp. 821–841.

Spence, A. M., 1983, "Contestable Markets and the Theory of Industry Structure: A Review Article," *Journal of Economic Literature*, 21, September, pp. 981–990.

Spence, A. M., and R. Zeckhauser, 1971, "Insurance, Information, and Individual Action," *American Economic Review, Papers and Proceedings*, 61, May, pp. 380–387.

Spiller, P. T., 1986, "Treble Damages, and Optimal Suing Time," *Research in Law and Economics*, 9, April, pp. 45–56.

Spulber, D. F., 1979, "Non-Cooperative Equilibrium with Price Discriminating Firms," *Economics Letters*, 4. pp. 221–227.

Spulber, D. F., 1981a, "Capacity, Output and Sequential Entry," *American Economic Review*, 71, June, pp. 503–514.

Spulber, D. F., 1981b, "Spatial Nonlinear Pricing," *American Economic Review*, 71, December, pp. 923–933.

Spulber, D. F., 1982, "Introduction: A Selective Survey," in *Essays in the Economics of Renewable Resources*, L. J. Mirman and D. F. Spulber, eds., Amsterdam: North-Holland, pp. 3–26.

Spulber, D. F., 1984a, "Competition and Multiplant Monopoly with Spatial Nonlinear Pricing," *International Economic Review*, 25, June, pp. 425–439.

Spulber, D. F., 1984b, "Nonlinear Pricing, Advertising and Welfare," *Southern Economic Journal*, April, pp. 1025–1035.

Spulber, D. F., 1984c, "Scale Economies and Existence of Sustainable Monopoly Prices," *Journal of Economic Theory*, 34, October, pp. 149–163.

Spulber, D. F., 1985a, "Effluent Regulation and Long-Run Optimality," *Journal of Environmental Economics and Management*, 12, June, pp. 103–116.

Spulber, D. F. 1985b, "Risk Sharing and Retail Inventories," *Journal of Economic Behavior and Organization*, 6, pp. 55–68.

Spulber, D. F., 1985c, "Capacity, Output and Sequential Entry, Reply," *American Economic Review*, 75, September, pp. 897–898.

Spulber, D. F., 1986a, "Second Best Pricing and the Core," *Rand Journal of Economics*, 17, Summer, pp. 239–250.

Spulber, D. F., 1986b, "Value Allocation with Economies of Scale," *Economics Letters*, 21, pp. 107–111.

Spulber, D. F., 1986c, "Contract Damages and Competition," Department of Economics, University of Southern California, Working Paper, October.

Spulber, D. F., 1987a, "Product Variety and Competitive Discounts," *Journal of Economic Theory*.

Spulber, D. F., 1987b, *Negligence, Contributory Negligence and Pre-Trial Settlement Negotiation*, University of Southern California, Working Paper, July.

Spulber, D. F., 1988a, "Bargaining and Regulation with Asymmetric Information about Demand and Supply," *Journal of Economic Theory*, 44, April, pp. 251–268.

Spulber, D. F. 1988b, "Products Liability in a Contestable Market," *Economica*.

Spulber, D. F., 1988c, "Optimal Environmental Regulation under Asymmetric Information," *Journal of Public Economics*.

Spulber, D. F., 1989, "The Second Best Core," *International Economic Review*.

Spulber, D. F., and R. A. Becker, 1983, "Regulatory Lag and Deregulation with Imperfectly Adjustable Capital," *Journal of Economic Dynamics and Control*, 6, September, pp. 137–151.

Steiner, P. O., 1957, "Peak Loads and Efficient Pricing," *Quarterly Journal of Economics*, 71, November, pp. 585–610.

Steiner, P. O., 1958, "Reply to Hirschleifer," *Quarterly Journal of Economics*, 72, August, p. 467.

Stewart, J. F., 1982, "Economic Efficiency and Automatic Fuel-Cost Adjustment Mechanisms: Theory and Empirical Evidence," in *Regulatory Reform and Public Utilities*, M. A. Crew, ed., Lexington, MA: Lexington Books, pp. 167–182.

Stigler, G. J., 1961, "The Economics of Information," *Journal of Political Economy*, 69, June, pp. 213–225.

Stigler, G. J., 1964a, "A Theory of Oligopoly," *Journal of Political Economy*, 72, February, pp. 44–61.

Stigler, G. J., 1964b, "Public Regulation of the Securities Market," *Journal of Business*, 37, pp. 117–142.

Stigler, G. J., 1966, *The Theory of Price*, 3rd ed., New York: Macmillan.

Stigler, G. J., 1968, *The Organization of Industry*, Homewood, IL: Irwin.

Stigler, G. J., 1970, "The Optimum Enforcement of Laws," *Journal of Political Economy*, 78, May/June, pp. 526–536.

Stigler, G. J., 1971, "The Theory of Economic Regulation," *Bell Journal of Economics*, 2, Spring, pp. 3–21.

Stigler, G. J., 1974, "Free Riders and Collective Action: An Appendix to Theories of Economic Regulation," *Bell Journal of Economics*, 5, Autumn, pp. 359–365.

Stigler, G. J., 1975, *The Citizen and the State: Essays on Regulation*, Chicago: University of Chicago Press.

Stigler, G. J., 1981, "Comment on Joskow and Noll," in *Studies in Public Regulation*, G. Fromm, ed., Cambridge, MA: MIT Press, pp. 73–77.

Stigler, G. J., and C. Friedland, 1962, "What Can Regulators Regulate: The Case of Electricity," *Journal of Law and Economics*, 4, October, pp. 1–16.

Stigler, G. J., and R. Sherwin, 1983, *The Extent of the Market*, Center for the Study of the Economy and the State, Working Paper No. 031.

Stiglitz, J. E., 1975, "The Theory of 'Screening' Education and the Distribution of Income," *American Economic Review*, 65, June, pp. 283–300.

Stiglitz, J. E., 1977a, "Monopoly, Non-Linear Pricing and Imperfect Information: The Insurance Market," *Review of Economic Studies*, 44, October, pp. 407–430.

Stiglitz, J. E., 1977b, "The Theory of Local Public Goods," in *The Economics of Public Services*, M. S. Feldstein and R. P. Inman, eds., London: Macmillan, pp. 274–333.

Stiglitz, J. E., 1984, *Information and Economic Analysis: A Perspective*, Stanford University, Hoover Institute, Working Paper No. E-84-16.

Stiglitz, J. E., 1987, "The Causes and Consequences of the Dependence of Quality on Price," *Journal of Economic Literature*, 25, March, pp. 1–48.

Stokey, N., 1981, "Rational Expectations and Durable Goods Pricing," *Bell Journal of Economics*, 12, pp. 112–128.

Sullivan, L. A., 1983, "The New Merger Guidelines: An Afterward," *California Law Review*, 71, March, pp. 632–648.

Susskind, L., and G. McMahon, 1985, "The Theory and Practice of Negotiated Rulemaking," *Yale Journal on Regulation*, 3, Fall, pp. 133–165.

Swan, P. L., 1970, "Durability of Consumption Goods," *American Economic Review*, 60, December, pp. 884–894.

Swan, P. L., 1971, "The Durability of Goods and Regulation of Monopoly," *Bell Journal of Economics*, 2, Spring, pp. 347–357.

Swan, P. L., 1980, "Alcoa: The Influence of Recycling on Monopoly Power," *Journal of Political Economy*, 88, February, pp. 76–99.

Sylos-Labini, P., 1969, *Oligopoly and Technical Progress*, Cambridge, MA: Harvard University Press.

Takayama, A., 1969, "Behavior of the Firm under Regulatory Constraint," *American Economic Review*, 59, June, pp. 255–260.

Teece, D. J., 1980, "Economies of Scope and the Scope of the Enterprise," *Journal of Economic Behavior and Organization*, 1, September, pp. 223–247.

Teece, D. J., 1982, "Towards an Economic Theory of the Multiproduct Firm," *Journal of Economic Behavior and Organization*, 3, March, pp. 39–63.

Telser, L. G., 1960, "Why Should Manufacturers Want Fair Trade," *Journal of Law and Economics*, 3, October, pp. 86–105.

Telser, L. G., 1964, "Advertising and Competition," *Journal of Political Economy*, 72, December, pp. 537–562.

Telser, L. G., 1966, "Cutthroat Competition and the Long Purse," *Journal of Law and Economics*, 9, October, pp. 259–277.

Telser, L. G., 1969, "On the Regulation of Industry: A Note," *Journal of Political Economy*, 77, November–December, pp. 937–952.

Telser, L. G., 1971, "On the Regulation of Industry: Rejoinder," *Journal of Political Economy*, 79, March–April, pp. 364–365.

Temin, P., 1981, *Taking Your Medicine: Drug Regulation in the United States*, Cambridge, MA: Harvard University Press.

ten Raa, T., 1983, "Supportability and Anonymous Equity," *Journal of Economic Theory*, 31, October, pp. 176–181.

ten Raa, T., 1984, "Resolution of Conjectures on the Sustainability of Natural Monopoly," *Rand Journal of Economics*, 15, Spring, pp. 135–141.

Thorelli, H. B., 1955, *The Federal Antitrust Policy: Origination of an American Tradition*, Baltimore: Johns Hopkins Press.

Tiebout, C. M., 1956, "A Pure Theory of Local Expenditures," *Journal of Political Economy*, 64, October, pp. 416–424.

Tietenberg, T. H., 1980, "Transferable Discharge Permits and the Control of Stationary Source Air Pollution: A Survey and Synthesis," *Land Economics*, 56, November, pp. 391–416.

Tietenberg, T. H., 1985, *Emissions Trading: An Exercise in Reforming Pollution Policy*, Washington, D.C.: Resources for the Future, Johns Hopkins.

Tirole, J., 1986, "Procurement and Renegotiation," *Journal of Political Economy*, 94, April, pp. 235–259.

Tolchin, S. J., and M. Tolchin, 1983, *Dismantling America: The Rush to Deregulate*, New York: Oxford University Press.

Tollison, R. D., 1982, "Rent Seeking: A Survey," *Kyklos*, 35, Fasc, 4, pp. 575–602.

Townsend, R. M., 1979, "Optimal Contracts and Competitive Markets with Costly State Verification," *Journal of Economic Theory*, 21, October, pp. 265–293.

Trebilcock, M. J., 1985, "Comment on Epstein," *Journal of Legal Studies*, 14, December pp. 675–680.

Trebing, H. M., 1976a, "A Critique of the Planning Function in Regulation," *Public Utilities Fortnightly*, 79, March, 15, pp. 21–30.

Trebing, H. M., 1976b, "Toward Improved Regulatory Planning," *Public Utilities Fortnightly*, 79, March, 30, pp. 15–24.

Trebing, H. M., 1976c, "Market Structure and Regulatory Reform in the Electric and Gas Utility Industries," in *Salvaging Public Utility Regulation*, W. Sichel, ed., Lexington: MA: C. D. Heath.

Tullock, G., 1965, *The Politics of Bureaucracy*, Washington, D.C.: Public Affairs Press.

Tullock, G., 1967, "The Welfare Costs of Tariffs, Monopolies and Theft," *Western Economic Journal*, 5, June, pp. 224–232.

Tullock, G., 1980, *Trials on Trial: The Pure Theory of Legal Procedure*, New York: Columbia University Press.

Tullock, G., 1982, *A (Partial) Rehabilitation of the Public Interest Theory*, Virginia Polytechnic Institute, Working Paper.

Turner, D., 1958, "The Validity of Tying Arrangements under the Antitrust Laws," *Harvard Law Review*, 82, November, pp. 50–75.

Turvey, R., 1963, "On Divergences between Social Cost and Private Cost," *Economica*, 30, August, pp. 309–313.

Ushio, Y., 1983, "Cournot Equilibrium with Free Entry: The Case of Decreasing Average Cost Function," *Review of Economic Studies*, 50, April, pp. 347–354.

Ushio, Y., 1985, "Approximate Efficiency of Cournot Equilibria in Large Markets," *Review of Economic Studies*, 52, October, pp. 547–556.

U.S. Code, 1974, *Congressional and Administrative News*, 93rd Congress, Second Session, vol. 4, Legislative History, St. Paul: West Publishing.

U.S. Department of Justice Merger Guidelines, 1982, June 14.

van Damme, E., 1986, "The Nash Bargaining Solution is Optimal," *Journal of Economic Theory*, 38, February, pp. 78–100.

van den Heuvel, P., 1986, "Nonjoint Production and the Cost Function: Some Refinements," *Journal of Economics*, 46, pp. 283–297.

Varian, H. R., 1978, *Microeconomic Analysis*, New York: Norton.

Varian, H. R., 1985, "Price Discrimination and Social Welfare," *American Economic Review*, 75, September, pp. 870–875.

Vawter, R. R., Jr., and S. B. Zuch, 1982, "A Critical Analysis of Recent Federal Appellate Decisions on Predatory Pricing," *Antitrust Law Journal*, 51, Summer, pp. 401–421.

Viner, J., 1931, "Cost Curves and Supply Curves," reprinted in *Readings in Price Theory*, G. J. Stigler and K. E. Boulding, eds., 1953, pp. 198–232.

Viscusi, W. K., 1979, *Employment Hazards: An Investigation of Market Performance*, Cambridge, MA: Harvard University Press.

Viscusi, W. K., 1980, "Imperfect Job Risk Information and Optimal Workmen's Compensation Benefits," *Journal of Public Economics*, 14, December, pp. 319–337.

Viscusi, W. K., 1983, *Risk by Choice: Regulating Health and Safety in the Workplace*, Cambridge, MA: Harvard University Press.

Viscusi, W. K., 1984, *Regulating Consumer Product Safety*, Washington, D.C.: American Enterprise Institute.

Von Hohenbalken, B., and D. S. West, 1984, "Predation among Supermarkets: An Algorithmic Locational Analysis," *Journal of Urban Economics*, 15, March, pp. 244–257.

Von Hohenbalken, B., and D. S. West, 1986, "Empirical Tests for Predatory Reputation." *Canadian Journal of Economics*, 19, February, pp. 160–178.

von Weizsäcker, C. C., 1980a, "A Welfare Analysis of Barriers to Entry," *Bell Journal of Economics*, 11, Autumn, pp. 399–420.

von Weizsäcker, C. C., 1980b, *Barriers to Entry: A Theoretical Treatment*, Berlin: Springer-Verlag.

Walras, L., 1897, "L'État et les Chemins de Fer," *Revue du Droit Public et de la Science Politique*, 7, Jan.–June, pp. 417–436, and 8, July–Dec., pp. 42–61.

Walras, L., 1936, *Études d'Économie Politique Appliquée: Théories de la Production de la Richesse Sociale*, Lausanne: F. Rouge.

Warren-Boulton, F. R., 1974, "Vertical Control with Variable Proportions," *Journal of Political Economy*, 82, July–August, pp. 783–802.

Warren-Boulton, F. R., 1978, *Vertical Control of Markets: Business and Labor Practices*, Cambridge, MA: Ballinger.

Weaver, S., 1977, *Decision to Prosecute: Organization and Public Policy in the Antitrust Division*, Cambridge, MA: MIT Press.

Weidenbaum, M. L., 1977, *Business, Government, and the Public*, Englewood Cliffs, NJ: Prentice Hall.

Weidenbaum, M. L., 1980, *The Future of Business Regulation: Private Action and Public Demand*, New York: AMACOM

Weimer, D. L., 1982, "Safe—and Available—Drugs," in *Instead of Regulation: Alternatives to Federal Regulatory Agencies*, R. W. Poole, Jr., ed., Lexington, MA: D. C. Heath, pp. 239–283.

Weingast, B. R., 1984, "The Congressional-Bureaucratic System: A Principal-Agent Perspective with Applications to the SEC," *Public Choice*, 44, pp. 147–192.

Weingast, B. R., and M. J. Moran, 1983, "Bureaucratic Discretion or Congressional Control? Regulatory Policymaking by the Federal Trade Commission," *Journal of Political Economy*, 91, October, pp. 765–800.

Weiss, L. W., 1974, "The Concentration-Profits Relationship and Antitrust," in *Industrial Concentration: The New Learning*, H. J. Goldschmid, H. M. Mann, and J. F. Weston, eds., Boston: Little, Brown, pp. 184–233.

Weiss, L. W., and M. W. Klass, eds., 1981, *Case Studies in Regulation: Revolution and Reform*, Boston: Little, Brown.

Weitzman, M., 1983, "Contestable Markets: An Uprising in the Theory of Industry Structure: Comment," *American Economic Review*, 73, June, pp. 486–487.

Wenders, J. T., 1971a, "Excess Capacity as a Barrier to Entry," *Journal of Industrial Economics*, 20, November, pp. 14–19.

Wenders, J. T., 1971b, "Collusion and Entry," *Journal of Political Economy*, 79, December, pp. 1258–1277.

West, D. S., 1981a, "Test of Two Locational Implications of a Theory of Market Pre-Emption," *Canadian Journal of Economics*, 14, May, pp. 313–326.

West, D. S., 1981b, "Testing for Market Preemption Using Sequential Location Data," *Bell Journal of Economics*, 12, Spring, pp. 129–143.

Westfield, F. M., 1981, "Vertical Integration: Does Product Price Rise or Fall," *American Economic Review*, 71, pp. 334–346.

Westhof, F., 1977, "Existence of Equilibria in Economies with a Local Public Good," *Journal of Economic Theory*, 14, February, pp. 84–112.

White, L. J., 1981, *Reforming Regulation: Processes and Problems*, Englewood Cliffs, NJ: Prentice Hall.

Wiggins, S. N., and G. D. Libecap, 1985, "Oil Field Unitization," *American Economic Review*, 75, June, pp. 368–385.

Wilde, L. L., and A. Schwartz, 1979, "Equilibrium Comparison Shopping," *Review of Economic Studies*, 45, July, pp. 543–553.

Williams, S., 1975, "Hybrid Rulemaking under the Administrative Procedure Act: A Legal and Empirical Analysis, *University of Chicago Law Review*, 42, Spring, pp. 401–456.

Williamson, O. E., 1966, "Peak-Load Pricing and Optimal Capacity under Indivisibility Constraints," *American Economic Review*, 56, September, pp. 810–827.

Williamson, O. E., 1968, "Wage Rates as a Barrier to Entry: The Pennington Case," *Quarterly Journal of Economics*, 85, February, pp. 85–116.

Williamson, O. E., 1974, "The Economics of Antitrust: Transactions Cost Considerations," *University of Pennsylvania Law Review*, 122, May, pp. 1429–1496.

Williamson, O. E., 1975, *Markets and Hierarchies: Analysis and Antitrust Implications*, New York: Free Press.

Williamson, O. E., 1976, "Franchise Bidding for Natural Monopolies—in General and with Respect to CATV," *Bell Journal of Economics*, 7, Spring, pp. 73–104.

Williamson, O. E., 1977, "Predatory Pricing: A Strategic and Welfare Analysis," *Yale Law Journal*, 87, December, pp. 284–340.

Williamson, O. E., 1979, "Williamson on Predatory Pricing II," *Yale Law Journal*, 88, May, pp. 1183–1200.

Williamson, O. E., 1983, "Vertical Merger Guidelines: Interpreting the 1982 Reforms," *California Law Review*, 71, March, pp. 604–617.

Williamson, O. E., 1985, *The Economic Institutions of Capitalism: Firms, Markets, Relational Contracting*, New York: Free Press.

Willig, R. D., 1978, "Pareto-Superior Nonlinear Outlay Schedules," *Bell Journal of Economics*, 9, Spring, pp. 56–69.

Willig, R. D., 1979a, "Customer Equity and Local Measured Service," in *Perspectives on Local Measured Service*, J. A. Baude et al., eds., Kansas City: Telecommunications Industry Workshop.

Willig, R. D., 1979b, "Multiproduct Technology and Market Structure," *American Economic Review*, 69, May, pp. 346–351.

Wilson, C. A., 1977, "A Model of Insurance Markets with Incomplete Information," *Journal of Economic Theory*, 16, December, pp. 167–207.

Wilson, C. A., 1979, "Equilibrium and Adverse Selection," *American Economic Review*, 69, May, pp. 313–317.

Wilson, C. A., 1980, "The Nature of Equilibrium in Markets with Adverse Selection," *Bell Journal of Economics*, 11, Spring, pp. 108–130.

Wilson, J. Q., ed., 1980a, *The Politics of Regulation*, New York: Basic Books.

Wilson, J. Q., 1980b, *American Government: Institutions and Policies*, Lexington, MA: D. C. Heath.

Wilson, R., 1985, "Multi-Dimensional Signalling," *Economics Letters*, 19, pp. 17–21.

Wittman, D., 1977, "Prior Regulation versus Post Liability: The Choice between Input and Output Monitoring," *Journal of Legal Studies*, 6, January, pp. 193–211.

Wittman, D., 1980, "First Come, First Served: An Economic Analysis of 'Coming to the Nuisance,'" *Journal of Legal Studies*, 9, June, pp. 557–568.

Wittman, D., 1981, "Optimal Pricing of Sequential Inputs: Last Clear Chance, Mitigation of Damages, and Related Doctrines in the Law," *Journal of Legal Studies*, 10, January, pp. 65–91.

Woj, C., 1985, "Property Rights Disputes: Current Fallacies and a New Approach," *Journal of Legal Studies*, 14, June, pp. 411–423.

Wolinsky, A., 1983, "Prices as Signals of Product Quality," *Review of Economic Studies*, 50, October, pp. 647–658.

Wooders, M., 1978, "Equilibria, the Core and Jurisdiction Structures in Economies with a Local Public Good," *Journal of Economic Theory*, 18, August, pp. 328–348.

Wooders, M., 1980, "The Tiebout Hypothesis: Near Optimality in Local Public Good Economies," *Econometrica*, 48. September, pp. 1467–1485.

References

Young, H. P., 1985, "Producer Incentives in Cost Allocation," *Econometrica* 53, July, pp. 757–766.

Zajac, E. E., 1970, "A Geometric Treatment of Averch-Johnson's Behavior of the Firm Model," *American Economic Review*, 60, March, pp. 117–125.

Zajac, E. E., 1972, "Lagrange Multiplier Values at Constrained Optima," *Journal of Economic Theory*, 4, pp. 125–131.

Zeckhauser, R., 1970, "Medical Insurance, A Case Study of the Tradeoff between Risk-Spreading and Appropriate Incentives," *Journal of Economic Theory*, 2, March, pp. 10–26.

Zerbe, R. O., Jr., and D. S. Cooper, 1982, "An Empirical and Theoretical Comparison of Alternative Predation Rules," *Texas Law Review*, 61, December, pp. 655–715.

Zupan, M. A., 1987a, *Cable Franchise Renewals: Do Incumbent Firms Behave Opportunistically?* School of Business, University of Southern California.

Zupan, M. A., 1987b, *Reneging by Cable Operators on Their Franchise Promises: Opportunism or Economic Necessity?* School of Business, University of Southern California.

Name Index

Subject Index